SAP PRESS e-books

Print or e-book, Kindle or iPad, workplace or airplane: Choose where and how to read your SAP PRESS books! You can now get all our titles as e-books, too:

- By download and online access
- For all popular devices
- And, of course, DRM-free

Convinced? Then go to www.sap-press.com and get your e-book today.

SAP® SuccessFactors® Recruiting and Onboarding

SAP PRESS is a joint initiative of SAP and Rheinwerk Publishing. The know-how offered by SAP specialists combined with the expertise of Rheinwerk Publishing offers the reader expert books in the field. SAP PRESS features first-hand information and expert advice, and provides useful skills for professional decision-making.

SAP PRESS offers a variety of books on technical and business-related topics for the SAP user. For further information, please visit our website: *www.sap-press.com*.

Marson, Mazhavanchery, Murray
SAP SuccessFactors Employee Central: The Comprehensive Guide (2nd Edition)
2018, approx. 675 pp., hardcover and e-book
www.sap-press.com/4480

Amy Grubb, Luke Marson
SuccessFactors with SAP ERP HCM: Business Processes and Use (2nd Edition)
2015, 644 pages, hardcover and e-book
www.sap-press.com/3702

Kandi, Krishnamoorthy, Leong-Cohen, Padmanabhan, Reddygari
Integrating SuccessFactors with SAP
2015, 551 pages, hardcover and e-book
www.sap-press.com/3723

Ringling, Smith, Wittmann
Concur: Travel and Expense Management with SAP
2017, 322 pages, hardcover and e-book
www.sap-press.com/4262

Amy Grubb, Kim Lessley

SAP® SuccessFactors® Recruiting and Onboarding

The Comprehensive Guide

Rheinwerk
Publishing

Editor Meagan White
Acquisitions Editor Emily Nicholls
Copyeditor Julie McNamee
Cover Design Graham Geary
Photo Credit Shutterstock.com/293904725/© etorres
Layout Design Vera Brauner
Production Kelly O'Callaghan
Typesetting III-satz, Husby (Germany)
Printed and bound in the United States of America, on paper from sustainable sources

ISBN 978-1-4932-1467-9

© 2017 by Rheinwerk Publishing, Inc., Boston (MA)
1st edition 2017

Library of Congress Cataloging-in-Publication Data
Names: Grubb, Amy, author. | Lessley, Kim, author.
Title: SAP SuccessFactors recruiting and onboarding : the comprehensive guide
  / Amy Grubb, Kim Lessley.
Description: 1st edition. | Bonn ; Boston : Rheinwerk Publishing, [2017] |
  Includes index.
Identifiers: LCCN 2017018377 | ISBN 9781493214679 (alk. paper)
Subjects: LCSH: SAP ERP. | Personnel management--Data processing. | Personnel
  management--Computer programs. | SuccessFactors (Firm)
Classification: LCC HF5549.5.D37 G778 2017 | DDC 658.3/111028553--dc23
LC record available at https://lccn.loc.gov/2017018377

Contents at a Glance

Dear Reader,

The arrival of more than 225 résumés in my inbox over a single weekend was more than a little alarming.

This wasn't the first time I'd coordinated the hiring of a new editorial assistant, but with the latest deluge of talented candidates submitting compelling applications, I was struck again by the importance of an effective HR workflow. The philosophical became tactical: How do you find the right people for your team? How do you ensure they see your job posting and apply? What practices help run the interview process smoothly and, once you have a signed offer letter, what's your plan for welcoming your new hire into the team?

For a lot of companies, SAP SuccessFactors is the recruiting and onboarding tool that boosts this key process. Between these pages, you'll find everything you need for the pre-hire portion of the process, from advertising the job posting and working with agencies to interviewing and creating offer letters. You'll also master the onboarding process, from streamlining the mountains of paperwork to using new hire buddy systems. As both SAP SuccessFactors experts and leaders in their own organizations, authors Amy Grubb and Kim Lessley know a thing or two about recruiting and onboarding with SAP.

What did you think about *SAP SuccessFactors Recruiting and Onboarding: The Comprehensive Guide*? Your comments and suggestions are the most useful tools to help us make our books the best they can be. Please feel free to contact me and share any praise or criticism you may have.

Thank you for purchasing a book from SAP PRESS!

Meagan White
Editor, SAP PRESS

meaganw@rheinwerk-publishing.com
www.sap-press.com
Rheinwerk Publishing · Boston, MA

Contents

PART I   SAP SuccessFactors Recruiting

1   Recruiting Overview

7   Recruiter Experience   253

8   Recruiting Management Admin Features   277

9   System Notifications and Email Options   321

10   Implementing Recruiting Management   355

11   Implementing Recruiting Marketing   377

12   Recruiting Data Migration   411

13 Language Translations

14 Integrating Recruiting with Employee Central and SAP ERP HCM

15 Integrating Recruiting with Third-Party Vendors 485

PART II   SAP SuccessFactors Onboarding

16   Onboarding Overview   517

17   Onboarding Processes   539

18   Onboarding Administrative Features

21 Onboarding Integration with Employee Central and SAP ERP HCM

631

Preface

In today's competitive labor market, the combination of state-of-the-art business processes and the best technology is critical for meeting ever-changing market trends and strategic business objectives. SAP SuccessFactors Recruiting and Onboarding solutions live at the intersection of high-impact HR processes and versatile business software, making this cloud system a valuable addition to competitive organizations' software landscapes.

In light of the high demand for information on this functionality, we have written this book to provide a consolidated reference for SAP customers, partners, and consultants as they work with these modules to achieve strategic business objectives. In these pages, we have provided an overview of the talent acquisition processes supported by SAP SuccessFactors Recruiting and Onboarding modules. We have identified industry challenges and trends that customers face in today's market: to identify top talent and bring them into your organization before your competitors do. From an HR perspective, process matters; once the desired candidate is identified, having an efficient and effective onboarding process is critical to their long-term success, and once candidates are onboarded, transferring valuable candidate data to your HR system of record is critical to your HR department's long-term success. Whether you run SAP SuccessFactors Employee Central or SAP ERP HCM, SAP SuccessFactors' tools and standard integrations support your new hire's transition from candidate to employee.

Who This Book Is For

This book is written for anyone interested in learning about the SAP SuccessFactors Recruiting and Onboarding solutions. This readership is diverse, and includes customers, partners, consultants, and business leaders or process owners from HR and other business units with an interest in talent acquisition who seek to evaluate or implement SAP SuccessFactors Recruiting or Onboarding modules. These modules offer a tremendous amount of functionality, so we have attempted to deliver the right mix of big-picture perspective and actionable detail that showcases how the modules function and are implemented. Of course, book publication has its temporal and spatial limits. It's difficult to capture a technology that is constantly changing (both modules experienced six quarterly releases while this book was in development!), and this book does not include complete step-by-step instructions on how to implement functionality in these modules. While we covered some of that in places, you should still refer to the SAP SuccessFactors documentation and training for the most detailed, up-to-date implementation instructions. This book does, however, give you a solid foundation in your developing understanding of the modules, how they interact with each other, and how they can support your critical recruiting and onboarding business processes.

How This Book Is Organized

We've organized this book in two sections: SAP SuccessFactors Recruiting and SAP SuccessFactors Onboarding.

Part I on recruiting extends from the applicant tracking capabilities found in Recruiting Management to the robust marketing and analytics tools in Recruiting Marketing. This block of chapters covers the business process concerns and capabilities of identifying and attracting talent and efficiently processing them for selection. We have organized this section sequentially based on the flow of the talent acquisition process: from identifying a hiring need, to developing and advertising a posting, to evaluating and selecting the candidates for hire. We cover topics such as integrating the modules with third-party products, providing candidate data to support the onboarding process, using administrative functions, and planning your implementation.

Part II on onboarding shifts the focus from acquiring talented candidates to onboarding them as employees. This process is key to each new employee's success and longevity with the company, yet overlooked by most organizations. In these chapters we discuss onboarding from a philosophical perspective and consider how to establish a well-rounded onboarding experience, and then drill into the capabilities that SAP SuccessFactors Onboarding offers. Likewise, we also discuss the administrative functions of Onboarding, how the module is implemented, and finally how to convert candidate data to new employee records.

We recommend reading this book sequentially from Chapter 1 onward; however, if you prefer, you can jump directly to any chapter and start reading about that topic. Let's review what is covered in each chapter of this book.

As the introduction to Part I of the book, **Chapter 1** provides an overview of talent acquisition processes and the key business challenges faced by enterprises operating in today's competitive labor market. We provide an introduction to how SAP

SuccessFactors Recruiting can enable businesses to attract and identify the best candidates and process them through interviews and evaluations.

Chapter 2 discusses how organizations can identify hiring needs and how SAP SuccessFactors Recruiting supports those efforts. We discuss the built-in tools that help you advertise those needs to the widest possible audience.

In **Chapter 3** we focus on the candidates' experience when searching for and applying for jobs through SAP SuccessFactors Recruiting. From job search options to job agents and from talent communities to candidate profiles, we discuss the features that create the best possible candidate experience, including both the web-based and mobile application options.

Once an organization identifies, opens, and posts openings and once candidates have applied, recruiters process candidates through the evaluation steps. **Chapter 4** discusses tools such as candidate search and the Candidate Workbench that enable this evaluation.

Chapter 5 explores additional features within SAP SuccessFactors Recruiting such as Employee Referral, Data Retention Management, and the Agency Portal. These features provide additional capability for managing recruiting processes and data. This chapter also covers tools such as Job Profile Builder and Competency Management.

Chapter 6 discusses all the ways SAP SuccessFactors Recruiting enables you to report on the valuable data collected in the talent acquisition process, including tools such as ad hoc reports, Online Report Designer, and the home page tiles that provide customized reports for meeting unique reporting needs.

Chapter 7 examines the features and functions within SAP SuccessFactors Recruiting that are focused on providing a good experience for recruiting users. These are topics such as the multiple ways to disposition candidates, searching the candidate database to source open jobs, and using the Recruiting Marketing Dashboard and other end user-focused features.

In **Chapter 8** we discuss the administrative features that customers can maintain within the Admin Center. This chapter covers email and offer letter templates, email triggers, the applicant status pipeline, and settings related to the Employee Referral Program and Agency Portal access. We examine the administrative features that are most often touched after the implementation has gone live.

Chapter 9 covers the options for communicating with candidates and recruiters via emails, from maintaining email templates that get sent automatically or on an ad-hoc basis to setting up standard system-wide notifications.

In **Chapter 10**, our focus is how to implement Recruiting Management. (Here we separate Recruiting Management from Recruiting Marketing since these are implemented slightly differently.) In this chapter we discuss the implementation methodology, roles and responsibilities, and key milestones, including potential impacts to your project timeline.

Chapter 11 explores the ins and outs of implementing Recruiting Marketing, covering both custom implementations and those built with Career Site Builder. Again, we consider the project methodology and how it is applied to this module, and highlight differences between Recruiting Marketing and Recruiting Management implementations you should consider.

Chapter 12 discusses options for migrating legacy recruiting data into SAP Success-Factors Recruiting. We explore the process, available tools, and pros and cons to consider when deciding whether to undertake this effort.

Some companies operate in multiple countries and languages. **Chapter 13** focuses on options for supporting multiple language translations, covering topics such as language packs and applying translations to custom fields in your Recruiting configuration.

In **Chapter 14** we discuss how data flows from SAP SuccessFactors Recruiting into both SAP SuccessFactors Employee Central and SAP ERP HCM to complete the hiring action. We discuss the standard integration available in both scenarios.

Our final chapter in Part I, **Chapter 15**, covers options for integrating SAP SuccessFactors Recruiting with third-party vendors. We discuss the standard integrations that SAP has built and maintains for ancillary business processes such as background checks and candidate assessments.

We begin Part II of the book in **Chapter 16** by overviewing an effective onboarding process and reflecting on its impact on both the new employee's success in their new role and also their employment longevity with the company.

In **Chapter 17** we move from generic onboarding into SAP SuccessFactors, focusing on the holistic onboarding business processes (onboarding, cross boarding, and off-boarding) within the SAP SuccessFactors Onboarding module.

Chapter 18 covers some of the more important administrative features within Onboarding. Because SAP has made nearly all of the module's functionality accessible from the administrative interface, it's important for customers, partners, and consultants to master these features.

In **Chapter 19**, we cover implementing Onboarding and the systems and tools that are involved. We cover how the project methodology is applied to this module and highlight variations on critical roles, responsibilities, and milestones.

The focus of **Chapter 20** is how Recruiting integrates with Onboarding to pass the critical candidate data that supports the onboarding process from one module to the other.

We complete the book in **Chapter 21** with a discussion of how Onboarding integrates with both SAP SuccessFactors Employee Central and SAP ERP HCM to transfer candidate data into the HRIS to support and complete the hiring process. We discuss the standard integrations available to tie these modules together.

Taken together, the chapters of this book give you not only a high-level understanding of how the SuccessFactors Recruiting and Onboarding modules work together, but also a close look at the features and functionality that support and enable your talent acquisition objectives. Approach this book as the foundation in your core understanding of these modules, and take advantage of the detailed documentation maintained by SAP and the training provided by SAP Education to build your knowledge of these modules, what they can provide to your organization, and how they are implemented.

Acknowledgments

Before we begin our journey through the world of talent acquisition with SAP SuccessFactors Recruiting and Onboarding, one final note: This book was a team effort and could not have been completed without some very hard work by several people.

Amy and Kim wish to thank, first and foremost, Emily Nicholls and Meagan White at Rheinwerk Publishing for shepherding this project through the arduous publishing process. They additionally would like to recognize the following people: Mark Ingram, Teresa Helt, Dwight Jones, David Ludlow, Arpit Nigam, Robin Michel, Joachim Foerderer, Brian Stiles, Jill Venable, Kelli Stock, Ruby Wilson, Andy Chan, Kim Glassman, Kelly Levine, Sharon Newton, Amy Sletten, Amy Broyles, and Elliot Wells.

Amy would also like to personally thank Don Grubb, Barbara Waddell, Leigh Kelleher, and Floyd and Sandy Rhoades for their inspiration, support, and encouragement.

Introduction to Talent Acquisition

Are you battling in the "war for talent"? In today's business environment, the companies that are making headway in this battle recognize the key to winning is having the right tools. There are many systems on the market, all purporting to have what you need to be successful. But the true key to winning is having the right tools and technology to support your talent acquisition strategy.

In today's business environment, companies recognize that to get ahead and stay ahead, they need the right talent. There is much talk in the industry about the "talent shortage," and whether you agree with that supposition or not, there is no denying that finding, engaging, and retaining the right talent is often challenging. Technology seems to move at the speed of light with updates, changes, and trends constantly changing. With hundreds of job-posting websites, venues such as LinkedIn, and informal recruiting channels (e.g., employee referrals), talent acquisition professionals are often overwhelmed with finding the right channels to advertise their openings and inundated with candidates without the right qualifications, while the right candidates have quickly moved on to other options. Recent statistics in recruiting have shown the following:

- In their job search, 79% of job seekers are likely to use social media.
- At least once a day, 45% of job seekers say they use their mobile device specifically to search for jobs.
- On average, each corporate job opening attracts 250 résumés. Out of those 250 applicants, only 4 to 6 will be called for an interview, and 1 is offered the job.
- Of Fortune 500 company career sites, 90% don't support a mobile apply solution.

These statistics show large pools of candidates competing for a small number of opportunities, candidates looking for jobs in new ways, and companies not necessarily tooled to handle that. All of those variables create a challenging environment for talent acquisition professionals.

If talent acquisition professionals make it through the hurdles of posting their jobs to the appropriate channels, they are then tasked with sorting through the voluminous applications that are submitted. Time is critical in recruiting top talent. If you hesitate, or are bogged down by sorting through reams of unqualified candidates, likely the candidate you want has moved on to other opportunities or has already been hired by another company. Maintaining momentum throughout the evaluation process is critical, from interviewing, background and reference checks, to the offer process, any delay could mean losing the ideal candidate.

After a qualified candidate is identified and selected, then comes the task of onboarding them for employment. Traditionally, onboarding meant many paper forms that need to be distributed, completed, signed, and provided back to HR departments before or on day one of employment. Often employee orientation sessions dedicate large blocks of time to new hires filling out all of this necessary paperwork. Time that could be spent on job-specific training or tasks is instead spent on generating paper. HR professionals can be inundated with numerous forms for each new hire, and keeping track of critical forms can be overwhelming. After all the appropriate forms are completed, the next issue is where to store them. Companies are increasingly looking for electronic alternatives to reduce time and paper in this process.

In this chapter, we'll look at the recruiting and onboarding processes and discuss the critical elements of each. We'll also begin discussing how SAP SuccessFactors Recruiting—specifically SAP SuccessFactors Recruiting Marketing and SAP SuccessFactors Recruiting Management—and SAP SuccessFactors Onboarding can support companies in these two critical business process areas.

Recruiting at a Glance

Competing in today's tight labor market starts with the talent acquisition process, also known as recruiting. This business process can be approached in a variety of ways, and many companies will develop their own flavor of recruiting process. At a high level, talent acquisition is about identifying open resource needs within an organization, fielding potential candidates for that position, evaluating those candidates, and then selecting the one to fill the need. These steps can be further broken down as follows:

- Identifying the need
- Developing or updating the position description

- Approving the opening
- Posting the position
- Reviewing and evaluating applicants
- Selecting the successful candidate and making the offer

We'll take a brief look at each step in the following sections.

Identifying the Need

The recruiting process begins with identifying a need, which can occur from someone vacating an existing position, a company reorganization, or growth plans that include adding to the head count. Hiring needs are often addressed during the budgeting process, as business units plan for their needs for the coming fiscal year and how that impacts human resource numbers. These hiring needs are ongoing throughout the year as companies experience attrition. Hiring needs are also identified by several different players. Hiring managers that are experiencing the need are often the most frequent identifiers as it has the most impact on their teams.

Developing or Updating the Position Description

After the need has been identified, it's critical to update the position description when filling an existing position or to create the position description if it's a new position. This critical step in the recruiting process is often overlooked or neglected altogether, despite its criticality to finding the right talent to hire. Existing positions can change over time as the business needs change and organizations adapt to those changes. Needed knowledge, skills, abilities, certifications, education, and other requirements will change as well. Taking time to review the position or job description prior to attempting to fill it will ensure that all day-to-day responsibilities and elements of the job are captured and communicated to candidates. Understanding actual job requirements is also critical to evaluating the candidates that apply. The job description review can be completed by the hiring manager, human resources (HR), or a combination of both.

SAP SuccessFactors can support this process through workflows attached to Job Profile Builder. For example, a manager could initiate creating a new job profile and send it through a workflow for approval, perhaps to their manager or department head and then to HR for approval. We'll discuss Job Profile Builder in more detail in Chapter 2 and Chapter 5.

Approving the Opening

Before a position can be filled, it's important to ensure that the hiring manager and talent acquisition departments have the appropriate approvals to do so. Many positions are approved during a company's budgeting process, but others may arise during the year and will need to be evaluated from a fiscal and organizational perspective before moving forward. Numerous parties typically are involved in approving an open position:

- Hiring manager
- Departmental/business unit leader
- Finance/compensation department
- HR/business partner/recruiting
- Executive

Positions may require some or all of these types of approval before moving forward. Justifications for the position are often required as the request moves through the approval chain so approvers understand the business reason for moving forward with the position. Sometimes, a position will open up through attrition and will be revised in level, compensation, responsibilities, or a combination of these. Of course, this revision is critical before beginning the search for potential candidates. Ensuring all interested parties and levels in the organization are in agreement with a need is critical to successful recruiting.

Posting the Position

After a position has been reviewed and approved as necessary, it's ready to be posted on various outlets to reach the most candidates. This may include an external posting page from the corporate website, any number of third-party job boards such as Monster or Career Builder, and industry-specific job boards. It can also be posted or announced internally so that employees may apply or refer qualified candidates to the position.

Job board aggregator services are also available to assist with increasing the reach of your postings while reducing the individual posting activity by recruiters. Some organizations will also have contracted services with search firms or hiring agencies to assist with sourcing qualified candidates.

Reviewing and Evaluating Applicants

When the opening has been posted through the appropriate channels, candidates will start to apply. At this point, recruiters and hiring managers will be busy evaluating the background and qualifications of the candidates, and they will start making decisions regarding which candidates should move forward. This is where that work in the first step, reviewing and revising the position description, comes into play. With that activity completed, all parties should have a clear understanding of the requirements of the job and have objective criteria against which to measure the applicants. Evaluation may include the following:

- Prescreening by reviewing application questions and the résumé
- Phone screens by the recruiting team
- Interviews by recruiters, hiring managers, and others
- Formal assessments of skills or knowledge
- Background checks and drug screening

Each company will have its own evaluation process, which may differ based on the kind of position being filled.

Candidate Selection and Developing and Extending an Offer

Having identified the qualified candidate, it's now time to develop an offer, which will rely heavily on the job data reviewed, revised, and approved earlier in the process. The final offer will be determined by numerous factors, such as the experience level of the selected candidate. It's not uncommon to find someone very highly qualified that warrants a starting salary in excess of what is graded for that position, or what was approved. Other elements of the employment offer will include vacation time, signing bonuses, and benefits such as relocation assistance. All of these elements will require approval to ensure what is offered is in line with organizational budgets.

When the offer elements have been compiled and approved, it's time to formally extend the offer to the candidate. Often this is done in two phases:

- **Verbal offer**
  The recruiter or hiring manager will extend an offer verbally, and some back and forth can occur while the offer is being negotiated and approved.
- **Formal offer letter**
  After all parties are in agreement, a formal offer letter is drafted and presented to the candidate. It's the candidate's responsibility then to accept the offer by signing

and returning the signed offer letter to the company. This last step is necessary before the onboarding activities kickoff.

Employee Onboarding at a Glance

Onboarding is a system of processes for integrating new employees into the social and performance aspects of their new jobs as quickly and smoothly as possible. This is also known as *organizational socialization*. Studies over the past several years have shown that in the United States alone, more than 25% of the workforce will experience a career transition either through obtaining a new position with their current company or joining a new organization. Nearly half of all hourly workers will leave their new job within the first 4 months, and half of all senior external hires fail within 18 months in their new position. Within the Fortune 500, approximately 500,000 managers will take on new roles every year. On average, managers will begin new jobs every two to four years. These are staggering statistics.

Where new employees are concerned, conventional wisdom provides that new employees are given about 90 days to prove themselves in their new roles. This suggests that the sooner new employees can feel assimilated to their new company, culture, and job responsibilities, the better they will perform. After an effective recruitment process, onboarding is one of the most important and impactful ways an organization can improve the effectiveness of their overall talent management strategy. However, onboarding as a process is often overlooked or poorly managed, creating a manual, labor-intensive process for all involved and often a negative first impression for the new hire.

Studies have shown that more than 80% of new employees decide whether or not to stay with a company within the first six months of being hired, and one in four do leave in the first year. An unorganized or incomplete onboarding process can cause those employees to rethink their decision to join the company just when they should be the most enthusiastic.

Onboarding is either informal or formal, and they both have a purpose to serve. *Informal onboarding* exists when employees learn about their new job without an explicit organization plan. This can also be thought of as the "sink or swim" method of onboarding. *Formal onboarding* refers to a written set of coordinated policies and procedures that are designed to assist new employees to adjust to their new job in terms of both tasks and socialization.

Not surprisingly, companies that engage in formal onboarding by defining and implementing detailed processes for new employees are more successful than those who only engage in informal onboarding. Within formal onboarding processes, there are several levels. At the most basic level, onboarding processes will cover compliance and company policies. The most advanced level of onboarding can be thought of as proactive, where they are systematically organizing onboarding activities with a strategic talent management approach. Onboarding processes can build on this basic level to include activities that are geared to clarifying an employee's role and expectations, addressing company culture, and connecting new employees with their new coworkers.

Onboarding has both short-term and long-term benefits. Following are some of the longer-term benefits:

- Higher retention rates among new hires
- Better job satisfaction and performance levels
- Career effectiveness

As with the recruiting process, each company will have its own unique process for onboarding new employees, but the basic steps will likely include the following:

- Gathering state and federal tax data
- Reviewing company policies and procedures
- Clarifying the role and setting goals
- Socializing with the new manager and team members
- Completing necessary training

We take a brief look at each of these areas in the following subsections.

Gathering State and Federal Tax Data

Covering that basic level of formal onboarding deals with compliance and gathering all of the necessary government required data. Federal and state/province specific forms must be accurately completed prior to the employee's first payroll to ensure that the employee is paid on time. While not exactly a value-added activity, gathering this data accurately is a critical part of onboarding new employees. It's also a cumbersome process that generates much paper and can often take considerable time to complete, submit, and then track that it has been completed.

Reviewing Company Policies and Procedures

Another critical activity in compliance-related onboarding is distributing company policies, procedures, and program documentation to new hires. These documents need to be reviewed carefully, and sometimes companies want acknowledgements that employees have read and understand the documents or agree to the provisions. Again, all of this means much paper is produced and needs to be distributed, collected, and stored. Although this time-consuming manual activity doesn't seem to add to an employee's time to productivity, it's critical to the overall success of the onboarding activity.

Clarifying the Role and Setting Goals

One of the first conversations new employees should be having with their managers regards expectations around performance goals and what competencies or other elements will be rated during the performance review. It's critical for employee engagement that they understand and agree with what they should be focused on not only in the first few weeks of employment but within the first year. Reviewing the employee's job description and the competencies assigned to the role, setting goals, and discussing regular one-on-one meetings will provide the new employees with a clear understanding of where they need to focus their attention.

Socializing with the New Manager and Team Members

One aspect of formal onboarding that is critical to new employees forming effective relationship bonds within their new environment is creating opportunities for the new employees to socialize with their new manager and team members. While this may seem frivolous, research has shown that the sooner new employees feel connected to their new team, the sooner they feel connected to the company as a whole and are able to perform at higher levels than those employees who aren't afforded the opportunity to form working relationships. There are several ways to accomplish this, but often companies will assign new employees to someone who is their main contact when questions and concerns arise. This can provide a sense of stability and can often help new employees feel empowered to step out and take risks, knowing there is someone available to assist if they run into trouble.

Developing strong working relationships and communication channels with new coworkers and managers is one of the best ways to increase time to productivity. Beyond developing comradery with peers, new employees will find benefit in developing relationships with other new employees. Connecting groups of new employees with each other is another effective way of strengthening the bond to the organization as well as new employees with each other.

Completing Necessary Training

Finally, we discuss here the completion of any necessary or required training. New employees may need to complete company-focused training, compliance training, or other training that will help them be productive in their role. Administrators or the manager often assign this training during the onboarding process, and the training often can be completed within the first few days or weeks of employment when new employees have more time to focus on it. Training can also be provided that assists employees in understanding their new role or that delivers information and skills that will result in higher performance levels.

These components are just examples of the kinds of activities that can be included in an employee onboarding process. Companies will have different elements in their programs as necessary for the type of job and the industry in which they operate. Let's now turn our attention to an overview of how SAP SuccessFactors Recruiting and SAP SuccessFactors Onboarding solutions can support a company's processes for attracting and hiring new talent.

Recruiting and Onboarding within SAP SuccessFactors

Talent acquisition is one of the most impactful HR processes to a business, and getting the right people in the organization has a dramatic, measurable impact on business performance. SAP SuccessFactors Recruiting (referred to as Recruiting) and SAP SuccessFactors Onboarding (referred to as Onboarding) modules enable organizations to source, engage, and hire the world's best talent. The solutions provide a comprehensive and integrated solution that can provide guidance at every step of the hiring process for everyone involved.

This book is focused on discussing the Recruiting and Onboarding modules in detail. In the next sections, we'll briefly highlight some of the features covered in subsequent chapters. These topics include applicant-tracking capability, marketing jobs through various posting channels, the candidate experience in Recruiting, and the principles upon which the SuccessFactors Onboarding solution is built: guiding, connecting, and developing. Let's start with Recruiting and how it can support an organization's talent acquisition goals.

SAP SuccessFactors Recruiting

With Recruiting, you can source the right talent globally with the following tools and methods:

- Accessing a central platform to manage requisitions
- Posting jobs to more than 3,000 sources across more than 80 countries, including job boards, colleges and universities, and social networks
- Using search engine optimization (SEO) career sites and landing pages to improve your site's ranking on major search engines around the world and to increase candidate flow
- Streamlining and simplifying the hiring process via detailed analytics by job, source, campaign, or any number of data points that get at the data quickly to optimize spend
- Easily identifying qualified candidates and moving them through the interview process to find the right candidate for the job
- Scheduling interviews and capturing competency-based feedback at the desk or from a mobile device to drive candidate ranking
- Developing offers, gaining approvals, and generating offer letters with electronic acceptance or eSignature capability to quickly hire candidates and begin the onboarding process
- Supporting form completion and gathering electronic signatures on various new hire forms, communicating company policies and procedures, and introducing team collaboration with an online onboarding process

The Recruiting module helps recruiters source, engage, and hire the world's best talent by providing data and guidance through every step of the talent acquisition process. Hiring needs can easily be identified, openings approved and posted to a variety of sources, and candidates managed in a user-focused interface that puts the most critical data at the fingertips of all those involved in recruiting.

Recruiting Management versus Recruiting Marketing

The SAP SuccessFactors Recruiting solution is comprised of two critical components: SAP SuccessFactors Recruiting Management and SAP SuccessFactors Recruiting Marketing. Recruiting Management contains all of the applicant-tracking capabilities such as requisition management, candidate evaluation, and support for the offer process. Recruiting Marketing provides robust tools for advertising job openings, marketing jobs to various job boards and talent communities of candidates, and running analytics on candidate sourcing. All of the features are combined to provide a holistic Recruiting solution. Let's take a brief look at these features.

Applicant-Tracking Capability

After a need is identified, Recruiting allows you to create requisitions and gain necessary workflow-driven approvals. Critical job data are captured and maintained for each job in the requisition and are made accessible throughout the process to provide input to emails to candidates and when developing offers. With flexible role-based permissions, you can involve any number of players in your recruiting process to streamline and expedite the evaluation of candidates. Requisitions, candidates, and applications can all be easily accessed and managed in dashboard-like screens, as illustrated in Figure 1.

Mobile capability supports approvals and capturing interview feedback so the evaluation process can continue moving forward. With various ways to communicate with candidates throughout the process, interviews quickly and easily scheduled, and clear presentation of data by all users throughout all steps in the process, your time to hire can reduce significantly.

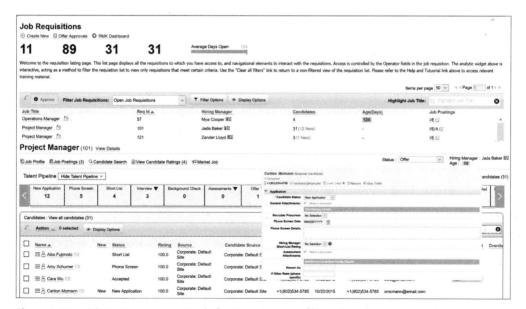

Figure 1 Recruiting Management Tools for Recruiters to Efficiently Manage Open Jobs and Candidates

Market Jobs via Multiposting Channels

With Recruiting multiposting options, recruiters can publish openings to numerous channels directly from within the Recruiting module. With channels such as job boards, aggregation sites, and thousands of universities, you can post to nearly unlimited sources. The Recruiting multiposting feature provides access to the following:

- More than 600 general and specialized job boards, such as the following:
  - Dice
  - Indeed
  - Monster
  - CareerBuilder
- More than 2,500 university job boards and alumni networks, including these:
  - Harvard Business
  - HEC Paris
  - NYU
  - Imperial College London
- Innovative channels such as LinkedIn, Twitter, and Viadeo
- Disability and other diversity channels such as America's Job Exchange and Agefiph (French acronym for Fund Management Organization for the Professional Integration of People with Disabilities)

SAP SuccessFactors brings together more than 3,000 partners globally in all regions. The job boards are categorized as General Job Boards and Specialized Job Boards. Recruiters can also identify certain job boards as Favorites for easy access and edit, manage, and delete postings to numerous channels in one tool.

Market Jobs and Candidate Experience

The Recruiting solution provides candidates with a robust experience and provides recruiters with analytics necessary to effectively manage recruiting budgets. With tools such as talent communities, featured jobs, saved job searches, and mobile apply capability, Recruiting helps to attract and engage your candidates. Recruiters can push jobs within talent communities to source candidates to critical jobs. Powerful recruiter-focused tools enable budget monitoring, inventory tracking, and reporting on source performance. All of this valuable data is provided in the Recruiting Marketing Dashboard, illustrated in Figure 2. With these tools, talent acquisition professionals can make more informed investment decisions on how to allocate sometimes-limited recruiting budgets.

Figure 2 Recruiting Marketing Dashboard with Numerous Tools to Identify, Track, and Report Candidate Sources

SAP SuccessFactors Onboarding

In today's competitive talent market, onboarding is just as critical as identifying the right talent to fill open positions. Companies can end up spending untold amounts of time and resources constantly recruiting for the same position when they could focus on improving the onboarding process.

The Onboarding module provides a platform that allows companies to define a comprehensive onboarding process that is user-centric and automates many currently manual processes—all while keeping the process personal and engaging the new hire with his new manager and team. This can decrease an employee's ramp-up time by focusing on three key areas:

- **Guiding**
  HR, the hiring manager, and the new employee are all guided through each step of the process to create consistency and a complete process each time.

- **Connecting**

  New employees are immediately connected with the right people and relevant content to support them not only on day one but before. Engaging new employees early initiates the bonding process with their new employer even before the first day of employment and can ultimately increase retention rates among new hires.

- **Developing**

  New employees are developed immediately by connecting the onboarding process with other talent management processes within the organization such as goal setting and learning.

Hiring managers, HR, and others can track new employees through all steps of the process via the Onboarding Dashboard, shown in Figure 3. Here you can view the work queue and manage tasks within it. Tasks can be filtered by criteria such as **New Employee Step**, **PostHire Verification Step**, or **Signature Step**. Completed documents can be accessed for viewing or downloading as well. The Onboarding Dashboard will be the focal point of Onboarding activities. Let's take a look at the guiding, connecting, and developing areas of onboarding and how the Onboarding module supports each.

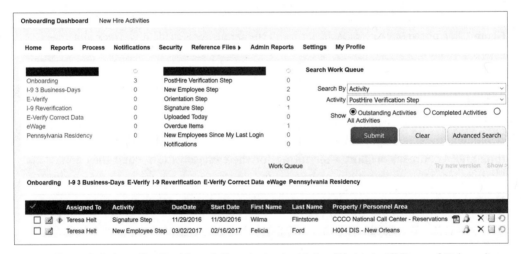

Figure 3 Onboarding Dashboard: Easy Access to All Candidates in All Steps of Onboarding Processes

Guiding

Of all the people involved in the onboarding process, the hiring manager has the greatest impact on new hires but is often the least engaged. Onboarding is often viewed as "HR's job," and this is most commonly reinforced by HR themselves. HR may be too busy to invest the time necessary to properly onboard the new employees. This also creates a negative first impression and doesn't set up the employee for success. Engaging the hiring manager in the onboarding process by making it easy to interact with the process results in an overall better onboarding process for all involved parties. Hiring managers and new employees are given the opportunity to engage and begin the bonding process before the first day of full employment. It sends a message to new employees that the company values them and creates excitement to get started with their new employers. It also eliminates burdensome manual tasks from HR and ensures that no steps are missed in this critical process.

With Onboarding, the process can be foolproof. Tools such as step-by-step wizards and easy-to-use dashboards lead hiring managers through every step of the process and can track completion along the way, ensuring no steps are missed, and all elements of the process are successfully completed. The new employees are also presented with step-by-step wizards asking simple questions that are used to complete sometimes-complicated paperwork. All required forms, both government and company-specific, are completed as part of the process so HR can be assured that nothing important is missed. All completed, signed forms are readily visible and accessible in the Document Center, so there is never a question about which forms have been completed and which have not.

Connecting

Starting a new job always involves some level of anxiety for employees, no matter what level they may be. New coworkers, office space, policies, procedures and processes, and company culture can be overwhelming for new employees to adjust to while also trying to excel at the job they have been hired to perform. The first week of any new job is about learning "the lay of the land," both physical and cultural. Onboarding provides a place for new hires to get connected and start to feel comfortable even before they start the job. Building connections with the new team and coworkers even before the first full day can kick-start employee engagement and decrease time to productivity. After new hires start, immediate access to the employee network gives them the ability to start learning at their own pace and to pick up conversations and content that are relevant to their roles. Getting new hires engaged with people and content early means they are more connected and are more likely to stay with the company longer.

Developing

Many studies have connected an improvement in the onboarding process to business results, including improved first-year retention, faster time to productivity, increases in profit growth, and revenue per employee. The Onboarding module combines the critical yet tactical aspects of onboarding, such as compliance and orientation, with the more strategic aspects, such as socialization and connection to other talent processes, to create an end-to-end process that drives better business results.

The Onboarding module takes a unique and more strategic approach to onboarding with the view that the onboarding process is a key starting point to fully integrated talent management and sets the stage for employee success in every area. With a robust set of workflow automation tools to improve compliance, the Onboarding module leverages the SAP SuccessFactors platform to integrate with all the talent processes, such as learning (formal and informal), goal setting, recruiting, and core HR. This transforms onboarding from an isolated HR process into a process at the center of a company's talent strategy, empowering new hires to ramp up quickly and contribute to corporate goals sooner.

Going Beyond

With Onboarding, you can do much more than just process new hire paperwork and engage new employees with the company and their team. You can also leverage the module to support other processes to crossboard or offboard employees. *Crossboarding* refers to when a current employee changes jobs within the organization, creating additional paperwork requirements. This could include taking an assignment in a different country or transferring to a different business unit. *Offboarding* refers to processing employees that have terminated. The offboarding process is often overlooked or not done well. Capturing signatures on exit paperwork, conducting exit interviews, and making sure terminating employees understand what resources may be available to them as alumni can all be supported using Onboarding.

We'll discuss both of these processes in more detail in Part II of this book.

Summary

In today's competitive market for top talent, how companies attract, engage, and retain resources begins with how they approach talent acquisition. Critical to finding the right candidate for your jobs is getting the opening in front of the right candidates at the right time. Marketing jobs through various channels increases the pool of qualified candidates, but it's also important to engage them early and not get bogged down in the evaluation process, or you risk losing that top talent.

After the successful candidate is selected, an effective talent acquisition strategy carries through to onboarding the new employee beginning before day one and following through into the first few weeks and months of employment. Approaching onboarding as a key part of an integrated talent management system not only improves the efficiency of the onboarding process but also leads to better employee engagement, higher retention rates, and faster time-to-productivity rates.

This book examines how SAP SuccessFactors Recruiting and SAP SuccessFactors Onboarding enable you to more efficiently and effectively manage open jobs, evaluate candidates to select the right one, and then create the best onboarding experience possible.

PART I

SAP SuccessFactors Recruiting

Chapter 1
Recruiting Overview

SAP SuccessFactors Recruiting provides robust tools to support talent acquisition professionals in finding, attracting, and engaging the best talent for the organization. With nearly unlimited marketing capabilities to ensure your openings reach the widest audience and mobile-enabled applicant-tracking capabilities, all players in your talent acquisition process are equipped to complete their tasks in the most timely and efficient way.

Talent acquisition in today's market is increasingly competitive with companies often competing for the same talent. If companies expect to hold their own, they must be armed with technology that enables their talent acquisition processes and increases the efficiency of evaluating those candidates who apply. Candidates search for jobs in new and different ways, continually making use of technology. You have seconds to grab their attention—the more time it takes candidates to find the jobs they want, the more likely they are to move on. Having an engaging and intuitive career site is critical to the goal of hiring the best talent into the organization.

The SAP SuccessFactors Recruiting module provides a very robust applicant-tracking functionality that supports recruiters in opening, approving, and posting positions to various channels. From flexible approval workflows to maintaining a library of job descriptions or profiles, requisitions can be quickly opened and prepared for posting. Once approved, jobs can be posted to a variety of channels through built-in job posting pages and various external channels such as agencies and job boards. After candidates have applied, recruiters can make use of robust features such as **Interview Central**, **Interview Scheduling**, and **Offer Letters** to quickly evaluate candidates and identify the most qualified candidate for the job. We'll discuss these features and many more in Part I of this book.

A company's career site is one of the most—if not the most—valuable resources a candidate uses when considering applying for a job. It's often the candidate's first impression of the company and should be attractive to candidates. The site should provide the following:

- Clear representation of the company's brand and culture
- An intuitive and easy-to-navigate interface
- Tools to assist candidates in finding jobs of interest

Having an outdated, clumsy career site without compelling and informative content will put you at a disadvantage in hiring top talent. The career site is the centerpiece of the Recruiting Marketing component of SAP SuccessFactors Recruiting. The Recruiting Marketing platform is a comprehensive one that includes career site optimization, multichannel job posting, social network integration, and mobile-enabled career sites.

The Recruiting Marketing platform also includes robust analytics that can help you develop highly effective, customized sourcing strategies and make more informed investment decisions on how to best allocate often-limited recruiting budgets. Tools such as talent communities, featured jobs, saved job searches, and mobile apply capability help to attract and engage your candidates.

Recruiting offers robust capabilities to manage open jobs, market them through various channels, capture candidate interest, solicit applications, evaluate candidates against job requirements, and initiate offers. In this chapter, we'll begin looking at the features within Recruiting that support initiating and advertising an opening, including the following:

- Approving a requisition and posting it through various channels
- Using the candidate search capability to source candidates to jobs and disposition applications through the evaluation process
- Optimizing the recruiting experience by collecting interview feedback and generating offer letters

We'll also take a detailed look at the key features available within Recruiting and discuss how they can be implemented and used to enhance a company's talent acquisition strategy.

1.1   Initiating and Advertising the Opening

The first step in any recruiting process begins with advertising an opening. Recruiting is a requisition-based system, and there are several ways that a requisition can begin. Figure 1.1 shows how users can open requisitions via the **Recruiting** tab in three ways:

- **Copy Existing Job Requisition**
  Copy a requisition from an existing requisition.
- **Browse "Families & Roles"**
  Browse job families and roles.
- **Create New Job Requisition From Blank Template**
  Create a new requisition from a blank template.

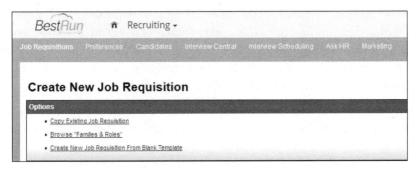

Figure 1.1 Three Ways to Create a Requisition

If you run SAP SuccessFactors Employee Central with position management, you can also configure the Employee Central to Recruiting integration and create new requisitions from **To Be Hired** positions on the position org chart.

Regardless of how the requisition is initiated, requisition fields must be completed, and then the requisition is sent for approval. The route map defines the approval workflow of the requisition and can contain numerous approvers. Some examples of types of approvers include the following:

- Hiring manager
- Recruiter
- Finance
- Compensation analyst
- Sourcing resource
- Executives

After the requisition has been approved by all users specified by the route map, the requisition can be posted. Once posted, the job opening is visible to candidates, both internally and externally, and applications will then be submitted. Let's look more closely at the ways in which requisitions can be created, followed by the options for posting the requisitions.

1.1.1   Creating the Requisition

A requisition may be created in several ways. We'll briefly review each one and discuss some advantages for each method.

Copy from an Existing Requisition

A quick way to open a requisition is to copy it from a requisition that has already been opened. Recruiting provides a search capability for users to find the appropriate requisition during the copy function. This is very similar to completing a **File • Save As** in Microsoft Word or Excel. You find the source requisition and copy it with a new requisition ID, thereby creating a new document in the system. After the document is created, fields can be updated as necessary for the new opening.

This method can be a real time-saver, especially for certain positions that are high volume where you might choose to manage the volume with new requisitions rather than multiple openings on one requisitions. Figure 1.2 shows how to search for existing requisitions during the copy process. You will select the appropriate requisition and then click **Copy Selected**.

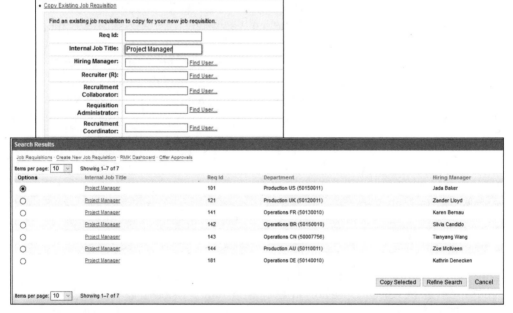

Figure 1.2 Copy Existing Open Requisitions and Search for the Source Requisition by Various Search Criteria

Browse Families and Roles

SAP SuccessFactors provides the ability to maintain a catalog of job descriptions or job profiles. When these are maintained in the SAP SuccessFactors foundation, they are visible within Recruiting and can be browsed and selected when creating a requisition. Using Job Profile Builder, the system allows various job profiles to be created and maintained. These job profiles can include short and long descriptions, sections with educational requirements, certifications, special skills required, and competencies required by the job, as shown in Figure 1.3. This information houses what is commonly referred to as the job description and is visible to candidates while searching for open jobs.

The advantage to maintaining a library of job profiles is to ensure consistency of the information communicated to candidates. It also prepopulates this information on the requisition during creation, thereby saving time when filling out the other requisition fields. We'll cover this functionality, as well as the job code entity feature, in Chapter 2.

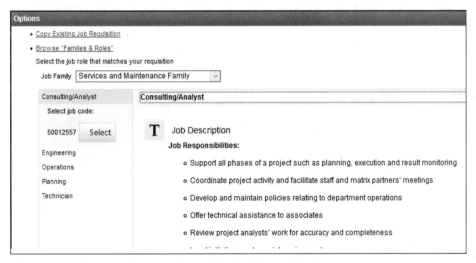

Figure 1.3 Browsing a Library of Job Families, Roles, and Profiles

Create from a Blank Template

A third method of creating a requisition is to do so from a blank template, which opens a requisition form with only a few fields populated:

- Any operators in the approval workflow
- Internal job title

All other fields, including the external job title and both internal and external job description fields (or the job profile, as applicable) must be completed. This is a less popular method of creating requisitions because it requires the most time.

Create from a Position on the Position Org Chart

When you have position management configured in Employee Central, there is a standard integration to Recruiting Management so that data from a requisition is copied from the position and populated on the requisition during creation, as shown in Figure 1.4. This integration requires configuration, and fields from the position are mapped to corresponding fields on the requisition. This method ensures data integrity between the position and the requisition and also can be used to ensure requisitions aren't initiated when they shouldn't be. Many companies will dictate that this is the only way requisitions can be initiated to maintain their position hierarchy and data integrity.

Using this integration and requisition creation method should be thoroughly discussed before enabling because it's driven by how positions are maintained within the organization, making it quite restrictive and not always flexible to accommodate exceptions. We'll discuss this integration further in Chapter 14.

Figure 1.4 Passing Job Data from an Open Position to Create a Requisition in Position Management

1.1.2   Advertising the Opening

After the requisition is initiated and has gone through the approval workflow, it's ready to be posted. This can happen in two ways, depending on whether companies have Recruiting Marketing deployed or not. Requisitions can be posted to various channels:

- Intranet and external postings
- Private postings (both intranet and external)
- Agency and job board postings
- Market job via Recruiting posting channels

Intranet and External Postings

Every company that uses Recruiting receives an internal job posting page via a careers page (intranet posting) and an external job posting page. Postings can be staggered between the intranet and external postings, for example, if there is a requirement to post jobs internally for a certain number of days before opening the job for outside candidates. This can be set up at one time, and the system will automatically post the job on the date specified. Jobs can also be posted for a specified period of time by indicating a posting end date. Figure 1.5 illustrates how openings can be posted to the internal and external pages, both publicly and privately.

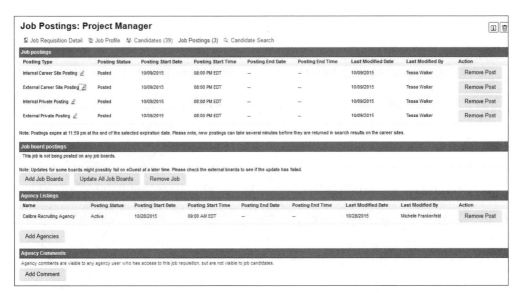

Figure 1.5 Posting Jobs to Various Channels from within the Recruiting Management Job Postings Page

Private Postings

Recruiting also has a private posting capability, which is useful for confidential requisitions that need to be filled but should not be openly available to all candidates. Just as there are intranet and external postings, private postings can be posted both internally and externally. The job posting sits on the respective posting page so that it can receive applications, but it isn't visible to candidates. To receive applications against private postings, recruiters must share the specific link with candidates via email (see Figure 1.6). After selecting the link, the candidate is taken to the job posting and may submit an application.

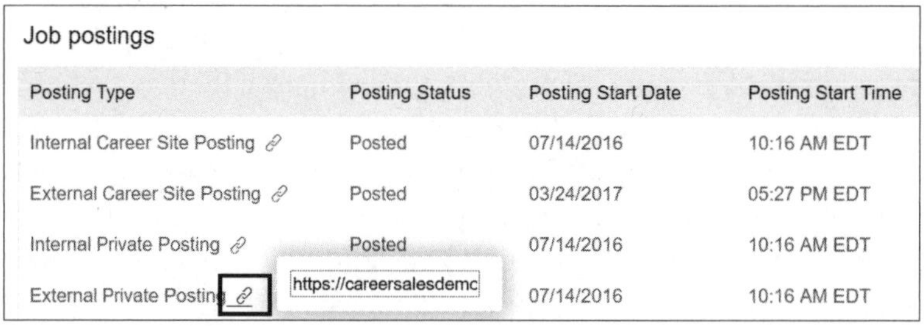

Job postings			
Posting Type	**Posting Status**	**Posting Start Date**	**Posting Start Time**
Internal Career Site Posting	Posted	07/14/2016	10:16 AM EDT
External Career Site Posting	Posted	03/24/2017	05:27 PM EDT
Internal Private Posting	Posted	07/14/2016	10:16 AM EDT
External Private Posting	https://careersalesdemc	07/14/2016	10:16 AM EDT

Figure 1.6 Recruiters Accessing Links to Private Postings to Share with Candidates

Agency and Job Board Postings

SAP SuccessFactors supports two other additional posting channels from the **Postings** page. First, there is built-in integration between Recruiting and eQuest, a global job board aggregator. With eQuest and a package of postings, recruiters can create and manage job postings to job boards such as Indeed, CareerBuilder, Monster, and a host of industry-specific job boards all from within the Recruiting **Postings** page.

The second channel is the agency portal supplied by SAP SuccessFactors to enable posting jobs to external agencies that may support your recruiting efforts. Openings can be selectively posted to the Agency Portal and any number of individual agencies that have been set up in Admin Center. Agencies can submit candidates to the postings for consideration by recruiters. Figure 1.7 shows how a posting can be added to one or more agencies via the agency portal. Recruiters can set the posting date by agency and add any comments that they want the agents to see on this particular opening. Note that these comments are only visible to agents via the agency portal and not to candidates.

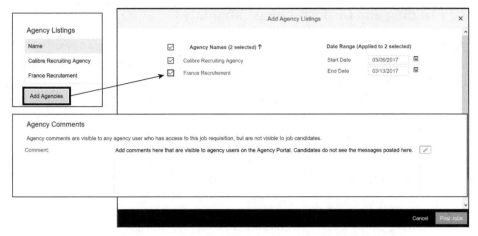

Figure 1.7 Recruiters Posting Jobs to One or More Agencies via the Agency Portal

Recruiting Posting

The SAP SuccessFactors Recruiting Posting solution is a new offering within the Recruiting functionality of SAP SuccessFactors that offers thousands of posting channels for jobs. With Recruiting Posting in place, recruiters have another dashboard from which to manage postings to numerous channels, including industry-specific job boards and university boards. By choosing the **Market Job** selection on the **Requisition Actions** menu for a particular job, recruiters can access the posting channels available through Recruiting Posting and push a job to a large number of job boards at one time. Figure 1.8 shows where to access the Recruiting Posting options for a requisition.

Figure 1.8 Posting a Requisition to Various Channels via Recruiting Posting

1.2   Finding and Dispositioning Candidates

After openings are posted and candidates begin applying, recruiters can evaluate the applicants through the talent pipeline and advance or disqualify candidates based on their qualifications against the open position. Recruiters may also conduct searches of the candidate database and push jobs to candidates based on their profiles. Recruiting offers numerous tools that enable recruiters to fill open positions quickly and efficiently.

Now, let's briefly discuss candidate search as a means for sourcing jobs, followed by dispositioning applicants through the talent pipeline.

1.2.1   Finding Candidates via Candidate Search

As candidates create profiles in SAP SuccessFactors, they have a candidate profile that can be actively searched by recruiters. This is a great way for recruiters to access the pool of talent in the database, add candidates to job requisitions, and then invite candidates to apply. There are two types of searches on the **Candidates** search page in Recruiting:

- KEYWORD AND ITEM SEARCH
- CONCEPTUAL SEARCH

Keyword and Item Search

This type of search provides numerous variables by which to search candidates in the database. You can add any number of search criteria to conduct your search to find the most suitable candidates, for example:

- Keyword search of résumé or cover letter
- Tags
- Employee referral
- Basic information such as country, state, and email
- Background information from the candidate profile
- Specific candidate by name

Additionally, you can choose whether to search for internal candidates (employees), external candidates, or both. If you conduct the same search multiple times, the search criteria can be saved and easily accessed for quick searching in the future. Candidates that meet the criteria entered are returned for further viewing and comparison, as shown in Figure 1.9. From here, you can view individual candidate profiles or select several for viewing at one time. You can also view résumés and forward candidates to a colleague or to a specific job requisition.

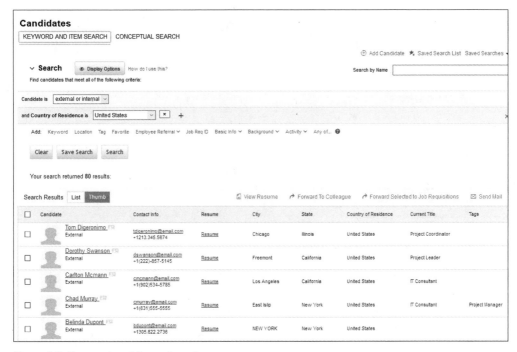

Figure 1.9 Keyword and Items Search

Conceptual Search

This feature is used to match a large quantity of text to other large quantities of text. Conceptual search matches candidates to selected match criteria based on the résumé. At the time of publication, the résumé is the only attachment available for conceptual searching, and U.S. English is the only language supported.

> **Note**
>
> Other languages for use with the conceptual search feature are coming in future releases. The conceptual search runs in other language packs, but because they aren't formally supported, results aren't always accurate.

Conceptual candidate search works in three ways:

- Search requisition job description
- Search candidates against other candidates' résumés
- Search candidates against a block of text

As with the keyword search, you can choose to search internal candidates, external candidates, or both. Figure 1.10 shows the search criteria for **CONCEPTUAL SEARCH**. Search results are returned based on relevancy and are listed from highest to lowest.

Figure 1.10 Conceptual Candidate Search Criteria

Candidate Search within a Job Requisition

When conducting a candidate search, recruiters can do it either from the **Candidates** tab, which will search the entire candidate database and allow forwarding to selected job requisitions based on a search, or, they can initiate a candidate search from within a job requisition. **KEYWORD AND ITEM SEARCH** and **CONCEPTUAL SEARCH** options are available in both scenarios. If a candidate search is initiated from within a job requisition, any candidates selected are forwarded to that job requisition. The recruiter can select from the **Forwarded** or **New Application** status to place the candidates into. Figure 1.11 shows how to forward candidates after a search from the **Candidates** tab and from within a job requisition. If you search from the **Candidates** tab, candidates are forwarded to selected requisitions. If you search from within a requisition, candidates are automatically forwarded once you set the status to **Forwarded**.

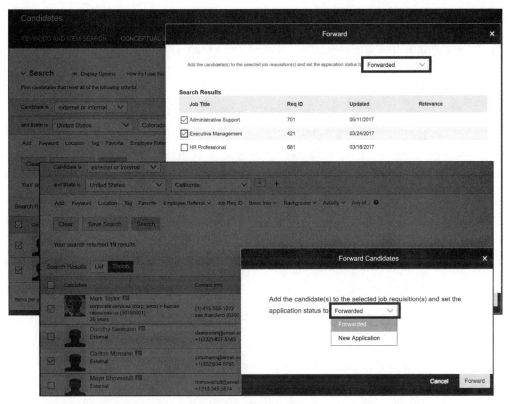

Figure 1.11 Forwarding Candidates to Job Requisitions after a Search or to a Specific Requisition if the Search Is Initiated from within the Requisition

1.2.2 Dispositioning Candidates

After candidates have applied to a requisition, the recruiter can disposition, or process, them through the talent pipeline. The talent pipeline is the group of statuses defined for a particular requisition template. Multiple talent pipelines are supported by SAP SuccessFactors, but its best practice to identify as few as possible. There is a 1:1 relationship between a talent pipeline and a requisition template. If a second talent pipeline is required, it will necessitate a second requisition template.

Talent Pipeline	Hide Talent Pipeline ∨										
Forwarded	Invited To Apply	New Application	Phone Screen	Short List	Interview ▼	Background Check	Assessments ▼	Offer ▼	WOTC ▼	Ready for Hire	Hired
1	0	15	4	2	5	0	1	4	0	2	2

Figure 1.12 An Example of Part of a Talent Pipeline

The **Talent Pipeline** screen area is divided into several sections with statuses that represent different parts of the process (see Figure 1.12). The main sections are **In Progress** and **Disqualified**. These sections of the pipeline can have as many statuses as needed to adequately capture and track candidates through evaluation. Following are a few highlights about talent pipeline statuses:

- Statuses can be grouped together for better user navigation and use.
- Each status can have various email templates assigned to automatically communicate with candidates and various other recruiting users.
- Statuses can be required or optional, and the system logs an audit trail of candidates through each status in the pipeline.
- Each status can capture comments, which can be optional or required, and the comments are auditable.

We'll discuss the talent pipeline and how to maintain it in greater detail in Chapter 4.

1.3   Optimizing the Recruiting Experience

Recruiting offers numerous functionality features that help to optimize the talent acquisition process and the experience of all Recruiting users from recruiters to hiring managers and others. These features combine to reduce the amount of time it takes to evaluate candidates and move them through the process until the right candidate is selected. We'll discuss these features at length in the chapters in Part I, but we'll also introduce a few concepts in the following sections.

1.3.1   Interview Central

As candidates are interviewed and their qualifications and performance evaluated against other candidates, the results of the interviews are captured in Interview Central. Interview Central leverages competencies and the Stack Ranker capability in the SAP SuccessFactors foundation and SAP SuccessFactors Performance & Goals to rate candidates against each other. Interview results are displayed in the Candidate Workbench for easy viewing by recruiters and others with access to the workbench. Interview results can be entered via the SAP SuccessFactors mobile app for easy tracking.

1.3.2   Interview Scheduling

Requisitions with candidates in an interview status can be managed in the **Interview Scheduling** screen. This serves as a dashboard for all requisitions that need interviews scheduled and is a very helpful view for recruiters. Interviews can be scheduled for several candidates at once, reducing the time to get this critical aspect of the talent acquisition process completed. Additionally, recruiters can set up blocks of time for each requisition and have candidates book themselves into open interview slots via the candidate portal. Moving this to a candidate self-service capability significantly reduces the coordination and time that recruiters and coordinators spend trying to get interviews scheduled.

1.3.3   Offer Approval and Offer Letters

After a successful candidate is identified, it's necessary to draft the details of an offer and get it approved. Recruiting provides an offer approval functionality that pulls data from the requisition, application, and candidate profile into a template and allows Recruiting users to enter other candidate-specific information to craft the offer. A workflow is tied to the offer to support sending it through various levels of approval. The workflow can be predefined or completely ad hoc.

After all necessary parties approve the offer details, an offer letter can be drafted from the details of the offer. SAP SuccessFactors provides a library of offer letter templates to choose from, and the particulars are dynamically populated into the candidate-specific offer letter via tokens. Options such as electronic acceptance and electronic signature with DocuSign integration support easy management of the offer acceptance.

1.3.4   Employee Referral

One of the best sources of qualified candidates is often your existing employees. With an employee referral program, a company's employees can recommend qualified candidates for openings and be compensated if they are eventually hired. The SAP SuccessFactors employee referral capability supports tracking program payouts and also allows recruiters to easily identify candidates as an employee referral for proper disposition. Employees can track their referrals all the way through the process easily via the **Referral Tracking** tab on their candidate portal on the careers page as shown in Figure 1.13.

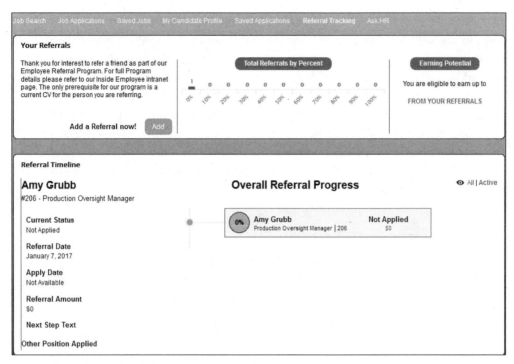

Figure 1.13 Referral Submission and Tracking

1.4 Candidate Features

Companies today understand that their employer branding must be compelling and that candidate experience is critical. In a competitive talent market, every click and every second counts to draw in those highly sought-after candidates. Often the first interaction a candidate has with an organization is through the career site. It's important to make a great first impression and back that up with useful content and easy navigation. Candidates are often also your customers or potential customers, and bad candidate experience can lead to losing out on great employees as well as losing customers. The more time it takes candidates to get to the application, the more likely they are to lose interest and move on.

The design principles that drive the look and feel of a career site should always bear the candidate experience in mind. Recruiting Marketing contains several features that help ensure a good candidate experience. In this digital age, web surfers lose interest within seconds; the candidates you desire will come to your site with specific needs and will be looking for certain things. You must grab their attention immediately and make it as easy as possible to set up a profile and apply for jobs. Increasingly, candidates are using their tablets and mobile devices and searching for jobs on the go. Recruiting Marketing offers optimized career sites that support mobile job search and application. This not only significantly broadens your reach to top candidates but also speaks to the technology focus a company has with keeping up to date with latest advancements.

When building your career site, good design principles should touch on the following:

- Targeted content
- Job searches
- Talent community
- Application process

Let's review each one in more detail.

1.4.1   Targeted Content

Career site content is critical in garnering candidate attention and making the case for why they should apply for a job. The Recruiting Marketing platform makes it easy for candidates to find what they are looking for from the moment they hit the site. Elements such as strategy pages will easily direct candidates to the jobs they are seeking. Recruiting Marketing offers consistent navigation throughout the site, with job search options on every page. This ensures that candidates can always search for jobs. After all, that's the main reason candidates visit a career site! Consistent headers and footers are used to ensure smooth navigation so candidates don't get frustrated and give up before they apply or join a talent community. The career site framework includes pages for general company content, such as benefits, culture, values, and beliefs, as well as targeted jobs pages that group similar jobs and job description pages. Other typical elements of a Recruiting career site include the following:

- Home or main landing page
- Interactive job map page
- Ability to join the company's talent community

- Strategy pages to highlight specialized or high-volume jobs
- Company pages
- Search engine optimization (SEO) pages
- Job description pages
- Subscribe and apply business cards
- Talent community emails
- Mobile site

With these components and easy to add and maintain *widgets,* you can build a career site that provides an optimal experience for your candidates. Figure 1.14 provides an example of a careers page with multiple widgets that allow candidates an easy jumping off point for what they are looking to do.

Figure 1.14 Example of Recruiting Marketing Career Pages with Numerous Widgets to Engage Candidates in Finding Jobs

1.4.2   Job Searches

Candidates have thousands of ways to search for jobs today. The Internet is full of job posting services such as Monster, CareerBuilder, LinkedIn, and other industry-specific channels. Jobs are also posted directly on company sites. Even before candidates land on your career site, they may be finding your jobs based on Internet searches. Recruiting Marketing includes search engine optimization (SEO) features that help your jobs get found through Internet searches and that drive candidates to your career site. On the career site, candidates can find jobs in multiple ways. Candidates can start a search for jobs by keyword and/or location. They can then further filter the search results by additional criteria, such as title and date posted. Candidates can also use the option to view all jobs that are currently posted and then filter the results from there.

Depending on how you implement your Recruiting Marketing site, candidates can also search for jobs using a map and drill down by location to find available jobs. You can also design your career site to group open jobs together on what are called strategy pages. Strategy pages are generally used for high-volume or difficult-to-fill positions. Examples of strategy pages where jobs are grouped include professionals, recent graduates, sales, professional services, and so on. Candidates can navigate to these pages to learn more about these types of positions and see all jobs currently open in that area. Candidates can also further filter the jobs by criteria such as job title, location, and date posted.

1.4.3   Talent Community

Joining a company's talent community has benefits both for the company and the candidate. Candidates can register in the talent community by creating a very basic profile. After becoming a member, candidates can define job alerts so they are emailed when jobs in their areas of interest become available. Figure 1.15 shows two ways candidates can join the talent community, either from a widget by entering their email address or from a talent community page. They can also subscribe to marketing emails, which may contain information about careers or the company. Companies can then market very specific jobs and campaigns to the candidates in these talent communities. They can push notifications about certain new job postings, candidate job interests, and any upcoming events or relevant news.

Figure 1.15 Joining the Talent Community

1.4.4   Application Process

After a candidate finds a job of interest, it should be easy to apply. Candidates can be given the option to apply directly, apply with LinkedIn, or apply with Facebook. When applying directly for a job, candidates are prompted to enter their email address. If they are already a member of the talent community based on that email address, candidates are prompted to log in and begin the application process. New users are directed to the Business Card to enter their personal information and be added to the talent community. If candidates choose **Apply with LinkedIn** or **Apply with Facebook**, the system will prompt them to log in and will extract data from their social media profiles to map to their candidate profile in Recruiting.

SSO is used to seamlessly pass external candidate data from the **Marketing Career** page to the candidate database within Recruiting for searches and more detailed profile information, as well as for candidates to complete the application process.

1.5   Recruiter Features

Recruiting Marketing gives companies the ability to build up a large database of candidates who are interested in working for the company. This can be a huge advantage when sourcing candidates for specific positions. Recruiters can leverage this database in multiple ways. In this section, we'll briefly review tools such as analytics, talent community groups and marketing, and the URL builder, and then we'll touch on how these can be used to more effectively execute a talent acquisition strategy.

1.5.1   Analytics

The Recruiting Marketing Dashboard is a key feature of the product that allows you to view data collected on the people who come to your career site—whether they just visit, join the talent community, or apply for a position (Figure 1.16). Recruiters can run reports on this information, set up alerts, and mine data from the talent community, including when and how many people are coming to the career site and where they are coming from.

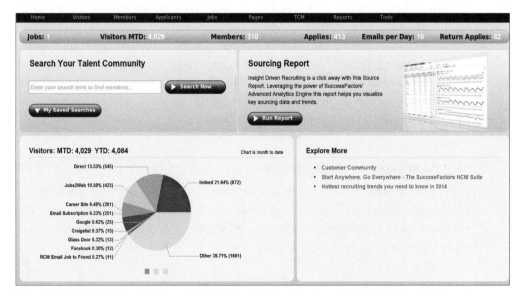

Figure 1.16 Valuable Candidate and Application Data on the Recruiting Marketing Dashboard

The dashboard allows recruiters to analyze, for example, which sources are most effective in bringing in candidates to the career site. Following are examples of Recruiting Marketing Dashboard reports:

- Visitors by location
- Visitors by day and time
- Members overview
- Applicants overview
- Applicants by job
- Jobs overview
- Most visited pages

1.5.2 Talent Community Groups

A company's talent community can, and should, grow quite large over time as more and more visitors come to the career site and register or apply for jobs. You can make the talent community more manageable by creating member groups to broadly group talent community members. Creating a group is as simple as defining a name for the group and a keyword. The system searches the talent community for all candidates with that keyword associated, either via a keyword search or a job application. After you create a member group, the group can be defined so that new members are automatically assigned to the group as they join the talent community or apply for jobs. Member groups tie in with talent community marketing (TCM) because TCM emails are generally sent to groups of candidates.

1.5.3 Talent Community Marketing

TCM allows you to create branded email communications and send them to candidates or groups of candidates in the talent community. You can also measure the effectiveness of these communications, including the number of recipients, views, clicks, undeliverables, and unsubscribed.

1.5.4   URL Builder

The URL Builder enables you to create coded, source-tracked URLs that drive visitors directly to the career site, to a specific landing page, to a job description, or to join the talent community page. These URLs can be used as links in email signatures, banner ads, or email campaigns. When you create the URL, you define the source and campaign associated with the link, which is used to track visitors who come to the site via that URL.

1.6   Administrator Features

As with other modules of the SAP SuccessFactors suite, Recruiting offers a host of administrative features available via the Admin Center. From the Admin Center, administrators with appropriate permissions can access the tools available to build and maintain the Recruiting Marketing careers page as well as advanced Recruiting analytic data. Let's briefly discuss both of these features next.

1.6.1   Career Site Builder

Career Site Builder allows Recruiting Marketing sites to be built and managed by non-technical users. In other words, the work doesn't need to be done by SAP SuccessFactors professional services. After the wire frame is established by SAP, and appropriate connections are made to integrate the site to the SAP SuccessFactors platform, all of the tools to build and maintain the site are accessible via the Admin Center. Administrators can manage page creation, colors, image uploads, and content through the Career Site Builder user interface. Career Site Builder uses templates and predelivered components as a starting point for building and managing sites. These templates can then be customized to business requirements. Delivered components include search, text, image, scrolling image, and so on.

Most of the configuration takes place directly in the **Manage Career Site Builder** screen in admin tools, allowing administrator self-service for career site updates, edits, and changes. Figure 1.17 shows some of the options available from within Career Site Builder, accessible under the Recruiting options in Admin Center.

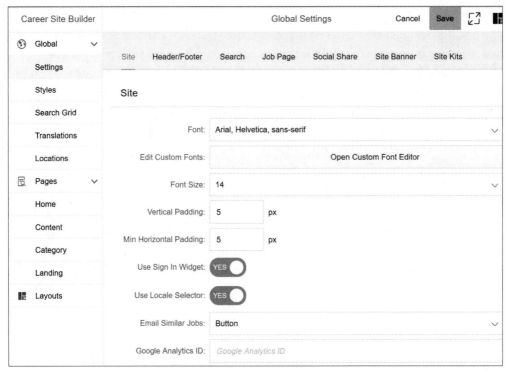

Figure 1.17 Career Site Builder Self-Service Options for Administrators to Build and Maintain External Career Pages

1.6.2   Advanced Analytics

Advanced Analytics in Recruiting Marketing is an online tool for companies to view data collected on visitors, members, and applicants who visit their Recruiting Marketing site. Cost data can also be loaded into the system to allow you to drill down to cost per hire.

Advanced Analytics combines the data from the applicant tracking system (ATS) and the Recruiting Marketing system to create full line-of-site data from a candidate's first visit to the career site to the eventual hire.

Advanced Analytics has more sophisticated reporting than the Recruiting Marketing Dashboard, including reports on candidate quality, quantity, cost per hire, time to fill, source behavior, and more.

1.7   Summary

The Recruiting module provides applicant-tracking functionality that allows you to open, approve, and post positions. After the job is approved, it needs to be posted and advertised through various channels to reach the most candidates. When candidates reach your career site, it's one of the most, if not the most, valuable resource a candidate uses when considering working for a company.

Robust marketing analytics can help you develop highly effective, customized sourcing strategies and make more informed investment decisions on how to best allocate often-limited recruiting budgets. Tools such as talent communities, featured jobs, saved job searches, and mobile apply capability help to attract and engage your candidates. SEO tools ensure your jobs are seen by the most candidates and that you receive accurate data about where your jobs are posted. Filling your career site with targeted content and an intuitive design will create the best user experience possible and enable your candidates to find the jobs they are looking for quickly.

In the next chapter, we'll discuss the tools offered by SAP SuccessFactors Recruiting that support initiating and advertising an opening.

Chapter 2
Initiating and Advertising an Opening

The battle for talent begins the moment a job opening is identified. Companies that post their openings quickly to the widest audience will have the advantage in attracting and engaging the best talent in the market. SAP SuccessFactors Recruiting features enable you to build, approve, and post job openings quickly and then push them to the most candidates to give your company that crucial advantage when seeking talent.

Requisitions are the documents SAP SuccessFactors Recruiting uses to store all necessary and desired data on a job opening. The requisition will contain data such as the following:

- Job title
- Job description
- Salary-related information
- Organizational unit and reporting data
- Approvers
- Other data required for approval or reporting
- Posting-specific data such as location and job type

Figure 2.1 provides an example of a portion of a requisition. You define requisition *templates* during the implementation process. Each template contains specific fields, and requisitions are then created against the template. Templates are assigned to a workflow, known as a *route map*, which contains the roles that need to review and approve each requisition. The route map defines who will receive, review, and approve the requisition and in what order.

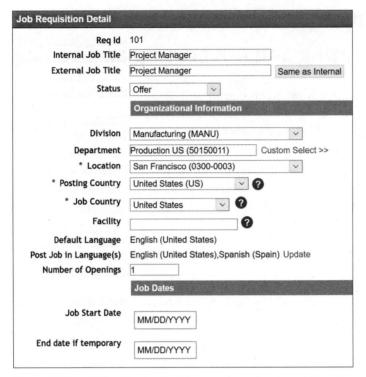

Figure 2.1 Requisition Containing Various Data about a Job Opening

In this chapter, we'll discuss the role requisition templates play in a Recruiting configuration, including considerations such as statuses and field-level permissions. We'll look at requisition workflow and the roles that are configured in Recruiting. Options for prepopulating data attributes onto the requisitions are discussed, including integration from SAP SuccessFactors Employee Central and SAP ERP Human Capital Management (SAP ERP HCM) position management to Recruiting. Options for pre-screening candidates are covered as well as posting the opening after it has been approved.

2.1   Requisition Template, Statuses, and Field-Level Permissions

As with other areas of the SAP SuccessFactors suite, Recruiting is template-based. The requisition template defines the fields that will be included on each requisition, the type of field (e.g., text or picklist), and the field-level permissions available for each of the Recruiting roles in each system status. This template is called the job requisition data model (JRDM), or just the requisition template. In this section, we'll discuss the JRDM first, followed by the requisition statuses and field-level permissions.

2.1.1   Job Requisition Data Model

The system allows you to define numerous JRDMs as your requirements dictate. Requisition templates contain all the fields of data needed in the approval, posting, and filling of open jobs. Requisition templates typically include the following data:

- Approvers and others that need to access the requisition (these are called operators)
- Job-specific data such as job codes
- Salary grade and pay range information
- Detailed job description
- Posting details

Requisition templates can contain different fields or the same fields, depending on what drives the need for an additional template. Requisition templates have a 1:1 relationship to the following elements of the Recruiting configuration that will dictate when an additional template is required:

- Route map
- Application template
- Applicant status pipeline

A few guidelines govern when an additional requisition template is needed, as follows:

- **Route map**
  A requisition template is assigned to one route map. Because there is a 1:1 relationship between requisition templates and route maps, that is the approval workflow. Any time a different approval workflow is required, a new requisition template will be required. This second requisition template can be identical to the original template, or it can contain different fields or permissions, as required.
- **Application template**
  Although features such as country-specific fields and multistage applications allow for many uses of one application template, occasionally there is a need to define additional application templates. Due to the 1:1 relationship between a

requisition template and an application template, defining an additional application template will necessitate an additional requisition template.

- **Applicant status pipeline**
  The applicant status, also known as the talent pipeline, is the process used to evaluate candidates. Again, there is a 1:1 relationship between requisition templates and applicant status pipelines, which will drive needing additional requisition templates if more than one applicant status set is required. An example of this is defining different applicant processes for salaried positions versus hourly positions.

- **Different fields**
  Finally, there is often a need to define different fields from one requisition to another. Obviously, in this case, there will be an additional requisition template required. These additional requisition templates may use the existing route map, application template, and applicant status pipeline, or they can have different elements as requirements dictate.

There is no system limitation to the number of requisition templates that can be supported. However, it's important to keep in mind that additional requisition templates impact not only the configuration needed during implementation but also reporting, available custom fields, mapping to Recruiting Marketing and Onboarding, and ongoing maintenance. It's a best practice to configure to the lowest common denominator with all recruiting templates and try to maintain the same fields for all job openings, keeping the number of templates to the necessary minimum.

2.1.2   Requisition Statuses

Several types of statuses are at work in the Recruiting module. One of the most important types of status is the JRDM system statuses, of which there are three, as follows:

- **Pre-Approved**
  This is the status of the requisition from the moment of creation until the requisition is through the entire route map and has obtained the last approval.

- **Approved**
  Requisitions spend most of their time in **Approved** status. This status occurs after the requisition is approved but before it's closed out.

- **Closed**
  After an opening is filled, the requisition can be closed out.

The three system statuses drive field-level permissions. Each status is permissioned in the JRDM and allows you to define very specific permissions for each recruiting operator role in the three statuses. Figure 2.2 provides an example of the three system statuses within a JRDM.

Figure 2.2 Field-Level Permissions Defined in the JRDM in Pre-Approved, Approved, and Closed Statuses

How does this work practically? When a requisition is in the **Pre-Approved** status, often the roles involved in the approval route map are required to enter or modify data into various fields for it to be approved. In the **Approved** status, it's common to have most fields permissioned to read-only access so that the data can be seen but not updated. In this case, a business will often have at least one role permissioned to edit the fields in case updates are required for any reason. After the position is filled, it's rare to have a need to edit fields on the requisition, so fields are typically permissioned for read access once closed. Let's discuss in more detail how field-level permissions work with the system statuses within the JRDM.

2.1.3   Field-Level Permissions

As mentioned in the previous section, the role of the three system statuses is to enable field-level permissions on the requisition. There are three types of field permissions in the requisition template:

- **Read**
  Fields are visible but can't be edited.

- **Write**
  Fields are visible and available to edit.

- **None**
  Fields have neither read nor write access. This is the default level of permission on the requisition.

Field-level permission means that each field defined on the requisition template can have a different permission depending on what recruiting role is viewing the requisition. For example, all requisitions have an internal and external title as two standard fields. Through field-level permissions, it's possible to permission the recruiter role to write to each field while the hiring manager may only have permission to view (or read) the fields.

To take the field-level permissions even further, you can permission the internal job title and external job title fields differently while the requisition is going through approval (**Pre-Approved** status), after its approved and is "open" (**Approved** status), and then when the position has been filled and the requisition is closed (**Closed** status). In other words, recruiters might be able to write to both fields in the **Pre-Approved** status but to only view these fields in the **Approved** and **Closed** statuses. The hiring manager may only be able to read the fields in all three statuses.

Every field defined on the JRDM is subject to permission within each requisition status and to each recruiting role. Remember that the default level of permission is none, so if a field exists on the requisition template but isn't specifically given a read or write permission in each status to at least one recruiting role, this field will be unavailable.

Field-level permissions within the JRDM is a powerful tool that provides much flexibility in keeping specific data confidential from certain players in the recruiting process while still maintaining it on the same requisition. Let's now discuss approval workflow and the role of operators on the requisition.

2.2 Requisition Workflow and Operators

As mentioned in the chapter introduction, requisitions are documents that have assigned workflows called *route maps*. These route maps define the users that are required to approve the requisition. The operators used in route maps are critical to their function. In Recruiting, six operators are available for use in granting approvals as well granting users access to a requisition once approved. A seventh operator role can be used to grant an ad hoc approver access to view the requisition. Let's discuss workflows, operator roles, and their relation to each other in more detail.

2.2.1 Workflows

Recruiting uses route maps to define approval workflow. This is the same functionality that drives performance management and compensation forms. This *document approval workflow* is different from workflows that are used in Employee Central. Route maps are built in Admin Center and assigned to requisition templates. They are fairly easy to create to support the your needs. The route maps use the Recruiting operator roles that we'll discuss in the next section.

Route maps are comprised of several "steps" that define the path of the requisition, as illustrated in Figure 2.3. Each requisition route map needs to be created or copied in Admin Center and then associated with the appropriate requisition template within the **Form Template Settings** area of Admin Center.

Figure 2.3 Route Map Defining the Approval Workflow of the Requisition

Route map steps can be of two types: a single user step or an iterative step. A single user step involves only one of the Recruiting operator roles, such as the hiring manager. An iterative step can involve two or more users (hiring manager and recruiter) where the document will pass between the users before moving forward. In iterative route map steps, it's necessary to define both an entry user (where the step begins) and an exit user (who can move the step forward). The purpose of the iterative step is to provide more than one role to have input into a requisition before it moves forward in the process.

For example, you may need someone to initiate the requisition and send it to the hiring manager for review, input, or comment before it's sent forward for approval. You can create an iterative route map step with the originator as the entry user, which means it starts with that user, and the hiring manager as the exit user. The requisition can move back and forth between these two users as many times as necessary before the hiring manager decides to "exit" the step and send the requisition on for approval. Each step within the route map can be either **Single Role** or **Iterative**, as shown in Figure 2.4.

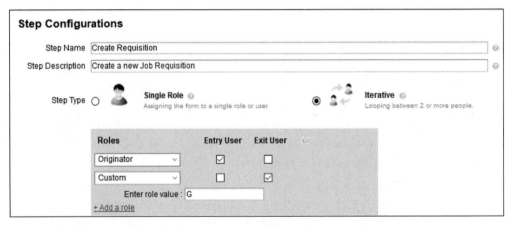

Figure 2.4 Route Map Steps: Single Role or Iterative

2.2.2   Recruiting Operators

Within Recruiting, specific roles have been defined to drive approval and access to the requisition and the data contained within it. These roles are called *recruiting operators* and they are very unique to Recruiting. As stated earlier, there are seven operator roles that can be used within the JRDM configuration. In this section, we'll discuss these roles and how they are used within the recruiting process and configuration.

Operator Roles Available

Up to seven operators can be leveraged across requisition templates to provide user access to the requisition:

- Recruiter (R)
- Hiring manager (G)
- Sourcer (S)

- Coordinator (T)
- Second recruiter (W)
- VP of staffing (Q)
- Approver (V)

Additionally, an originator (O) role is assigned to anyone who creates the requisition, as that user is the originator of the requisition. The originator role can be specifically called out, as shown previously in Figure 2.4, or can be automatically assigned to whomever creates the requisition.

The letters in parentheses after each role name designate each role used in field-level permissions in the JRDM. These letters are very important and must be used as specified. These roles are used to grant access to users in the system to requisitions at various points in the recruiting process. The seven roles are used across all requisition templates that are in place. For example, if you have three requisition templates, you must use the recruiter (R) role consistently on all three templates. The operator roles are standard fields, and their labels are set in provisioning; therefore, it isn't possible to use the R role on one requisition template as "Recruiter" and the R role on another requisition template as "Hiring Manager." When you're designing your requisition templates, it's critical to understand how operator roles are used and their limitations. Operator roles on a requisition are shown in Figure 2.5.

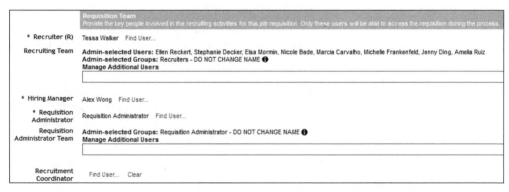

Figure 2.5 Operators Selected to Approve the Requisition with Access to the Requisition and Candidates after Approval

Note that an exception to the use of operator roles is the approver (V) role. This role is specifically designed for users that are added as approvers to the route map using the **Add Approver** feature that can be enabled on the requisition template. It's best practice to include permissions for both the originator (O) and approver (V) in the permission sets within the JRDM. You can also leverage the derivative roles such as second-level and matrix reporting relationships, similar to how you might use these roles in performance management. For example, you may want to send requisitions from the hiring manager to his direct manager for approval before sending on to the recruiter. In this case, you could define a route map step for GM, that is, the hiring manager's (G) manager. The system would then look at what user is defined as the hiring manager and place that user's manager in the **Second Level Manager** field.

You can also leverage matrixed reporting relationships; however, it's important to note that for this to work as desired, users must have matrix managers defined in their user record in SAP SuccessFactors. These derivative roles can be used to extend the seven named operator roles, as required and supported by employee data.

Using Operator Roles

Two types of Recruiting operators are used on the requisition. Operators are involved in the approval process for a requisition, but they are also used after the requisition is approved to grant access to the requisition and the applicants. You can have a recruiter (R), hiring manager (G), and talent acquisition executive (Q) involved in approving requisitions, but then also have an interview coordinator (T) who will need access to the requisitions and applicants after they are approved and posted to schedule candidate interviews. In both cases, operator roles must be defined, and users must be assigned to each role. If a user isn't specifically given a role on a requisition, the user will have no access to view the requisition data, see the applications, or take any action against the open job. Operators are permissioned for fields on the requisition, application, and candidate profile and also for various statuses in the applicant status pipeline.

Unless an operator field is restricted to a defined group of users, any user in the employee database can be selected as any operator on the requisition. The permissions for the requisition are built-in to the JRDM, so no other permissions are required for a user to participate in the recruiting process.

> **Tip**
> The initiator of the requisition will need to have permission to create the requisition template granted in role-based permissions.

While this provides a great amount of freedom, it's best practice to use recruiting groups to limit the pool of users that can be selected for roles other than the hiring manager. Figure 2.6 provides an example of a finite group of users that can be selected to fill the recruiter role on a requisition. This reduces the chance of user error in assigning a user to access a requisition that should be involved in the recruiting process. For example, if there are 100 recruiters within your company, you'll want to define a group of these 100 people and tie it to the **Recruiter (R)** field on the requisition so that no one other than those 100 users may be selected as the recruiter.

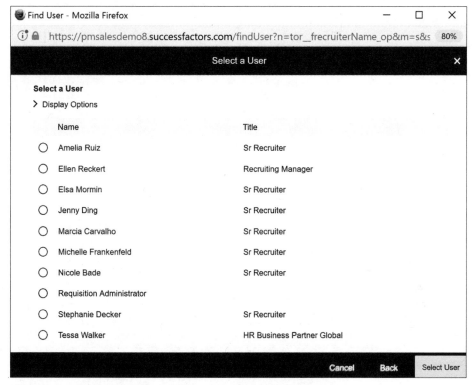

Figure 2.6 Using a Dynamic Group to Limit the Possible Recruiters

Recruiting Team

The *named operator* role enables a single user to access a requisition. This role can be restrictive as many companies manage their recruiting process in a team-based approach with several recruiters or coordinators working the same requisitions. To address this, Recruiting offers the Recruiting Team functionality. This feature provides a corresponding "team" role for each of the main recruiting operator roles. A dynamic recruiting group is used to define the users that are included in each team, and then groups are assigned to requisitions in **Manage Recruiting Team Settings** in Admin Center (see Figure 2.7).

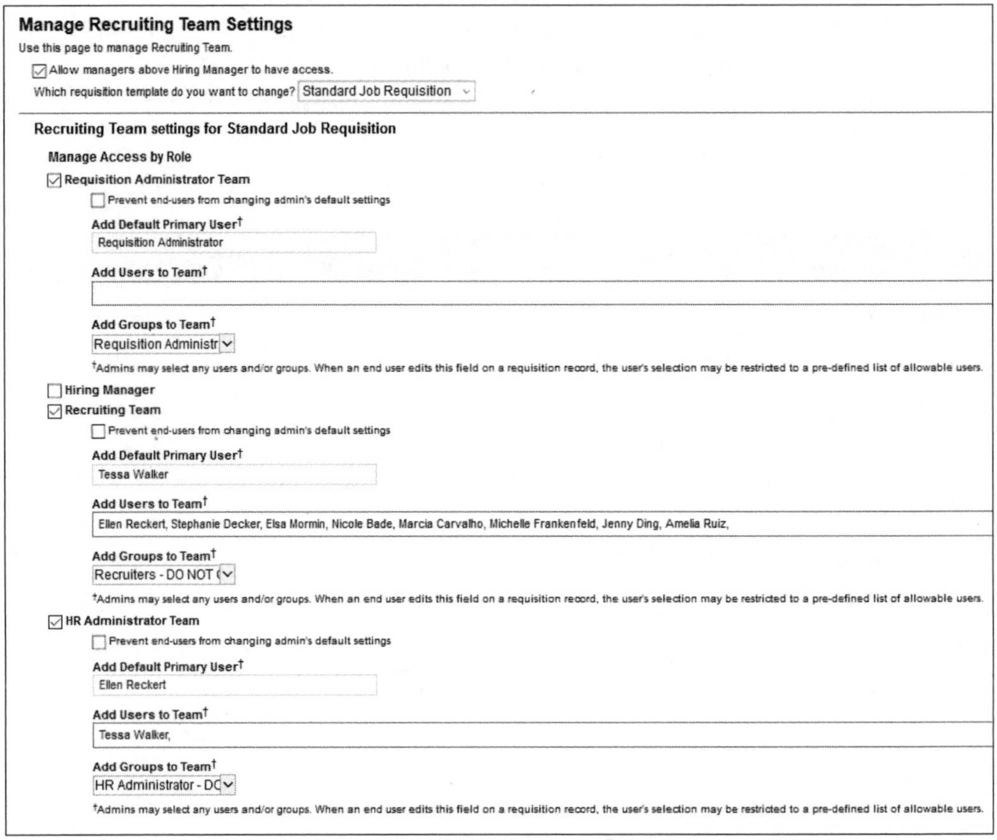

Figure 2.7 Recruiting Team Settings Maintained by JRDM in Admin Center

In addition to assigning recruiting groups to each named operator role, you can also define a default primary user for each role. This user will default in that operator field during the requisition creation process; however, it can be overridden if desired. Additional individual users can also be added to each team role by adding them in the **Add Users to Team** field. It's possible to permission operators to write the **Add Users to Team** field on requisitions so additional users can be granted access on a requisition-by-requisition basis. You should keep tight control on this ability, however, because any user added to the group will have the same access to the requisition and any resulting applications as the named operator.

Permissions for the team role flow from the named operator role. For example, recruiter team permissions within the JRDM adopt the recruiter (R) permissions that are defined; you don't specifically define permissions for any team role. This means that anyone who belongs to the recruiter team Dynamic Group, for example, will have the same permissions as the named recruiter on every requisition. If additional users are added to the team, as just discussed, these users will also have the same permissions as the named operator role. Understanding how the team permissions flow from the operator is critical when designing the JRDM and configuring permissions. Recruiting team permissions apply to approved requisitions, although members of the team can see requisitions in the **Pre-Approved** status. Only the named operators in the route map can approve the requisition.

2.3   Populating Data onto the Requisition

When a requisition is first created, there are several ways to prepopulate data into its fields. This is a huge time-saver for recruiters, hiring managers, and anyone else tasked with initiating the requisition as well as increasing data integrity by eliminating manual entry of critical job data. Maintaining and using data centrally ensures that all requisitions have accurate data with just one place needed to make updates over time. In this section, we'll briefly discuss job profiles within Job Profile Builder, competencies, and job code entity, as well as how each of these can be used to prepopulate data onto a new requisition. Let's begin by looking at job profiles.

2.3.1   Job Profiles via Job Profile Builder

Job Profile Builder is a feature within the platform that replaces the legacy families and roles functionality whereby you could create and maintain a library of job families, roles, and job descriptions. Although you still build a library of job families and roles, Job Profile Builder expands the families and roles capability to allow you to build complete job profiles with multiple content types. Recruiting leverages Job Profile Builder, enabling definition of robust profiles for each job within the organization to be used in talent acquisition. This is especially useful as the standard job description fields on the JRDM are limited in space (4,000 characters) and capability. With job profiles, companies can present a full view to candidates of the requirements of every job by calling out educational requirements, competencies required, certifications necessary, and other descriptive information.

Job profiles are built against templates that drive their look and feel. The templates don't contain content; instead, they define the content types, order of sections, which sections are required, and other formatting. Job profile templates are assigned to job families and can contain any of the following types of information:

- Short description
- Long description
- Certifications*
- Compensation data
- Competencies*
- Conditions of employment
- Education*
- Interview questions*
- Job responsibilities*
- Physical requirements*
- Relevant industries*
- Skills*
- Header
- Footer

Note

The sections marked with an asterisk (*) are populated by selecting from values pre-defined in the **Manage Job Profile Content** section of the Admin Center. They aren't free-form text fields.

Several job profile templates can be defined to fit various needs. As Job Profile Builder resides in the platform, it's shared across multiple modules of the suite, including Recruiting. Accordingly, it's possible to define job profile templates that meet the specific needs of talent acquisition. Figure 2.8 provides an example of a job profile template with various sections of content defined. When building your job profile templates, select the Recruiting options—**Show in Job Requisition** (**Show in internal posting** and **Show in external posting**)—to ensure you can view the profiles when creating requisitions.

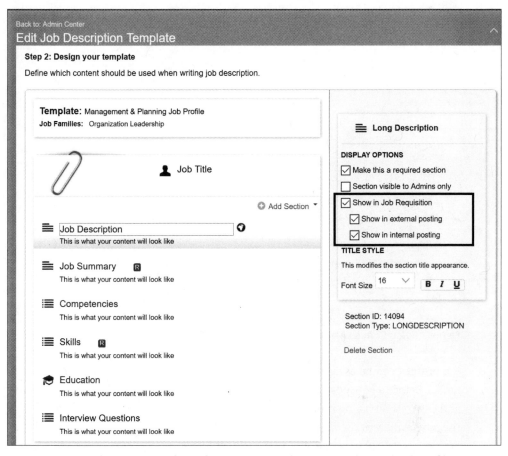

Figure 2.8 Job Profile Templates for Defining the Type of Content within Each Job Profile

After the job profile template is defined, corresponding job profiles are created against the template. While Job Profile Builder replaces the legacy Families & Roles functionality, it's still necessary to build out a structure of job families and job roles. Job profiles are then created and associated to families and job roles as shown in Figure 2.9. After they are activated, the profiles are available to browse from within the requisition creation process. Families, roles, and job profiles can be created manually via the user interface (UI), or they can be imported via a series of import templates. You can also download families and roles from the Success Store, accessible from within Admin Center.

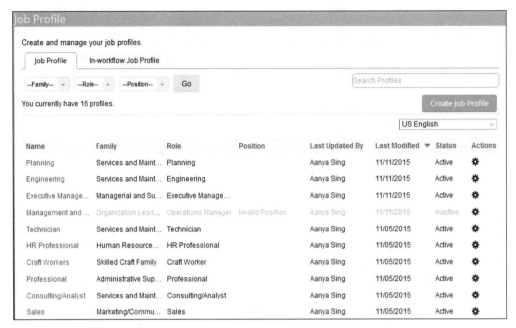

Figure 2.9 Job Profiles Associated with Families and Job Roles

Job profiles can be assigned to a workflow for either initiation/creation or maintenance. Before a new position is posted, it's common to review the job requirements
and ensure everything is up to date and any needed changes have been made. Using
the job profile workflow, it's possible to enable hiring managers, departmental leaders, or those in HR to create or update a job profile as the start of the talent acquisition
process. This helps ensure that all new profiles and all updates are approved by the
necessary parties, and all who need to be made aware are adequately informed. Profile workflow tasks are accessible from the users' to-do list on the home page.

If you choose to use job profiles in your recruiting process, it's advised to discuss the
creation and maintenance requirements for ongoing needs extensively to ensure
this isn't overlooked during implementation. It's also necessary to consider the use
of job profiles across the organization for process areas such as performance management. Because Job Profile Builder is used across the SAP SuccessFactors suite, it's
advised to approach this feature with a broader view than just talent acquisition.

> **Tip**
>
> Job Profile Builder provides an acknowledgement setting that can be used in regulated industries to assure regulatory bodies that employees have been notified of their job description details and have acknowledged receipt of the information. The Job Profile Acknowledgement Report provides key information that can be used to fulfill reporting requirements.

2.3.2   Competencies

Another element from the SAP SuccessFactors platform that is crucial to Recruiting Management is the competency functionality. Competencies are used within Recruiting to facilitate gathering interview feedback on candidates in Interview Central. Competencies against which candidates will be evaluated can be populated on the requisition as it is created by either mapping to the job profile or mapping against roles.

In Section 2.3.1, we discussed the job profile features and how competencies can be defined as a section within a job profile template. If the Recruiting job profile template being used contains a competency section (it should, or you won't be able to use Interview Central), then the individual competencies must be assigned to each job profile as shown in Figure 2.10. Again, this can be done via the UI or an import file. If permissions allow, some operators can edit the competencies on individual profiles on the requisition. This isn't advisable because it allows deviation from the central library of profiles and data contained therein.

If Job Profile Builder isn't being used, competencies are mapped to roles in **Manage Families & Roles** in Admin Center. Again, they can be maintained via the UI or a series of import files. At this point, its best practice to use Job Profile Builder because of the robust capability of defining a full profile rather than just a job description. However, as of publication, the import files for Job Profile Builder can't be automated via a scheduled job, and some businesses opt to remain with the legacy Families & Roles functionality so the family, role, competency, and job description information can be imported automatically via scheduled jobs in the Quartz scheduling tool within provisioning.

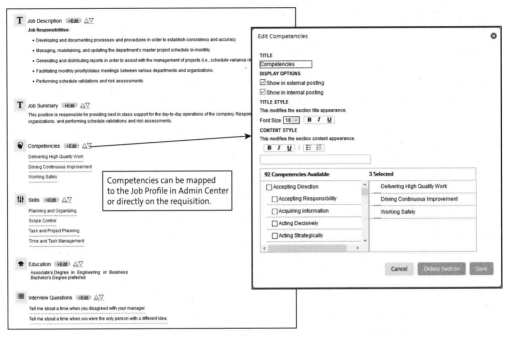

Figure 2.10 Mapping Competencies to the Job Profile and Editing Directly on the Requisition

As demonstrated in Figure 2.10, competencies are mapped from the competency libraries to individual job profiles (or roles). You also see additional sections of the job profile such as **Skills** and **Interview Questions** that are also pulled from a central repository. All of the information within the job profile is displayed to the candidate on the **Job Posting** page. You can see the advantage of using job profiles over a simple **Job Description** field that is just a block of text. Candidates can access more information about the position, can see the requirements for the position, and can make better informed decisions on whether to apply.

2.3.3   Job Code Entity

Job code entity refers to the capability to populate selected job attributes in fields on the requisition when it's created. It works in conjunction with Job Profile Builder, which will populate the job title and description information as discussed in the previous section. Job code entity leverages the job classification foundation object that resides within Employee Central but is available for use for non-Employee Central customers. Typical job attributes configured with job code entity include salary range, pay grade, and organizational structure. However, any type of data may be used to support business requirements. There is no restriction within the functionality to the kind of attributes that are configured. Job code entity fields are limited in number and apply across all requisition templates, just as operator roles do, so it's critical to be discerning when designing the functionality.

When operators create a requisition by the **Browse "Families & Roles"** method, they search the catalog of job families, roles, and then profiles (if using Job Profile Builder). Selecting the job code, as shown in Figure 2.11, determines which row of data will be used to populate the job code fields on the requisition. Note that each role may have one or more job codes mapped to it. When the requisition is opened, not only will the job title and profile (or description) be populated, but also the corresponding job code fields. In this way, the integrity of critical job information is ensured rather than having operators selecting from picklists and entering text that could be incorrect. Correct data on the requisition becomes critical in reporting, onboarding, and processing the new hires into the human resources information system (HRIS).

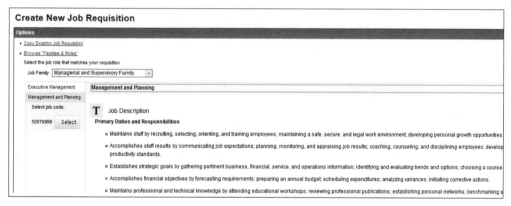

Figure 2.11 Activating the Corresponding Table Entry in the Job Classification Table by Selecting the Job Code

Let's take a more detailed look at job code entity by discussing its configuration, implementation, and limitations.

Configure Job Classification

As previously mentioned, job code entity leverages the job classification foundation object within Employee Central. When this feature is enabled, fields are configured on the job classification object to store the necessary data and are then mapped to corresponding fields on the requisition. The job classification object is a Metadata Framework (MDF) foundation object and must be configured in **Configure Object Definitions** before any data can be loaded into the table. Configuring the job classification object determines the headers for the data import template used to import all of the related job information.

There are 15 `customString` fields available to configure on the JRDM that map to corresponding `custom_string` field definitions on the job classification object. Figure 2.12 shows six `custom_string` fields that have been configured to house job-related data for requisitions. It can't be overstated that because there is one job classification object, the job code fields need to be used consistently across requisition templates. Some `customDate` and `customLong` fields are also available. See Table 2.1 in the next subsection for more information.

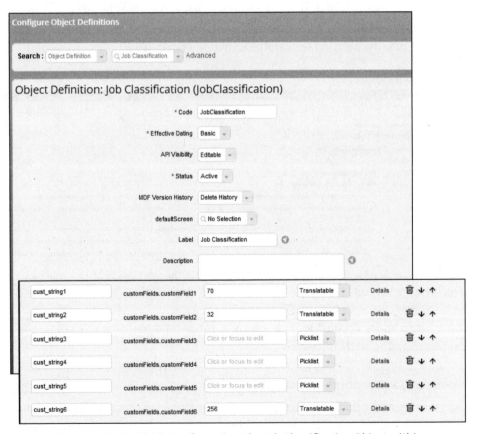

Figure 2.12 customString Fields Configured on the Job Classification Object within Configure Object Definition

Implementing Job Code Entity

Detailed instructions on how to implement job code entity within a Recruiting configuration are provided in the Recruiting Implementation Guide. Here we'll briefly discuss what is required to implement this feature. High-level activities include the following:

- Enable provisioning settings:
  - **Recruiting • Enable Job Code**
  - **Employee Central Foundation Objects**
- Configure the job classification object in **Configure Object Definition**.
- Set up families and roles.
- Set up Job Profile Builder (if necessary).
- Configure job code fields on the JRDM.
- Generate data import templates and load necessary data for the following:
  - Job families, roles, and profiles
  - Job classification
- Schedule automated data imports, as required.

The types and number of fields available to configure within the job code entity feature are listed in Table 2.1.

Field Definition	Field Type
Description	Text (100-character limit)
customString1-15	Text or picklist (100-character limit)
customLong1-5	Integer (no decimals)
customDate1-5	Date

Table 2.1 Types of Fields Available to Configure for Job Code Entity

Job code fields can be locked down from editing after requisition creation. This setting in **Manage Recruiting Settings** works in conjunction with the field permissions in the JRDM. Because the main business driver for implementing job code entity is to maintain data integrity, you should enable this setting. If necessary, allow a super user or administrative role to have write permissions to these fields in case of extraordinary circumstances. If the data is incorrect for a particular job code, it should be updated directly to the job classification object via an accurate import file, not updated on the requisition.

Job Code Entity Limitations

Although there are several benefits to using job code entity, there are also some limitations that should be understood before deciding to use it. First, job code fields are limited to those listed in the Table 2.1. After those fields are expended, you can't define additional fields, which can be limiting if the JRDM contains many data attributes. Because the job code fields are used consistently across all templates, this can be further limiting to the use of this feature.

Secondly, if the values for a given job code are updated in the job classification table after a requisition is created, the changes don't flow to the existing requisitions. Updates will only be reflected in new requisitions created after the update. Additionally, the use of decimals isn't supported in customLong fields, which can impact the formatting of fields in email templates, offer approvals, and offer letters. Finally, job code fields aren't visible for requisition approval via a mobile device, which can hinder the effective use of the mobile requisition approval, as typically the job code data is critical and that's why it has been selected to prepopulate.

Understanding these limitations will help you determine whether this feature will provide value to the Recruiting configuration. Note that if you're already live with Recruiting and aren't using job code entity, this can be configured in your existing configuration.

Job Code Entity versus Mapping Position Data

When we discuss prepopulating job attributes to the requisition during creation, we're not including in this when a requisition is opened from an open position in the position management hierarchy. This method of requisition creation will be discussed further in the next section. Job code entity isn't supported in creating requisitions from an open position because the triggering event is choosing a job code from the library of families, roles, and profiles. This tells the system to access the corresponding row of data in the job classification table and populate those fields accordingly. This doesn't occur when a requisition is opened from the position.

When a requisition is created from the position org chart, no job code is ever selected. Further, the job code entity feature isn't required with this creation method because job attributes are being mapped directly from the position itself. Understanding the differences between these two features is also critical in deciding how either, or both, will play a role in your Recruiting Management configuration.

Let's discuss in more detail the options in using the position management integration with Employee Central position management.

2.4   Creating a Requisition from an Open Position

In addition to the methods already discussed in this chapter, another way for job attributes to prepopulate on a requisition is to enable integration with position management. This integration can be from Employee Central or SAP ERP HCM. We'll discuss the options for integrating Recruiting with both elements from a functional perspective in this section. This won't include a configuration discussion, as that will be covered in Chapter 14.

Different from populating job attributes from the job profile or job code entity, position management integration allows for mapping data housed on the position object to fields on the requisition. This not only populates requisition fields but also initiates the requisition creation.

Businesses using Employee Central will leverage the built-in integration between Employee Central position management and Recruiting. There are no integration packages or middleware required to configure this integration. For businesses that run a hybrid deployment with core HR processes maintained in SAP ERP HCM on premise solution and talent processes maintained in SAP SuccessFactors, SAP delivers a standard integration package to enable SAP ERP HCM to Recruiting integration for creating requisitions from open positions within SAP ERP HCM. This integration requires a middleware connection, such as SAP Process Integration (SAP PI) or SAP Cloud Platform Integration, and is more time consuming to install, configure, and test. In either scenario, the end result is the same: a position becomes open in the organizational structure, and a requisition can then be created. Let's discuss each option.

2.4.1   Employee Central Position Management Integration

The integration between Employee Central position management and Recruiting offers several benefits. Obviously, the prerequisite is that you have position management implemented within your Employee Central landscape. With this integration, requisitions are created not within Recruiting but from the position org chart. The rules engine is used to determine which requisition template should be chosen (if using more than one) and to define the field mapping between the position data and the fields on the JRDM. The system will automatically determine which job profile to assign to the new requisition based on what is maintained on the position.

Requisitions may be created on the current date, immediately making a requisition available within Recruiting. Requisitions may also be created as of a future date, which creates a job requisition processing request in Quartz scheduler. When the future date is reached, the scheduled job will run and create the requisition in Recruiting Management. Be sure to set up the schedule job that runs to create these future dated requisitions in the Quartz scheduling tool in provisioning.

Creating a requisition from an open position has several benefits. First, it ensures the integrity of the data within the requisition because it's populated directly from the job attributes maintained on the position. This reduces the risk of data errors in the recruiting process from operators making incorrect selections while creating the requisition, resulting in fewer downstream data impacts to processes such as onboarding and hiring. Second, when a requisition is created from the position, the subsequent candidate hired will be automatically assigned to the source position in the **Pending Hires** queue in Employee Central.

On the position side, after a requisition has been created, the assigned job requisition (or requisition processing request, if created for a future date) is visible on the **Position** tile. This assumes v12 of the position org chart is in use. It's also possible to display additional job requisition data in the **Position** side panel on the org chart. Let's look at some of the configuration specifics for integrating Recruiting with position management within SAP SuccessFactors as well as SAP ERP HCM.

Configuring Employee Central Position Management to Recruiting Management Integration

The prerequisite to configuring this integration is having a system where both modules are enabled and configured. This integration can be configured completely within Admin Center in the UI. The first step is to enable the integration in **Position Management Settings**. Set the **Use Recruiting Integration** setting to **Yes,** and then select the appropriate entries in the **Rule for Deriving the Job Requisition Template ID** and **Rule for Mapping Fields Between Position and Job Requisition** dropdown lists (see Figure 2.13).

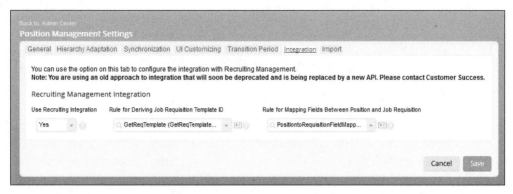

Figure 2.13 Enabling the Position Management to Recruiting Integration

If more than one requisition template is in use, you can use attributes on the position to determine which requisition template will be used to create the requisition. For example, if there is a **Standard Job Requisition** template, you can set a rule to derive this template if the position has a company value of ACME. If there is a **Professional Job Requisition** template, a rule can be set that will derive this requisition template if the position has a job code value of **Consultant** or **Executive**. It's also possible to have a user select the job requisition template from a dropdown menu while initiating the requisition creation.

Use the rules engine to define the field mapping between the position and the JRDM. Note that if you want to use custom fields from the JRDM in the integration, these fields must be visible. Ensure the `custom` attribute in the JRDM is set to `custom="true"` in the XML, or these fields won't be available for mapping. Use the **Map Fields from Position to Job Requisition in Recruiting Integration** option within **Configure Business Rules**. There are requirements to follow to map fields of type date, Boolean, number, country, and foundation object, so be sure to refer to the most recent Implementation Guide for these steps.

All required fields on the requisition must be mapped from the position; otherwise, the requisition won't be created. This should be considered both when designing the attributes maintained on the position as well as when identifying the required fields on the JRDM.

Note

The JRDM templates used for this integration must always have the following standard fields:

- numberOpenings
- positionNumber

Note that these fields don't need to be mapped using a rule because the system fills them automatically.

After the fields have been mapped, the system is in the default setting. Appropriate permissions must be provided in role-based permissions to all impacted roles before any user will be able to successfully create a job requisition from the position. From the **Manage Position** area in role-based permissions (Figure 2.14), select any of the following permissions as appropriate for the role:

- **View Job Requisition in Position Organization Chart**
- **Create Job Requisition in Position Organization Chart**
- **Select Job Requisition Template in Position Organization Chart**

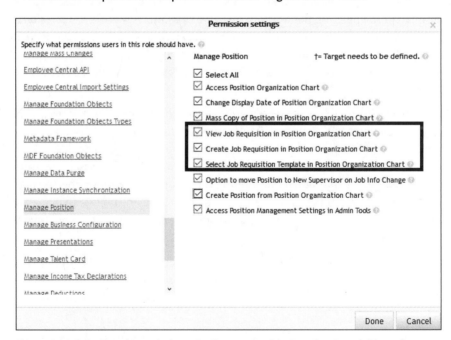

Figure 2.14 Role-Based Permissions Settings to Enable Creating Requisitions from the Position

Creating Requisitions from the Position Organization Chart

After the configuration has been completed, all rules have been built, and appropriate permissions have been granted, requisitions can now be created from the position org chart. Rather than going to Recruiting to create the requisition, users must navigate to the **Position Org Chart** option under the **Company Info** menu. Select the **Position Org Chart** subtab, and then search for the position for which you desire to create a requisition. Positions may be searched by **Position ID** or by the incumbent who holds the position.

Select the **Position Title** to display the position details and options. In the top-right corner of this box, select the icon (three parallel lines) to display the action menu, as shown in Figure 2.15. If the user has the appropriate permissions, the **Create Job Requisition** option will be displayed. Select this option, and the system creates the requisition based on the configuration.

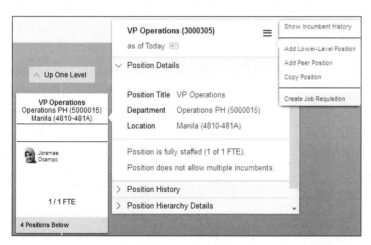

Figure 2.15 Creating a Requisition from a Position on the Position Org Chart

The system flashes a quick message that the requisition was successfully created, and the position org chart will refresh with requisition details now available in the **Position Details** window (Figure 2.16). This information will be updated as the requisition progresses through its lifecycle. The requisition details provided include the following:

- Requisition ID
- Template name
- Job title
- Status (will always be **Pre-Approved** when first created)

- Number of openings
- Number of candidates
- Job requisition originator
- Hiring manager
- Job requisition creation date

After the requisition is created, the operators in the route map must be added so the system knows to whom to send the requisition. This should be considered when defining not only the route map steps and whether they are single-user or iterative but also within the JRDM permissions. If the initial operator doesn't have permissions to write to the operator fields, or you haven't permissioned the originator (O) role appropriately, the requisition won't be able to move forward. Open the requisition, either directly from the position org chart or by navigating to the **Recruiting** page, and fill in the operator fields. Save the requisition to populate the approvers in the route map.

Figure 2.16 Requisition Details from the Position Details Tile

2.4.2   SAP ERP HCM Integration Add-On for Recruiting Management

If you run a talent-hybrid landscape with core HR processes maintained in SAP ERP HCM and leveraging Recruiting Management, there is also an integration that will bring position data from SAP ERP HCM over to SAP SuccessFactors to initiate requisitions. Detailed information about this integration package can be accessed at *https://uacp2.hana.ondemand.com/viewer/p/SFIHCM* by choosing **Integration Add-On for SAP ERP HCM and SuccessFactors HCM Suite**. Be sure to reference the most recent service pack when accessing the information. If customers maintain open positions within SAP ERP HCM, position data can be exported from the SAP ERP system and mapped to fields on the requisition template in Recruiting. The benefits of using an open position to initiate a requisition were discussed in the previous section, and there is no difference in these benefits if a business uses Employee Central position management or SAP ERP HCM for its core HR processes.

In the integration add-on, there are fields used by default to transfer job requisition data from positions within SAP ERP over to SAP SuccessFactors. These fields map to standard fields in Recruiting and are assigned to the SAP_REQ_DEMO field set. After the requisition is created in Recruiting, the requisition ID is transferred back to the SAP ERP system. The requisition ID is stored in Infotype 1107 (SFSF Job Requisition).

> **Tip**
>
> When configuring this integration, be sure to add the originator (O) role to the route map workflow as the first step and permission O for all write permissions in **Pre-Approved** status. It's also advised to map the hiring manager **UserID** field in SAP ERP to both the `originator` and `hiringManagerName` fields within SAP SuccessFactors.

Numerous fields within SAP ERP can be mapped to the SAP SuccessFactors requisition. These are general fields and fields from Infotype 1005 (Planned Compensation). Table 2.2 shows the required fields that must be mapped from SAP ERP HCM to SAP SuccessFactors to support the integration with the destination field ID in Recruiting Management.

SAP ERP HCM Field	SAP SuccessFactors Field ID
GUID of Job Requisition	Guid
Requisition Originator	Originator
Position ID	sapPositionID
Job Name	Title
Requisition Creation Date	dateCreated
Requisition Closed Date	jobCloseDate

Table 2.2 Required Fields to Be Mapped between SAP ERP HCM and SAP SuccessFactors

SAP ERP HCM Field	SAP SuccessFactors Field ID
Job Requisition State	jobReqStatus
Job Requisition Status	Status

Table 2.2 Required Fields to Be Mapped between SAP ERP HCM and SAP SuccessFactors (Cont.)

Refer to the Integration Add-On documentation for a full listing of available fields that can be used in the integration.

2.5   Prescreening Questions

One of the usability features of Recruiting is the ability to prescreen candidates based on a predefined set of criteria. Prescreening questions can be included on the requisition and are presented to candidates in the application process. These prescreening questions may be used to gather information, score the applicant, and automatically disqualify them from consideration. Prescreening questions are assigned to the requisition and are presented at the bottom of the application form during the initial application process. Let's look at how you can maintain and assign these questions as well as how applicant responses may be viewed.

2.5.1   Maintaining and Assigning Questions

Questions are maintained in a library and are accessible to permissioned operators on the requisition. Questions may be created directly on the requisition or pulled from a central library maintained in Admin Center. All questions should be maintained centrally in one or more libraries and then added to requisitions as needed to ensure consistency in how the questions are presented to all applicants. Because the questions can be scored and used to automatically disqualify applicants, its best to ask the question the same way, with the same possible responses, for every applicant. You can create several different "libraries" of questions that can be used to categorize the types of questions within each library, as shown in Figure 2.17. This is helpful to guide operators regarding which questions to add to requisitions. Examples are required questions, basic screening, minimum qualifications, and so on; there is no limitation to the number of sublibraries you maintain to organize questions.

Questions are assigned on the requisition and set as **Required, Disqualifier,** or **Score**. For a question to be used as a disqualifier, it must also be required. You can browse from the question library to find, select, and add all the questions to the requisition at once.

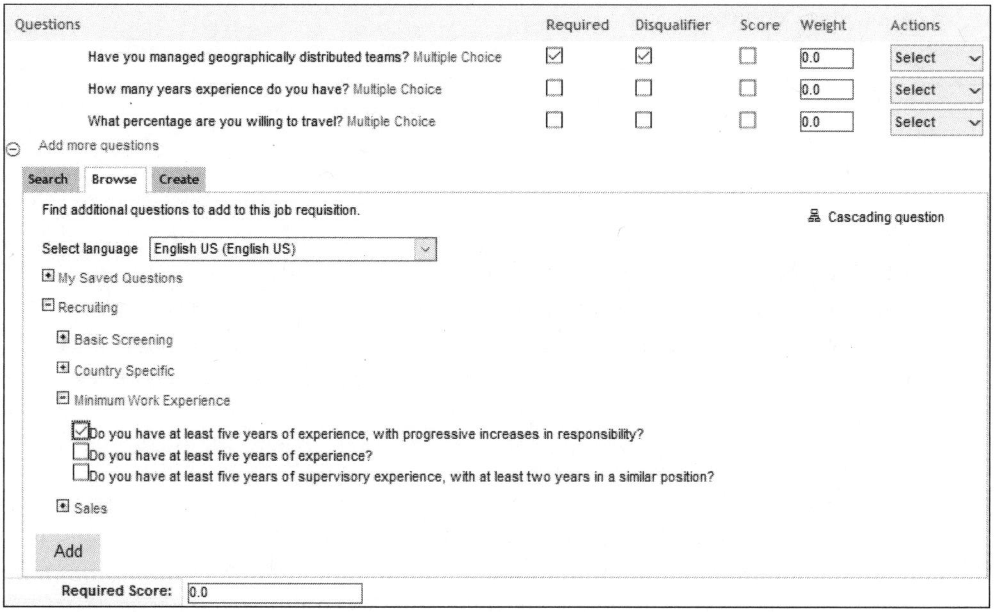

Figure 2.17 Questions Assigned on the Requisition and Set as Required, Disqualifiers, or Scored

Questions can't be prepopulated on the requisition the way competencies can be. They must be individually added to each requisition. A user with write permission to the question field can use the **Add more questions** link to select from the library and add individual questions to the requisition. If a requisition is copied from an existing requisition, the same questions are used on the new requisition. It's best practice to permission questions as read only after the requisition has been approved.

If questions are changed after the requisition has been posted and applicants have applied, the user changing the question will be prompted upon save to allow existing applicants to be reevaluated and those that have been disqualified may possibly be un-disqualified based on the new criteria. To receive the prompt to reevaluate existing applicants, the user saving the requisition with changes to questions must have permission to status the applicants in the talent pipeline. This could obviously lead to charges of unfair hiring practices or discrimination and could cause unintended consequences, so it's best to leave questions untouched after requisitions have been posted.

Questions can be set up in various types, as follows:

- Multiple choice
- Rating scales
- Numeric
- Free text

Questions may be marked as required, meaning the applicant must answer before submitting their application. Required questions can also be selected as disqualifiers, where choosing the incorrect answer will filter the applicant to the automatic disqualified status. Finally, questions may be scored to produce an average rating. If the questions are scored, use the weight attribute to determine the number of "points" the applicant will receive for the response. In addition to making individual question disqualifiers, you can set a required score for all questions. If the applicant's total score of all questions doesn't meet this threshold, the applicant is automatically disqualified.

You can also have *cascading* questions. These are questions with parent-child relationships where the candidate's response to the parent question will present an additional question. These cascading questions can only be set up with one level of child relationship and must be created via the import file. You can't create cascading questions via the UI within Admin Center. These types of questions can be helpful in gaining clarifying information from candidates on the initial question. For example, you may want to ask applicants if they have experience relevant to the job with a "yes" or "no" answer. If they respond "yes" to this parent question, you inquire further with a child question regarding their years of experience.

2.5.2   Viewing Question Responses

After applications have been submitted, operators with read permission to the `questionResponse` field on the application will see a section called **Screening Details** in the Candidate Workbench, listing the applicant's responses to the prescreening questions (see Figure 2.18). If operators also have permission to view the `averageRating` field, a **Rating** column will be displayed in the Candidate Workbench dashboard that contains the sum of all points assigned to weighted questions. The **Average Rating** column can be sorted from highest to lowest to rank applicants by prescreening results.

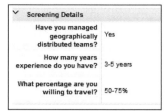

Figure 2.18 Screening Details Portlet from the Candidate Details Screen

2.6   Advertising the Opening

In Chapter 1, we briefly introduced the methods of posting jobs to various channels for internal employees and external candidates. As every talent acquisition professional can attest, the secret ingredient to finding the best candidates is putting your job openings where they are. SAP SuccessFactors has a variety of options that can be used as standalone, or in concert, to advertise your openings to the widest possible audience of candidates. In this section, we'll take a closer look at the options Recruiting offers to advertise openings, both internally and externally.

2.6.1   Internal Candidates

In Recruiting terms, every employee is an internal candidate. Each employee has an employee profile (or people profile if that is in use) that contains information about the employee's experience, skills, capabilities, and professional affiliations. This information comprises the employee's résumé for talent management purposes and is searchable via Talent Search. Because employees often want to change jobs and look for new opportunities within the company, they are also candidates, and, in Recruiting, they will also have a candidate profile. This candidate profile will contain much of the same data that are on the employee/people profile, but it may also contain information that is more applicable for Recruiting purposes. While the people/employee profile makes up the employee's talent résumé, the candidate profile houses their professional résumé where the actual résumé file is uploaded and stored.

Employees will search for openings on the careers page within SAP SuccessFactors. This is where all the jobs that are posted to the **Internal Career Site Posting** field are displayed. Because this is actually a separate page from where external job postings are displayed, it can have its own set of search filter criteria. Companies commonly include criteria that are meaningful for employees to enable them to find the jobs they seek, whereas the external search criteria are focused on helping external candidates find the right jobs. Companies will often choose to display the name of the hiring manager on the careers page to help employees know to whom they would report (see Figure 2.19).

Figure 2.19 Hiring Manager Name Provided in the Search Results on the Careers Page for Internal Candidates

Many companies will have a policy that jobs must first be advertised internally before looking outside. The system supports this policy very well and allows recruiters the option of setting up these staggered dates at one time rather than having to remember to go back and post a job externally after a period of time. This option also applies to agency postings, as will be discussed in Chapter 5.

> **Note**
>
> The candidate profile is designed to be synced with the employee profile so that employees need only enter and update information in one place while making the information available in both. This is best practice.

SAP SuccessFactors also understands that sometimes recruiters need to fill a job that hasn't been vacated yet or is otherwise confidential, and so having it posted publicly isn't possible. The internal private posting feature enables you to post the job and then invite select internal candidates to apply for it. The job is still posted on the careers page, but it isn't visible to the public. The only way to view the job is to have the actual URL to the job posting. Recruiters can email this link to internal candidates where they can view the job profile and submit an application (as discussed in Chapter 1).

To use this feature, the **Internal Private Posting** field must be added to your JRDM and permissioned for write access to appropriate recruiting roles so jobs may be posted there.

2.6.2   External Posting Options

One of the most robust features of Recruiting is the almost unlimited options companies have available to post jobs outside of their company. In this section, we'll look at each of the options available to post jobs to external candidates, to external Recruiting users, and to multiple job boards.

External Postings via the External Careers Page

Any jobs that are posted to the external career site will be pushed to the careers page. From there, external candidates can view the jobs, join talent communities, set up job alerts to automatically be notified of jobs that interest them when they are posted, and apply via mobile apply. Refer to Chapter 1, where we discussed elements of the careers page and the options that candidates have for searching for jobs.

External Private Posting

Just as private postings are supported for internal candidates, private postings can be made accessible to external candidates as well. The feature works the same as internal private postings, but the job is pushed to the external page and will have a different URL. When recruiters provide this URL to candidates, they are taken to the external posting page to view the job profile and submit an application through the normal process. When a job is posted privately, there is a link icon to the right of the posting type where the URL is accessed.

External Private Posting is a separate field, just like **Internal Private Posting**, and it also must be configured on all applicable JRDM templates and permissioned for write access. If you don't see these fields on the **Job postings** page, as shown in Figure 2.20, you either don't have permission to this field, or it has not been configured in your JRDM.

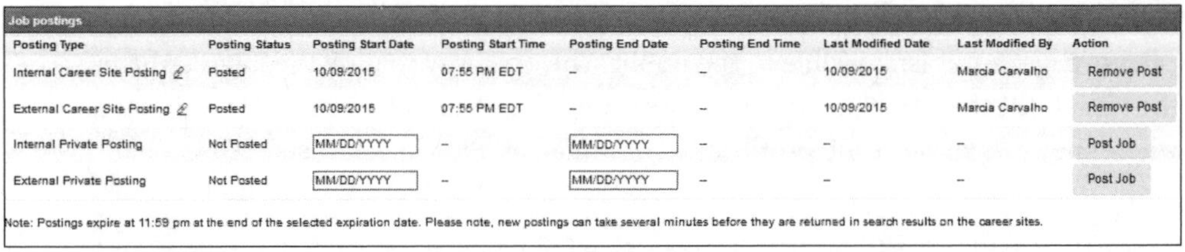

Figure 2.20 Job Postings Page Showing Internal and External Private Postings

SAP SuccessFactors Recruiting Posting

Late in 2015, SAP acquired Multiposting, a French company that was a European leader in job posting solutions. The Multiposting product has now been integrated into the Recruiting offering as SAP SuccessFactors Recruiting Posting to provide you with an integrated method of efficiently posting jobs to a global network comprising thousands of channels. With the Recruiting Posting offering, you have access to the following:

- More than 1,000 general and niche job boards globally
- 2,500 university job boards and alumni networks
- Social networks

Recruiting Posting is based on credits and slots. Each credit allows you to post one job to as many job boards as you need for 30 days. Credits can be easily managed from within the tool where you can maintain all the contract information for the job boards with which you interface. Job board credits can be allocated easily among users or groups of users.

In total, Recruiting Posting offers you a choice of more than 4,000 integrated sources around the globe in more than 80 countries that you can access from the job board marketplace and easily make available for posting. The multilingual capability of Recruiting Posting supports the ability to post the same job in multiple languages as required.

With Recruiting Posting, companies will have extended visibility of the effectiveness of the source channels and can take advantage of advanced analytics and candidate tracking. Detailed cost analysis is available on the following:

- Cost per résumé per click for each job board used
- Number of applications received to evaluate whether any improvements are needed to increase job performance

With Recruiting Posting in place, recruiters have access to Marketing Central where the Recruiting Posting platform is accessed and where the workflow for each job starts. After the Recruiting Posting platform is accessed by choosing **Market Job** in the **Requisition Actions** area (see Figure 2.21), recruiters select the general and specialist job boards where the job should be posted. Posting information is pulled from SAP SuccessFactors and populated in the Recruiting Posting fields. Jobs can be posted immediately or scheduled for a later time.

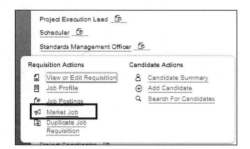

Figure 2.21 Choosing Market Job from the Requisition Actions Menu in Recruiting Posting

Jobs are posted with a SAP SuccessFactors-specific URL so that candidates are returned to SAP SuccessFactors to submit their application. After candidates submit applications, the **Source** column in the Candidate Workbench is updated with the specific job board from where the candidate found the job. Recruiting Posting analytics are tracked and available within Recruiting Marketing.

With the Recruiting Posting offering as part of the Recruiting suite, you have a huge network of channels within which to advertise their open jobs, increasing their opportunities to attract the best candidates.

At the time of publication, Recruiting Posting was implemented only by SAP Professional Services and is estimated to take six to eight weeks. This should be considered when embarking on a Recruiting implementation that includes Recruiting Posting so it can be built-in to the overall project timeline and detailed plan.

Job Board Posting via eQuest integration

If you use eQuest to manage job board postings, SAP SuccessFactors offers prebuilt integration so jobs can be posted to eQuest directly from the **Job postings** page. We briefly discussed this in Chapter 1, but we'll look at the specifics of the configuration in this section. The integration is very straightforward to configure, but you must have an existing relationship with eQuest and have purchased postings to use in your eQuest account. Enabling this integration allows you to select which job boards you want eQuest to post to, and you can manage these from within the Recruiting **Job postings** page.

Standard fields need to be configured on the JRDM to capture the data required by eQuest to support the job postings. Note that the standard **Country** field is an eQuest integration field, but it's leveraged for other functionality within SAP SuccessFactors such as configuring country-specific overrides on application fields.

After the JRDM has been properly configured, set up is required in Admin Center under the **Set Up Job Board Options** area of Recruiting. Note that eQuest does provide a test environment so this integration can be configured and tested in your test instance. Refer to the latest version of the Recruiting Implementation Guide for specifics on configuring this integration.

Agency Posting

SAP SuccessFactors provides a portal to enable companies to post their jobs and grant access to recruiting agencies and other external recruiters. The agency portal supports these postings and is discussed in Chapter 5.

2.7   Summary

In this chapter, we discussed the elements of Recruiting related to initiating and advertising an opening. JRDM templates define the fields of data that are needed for approval. The number of templates required will be determined by the number of unique approval workflows, talent status pipelines, and application templates needed. Recruiting leverages discreet operator roles that are baked into the templates and drive field-level permissions.

Various data attributes can be prepopulated onto the requisition at the point of creation, depending on the kind of data. Tools such as Job Profile Builder enable robust descriptions and requirements to be built and presented to candidates, including elements such as competencies required for the job. Maintaining this information centrally not only ensures that it's consistent across the organization but also that it can be populated when the requisition is created. Job code entity is used to populate critical pay range, salary grade, and organizational structure data onto requisitions by leveraging the job classification foundation object within Employee Central.

If you use position management, either within Employee Central or in SAP ERP HCM, integration exists to create requisitions from open positions within the employee data. With this integration in place, data are shared from the position and populated onto the requisition when it's created. This eliminates the risk of data entry errors and ensures that when candidates are selected for hire, there are already open, approved positions in which to hire them.

Recruiters can begin evaluating candidates even from the initial application by using prescreening questions on the requisition. These questions can be used to automatically disqualify candidates based on incorrect answers or to generate a rating that can be used to compare candidates against each other and the data gathered in the questions. This can be a valuable and time-saving feature for recruiters who often have to sort through hundreds of candidates for a single opening.

Finally, we discussed all the avenues that SAP SuccessFactors provides for advertising open jobs. From making openings available to internal employees by posting them on the careers page, to leveraging the external page supported by Recruiting Marketing or using the agency portal, SAP SuccessFactors makes it easy and accessible for recruiters to post and manage their postings from one location. With tools such as eQuest integration (for Recruiting Management-only users) and the newer Recruiting Posting offering, companies have almost unlimited avenues through which to push their jobs to multiple channels.

In the next chapter, we'll discuss the candidate experience within Recruiting.

Chapter 3
Candidate Experience

Poor candidate experience negatively affects employers' ability to hire good talent. According to a 2016 study by Future Workplace and CareerArc, 80% of job seekers said they would be unlikely to consider other job openings at a company that failed to notify them of their application status. However, they would be 3.5 times more likely to reapply to a company if they were notified.

Although both internal and external candidates will interface with SAP SuccessFactors Recruiting in their search for new opportunities, their experiences will be very different. Internal candidates, your current employees, will go directly to the job search page from within SAP SuccessFactors. External candidates will access your career site from a variety of avenues as they search for jobs and hopefully submit applications. SAP SuccessFactors Recruiting Marketing offers a series of features focused on enhancing a candidate's experience while interacting with the career site, including talent communities, business cards, and job search options.

When candidates start job hunting, they search for jobs and research companies. The marketing tools within Recruiting can give companies an edge in competing for talent by making it easier for candidates to find their career sites, by providing quality content in an intuitive layout, and by providing a way for candidates to stay in touch with the company.

In this chapter, we'll discuss the candidate experience, both internal and external, while interacting with your Recruiting system. We'll discuss the use of talent communities, the business card and candidate profile, responsive design through mobile apply, job search options, and language translations.

Let's begin by discussing the experience of internal candidates.

3.1 Internal Candidate Experience

When we talk about internal candidates, we're referring to your current employees. Recruiting views all employees as "candidates" and assigns them a candidate profile that likely leverages data from their employee profile. SAP SuccessFactors recognizes that these candidates often have needs unique from external candidates seeking jobs within your organization, and it provides tools to interact with internal candidates differently from externals. Every internal candidate resides in the candidate database and can be searched in candidate search. They also are distinguished from external candidates for purposes of communicating with them via automatic emails tied to an applicant status. You can specify email templates for internal candidates that are different from those you use for external candidates. Additionally, you can communicate with an internal candidate's current manager.

Let's look at the experience an internal candidate has within Recruiting, including the following:

- Searching for jobs
- Maintaining the candidate profile
- Submitting employee referrals

3.1.1   Internal Candidate Job Search

If internal candidates want to seek additional opportunities within the organization, they log in to SAP SuccessFactors and select the **Careers** tab. This is where all of their candidate activity will occur, including searching for jobs, maintaining their candidate profile, viewing submitted applications, scheduling interviews, and managing any employee referral activity. The **Careers** tab and **Job Search** page are shown in Figure 3.1.

Access to the **Careers** tab is managed within role-based permissions so you can select which employees can access it and which can't. When candidates access the **Careers** tab, they are brought immediately to the **Job Search** page. Here they can enter any combination of search criteria to help them find jobs of interest. There is space on this page for you to provide messaging to your internal candidates through graphics, links, and other communications. This page is maintained within Admin Center and will be discussed further in Chapter 8.

Because Recruiting supports posting jobs to the internal page separately from your external site, there may be jobs available to internal candidates that aren't available to externals or vice versa. Candidates can peruse open jobs, view the job description or profile, and take action accordingly. Figure 3.2 provides an example of internally posted openings and the actions internal candidates can take against them. Let's briefly discuss each of these.

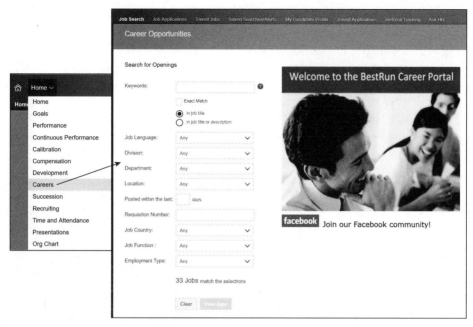

Figure 3.1 Internal Candidates: Accessing Job Searches from the Careers Tab

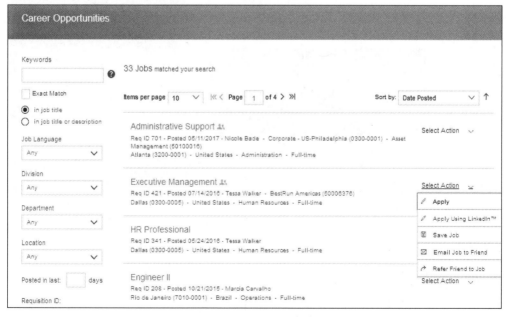

Figure 3.2 Searching for Open Jobs and Using the Select Action Options

Internal Candidate Actions

From the **Job Search** page, internal candidates have several options available to them in the **Select Action** list:

- **Apply**
  Immediately choose to submit an application for the job.

- **Apply Using LinkedIn™**
  Apply for the job using information pulled from the candidates' LinkedIn profile. If candidates select this feature, they are prompted to log in to their LinkedIn profile and enter a security code, as shown in Figure 3.3.

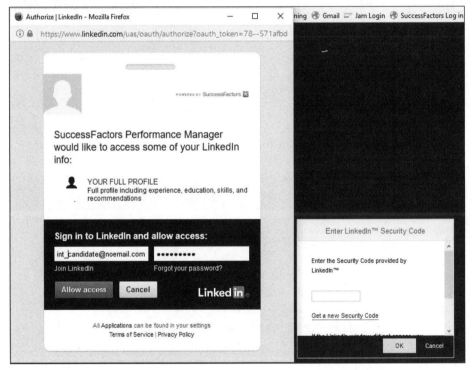

Figure 3.3 Logging In and Retrieving a Security Code to Access a LinkedIn Profile

- **Save Job**
  Save jobs of interest to their **Saved Jobs** page to review at a later time.

- **Email Job to Friend**
  Email job descriptions to colleagues who might be interested. This isn't the same as submitting a formal employee referral.

- **Refer Friend to Job**
  Submit a formal employee referral that can be tracked on the **Referral Tracking** page.

Saved Searches and Job Alerts

Just as external candidates can create job agents, where they are notified by email of jobs that meet particular criteria, internal candidates may also create saved searches for easy access at any time, as well as job alerts. These are managed on the **Saved Searches/Alerts** tab within **Careers**. The candidate will enter the following information to create a job alert:

- Name of the alert (required)
- How frequently to be notified (required):
  - **Daily**
  - **Weekly**
  - **Every Two Weeks**
  - **Never**
- Any specific search criteria such as **Keywords**, **Job Language**, **Department**, **Location**, or **Requisition Number**

The criteria that can be specified in a job alert depends on the search criteria configured for the internal career page in provisioning. An example of a job alert is provided in Figure 3.4.

Figure 3.4 Setting Job Alerts to Stay Notified of Openings of Interest

3.1.2   Maintaining the Internal Candidate Profile

Internal candidates will have two profiles: the employee profile (or people profile, if in use) and a candidate profile. These two profiles work in concert to provide the most up-to-date information about your employees/internal candidates as possible. It's best practice to configure the candidate profile so that data residing on the employee profile will sync over to the candidate profile. This will be data such as name, email address, title, phone number, and background information such as internal work history, external work history, education, and any other background information that may be of value.

Employee Profile Syncs to Candidate Profile

Because of the syncing of data between the two profiles, much of the data on the candidate profile may not be available for internal candidates to edit. Prime examples of this are demographic information such as name, title, and contact information. Because this information resides on their employee record within SAP SuccessFactors, you don't want them updating this information on the candidate profile.

Other information, such as the background data, will sync from the employee profile but will also be available to edit. The syncing works in both directions so that any updates or new entries made on the candidate profile will be reflected as well on the employee profile.

Role of the Internal Candidate Profile

You may be asking why a candidate profile is required if an internal candidate already has an employee profile. Although the employee profile and candidate profile contain much of the same data (perhaps they are mirrors of each other), they actually perform different functions within the system. The employee profile is used throughout the SAP SuccessFactors suite and is leveraged by many different modules. The employee profile is accessible by other employees to view publicly available information such as location, phone number, and email address. The employee profile also represents an employee's talent résumé and is searchable in talent search for performance, development, and succession planning functions.

The candidate profile, on the other hand, represents the employee's recruiting résumé. This is where employees upload their actual résumé file. The candidate profile isn't widely accessible outside of Recruiting users, and you can't permission it to be so. The candidate profile plays a specific Recruiting purpose and doesn't have a wider reach. Finally, the candidate profile is what is searched while doing a candidate search. The employee profile isn't used or accessible during the candidate search function, outside of sharing information to the candidate profile.

3.1.3   Employee Referral Experience

If you've deployed the employee referral feature within Recruiting, internal candidates will have the ability to submit external candidates to job openings. When they select the **Refer Friend to Job** action from the **Job Search** page, they are actually creating an external candidate and placing that candidate in the forwarded status of that job. After an employee has submitted an employee referral, the employee can view that referral and track its progress on the **Referral Tracking** tab of the **Careers** page (see Figure 3.5). Employee referrals also can be added directly from this page rather than just from the **Job Search** page.

Upon adding the referral, candidates referred will receive an email informing them of the referral, which should include instructions on how to log in and complete their candidate profile, view the job description, and hopefully apply for the job.

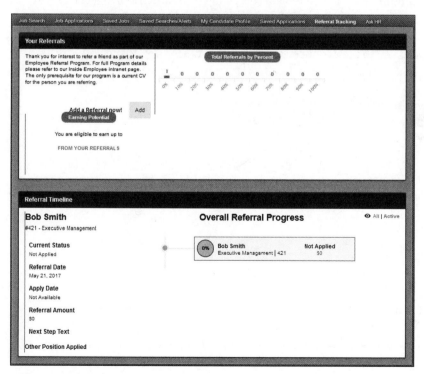

Figure 3.5 Tracking Progress of All Employee Referrals on the Referral Tracking Page

We'll discuss employee referrals in greater detail in Chapter 5. Now, let's explore the experience of external candidates by discussing talent communities.

3.2 Talent Communities

Candidates that are external to your organization will interact with your external-facing career page via the Recruiting Marketing platform. They will arrive on your site from a variety of avenues: your corporate website, a Google search, or any number of job board postings. Not every candidate that visits your career site is ready to apply for a job at your company. They may have only just started considering a move and are looking for more information, or maybe they just don't find an opening on your site that matches their skills and interests at the moment. You want to be able to capture these visitors who have already shown enough interest in your company to visit your career site. These career site visitors can fill out a simple form to join your talent community and stay informed of what's going on in your company.

Talent communities are a great tool for companies to use when looking for talent. When handled correctly, talent communities can have a multiplier effect, giving you quick and easy access to passive candidates and their networks. People in your talent community can lead you to their connections. People trust their friends and are more likely to consider working for a company that their friends or trusted contacts can vouch for.

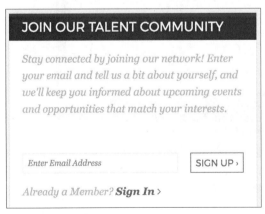

Figure 3.6 Candidates Can Join the Talent Community to Stay Informed of Opportunities

The key to executing and building your talent community correctly is to make it as simple as possible for your site visitors. You've *attracted* them, and now you want to *engage* them. Engaging visitors in your talent community can be as easy as entering their email address in the talent community widget, hopefully located prominently on your career home page, as illustrated in Figure 3.6. This is quick and easy for candidates and provides you with a predefined pool of people who are interested in employment opportunities. The prompt to join the talent community is also available as a link in the **Not Finding a Job** menu.

After you start to build up your talent community, you can take advantage of having this self-selected pool of people interested in your organization. Recruiting Marketing allows you to segment your talent into groups of individuals with similar interests so that you can provide them with targeted content. When they first register, you can ask them specific questions to help you categorize them appropriately. This will guide you in how best to interact with them on an ongoing basis. The interaction with the talent community is bidirectional. Not only do you interact with them as recruiters, but they can also interact with you. Let's look at the ways candidates can interact with the talent community.

Candidates interact with the talent community in different ways, both candidate driven and organization driven. When candidates define their own specific job agents, they are interacting with the talent community and giving you, as recruiters, valuable information about their interests. A job agent is really just a saved search that candidates can set up based on their own criteria and specify how frequently it should run. This is the external equivalent of the job alert discussed in Section 3.1.1. When the search is conducted, the candidate is sent an email with the open jobs found that match the search criteria. In this way, you're continually engaging them by keeping them informed of openings that are of interest to them. Figure 3.7 illustrates how a candidate can create a job agent. Candidates can have multiple job agents for different interests.

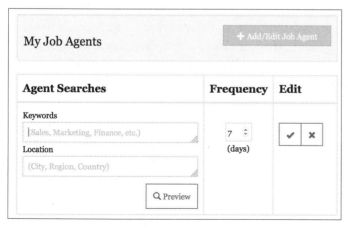

Figure 3.7 Job Agents to Notify Candidates of New Openings That Match Their Interests

The second way candidates interact with the talent community is company driven. As candidates join your talent community and provide information on their interests by creating job agents, this provides valuable information that recruiters can use to develop targeted messaging and campaigns for various segments of the talent community. They key to effectively managing the talent community is to always be communicating with the members, letting them know that you're interested and that there are opportunities for them.

This requires commitment on behalf of the organization to devote the time and resources needed to nurture relationships in the talent community. Some best practices for growing and maintaining your talent community include the following:

- **Communicate**
  Respect the fact that candidates have taken the time to express interest in your company. If they reach out to you, make sure you respond promptly. Don't make the talent community another black hole where after a person joins, they never hear anything again. According to the Glassdoor U.S. Site Survey from January 2016, 90% of job seekers say that it's important to work for a company that embraces transparency. Lack of communication or information will frustrate candidates and lead to increased drop-off rates.

- **Make it relevant**
  Communication on its own isn't enough. Make sure that when you do communicate with the members of your talent community, the information you provide is relevant to them. If a person registers in your talent community as a seasoned professional, don't send them information about college career fairs or entry-level positions. That is just spam and shows candidates that you didn't take the time or effort to target your communication to make it relevant for their needs. Remember, a person who joins your talent community is interested in you as an employer but only for jobs and areas that match their interests. They don't need or want to know about jobs that are totally uninteresting to them.

- **Be honest**
  Don't try to be something you're not. If you're a manufacturing company with a t-shirt and jeans dress code, don't present yourself as a suit and tie organization. Embrace your culture and celebrate it. Make sure your culture comes through in all your communications and in your career site. Always be genuine in your communication with candidates. They will be much more likely to be patient with a

long hiring process if they are told what to expect instead of just hearing nothing. According to the Harris Interactive Survey for Glassdoor from 2014, more than two-thirds (67%) of employers believe retention rates would be higher if candidates had a clearer picture of what to expect about working at the company before taking the job. So make sure you clearly represent the company culture in all interactions with the candidate.

3.3 Candidate Business Card and Profile

The first step in joining the talent community involves the candidates completing what is referred to as the *business card*. The business card feature consists of just a few fields that feed into the candidate profile where candidates can manage their information and subscriptions. Let's look at the business card and candidate profile and discuss how they both play an important role in capturing critical information about your external candidates.

3.3.1 Business Card

Figure 3.8 provides an example of the business card's basic fields. Some of the business card fields are always required, and some can be defined as required or optional by the client during implementation. The following fields are part of the standard business card:

- **Email**
- **Create Password/Confirm Password** (always required)
- **First Name** (always required)
- **Last Name** (always required)
- **Phone Number**
- **Current Employer**
- **Current Title**
- **Interest Level**
- Customer-defined yes/no question (optional)
- Customer-defined multiple choice question (optional)

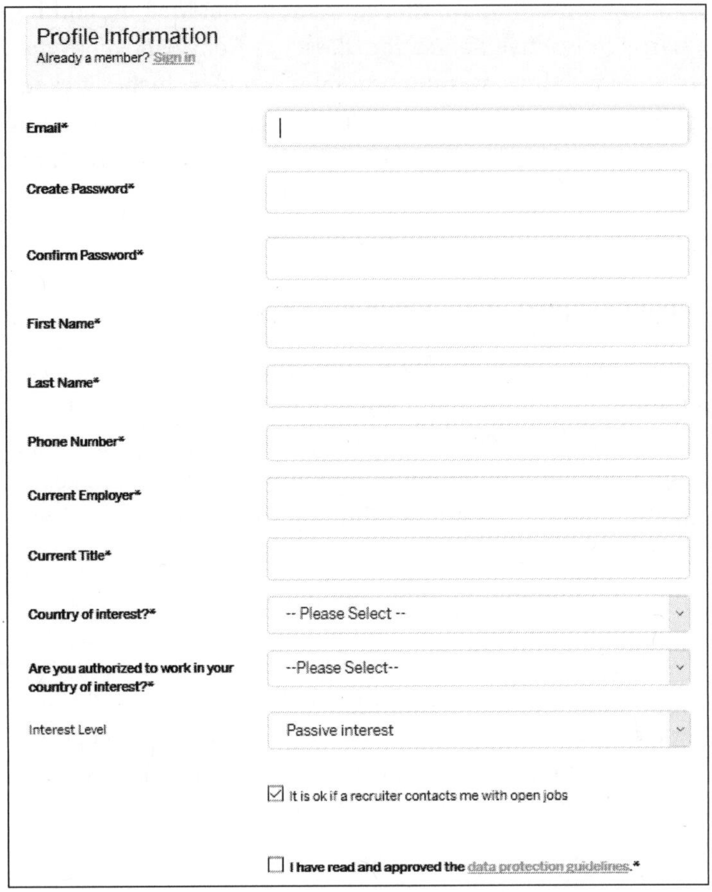

Figure 3.8 Completing the Business Card to Begin Creating External Candidate Profile

Candidates can either enter this information manually or use their LinkedIn profile to join the talent community. Refer to Section 3.1.1 to review how internal candidates can populate data from their LinkedIn profile as the process is the same for external candidates.

3.3.2   Candidate Profile

The candidate profile in the Recruiting Marketing platform captures basic information and preferences from the candidate. After logging in, users can access their profile page by clicking the **Your Profile** link. The profile page is organized into the following different areas, which are described in this section and shown in Figure 3.9:

- **Contact Preferences**
- **Saved Jobs**
- **My Job Agents**
- **Email Subscription Management**
- **Language**

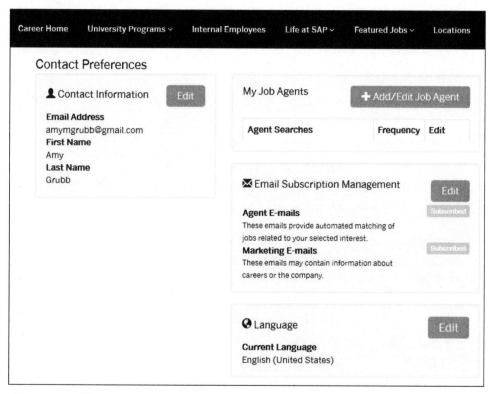

Figure 3.9 Profile Page: Built and Updated from the Business Card

The **Contact Information** area of the profile displays information that was entered on the business card when the candidate joined the talent community. Candidates can edit this information by clicking **Edit** in the **Contact Information** area as shown in Figure 3.9. Editing the **Contact Information** is shown in Figure 3.10.

Figure 3.10 Candidate Editing Contact Information

The **Saved Jobs** area displays any jobs the candidate has saved in the past, showing the title and location of saved jobs and the date the job was saved, as shown in Figure 3.11. It also includes a link to the job posting so the candidate can review the posting description and apply for the job when ready.

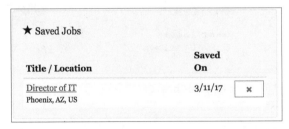

Figure 3.11 Saved Jobs for Later Viewing or Application

The **My Job Agents** area displays any job agents set up by the candidate. Here candidates can edit or delete existing agents, change the frequency of the agents, or create new agents, as shown in Figure 3.12.

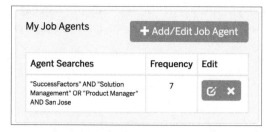

Figure 3.12 Managing Saved Searches (Job Agents)

The **Email Subscription Management** area allows candidates to subscribe or unsubscribe from both job agent emails and marketing emails, as shown in Figure 3.13. This gives candidates control over whether or not they want to receive emails from the company.

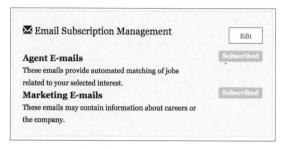

Figure 3.13 Managing Email Preferences

The **Language** section allows candidates to see the language they currently have set for the site. If the company configured the career page to support multiple languages, candidates can change their preferred language. Clicking **Edit** allows candidates to choose a new language from a dropdown populated with the languages configured for the site, as shown in Figure 3.14.

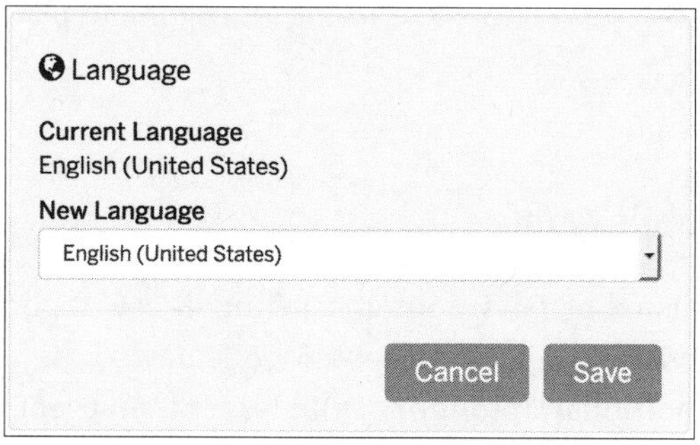

Figure 3.14 Changing Language Preference

Updating the language here immediately refreshes the browser session language, allowing candidates to see translated elements of the site in the chosen language right away, as shown in Figure 3.15.

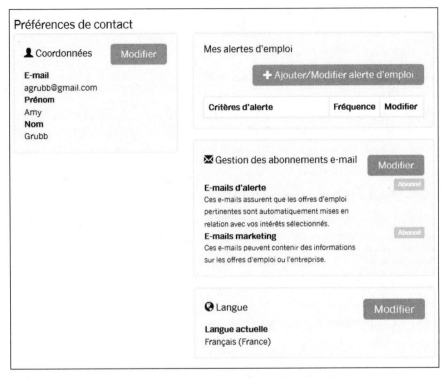

Figure 3.15 Profile after Changing Language Preference to French

After going through the process of finding a job in the careers page and completing the application, candidates can also see their job activity from this profile, as well as the candidate profile page with the SAP SuccessFactors Recruiting Management platform.

3.4 Responsive Design and Mobile Apply

In separate independent studies conducted by Glassdoor and Kelton, it was found that 9 in 10 job seekers use mobile devices to search for jobs. Mobile devices have quickly become more common than traditional laptops or computers in many geographies and demographics. Consumers, including job applicants, are demanding that they be able to carry out more and more complex processes using their phones and tablets. That's where responsive career site design and mobile job applications come into play. Let's discuss both of these developments and how Recruiting addresses each need.

3.4.1   Responsive Design

Having a career site that is designed to work on any device is vital in today's job market. Responsive design is the term used to describe sites whose layout automatically responds and adapts based on the device used to consume it, whether a browser, smartphone, or tablet. Recruiting external sites are designed to be responsive so that the layout and navigation dynamically adapt based on the device. Figure 3.16 shows the SAP careers page as viewed on an iPhone. The screens shown left to right are displayed as a continuous scroll top to bottom on the device. Notice how the panels, graphics, and widgets are centered within the parameters of the screen, and no right or left scrolling is required to view the content.

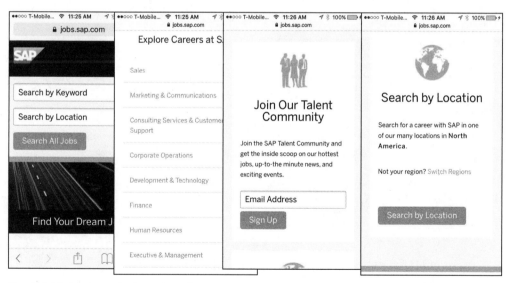

Figure 3.16 A Responsively Designed Career Site as Viewed on an iPhone

3.4.2   Mobile Apply

A study by the Pew Research Center found that 70% of applicants want to apply for jobs directly from their mobile device, and 55% of candidates want to upload their résumé to a career site from their mobile device. Think about it—if 90% of job seekers are searching for jobs on mobile devices, you want to make sure they can complete the application process from a mobile device. Interrupting the process by forcing a candidate to complete a job application on a browser that they started on their phone is a lousy candidate experience and will lead to significant candidate drop-off.

The SAP SuccessFactors Recruiting mobile apply feature enables candidates to use mobile devices such as a smartphone or a tablet to search for jobs, create and manage a profile, and complete the job application process. Mobile apply seamlessly integrates the job search features with the application process and presents it in a responsively designed user interface.

With mobile apply, the profile creation and application process are consolidated into a single page. Figure 3.17 provides just a few examples of what the mobile apply process is like for candidates. Fields that are common between the candidate profile and application are only displayed once to the candidate. This simplifies the application process because the candidate won't have to enter the same data more than once.

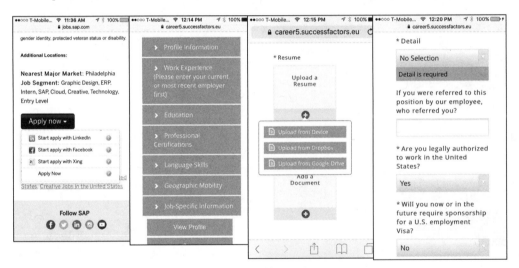

Figure 3.17 Screens Showing the Mobile Apply Process from an iPhone

When mobile apply is deployed, it also impacts the view of the application when viewed in a browser. The responsive design lays out the fields across the screen rather than from top to bottom. The information is divided into logical sections with headers. The candidate profile sections are displayed within the same screen, and candidates can update this information as they progress down the page, ensuring they are providing the most up-to-date information.

Figure 3.18 provides an example of such an application viewed in a browser. In this example, the application fields are contained within the header **Job-Specific Information**. When this is expanded, candidates can complete the fields that are configured on the candidate data model.

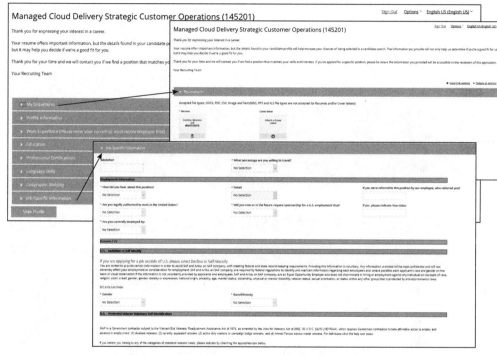

Figure 3.18 Mobile Apply: Impacting the View of the Application in a Browser

3.5 Job Search Options

Your career site is your most important recruiting channel, and the job search function is the most important feature on your career site. Of course, the content on your career site must be relevant and engaging, but if a candidate can't find a job to apply for, then all the time and effort you've put into your career site is useless. Recruiting Marketing offers candidates a number of ways to find jobs through tools such as the job search widget, location search, strategy pages, job listing and description pages, and social apply. Let's look at these in more detail.

3.5.1 Job Search Widget

Recruiting provides a search widget that is integrated into nearly every page of the career site by design. You have a captive audience of people on your career site considering your company as an employer so you want to make sure it's easy for them to find jobs. Not only is this widget incorporated into most pages of the career site, but the widget code is also provided to you to embed anywhere else on your corporate site. The standard widget allows candidates to search for jobs based on keyword and location. Figure 3.19 displays the job search widget from the main **Career Home** page (top) as well as on a strategy page focused on development and technology jobs (bottom).

Figure 3.19 Job Search Widget on the Main Career Home Page and a Strategy Page Focused on Development and Technology Jobs

3.5.2 Search by Location

One of the most common ways candidates search for jobs is by location. They often look for jobs that are available near where they currently live or where they are looking to relocate. The interactive job map page allows candidates to search for jobs by location on a map. This is a popular option for organizations with jobs distributed across one or multiple countries. If an organization has the majority of jobs clustered in one location, the map search functionality may not provide a lot of value to candidates.

Clicking on the **Jobs by Location** link takes candidates to an interactive Google Maps page as shown in Figure 3.20.

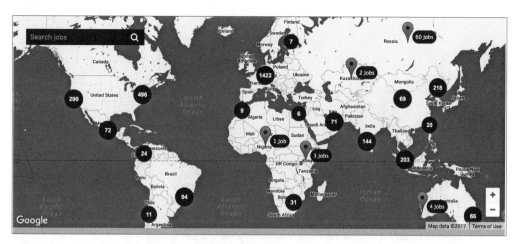

Figure 3.20 Interactive Job Map Using Google Maps

The map provides the standard controls you expect from Google Maps. You can zoom into the map using the standard zoom controls or by clicking on one of the job clusters. After you've drilled down to a specific location, you can view the list of jobs open in the location, navigate to the job descriptions from there, and start the application process.

3.5.3   Featured Jobs/Strategy Pages

Job strategy pages allow companies to highlight particular types of jobs, thereby further focusing candidates where they want to go quickly and easily. Up to 10 strategy pages are available by default. More pages are available but require additional service by SAP. Strategy pages are sometimes known as featured jobs pages. The intention behind featured jobs pages is to logically group types of jobs and to highlight hard-to-fill positions. Candidates can quickly see by the title of the featured jobs page whether those jobs might be of interest.

Strategy or featured jobs are prominently displayed on the career home page so candidates can clearly see them. When a page is selected, the candidate will see not only additional information about these types of jobs, but also all of the jobs related to that page will be available to peruse and apply. It's important to understand what the strategy pages will be early on when implementing the product, as the information the system uses to post jobs appropriately is set on the requisition. Figure 3.21 provides an example of strategy pages as displayed on the **Career Home** page and then the detailed strategy page once selected and the jobs available on that page.

Figure 3.21 Strategy Pages Providing Additional Information and Filtered Search for Jobs Related to the Particular Topic or Field

3.5.4   Job Listing Pages

Regardless of how the candidates navigate to a list of jobs, whether from a job search or navigating directly to a jobs page, the jobs listing page is consistent. The jobs page lists jobs by title, location, and date posted, and it allows the candidate to sort and filter the list as needed. Figure 3.22 shows a jobs listing page as viewed from a browser. Figure 3.23 provides an example of the same jobs listing page from a mobile device.

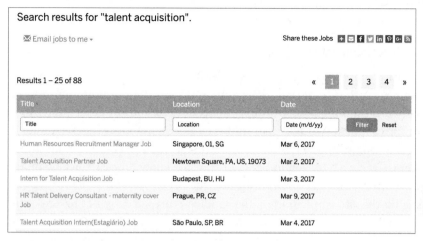

Figure 3.22 Job Listings as Viewed in a Web Browser

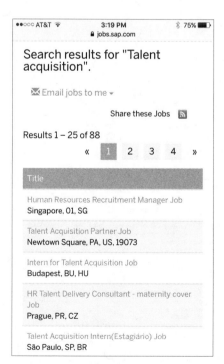

Figure 3.23 Job Listings as Viewed on a Mobile Device via Responsive Design

Candidates can share the jobs found via the social channels defined during implementation (e.g., Twitter and LinkedIn), email the jobs to themselves, or click on a job title to display the corresponding job description.

3.5.5   Job Description Page

The job description page displays the job description or job profile (if used) and should convey to the candidates the main responsibilities, educational requirements, particular skills required, work experience desired, and any other information necessary for candidates to make an informed decision about whether to apply. There is an option for candidates to share the job via social channels, email similar jobs to themselves, save the job for later, or start the apply process. Clicking on the **Apply now** button (see Figure 3.24) brings up the list of ways to apply for the job. Depending on the site configuration, the candidate may or may not be presented with social apply options. If they choose **Apply now** without linking to a social media profile, they will be taken directly to Recruiting to complete the application.

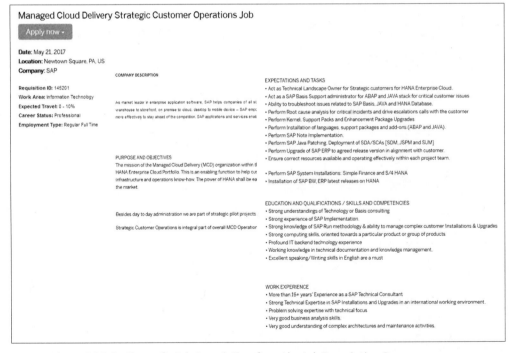

Figure 3.24 Portions of a Job Description from the Job Description Page

3.5.6   Social Apply

The social apply feature allows candidates to use profiles they have already established on certain social sites, such as LinkedIn, Facebook, and Xing, as a shortcut in the apply process. When users click the **Start apply** option for one of the social networks, they are prompted to supply their credentials for that site to validate who they are. When a candidate uses social apply from a recruiting site, their basic information will be passed and populated into their recruiting candidate profile. The Recruiting system will attempt to pass and populate the following fields, where available:

- email
- password
- phone
- partnerSource
- partnerMemberId
- locale
- country
- candidateSource

- jobReqId
- firstName
- lastName
- address
- homePhone
- cellphone
- dateOfBirth
- profileUrl

Recruiting will attempt to extract the following information about a candidate's employment history from the social profile (LinkedIn or Facebook) and place it into the candidate profile:

- startDate
- endDate
- title

- description
- company
- current

Recruiting will attempt to retrieve the following information about a candidate's education history for the candidate profile:

- startDate
- endDate
- name

- degree
- fieldOfStudy

The candidate can verify and correct the data imported and complete the application process in Recruiting.

3.6   Language Translations

Recruiting provides the framework for companies to provide multiple language versions of their career site. This allows candidates to search for jobs based on their local language and location. It's up to the company that sets up the Recruiting site to determine which languages to enable and to provide translated versions of the site content in the appropriate languages. All standard navigation and buttons have presupplied translations; it's actually the marketing content that you need to translate. Candidates will be able to change their preferred language. Candidates can define their preferred language for the site from their profile. Figure 3.25 provides an example of the candidate profile displayed in French.

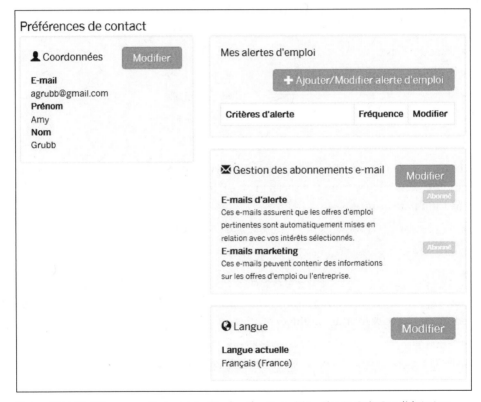

Figure 3.25 Multilanguage Support to Display the Recruiting Site to Suit Candidate Language Preferences

3.7 Summary

Candidate experience is crucial for finding top talent. There are some hidden, and some not so hidden, costs to poor candidate experience. For example, poor candidate experience negatively impacts your brand as an employer. According to a recent Talent Board study, 66% of job seekers share their negative interview experiences with their inner circle, and 51% share these via social media as well. Bad reviews get around.

Poor candidate experience also makes it more difficult to reengage previous candidates, and the people you don't hire today may be the very people you need in a year or two. If you don't treat them right the first time, it will be an uphill battle to get them to consider you now that you need them. A clearly designed career site with rich content can certainly help with good candidate experience. Make sure the content is relevant, you communicate with your talent community in a thoughtful way, and you make it easy for job seekers to actually find your jobs.

In this chapter, we discussed the various tools and methods that Recruiting provides to enable companies to market open jobs to the widest audience of internal and external candidates. With tools such as talent communities, companies can capture even the most passive candidate and market to them any available jobs for which they are a good fit. Tools such as the business card make it easy for candidates to provide their information even without applying for a job. Providing various tools to help focus candidate job searches will increase their time on your site and improve the odds of candidates submitting applications. Strategically placing the job search widget throughout your site, and using strategy/featured job pages, will also help focus your candidates' activities on your site. Using integration with social sites to pass profile information into SAP SuccessFactors makes the application process even easier. With the entire site responsively designed to support mobile applications, your candidates can search and apply for jobs from nearly anywhere. All of these tools give you a strong arsenal to attract and engage the best talent for your open positions.

In the next chapter, we'll look at how recruiters find and disposition candidates in their sourcing endeavors.

Chapter 4
Finding and Dispositioning Candidates

After requisitions are approved and posted, recruiters will spend the most time searching for and evaluating candidates. Using tools that increase the efficiency and speed with which candidates are evaluated means your recruiters can work smarter and identify those desired candidates right away.

After a requisition is created, approved, and posted, candidates will begin applying. Sometimes you may want to source candidates to requisitions from the candidates in your database. SAP SuccessFactors Recruiting Management offers many ways that you can source and disposition candidates on your open jobs. These features are geared toward equipping recruiters with as many tools as possible to thoroughly and quickly evaluate candidates and move them on in the process or remove them from consideration. The longer it takes to evaluate candidates, the greater the drop-off rate will be and the higher the risk of losing talent. In this chapter, we'll discuss the following features in Recruiting Management that support recruiters in evaluating candidates:

- Working with the candidate profile
- Using the application
- Using the Candidate Workbench
- Evaluating candidates through the talent pipeline
- Scheduling interviews
- Documenting interview feedback
- Approving an offer and managing offer letters
- Conducting a candidate search

Let's begin by discussing the candidate profile.

4.1 Candidate Profile

The candidate profile stores information about candidates independent of a specific job. The candidate profile is sometimes referred to as the online résumé of a candidate. It allows you to capture data about a candidate that remains fairly static over time, such as address, contact information, education, and work history, as shown in Figure 4.1. Recruiters can search for candidates based on profile information, and candidates can use their profile as part of the application process.

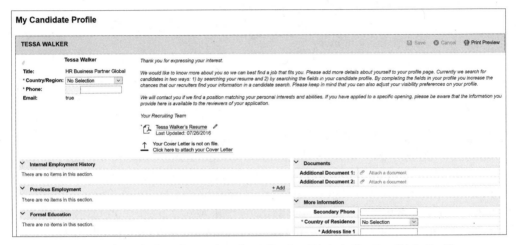

Figure 4.1 Résumé-Like Information about the Candidate in the Candidate Profile

The application, on the other hand, is specific to an opening and is used to collect data needed specifically to evaluate a candidate for the position to which they have applied. The application associates a candidate to a requisition and includes data relevant to that particular requisition-candidate relationship and process. The application is always associated to a status in the talent pipeline and is in one status at any given time.

The candidate profile and application both contain critical information necessary for recruiters to adequately evaluate a candidate's fit for a job, and it's important to understand the relationship between these two elements when designing them in an implementation. We'll discuss the application in greater detail in Section 4.2.

Let's look at the components of the candidate profile and its role in the recruiting process, including the different data elements, the ways in which the profile is created and maintained, and the impact of data privacy settings on the profile data.

4.1.1   Candidate Profile Data Elements

When candidates hit your career site and create an account, the next step should be to complete their candidate profile. The candidate profile should be completed prior to applying for a job; however, candidates can create an account and profile without applying for a job. Candidates may do this, for example, if they are preparing to apply for a job but aren't quite ready to submit the application, or if they are looking for a specific job but don't find an opening available. In this case, they can create an alert which will notify them via email of jobs that meet specified criteria.

The candidate profile comprises two types of data: live profile and background data elements. Each type of data has unique characteristics and plays a specific role in the recruiting process.

Live Profile Data Elements

Live profile data are individual fields of data. The most common use of live profile data elements is to capture contact information such as name, address, email, and phone number, as shown in Figure 4.2. These fields are located along the right side of the candidate profile and can be mapped to fields on the application so data are shared between the two templates, and candidates don't have to enter the same data twice. Live profile data are searchable in candidate search and can also be used to populate email and offer letter templates via tokens. They can also be leveraged as custom display columns on the Candidate Workbench.

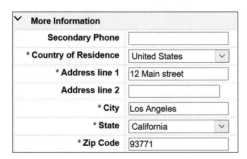

Figure 4.2 Live Profile Data under More Information

During the design phase of an implementation, it's common to define live profile fields that may be permissioned for recruiter use and not visible to the candidate. These fields can then be used in reporting or can populate data in email templates.

Background Element Data

The other type of data used on the candidate profile is called background data, or portlets. A background data element is two or more fields grouped together in a row of data, as shown in Figure 4.3. These portlets of data are used to capture information such as work history or education, where multiple data are required to convey the information. Background elements are leveraged from the employee profile. All available background elements on the employee profile can be used on the candidate profile. Following are examples of employee profile background elements commonly used on the candidate profile:

- Internal work history
- External work history
- Education history
- Languages
- Certifications
- Professional memberships
- Geographic mobility

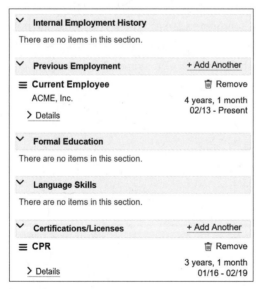

Figure 4.3 Background Elements Capturing Groups and Multiple Rows of Data

When employee profile background elements are used on the candidate profile, they are synced so that data entered are shared across both profiles for internal candidates. This creates a better user experience for internal candidates (employees), as they only have to enter data in one place. To enable this syncing, the fields within each background element must be the same between the employee profile and candidate profile, including field type and picklist values, as applicable.

In addition to employee profile background elements, custom background elements can be configured to capture business-specific required data. A common example of a custom background element is to capture reference information. Candidates can enter their reference names and contact information and update the information as required.

Finally, just as you can configure live profile fields for recruiter-only use, you can configure background elements that only recruiters can see and edit. This is accomplished with permissions configured into the candidate profile template. An example of a recruiter-accessible background element may be to capture reference feedback.

There is one candidate profile template that can be configured, and it must support the data needs of all internal and all external candidates across all geographic regions. You can use permissions to affect the view of the candidate profile from internal and external candidate perspectives. For example, a common background element used is the internal work experience portlet that is mapped from the employee profile. This is used to capture information about an employee's roles within the organization. This information doesn't apply to external candidates, so presenting it to them wouldn't create a good user experience. Using permissions, you can make this portlet visible and editable only by internal candidates.

Recruiting users can search candidate profile records to locate potential matches for job requisitions. During implementation, it's important to consider the data that might be used to find candidates. This information should be captured in either a live profile or background element data element to support searching needs. Candidate search was discussed in more detail in Chapter 1.

4.1.2   Creating a Candidate Profile

The first step for candidates after hitting the career site is to create a candidate profile, which can be done in the following ways:

- An external candidate creates profile in Recruiting Management.
- An external candidate is added to Recruiting Management by a Recruiting user.
- An external candidate is created in SAP SuccessFactors Recruiting Marketing and passed to Recruiting Management.
- An external candidate is created via data migration.
- A new user account is created that results in an internal candidate profile.

Let's look at each method in more detail in the following sections.

External Candidate Creates Profile in Recruiting Management

When a business deploys Recruiting Management not integrated with Recruiting Marketing (this isn't typical, but is possible), the primary way for external candidate profiles to be created is for candidates to create a profile themselves. Typically, candidates will create a profile at the same time they are applying for a job. Candidates access a job description on the company's external career site, either by navigating directly to the career site from the company's public website or by following a link in a search. Candidates click the **Apply** button on the job description and are brought to the **Career Opportunities: Sign In** screen, as shown in Figure 4.4.

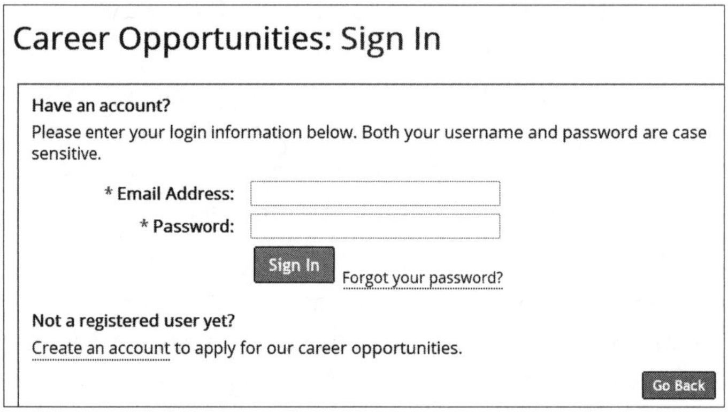

Figure 4.4 Choosing to Sign In or Create an Account from the Sign In Page

If the candidates haven't yet created an account in the system, they click **Create an account**. On the subsequent screen, they enter some basic information about themselves as shown in Figure 4.5. Depending on the company's data privacy settings, candidates may or may not be presented the profile visibility options and the data privacy statement. After the candidates are registered, they can complete additional elements of the profile, which are discussed later in the chapter.

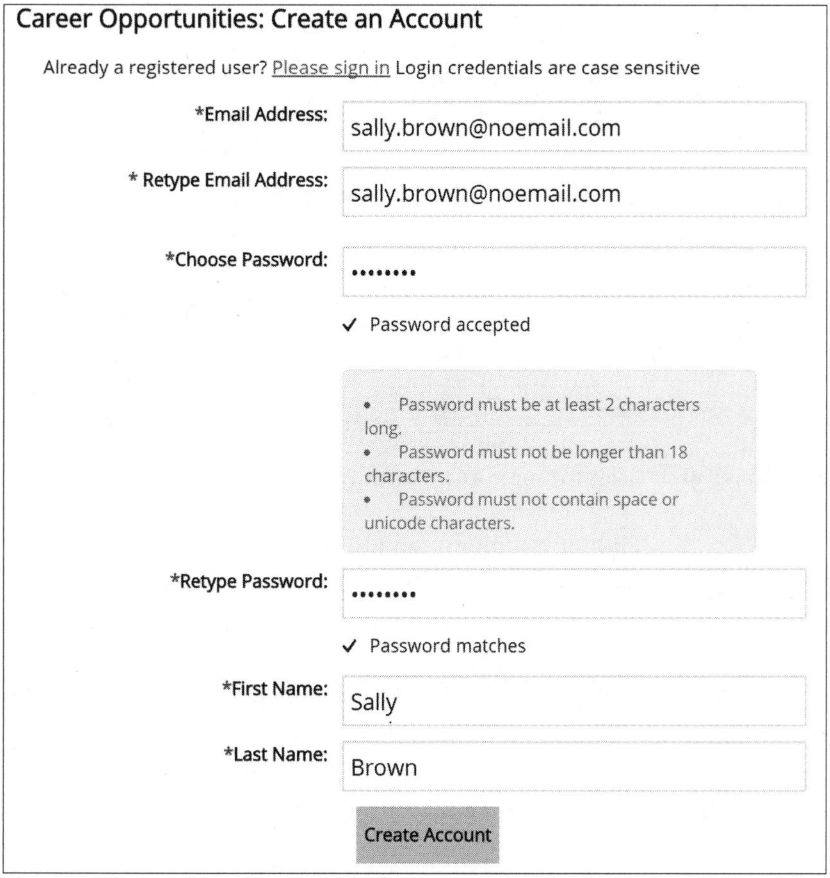

Career Opportunities: Create an Account

Already a registered user? <u>Please sign in</u> Login credentials are case sensitive

*Email Address: sally.brown@noemail.com

* Retype Email Address: sally.brown@noemail.com

*Choose Password: ••••••••

✓ Password accepted

- Password must be at least 2 characters long.
- Password must not be longer than 18 characters.
- Password must not contain space or unicode characters.

*Retype Password: ••••••••

✓ Password matches

*First Name: Sally

*Last Name: Brown

Create Account

Figure 4.5 Entering Basic Information to Create a Profile

External Candidate Added to Recruiting Management by Recruiting User

Recruiting users with the appropriate permissions can manually add candidates directly to the external candidate database. To add a candidate directly to the database, the Recruiting user navigates to Recruiting and clicks **Candidates** and then **Add Candidate**. Recruiters may also add candidates to the database and directly to a job requisition at the same time. To do this, the Recruiting user navigates to the list of candidates assigned to a requisition and clicks **Candidate Search** and then **Add Candidate**.

The pop-up shown in Figure 4.6 appears in both cases. All fields must be completed to create the profile.

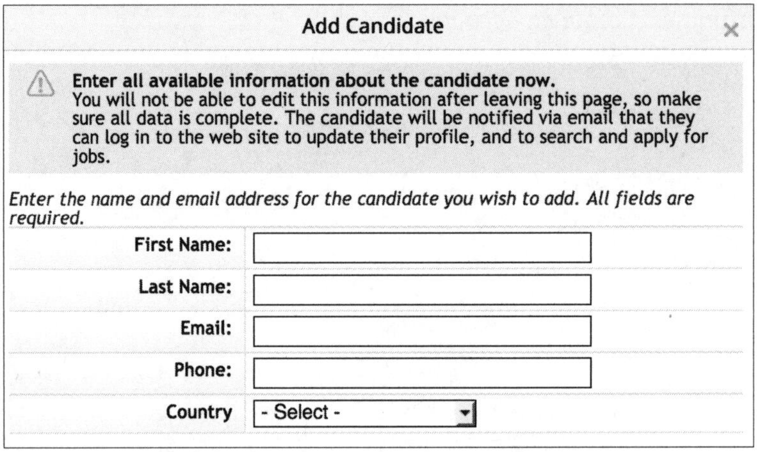

Add Candidate	✕

⚠ **Enter all available information about the candidate now.**
You will not be able to edit this information after leaving this page, so make sure all data is complete. The candidate will be notified via email that they can log in to the web site to update their profile, and to search and apply for jobs.

Enter the name and email address for the candidate you wish to add. All fields are required.

First Name:	
Last Name:	
Email:	
Phone:	
Country	- Select - ▼

Figure 4.6 Required Basic Fields to Create a Candidate Profile

After the basic profile is created, the Recruiting user can then upload a résumé and cover letter on behalf of the candidate and maintain additional elements of the candidate profile. Candidates can receive an email informing them of their new profile along with information on how to access the system. A standard email notification can be enabled or disabled in **System Email Notification Template Settings**. This email template is configurable, so you can add any text they like.

External Candidate Created in Recruiting Marketing and Passed to Recruiting Management

External candidate profiles are created differently for companies that have implemented both Recruiting Marketing and Recruiting Management. In this case, external candidates create an account in Recruiting Marketing through the business card feature or by joining a talent community. When they choose to apply for a job, their data are passed over to the candidate database, and they will access the detailed profile discussed in the previous section.

> **Note**
> Internal candidates only have profiles in Recruiting Management and not in Recruiting Marketing.

External Candidates Created through Data Migration

External candidates can be loaded into the system through data migration as part of the initial implementation. This is typically done by companies that want to move external candidates from a legacy recruiting system into SAP SuccessFactors. This complex process involves mapping data from the fields in the legacy system to the candidate profile fields configured in SAP SuccessFactors. Data migration is discussed in more detail in Chapter 12.

Note, however, that if you do choose to create candidate profiles through data migration, no automated notification is sent to candidates created through data import. You have to email those candidates informing them they have been migrated and asking them to log in to the new Recruiting system to verify and update their profile information. You must be sure that the contactEmail field is configured and data has been imported into this field so migrated users can retrieve their password.

New Internal User Account Created Resulting in an Internal Candidate Profile

An internal candidate profile is created when a new internal user account is created via the hire action in SAP SuccessFactors Employee Central, or when an employee record is created via an integration with the a business's Human Resources Information System (HRIS) system of record. After a new user account is created, a conversion process is run to convert the candidate's external candidate profile to the internal employee profile, which will then sync data to the new internal candidate profile. To set up this conversion process, choose **Manage Recruiting Settings • External to Internal Candidate Profile Settings**, and select the fields to use to identify and link the internal and external profiles as displayed in Figure 4.7. After you make these settings, a sync job must be set up in Quartz scheduler and run on a regular basis.

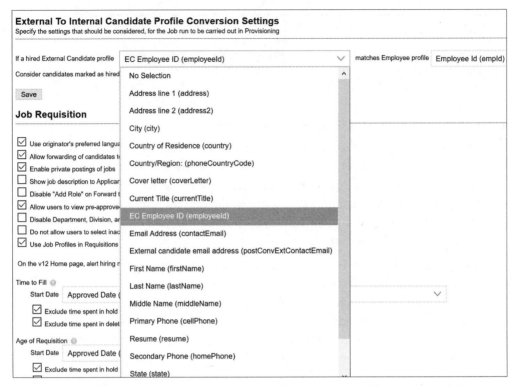

Figure 4.7 Choosing the Fields That Will Link the External Candidate Profile with the New Employee Profile

4.1.3   Data Privacy and the Candidate Profile

If a business has implemented the data privacy consent statement functionality, the first time external candidates register or internal candidates attempt to maintain their candidate profile, they are presented with the company's data privacy statement. The data privacy statement details how the company handles the candidate's personal data. Candidates must view and accept this statement and then choose how their personal data should be handled during the job search process before their profile is created and they can apply for jobs. The options for how a candidate's data can be handled are shown in Figure 4.8.

Refer to Chapter 5, Section 5.2, for more detailed discussion of the data privacy consent statement functionality.

Figure 4.8 Selecting the Data Privacy Settings When Creating an Account

4.1.4   Candidate Profile Elements

In Section 4.1.1, we discussed the two types of data elements in the candidate profile. In addition to these types of data, there are also a few components in the profile:

- Business card
- Welcome message
- Résumé and cover letter
- Data privacy visibility settings
- Background information
- Documents
- More information
- Footer
- Comments
- Tags
- Jobs applied portlet

The following sections walk through each of these and how they can be configured.

Business Card

As the name suggests, the business card feature contains the candidate's name, email address, phone number, and, optionally, their title and company, as shown in Figure 4.9. The business card appears in the upper-left corner of the profile and can't be hidden or moved. This information is also displayed in the Candidate Workbench, as you'll see in Section 4.3.

* First Name:	James
Middle Name:	D
* Last Name:	Wilson
* Title:	Marketing Director
* Company:	Pacific Coast Industries
* Phone:	206 555-9999

Figure 4.9 Contact Details and Current Position Information in the External Candidate Profile Business Card

Welcome Message

The welcome message, which appears in the top-right area of the profile, provides a space for customized content welcoming candidates to the profile and providing some instructions. Although there is no character limit for text in this area, a long message will push the data fields to the bottom of the screen, so you should keep this text as succinct as possible. The welcome message can use HTML formatting to provide larger fonts in different colors, and links may also be provided to other areas of the system as long as the `<mime-type>` attribute is set to `<mime-type="text-html">`. Figure 4.10 provides an example of the welcome message.

Thank you for expressing your interest in ACE Company!

We would like to know more about you so we can best find a job that fits you. Please add more details about yourself to your profile page. Currently we search for candidates in two ways: 1) by searching your resume and 2) by searching the fields in your candidate profile. By completing the fields in your profile you increase the chances that our recruiters find your information in a candidate search. Please keep in mind that you can also adjust your visibility preferences on your profile.

We will contact you if we find a position matching your personal interests and abilities. If you have applied to a specific opening, please be aware that the information you provide here is available to the reviewers of your application.

Your Recruiting Team

Figure 4.10 Welcome Message on the Candidate Profile Displaying Information and Instructions to Candidates

Two types of headers can be configured on the candidate profile: candidate header and Recruiting user header. The *candidate header* is displayed to both internal and external candidates; you can't configure different messages for internal and external candidates. This header is used to provide information and instruction to candidates.

The *Recruiting user header* is specifically for Recruiting users when they are adding a candidate via **Add Candidate** and the candidate profile is viewed for the first time. The `<operator-instruction-header>` tag must be used to call out this header. Again, HTML is supported as long as the `mime-type` attribute is set accordingly. This header might be used to provide instructions to recruiters on what to complete when creating an external candidate manually.

Résumé and Cover Letter

This area contains two standard fields that allow for attachments to upload a résumé file and a cover letter file, respectively. These fields can't handle multiple attachments, so only one document per field is permitted. These fields can be updated by candidates at any time. Accepted file types for résumé and cover letter uploads are Microsoft Word/PowerPoint, PDF, HTML, XLS, CSV, image, and text. No other files types are supported.

All attachments are scanned for viruses by the SAP SuccessFactors platform. If any viruses are found, the documents won't be sent to the server. These fields sync to the same field definitions on the application so that any files attached one place will update the other.

Data Privacy and Visibility

If the data privacy consent statement functionality is enabled, the data privacy statement and the visibility settings will always be displayed for candidates on their profile. Candidates may view the consent statement at any time by selecting the link to the company's data privacy statement. In addition, candidates may always revoke their consent or update their profile visibility settings. Refer to Chapter 5, Section 5.2, for additional information on data privacy consent statements.

Background Information

The background information area contains all of the background elements or portlets that are configured on the candidate profile. Remember that this type of data represents multiple fields in a row and allows for multiple rows of data as shown in Figure 4.11. This information always appears on the left side of the candidate profile, directly under the business card. Permissions can be applied to make visible, hide, or allow editing by internal candidates, external candidates, or Recruiting users (most often the recruiter role).

Figure 4.11 Background Elements Capturing Multiple Fields in Multiple Rows of Data

Documents

The **Documents** area provides fields that can handle multiple attachments to allow candidates to upload additional documents other than a résumé and cover letter. The **Documents** area appears on the right side of the profile below the welcome message and can't be hidden, as shown in Figure 4.12. The two fields in this area can be relabeled as desired.

More Information

The **More Information** area is a continuation of the business card and contains the live profile data elements discussed earlier. Here you can capture information such as address, additional email address, and secondary phone number. You can also configure any custom fields that may be needed. Remember you can add additonal contact information. It also contains any custom fields configured as viewable or editable by Recruiting users only. The **More Information** area appears on the right side of the profile below the **Documents** area and can't be hidden (see Figure 4.13).

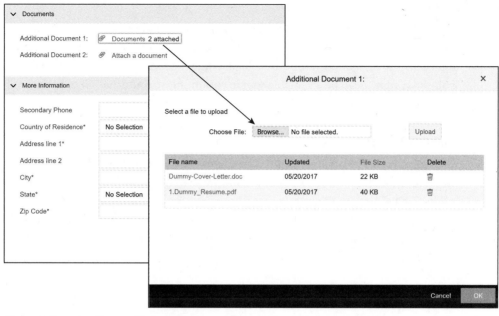

Figure 4.12 Uploading Multiple Documents in One of Two Document Fields

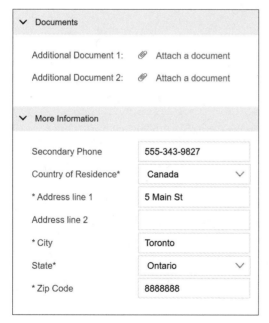

Figure 4.13 Live Profile Data to Capture Address and Other Information

157

Footer

The footer can be configured to display any compliance information or instructions for candidates or Recruiting users. It displays at the bottom of the candidate profile and be displayed, hidden, or not used at all. While the footer on the candidate profile isn't used often, it can be a valuable tool to communicate information to both candidate and recruiter audiences.

Comments

Also called recruiter comments, the **Comments** area is available to Recruiting users only and allows them to provide comments about a candidate (see Figure 4.14). Comments can be seen by other Recruiting users, but only the user leaving a comment may edit or delete it. This portlet works in conjunction with comments on the application, and you may choose to make comments left there visible on the candidate profile as well.

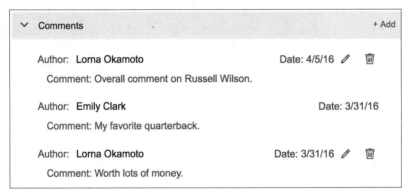

Figure 4.14 Leaving Recruiter Comments on the Candidate Profile That Are Visible to Other Recruiters

Tags

Tags are a way to identify candidates at a later time, such as in a candidate search. They are only available to Recruiting users and will display on the candidate profile as well as the application. Figure 4.15 shows the **Tags** area with tags that have been assigned to a candidate. Tags are completely ad hoc—any Recruiting user may create any kind of tag. Along with tags, you can also mark a candidate as a **Favorite**.

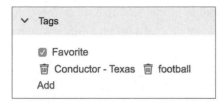

Figure 4.15 Tags Used to Identify and Search for Candidates

Jobs Applied

This portlet provides critical information to recruiters while evaluating a candidate for a job. It provides information on other jobs for which the candidate has submitted an application, as shown in Figure 4.16. This portlet is only visible to Recruiting users and displays the job title, requisition ID, recruiter name, and current status of that candidate for that job. If the Recruiting user has access to the requisition, the title will appear as a link that will take them to the requisition details. You can configure which internal users have access to the **Jobs Applied** portlet by permissioning the jobs-applied field in the candidate data model (CDM) XML template.

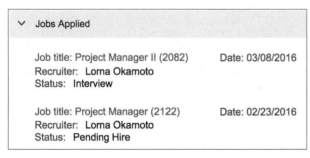

Figure 4.16 Viewing Other Jobs for Which a Candidate Has Applied and Is Being Considered

4.2   Application

Candidates express interest in a position by submitting an application. The application associates the candidate with a specific requisition. The application works in conjunction with the candidate profile to capture and convey all pertinent information about a candidate's qualifications for a job. Similar to the requisition, an application is defined in a template known as the candidate data model (CDM). Application templates have several features that allow you to present different fields to different users based on whether they are internal or external candidates or present country-specific information based on where the job is located. The data collected on the application is presented together with the candidate profile so Recruiting users have the full picture of every candidate to make informed hiring decisions.

The candidate view of the application is presented as a single page with no separate portlets as you find on the candidate profile. In the following sections, let's take a more in-depth look at the features of the application in SAP SuccessFactors, including the application template, single-stage and multistage applications, and how the application interacts with the candidate profile.

4.2.1   Application Template

As mentioned in the preceding section, applications are defined by templates, and each application template is associated with one requisition template. The application template is designed to capture job-specific information from candidates and facilitate capturing information from recruiters throughout the evaluation process, for example, results of background checks or drug screens. The candidate view of the application is presented as a single page with fields listed from top to bottom (see Figure 4.17) and with no portlets as there are on the candidate profile. The application supports field types including:

- Free text
- Picklist fields
- Text area fields
- Instructional headers
- Date fields
- Radio buttons

You can define header fields with colors to break up the flow of the application and organize fields in logical sections. Fields on the application will sync with the candidate profile so that data such as name, address, and email address will be carried over from the candidate profile when a candidate submits an application.

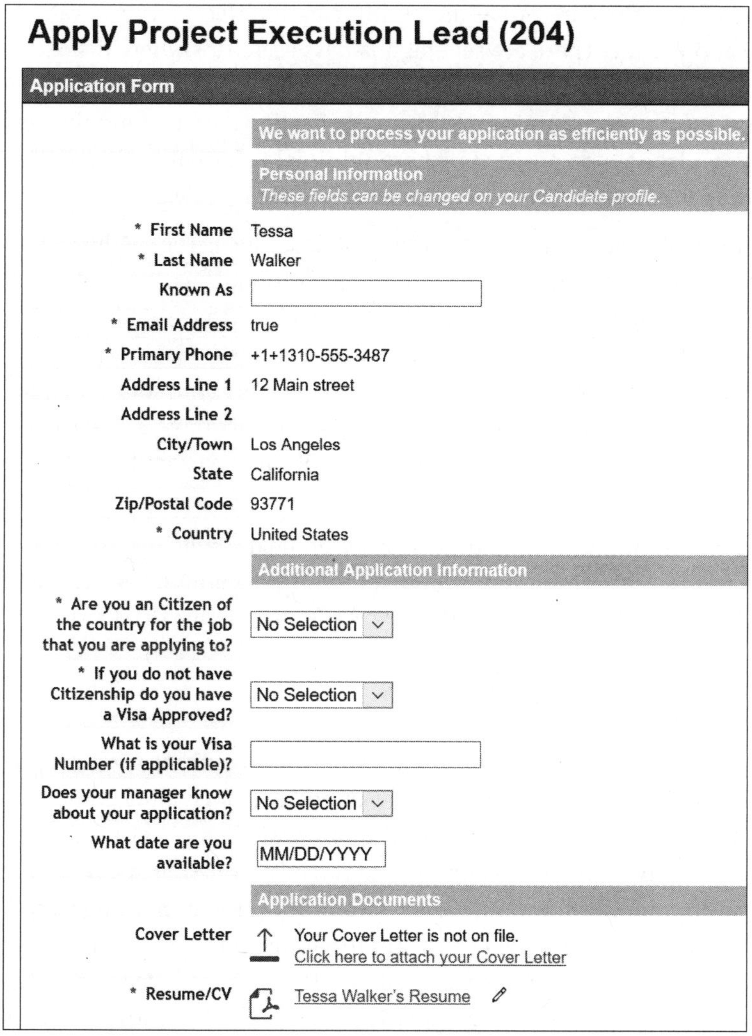

Figure 4.17 Application with Headers in Recruiting

4.2.2 Basic Single-Stage Application

The basic application template presents all fields to the candidate at once. This is referred to as a *single-stage application,* as opposed to a multistage application, which will be discussed in the next section. This is the simplest process candidates can experience because they are providing all information necessary to evaluate their candidacy at one time. There are several business scenarios where it's necessary to extend the application process, but businesses can manage using a single-stage application most of the time. Single-stage applications are commonly used for hourly or direct-labor type positions where minimal information is required and the application process should be as quick and easy as possible.

The best user experience will capture most of the candidate data on the candidate profile while collecting job-specific information on the application. Thus, the application itself is fairly short with contact information being synced from the candidate profile, the résumé and cover letter being captured or carried over from the candidate profile, followed possibly by an acknowledgement, and then prescreening questions, as applicable. After a candidate submits the application, the process is complete, and evaluation can commence. Data on the application isn't editable by the candidate after the submission.

In single-stage applications, Recruiting users can see all fields in all application statuses as long as they have view permission for that field. Permissions to view and edit application fields on a single-stage application are maintained in the CDM XML.

4.2.3   Multistage Application

In a multistage application configuration, the candidate and Recruiting users are presented with different fields in the application to view and edit depending on the current status of the application. In other words, the candidate completes a subset of application data at the initial point of applying and can be permissioned to edit that data and/or complete additional fields in a later status. For example, in the new application status, the candidate will provide basic information and a résumé. In a later stage of the evaluation process, perhaps after a phone screen or interview status, the candidate will be asked to return to the application, be presented with additional fields, and will be asked to provide additional information.

With multistage applications, the permissions to view and edit fields are maintained in the job requisition data model (JRDM) XML instead of the CDM XML. The exceptions are three fields: statusId, resume, and coverLetter. These fields are still permissioned in the CDM.

Some common use cases for collecting information from applicants at different points in the process include the need to ask for references prior to the interview, to collect the Social Security number and date of birth prior to the background check, or simply to keep the initial application as streamlined as possible. The additional information only needs to be collected from applicants who reach a certain stage in the process, such as the interview or offer stage. Collecting this information upfront at the initial application stage would lead to a higher candidate drop-off and may also put the company at some risk in asking for and storing sensitive data on all applicants.

In a multistage application environment, Recruiting users can also be permissioned to view and edit different fields depending on the status of the application. Let's look at three examples of how this might be used:

- In a screening or interviewing status, you could configure fields to capture the date and notes on a phone screen. These fields would only appear when a candidate is placed into the identified status.

- You could configure a start date field on the application, making it required and visible to recruiters only after the candidate reaches an offer status. This would allow you to track an accurate start date without having to edit the offer approval form if the start date changes after the offer has been negotiated.

- Similar to the start date field, you could configure an offer acceptance date on the application, making it required and visible to recruiters only after the candidate reaches an offer status. You could then use this date as a trigger for calculating time to fill.

Making these fields required ensures that you collect this data from the recruiters because they won't be able to advance the candidate to the next status until all required fields have been completed. In a multistage application, for candidates moving to any **In Progress** status, all required fields for all status operators must be filled out. An applicant can be moved to a **Disqualification** status at any point, regardless of whether or not the required fields are completed.

4.2.4 Country-Specific Functionality and Overrides

Companies that operate and recruit globally need to be able to differentiate the information they collect from applicants based on the country of the position with a single application template. In the United States, for example, companies subject to Equal Employment Opportunity Commission (EEOC) regulations are required to request gender and race/ethnicity information from applicants. In other countries, it's against the law to do so. Many companies also want to have a different application experience for internal applicants versus external applicants. Both of these requirements can be handled with what is known as *overrides* in the CDM. This feature basically defines business rules that govern when and to whom fields are displayed, whether they are candidates or Recruiting users. In this way, you can configure a single application template that covers requirements of different countries and internal versus external candidates.

Overrides can also be configured to hide country-specific or candidate-type specific information from Recruiting users. For example, in some countries, it's customary to collect information on marital status and nationality and display this information to recruiters in those countries. In other countries, you can't ask for that information from applicants or display it to Recruiting users. In such cases, an override could be configured to display it only when necessary per country requirements and regulations.

To configure overrides, you first define the fields in the CDM and permission them appropriately, either in the application for single-stage scenarios or the job requisition for multistage scenarios. Then you define the override in the application template. Overrides must be placed immediately following the `field-permission` element. The proper method of setting up an override is as follows:

1. Define the application field definition.

2. Set the public attribute on the field definition to `<public="false">` so the field doesn't appear.

3. Set up the attribute conditions to state when the field(s) should appear and to whom:

   – Configure overrides for external candidates separately from internal candidates.

   – List each country separately (using the asterisk to reflect all countries won't work for overrides).

So if you wanted to display the **Gender** field to external candidates applying to jobs in the United States, it would look like Listing 4.1.

```
<field-attr-override>
  <override>
    <description><![CDATA[For external applicants in the US only.]]></description>
    <country><![CDATA[US]]></country>
    <field-attr attribute="public" value="true" applicant="external"/>
```

```
    </override>
    <field refid="gender"/>
</field-attr-override>
```

Listing 4.1 Configuring Overrides for the Gender Field to Display to External Candidates Applying to a Job in the United States

The override feature uses the standard eQuest country field on the requisition. If you want overrides to work properly, you must use this standard field and define the country values in **Set Up Job Board** options in Admin Center. Using a custom picklist for country won't drive this functionality. You also need to be careful not to repeat the attribute configuration in the field definition or declare two overrides that conflict with each other.

Overrides can be a powerful feature to support the data needs of multiple countries, but they will increase the configuration complexity and the testing duration. The more countries that are in scope, the greater the amount of testing is required. Testers should not only do positive testing to ensure that fields are appearing to users in countries as configured, but *negative* testing should also occur to ensure unintended users aren't seeing fields they aren't meant to see.

Let's complete our discussion of the application by looking at how the candidate profile and application interact.

4.2.5   Interaction between the Candidate Profile and Application

The application consists of the information submitted by the candidate at the point of application, a snapshot of the candidate's profile taken the moment a Recruiting user first views the application, data added to the record by the Recruiting user, and possibly additional data added to the record by the candidate after the initial apply. Permissions in the application control what the candidate sees during and after applying for a job, and what a Recruiting user sees when viewing candidates who have applied for a job.

When applying for a job, candidates are first taken through the candidate profile. The candidates can review and update their information if they have created a profile in the past or create a new profile if it's the first time. Certain data specified on the profile can be passed from the candidate profile to the application as long as both the application XML and candidate profile XML have the same field ID and configuration. Data are passed from the candidate profile to the application only at the point when the candidate initially applies to a job. If candidates update their candidate profile after applying, the updated information won't be passed to the application.

Data are synched from the application back to the candidate profile any time it's changed on the application; the system assumes the most recent updates should always be fed back to the candidate profile.

4.3 Using the Candidate Workbench

The Candidate Workbench displays all candidates assigned to a requisition. This includes those that applied directly, those submitted as employee referrals, and those forwarded or added to the requisition by a Recruiting user. The Candidate Workbench can be filtered to show all candidates or only active candidates. Active candidates are those that haven't withdrawn from consideration or been dispositioned by a Recruiting user. You can access the Candidate Workbench by clicking the number displayed in the **Candidates** column when viewing your list of requisitions or by clicking the **Candidates** option from the job requisition detail screen.

Recruiting users have a slightly different view of the application. The header at the top of the application includes candidate contact information, links to the applicant's cover letter, résumé, and profile, as well as an email button and link to the **Take Action** menu (see Figure 4.18).

Figure 4.18 Application Header: Candidate Snapshot Information and Action Options

In the following sections, we'll look at the different portlets that make up the Candidate Workbench, the different columns that appear within it, and how to sort and highlight candidates.

4.3.1 Portlets

The rest of the application is made up of different portlets of information. Note that you can't reorder, rename, or create new portlets on the application. The portlets are as follows:

- **Application**

  This portlet includes fields editable by Recruiting users that are hidden from candidates as well as the application information provided by the candidate (see Figure 4.19). This portlet is always displayed. The fields that are shown can be controlled by permissions.

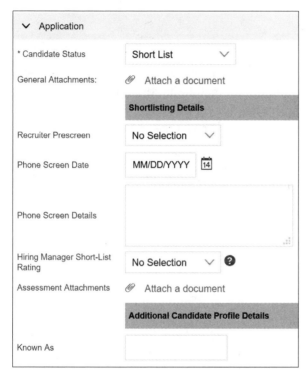

Figure 4.19 Application Portlet: Editable Fields Specifically Meant for Recruiting Users on the Application

- **Comments**

  This portlet displays free-form comments made by Recruiting users about the application. Comments are date stamped and include the author's name, as shown in Figure 4.20. This portlet tracks comments made by any Recruiting user who can access the portlet. Users can only edit or delete their own comments. This portlet can be configured as hidden or visible based on the permissions to the comments field in the application template.

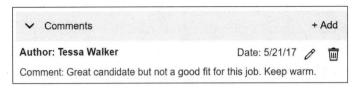

Figure 4.20 Comments Portlet: Tracks Comments Made by Various Recruiting Users

- **Interviewers**
  This portlet displays information about scheduled interviews as well as provides the ability to set up a new interview. Note that this portlet assumes the company isn't using Interview Scheduling or Interview Scheduling with Outlook. This portlet can be configured as hidden or visible based on the permissions to the `interviewAssessment` feature in the application template.

- **Screening Details**
  This portlet displays the prescreening questions and responses, as shown in Figure 4.21. This portlet can't be permissioned or hidden; it's always displayed.

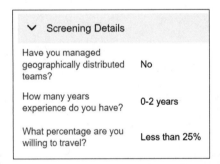

Figure 4.21 Screening Details Portlet: Displays Candidate Answers to Prescreening Questions

The following portlets are the different background elements that were configured on the candidate profile, such as education and previous employment. This section can't be permissioned or hidden; it's always displayed.

- **Jobs Applied**
  This portlet displays the job title, requisition ID, recruiter name, current candidate

status, and last modified date of the candidate pipeline status. If the Recruiting user has access to the requisition, the title will appear as a link to the requisition details. This portlet is permissioned in the Admin Center.

- **Correspondence**
  This portlet displays information about email notifications sent to the applicant from the system, including the date the notification was sent, who sent it, and a link to the notification itself, as shown in Figure 4.22. To view the notification, select the active link of the notification subject. This portlet can't be permissioned or hidden; it's always displayed.

Figure 4.22 Correspondence Portlet: Tracks All Email Communication Sent from the System to a Candidate

- **Onboarding**
  This portlet displays after an applicant has been sent to the SAP SuccessFactors Onboarding module. The portlet shows the date the applicant was transferred, by whom, and whether the transfer of data to Onboarding was successful or not. If successful, the portlet also contains a link directly to Onboarding. This portlet can be configured as hidden or visible based on the permissions to the onboarding feature in the application template.

- **Offer Letter**
  This portlet displays information about offers sent to the applicant, including the date the offer was sent, how it was sent, who sent it, and a link to the offer letter itself, as shown in Figure 4.23. This portlet can't be permissioned or hidden; it's always displayed. If the **Online Offer** option has been enabled, the portlet will also show whether the candidate has viewed the offer letter and accepted or declined it.

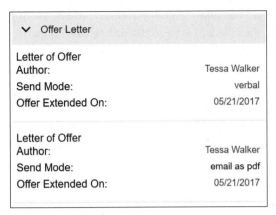

Figure 4.23 Offer Letter Portlet: Tracks All Forms of the Offer

- **Application Status Audit Trail**

  This portlet displays the statuses the applicant has moved through on this specific requisition, including the status name, the date the status was changed, and who changed the status, as shown in Figure 4.24. This portlet can't be permissioned or hidden; it's always displayed.

Figure 4.24 Application Audit Trail Portlet: Tracks All Activity Taken against a Candidate

- **Tags**

  This portlet displays tags previously assigned to the candidate. Recruiting users with appropriate permissions can add new tags. This feature must first be enabled in provisioning and permissioned in role-based permissions.

- **More Information**

  This portlet displays contact information and any custom fields configured as viewable or editable by Recruiting users. This portlet is always displayed. The fields that are shown can be controlled by permissions.

4.3.2   Understanding the Columns in the Candidate Workbench

The Candidate Workbench displays the list of candidates assigned to a requisition with specific columns of information. There are standard predelivered columns, but you can configure custom columns as well.

Standard Columns

The standard columns in the Candidate Workbench are as follows:

- **Name**

  This column displays the name of the candidate, with a hyperlink to the candidate's application. A color-coded business card based on candidate type is displayed to the right of the candidate's name. Additional information about the candidate is displayed when you hover over the business card:

  - **Internal Candidate**

    This business card is colored blue and contains the candidate's name with a link to the candidate's employee profile, position and location in the organization, résumé and email address.

  - **External Candidate**

    This business card is colored yellow and contains a link to the candidate's résumé, phone number, and email address.

  - **Agency Candidate**

    This business card is colored green and contains a link to the candidate's résumé, phone number, and email address. It also contains information about the agency that submitted the candidate, including the agency name, date the agency's ownership of the candidate expires, and the date the candidate was last updated.

  If a candidate was referred by an employee, an employee referral icon will appear to the right of the business card.

- **New**

  This column contains one of three values:

- **New**

  This value appears next to an applicant until a Recruiting user displays the application. As soon as a Recruiting user opens the application, the **New** flag disappears.

- **Updated**

  This value is only available in environments where multistage application functionality is enabled. The **Updated** flag appears when the candidate has edited the application since the last time a Recruiting user viewed it. The **Updated** flag disappears after a Recruiting user opens the updated application.

- Blank

  When no value is shown in this column, this means the application has been viewed by a Recruiting user since the applicant edited it.

- **Status**

  This column displays the current step of the candidate pipeline where the candidate is. If the candidate was added to the requisition by a Recruiting user or as an employee referral, the **Status** column will display the **Forwarded** status.

- **Rating**

  This column displays the total sum of all points assigned to the candidate's response to weighted questions. If a candidate was manually added to the requisition and hasn't yet completed the application, the score will show as **0.0**. If there are no weighted questions assigned to a requisition, then the column will show **N/A**.

- **Source**

  This column displays a high-level view of the how the candidate was assigned to the requisition. Examples of sources you'll see in the **Source** column include **Internal Site, Corporate: Site Name**, and **Forwarded**. If you use Recruiting Marketing, you'll also see **Recruiting Marketing: Source 1** and **Recruiting Marketing: Source 2**.

- **Candidate Source**

  This column includes more details about how the candidate was assigned to the requisition than the **Source** column. Some of the source names are repeated, but additional values you may see in the **Candidate Source** column include **Agency Name, Recruiter Sourced**, or **Employee Referral**.

- **Phone Number**

  This column lists the phone number from the candidate's employee profile.

- **Last Updated**

  This column displays the date the application was last updated.

Custom Display Columns

You can define custom display columns for the Candidate Workbench. These are configured in the candidate profile XML with the `candidate-summary-display-options-config` element. This element allows you to define which candidate profile and application fields are available as display options on the candidate summary page for a requisition. Some examples of custom display columns include a **High Potential** indicator (defined as a custom field on the candidate profile) and a **Recruiter Rating** (defined as a custom field on the application). These custom display options can be grouped into categories to make it easier for Recruiting users to personalize. Note that the `candidate-summary-display-options-config` element doesn't support background elements from the candidate profile.

If you configure a field to be available as a display column in the Candidate Workbench, all users with access to the Candidate Workbench will be able to see data in that column. You should therefore think carefully before configuring a field as a display option if it could contain sensitive data that needs to be hidden from certain users.

Personalizing Display Columns

End users can choose to hide or display the following standard columns: **Rating**, **Source**, **Candidate Source**, **Phone Number**, and **Last Updated**. Custom display columns can be defined as visible by default to all users or not. All custom display columns can be hidden or displayed by the end user. Users can modify their personal view to display the candidate information that is most helpful to them, as shown in Figure 4.25. To hide or display the display columns, click on the **Display Options** button above the list of candidates.

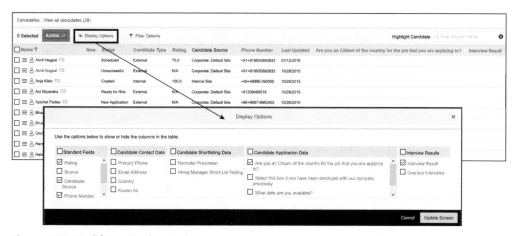

Figure 4.25 Modifying Display Options

4.3.3   Sorting Candidates

Most columns in the Candidate Workbench can be sorted by simply clicking the column header. However, you can't sort by two columns at the same time. The **Name** column consists of both the first and last name of the candidate. Clicking on the column header will sort the column by first name. If you want to enable Recruiting users to sort the list by last name, you need to add **Last Name** as a custom display column for the Candidate Workbench. **Last Name** will appear as an additional column to the standard **Name** field that displays first and last name.

4.3.4   Highlight Candidates

When you have a lot of applicants on a requisition, it can sometimes be challenging to quickly find a specific candidate. The **Highlight Candidate** field allows recruiters to search for candidates assigned to a specific requisition by keyword. Simply type in the keyword in the **Highlight Candidate** field, and click the **Search** icon. Any candidates found matching the keywords are highlighted in the list.

4.4   Evaluating Candidates through the Talent Pipeline

The talent pipeline documents the statuses, sometimes referred to as the workflow, that candidates should be taken through as part of the recruiting process. You define the steps or statuses that make up the talent pipeline as part of the implementation process. Part of that setup includes defining which roles have permission to see candidates in which statuses as well as which roles have permission to move candidates into which statuses. This section explains the layout of the talent pipeline and how you can take action on candidates, including emailing them and moving them into different statuses.

4.4.1   Overview

You access the talent pipeline for a requisition by clicking the number displayed in the **Candidates** column when viewing your list of requisitions or by clicking the **Candidates** option from the job requisition detail screen. The talent pipeline visual is displayed above the list of candidates assigned to the requisition and contains the statuses that candidates go through during the evaluation process, as shown in Figure 4.26. Depending on how many statuses are included in your talent pipeline, you may be able to scroll right and left to see all statuses. You can hide and display the talent pipeline visual by clicking the **Talent Pipeline** option above the list of candidates.

Figure 4.26 Talent Pipeline Containing the Candidate Statuses

As mentioned, you can filter candidates assigned to the talent pipeline by active candidates or all candidates. You can also sort the list of candidates by the display columns to help prioritize which candidates you evaluate first, for example, those who rate highly in prescreening questions or are employee referrals.

The talent pipeline displays the list of statuses in a bar above the Candidate Workbench. When looking at the talent pipeline, each status the Recruiting user has permission to see is visible along with a number indicating how many candidates are in each status.

You can review candidates in the pipeline one by one or as a group. To review candidates one by one, you click on their name in the candidate list. This brings up their application record, which shows the following details:

- **Application Status**
- **Contact Information**
- **Candidate Profile Information**
- **Responses to Prescreening Questions**, if applicable
- **Attachments** (résumé/cover)
- **Comments**
- **Jobs Applied For**
- **Correspondence**
- **Application Status Audit Trail**

To review a group of candidates, you select multiple candidates from the list of candidates by clicking the checkbox to the left of their names, click the **Action** menu, and then click **View Résumé**. This brings up the **Résumé Viewer** window, which allows you to quickly page through the résumés of multiple candidates. However, with this method, you only see the candidate's résumé and not the additional details you would see if you click on the candidate's name to display the full application record.

After the Recruiting user reviews an applicant, he moves the applicant to the next logic step or status in the talent pipeline. There are multiple ways to move candidates in the talent pipeline as outlined later in the chapter. Prerequisite for moving candidates is permission to the `statusId` field on the application template XML as well as permission to move a candidate as defined within the application status set itself.

4.4.2   Emailing Candidates

If the end user has permission, he can email candidates directly, either individually or in a group. By default, all operators have permission for the **Email** button on the application. You can, however, restrict the permission to email candidates by role using the `<candidate-email-permission type="candidateEmail">` element in the JRDM XML.

Click on the **Email** button to access the email screen where you can select from the library of predefined email templates or draft your own email message. Emails are stored against each application so that you can always audit the communication sent to candidates.

4.4.3   Dispositioning Candidates

Properly documenting the steps that each candidate is taken through as part of the recruiting process is very important for a couple of reasons. One is for compliance. An organization needs to be able to defend itself with hard data if an applicant sues for unfair hiring practices. Being able to clearly demonstrate that each candidate is taken through the same process, as well as being able to show the specific steps the candidate in question was taken through, helps the company in its defense. Another reason is for operational efficiency. If you track each step candidates are taken through as part of the hiring process, you're able to analyze potential bottlenecks in the process and implement process improvements.

Unfortunately, dispositioning candidates can be tedious and time-consuming. Recruiting simplifies the process by offering numerous ways to disposition candidates as well as the ability to automatically disposition candidates in certain circumstances, as will be discussed in the following sections.

Drag and Move

Select the applicant you want to move by clicking the icon (three horizontal lines) to the left of the candidate name and dragging the candidate to the relevant status.

Use Status Dropdown

Click on the candidate's name to access the application details (see Figure 4.27). Select the relevant status from the **Candidate Status** dropdown, and click **Save**. If status groups are used, first select the group, and then choose the particular status in the second field.

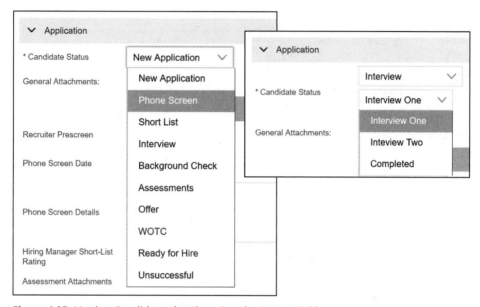

Figure 4.27 Moving Candidates by Changing the Status Field

Move Candidate Button

Click on the candidate's name to access the application details. Scroll to the bottom of the application details, and click **Move Candidate**. Select the relevant status in the **Move Candidate** pop-up that appears, and click **Apply Updates**.

Action Menu

Select one or more candidates from the list by clicking the checkbox to the left of their names, click the **Action** menu, and then click **Move Candidate** (see Figure 4.28). Select the relevant status in the **Move Candidate** pop-up that appears, and click **Apply Updates**. This moves all selected applicants to the chosen status. Alternatively, you can select **Advance Candidate** from the **Action** menu. This will advance each selected candidate to the next status that follows the one they are currently in.

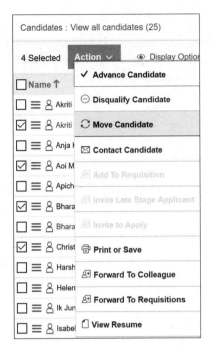

Figure 4.28 Action Column Options

Résumé Viewer

Select multiple candidates from the list of candidates by clicking the checkbox to the left of their names, click the **Action** menu, and then click **View Résumé**. From the **Résumé Viewer** window, click **Move Candidate**. Select the relevant status, and click **Apply Updates**.

Automatic Dispositioning

In a few instances, the system can automatically move candidates into one of the predefined final statuses. If you use prescreening questions to rate candidates' suitability for a position, those candidates who are deemed unsuitable based on their responses to the questions are moved into the system status **Auto Disqualified**. If candidates delete their profile after applying for a job or ask the administrator to delete their profile for them, the candidates will be moved into the **Deleted On Demand by Candidate** or **Deleted On Demand By Admin** status. If candidates withdraw their application, they are moved into the **Withdrawn By Candidate** status. If the organization has configured data privacy functionality, and candidates revoke their acceptance of the company's data privacy statement after applying, they are moved to the **Declined DCPS** status.

After the final candidate is selected, and there are no more openings on a requisition, recruiters generally want to move on to working on filling another open position and not have to go through all remaining candidates on the requisition to move them into a final status. In SAP SuccessFactors, you can configure the system to automatically move any candidates on the requisition who didn't reach a final status into the **Requisition Closed** system status. Furthermore, you can also configure the system to automatically move candidates who have applied to multiple positions but hired on one of them to the **Hired On Other Requisition** system status. This configuration is done in Admin Center under **Manage Recruiting Settings**.

4.5   Scheduling Interviews

Scheduling candidates for interviews is a key component of the hiring process. The task of scheduling and managing interview dates and times can be very time-consuming and tedious, especially in organizations that conduct a lot of interviews. In fact, the interview-scheduling task is often managed by a separate role within the organization or even outsourced because it can take so much time and back and forth. Having a recruiting system that helps you organize and schedule interviews can go a long way toward streamlining the recruiting process.

Recruiting offers three different options for scheduling interviews. There are no agreed-upon standard names for the three options, so we'll refer to them here as follows:

- Basic interview scheduling
- Interview scheduling with native calendar
- Interview scheduling with Outlook integration

All three options have advantages and disadvantages, so we'll discuss the details of each in the next sections.

4.5.1   Basic Interview Scheduling

Basic interview scheduling allows you to record interview dates and times as well as send notifications to interviewers. It doesn't include built-in calendar functionality or integration to external calendars like Microsoft Outlook. If using the basic interview scheduling option, you'll need to check interviewer and interviewee availability outside of Recruiting. The benefits of using this option include integration to Interview Central, where your interviewers can record feedback on interviewees, define a reusable interview panel, and send standardized notifications to interviewers.

Prerequisite for using basic interview scheduling is to configure and permission the `interviewAssessment` feature in the JRDM XML for at least one candidate status and requisition operator.

When using basic interview scheduling, an **Interviewers** portlet will appear in the application, as shown in Figure 4.29. The **Interviewers** portlet will appear in only those statuses for which the `interviewAssessment` feature is permissioned and to Recruiting operators that have been assigned `interviewAssessment` permission. This is where you record interview information.

Figure 4.29 Interviewers Portlet with Set Up Interviewers Link

Click **Set up Interviewers** to display a pop-up where you can define the interview team, along with dates and times for each interviewer (see Figure 4.30). Interviewers must exist in your SAP SuccessFactors system. In other words, you can't add interviewers outside of the system.

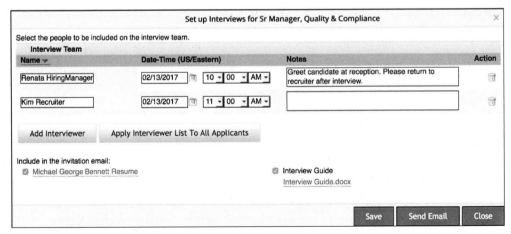

Figure 4.30 Adding Interviewers and Setting Dates and Times

If desired, you can also include the candidate's résumé and the interview guide attached to the requisition in the email notification. These will be included as attachments in the email to interviewers. If you add information in the **Notes** section, these notes will be included in the email to interviewers as well.

The **Apply Interviewer List To All Applicants** button creates a default interview slate that will be proposed for all future interviews scheduled on this requisition. You can delete users from the proposed slate or add new interviewers, but this feature can help provide consistency and a shortcut when scheduling multiple interviews for a position.

Click **Save** to save the interview schedule without sending a notification. If you click **Send Email**, a summary email will be sent to all interviewers on the slate. The email lists the dates and times for each interviewer, the job description as defined on the requisition, the competencies defined on the requisition, the candidate's résumé if it exists, and the interview guide uploaded to the requisition.

4.5.2   Interview Scheduling with Native Calendar

One of the ways interview scheduling can be greatly simplified is by giving candidates the ability to self-schedule their own interview dates and times. This eliminates back and forth emails or phone tag between the candidate and scheduler. When recruiters spend less time on the phone scheduling, canceling, and rescheduling candidate interviews, they can focus on actual value-adding recruiting tasks such as sourcing.

Interview scheduling with native calendar functionality makes this possible. Candidates can review and select from open interview slots, and recruiters check interviewers' calendar availability prior to scheduling interviews. You can schedule individual, panel, and back-to-back interviews, where one interviewer does the first part of the interview, and another interviewer does another part. Numerous standard notifications can be sent out to support the process as well, such as to remind interviewers of upcoming interviews.

Before using this option, you must turn on interview scheduling in Admin Center, map interview location picklists in Admin Center, configure the email triggers related to interview scheduling, permission the calendar for interviewers, and configure and permission the `interviewAssessment` feature in the JRDM XML for at least one candidate status and requisition operator.

When you enable interview scheduling, the **Interviewers** portlet on the application that was discussed for basic interview scheduling is no longer displayed. All interview setup information is managed on the interview **Scheduling** tab, as shown in Figure 4.31.

Interview scheduling with native calendar relies on interviewers entering their availability directly into the calendar in Recruiting. This option doesn't include integration to an external calendaring system, such as Microsoft Outlook, to look up interviewer availability or pull interview availability information into Recruiting.

For recruiters and schedulers to see an interviewer's availability on the native calendar, the interviewers need to maintain their availability from within Recruiting. They can do that by going into Recruiting and clicking on **Interview Scheduling** and then **My Calendar**. From there interviewers can click on the calendar or the **Add Availability** button to define times they are available for interviews. Maintaining this availability makes it possible for recruiters to easily schedule interviews with candidates without leaving the system and for candidates to select their own interview slots.

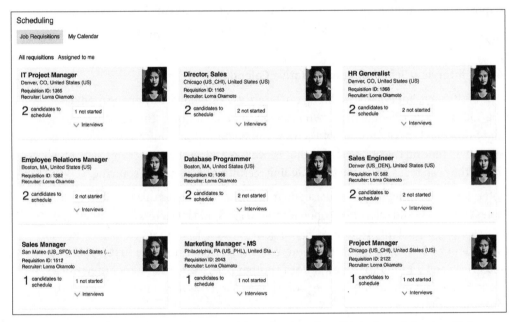

Figure 4.31 Interview Scheduling Dashboard: Managing All Jobs in an Interview Status

4.5.3   Interview Scheduling with Outlook Integration

Interview Scheduling with Outlook integration offers the same advantages as interview scheduling with native calendar but with the added benefit of integrating directly to the Microsoft Outlook calendar. You can book people and rooms into a user's Outlook calendar without having to leave Recruiting.

Interview Scheduling with Outlook integration supports Outlook Web App, Exchange 2010, Office 365, and it doesn't require professional services support to implement. Interviewers don't need to install anything for Outlook integration. They simply need to make sure that default level of access to their calendar is set to free busy time, which is the Exchange default. Using the Outlook integration within Interview Scheduling has several advantages:

- Visibility into Outlook calendar information is possible without leaving Recruiting.
- Predefined templates help standardize notifications.
- Candidates can self-schedule interviews.
- Meeting rooms and interviewers can be booked through the Outlook integration.
- Professional services support isn't required to configure Outlook Interview Scheduling.
- Functionality is actively being developed and enhanced by SAP SuccessFactors.

Along with the many pros for using Outlook integration, there are also some drawbacks:

- You can't refine potential interview dates until after you click **Find Availability** (default is to start with the current week).
- Only one interview room can be booked for entire interview duration.
- Only one interview can be booked per day per candidate.
- The Outlook invitation sent to interviewers is based on a predefined letter template and can't be edited at the time of interview booking.
- Interview rooms must be manually loaded and kept up to date in SAP SuccessFactors.
- After an interview has been sent, you can't change the duration or the interviewers. If a change is necessary, the organizer must delete the candidate from that schedule and set up a new interview schedule. The candidate will be notified via email.

Table 4.1 provides an overview of the various scheduling options and what is supported in each.

	Basic Scheduling	Native Calendar	Outlook Integration
Supports panel interviewers	Yes	Yes	Yes
Supports sequential interviewers	Yes	Yes	Yes

Table 4.1 Comparison of Interview Scheduling Options

	Basic Scheduling	Native Calendar	Outlook Integration
Email notifications to interviewers	Yes	Yes	Yes
Integration to Interview Central	Yes	Yes	Yes
Calendar (native Recruiting Management)	No	Yes	No
Calendar (Outlook integration)	No	No	Yes
Candidate self-scheduling	No	Yes	Yes
Outlook interview invitation	No	No	Yes
Book meeting rooms	No	No	Yes

Table 4.1 Comparison of Interview Scheduling Options (Cont.)

4.6   Documenting Interview Feedback

After a candidate has been interviewed, it's important to properly document the results of the interview. This not only helps in determining which candidate to offer the job to, but it can also help a company defend itself if audited or accused of unfair hiring practices. Interview feedback is collected from all interviewers and is stored centrally in Recruiting in Interview Central. The rest of this section discusses how you can view interview information, rate candidates, and view consolidated interview feedback.

4.6.1   Viewing Interview Information

Interview Central lists all open and closed interviews assigned to an interviewer. After an interview is scheduled in Recruiting using one of the methods described in Section 4.5, a new **Interview Assessment** form is placed on the **Interview Central** tab for each interviewer. The interviewer will then see the **Recruiting** option on their home menu. There is no need to explicitly grant interviewers permission to Recruiting; they will implicitly be granted permission after being assigned as an interviewer.

The main **Interview Central** screen shows basic information about each interview, such as the **Job Title**, **Req ID**, **Hiring Manager**, and **Job Description** (link), as shown in Figure 4.32. Clicking on the job title opens up further information, including notes from the hiring manager, an interview guide if one was attached to the requisition, and the list of candidates the interviewer is set to interview for that position.

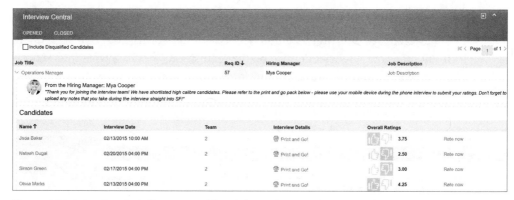

Figure 4.32 Interview Details Managed from the Main Interview Central Screen

Interviewers can drill down into further information about the candidates they are scheduled to interview, view the interview date and time, and see who is on the interview team. Interview Central also includes a **"Print and Go" pack**, which summarizes the interview information into a printable format so that interviewers can take it into an interview with them for reference (see Figure 4.33).

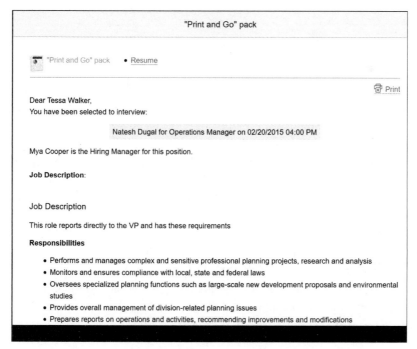

Figure 4.33 "Print and Go" Pack: Helpful Information for Interviewers

4.6.2   Rating Interviewees

Interview feedback is recorded in interview assessment forms. Interview assessment forms use the competencies defined on the requisition. These are what interviewers rate candidates against. If no competencies are defined on the requisition, the interview assessment form won't display properly. It's therefore best practice to make **Competencies** a required field on the requisition template.

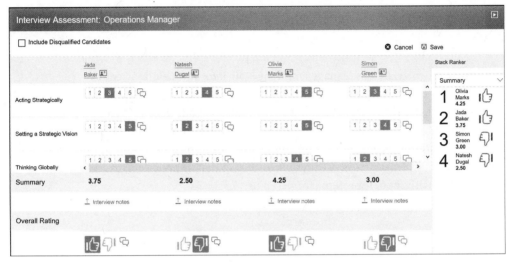

Figure 4.34 Interview Feedback Captured for Each Candidate

Interviewers navigate to Recruiting, click on the **Interview Central** tab, and then click the **Rate Now** link for a candidate to provide interview feedback. As seen in Figure 4.34, interviewers can assign a numeric rating of how well the candidate fulfills each competency as well as add comments for each individual competency. Additionally, interviewers can provide an overall thumbs-up or thumbs-down rating of the candidate, add overall comments, and attach documents to support their interview feedback.

4.6.3   Viewing Consolidated Interview Feedback

Users can see interview feedback on the candidate summary page in the **Interview Result** column. Hovering over a value reveals more detailed information about the interview feedback, as shown in Figure 4.35.

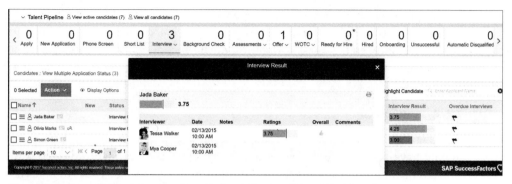

Figure 4.35 Consolidate Interview Results from the Candidate Workbench

Depending on permission, the user can also click on the **View Candidate Ratings** link from the Candidate Workbench to review the interviewers' ratings and feedback on the candidates. Candidates' individual and overall ratings are displayed for each interviewer. Hovering over a candidate's competency rating shows how each interviewer rated the candidate against that competency and any comments they may have made, as shown in Figure 4.36.

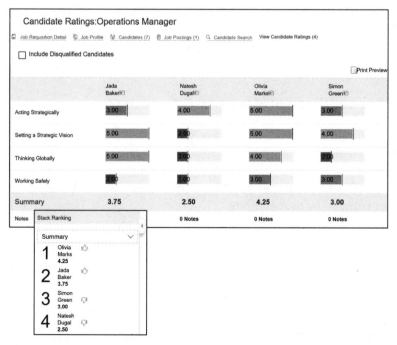

Figure 4.36 Viewing Candidate Ratings for All Candidates

You can also use the **Stack Ranking** dropdown menu to compare the consolidated rating of all interviewers for candidates against individual competencies and to order candidates by overall ratings. Overall candidate recommendation is displayed as thumbs up or thumbs down. See Figure 4.36 for an example of the candidate rankings.

4.6.4   Configuration Tips

Assign the `interviewAssessment` feature permission to the appropriate roles that should have access to interview results in the desired statuses in the JRDM XML. There is no difference between the access for interview setup and access to interview results. It's therefore best practice to permission the `interviewAssessment` feature in all interview statuses and statuses beyond interview.

If you want to include an interview guide in Interview Central, be sure to define the standard `interviewGuide` attachment field in the JRDM XML. The **Notes from Hiring Manager** is a standard field in Interview Central that always appears. If you want to include notes for interviewers in Interview Central, you need to define the standard `hiringManagerNote` field in the JRDM XML and grant permission to the hiring manager role to edit the field.

On the application XML, you should define the standard fields `interviewResult` and `overdueInterviews` so that you can define interview-related data on the application record and make some interview information reportable.

4.7   Approving an Offer and Managing Offer Letters

After a recruiter, hiring manager, or other authorized user decides to hire a candidate to fill a job requisition, the offer process consists of assembling details of the offer that will be extended to the candidate; routing these details for approval; generating an offer letter using tokens from the requisition, application, and offer details form; and extending an offer letter to a candidate.

To enable the offer process, you must configure the offer details component in the JRDM. Then you must configure the offer details template XML. In this section, we'll discuss the offer approval process as well as the offer letter capability within Recruiting.

4.7.1   Offer Approvals

The first step in the offer process is to initiate an offer and send it for approval. This feature should be configured to be available in any offer status. When there is a candidate in an offer status, the **Offer Approval** option is available from the **Action** menu. Select **Offer • Offer Approval** from a candidate's details. You need to select the offer approval template, and then you can review the data that are automatically populated and enter offer-specific data, as shown in Figure 4.37. It's possible to have more than one offer details template in the system. For example, you may have one offer details template for salaried positions and another for hourly positions.

The approval workflow for the offer details can be ad hoc, predefined, or a combination of both. By default, Recruiting users can add approvers to the offer details as required for the position. Using the **Add Another** link, you can type the name of any user in the system to be an approver on the offer.

It's also possible to predefine the approvers based on several criteria:

- Roles on the requisition such as recruiter or hiring manager
- User-specific approvers by specifying a user ID
- Groups of approvers, such as finance users

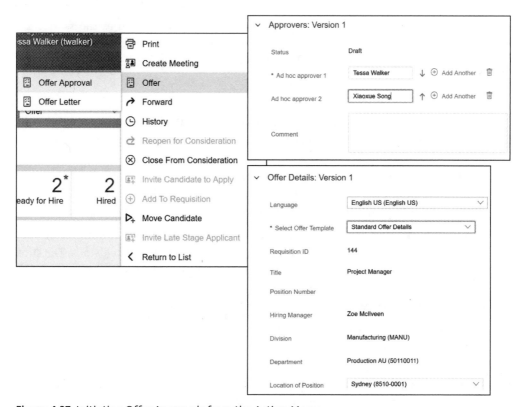

Figure 4.37 Initiating Offer Approvals from the Action Menu

The predefined approvers can be locked down so that they can't be edited. However, a configuration option is to predefine a list of approvers and allow users to add or remove approvers as required. Offer details must have at least one approver. The approval process proceeds linearly from the first approver on the list to each subsequent approver, unless the offer details are declined. If this happens, the approval returns to the user that initiated it for editing and sending it back out for approval. Note that when an offer is declined, the user declining the offer must provide comments. Comments are optional if the offer is approved and sent forward. Every time the offer is edited, the system will create a new version of the offer. This is great for auditing purposes and keeping track of the offer negotiations. Every version of the offer approval is saved by the system and accessible by the user that generated it.

After the offer is approved, the offer letter can be generated.

4.7.2   Offer Letters

Recruiting provides the ability to create and send offer letters using information dynamically generated from various places in the system, such as the requisition, application, offer details, and candidate profile. Offers can also be conveyed via various methods. In this section, we'll discuss creating and sending offers within Recruiting.

Creating Offer Letters

Recruiting provides the ability to maintain a library of offer letter templates that are used to generate candidate-specific offer letters. These letters use data pulled from various areas of the system to dynamically populate information, using tokens placed within the templates. The templates are defined and maintained in Admin Center and selected from the offer letter interface for a selected candidate. Offer letters can be defined by country and language, as shown in Figure 4.38.

When an offer has been approved, and you're ready to generate the offer letter, you make that selection from the **Action** column within the candidate details. The **Offer Letter** screen appears where you'll choose the appropriate template. The offer letter template is displayed with all of the text and tokens as established in the **Manage Offer Letter Templates** area of Admin Center.

When generating the offer letter, you can make adjustments to the body of the offer letter in the **Offer Letter** screen, including adding and removing blocks of text and tokens. Any changes made in this screen will only apply to the individual offer letter being generated and not to the template itself. If you want to make permanent changes, you should adjust the offer letter template in Admin Center.

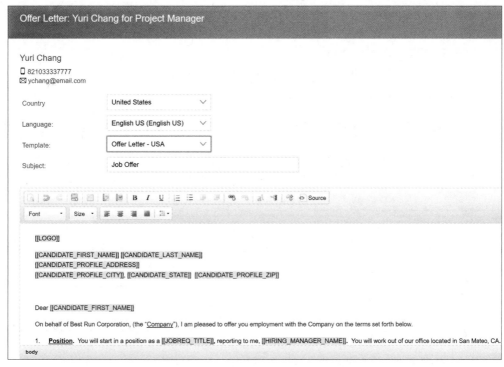

Figure 4.38 Generating Offer Letters from Templates and Populating Data Where You Place Tokens

Methods of Sending an Offer

When the offer letter is generated, the offer letter can be transmitted to the candidate in several ways. All of these methods are available from within the offer letter creation process. When you choose to preview the offer letter or move to the next step in the process, you'll see the offer letter with all the tokens completed with candidate-specific data. You'll also see at the bottom of the page the various methods that are available to send the offer letter (see Figure 4.39):

- **Online Offer with eSignature**
  Use DocuSign to capture an electronic signature.
- **Online Offer**
  The candidate views the offer letter from the candidate profile and accepts or declines it.
- **Verbal Offer**
  Date stamp is used to show that a verbal offer was communicated to the candidate.

- **Email as text**
  While not used much often, send the offer letter as text within an email.

- **Email as PDF attachment**
  Generate a PDF file of the offer letter and send it with an email.

You can also print the offer letter from this screen, if necessary.

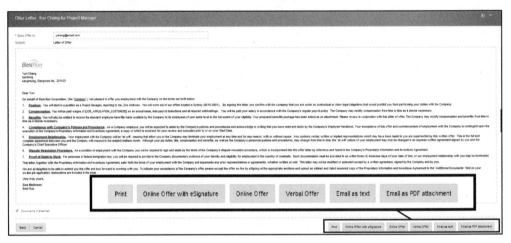

Figure 4.39 Various Methods of Communicating an Offer Letter

4.8   Conducting a Candidate Search

Candidate search enables Recruiting users to search the Recruiting database of candidates for qualified individuals based on experience, career interests, and posted profiles. Recruiting users can apply multiple criteria to identify qualified internal and external candidates.

Users who have permission for candidate search can search through the candidate profile database. The candidate search feature searches candidate profile information, including uploaded résumés, but not application information or responses to prescreening questions.

Candidate search results supports displaying 10, 20, 50, or 100 candidates per page. Viewing all candidates in the list isn't supported due to the impact on system speed when displaying a large number of candidate profiles on a single page.

Several search criteria can be used to build a candidate search, including the following:

- Name search
- Keyword
- Background elements
- Tags

Candidates are added to the search index based on data privacy consent statement settings and candidate data privacy options. If a business doesn't enable data privacy consent statement settings, all internal and external candidates can be found in searches. If a business enables data privacy consent statement settings 2.0, internal and external candidates who haven't accepted the data privacy statement can't be found in searches. The system prompts internal candidates to accept the data privacy statement whenever they click the **My Candidate Profile** or apply for a job. The system prompts external candidates to accept the privacy statement when they register.

Candidates can also define candidate visibility options, which impact how they can be found in searches, as follows:

- **Any company recruiter worldwide**
  Candidate can be found by any Recruiting user with candidate search permission. This is the default setting if the privacy feature isn't turned on.

- **Only recruiters managing roles in my country of residence**
  A Recruiting user in the candidate's country of residence will be able to find the candidate in a candidate search. The system checks to match the Recruiting user's country found in their employee data file with the candidate's country of residence. Recruiters without a country on their employee profile will receive an error when they try to search for candidates. Candidates can't be forwarded to colleagues; attempts to forward candidates will prevent colleagues from being found in the search but won't provide an explanation.

- **Only recruiters managing jobs I apply to**
  This is the most restrictive setting. Candidates with this selected will never be found in candidate search. Candidates will only visible on the requisitions to which they have applied. Candidates can't be forwarded to colleagues; attempts to forward candidates will prevent colleagues from being found in the search but won't provide an explanation.

Candidate search was also discussed in Chapter 3.

4.9   Summary

In this chapter, we discussed many features provided by Recruiting that are available to support the process of finding candidates for open positions and dispositioning them through the talent acquisition process. By using features such as the candidate profile and candidate search, recruiters can actively source their jobs with qualified resources within the candidate database by using the data provided on their candidate profiles. They can then forward these candidates to particular jobs and solicit them to submit an application. The application can capture critical information all at once or in logical phases, and combined with the candidate profile, it presents a holistic view of applicants so educated hiring decisions can be made.

The Candidate Workbench offers numerous tools and features to support Recruiting users as they review, evaluate, and move applicants through the process. Information is continuously updated and displayed through portlets in the candidate detail screen, and action can be taken on candidates in various ways, as best fits the recruiter's preferences. Interviews can be scheduled for candidates and interviewers, or candidates can use self-service features to schedule themselves into interviews via the Interview Scheduling feature. This eliminates much manual work and back and forth between the candidate and scheduler as the responsibility for scheduling is placed with the candidate. When a successful candidate is identified, offers can be quickly and easily generated and sent for approval, and offer letters can then be created and sent in any number of ways.

In the next chapter, we'll look at some additional features in Recruiting that can be leveraged to further build out the applicant-tracking capabilities of your talent acquisition program.

Chapter 5
Additional Recruiting Management Features

SAP SuccessFactors Recruiting Management offers additional features that can help you in your talent acquisition process. Although you can successfully run Recruiting Management without these features, they can help smooth out your processes.

In the previous chapter, we discussed at length the features available within SAP SuccessFactors Recruiting that users have available in their daily quest to source the best candidates for their jobs and move them through the process as quickly and efficiently as possible. Robust tools such as candidate search allow recruiters the opportunity to actively search through profiles already existing in the candidate database and identify potential fits for open jobs.

Features such as prescreening assessments and capturing interview feedback within Interview Central also help recruiters get an overall picture of a candidate's qualifications as compared against other candidates, which assists in making informed hiring decisions.

In this chapter, we turn our attention to some additional features within Recruiting that aren't always used by companies in their talent acquisition activities but are important to understand so that you can evaluate whether you're fully optimizing the system to help meet your talent acquisition objectives. These features include the following:

- Employee referral
- Data privacy and data retention management (DRM)
- Agency portal
- Job Profile Builder
- Competency management

While Job Profile Builder and competency management aren't strictly Recruiting features, they both play a significant role in the recruiting capabilities of the system and its worth furthering the discussion of how they can be leveraged within Recruiting.

Let's begin with a deeper look at the employee referral capability within SAP Success-Factors and discuss this as a valuable source of high-quality candidates.

5.1   Employee Referral

One of the most effective ways to source candidates is via an employee referral program. These programs turn every employee in the company into a kind of sourcer and alleviate the burden of sourcing candidates falling solely on the talent acquisition department. Studies have shown that referred candidates, if hired, stay in their jobs longer than nonreferred hires, and referral programs improve an organization's employee retention rate. A strong employee referral program can be an organization's top way to identify the best talent in the market and attract them to the right jobs. Having a program that is robust yet easy to participate in is a key to success. Communicating the organization's talent needs and the objectives they may be trying to achieve (e.g., increasing diversity by hiring more minorities), and then enabling employees to quickly and easily connect qualified candidates with the right postings, is paramount.

Three parties are involved in any employee referral:

- Referring employee
- Recruiter
- Referred candidate

Recruiting provides a platform to support each of these players in the recruiting process. We'll examine the capabilities of this feature from the perspective of the referring employee and the recruiter. The referred candidate experience is discussed in both of these topics.

5.1.1   Referring Employee Experience

Your existing workforce can often be the best channel to the most qualified candidates. Not only do they know the organizational culture and needs, they have professional networks that can be invaluable to your talent acquisition team. The Recruiting employee referral program allows employees to search for openings and suggest potential candidates for these positions by adding some basic information about the candidate to the database and uploading their résumé. Just as recruiters can add candidates to the external candidate database, employees simply need to enter the following information about a candidate:

- **First Name**
- **Last Name**
- **Email**
- **Phone**
- **Country**

From the **Job Search** page, employees can choose to **Refer Friend to Job** and enter the candidate details to submit the candidate to a particular job, as shown in Figure 5.1.

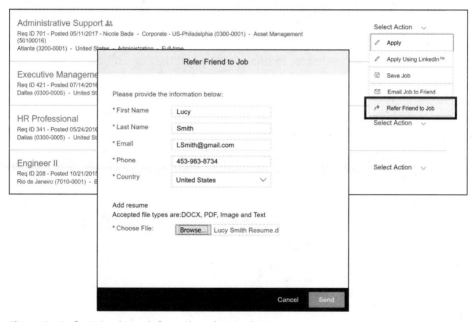

Figure 5.1 Refer Friend to Job from the Job Search Page

The **Add resume** field can be made required or not required in the employee referral settings in Admin Center. Employees won't always have a copy of a candidate's résumé, so making this field required should be discussed thoroughly. The **Phone** field will be required if this field is required on the candidate profile template. If a job is posted both internally and externally, it will have an **Employee Referral** icon next to it, indicating that it's open for a referral. It's important to think through the kind of information that referring employees will have on hand most often when submitting an employee referral. To have a successful program, you want the experience to be as simple and streamlined as possible for your employees. Keeping the required fields to a minimum will help.

When employees make a referral, they must understand the rules that govern the "ownership" of referred candidates and how these impact their ability to make the referral. In the following sections, we'll look at both referral ownership and the process of tracking referrals.

Referral Ownership

The system provides two methods of "owning" a candidate referral. Basically, when an employee submits a referral, the system will run a check against the candidate based on the ownership settings made in Admin Center to determine if the referral is accepted. The mechanics of these settings are discussed later in this section.

Employees can refer candidates in one of two ways. They can submit a referral to a specific requisition, or they can make a general referral, which will add the candidate to the external candidate database where they can be found during candidate search. General referrals are made from the **Your Referrals** area of the **Referral Tracking** page as shown in Figure 5.2.

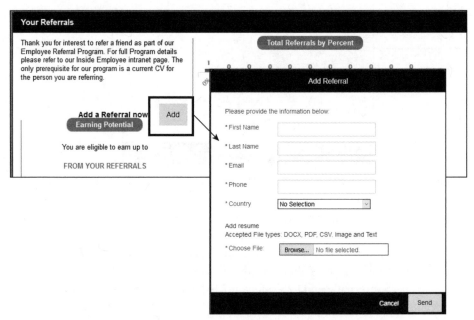

Figure 5.2 Adding General Referrals Directly from Referrals Tracking

If a general referral is made, the candidate will receive an email with the credentials to log in and create a candidate profile. From there, the candidate can search for posted jobs and apply to any of interest.

If a candidate is referred to a specific job by using the **Refer Friend to Job** feature discussed previously, the candidate will be assigned to the **Forwarded** status in the talent pipeline. Referred candidates will receive an email informing them they have been referred and providing their username and a URL to set their password. After they log in, they will be taken to the job description page of the referred job and from there they can complete their candidate profile and apply for the job. If candidates submit an application, they are moved from the **Forwarded** status to **New Application**. Alternatively, the recruiter may review their résumé and invite them to apply for the job.

Tracking Referrals

Employees who submit referrals may track the progress of their referrals from their careers page on the **Referral Tracking** tab as shown in Figure 5.3.

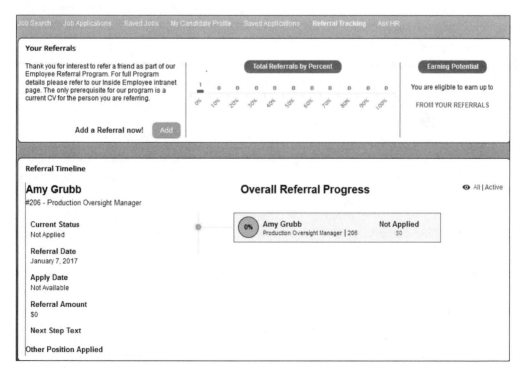

Figure 5.3 Employees Tracking the Progress of Their Referrals

This page is divided into two areas. The **Your Referrals** area provides an overview of all referrals, whereas the **Referral Timeline** shows the progress of specific referrals. Let's look at each element:

- **Your Referrals**

  This area displays a configurable message from talent acquisition that typically provides information about the employee referral program. Employees can also add new referrals here as well as from the **Job Search** page, as discussed in the previous section.

- **Total Referrals by Percent**

  This bar graph shows how far referrals have progressed in the application progress. Percentages are calculated based on the number of applicant statuses visible to employees. This is configured in the applicant status set.

- **Add a Referral now!**

  Referrals can be added directly from the **Referral Tracking** page. These are general referrals and not specific to any particular requisition. When a candidate is referred via this method, if the candidate's email address already exists in the database, the referral isn't allowed. If they exist, the system will prompt you to refer them to a job. Any referrals added this way are searchable in candidate search.

- **Earning Potential**

  This is the sum of all referrals an employee has made. If an employee makes referrals for jobs with varied currencies, the sum for each currency is displayed separately. So, if an employee has referrals in both US dollars and euros, the employee will see a total for both currencies.

- **Referral Timeline**

  This area displays a summary of a selected referral. If no referral is selected, this will display a summary of the referral with the highest percentage of completion.

- **Overall Referral Progress**

  This area displays progress for either all referrals or active referrals. **All** referrals will include disqualified candidates while **Active** includes referrals still in **Forwarded** status who haven't yet applied. Disqualified and hired referrals are excluded from **Active**.

5.1.2   Recruiter Experience

Recruiters can identify candidates that are employee referrals in numerous ways. The application and candidate profile both have an **Employee Referral** portlet that displays information about what job(s) the referred candidate has been referred to, when, and what employee submitted the referral. Second, each employee referral has an icon next to their name in the Candidate Workbench summary page so recruiters can easily identify which candidates have been referred and take immediate action regarding them.

The **Candidates** summary display has two source columns: **Source** and **Candidate Source**. For employee referrals, the **Source** column will contain the value **Forwarded**, while the **Candidate Source** column will contain **Employee Referral** during the preapplication stage (see Figure 5.4). After the candidate applies for the job, the **Source** column displays where the candidate actually applied for the job (e.g., **Corporate: Default Site**).

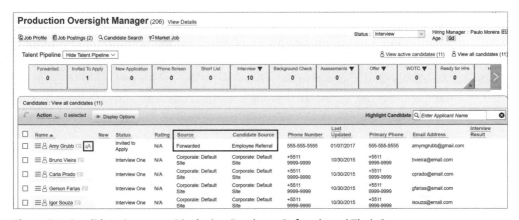

Figure 5.4 Candidate Summary Displaying Employee Referrals and Their Source

5.1.3   Implementing Employee Referral

To implement the employee referral capability, you must first enable the setting in provisioning, as shown in Figure 5.5, to make the settings available within the Admin Center. After it's enabled, the standard erpAmount field must be added to any job requisition data models (JRDMs) to capture the employee referral payout amount. This field is necessary to feed the **My Earning Potential** area of the **Referral Tracking** portlet. Your implementation consultant will enable this setting and add any permissions necessary for the field on the JRDM.

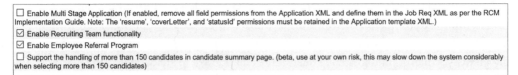

☐ Enable Multi Stage Application (If enabled, remove all field permissions from the Application XML and define them in the Job Req XML as per the RCM Implementation Guide. Note: The 'resume', 'coverLetter', and 'statusId' permissions must be retained in the Application template XML.)
☑ Enable Recruiting Team functionality
☑ Enable Employee Referral Program
☐ Support the handling of more than 150 candidates in candidate summary page. (beta, use at your own risk, this may slow down the system considerably when selecting more than 150 candidates)

Figure 5.5 Enabling Employee Referral in Recruiting Company Settings

After this configuration has been completed, all employee referral program settings are made within Admin Center. These settings are discussed in detail in Chapter 8.

5.2   Data Privacy and Data Retention Management

In today's environment, data security and privacy are of utmost concern for candidates providing their information and companies that are accepting the information. SAP SuccessFactors offers functionality to manage data privacy statements by country for the general application and also specifically for Recruiting. This capability determines whether an external candidate can create a candidate profile in your Recruiting system and how the data will be managed. In this section, we'll examine these features.

5.2.1   Data Privacy Consent Statements for Internal and External Candidates

SAP SuccessFactors supports companies distributing data privacy statements that notify candidates of what will be done with the data they submit in the job search process. These statements are supported for both internal and external candidates and for all countries and in different languages. Maintaining consent statements for external candidates is most common. When configured, external candidates are required to view and accept the data privacy consent statement before creating their profile. If they choose not to accept the consent statement, they aren't able to create a profile.

Data privacy consent statements can apply to all countries, or you can maintain country-specific statements to allow for different policies among different countries. There is also a default statement presented to candidates in countries that don't have their own statement assigned. See Figure 5.6 for an example of setting up a consent statement for the United States.

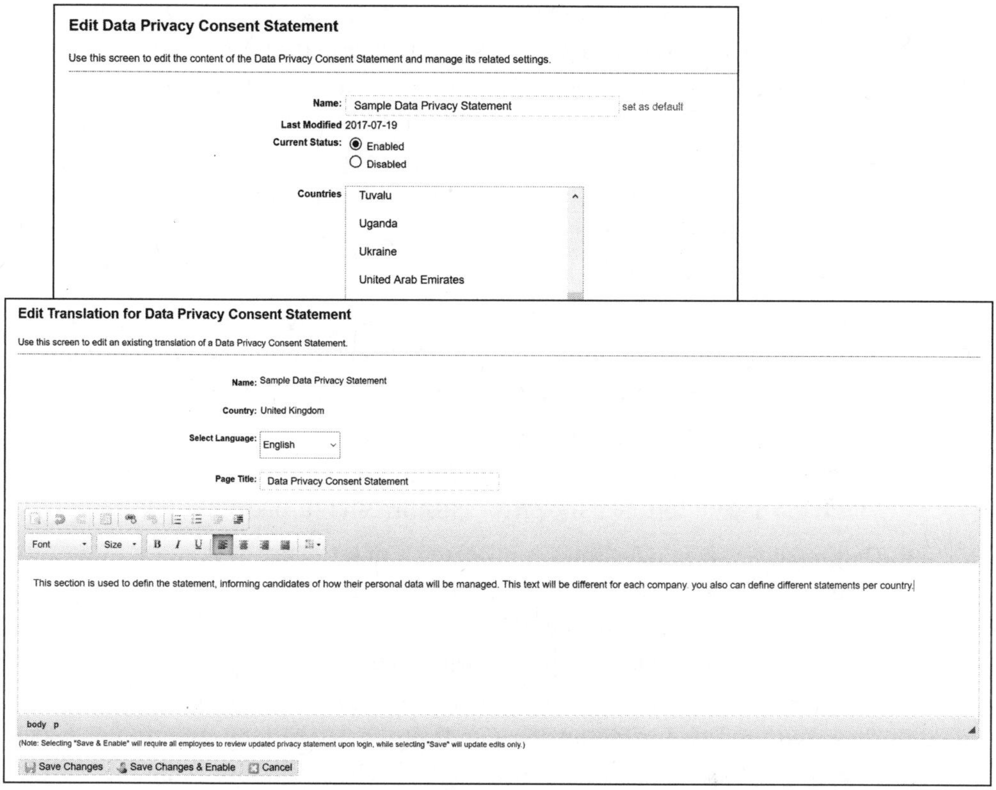

Figure 5.6 Choosing to Set Up Data Consent Statements for All Countries or Specific Countries

Having a default statement is optional; however, if you don't maintain a default statement, and candidates from a country not represented by an assigned statement will be impacted.

Consent statements may also be maintained in various languages that have been assigned in **Manage Recruiting Languages**. If candidates use one of the Recruiting languages enabled in your system, the consent statement will be presented in that language (assuming it has been translated). If the candidate's language isn't available, the statement will be presented in the default language.

After candidates view and accept the consent statement, they always have the option of revoking their consent. They also can choose to delete their candidate profile at any time. It's important to understand the impact of data privacy configuration to candidate data and accounts, and to make clear to your candidates what the consequences are of declining or revoking their acceptance of the terms. First, if candidates choose not to accept the statement, they won't be able to finish completing their profile. If they accept and then at a later time choose to revoke that acceptance, their candidate profile will immediately be inaccessible to them. If candidates have an active application at the time they choose to revoke the data privacy consent, they are immediately moved to the **Declined DPCS** status. They also will no longer be found in searches or be able to apply for jobs.

Short of revoking their acceptance of the data privacy consent statement, candidates may update their settings from their candidate profile at any time. The following settings govern how their data will be used and who can see their data:

- **Any company recruiter worldwide**
  Candidate can be found by any Recruiting user with candidate search permission. This is the default setting if the privacy feature isn't turned on.

- **Only recruiters managing roles in my country of residence**
  A Recruiting user in the candidate's country of residence will be able to find the candidate in a candidate search. The system checks to match the Recruiting user's country in their employee data file with the candidate's country of residence. Recruiters without a country on their employee profile will receive an error when they try to search for candidates. Candidates can't be forwarded to colleagues; attempts to forward candidates will prevent colleagues from being found in the search but won't provide an explanation.

- **Only recruiters managing jobs I apply to**
  This is the most restrictive setting. Candidates with this selected will never be found in candidate search. Candidates will only visible on the requisitions to which they have applied. Candidates can't be forwarded to colleagues; attempts to forward candidates will prevent colleagues from being found in the search but won't provide an explanation.

See Figure 5.7 for an example of how these settings are displayed on the candidate profile.

You can enable data privacy for internal candidates, external candidates, or both. If data privacy is enabled for internal candidates, your employees will be prompted to review and accept the statement when they log into SAP SuccessFactors.

Data privacy consent is reportable. You can use this reporting to demonstrate that candidates have been duly notified of how their data will be handled and have agreed to such handling. You can also use this reporting to better understand how the candidate personal data are used.

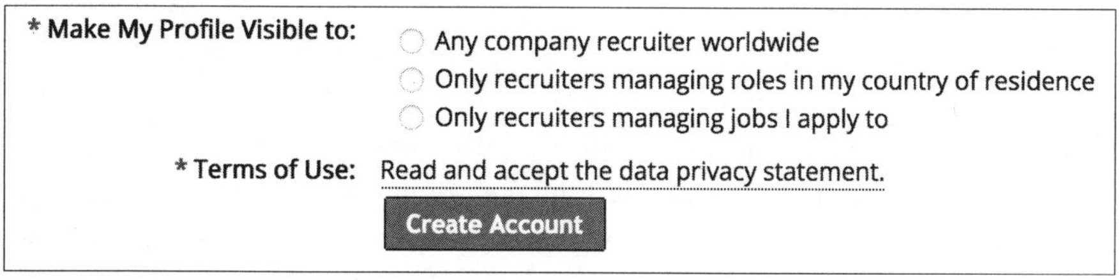

* Make My Profile Visible to:	○ Any company recruiter worldwide
	○ Only recruiters managing roles in my country of residence
	○ Only recruiters managing jobs I apply to
* Terms of Use:	Read and accept the data privacy statement.
	Create Account

Figure 5.7 Candidates Choosing How Their Data Will Be Handled When Creating an Account

The selections candidates make during the profile setup will impact how their data will be handled and who can find them. The more restrictive their choice, the fewer users can find them. This impacts how the candidate data are returned during a candidate search as well. These options may be updated by candidates at any time from their candidate profile.

5.2.2 Implementing Data Privacy Consent Statements

If you already have a live Recruiting system, you can still implement data privacy consent statements. When implemented, candidates will be presented with the consent statements and asked to determine how their data should be managed the next time they log in to the system. Again, if the candidates don't accept the statement, they won't be able to access their accounts. If you're considering implementing this feature, you should think through how to handle candidates that choose to decline and how this will impact candidates who have already applied for jobs.

Candidates need only agree to the data privacy terms once. If you make updates to the statements, you can choose whether you want all candidates to agree to the new statement or just have new candidates affected. If you choose to have all candidates agree to the updated content, they will be presented with the statement at their next login.

Enabling data privacy consent statements will have an impact on how candidate data are available to recruiters and others in the talent acquisition process. If you choose to implement this feature, it's critical that you understand the implications fully so that you know the impacts on things such as candidate search and dispositioning candidates.

5.2.3   Data Retention Management

Data retention management (DRM) is a tool that allows users to purge inactive internal or external user data from the SAP SuccessFactors system for the purpose of complying with country-specific regulations or to adhere to security best practices. DRM applies to modules other than Recruiting Management. Within the Recruiting module, data can be purged for inactive candidates and their respective applications. As various countries have differing regulations regarding data retention periods, SAP SuccessFactors supports setting different durations by country. Settings are made by application and candidate profile data.

After the feature has been enabled and configured by country, purging is a two-step process. First, a purge rule must be established that supports one object type by request. This means that if you want to purge candidate application data and candidate profile data, you need two different purge rules. Figure 5.8 provides an example of a purge rule for purging inactive candidate profiles for candidates who have been inactive for 180 days in all countries. After a purge rule is set up, the second step is to approve it. Purge requests must be approved by at least one approver before running. Approvers are set while creating the purge request. Purge requests can be entered manually or scheduled. Either way, they must be approved before running.

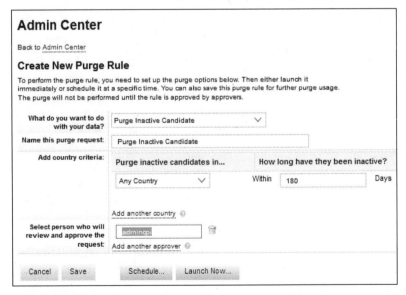

Figure 5.8 Purge Rules Used to Govern Data to Purge and Approvers

When using DRM and purging candidate and application data, you must deal with the issue of anonymization of data and legal minimum obligation periods, as discussed next.

Data Anonymization

Not all data captured during the recruiting process is considered personally identifiable information (PII) data that needs to be removed. With the newest version of DRM, data can be anonymized rather than purged from the system so that it's retained for reporting purposes. You can decide on a field-by-field basis whether data should be anonymized. The anonymize attribute is configured in the field definition in the XML templates. When a field's anonymize attribute is set to "true", then the data in that field will be anonymized, or "X'ed" out by the system so it's no longer legible.

There are three purge actions relevant to Recruiting:

- **Purge Inactive Candidate**
  This action anonymizes inactive external candidates.

- **Purge Inactive Job Application**
  This action anonymizes data from inactive applications. Only closed applications are anonymized in this action.

- **Purge Inactive User**
  This action anonymizes data from inactive internal candidates. Note that this option anonymizes data for the SAP SuccessFactors suite, not just Recruiting Management, so this should be used with extreme caution.

Not all fields configured on the application and candidate profile support anonymization. Your implementation consultant will help you understand what fields may and may not be anonymized, as this is critical in how to manage data retention within your organization.

Legal Minimum Obligation Period

As mentioned earlier, different countries have different regulations regarding retention of data. As part of configuring DRM, you can configure the **Legal Minimum Obligation Period** for each country in which you operate. See Figure 5.9 for an example of different settings by country. Note that this setting can be made globally to apply to all countries, or you can add all the specific countries in which you do business. In terms of Recruiting data, this obligation period is set in relation to candidate and application data, and it applies to how long inactive data will be retained before it's subject to purge/anonymization.

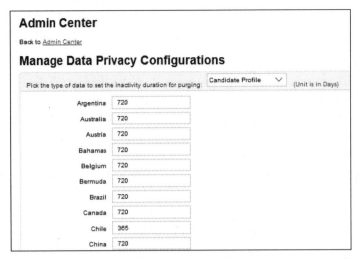

Figure 5.9 Setting the Number of Inactivity Days on Candidate Profile and Application Data

> **Warning!**
> When setting the **Legal Minimum Obligation Period**, don't configure the period as one day. If you do, all of your candidate data will be purged!

5.3   Working with Agencies via the Agency Portal

Some companies use external recruiters or agencies to source candidates for their job openings. To support this type of external involvement, Recruiting Management has an agency portal and supports posting requisitions to individual agencies and allowing them to submit candidates to posted jobs. There is one agency portal for each SAP SuccessFactors datacenter, and it supports all customers on that datacenter. It can't be branded for any business. You may be concerned about the security of this, but no users can access the portal unless they have specifically been granted access to the portal and to an individual company's section of the portal. In this section, we'll discuss how to manage agency access, post job requisitions to the portal, and manage candidates submitted by agency users.

5.3.1   Managing Agency Access

Companies and users within each company that can access your jobs within the agency portal are easily managed within Admin Center. No configuration is required; only master data setup is involved. Within the administrative functions listed on the **Recruiting** page, choosing **Set up Agency Access** allows you to enter agencies that you work with and want to provide access to the portal. Figure 5.10 shows where to find this in Admin Center.

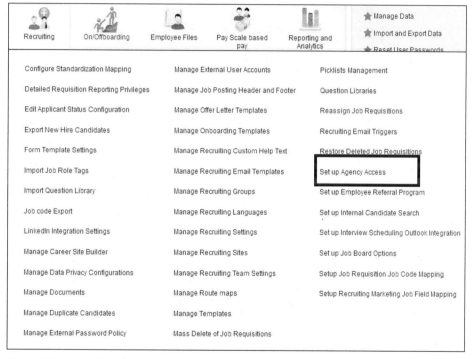

Figure 5.10 Accessing the Agency Capability within Recruiting in Admin Center

First, you'll enter the agency, and, once saved, you can add one or more users within each agency (see Figure 5.11).

There are numerous fields to complete, but only some are required:

- **Agency ID**
- **Agency name**
- **Address and Phone**
- **Candidate ownership**

- Candidate self-ownership
- Agreement Text

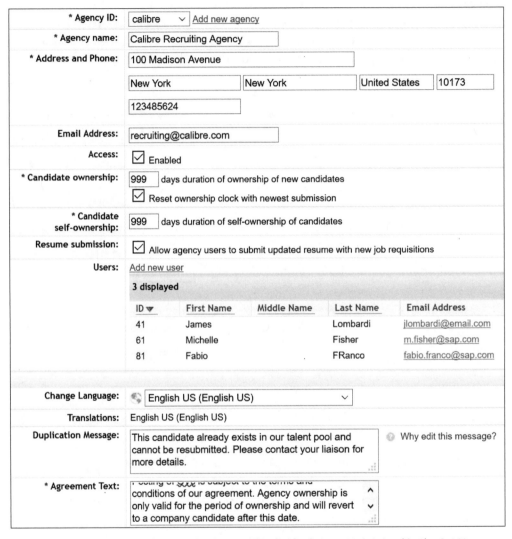

Figure 5.11 Agencies, Agency Settings, and Individual Users Maintained in the Set Up Agency Access Functionality

The **Agency ID** is critical because agency users will use this to log in to the portal. After it's created, the ID can't be changed and shouldn't contain spaces or special characters.

The other two important fields deal with candidate ownership. If the relevant provisioning setting is enabled, the **Candidate ownership** by duration will appear. The duration in days governs the length of time that the agency will own any new candidates submitted in the system. After the duration elapses, the ownership will show as expired.

If ownership is set at the requisition level, unique agencies can submit the same candidate for unique job requisitions. Often, candidates will be submitted by an agency that already has a candidate profile in the system. The **Candidate self-ownership** setting sets the number of days that such candidates will own themselves and won't be eligible to be submitted by the agency.

Finally, there is an area to enter text related to the agreements in place between the company and the agency. This text will display to any agency user who accesses the portal. Each agency user must accept this agreement before submitting a candidate. The **Agreement Text** field is limited to 512 characters and isn't meant to contain the entire agreement between the parties. However, it's possible to provide a link to the full agreement, if desired.

After saving the new agency, you can add one or more users to each agency. Use the **Add new user** link in the **Users** area of the screen. Add users in the **Add New User** box that appears, as shown in Figure 5.12.

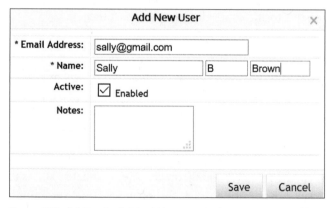

Figure 5.12 Adding Individual Users to Each Agency to Enable Log In

After agencies are added to the system, they can be maintained by selecting them from the dropdown list in the **Agency ID** field. Agencies are displayed in the list alphabetically. All of the data, except the **Agency ID**, can be updated.

5.3.2 Posting Jobs to the Agency Portal

If you're using the agency feature in your Recruiting system, after you've set up all the agencies and related users, you can post your jobs to the agency portal. When using the agency feature, you should see a section for **Agency Listings** on the **Job Postings** page, if you're permissioned to post to the agency portal. Note this is a field-level permission within the JRDM. Posting to agencies is shown in Figure 5.13.

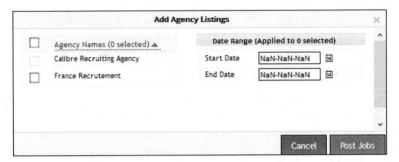

Figure 5.13 Posting Jobs to One or Many Agencies from the Job Postings Page

To post a job to the agency portal, you select **Add Agencies** and then select from the list of agencies set up in your system. You can set a start and end date for the posting, but it's not required. This is helpful if you have a policy for how long jobs are posted with agencies, as you can use this to automatically post or unpost the job.

After the job is posted to the portal, the agencies that received the post will view your job and can submit candidates accordingly. Agency candidates will be clearly identified as such, are separate from internal and external candidates, and will appear in the **Forwarded** status on the job in question. After submitted, the ownership rules configured for the submitting agency will take effect. Refer to the Section 5.3.1 for establishing agency ownership criteria.

Recruiters can view the agency candidate's résumé and determine if they are interested in moving forward. If so, the recruiter should update the candidate's status to **Invite to Apply** so the candidate can be notified, view the job description, and submit an application. Recruiters can disqualify agency candidates from the **Forwarded** status if they aren't interested in pursuing them. Throughout the process, recruiters are presented with important information that is always visible to them, as shown in Figure 5.14. This information is visible whether they are viewing the Candidate Workbench summary screen or viewing a candidate's details:

- A green quickcard next to the name indicates an agency candidate.
- The **Candidate Source** column on the summary screen displays the submitting agency.
- The candidate details clearly identify the candidate as agency-owned as well as the submitting agency and ownership period.
- The **Jobs Applied** portlet keeps the recruiter informed of other activity for this candidate.

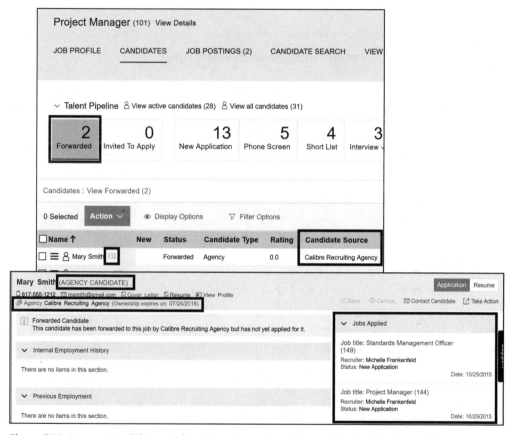

Figure 5.14 Agency Candidates, Submitting Agency, and Ownership Period Information Readily Visible to Recruiters

Note

Recruiters can easily identify agency candidates by their green quickcard from the Candidate Workbench summary screen.

Via the agency portal, all agency users are kept up to date with what is happening with the candidates they have submitted. This helps eliminate phone calls and email updates typically required to communicate with the agency users and allows recruiters to focus on evaluating the best candidates.

If you choose not to use the agency feature, it's advised that you request your implementation consultant not permission the agency posting field. This will remove that block from your **Job Postings** page and eliminate any confusion on the part of your Recruiting users.

5.4   Using Job Profile Builder with Recruiting

In Chapter 2, we discussed the use of Job Profile Builder within Recruiting and how it can expand job descriptions beyond 4,000 characters to build and present full profiles to candidates. These profiles can include numerous elements such as the following:

- Description
- Job responsibilities
- Educational requirements
- Skills needed
- Competencies
- Other elements

Job Profile Builder is part of the SAP SuccessFactors platform (also called the SAP SuccessFactors foundation) and is used by various modules within the SAP SuccessFactors suite. For example, job profiles are used within SAP SuccessFactors Succession & Development as employees browse the available roles within the career worksheet and provide an overview of the job for which you're naming successors. As we've discussed, job profiles in Recruiting are used to present a full picture to candidates of what a job entails from a job responsibility and requirements perspective. Expanding on the 4,000 characters available in the standard internal and external job description fields within the requisition template, Job Profile Builder provides an expansive area to fully communicate your job openings.

Job Profile Builder is a replacement for the legacy Job Description Manager tool. If you have Job Profile Builder already enabled in your SAP SuccessFactors landscape, you may use it in conjunction with skills management, which allows employees to maintain a list of skills maintained on the profile.

It's necessary to enable Job Profile Builder within provisioning. After this is done, the legacy Families & Roles and competency management interfaces are replaced with Job Profile Builder. This feature can be turned on and off within provisioning, so if you enable it and decide it's not meeting your needs, you can also switch back to legacy functionality. To enable Job Profile Builder, you need to configure a few settings within **Company Settings**:

- **JDM v2.0/Skills Management**
- **Role-based Permissions** (prerequisite)
- **Generic Objects** (prerequisite)

When these features are activated within provisioning, you can complete the setup of Job Profile Builder within Admin Center. Several components of maintaining Job Profile Builder should be understood:

- Job profile templates
- Job profile content
- Families and roles

Let's briefly discuss each one of these.

5.4.1   Job Profile Templates

All job profiles are built off of a template. Sound familiar? You can maintain any number of job profile templates within the system that can support a variety of needs within Recruiting as well as other modules. We just mentioned how job profiles are used within the SAP SuccessFactors Succession & Development module. The profiles used in these business scenarios are likely different from those that will be used to advertise job openings within Recruiting. By creating various job profile templates with different structures, you can accommodate all of the organization's needs. Figure 5.15 shows two different job profile templates that comprise different sections. The **Management & Planning Job Profile** template is assigned to one family and has six sections of content. The **Administrative** template is assigned to multiple families and comprises just two content sections.

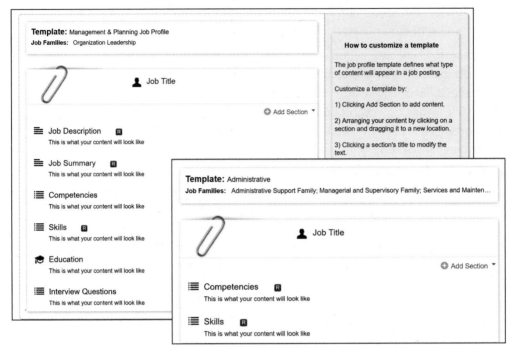

Figure 5.15 Different Job Profile Templates Created with Different Sections to Support Various Organizational Needs

5.4.2   Job Profile Content

When Job Profile Builder is enabled and the job profile templates are built, the next step is to add the content to the various sections. From job descriptions to educational requirements to competencies, this content is added in one of two ways:

- **User interface (UI)**
  Add content to a job profile directly in the UI. This allows users to build and maintain profiles at any time as needed.

- **Templates**
  Import content to a job profile using templates.

Let's look at both methods in a bit more detail.

Add Content via the User Interface

Users with permissions to create job profiles can do so in **Admin Center • Manage Job Profile Content**. Job profiles leverage content maintained in libraries, such as the Competency Library or Interview Questions Library, or the content can be added in text area boxes. These are required before building the profile. The library content includes the following:

- Certification
- Competency
- Employment Condition
- Education – Degree
- Education – Major
- Interview Question
- Job Responsibility
- Physical Requirement
- Relevant Industry
- Skill

> **Note**
>
> Job profiles are associated with roles, which are assigned to a family. These are pre-requisites to creating the job profile. It's common practice for the job profile name to mirror the role name.

Import Content

If you have a large number of job profiles to create or edit, the better option is likely importing the content. There is a template for importing each type of content to a job profile. These templates are easily accessible in the **Import/Export Content** area of Admin Center. It's import to understand the dependency of the objects involved in job profiles so that data are imported correctly. The template for each content type will have a slightly different format, but you'll need to know the job profile GUIDs involved and any related external codes to complete the template properly. Figure 5.16 illustrates two import templates: the top one is importing families, and the bottom template is importing roles. Note that the role import template references the family GUID.

Family Import Template

[OPERATOR]	name.en_US	name.defaultValue	name.de_DE	name.en_DEBUG	createdLocale	status	externalCo subModule
Supported operators: Delimit Clear	US English	Default Value	German (Germany)	English (DEBUG)	createdLocale	Status(Valid Values : A/I A for Active I for InActive)	GUID subModule
	Talent Services	Talent Services			en_US	A	1000060
	SAP	SAP			en_US	A	1000070

Role Import Template

name.en_US	name.defaultValue	name.de_D	name.en_D	family.extern	createdLocale	status	externalCo subModule
US English	Default Value	German (G	English (DB	Family.GUID	createdLocale	Status(Vali	GUID subModule
Application Programmer/Developer Associate Consultant	Application Programmer/Developer Associate Consultant			1000060	en_US	A	1000070
Application Programmer/Developer Consultant	Application Programmer/Developer Consultant			1000060	en_US	A	1000072
Application Programmer/Developer Senior Consultant	Application Programmer/Developer Senior Consultant			1000060	en_US	A	1000074
Application Programmer/Developer Principal Consultant	Application Programmer/Developer Principal Consultant			1000060	en_US	A	1000076
Solutions Architect Sr. Consultant	Solutions Architect Sr. Consultant			1000060	en_US	A	1000078
Solutions Architect Principal Consultant	Solutions Architect Principal Consultant			1000060	en_US	A	1000080

Figure 5.16 Job Profile Template Information Being Imported in a Series of Templates

After the templates have been created, they are imported in **Admin Center • Manage Job Profile Content Import/Export**.

5.4.3   Families and Roles

Families and roles are the foundation of the job structure within SAP SuccessFactors. It's necessary to define your families and roles before you build your job profiles. Let's define the critical elements and begin to see how they relate to each other:

- **Family**
  A family is a collection of roles that share like attributes such as skills, competencies, job responsibilities, functional area, and more. A family will have multiple roles.

- **Role**
  A role defines the responsibilities and expected behavior assigned to a position. Roles are assigned to families and will have at least one job code that identifies the role throughout the system. A role may also have multiple job codes.

- **Job codes**
  Job codes are used to map competencies to an employee for purposes of performance management, development planning, and others. Job codes are assigned to employees, and the same job code may be assigned to multiple employees.

5.5   Competency Management in Recruiting

Another component of the SAP SuccessFactors platform is competency manage-ment. SAP SuccessFactors is a competency-based system with competencies touch-ing numerous modules within the suite such as Performance & Goals, Succession & Development, and Recruiting. In this section, we'll briefly discuss competencies within SAP SuccessFactors and how they interact with Recruiting.

Competencies are the skills and behaviors required to perform a job role. They describe the contributing factors that enable employees to function successfully in their role, such as knowledge, skill, attitude, and so on. If goals are the "what" aspect of an employee's job, competencies are the "how" they perform. The most common use of competencies within SAP SuccessFactors is in the SAP SuccessFactors Perfor-mance & Goals module where employees are rated against either core competencies, role-specific competencies, or both. You'll also see role-specific competencies within Succession & Development as new development objectives are created and tied to one or more competencies that an employee is working toward developing.

5.5.1   Competency Libraries and Mapping

SAP SuccessFactors provides a best-practice competency library that can be used by businesses as those competencies match the company's needs. It's also very easy to create custom competencies within custom libraries to meet the organizational needs as well. Competencies get mapped to job codes, which we discussed in the pre-vious section and elsewhere in this book, and job codes are then tied to roles. When an employee is assigned to a particular job code within SAP SuccessFactors, the role and any mapped competencies are also linked to that employee.

Competencies are mapped differently depending on whether Job Profile Builder is in place or you're using legacy Families & Roles. Figure 5.17 shows how to manage com-petencies when Job Profile Builder is in use. You can see that the **SuccessFactors 2.1 Competency Library** is available, as well as a custom library called **Suggested Inter-view Questions**, used specifically for Recruiting. These competencies are geared toward guiding conversation within an interview. We'll discuss this further in the next section.

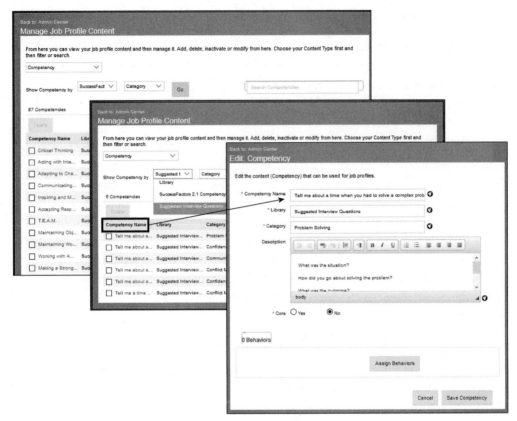

Figure 5.17 Maintaining Competencies within Job Profile Builder

5.5.2   Competencies within Recruiting

Competencies impact Recruiting in several ways. First, as we mentioned in our Job Profile Builder discussion, there is a standard **Competency** section that can be included in the job profile template. This is where the competencies per job profile are mapped. These competencies can be displayed to the candidates so they understand the knowledge, skills, and abilities required for the job.

Competencies are also used to drive Interview Central, which captures feedback on candidates during the interview process and can rank candidates against each other. Because Interview Central leverages the Stack Ranker functionality from SAP SuccessFactors Performance & Goals, it's necessary to assign competencies to a role or profile so that interviewers can capture feedback against a rating. The rating can be the standard five-point performance rating scale, or you can define a rating scale specific to Recruiting during implementation. Figure 5.18 shows competencies within Interview Central using a five-point rating scale. Notice the **Stack Ranker** column on the right.

Figure 5.18 Competencies Driving Feedback via Ratings and Comments in Interview Central

> **Note**
>
> The rating scale used in Interview Central is specified in the JRDM so the same rating scale must be used for all jobs against a requisition template.

A little known connection between Recruiting and SAP SuccessFactors Performance & Goals is the ability to do gap assessment on new hires. If you use the same competencies to evaluate candidates for a job that you do to evaluate performance of employees, for example, with core competencies, the system will recognize the competency ratings captured during the interview process after that candidate becomes an employee. You could then do a 90-day performance review, for example, and rate the new hires against those same competencies to see how they are performing after a period of time in the job. This can provide valuable data and insight into how employees are being onboarded as well as areas for further development to get them to maximum productivity.

5.6   Summary

With the competitive job market companies face today, they often look for as many vehicles as possible to advertise their jobs and source good candidates. Employee referral programs have existed for quite some time but are often administered manually, causing additional burden on the part of talent acquisition or HR to keep track of all the various data elements involved. In addition, working with outside agencies, while a good source of quality candidates, can add extra time to recruiters in having to communicate with agencies regarding open jobs and submitted candidates. With features such as the employee referral program and agency portal, SAP SuccessFactors offers businesses good solutions to many of the problems faced by maintaining this program and sources outside the system.

The data privacy consent statement and data retention management (DRM) capabilities likewise offer businesses automated options for communicating with candidates, allowing them the option of how their personal data should be managed, and expelling sensitive data from your system when data are no longer required or needed. These tools help reduce a company's exposure in handling and maintaining a nonemployee's sensitive data.

Components of SAP SuccessFactors platform will provide companies even more powerful tools to use in their talent acquisition activities. Building and communicating robust job profiles that clearly outline the duties and responsibilities as well as the educational and skill requirements of a job will allow candidates to determine whether they are a fit before submitting an application. Leveraging the competency management capabilities to capture interview feedback on candidates not only supports consistent evaluation of all candidates against objective criteria but also supports detailed performance and gap reporting of new employees after they are onboard and performing their daily duties. Using this information can drive very specific employee development objectives and activities that will increase overall performance and time to productivity.

In the next chapter, we'll discuss the critical topic of reporting and explore the options Recruiting Management offers companies to report on critical metrics within talent acquisition.

Chapter 6

Reporting on Recruiting Data

The age of big data is upon us. Companies have been collecting data on business transactions for years, and recruiting is no different. Tools within SAP SuccessFactors Recruiting put the power of big data in the hands of the recruiters by giving them insight into end-to-end analytics that track a candidate from visitor to hire, along with the ability to slice and dice this information by source, location, job type, and other factors.

All modules within the SAP SuccessFactors suite capture huge amounts of valuable data that can be mined to help make intelligent business decisions regarding talent. SAP SuccessFactors Recruiting not only captures significant data related to talent acquisition activities, but there are also built-in tools within the SAP SuccessFactors Marketing platform to arm recruiting professionals with metrics and source data not available in other applicant-tracking system solutions.

In this chapter, we'll discuss the various reporting options available within Recruiting and how to choose a report for a given task. The main reporting areas we'll cover are as follows:

- Ad hoc reporting
- Standard U.S. compliance reporting for federal contractors (Office of Federal Contractor Compliance Program [OFCCP]) and veterans (Veterans Employment and Training Service [VETS])
- Reporting in the Online Report Designer (ORD)
- Displaying reports in dashboard tiles

All reporting solutions within SAP SuccessFactors use the same view of recruiting data, and most recruiting data are available to reporting. Standard fields are automatically available; custom fields need to be made reportable in provisioning.

There are two flavors of recruiting domains for reporting: Recruiting V2 and Recruiting V2 Secured. Recruiting V2 gives access to all Recruiting data, and Recruiting V2

Secured only gives access to data where the user has a role on the requisition. For example, if a report uses the Recruiting V2 Secured domain, a specific recruiter will only see data from requisitions on which that recruiter has a role. This distinction is critical to understand when building reports, as it greatly impacts the data returned!

Reporting on Recruiting typically includes many different tables of data. At times, it may be necessary to use other reporting solutions to specify table joins, but within the Recruiting solution, these considerations have already been baked into the reporting solution. This particularly impacts reporting filter criteria, as filters need to be applied to primary tables such as candidates, applications, offers, and requisitions before dependent objects such as candidate education, requisition location, and so on can be selected.

Following is a quick overview of the different reporting options:

- **Ad hoc reporting**
  Basic, easy-to-use reporting with a tabular output with export options.

- **Online Report Designer (ORD):**
  - **Detailed Reporting**
    This ORD tool provides enhanced capabilities over ad hoc to include calculations, formatting, and dynamic dates (e.g., last quarter) versus fixed dates. The output is a list, which can be distributed automatically to recipients on a regular basis.

  - **Report Designer**
    This ORD tool provides produces a formatted multipage report with the same capabilities as detailed reporting but allows pivot tables, pivot charts, and WYSIWYG capabilities to define the exact layout of the report. May be more suitable for delivering high-level analytics.

- **Tile-based dashboards**
  Simple graphical representation of Recruiting with some drilldown capabilities. Shown in real time in various places in SAP SuccessFactors, including the home page and within the Recruiting application.

Though the SAP SuccessFactors reporting solutions are very powerful, you can use another solution for all of your enterprise reporting. In this case, SAP SuccessFactors has a powerful set of application interfaces called OData Application Programming Interfaces (APIs) that can extract most data from SAP SuccessFactors Recruiting Management and other modules.

Let's focus our discussion on the different reporting options available within Recruiting, beginning with ad hoc reporting.

6.1 Ad Hoc Reporting

Recruiting comes with a powerful ad hoc reporting tool that enables you to build reports to meet your needs. These reports can pull data from nearly every field within Recruiting, both standard and custom. SAP SuccessFactors has published some example ad hoc reports in the past for Recruiting. In most implementations, consultants will load these sample reports for clients to tailor and use as needed. Examples include time-to-fill and applicant status tracking reports.

Ad hoc reports are generally used to display operational field-level data. These reports are recommended when a detailed list of information is required and are most commonly used for transactional reporting and as a means to generate data for export into another system or tool, such as Microsoft Excel.

You can navigate to **Ad Hoc Reports** page from the **Home • Analytics • Reporting • Ad Hoc Reports** menu, as shown in Figure 6.1. Note that the navigation and naming of links/tabs may differ in your system, as these tabs can be labeled per business requirements.

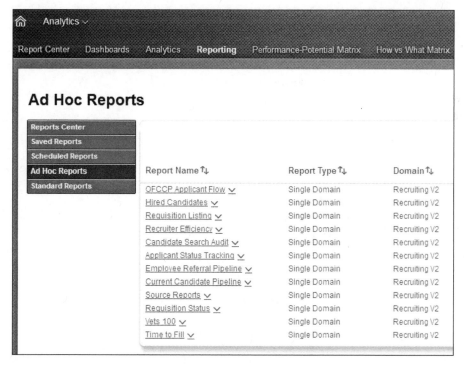

Figure 6.1 Ad Hoc Reports

When building ad hoc reports, there are some concepts that are important to understand to find the data you're looking for and build a report that meets your requirements. In the next sections, we'll discuss the role of domains within ad hoc reporting, as well how to build a report.

6.1.1 Ad Hoc Reporting Domains for Recruiting

Domains are categories of data within SAP SuccessFactors. They are important to understand when building your ad hoc report because it's the first selection made, and the domain selected determines the available tables and resulting data available to the report. As mentioned earlier, within Recruiting, the Recruiting V2 and Recruiting V2 secured domains are available. The "V2" referenced in the domain name simply refers to the second version of Recruiting, which was used to distinguish from Recruiting V1, which has been sunset.

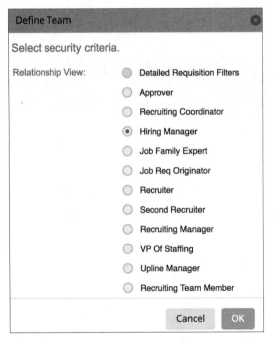

Figure 6.2 Defining the Relationship to a Recruiting V2 Secured Report

The Recruiting V2 domain provides the user full access to all Recruiting data defined in the report, regardless of whether the user is assigned to a role on the requisitions for which data are displayed on the report. Users with create permission for Recruiting

V2 reports can create a report with any columns from any Recruiting form and view all data in the results. This level of access is usually only granted to an administrator or to recruiters in organizations that have a more relaxed data access policy. This access can't be divided up—that is, if a user can build a Recruiting V2 report, he has access to all tables and data—so assign this ability wisely.

The Recruiting V2 Secured domain is similar to Recruiting V2 but with an extra layer of security. You can define Recruiting V2 Secured reports to only display data to the person running the report based on their relationship to the data in the report. For example, you can restrict it by whether the user running the report is assigned to the hiring manager or recruiter role or another role on the requisition, as shown in Figure 6.2.

6.1.2   Manage Ad Hoc Reports

Role-based permissions are used to define which users have permission to create ad hoc reports and which users can run ad hoc reports. This can be further narrowed down by module, so that, for example, users are limited to only creating or running Recruiting-related reports. Figure 6.3 shows a role being permissioned to create ad hoc reports for only the **Recruiting V2** and **Recruiting V2 Secured** domains.

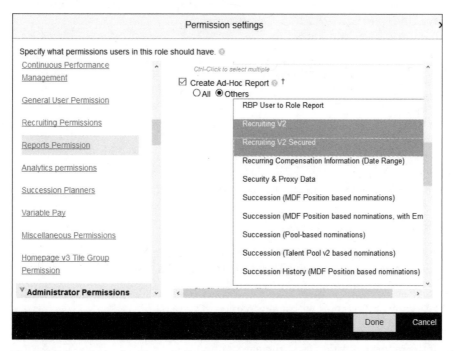

Figure 6.3 Permissioning Users to the Domains in Which They Can Create Ad Hoc Reports

The main **Ad Hoc Reports** screen lists all reports you're permissioned either to run or edit and any reports that have been shared with you. The reports are listed by name, type (single or multidomain), domain (roughly equivalent to module), owner, creation date, and last modified date. Figure 6.4 shows the **Ad Hoc Reports** list for a user. You must be the owner of a report to edit it. Otherwise, you can only run the reports you find here. This means you must have created the report. You can't edit a report that has been shared with you. You must first save the report as one of your own, and then you can edit it.

Figure 6.4 Accessing All Ad Hoc Reports from the Ad Hoc Reports Page

The action menu for reports for which you're the owner includes several options, as displayed in Figure 6.5.

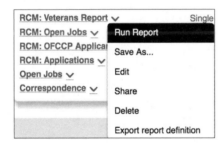

Figure 6.5 Accessing Options for Ad Hoc Reports from the Action Menu

The possible actions are as follows:

- **Run Report**
  Runs the report query and displays the current results online.

- **Save As...**
  Save a copy of the report with a new name.

- **Edit**
  Edit the report definition (report creators only).

- **Share**

  Share the report with others (report creators only). Shared reports automatically appear in the user's list of available ad hoc reports after they are shared with them.

- **Delete**

  Delete the report from the system (report creators only).

- **Export report definition**

  Export the report definition as an SFR file. This file can then be sent to another user who can import it and edit the report definition or import it into another instance.

You can upload SFR files here from your computer and then tweak them as necessary. Most Recruiting implementation consultants will have access to sample Recruiting ad hoc reports that they can load here.

6.1.3   Create New Report

If you want to build a new report, you begin by selecting the **Create New Report** button from the main **Ad Hoc Reports** page. Then you select the **Report type—Single Domain Report**, **Multi Dataset Report**, or **Cross Domain Report**—as well as the **Report Definition type**. **Multi Dataset Report** and **Cross Domain Report** options aren't really applicable to Recruiting. Multi dataset reports will allow you to report on more than one dataset, for example, if you wanted to build a report on goals for the past three years and needed to select three goal plan templates. Cross domain reports involve more than one domain, for example, performance management and employee profile. Figure 6.6 shows the settings to create a Recruiting V2 report (this is what you'll select most of the time).

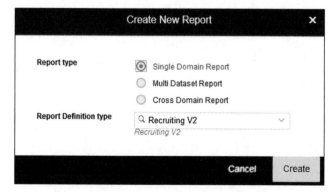

Figure 6.6 Initial Settings to Start Creating the Report

After you make the appropriate selections, you click the **Create** button.

In the next screen, you'll name the report, give it a description that is visible from the main **Ad Hoc Reports** listing page, and set the priority, as shown in Figure 6.7. Use the navigation across the top to step through all of the components of building the report:

- **General Info**
- **Columns**
- **Configuration**
- **Filters**

After you've set the general information for the report, you'll choose the columns of data to add. Select the **Columns** tab and then **Select Columns** to select almost any in Recruiting for your report (see Figure 6.8).

Figure 6.7 Stepping through Various Screens to Build and Test the Report

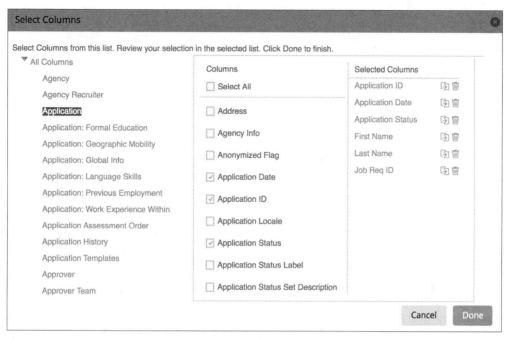

Figure 6.8 Selecting Columns in an Ad Hoc Report

In the **Select Columns** window, there are three main panels. The far left panel provides filters or sorts for the columns of data. Here you can select from options such as **Application**, **Requisition**, and **Candidate Profile** background portlets to refine the columns you're searching. Note that all standard fields within Recruiting are available to select in reporting even if they aren't used in your configuration. There are also similar fields among the various templates used, such as address or phone, and all of these will be displayed as well. Building Recruiting reports is often an exercise in trial and error.

After you've selected the columns to include in the report, you can rearrange the column sequence and define sorting and grouping rules. You can also define report filters. Examples of report filters on requisition-related reports are requisition status, division, department, and so on. You can define whether the filters are user prompted or fixed. If they are user prompted, this means when users run the report, they can change the filter selection at runtime, for example, to select a different requisition status or division.

6.1.4   Execute Ad Hoc Reports

If you have permission to run Recruiting ad hoc reports and are either the owner of the report or one has been shared with you, you can run these reports from the main **Ad Hoc Reports** screen. Depending on how the report was defined, you may be able to refine the filter criteria when running the report, for example, to narrow the report to a certain date range, division, or department.

Reports can be run online within the browser window or offline for larger queries. You can also download formatted reports as PDF, XLS, and PPT, or the unformatted data can be downloaded as CSV.

Reports can be run offline and retrieved later from the **Scheduled Reports** menu when the reports are completed.

6.1.5   Standard Sample Recruiting Ad Hoc Reports

SAP SuccessFactors doesn't deliver built-in Recruiting ad hoc reports. However, over time, SAP SuccessFactors has provided sample reports for Recruiting that consultants or businesses can load and use. Table 6.1 describes the most common sample reports and what they do.

Report Name	Definition
Applications	Combines data from both the requisition and the application objects and is sorted by application date. The current application status of each applicant is displayed as well as the date the applicant reached that status.
Current Candidate Pipeline	Displays a count of applicants currently in each stage of the recruiting process, grouped by requisition.
Requisition Candidate Pipeline	Contains the number of candidates that are currently at each candidate status grouped by requisition. The results are limited to requisitions that aren't closed.
Employee Referral Pipeline	Provides a graphical view of candidate referral counts and percentages grouped by job requisition. Summary tables are provided with the same information regardless of the dataset size.

Table 6.1 Sample Recruiting Ad Hoc Reports

Report Name	Definition
Hired Candidates	Provides a list of candidates hired within a specified date range, ordered by ascending start date.
Hires	Combines data from both the requisition and the application and is sorted by hire date. "Hired" is defined as the application having a "hired on" date listed.
Requisition Status Report	Displays information about job requisitions, including requisition count by requisition status, number of openings versus positions filled, and a list of all job requisitions.
OFCCP Applicant Flow	Displays candidate data to aid in compliance reporting.
Applicant Flow Log	Displays candidate data to aid in compliance reporting.
Open Requisitions	Displays information about all job requisitions that are active within a user-defined date range. Requisitions are considered active if they were opened, posted, closed, or filled within the date range.
Source Report	Displays application activity grouped by application source, job board name, and referral key. It provides insight into where advertising spend is and isn't working well.
Time to Fill	Displays the average number of days between the application date and each status in the application process. Averages are grouped by location and job requisition number.
Veterans Report	Displays veteran information to aid in compliance reporting.
Cost Per Hire	Displays information about cost per hire. Includes a graphical chart display as well as a summary table. This report relies on the standard costOfHire field being defined in the requisition XML, and cost information being manually maintained on requisitions.

Table 6.1 Sample Recruiting Ad Hoc Reports (Cont.)

6

6.2   Reporting in Online Report Designer

Online Report Designer (ORD) is a detailed, metric-based reporting tool that is part of SAP SuccessFactors Workforce Analytics but is made available to businesses using SAP SuccessFactors to build enhanced reports absent the SAP SuccessFactors Workforce Analytics module. ORD has two report creation tools: Detailed Reporting and Report Designer. ORD also has the Report Distributor to run reports on a set time period and make them available through various means.

Detailed Reporting is a very powerful tool for formatted, tabular reports. The use of calculated columns is particularly useful in Recruiting, for example, to calculate the days between dates.

Report Designer supports multipage reports with charts, pivot tables, and detailed tables. Ad hoc reports or detailed reports can be used as the source of the data. Report Distributor can be used to schedule regular delivery of reports to users for reports created by Report Designer or Detailed Reporting.

Analytics are presented via the **Analytics** home page, as shown in Figure 6.9.

Figure 6.9 Analytics Home Page Providing a View of the Available Metric-Based Reports

6.2.1   Detailed Reporting

Detailed reporting is great at performing logic on Recruiting fields, sorting data, and performing basic calculations. It's not Excel, but it can automate a lot of reporting tasks. Detailed Reporting is very easy to use with a drag-and-drop user interface (UI). The results can be exported to Excel or can feed visual components such as table views, pivot tables, or pivot charts within Report Designer, where additional formatting can occur.

One key advantage of Detailed Reporting over ad hoc reporting is the use of calculated columns. Figure 6.10 shows an example of using a calculated column to create an application **Full Name** from **First Name** and **Last Name**.

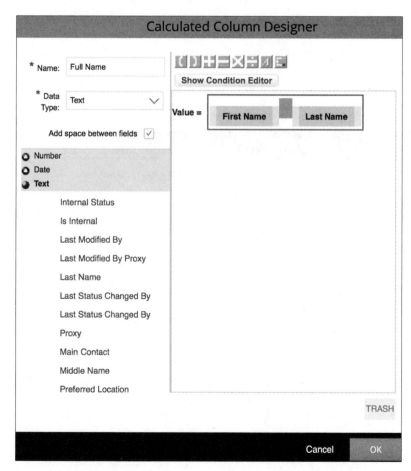

Figure 6.10 Building Calculated Columns in the Detailed Reporting Tool

Calculated columns can also be used to calculate days to measure recruiting activities. Figure 6.11 shows an example of **Application Date** to **Start Date**.

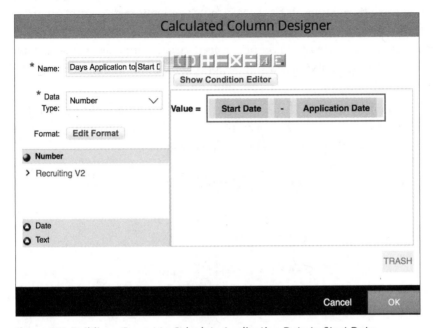

Figure 6.11 Building a Report to Calculate Application Date to Start Date

Calculated columns can also be used to define logic. Let's say you want to build a report to count the number of interviews over a period of time, but the applicant status needs to be evaluated to check if it's an interview. For example, **First Interview** and **Second Interview** are different statuses, but both should be counted as interviews. You can build a calculated column to define this, as shown in Figure 6.12.

Another key advantage to Detailed Reporting is the use of dynamic dates in filters. Ad hoc reports need a specific date range such as 01/01/2017 – 03/31/2017, and the dates need to be changed over time. With Detailed Reporting, you can specify "Between first day and last day of previous quarter," for example. This is especially necessary when the Report Distributor is used to automatically generate reports with no human intervention in running the report.

Figure 6.12 Using Calculated Columns to Define Logic within a Report

6.2.2   Report Designer

Report Designer allows the creation of visual reports with exact layout of charts, tables, images, and text. It's a visual report solution and not designed for extraction to Excel and further manipulation. Report Designer reports can be distributed as needed using the Report Distributor. Reports can have multiple pages, and each page has fixed visual components such as charts, pivot charts, graphical gauges, and list reports. Text and images can also be added. Report Designer is very much a presentation tool.

Figure 6.13 shows the design layout of the first page of the VETS-100 report. You can see it has four charts and some explanatory text at the top.

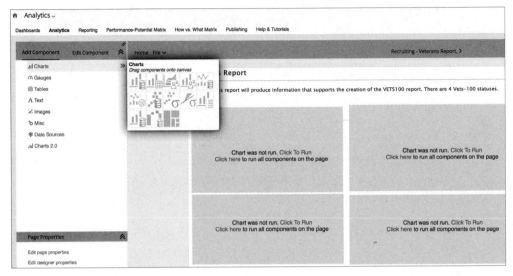

Figure 6.13 The VETS-100 Report as Viewed in Report Designer

If you edit one of the chart components, you can see the many options for finer control of the look of the chart (see Figure 6.14).

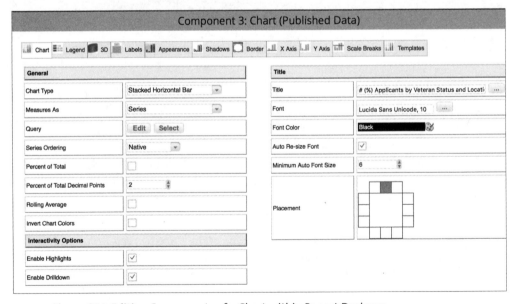

Figure 6.14 Editing Components of a Chart within Report Designer

When the first page of the report is generated, it looks like Figure 6.15.

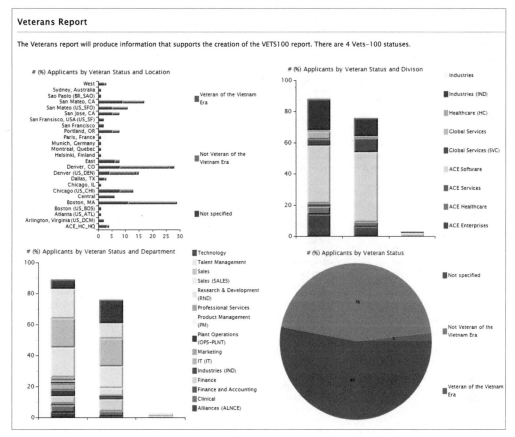

Figure 6.15 The VETS-100 Report after Editing the Chart Elements in Report Designer

It's common to have a separate report page with the details that are used in the report. Because the generated reports are documents, there are no drilldown capabilities, and any necessary details must be included in the design. Figure 6.16 shows a pivot table that feeds the preceding pivot charts.

			Not specified	Not Veteran of the Vietnam Era	Veteran of the Vietnam Era
Alliances (ALNCE)	Global Services	ACE_HC_HQ	3	1	
Clinical	ACE Healthcare	San Jose, CA	5	3	
Finance and Accounting	ACE Enterprises	Chicago, IL	1		
Finance	ACE Enterprises	San Mateo, CA	2		
	ACE Software	San Mateo, CA	3	8	
Industries (IND)	Healthcare (HC)	Boston (US_BOS)	1		
	Industries (IND)	San Mateo (US_SFO)	3	1	
IT (IT)	Global Services (SVC)	Helsinki, Finland	1		
	Industries (IND)	Atlanta (US_ATL)	1		
		Sydney, Australia	1		
Marketing	ACE Enterprises	San Mateo, CA	1		
Plant Operations (OPS-PLNT)	Industries (IND)	Denver (US_DEN)	1	1	
Product Management (PM)	Industries (IND)	Sao Paolo (BR_SAO)	1		
Professional Services	ACE Services	Munich, Germany	1		
		Paris, France	1		
Research & Development (RND)	Industries (IND)	San Mateo (US_SFO)		5	
Sales (SALES)	Global Services (SVC)	Denver (US_DEN)	3	9	1
	Global Services	Arlington, Virginia (US_DCM)	2		
	Industries (IND)	Chicago (US_CHI)	8	5	
		San Francisco	1		
		San Fransisco, USA (US_SF)	2		
		San Mateo (US_SFO)	2		
	Industries	San Francisco	1		
Sales	ACE Enterprises	Boston, MA	1	6	
	ACE Software	Boston, MA	2	1	
		Dallas, TX	2	1	
		Denver, CO		4	
		East	5	2	
		Montreal, Quebec	1		
		Portland, OR	5	3	
		San Mateo, CA	1		
		West	2	1	
		Central	6		
	ACE Enterprises	East	1		

Figure 6.16 Using Pivot Tables as a Data Source for Charts within Reports Built in Report Designer

6.2.3   Report Distributor

Report Distributor is a powerful tool to generate one-off or recurring reports and distribute them through the following means (see Figure 6.17):

- Email to a distribution list.
- Run offline and pick up from the job status queue for download.
- Send to an FTP server.

The Report Distributor is available under the **Tools** menu of Detailed Reporting. Reports are organized into a bundle that has the same distribution method, schedule, recipients (for email only), and format. The format can be Word, PowerPoint, and PDF. Page sizes can also be selected. Non-SAP SuccessFactors data can be added to the bundle by uploading an Excel or CSV file. Report Distributor will only distribute reports created through Report Designer. This means that if you want to use this tool for ad hoc reports or Detailed Reporting reports, then you need to create a report using Report Designer and reference the original report as the source in one of the report's visual components.

Home

Bundle Name	Items	Parts	Destination	Recipients	Suspended Recipients	E-Mail Override
AC bundle	1	1	E-mail	0	0	No
April 2016	1	1	E-mail	1	0	No
Aspen	2	1	FTP	0	0	No
ASW_Score_Download	1	1	Run Offline	0	0	No
Ben Test	2	1	E-mail	0	0	No
Bundle_TEST_MM	3	6	E-mail	3	0	No
CF	2	2	Run Offline	1	0	No
Christy Test	1	1	E-mail	0	0	No
Contingent	1	1	FTP	0	0	No
Demo CF	2	2	FTP	2	0	No

Items | Destination | Recipients | Schedule

○ **E-mail**
   Content will be sent to the recipients set up for this bundle.
   Edit Recipients

○ **Run Offline**
   Download link will be made available on the Job Status page when content is ready.
   Content will remain for 7 days.
   Show Job Status page

○ **FTP**
   Content will be sent to the FTP server setup for the organisation.

Recipients are ignored for Run Offline and FTP. These outputs run in the context of the user running the bundle.

Figure 6.17 Using Report Distributor to Manage the Running and Pushing of Reports Based on Specified Criteria

6.3   Tile-Based Dashboards

Tile-based dashboards are a great way to present real-time information in a simple graphical way, along with the ability to filter data and drill down into further detail.

They are very easy to create but are limited in their capabilities and layout control as compared to Report Designer. Let's look at some examples of how data can be deployed to users via tiles on the home page.

6.3.1   Examples of Tiles on Reporting Data

In this section, we'll provide some examples of common types of Recruiting data and how that data can be easily made available to various Recruiting users on their home page via tile-based dashboards.

Figure 6.18 shows a simple **Requisition Age by Division** dashboard tile on the bottom-right corner of the SAP SuccessFactors home page.

Figure 6.18 Requisition Age by Division Tile on the Home Page

Click on the tile to open it, and then click on a bar for details of the **Industries** (IND) division to get more information (Figure 6.19).

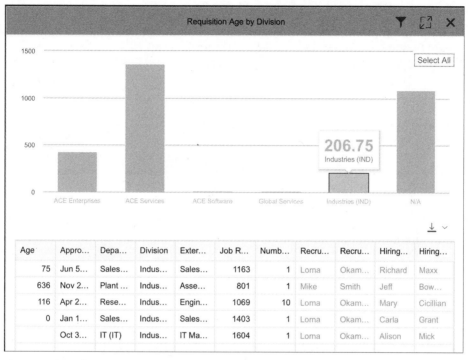

Figure 6.19 Drilling into the Dashboard to Reveal the Data for More Detailed Viewing

Figure 6.20 provides an example of two tiles in a non-SAP Fiori UI for **Offer Approval Status** and **Candidate Pipeline**.

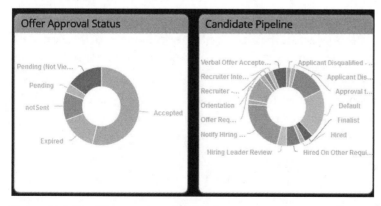

Figure 6.20 Two Tiles on a Non-SAP Fiori Home Page Showing Offer Approval Status and Candidates in the Candidate Pipeline

In addition to the home page, dashboard tiles can appear under **Analytics** and from within the SAP SuccessFactors Mobile app. A relatively new feature is to enable dashboard tiles under **Insights**, as displayed in Figure 6.21. This allows for embedded analytics within Recruiting as well as other modules.

Figure 6.21 Insights Providing Additional Reporting from the Recruiting Page

6.3.2   Creating and Managing Dashboards

Tile-based dashboards can be created and managed fairly easily by following a simple wizard within Admin Center. The navigation is **Admin Center • Manage Dashboards • Manage Standard Dashboards and YouCalc Files • Build Tile**.

Step through the categories across the top to build the components of the dashboard. The **Preview** tab, shown in Figure 6.22, gives you a peek at what the tile will look like.

Dashboard tiles can be assigned to groups of users through role-based permissions. This can deliver just the right tiles to the right users. If the information presented is based on where, for example, a recruiter is looking at his own metrics, the Recruiting V2 Secured domain should be used to restrict the data this are used.

> **Examples**
>
> There are so many great reporting tools within SAP SuccessFactors that the choice of tool can be confusing. Table 6.2 shows some example recruiting use cases and the suggested tool for each.

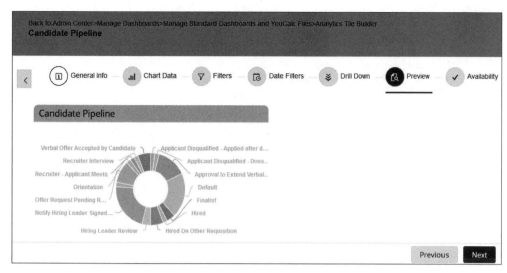

Figure 6.22 Building Custom Dashboards That Are Deployed in Tiles on Your Home Page

Use Case	Tool
My recruiting manager wants to see average requisition age by recruiter as a quick visual when logging in and may want to drill down to see which requisitions are skewing the average.	Tile-based dashboard
Once a month, I need to summarize recruiting metrics to management. I like to review data, highlight issues, and tell a story through data.	Ad hoc reporting and Excel (labor intensive)
Once a week, I want to email colleagues responsible for orientation a list of applicants that have an upcoming start date and ensure they have cleared background checks, drug tests, and so on. It helps them plan orientation class sizes and lets me know if we have any preemployment verification delays.	Report Distributor and Report Designer
My recruiters want to know when applicants have cleared preemployment checks so that they can send them to the SAP SuccessFactors Onboarding module. They need the information in real time and appearing prominently in their UI. They don't want to have to keep running a report.	Tile-based dashboard

Table 6.2 Use Cases for Recruiting Reporting Needs and How They Can Be Addressed with Reporting Tools

Use Case	Tool
I have a standard set of visual reports with some breakdown detail that I send to HR management once a week. It tells them if a number of parties such as background check vendor and Center of Excellence are meeting their Service Level Agreements.	Report Distributor and Report Designer
I want a straight dump into Excel of my applicant funnel numbers, but it sure would be nice if SAP SuccessFactors did some of the calculations and logic so I don't have to. Ad hoc reporting just doesn't seem up to the task.	Detailed Reporting

Table 6.2 Use Cases for Recruiting Reporting Needs and How They Can Be Addressed with Reporting Tools (Cont.)

6.4   Business Intelligence and Reporting Tool

When creating your own ad hoc reports within SAP SuccessFactors, you'll notice that there are no options to create the graphical charts that are available in the standard reports. If the ORD tool isn't an option for you, and if Visual Publisher is licensed through SAP SuccessFactors, then the open-source Business Intelligence and Reporting Tool (BIRT) can be used to add additional logic or create charts to expand your ad hoc reports in a powerful way. If you're not familiar with BIRT, it's an open-source project and add-on tool for Eclipse Foundation, a not-for-profit open-source community organization. BIRT has been used most extensively with the SAP SuccessFactors Learning solution. However, it can also be used to impact how the data within an ad hoc report are displayed.

To use BIRT to enhance Recruiting reports (or, really, any ad hoc reports within SAP SuccessFactors), you must have the tool available from within SAP SuccessFactors. This is where the additional licensing comes in to play. After you're set up, when you build your ad hoc reports, the data will be pulled into the SAP SuccessFactors Report Builder engine. By using BIRT to enhance ad hoc reports, you can add the following:

- Lists
- Charts
- Cross tabs
- Letters and documents

You also can build a compound report that combines all of the listed items into a single report. Figure 6.23 shows BIRT from within SAP SuccessFactors ad hoc reports.

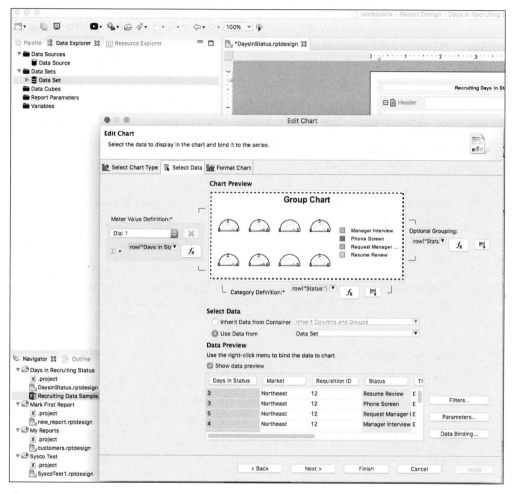

Figure 6.23 Using BIRT to Enhance Ad Hoc Reports

6.5   Standard Reporting for OFCCP and VETS-100

When implementing Recruiting, it's very important to involve the organization's legal or compliance team to determine what, if any, data needs to be collected on applicants and eventually reported on. In the United States, for example, there are certain regulations around applicant data collection and reporting that every federal contractor and subcontractor must comply with. This section discusses two of those compliance reporting needs—for Equal Employment Opportunities Commission (EEOC) or Office of Federal Contractor Compliance Program (OFCCP) compliance and for Veterans Employment and Training Service (VETS-100) veterans reporting compliance.

At their core, these programs are designed to make sure organizations don't discriminate in their hiring process. Special care should be given when defining who has access to these reports due to the sensitive data they include.

To report on this data, you need to first define what data you need to report and capture it on one or more of the Recruiting templates, such as the job requisition and application. It's best practice to use the standard SAP SuccessFactors fields to capture gender, race, ethnicity, veteran status, and EEO job category if you want to use the sample reports as is.

> **Note**
>
> This section isn't intended as a substitute for legal advice. It merely demonstrates the capabilities for capturing and reporting on sensitive compliance data.

6.5.1 OFCCP/EEOC Reporting

Every U.S. federal contractor and subcontractor is required to keep an applicant flow log that records the information needed for conducting adverse impact analyses. This log is used to determine what positions were open during a reporting period, who applied for them, and who was hired to fill the position. The applicant flow log includes gender, race, and ethnicity information about the applicants, among other things.

As mentioned in Section 6.1.5, there are two example reports that can be used. The OFCCP Applicant Flow Log sample report outputs the data into table format showing the number and percentage of applicants of each race/ethnicity and gender broken down by job category. It also includes a summary table with the data used in the report. See Figure 6.24 for the sample output.

OFCCP "Applicant Flow"

EMPLOYMENT DATA - Count of all applicants categorised by EEO Job Category, Gender and Ethnicity

Job Categories	Number of Applicants (Report applicants in only one category)														Total Col A-N
	Race/Ethnicity														
	Hispanic or Latino		Not-Hispanic or Latino												
			Male						Female						
	Male	Female	White	Black or African American	Native Hawaiian or Other Pacific Islander	Asian	American Indian or Alaska Native	Two or more races	White	Black or African American	Native Hawaiian or Other Pacific Islander	Asian	American Indian or Alaska Native	Two or more races	
	A	B	C	D	E	F	G	H	I	J	K	L	M	N	O
Administrative Support Workers	0	0	0	0	0	0	0	0	0	0	0	0	0	0	1
Executive/Senior Level Officials and Managers	0	0	0	0	0	0	0	0	0	0	0	0	0	0	7
First/Mid-Level Officials and Managers	0	0	0	0	0	0	0	0	1	0	0	0	0	0	4
Professionals	0	0	6	0	0	1	0	0	3	0	0	1	0	0	42
Sales Workers	0	0	0	0	0	0	0	0	0	0	0	0	0	0	17
Other	0	0	5	0	0	2	0	0	3	0	0	0	0	0	17
TOTAL	0	0	11	0	0	3	0	0	7	0	0	1	0	0	88

Figure 6.24 Example of the OFCCP Applicant Flow Log

The Applicant Flow Log report displays similar data to the OFCCP Applicant Flow Log but only in the detailed list form. There are no tables or graphical output. It's also easier for you to manipulate the reporting columns because there are no generated tables or graphs.

6.5.2   Veterans Reporting

This report displays veteran information provided by applicants within a specified data range. It can be used as input for the VETS-100 report mentioned previously. The sample report is output in four charts as well as a detailed list of the data used in the report.

The definitions of how veteran data needs to be collected have changed since the sample report was created, so the chart outputs may not render correctly. The sample report is looking for the veteran options **Veteran of the Vietnam Era** or **Not Veteran of the Vietnam Era**. Figure 6.25 shows the report output with the old veteran selections.

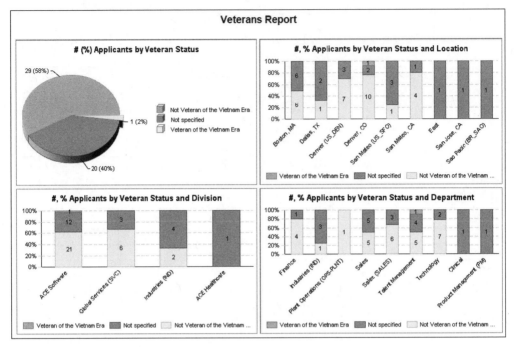

Figure 6.25 Example of the Veterans Report

6.6   Summary

Reporting is critical to any company successfully executing its talent acquisition strategy. Having the most up-to-data data available when you need it, and in a usable format, helps everyone tasked with hiring talent complete their jobs in the most efficient manner. As we've seen in this chapter, SAP SuccessFactors makes several different kinds of reporting tools available for companies to satisfy their reporting requirements. Whether you're running government-mandated reports, such as OFCCP or VET-100 reports, or wanting to make information available to users in tiles on their home pages, SAP SuccessFactors offers tools to meet the need.

Ad hoc reports can be created and run quickly and easily with the Report Builder and shared to other users who may not need, or shouldn't have access to, such a broad swath of data. To address security concerns, SAP SuccessFactors provides wide-open reporting through the Recruiting V2 domain or the ability to lock it down with the Recruiting V2 secured domain.

More advanced or complicated reports can be accommodated through tools such as ORD's Detailed Reporting or Report Designer and pushed out to users via the Report Distributor.

In the next chapter, we'll turn our attention to the recruiter experience in using Recruiting.

Chapter 7
Recruiter Experience

Your recruiters are on the front lines of the talent war every day, trying to gain ground and find the best resources to bring into the organization to further not just talent acquisition goals but overall corporate objectives. They are the power users of any recruiting system and should be armed with powerful and easy-to-manage tools that make their jobs easier and less time-consuming. SAP SuccessFactors Recruiting is focused on creating the best recruiter experience possible.

Opening new requisitions, posting jobs, scheduling interviews, searching for new sources of candidates, extending offers—your recruiters do all of these things and more every day. SAP SuccessFactors Recruiting is designed to not only create a great candidate experience but also a great recruiter experience. The more tools your recruiters have at their disposal to find and evaluate the best candidates, as well as take them through the interview process as quickly as possible, the more likely you are to capture those top-quality candidates that seem to be too few in number and wanted by all your competitors.

In this chapter, we'll discuss some of the tools that are directed specifically at your recruiters to enhance their efficiency and decrease time to fill. Throughout previous chapters, we've highlighted areas of the system that can improve the overall results of your recruiters, but it's worth reviewing those again here. We'll also look at the feature-rich dashboards and reports available in the SAP SuccessFactors Recruiting Marketing platform that give recruiters and other talent acquisition professionals critical data to make the best informed decisions.

Let's begin by reviewing some of the features of the system that can enhance a recruiter's daily tasks.

7.1   Recruiting User Feature Review

It's difficult to pinpoint the features within the Recruiting solution that make recruiters more efficient or improve their day-to-day jobs because there are so many! In the following sections, we'll discuss some features that are worth mentioning again so they aren't missed, in no particular order.

7.1.1   Personalized Display and Filter Options

On both the **Requisitions** page and the Candidate Workbench, all recruiting users have the ability to define and change the fields of data that can be displayed on the screen. Display options are predefined on the **Requisitions** page, but custom display options can be configured on the Candidate Workbench to make the most valuable data available to Recruiting users while evaluating candidates. Filters are also available on both pages to further refine the data that users are presented to streamline their day-to-day work. Both the display options and the filter options are "sticky," meaning that after they are set, they will remain that way until they are changed. In addition to being able to change the display and set filters on these pages, nearly every column is also sortable. This can be especially helpful if you're looking for a particular requisition or candidate and want to sort A to Z or Z to A.

Another very helpful tool that is often overlooked is the highlight feature. This is available on both the **Requisition** page and the Candidate Workbench and allows you to type a name or word in the **Highlight** field, and the system will highlight where that word appears on the screen. In Figure 7.1, you see an example of searching for the name "Christopher" in the **Highlight Candidate** field, and the system uses yellow highlighting to indicate where that candidate is found. On the **Requisitions** page, the **Highlight Job Title** field works the same way. This can be especially helpful on high-volume jobs with hundreds or possibly even thousands of candidates!

Candidates : View all candidates (39)								
0 Selected Action ∨ 👁 Display Options ▼ Filter Options						Highlight Candidate 🔍	Christopher	
☐ Name ↑	New	Status	Candidate Type	Rating	Candidate Source	Phone Number	Last Updated	
☐ ≡ 👤 Akriti Nagpal ✉		Scheduled	External	75.0	Corporate: Default Site	+91+919930893833	07/12/2016	
☐ ≡ 👤 Akriti Nagpal ✉		Unsuccessful	External	N/A	Corporate: Default Site	+91+919930893833	10/28/2015	
☐ ≡ 👤 Anja Klein ✉		Created	Internal	100.0	Internal Site	+49+49999 090000	10/28/2015	
☐ ≡ 👤 Aoi Miyanaka ✉		Ready for Hire	External	N/A	Corporate: Default Site	+81338489018	10/28/2015	
☐ ≡ 👤 Christopher Harrison ✉		Short List	External	100.0	Corporate: Default Site	+61404 445 567	10/28/2015	

Figure 7.1 Finding Candidates Easily with the Highlight Candidate Feature

7.1.2   Resume Viewer and Carousel

When recruiters are evaluating candidates for openings, they are most often comparing candidates against each other or taking action on several candidates at one time. At least, that's what they would like to do! This is where the Resume Viewer (also known as the resume carousel) is incredibly valuable. This feature allows Recruiting users to select multiple candidates and view their résumé details. By selecting multiple candidates and then choosing **View Resume** from the **Action** menu, recruiters can page through multiple candidates' résumés and disposition them right from that screen. You can move candidates forward in the pipeline, disqualify candidates, make comments on their record, or tag them for subsequent searches.

Figure 7.2 illustrates viewing one of four candidates in the resume carousel. Use the arrow buttons at the top right of the **Resume Viewer** screen to tab through each candidate.

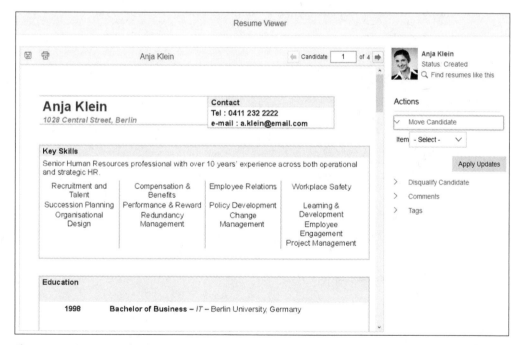

Figure 7.2 Viewing Multiple Candidates at Once with the Resume Carousel

7.1.3   Multiple Ways to Disposition Candidates

Recruiting offers the following various ways to move candidates through the pipeline or disqualify candidates, depending on where the user is and what they are doing:

- **Drag and drop**
  This method allows you to move candidates from the **Action** column to a status in the pipeline. Select one or more candidates, grab the three horizontal lines to the left of their name, and drag them where you want to put them. Let your mouse go, and their status has been updated.

- **Advance the candidate**
  Selecting the **Advance Candidate** option from the **Action** menu allows you to advance candidates to the next status in the pipeline. This can also be done to one or more candidates and will move them to the next status from where they currently reside, regardless of what that is. It doesn't matter if all candidates are in the same status because everyone just gets moved forward to the next step. Figure 7.3 shows the options for advancing candidates from the **Action** menu.

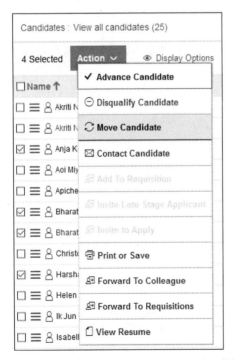

Figure 7.3 Take Action on Numerous Candidates at Once from the Action Menu, Including Advancing, Moving and Disqualifying Them

- **Move the candidate**

  Selecting **Move Candidate** from the **Action** menu allows you to move candidates to any status in the pipeline. Have a group of candidates you've evaluated and are ready to move to **Interview** status? Check their names, and select **Move Candidate** from the **Action** column. Use the **Status** dropdown to select the status you want to move them to and then save. All candidates need to be going to the same status, but it's a great way to act on numerous candidates in a few mouse clicks.

- **Update the Status field**

  This allows you to update the status field from within the **Candidate Details** screen. Are you working on a particular candidate's application? Just change the value in the **Status** field at the top, and save your changes. Your screen will refresh, and the candidate will be in the new status.

7.1.4 Candidate Search within the Job Requisition

Recruiters who are working on a particular requisition and not seeing the kind of applicants they are looking for can conduct a candidate search directly from the Candidate Workbench. All candidate search tools and search criteria are available if the search is initiated this way, but when candidates of interest are found, they are forwarded directly to the requisition they started from. No searching is necessary for the requisition. Recruiters can also choose to send the candidate to **Forwarded** status or add them directly to the requisition.

7.1.5 Interview Scheduling

One of the newest features in the system, the Interview Scheduling tool, provides recruiters with a high-level view of all jobs that have candidates who need to be scheduled for interviews. Previously, this information was buried not just within each job requisition but also within the candidate details of each application. Having the ability to view interviews in more of a dashboard helps keep this critical task on target and allows recruiting users to keep up to date with a quick glance, as shown in Figure 7.4.

Another feature that is a huge time-saver for recruiters is the online interview scheduling that allows candidates to set their own interviews. Moving this task to candidate self-service will free up a tremendous amount of your recruiting team's time. Add to that the integration with Outlook calendars to see interviewer availability, and interview scheduling just became fast and easy!

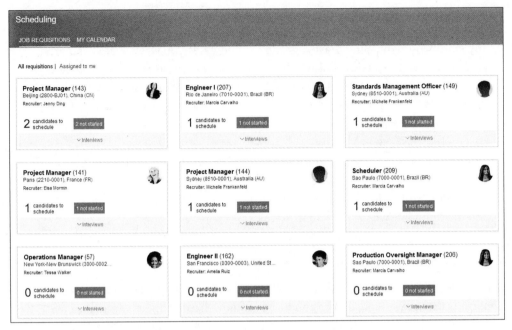

Figure 7.4 Keeping Tabs on All Interviews with a Quick Glance

These are by no means the extent of the features that enhance the recruiter experience; they are just a sample. Users will find those elements that make their jobs easier after they become familiar with the system, but these features are certainly a great place to focus attention.

Now let's discuss the tools included in the Recruiting Marketing dashboard that provide an enhanced recruiter experience.

7.2   Recruiting Marketing Dashboard

The Recruiting Marketing dashboard is divided into nine primary menus that recruiters can use to search for candidates, create reports, and assign permissions, among other tasks within the Recruiting Marketing. The Recruiting Marketing dashboard is accessible from the **Recruiting** page. This section will describe the following menus:

- **Home**
  Displays a quick snapshot of Recruiting Marketing activity.

- **Visitors**
  Displays information related to users who have visited Recruiting Marketing pages.

- **Members**
  Displays information related to users who have become members by applying to a job or joining the talent community.

- **Applicants**
  Displays information related to those who have started to apply for a job.

- **Jobs**
  Displays information about jobs in the Recruiting Marketing system.

- **Pages**
  Displays ranking information for search engine optimized (SEO) pages.

- **Reports**
  Provides access to reports and data managed by Recruiting Marketing.

The following sections will detail what you can do in each of those tabs.

7.2.1   Home

The **Home** tab displays a snapshot of Recruiting Marketing activity such as the number of **Jobs**, month to date count of visitors (**Visitors MTD**), total number of **Members**, **Applies**, average number of **Emails per Day** over the past 30 days, and **Return Applies** (see Figure 7.5). The **Home** tab also displays a revolving chart of key metrics, the ability to search the talent community, and a quick link to the **Sourcing Report**.

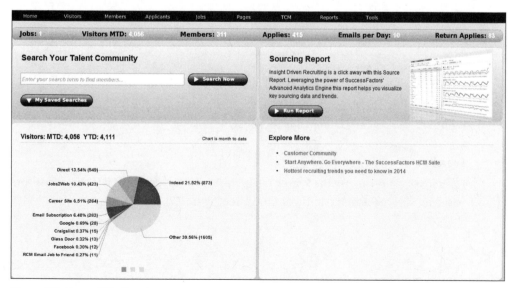

Figure 7.5 Home Tab Showing Recruiting Marketing Activity

7.2.2   Visitors

The **Visitors** tab displays information about users who have visited a Recruiting Marketing public site page (see Figure 7.6). There are six subtabs under the **Visitors** tab, which we'll explore in the following sections:

- Search
- Overview
- Map
- By Date & Time
- Segments
- Mobile Overview

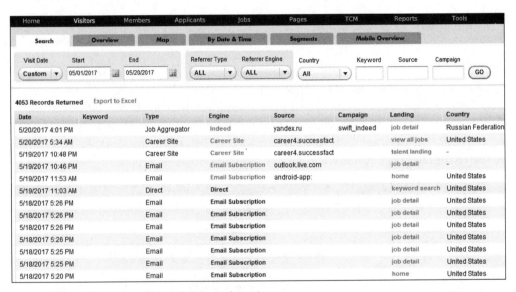

Figure 7.6 Visitors Tab Columns and Sections

Search

Dashboard users can use the **Search** tab in the **Visitors** page to display a list of visitors based on various search criteria or filters (see Figure 7.7).

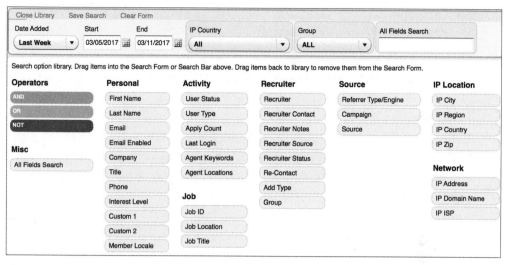

Figure 7.7 Recruiting Dashboard: Search

When conducting a search on visitors, you can use the following search filter criteria:

- **Visit Date**
  Select from a predefined set of date ranges, or define your own custom date range. The visit date is defined as the day the person visited the business's Recruiting Marketing career site.

- **Referrer Type**
  Select from an alphabetically sorted list of actively used referrer types. Examples of referrer types are **Search Engine**, **Social Network**, **Email**, **Banner Campaigns**, **Job Boards – Major**, **Job Boards – Niche**, and **All**.

- **Referrer Engine**
  Select from an alphabetically sorted list of actively used referrer engines. Referrer engines are related to the referrer type. For example, the referrer type **Social Network** could have referrer engines such as **Facebook**, **Twitter**, **LinkedIn**, and so on.

- **Country**
  Filter the view based on the country associated with the visitor's IP address.

- **Keyword**
  Filter the list of visitors based on keywords entered by visitors when searching for jobs.

- **Source**
  Filter visitors by the source URL of the visitor. You can enter a full or partial URL.

■ **Campaign**

Filter visitors by campaign code.

The results are displayed in a flat list that can be exported to Excel. The list includes columns for **Date**, **Keyword**, **Type**, **Engine**, **Source**, **Campaign**, **Landing**, and **Country**.

Overview

The **Overview** tab displays a graphical representation of the percentage of visitors by source, type of search, and cumulative visitor traffic, as shown in Figure 7.8. You can filter the charts by selecting from a predefined date range or defining your own custom date range. Following are the areas of the screen:

■ **Source of Visitors**

Displays the percentage of visitors by source. Visitors who don't belong to the top 10 sources will be aggregated into the **Other** category.

■ **Type of Searches**

Displays the percentage of visitors by type of search. Visitors who don't belong to the top 10 sources will be aggregated into the **Other** category.

■ **Inbound Visitor Traffic**

Displays the total number of visitors by day.

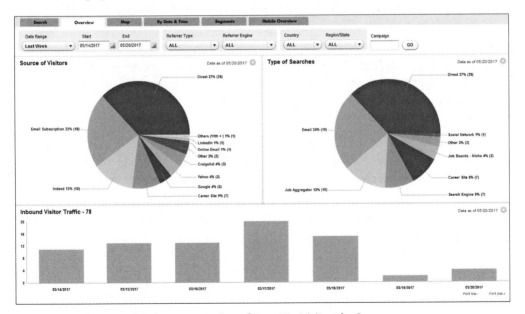

Figure 7.8 Graphical Representation of Your Site Visitors by Source

Map

The **Map** tab represents the number of site visitors in the form of a world heat map. The view can be filtered by date range as well as **Segment Category**, **Segment Subcategory**, and **Keyword**. **Segment Category** and **Segment Subcategory** allow you to select the primary category and subcategory defined for the job in the Recruiting Marketing segment engine. The more visitors that originated from a country based on the visitor's IP address, the darker the country on the map. You can drill down by clicking on the map to see more details by region, country, or state. See Figure 7.9 for an example of a heat map of the United States.

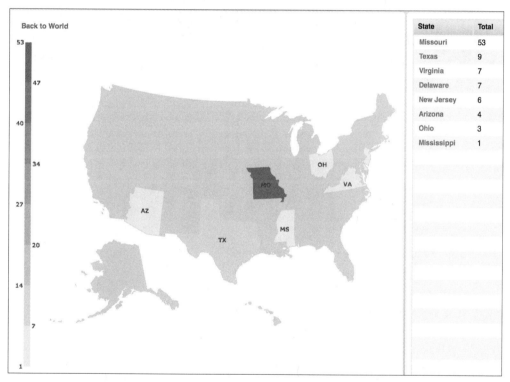

Figure 7.9 Example of Heat Map of Site Visitors

Hovering over a specific section of the map legend on the right highlights countries and their corresponding visitor count in the list on the left. Clicking a country displays more detailed visitor counts by state or region, and a user can drill down to more specific counts by city. Visitor counts by location are based on the availability of the visitor's IP address and accuracy of the visitor's network provider.

By Date & Time

The **By Date & Time** tab displays the count of visitors by the day of the week and time of day. This can help recruiters decide, for example, which days are best to post new jobs to get the most attention. See Figure 7.10 for an example of these bar charts.

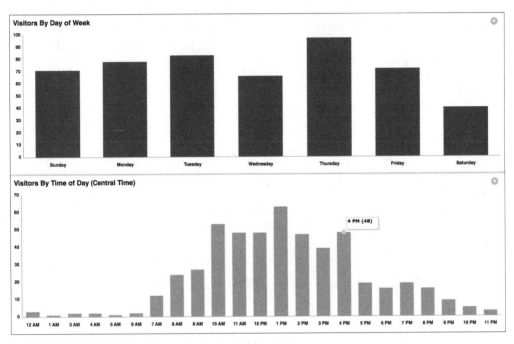

Figure 7.10 Visitors Viewed by Date and Time

Segments

The **Segments** tab displays the visitor count by job category and two charts. The first shows the number of visitors searching for jobs in each segment category. The second chart shows the count and percentage of visitors searching for jobs in each segment category, based on the selected primary category from the first chart.

Mobile Overview

The **Mobile Overview** tab displays information about visitors who visited the Recruiting Marketing career site from mobile devices, as shown in Figure 7.11. The tab shows three charts:

- **Source of Mobile Visitors**
  Displays the top 10 sources of mobile visitors. Examples of sources are direct, Google, and so on.

- **Type of Mobile Searches**
  Displays the top 10 sources of mobile visitors by type of search, such as search engine, direct, and so on.

- **Inbound Mobile Traffic**
  Toggle the chart to display either the percentage of visitors tracked from mobile devices or the absolute number of visitors from mobile devices.

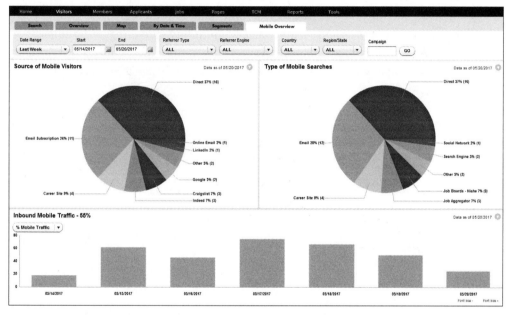

Figure 7.11 Understanding Who Is Visiting Your Site from Mobile Devices

7.2.3   Members

The **Members** tab displays information about users who have applied for a job through Recruiting Marketing or joined the talent community. There are seven subtabs under the **Members** tab:

- Search
- Overview (New)
- Referrals

- Map
- Groups
- Overview
- Member Detail

Search

You can use the **Search** tab on the **Members** page to find site members based on various search criteria or filters. There are a large number of options to use when searching for candidates, as was shown in Figure 7.7.

After you find members, you can select some or all and add them to or remove them from groups, as well as add them to talent community marketing (TCM) emails. You can also manually add members to the community from the **Members Search** tab by clicking the **Add New Member** link. The **Member Details** tab then opens where you can specify the new member's information, as shown in Figure 7.12.

Figure 7.12 Manually Adding a Talent Community Member

Overview (New)

The **Overview (New)** tab displays a graphical representation of the percentage of members by source, type of search, and member traffic (see Figure 7.13). You can filter the charts by selecting from a predefined date range or defining your own custom date range, as follows:

- **Source of Members**

  Displays the percentage of visitors by source. Visitors who don't belong to the top 10 sources will be aggregated into the **Other** category.

- **Type of Searches**

  Displays the percentage of visitors by type of search. Visitors who don't belong to the top 10 sources will be aggregated into the **Other** category.

- **Members By Date**

  Displays the total number of visitors by day.

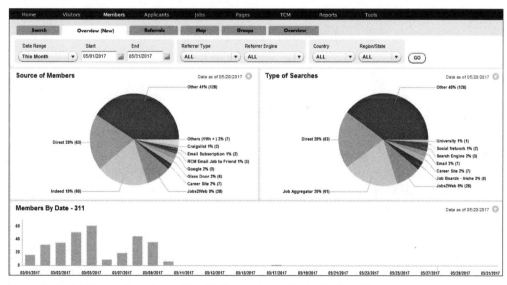

Figure 7.13 Getting an Overview of the Visitors to Your Site in Various Charts

Referrals

The **Referrals** tab displays a detailed list of members and the person who referred them to the talent community. The left side of the screen shows the **Referred Members**, and the right side shows the **Referring Members**.

Map

The **Map** tab represents the number of members in the form of a world heat map. The view can be filtered by date range as well as keyword and group. See Figure 7.14 for an example of the members map.

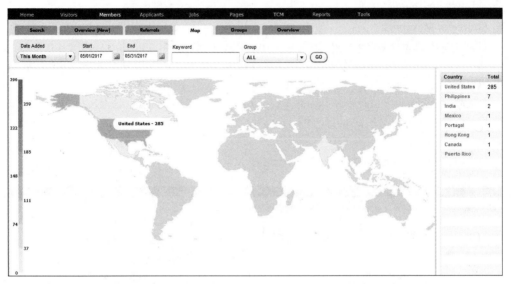

Figure 7.14 Viewing Where Your Members Are Located Geographically

Groups

The **Groups** tab shows the name of each user-defined member group and the number of members in the group. You can select and add groups to TCM emails. You can also add or delete member groups from this tab.

Overview

The **Overview** tab displays a graphical representation of the percentage of members by source, type of search, and member traffic. You can filter the charts by selecting from a predefined date range or defining your own custom date range. The **Overview** tab is nearly the same as the **Overview (New)** tab, as you can see in Figure 7.15.

Figure 7.15 Getting Another Graphical Overview Similar to the Overview (New) Tab

Member Detail

The **Member Detail** tab is only visible when a user clicks on a member's name in one of the other tabs or when a user adds a new member to the community. The **Member Detail** tab shows detailed information for each member, such as the agents they have defined, TCM emails they are associated with, jobs they have applied to, and so on.

7.2.4   Applicants

The **Applicants** tab displays information about users who have clicked the **Apply Now** button from your Recruiting Marketing career site to begin a job application. If you want to report on applicants that have completed the apply process, you need to either build an ad hoc report or use advanced analytics, which combines the visitor and apply start information with the applicant status pipeline steps in Recruiting.

There are seven subtabs under the **Applicants** tab:

- Search
- Overview
- Referrals

- Map
- Applicants by Job
- Unique Applicants Overview
- Applicants by Job Overview

The **Search**, **Overview**, **Referrals**, and **Map** tabs are essentially the same for applicants as for members. The difference is, in this case, the charts are showing people who actually applied to jobs and not just members of the community.

Applicants by Job

The **Applicants by Job** tab displays the total number of applicants and their associated apply starts. The system displays a line for each applicant and job combination. If an applicant clicks on the **Apply Now** button more than once for a job, the system will display the number of additional apply starts in brackets. You can sort and filter the list by different criteria and export it to Excel for further processing.

Unique Applicants Overview

The **Unique Applicants Overview** tab displays two pie charts and one bar graph showing the source of applicants, the type of searches performed, and unique applicants by date.

Applicants by Job Overview

The **Applicants by Job Overview** tab displays two pie charts and one bar graph showing the source of applicants, the type of searches performed, and applicants by date.

7.2.5   Jobs

The **Jobs** tab allows you to search, edit, manage, and share jobs posted through Recruiting Marketing. The **Jobs** tab is divided into four subtabs, as shown in Figure 7.16:

- Search
- Overview
- RSS
- Craigslist Search

Figure 7.16 Jobs Tab: Search Subtabs

Search

You can use the **Search** tab to find active jobs in Recruiting Marketing based on various search criteria or filters. You can see information on each job such as its title, location, when created, ID, how many times it has been viewed, how many apply starts there have been, and so on. You can also export the list to Excel for further processing.

Clicking on the link icon for a job takes you to the **URL Builder** tab in the Recruiting dashboard and prepopulates it with the job information.

Overview

The **Overview** tab displays two charts showing active jobs by Recruiting Marketing job category, such as **Human Resources**, **Facilities**, and **Hospitality**. The first chart shows the count of jobs in each Recruiting Marketing category. Clicking on an individual bar or job category in the chart displays the subcategories for the selected segment in the second chart. For example, clicking on the job category **Hospitality** could bring up subcategories such as **Food Service**, **Kitchen**, **Bartender**, and so on in the second chart.

For each chart, you can switch between the graphical representation and a data grid with a list of items with totals and percentages.

RSS

Real Simple Syndication (RSS) is an Internet standard technology that makes it easy to share new content. RSS feeds allows your company to automatically market jobs across your media channels (social networks, blogs, personal RSS readers, and other web applications) while maintaining consistent messaging and enhanced usability. Dashboard users can create custom RSS feeds for tracking using the **RSS** tab.

Craigslist Search

The functionality has been reduced due to recent Craigslist security updates. For that reason, that tab isn't covered here.

7.2.6 Pages

The **Pages** tab displays all of the SEO pages that have been created for the business's Recruiting Marketing career site. SEO pages are generated based on keywords and locations. You can see different information about each SEO page, as shown in Figure 7.17.

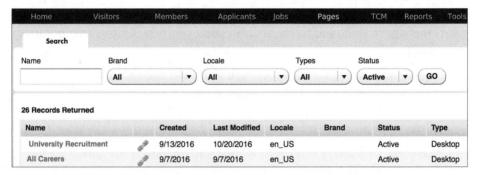

Figure 7.17 Pages Tab in the Recruiting Dashboard

You can click on the name of an SEO page to navigate directly to it. Clicking on the link icon takes you to the **URL Builder** tab in the Recruiting dashboard and prepopulates it with the SEO page information.

7.2.7 Reports

The **Reports** tab is divided into the following four subtabs:

- **Reports**
- **Conversions Overview**
- **Email Activity**
- **Source Report**

Reports

The **Reports** subtab consolidates and provides links to the reports managed in the other tabs of the Recruiting dashboard discussed earlier in this chapter. This gives you an easy overview of all the reports without navigating between tabs (see Figure 7.18).

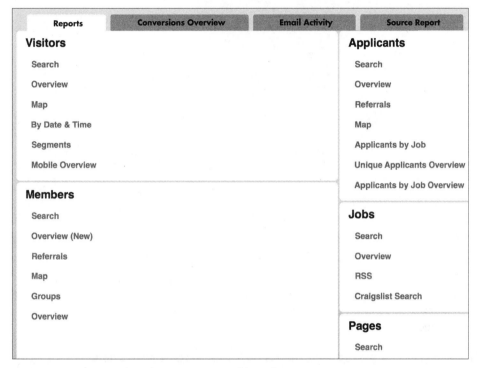

Figure 7.18 Reports Tab in the Recruiting Dashboard

Conversions Overview

The **Conversions Overview** tab displays a funnel chart showing the number of visitors, members, and applicants. This allows you to see how well you're converting career site visitors to applicants (see Figure 7.19).

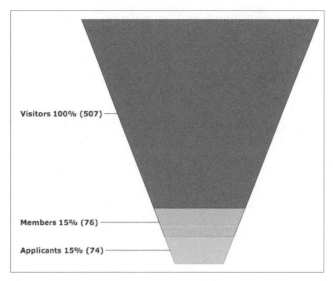

Figure 7.19 Conversions Overview Funnel

Email Activity

The **Email Activity** tab displays the number of job alert emails sent for the selected date range. You can toggle between a **Standard Graph**, which shows a bar chart of the total number of job alert emails by day, or the **Clustered Graph**, which shows a bar chart of the total number of job alert emails by day broken down by user type (subscriber, employee, past applicant, text to apply). An example of this report is provided in Figure 7.20.

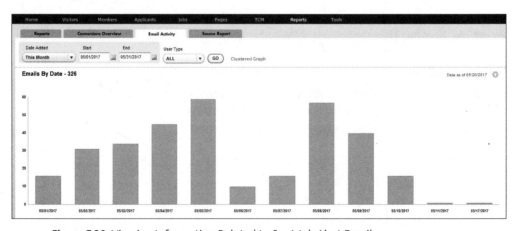

Figure 7.20 Viewing Information Related to Sent Job Alert Emails

Source Report

The **Source Report** tab is similar to the conversion funnel but provides more details. It shows the progression from visitor to subscriber to apply start by source and also shows the percentage of each (see Figure 7.21).

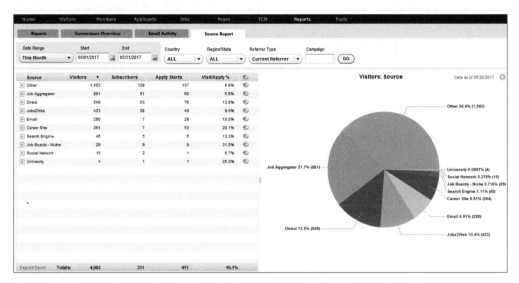

Figure 7.21 Viewing Conversion Data by the Progression of Candidates to Your Site

7.3   Summary

Recruiting provides a wide array of tools and features to recruiters, hiring managers, and other Recruiting users to facilitate them in completing day-to-day activities related to executing the organization's talent acquisition strategy. From feature-rich tools such as display and filter options, sorting, and highlighting data on a page, to providing multiple ways to disposition candidates individually and in groups, SAP SuccessFactors is designed with recruiters' efficiency in mind. Presenting information throughout the solution in a dashboard-like manner helps users keep up with critical information with just a quick glance so they know where to focus their attention most.

Having the ability to review and action candidates in the résumé carousel and conducting candidate searches from within a job requisition work to decrease time spent evaluating candidates so that jobs are filled quickly with the best talent available.

Within the Recruiting Marketing dashboard, recruiters have a host of views of data not previously available on where their candidates are coming from, both geographically and from a job board perspective. They can evaluate the quality of the sources of candidates quickly and continually improve posting decisions based on the latest decisions. Information is presented in a pleasing and easy-to-digest graphical format that translates nicely into executive reports and updates to keep all levels of talent acquisition up to date on recruiting activity.

In the next chapter, we take a look at the most commonly used administrative features within Recruiting.

Chapter 8

Recruiting Management Admin Features

After SAP SuccessFactors Recruiting is implemented and live in a business's environment, numerous features can be maintained in Admin Center. Understanding these features and how to use them is critical for maintaining the system to full optimization after go-live.

SAP SuccessFactors Recruiting Management has more than 30 options within the Recruiting area of Admin Center. Not all of these features will be used by all businesses; some deal with very specific features such as setting up and managing eQuest integration, whereas others such as Manage Route Maps are shared functions with other modules (SAP SuccessFactors Performance & Goals). Others will be used during implementation and then not needed on an ongoing basis. In this chapter, we'll look at the most common features that SAP SuccessFactors Recruiting administrators will work with after implementation, including the following:

- Recruiting settings
- Recruiting email templates
- Offer letter templates
- Edit applicant setting configuration
- Data privacy consent statements
- Question libraries
- Duplicate candidates management
- Job requisitions reassignment
- Agency portal access
- Employee referral program
- Recruiting group management
- Job posting headers and footers

- Custom help text management
- Document management

Additional features in the Recruiting area of Admin Center are typically used only during implementation. We'll take a brief look at these features in the last section of this chapter. SAP continues to build out the administrative capabilities of Recruiting so new features will continue to be added with each new release cycle.

8.1   Manage Recruiting Settings

The **Manage Recruiting Settings** area in Admin Center contains a variety of settings that impact how Recruiting behaves. In the following sections, we'll discuss some of the most critical settings, as follows:

- **Return Email Address Information**
- **Candidate Profile Settings**
- **Applicant Profile Settings**
- **Job Requisition**
- **Interview Central**
- **Offer Approval/Offer Letter**
- **Career Site Settings**

8.1.1   Return Email Address Information

In this area, shown in Figure 8.1, you'll specify a display name and email address for system-generated emails that are sent from the system to candidates. You can also choose whether to allow the return email address editable. Probably the most important setting in this area is **Delay Emails to Disqualified Candidates (in hours)**. This setting will delay emails that are sent out to candidates who are moved into a **Disqualified** status. This is most important for candidates that are automatically disqualified by incorrectly responding to a disqualifying prescreening question. If this isn't set, a candidate who submits an application and is automatically disqualified would receive both the application confirmation and the disqualified email within a span of minutes. Note that this setting is set in hours, not days.

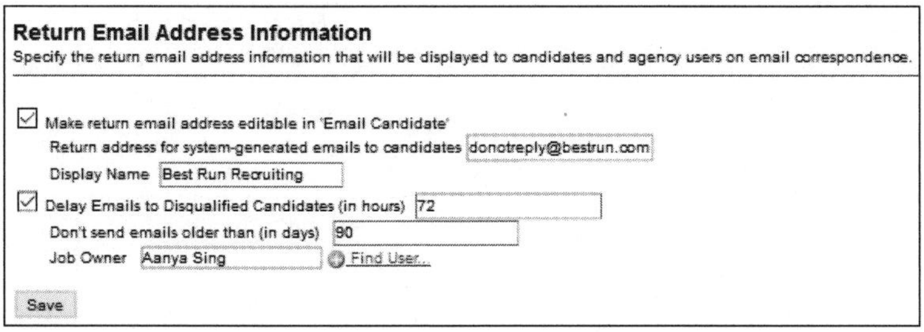

Figure 8.1 Settings for Emails Sent to Candidates from the System

8.1.2 Candidate Profile Settings

This area, shown in Figure 8.2, is where résumé parsing is enabled. Résumé parsing is the feature that will read the candidate's résumé and populate fields on the candidate profile into fields such as name, email, address and background elements for the **Work History and Education** area. Once enabled, field mapping must be configured in standardized mapping for résumé parsing to work.

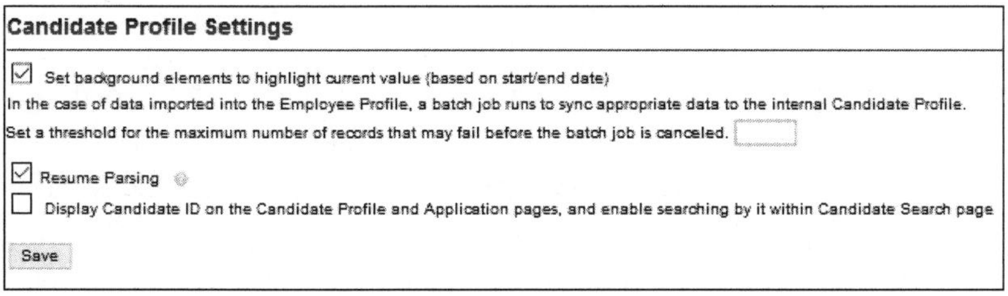

Figure 8.2 Résumé Parsing Setting in the Candidate Profile Settings Area

8.1.3 Applicant Profile Settings

In the **Application Profile Settings** area, there are numerous settings that impact how applicant data are handled and some options that automate dispositioning. We'll look at each of these important settings as shown in Figure 8.3:

- **Hide skipped statuses in application audit trail**
  By default, the system tracks every status that an applicant is placed in and every skipped status. If this setting is enabled, the system won't track any status that is skipped while dispositioning candidates. This impacts the **Application Audit** portlet that tracks activity against a candidate.

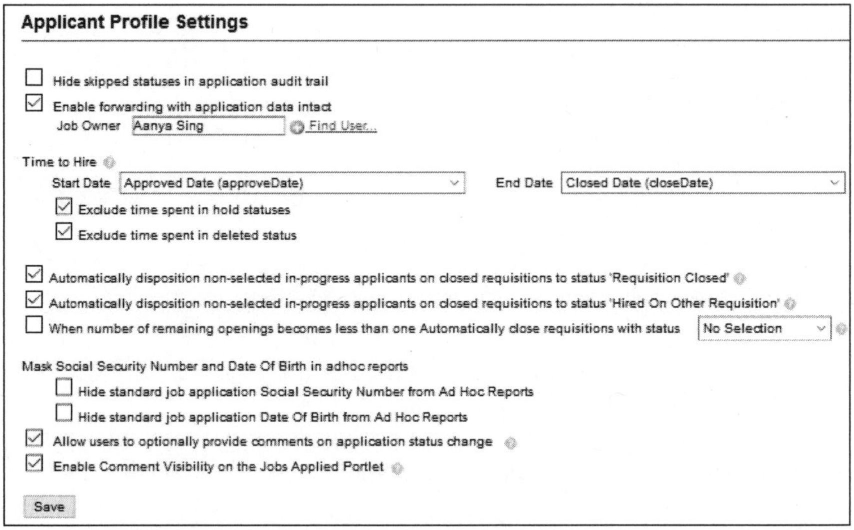

Figure 8.3 Applicant Profile Settings Addressing How Applicant Data Are Handled and Automatic System Actions Based on Certain Actions

- **Enable forwarding with application data intact**

  This setting impacts the situation when a candidate is forwarded from one requisition to another. Sometimes, recruiters will deem a candidate who has applied for one job to be a fit for another. In this case, they can forward the applicant to that job. When this setting is enabled, and a candidate is forwarded, the system will populate similar fields on the application of the new job with what was already submitted. Candidates will be presented with this information when they apply and can confirm or update it before submitting their new application.

- **Time to Hire**

  These settings impact how the system calculates time to hire. From the dropdown menus, you select the options you want to use to indicate both the **Start Date** and **End Date** for time-to-hire purposes. You can optionally choose to exclude any time a candidate may spend in any status that is used as a holding status. If this is selected, time to hire will be calculated retroactively.

- **Automatically disposition non-selected in-progress applicants on closed requisitions to status 'Requisition Closed'/. . . to status 'Hired On Other Requisition'**

  These two settings impact how nondispositioned candidates will be treated when a requisition is closed. The first setting manages applicants that are in an **In Progress** status when the requisition is closed; this can automatically move these candidates to the standard status of **Requisition Closed**. The second setting deals with applicants that are being dispositioned on more than one active requisition. If they are hired on another requisition, this setting automatically dispositions their record on any other active applications to the standard status **Hired on Other Requisition**. It's best practice to select both of these options.

> **Note**
>
> These settings impact candidates in any **In Progress**, **On Board**, or **Hired** status that doesn't have the **Hireable** option selected. Any candidate in a **Hireable** status won't be moved.

- **When number of remaining openings becomes less than one Automatically close requisitions with status**
  This setting will assist in requisition maintenance. When a requisition's number of openings is zero, this setting automatically closes the requisition and sets the status to the value selected in the dropdown menu. This setting works in concert with the two previous settings on what happens when a requisition is closed.

- **Mask Social Security Number and Date of Birth in adhoc reports**
  When these settings are enabled and the standard fields for **Social Security Number** and **Date of Birth** are used, these settings will hide these values in ad hoc reports. The data is still visible via the SFAPI (SAP SuccessFactors web service) and the New Hire Integration report.

- **Allow users to optionally provide comments on application status change**
  When this is enabled, the system adds a text box where recruiters can add comments when an applicant is moved from one status to another. Comments are optional unless required on the status in **Edit Applicant Status Settings**.

- **Enable Comment Visibility on the Jobs Applied Portlet**
  This makes visible any application comments made upon status change within the **Jobs Applied** portlet, which displays other jobs that candidates have applied for.

8.1.4   Job Requisition

This area also has numerous settings that impact how and what users can do when working with requisitions (see Figure 8.4). We'll also look at each setting in this section, as all are important to understand:

- **Use originator's preferred language as the default language of a new job requisition**
  In a multilanguage instance, when job requisitions are created, a default language must be selected. This can be set in the XML template, or this setting can be used. If this is enabled, the system automatically assigns the creating user's selected language pack as the default language of the job requisition. This can be useful in multilanguage situations so users don't need to remember to set **Language**.

- **Allow forwarding of candidates to unposted jobs**
  This setting allows Recruiting users to forward candidates to requisitions regardless of whether they are currently posted. This applies when doing a candidate search or dispositioning a candidate who has applied to another requisition. It's recommended to enable this setting.

- **Enable private postings of jobs**
  This will allow requisitions to be posted privately, as discussed in Chapter 2. This setting must be enabled even if the internal and external posting fields are included in the job requisition data model (JRDM), and permissioned or private postings won't be supported.

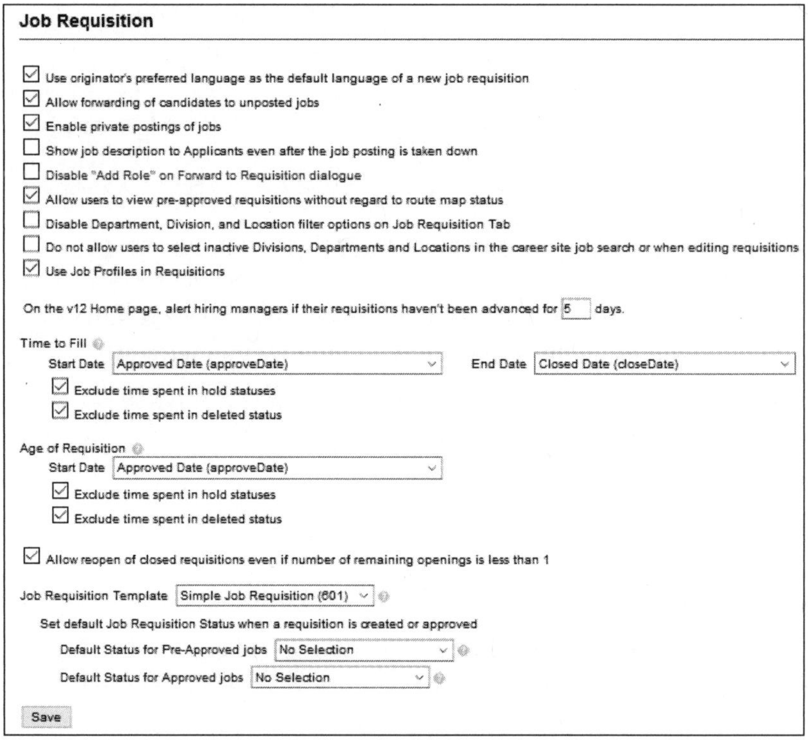

Figure 8.4 Job Requisition Settings for Managing Requisitions

- **Show job description to Applicants even after the job posting is taken down**
  By default, when a requisition posting is removed or expires, the job description will no longer be accessible, even to candidates who have applied for the job. If this setting is enabled, candidates with active applications will be able to access job descriptions from the **Job Applications** tab even if the job has been unposted. Candidates doing a job search, or attempting to view the job from **My Saved Jobs,** won't be able to access the job description.

- **Disable "Add Role" on Forward to Requisition dialogue**
  When forwarding candidates to other requisitions, there is an **Add Role** option that allows users to select from families and roles in their search criteria. Selecting this option disables the **Add Role** option from the search dialog.

- **Allow users to view pre-approved requisitions without regard to route map status**
  This setting allows users who are operators on a requisition to view requisitions regardless of the route map step or whether the requisition has been approved.

- **Disable Department, Division, and Location filter options on Job Requisition Tab**
  This setting applies to the **Department**, **Division**, and **Location** fields that are standard filters. Often the values in these fields aren't applicable to Recruiting, so custom fields are defined. In this case, you'll want to disable these fields as a filter option to avoid confusing your users.

- **Do not allow users to select inactive Divisions, Departments and Locations in the career site job search or when editing requisitions**
  Just as the standard **Division**, **Department,** and **Location** fields can be used as standard filters on the **Requisition** page, they can also be selected as candidate search criteria on the **Job Search** page. If this is enabled, any inactive values in these fields won't be available to select either when searching for jobs or editing requisitions.

- **On the v12 Home page, alert hiring managers if their requisitions haven't been advanced for "number" of days**
  This setting provides an alert on the home page of hiring managers if their requisitions become stalled. The recommended setting is three days.

- **Time to Fill**
  These settings determine how the system calculates time to fill for requisitions. Just as with time to hire in the applicant settings, you select how to determine the **Start Date** and **End Date** and can exclude time spent in hold statuses. The Time to Fill report is available in the **Ad Hoc Reports** page.

- **Age of Requisition**
  These settings are used to determine how requisitions are aged by the system. Make a selection for how to determine **Start Date,** and choose whether to exclude time spent in a hold status.

- **Allow reopen of closed requisitions even if number of remaining openings is less than 1**
  This setting allows users with button permissions to **Reopen Requisition** to be able to reopen requisitions with zero openings.

- **Default Status for Pre-Approved jobs/Default Status for Approved jobs**
  By requisition template, you can set the default status the system will assign for requisitions in **Pre-Approved** and **Approved** statuses. Make the applicable selections in the dropdown menus.

8.1.5 Interview Central

These settings address whether attachments can be added for interview notes and enabling Interview Scheduling, as you can see in Figure 8.5. If the attachments setting is enabled, interviewers will have an **Attachment** field available in Interview Central to upload any notes taken in document form.

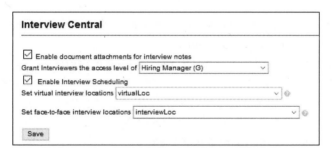

Figure 8.5 Make Settings Related to Interview Central

Interview Scheduling is enabled here, and locations for virtual and face-to-face interviews are selected. Note that these two picklists must be created in picklists management before these settings can be made.

8.1.6 Offer Approval/Offer Letter

In the **Offer Approval** area, displayed in Figure 8.6, you select whether any job code entity fields are editable. Refer to the discussion of job code entity in Chapter 2 before making this setting. The second **Offer Approval** setting disables pulling updated job application and requisition field data onto the offer approval when the offer approval is edited or a new version is created.

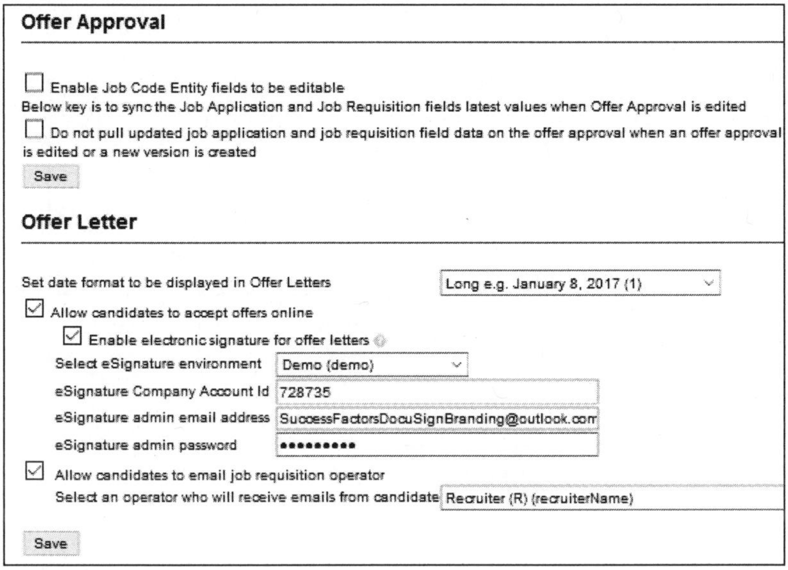

Figure 8.6 Settings for Offer Approvals and Offer Letters

The **Offer Letter** settings enable electronic acceptance of offers, enable electronic signature (via DocuSign integration, which requires further configuration), and determine whether candidates can email the selected job requisition operator (choose from the dropdown menu).

8.1.7 Career Site

The settings under **Career Site** are related to the **Internal Job Posting** and **External Job Posting** pages. These settings, provided in Figure 8.7, will enable the **Apply with LinkedIn** capability for the internal and external sites and disable the CAPTCHA verification when candidates choose to email a job or when an account is created.

The other two areas allow users to customize the job application submission message on both the internal and external career sites. If custom messages aren't configured, the standard message will apply on both pages.

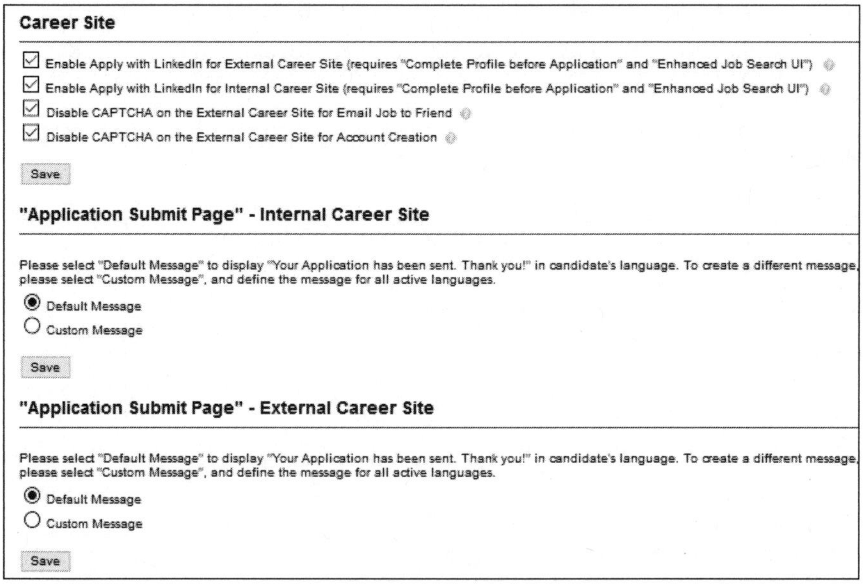

Figure 8.7 Settings for the Internal and External Career Pages

Recruiting settings are added frequently with quarterly enhancements so be sure to keep up to date with the Release Readiness information to make sure you're aware of the latest and greatest settings.

8.2   Email Templates

Using the system, you can communicate with candidates during the Recruiting process in several ways. Operators can email candidates at any time during the process by using either predefined email templates or ad hoc emails. Email templates can also be attached to statuses in the applicant status pipeline to automatically communicate with candidates and other Recruiting players when a candidate is moved into a status. A library of email templates is maintained in Admin Center. Under **Manage Recruiting Email Templates**, users can define email templates for use throughout the system (see Figure 8.8).

Templates can only be enabled or disabled; they can't be deleted. The email templates are also presented in alphabetical order within the user interface (UI), so thought should be given to how the templates are named. Additionally, all email templates will be presented regardless of whether email templates are applicable to the given action. For example, when choosing to email a candidate from the Candidate Workbench, recruiters will see email templates related to sending electronic offers and offer letters, as well as email templates that are attached to applicant statuses. Developing guidelines around how to name email templates is advised, especially if administration of email templates is shared across regions or countries.

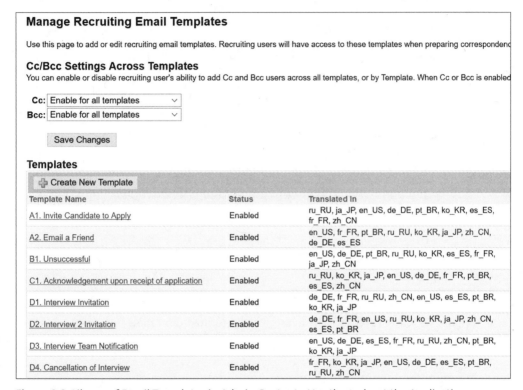

Figure 8.8 Library of Email Templates in Admin Center to Use throughout the Application

Tokens can be used to dynamically populate emails with data pulled from the requisition, application, candidate profile, and offer approval. Each email template can be translated into various languages within the UI. See Figure 8.9 for the edit options for email templates. Email templates can be edited when sending, if sending ad hoc emails, but if permanent updates are needed, the template should be updated.

Email templates can have carbon copy and blind copy capability enabled in this area. You can enable these features for all email templates or individual email templates. It's best practice to enable at least carbon copy capability for all email templates so this can be used as needed when emails are sent from within the UI. You can also define text for SMS communication to candidates. Although this feature isn't shown in Figure 8.9, it's available for each email template. (Emails are addressed in greater detail in Chapter 9.)

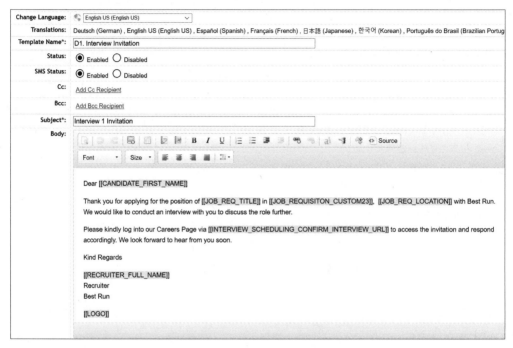

Figure 8.9 Using Tokens to Dynamically Populate Data from Various Templates within Recruiting

8.3   Offer Letter Templates

Offer letter templates work similarly to email templates. In **Manage Offer Letter Templates**, you build and maintain a library of templates that are used to make offers of employment, as you can see in Figure 8.10. Offer letter templates also can only be enabled or disabled, just like email templates. Just like email templates, tokens are used to dynamically populate data from the following templates:

- Job requisition
- Application
- Candidate profile
- Job offer details (approval)

Any user who has permission to manage offer letter templates has access to all offer letter templates; it isn't possible to permission access to templates within this area. As with email templates, guidelines are recommended for managing the naming of offer letters so they are easily identifiable to users.

Businesses take different approaches to managing offer letter templates. Some will define templates that are country-specific, whereas others will define templates for the type of job or the extra incentives included, such as sign-on bonus or relocation assistance.

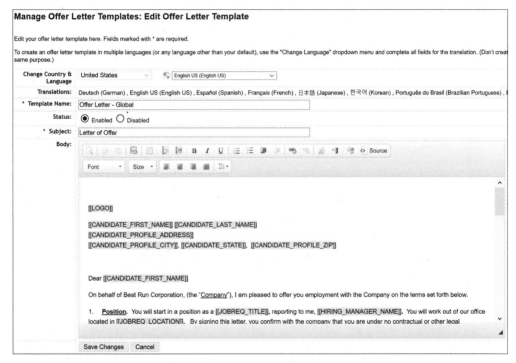

Figure 8.10 Tokens Used in Offer Letter Templates to Populate Candidate-Specific Data into the Offer Letter

8.4   Edit Applicant Status Configuration

The applicant status set is the system name of the talent pipeline. This contains all the statuses that comprise the process you use to evaluate your candidates. Your applicant status set will be configured during implementation. However, several features are maintained in Admin Center and may be advantageous for you to use to better manage your process and communicate to players in the Recruiting process. For each status in the pipeline, the following settings can be made:

- Setting the language
- Making a status required
- Setting the internal label to recruiting users
- Setting the candidate label for candidate view
- Setting next step text to communicate to candidates on the job applications portal
- Making employee referral settings (if applicable)
- Enabling the status for internal and/or external candidates
- Hiding the status from users who don't have view privileges
- Hiding the applicant count from users who don't have view privileges
- Collecting a comment if the status is skipped
- Setting email templates to various players in the process to automatically send email communication when a status is triggered
- Setting viewing and selecting permissions

The most critical of these settings are discussed in the following list and shown in Figure 8.11:

- **Language to Translate**
  If multiple languages are in use, this field will select each language for all applicable translations. The settings for **Internal Label**, **Candidate Label**, and **Next Step Text** must be set for each Recruiting language that is being used.

- **Required**
  Selecting this box will make that status required, which means that before candidates can move past it in the pipeline, they must first be moved to that status. Required statuses are indicated with an asterisk on the status in the talent pipeline.

- **Internal Label**
  This is what Recruiting users will see when viewing the status in the pipeline.

- **Candidate Label**
  This is displayed to candidates on the **Jobs Applied** page on the portal. They will see this label for all statuses in which they are placed. It's common practice to keep this label very high level and generic, such as "Thank you for applying," and to use email templates to communicate detailed information with candidates.

- **Next Step Text**
  This is also displayed to candidates on the **Jobs Applied** page. As with the **Candidate**

Label, it's recommended that this be kept very high level and generic. A common message is to remind candidates to keep an eye out for additional openings on the **Job Search** page.

- **Employee Referral Program Settings**

  If the employee referral feature is enabled, you have options on what to communicate and display to the referring employee. You can choose to display the status or not, and you can also set a status label and **Next Step Text** that they will see in the **Employee Referral** portlet. You can also choose to communicate with the referring employee by using an email template.

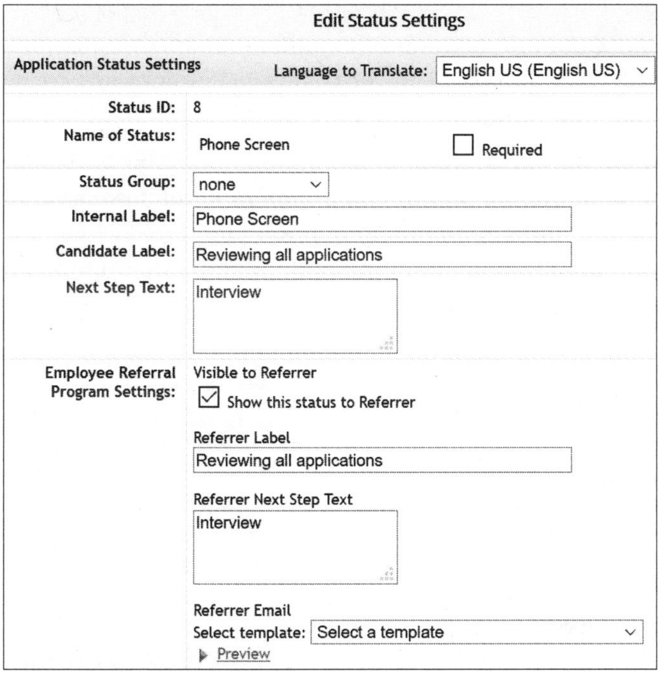

Figure 8.11 Applicant Status Settings

- **Options**

  There are various settings under **Options**, as shown in Figure 8.12, which determine how the status will be used:

  - **Enable this status for internal candidates**

    If this is enabled, the status is available for Recruiting users to select for any internal candidate. Note that this enables you to have statuses that are just applicable to internal candidates.

– **Enable this status for external candidates**
If this is selected, the status is available for Recruiting users to select for any external candidate. Note that this enables you to have statuses that are just applicable to external candidates.

– **Hide the status from users who don't have application status Visible To privilege**
If this is selected, Recruiting users who don't have the requisite **Visible To** privileges set on the status won't see it in the talent pipeline (**Visible To** options are discussed later in this list).

– **Hide applicant count from the users who don't have application status Visible To privilege**
If this is selected, Recruiting users who don't have the requisite **Visible To** privileges set for the status will see the status in the talent pipeline but won't see the number of candidates in the status.

– **Collect comment if this status is skipped**
This option will provide a comment box when moving a candidate so comments can be made if the status is skipped for any reason.

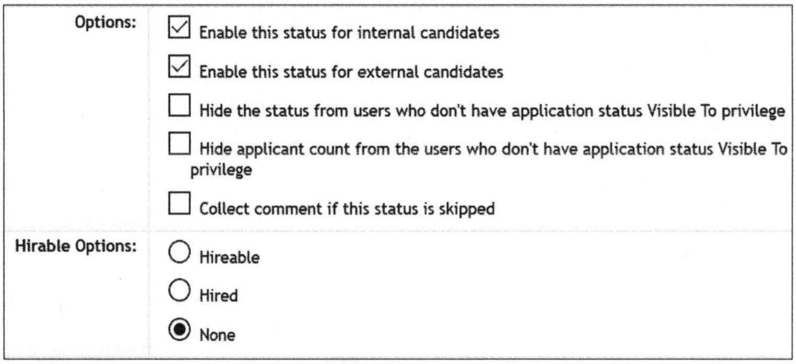

Figure 8.12 Various Options for Enabling and Viewing the Status and Indicating a Hirable Option

- **Hirable Options**
These settings indicate how the status behaves when integrating with Employee Central or SAP ERP Human Capital Management (SAP ERP HCM) in a hybrid situation. These settings are only made on one status in a status set. If the **Hireable** option is selected, the system will know that when a candidate is moved into this status, the candidate should be queued to Employee Central pending hires. If **Hired** is selected, this will queue a candidate to the integration with SAP ERP HCM to

send new hire candidates over to be hired in that hire action. For most statuses in a status set, the **None** setting will be selected.

- **Email Template Settings**

  The next section allows you to identify email templates that can be associated with the status to automatically communicate information to various players in the process. You can see these email settings in Figure 8.13. The templates must first be defined in **Manage Recruiting Email Templates** as discussed in Section 8.2. For a status that has an email template associated with a role, when a candidate is moved into that status, the system will automatically send the email template to the specified users. In addition to all of the Recruiting operator roles that may be in use, you may also define an email template for these roles:

  - **Internal Candidate**

  - **Internal Candidate's Current Manager**

  - **External Candidate**

  - **Agency User**

  - Any Recruiting team role in use

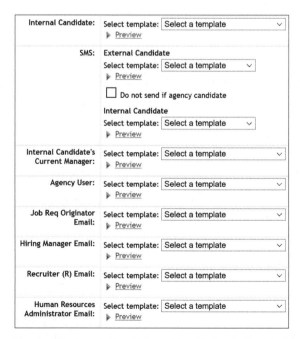

Figure 8.13 Associating Roles with a Status to Enable Automatically Sending Emails to Various Roles

The last area of the applicant status settings are the permissions, as shown in Figure 8.14. For each status, you must select the roles that can select the status, which is called the **Selectable By** permission. You must also set who can view the status by setting the **Visible To** permissions. Only those roles that have checkboxes selected will be able to see and/or select that status. Note that there is an option to permission **Upline Managers** to the status as well.

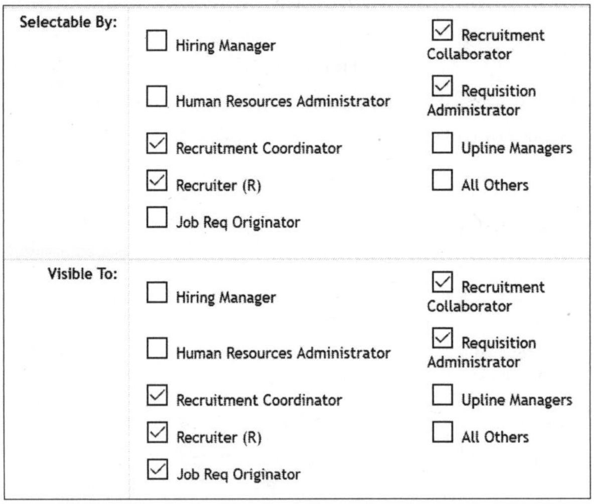

Figure 8.14 Setting Permissions on Each Status to Determine Who Can Select and View the Status

8.5   Question Libraries

The system provides applicant-prescreening capabilities during the application process. If questions are added to the requisition, these questions display to applicants during the application process. These questions may be used to calculate a rating of applicants or to automatically disqualify applicants based on incorrect responses or not meeting a minimum score. Refer to Chapter 2 for further explanation of prescreening questions.

Any number of question libraries can be maintained centrally in Admin Center to manage different types of questions that can be added to requisitions. It's best practice to maintain question libraries in Admin Center so that all requisitions use the same question wording and the same answers. This is important to maintain consistency in evaluating applicants against these prescreening questions, especially if the questions will be used to disqualify applicants or calculate an average score. Let's look at how question libraries can be imported and maintained within the UI.

8.5.1   Importing Question Libraries

When a Recruiting instance is first configured, there are no question libraries in the instance. At least one library should be imported so there are questions available (see Figure 8.15). To import a question library, follow these steps:

1. Navigate to **Question Library Import** in Admin Center.
2. Browse for the **Question Library File**.
3. Enter a name for the library in the **Library Name** field; this is how the library will be displayed in the instance.
4. Select whether the library will be **Editable** (recommended) or **Read-only**.
5. Choose the **Character Encoding**. If the file contains language translations make sure that **Unicode (UTF-8)** is selected in this field. If a library file with translations is imported with encoding as Windows/ISO, there will likely be issues with any special characters in the file being displayed with errors in the instance.
6. Click the **Import** button.
7. Repeat these steps to import additional libraries as needed.

Figure 8.15 Adding Question Libraries via Question Library Import in Admin Center

Note that the only way to add a new library to the instance is via the **Question Library Import** screen. After a library has been imported, question categories can be added, modified, or created in the UI. We'll review this in the next section.

8.5.2   Maintaining Questions in the User Interface

Figure 8.16 displays questions within libraries in the UI. These questions can be edited here, or you can create new questions. To create questions in the UI, follow these steps:

1. Choose the library in which you want to add or edit the question. When you select a library, you can see all the questions available in that library.

2. In the **Create new question** field, enter the question you want to create.

3. Choose a category for the question, and click **Create**. The question is added to the library, and you can now select it and edit the type of question and any answers.

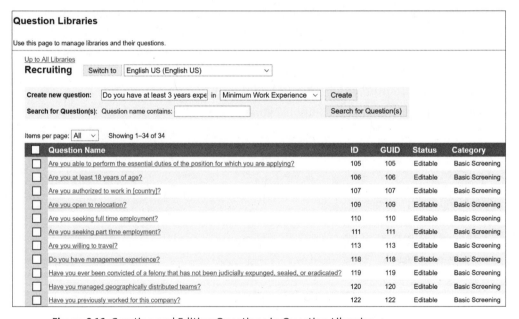

Figure 8.16 Creating and Editing Questions in Question Libraries

The system supports several types of questions, including questions that are associated with a rating scale. However, the most common types of questions are multiple-choice and free-text questions. When a multiple-choice question is created, you must add the various possible answers to the question. Note that while this will appear like a picklist to candidates, the answer values are actually maintained on the question itself. You must also select the correct answer.

If **Rating Scales** is selected as the question type, you must select from a rating scale defined in **Admin Center • Rating Scales**, as you can see in Figure 8.17. Correct answers can be specified as anything higher or lower than the selected value. This feature doesn't provide a true multiple-selection functionality but does allow multiple correct answers to be specified.

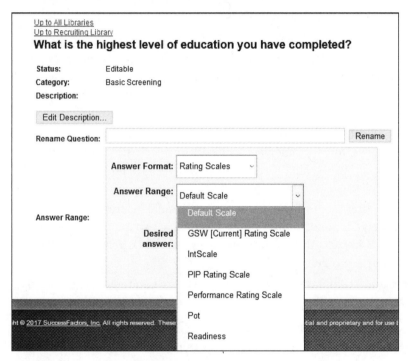

Figure 8.17 Choosing a Rating Scale

Numeric questions solicit a numeric answer. You can specify any number five digits or fewer, including decimals, as the correct answer. The candidate can enter a value higher or lower than the specified value. No formatting constraints can be applied to this question type. For example, there is no way to restrict the candidate to entering only a four-digit year.

8.6   Managing Duplicate Candidates

Unfortunately, there is no way to prevent candidates from creating multiple accounts. Although each account must have a unique email address, often candidates will forget their password, so they will just create a new account with a different email address. SAP SuccessFactors offers a solution for managing duplicate candidate profiles. In this way, you can merge two profiles from the same candidate into one profile. This feature must first be enabled in provisioning. Once enabled, duplicate profiles can be managed in Admin Center. The following guidelines are important to understand before working with this feature:

- After candidate profiles are merged, they can't be undone.
- Only one pair of candidates can be merged at one time. There is no mass merge feature, and it's not possible to merge all candidates found by the duplicate search at once. If a candidate has created more than two profiles, you must merge the first two and then proceed to merge the duplicates two at a time.
- Duplicate candidates can only be merged within Admin Center. It's not possible to merge the profiles from the candidate profile UI. However, the system will provide an alert to Recruiting users in the candidate profile view if a profile is identified as a potential duplicate.
- Internal candidates can be merged with external candidate profiles. External profiles can be merged to another external profile. But no two internal profiles can be merged, as this impacts the Human Resources Information System (HRIS) data and the employee profile.
- The system uses a combination of first name, last name, and address fields to identify potential duplicates.

In the **Manage Duplicate Candidates** area of Admin Center, you'll see two tabs: **Potential Duplicate Candidate List** and **Manually Merge Duplicate Candidates**. You'll search for possible duplicate candidates and then choose a "master" candidate that will represent the official candidate record that will be merged into.

8.6.1   Potential Duplicate Candidate List

On this tab, potential duplicate profiles are presented (see Figure 8.18). If a search has already been run, the results of the last search will be displayed with a message that includes the date and time of the last search. Selecting **Update List** will run the search again through the entire candidate database and attempt to find duplicate candidate profiles.

The entire candidate database is searched, so the search can take quite a long time. It's a good idea to initiate this search as part of regular system maintenance so that the data are available when it's time to maintain the candidate profiles.

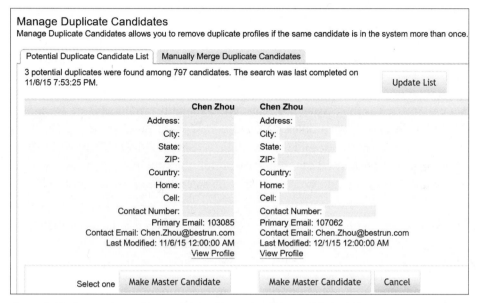

Figure 8.18 Comparison of Potential Duplicate Candidates Side by Side

When you select a pair of matched candidates, you see a side-by-side view of basic data to help you confirm whether the two profiles presented are in fact duplicates. You'll then be presented with a question: **Are these duplicate candidates?** If you select **Yes**, two additional buttons are provided.

To merge two candidate profiles, you must select one profile to be the master profile. Choose which of the two candidate profiles you want to be the master and select the **Make Master Candidate** button. If **No** is selected, meaning the candidate profiles aren't duplicates, the profiles are marked off so they are removed from the **Potential Duplicate Candidates List**.

8.6.2 Manually Merge Duplicate Candidates

On this tab, you manually search for duplicate candidates you already know of. The keys are either the **Primary Email** (username) or **Contact Email** address. You'll select if you're searching for external or internal candidates. You must also enter a search criteria such as a name or email domain. When the two profiles are presented, the same process as outline in the previous section is followed. You view the candidate information side by side and select a master candidate.

8.6.3   Master Candidates

Before merging profiles, a master candidate must be selected. This is the profile into which the duplicate profile will be merged. The merged profile will no longer exist. When merging an external profile into an internal profile, only the internal profile may be selected as the master candidate. When merging profiles, if there is conflicting data between the two profiles, such as different phone numbers in the same field, the data from the master record will be retained. For fields that are blank on the master profile but have data on the secondary profile, the system will populate the master profile fields with data from the duplicate so the maximum amount of data is retained.

Before merging the profiles, you can choose to notify the candidate of the merge action via email. The standard email presented can be modified before sending out to the candidate. There are options to notify the master candidate email, the secondary profile email, or both.

8.7   Reassigning Job Requisitions

Sometimes it's necessary to reassign job requisitions from one specific user to another. The **Reassign Job Requisition** feature screen in Admin Center allows you to assign one or more requisitions to multiple users. You can search for requisitions by requisition template (**Select Template**) or by specific job requirement ID (**Search Job Req ID**). After the job requisitions are displayed, you can select one or more and then choose **Select** to display the roles that can be reassigned. Note that all of the recruiting operator roles can be reassigned here. Type the user's name in the specific field, or click **Find User** to search for the correct user. After all the roles are completed, click the **Reassign** button (see Figure 8.19).

Requisitions that are pending approval when reassigned will be routed to the new *currently with* approver. Operators who have been reassigned to the requisitions will receive an email notification with information about the change. The administrator will also receive an email confirmation. When recruiting teams are configured, if the hiring manager is changed and that hiring manager has preferences set for a Recruiting team, those preferences will populate into the operator fields on the reassignment screen. These preferences can be edited or can remain as they are. Team preferences for any operator will be applied to the reassignment screen by default.

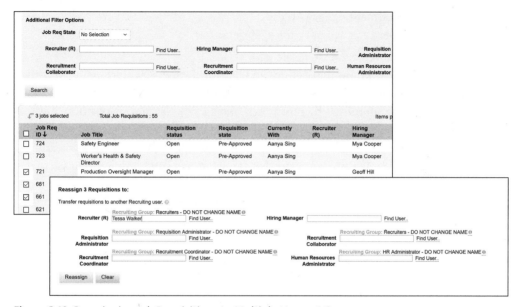

Figure 8.19 Reassigning Job Requisitions to Multiple Users at Once

8.8   Agency Portal

Businesses often work with various recruiting agencies to support their candidate sourcing and find qualified applicants for key jobs. Recruiting provides a convenient, online method for external recruiters at these agencies to view job postings and submit potential candidates for consideration. This feature is called the agency portal, and we discussed posting jobs to the agency portal in Chapter 2. SAP maintains one agency portal URL for each datacenter. The portal is shared across all businesses on a datacenter, with customer-specific space on the portal where individual businesses will post their jobs that are accessible only by those agency users who have been provisioned in Admin Center.

Let's discuss the agency portal in more detail, including an overview discussion and how to work with agencies with access to the agency portal.

8.8.1   Overview of Agency Access

For a business to use the agency portal, the feature must first be enabled in provisioning. The following settings, as shown in Figure 8.20, are required to use the agency portal:

- **Enable Recruitment Agency Access**
  This setting enables access to the agency portal.

- **Agency advanced ownership setting**
  There are two options that define candidate ownership: **Ownership for requisition** and **Ownership for duration**. First, ownership for requisition means that a candidate may be submitted by more than one agency for various position, but that only one agency can have ownership of that candidate for a specific requisition. Second, ownership can be defined by duration, which defines a time period during which only the agency that owns that candidate can submit that candidate to requisitions.

There are also some optional provisioning settings that can be set for Agency Access (also shown in Figure 8.20):

- **Disable Agency filtering by locale (show all jobs regardless of posting locale)**

- **Agency - Display Powered By SuccessFactors Logo**

- **Enable Posting to specific agencies**

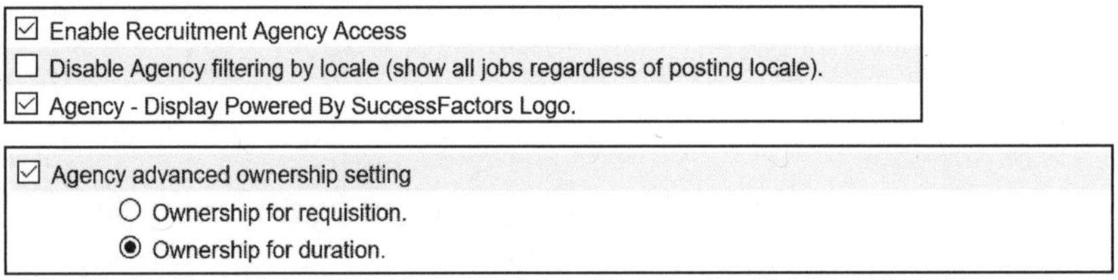

Figure 8.20 Agency Settings in Provisioning

> **Note**
>
> If the **Enable Posting to specific agencies** option is enabled, a user can choose to post to any of the configured agencies separately. If not enabled, jobs are posted to all configured agencies. This feature can't be disabled once enabled, so it's important to explain how this feature works to businesses and gain their decision.

When the **Agency** feature is enabled, you can set up both agencies and agency users to access the agency portal shown in Figure 8.21, and each datacenter has an agency portal. You can't restrict viewing of agencies using role-based permissions, so if administrators have access to **Agency** in Admin Center, they can view and maintain all entries there. This also means that when posting to agencies, Recruiting users are going to see every agency and can post to every agency. An agency can have multiple users who can log in to view the jobs posted there, but when posting jobs to an agency, the job will be available to all users within that agency, and the jobs will all have the same start and end dates.

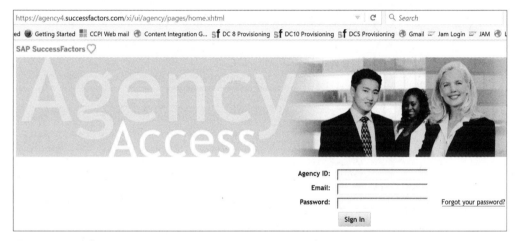

Figure 8.21 Performance Manager Datacenter Agency Portal

8.8.2   Working with the Agency Portal

Recruiting administrators can set up agencies and their respective users within Admin Center. When navigating to **Set Up Agency Access,** a user will see the first agency in the list (if agencies have already been created), as shown in Figure 8.22. To toggle between different Agencies choose the **Agency ID** dropdown, and select the agency desired. To add a new agency, select the **Add new agency** link next to the **Agency ID** field. After an agency is added, individual users must be added. The users are the ones that will log in to the agency portal. Select the **Add new user** link to the right of the **Users** field. Administrators will create and manage the agents' passwords in this screen.

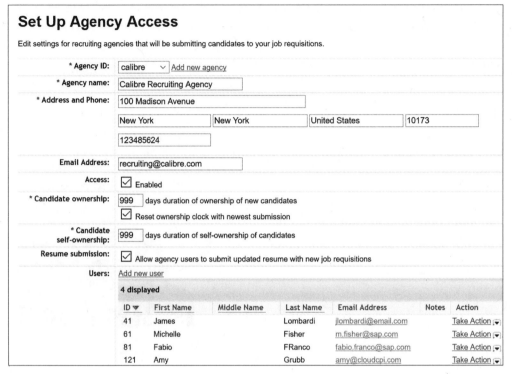

Figure 8.22 Maintaining Agencies and Their Users in the Set Up Agency Access Screen

When creating an agency, the following fields should be completed:

- **Agency ID**
  This is unique per agency and is used to log in to the portal. This **Agency ID** will identify agents to the jobs posted to them. An **Agency ID** can't contain any special characters.

- **Agency name**
  This is the name of the agency that is visible on the **Job Postings** page.

- **Address and Phone**
  This is the address and phone number of the agency; if an agency has more than one location, select the company headquarters or a main location to enter here.

- **Email Address**
  Enter an email address for the agency. Note that emails for individual users will be entered for each agent.

- **Access**

  If this agency is active, check this box to enable access to the portal for users.

- **Candidate ownership**

  A numeric value in days that the agency will own candidates, for example, "365". This is only for agency ownership by duration; if ownership by job requisition is enabled, this option isn't available. If ownership is set at the requisition level, then the same candidates can be submitted to unique requisitions by unique agencies.

- **Reset ownership clock with newest submission**

  This accompanies the **Candidate ownership** setting, if enabled.

- **User most recent submission as starting date for agency ownership duration period**

  When agency ownership by duration is in place, you can choose whether the duration period uses the first submission date or the most recent submission date as the starting date for the duration.

- **Candidate self-ownership**

  Candidates can "own themselves" meaning they can't be submitted by an agency for a set time period. The time period will restart every time a candidate applies to a job and, if no job applications are submitted, will use the date the candidate created their profile. This is a useful feature as many agencies will submit candidates that likely have profiles already.

- **Resume submission**

  Checking this box enables agency users to submit an updated résumé for existing candidates when submitting them to new jobs.

- **Duplication message**

  Here you can provide text that will be displayed to agencies when they try to add a duplicate candidate in the system. Remember that you can't add two candidates with the same email address.

- **Agreement Text**

  Here you enter a message that agents need to agree to before submitting candidates.

To add new agency users, you must provide the email address, and first and last name. Make sure the **Active** box is checked so this user can access the agency portal. When created, the user will receive an email with information on how to access the portal. Note that unlike candidates, you can enter users with the same email address for any configured agency.

8.8.3   Agency Experience

When agents access the agency portal, they must enter their username and password, along with the **Company ID** with a colon and the **Agency ID**, so that the system knows which jobs to present to the agent.

Upon entering the agency portal, there are two tabs as you can see in Figure 8.23. The **Candidates** tab displays any candidates that the agent has submitted to open jobs. You can view the name and phone number of the candidate, the date the candidate was added, the date the agency's rights to that candidate expire, and the last updated date. Also visible is the status that candidate is sitting in on the job to which they were submitted. What is displayed here is the **Agency** label entered on that status in applicant status configuration, as discussed in Section 8.4.

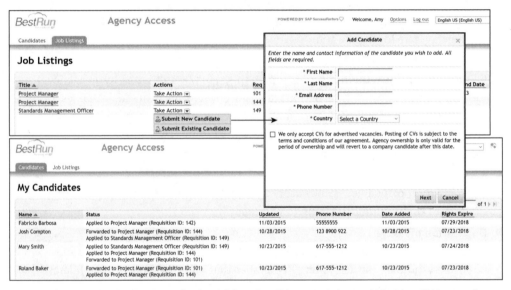

Figure 8.23 Viewing Posted Jobs, Adding Candidates to Jobs, and Viewing Statuses of Submitted Candidates

To view jobs posted to the agency, select the **Job Listings** tab. Candidates can be submitted to these jobs under the **Take Action** link. An agent can submit an existing candidate or a new candidate after entering basic information about the candidate.

Agents may also set up job alerts, which are saved searches that can be run on a specified time frame and email jobs to the agent. This is similar to the feature available to candidates. This is a good way for agents to keep notified of when new job openings are posted to the portal without having to check back regularly.

8.9   Employee Referral Program

The employee referral functionality was discussed from an end-user perspective in Chapter 5. To use the employee referral capability, settings need to be made first in provisioning and then in Admin Center. After employee referral is enabled in provisioning and the necessary configurations are done in the JRDM, the remaining setup for employee referral takes place in Admin Center. From the **Employee Referral Program Setup** page, you'll set the business rules that will govern the employee referral capability within the system. The business rules are broken down into three areas:

- **Ownership Options**
- **Employee Referral Program - Program Information**
- **General Options**

We'll take a brief look at each area.

8.9.1   Ownership Options

For an employee referral program to run effectively, all participants need to understand the rules around who owns the candidate submission and for what period of time. Often, you may have more than one employee submit the same candidate for different positions. Understanding how you'll manage this, or whether it will be allowed at all, will be key to making the ownership settings within SAP SuccessFactors.

Ownership can be determined in one of two ways:

- **Ownership by Requisition for Employee Referral Program**
- **Ownership by Duration for Employee Referral Program** (number of days)

Note that this is very similar to the ownership settings made to agency users. Ownership options are provided in Figure 8.24.

When the referred candidate's information is submitted, the system will do a check to determine ownership based on the settings made. If **Ownership by Requisition for Employee Referral Program** is selected, the system will check the job requisition to see if the referred candidate already exists on the selected requisition. If the candidate does exist, the referral won't be added. If it doesn't exist on the requisition, the candidate will be added to the job requisition in the **Forwarded** status. With this setting enabled, it's possible for more than one employee to refer the same candidate to different jobs.

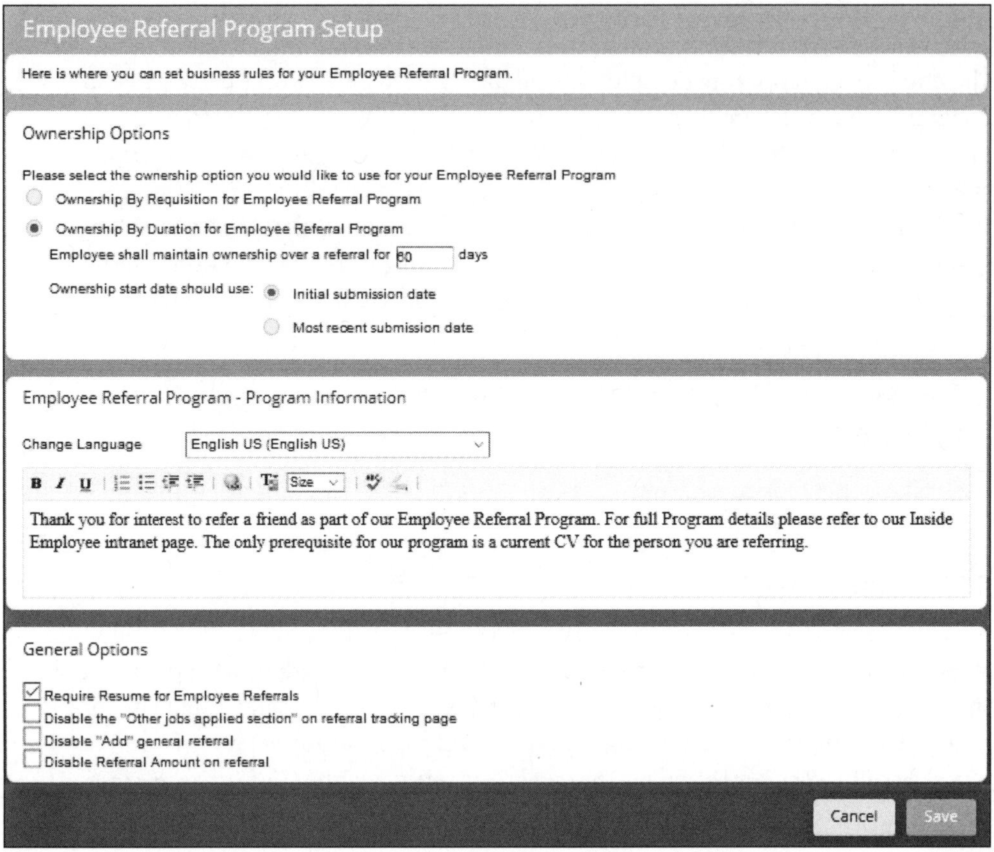

Figure 8.24 Employee Referral Program Setup Options in Admin Center

If **Ownership by Duration for Employee Referral Program** is selected, as shown in Figure 8.25, upon submission, the system will check to see if the referred candidate is currently owned. If the referral is currently owned by the referring employee, the system will check to see if the candidate already exists on the requisition. Referred candidates will be added if they don't already exist on the job requisition. If they are owned by another employee, the referral won't be added. Note that if you choose this ownership method, you must also choose what date will be used to start the duration: **Initial submission date** or **Most recent submission date**.

It's important to understand the impact of these settings so that the details of how the employee referral program, and specifically the referral tracking, will be managed so you can communicate this to your employee population.

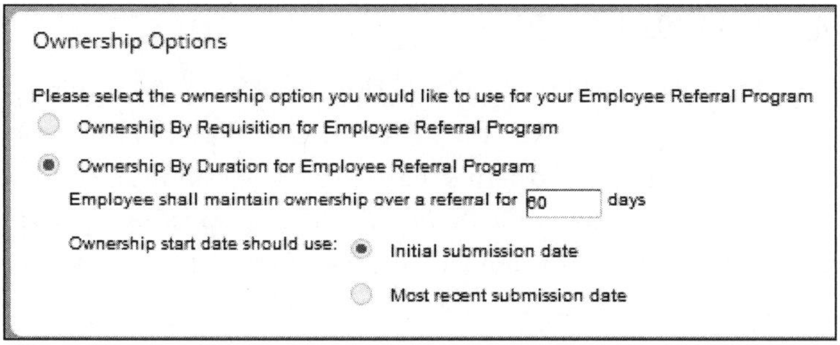

Figure 8.25 Two Options for Determining Referred Candidate Ownership

8.9.2   Referral Program Information

This is an area to provide program details to your employees. Use this area to provide high-level details, important points about the program, and other reminders. Because this area is limited in space, it's advisable to provide a link to a more complete program page somewhere on your intranet or make available the employee referral program document.

8.9.3   General Options

The last group of settings will enable and disable the following things:

- **Require Resume for Employee Referrals**
  Check this box if you want employees to provide the candidate's résumé to submit. Remember that they may not always have access to the résumé, and selecting this option will limit employees' ability to make referrals.

- **Disable the "Other jobs applied section" on the referral tracking page**
  By default, employees will be able to see other jobs their referral has applied to. Check this option to turn that feature off.

- **Disable "Add" general referral**
  By default, employees will be able to make general referrals of candidates to the database. If you only want employees to refer candidates to specific jobs, check this box.

- **Disable Referral Amount on referral**
  By default, employees will see the referral amount on their referrals. If you don't want employees to be able to see that information, check this box.

8.10   Managing Recruiting Groups

Recruiting groups are dynamic groups that have specific application to Recruiting. They can be used to restrict the pool of users who can be selected as a recruiting operator on a requisition. They are also used to define the groups of users who are used in recruiting teams. Figure 8.26 shows the **Group Definition** screen of a recruiting group where the **People Pool** is defined by **Title** and will include those that have a title of **Recruiter** or **Sr. Recruiter**.

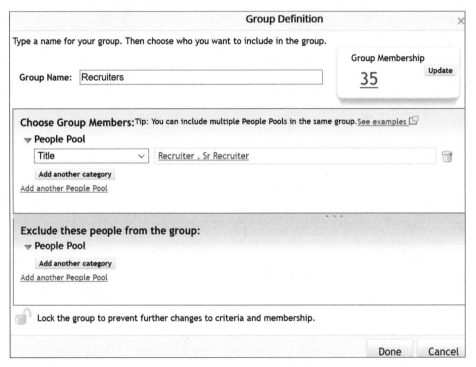

Figure 8.26 Recruiting Groups Requiring People Pools and Excluding Groups of Users

As user data are added and updated in the system, changing titles to and from **Recruiter** and **Sr. Recruiter**, the membership of the group will also be updated. This is the best way to define the group membership because they can be updated dynamically and not manually.

Recruiting groups work just like groups in role-based permissions. You set up groups and define a people pool and any users who should be excluded. The **Manage**

Recruiting Groups screen is specific to manage Recruiting admin features, however. From **Manage Recruiting Groups**, you can create new groups or edit existing groups. If creating a new group, you need to enter a group name and select how to define the people pool. Each Recruiting group can include multiple people pools, for example, **Job Title**, **Location**, and **User**.

Recruiting groups are visible and can be maintained by all admin users who have permission to manage recruiting groups. Just as with agency access, this access can't be filtered to specific groups. If a user can access this area, the user has access to all Recruiting groups.

After the Recruiting groups are saved, they can be added to team roles in **Manage Recruiting Team** settings or configured into the JRDM on an operator field. While Recruiting groups can be renamed, it's important to understand which groups are configured in the JRDM because if the group name is changed, the functionality will cease working correctly.

8.11   Job Posting Headers and Footers

Headers and footers are rich text fields that store content appended to the top and bottom of a job posting. Headers and footers are most commonly used when Job Profile Builder isn't used, and they can extend the character count of a job description. Header and footer content can't be automatically populated onto a requisition. Users must select the header/footer combination to add to the requisition. The operator user adding the header/footer must have write permissions to the requisite header and footer fields.

To use posting headers and footers, the feature must first be enabled in provisioning. Next, there are four fields that must be configured on the JRDM:

- `intJobDescHeader`
- `extJobDescHeader`
- `intJobDescFooter`
- `extJobDescFooter`

These fields must also be properly permissioned. To add a header or footer, an operator must have write access to the preceding fields. These four fields always go together and represent internal and external headers and internal and external footers.

The content for headers and footers is maintained in **Admin Center • Manage Job Posting Header and Footer**. Here you can define any number of header and footer content that can be selected to add to the requisition. As you can see in Figure 8.27, you define internal and external header content. Below that is the footer content (see Figure 8.28). In that example, the footer contains SAP SuccessFactors Recruiting Marketing posting tokens. Note that you don't have to define text in all areas. For example, you can have an external header without having an internal header. This means that when the job is posted, external candidates would see a header while internal candidates would not.

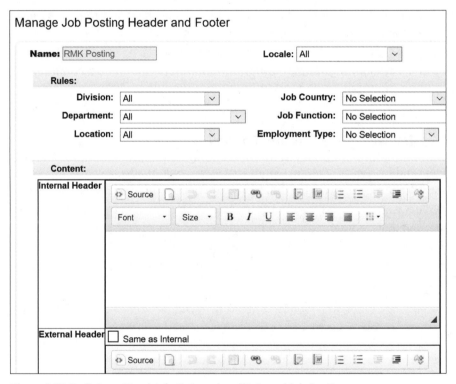

Figure 8.27 Defining a Header for Internal and External Job Postings

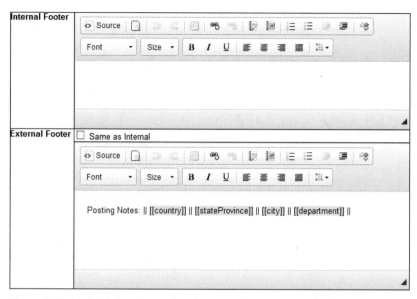

Figure 8.28 Maintaining Internal and External Footers Separately

8.12   Manage Custom Help Text

Sometimes it's helpful to provide users with some guidance or additional information on various Recruiting templates to enable them to complete those templates correctly. To support this need, you can define custom help text in Admin Center. The **Manage Recruiting Custom Help Text** page in Admin Center provides an easy interface for administrators to create or maintain field-level help text on the following templates:

- Requisition
- Application—candidate view
- Application—recruiter view
- Candidate profile
- Offer detail

To add custom help text to a template as shown in Figure 8.29, follow these steps:

1. Select the appropriate template from the tabs across the top of the page.
2. Once there, edit the help text already defined or delete it. You can also add new field help text.

3. Choose the **Select Field** button to display all available fields on the respective template.

4. Choose fields by checking their boxes, and then click **OK**.

5. After the fields are added to the template, you can define the help text in the Rich Text box. Formatting is available as well using the tool bar.

6. When the text is defined as desired, click **Save**. The changes will be reflected on the template immediately.

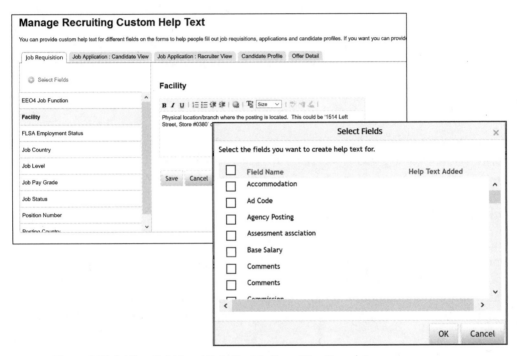

Figure 8.29 Adding Field-Level Help Text to Recruiting Templates

8.13   Manage Documents

In the **Manage Documents** area of the **Manage Recruiting** screen, displayed in Figure 8.30, you can view the attachments submitted by candidates on their candidate profile or applications. These documents can be downloaded easily into a ZIP file for other uses or archiving. In addition, you can easily see your storage limits and usage so you can manage these areas. If you use all of the allocated storage for your system, no candidates will be able to submit any more documents. If you have a large volume of candidate activity, you can quickly expend your storage.

It's good practice to review the settings for how documents are handled when a candidate profile is deleted, either by the candidate or due to inactivity. You should delete those documents so your storage isn't taken up by files from deleted candidates.

Manage Documents has a search feature to help you quickly find the documents you're looking for. You can search by the following:

- **File Name**
- **Updated By** (user)
- **Internal** or **External**
- **File Size**
- **Status** (of the profile)
- **File Type**

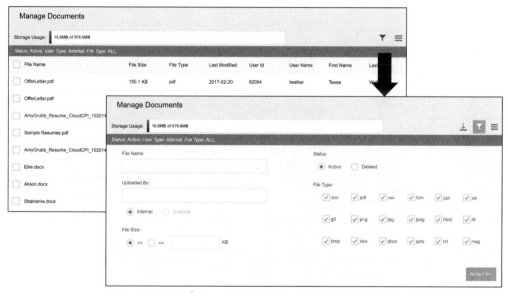

Figure 8.30 Managing and Searching Documents Uploaded by Candidates Using Search Filters

8.14   Miscellaneous Administrative Features

Numerous administrative features are available in **Manage Recruiting** that are only accessed during implementation. Others are older features that have been obsoleted with other features but haven't yet been completely retired from the administrative interface. We'll briefly cover these in this section.

8.14.1   Implementation Features

The following features are typically only used during implementation. Although some updates may be made on occasion, typically these will be done by the implementation partner.

Configure Standardization Mapping

In this area, you set up the mapping that supports résumé parsing on the candidate profile. There are two background elements that can be mapped to parse data from the résumé file into fields on the candidate profile. These are the **Work Experience** and **Education** portlets. Although there are numerous fields available to be mapped, not all available fields will have a mapping. As you select fields from the dropdown list in your configuration, you'll see the available options. Any available fields that aren't mapped will display **Not Mapped** in red text, as shown in Figure 8.31.

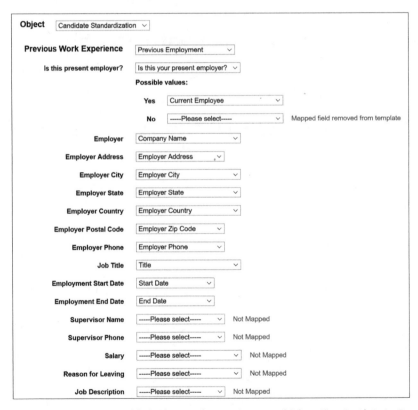

Figure 8.31 Mapping Fields in the Work Experience and Education Portlets to Parse Data from the Résumé

Set Up Internal Candidate Search

It's possible to completely disable searching for internal candidates or to limit the search to where a date field on the employee profile is *X* number of days from today or earlier. A use for this might be when you only want to search internal candidates who have a "ready to develop" date on their profile. This feature isn't used extensively but could have valuable use in an overall talent management strategy where succession planning is also implemented.

Set Up Job Board Options

In **Set up Job Board Options**, shown in Figure 8.32, you set values for the **Function**, **Country**, and **State** fields on the requisition. These are fields of type enum, which appear like picklist fields, but the values are actually maintained here in this feature.

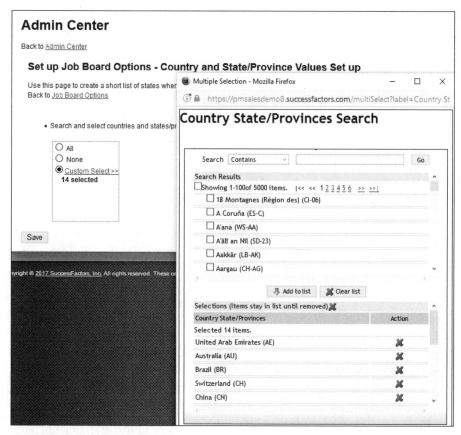

Figure 8.32 Setting the Values That Display in eQuest Standard Fields in Admin Center

These fields support eQuest integration from Recruiting Management, but they can also have additional uses. For example, to configure attribute overrides on the application to display different fields to internal or external candidates or candidates applying to jobs in different countries, you use the eQuest field for country. You select the values to make available on that field in **Set up Job Board Options**.

Onboard Integration Setup

When SAP SuccessFactors Onboarding is in play, the integration between Recruiting and Onboarding is enabled in Admin Center, as you can see in Figure 8.33. In this feature, you'll make the initial settings, choosing to apply Onboarding to either all job requisitions or to requisitions that meet certain criteria. You can also manage updates to Onboarding on the tab of the same name.

After the initial settings are made, you'll map fields from the three main Recruiting templates:

- **Job Application**
- **Job Requisition**
- **Job Offer**

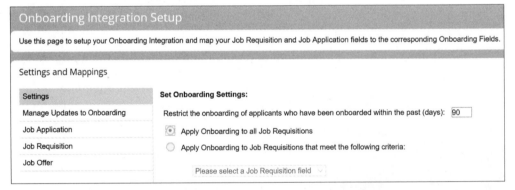

Figure 8.33 Onboarding Integration Settings to Map Data from Recruiting Management Templates

Set Up Recruiting Marketing Job Field Mapping

To post jobs to the appropriate pages within the external career site, it's necessary to map data from certain fields on the requisition templates in Recruiting Management to fields in Recruiting Marketing. You can see an example of this mapping in Figure 8.34. This mapping is done by requisition template, so if more than one template is configured, be sure to set up the field mappings for all requisition templates. Just as with the **Standardization Mapping** page, not all fields available will have mappings. This step is necessary for external jobs to be posted correctly in Recruiting Marketing.

Figure 8.34 Mapping Fields from the Requisition to Fields in Recruiting Marketing for External Job Postings

8.14.2   Other Miscellaneous Features

There are other features you may see in **Manage Recruiting** that no longer have application to new implementations:

- **Detailed Requisition Reporting Privileges**
  Replaced by reporting in the ad hoc Report Builder and advanced reporting.

- **Export New Hire Candidates**
  Replaced by integration with Onboarding or Employee Central. If neither Onboarding nor Employee Central are present, an ad hoc report is usually built to capture requisite new hire fields to send to the applicable HRIS. This is the preferred method as different HRISs will have different fields for a new hire action, and businesses will use various fields in their Recruiting Management configuration.

- **Manage Onboarding Templates**
  This feature was used prior to the introduction of the Onboarding module to help manage information captured during an Onboarding process. It is recommended to use email templates rather than Onboarding templates if Onboarding isn't in play.

You may choose not to permission any of these features and several of the ones in the previous section so that there is no confusion among your administrators. This can be managed nicely in role-based permissions.

8.15   Summary

The **Manage Recruiting** area of Admin Center offers you a great amount of control over various components of the Recruiting Management module. While some of the features are a one-time setup during implementation, other features will be maintained on a regular basis. Examples include email and offer letter templates, as well as **Manage Recruiting Settings**. As this area continues to expand in capability with new releases, it's important to keep up to date on opt-in enhancements and role-based permissions to ensure your Recruiting administrators always have the most recent features available.

Let's now turn our attention to a deeper discussion of system email notifications and email options within Recruiting.

Chapter 9
System Notifications and Email Options

The key to engaging talent and keeping them interested in working for your company is to continually communicate with them throughout the process. It's a balance of keeping candidates up to date with relevant information in multiple modes. Having a system that supports multiple communication mechanisms will help you find this balance.

You've published your job opening and are now fielding applicants on your job. This necessitates the need to communicate with candidates to help them understand the process and what is expected of them, as well as to keep various other players in the recruiting process informed, such as the hiring manager. With many people needing communication on every job opening in numerous steps of the process, recruiters can feel overwhelmed. SAP SuccessFactors Recruiting offers several communication mechanisms that can be used throughout the process to actively and passively keep the right people informed at the right times.

Managing notifications can be a bit tricky when it comes to Recruiting because there are so many places in the system where you can either define notifications or define when they are sent. There are e-mail notification templates, which are predelivered notification templates shared across multiple modules; Recruiting email templates, which are notifications specific to the Recruiting module; the **Next Step Text** field, which can be defined on your applicant statuses to communicate via the candidate portal; and offer letter templates, which are specific to the offer process in the Recruiting module. These notification templates and mechanisms are maintained in different places in the Admin Center.

SAP SuccessFactors delivers content for some of these notifications to give you a head start with notifications. The wording of all types of notifications can be tailored to meet the specific terminology or needs of your organization. All of these email templates also allow you to use tokens, which will dynamically populate candidate or job-specific information into a template when sent.

In this chapter, we'll discuss the following communication methods that Recruiting supports:

- System email notifications
- Recruiting emails and triggers
- **Next Step Text** field
- Offer letter templates

Let's begin with a look at system email notifications.

9.1   System Email Notifications

SAP SuccessFactors comes predelivered with a number of notification templates that can be shared among the different SAP SuccessFactors modules, such as Performance & Goals and Recruiting. These types of templates are known as system notifications or email notification templates. These templates have built-in trigger points and can be enabled or disabled as necessary to meet your communication needs. This section details the predelivered templates that are relevant for Recruiting, including how to enable, edit, and tailor them so that the wording can be different by template.

9.1.1   Email Notification Templates

Having predelivered templates helps customers quickly set up notifications with pre-defined content. These shared system notifications also come with translations in all languages, so you'll have that available for any language pack in use.

System notifications are automatically sent out when certain conditions are met, such as when a requisition is routed for approval.

The following email notification templates are most relevant for Recruiting:

- Document Creation Notification
- Document Routing Notification
- Document Due Notification
- Document Late Notification

- External To Internal Candidate Profile Conversion Success Notification
- Internal To External Candidate Profile Conversion Success Notification
- New Recruiting Operator Notification
- Recruiting Interviewer Notification
- Recruiting Event Interviewer Notification
- Recruiting Manual Candidate Creation Notification
- Recruiting Imminent Candidate Purge Notification
- Recruiting Agency
- Share Candidate Search

Table 9.1 describes each of these templates in more detail and lists out which tokens are supported by template.

Notification	Description	Tokens Supported
Document due notification	Document due notification will be sent to a user when the documents in his/her inbox are approaching the due day. Documents relevant for recruiting are requisitions and offer approval forms.	■ [[DOC_TITLE]] ■ [[IS_WAS_DUE_ON]] ■ [[DOC_ACCESS_URL]] ■ [[SIGNATURE]]
Document late notification	Document late notification will be sent to a user when the documents in his/her inbox are already late for completion. Documents relevant for recruiting are requisitions and offer approval forms.	■ [[DOC_TITLE]] ■ [[IS_WAS_DUE_ON]] ■ [[DOC_ACCESS_URL]] ■ [[SIGNATURE]]
Document routing notification	Document routing notification will be sent to a user when a form is available in his/her inbox. Examples of recruiting forms include requisitions and offer approval forms.	■ [[DOC_TITLE]] ■ [[DOC_ACTION]] ■ [[SENDER]] ■ [[IS_WAS_DUE_ON]] ■ [[DOC_COMMENT]] ■ [[DOC_ACCESS_URL]] ■ [[SIGNATURE]]

Table 9.1 Standard Email Notification Templates Relevant for Recruiting and Their Supported Tokens

Notification	Description	Tokens Supported
External to internal candidate profile conversion success notification	Sent to the job owner when the external to internal candidate profile conversion process has run successfully.	<ul><li>`[[RECRUITING_CANDIDATE_FIRST_NAME]]`</li><li>`[[RECRUITING_CANDIDATE_LAST_NAME]]`</li><li>`[[RECRUITING_CANDIDATE_USERNAME]]`</li></ul>
Internal to external candidate profile conversion success notification	Sent to the job owner when the internal to external candidate profile conversion process has run successfully.	<ul><li>`[[RECRUITING_CANDIDATE_FIRST_NAME]]`</li><li>`[[RECRUITING_CANDIDATE_LAST_NAME]]`</li><li>`[[RECRUITING_CANDIDATE_USERNAME]]`</li><li>`[[RECRUITING_CANDIDATE_SITE_URL]]`</li><li>`[[RECRUITING_CANDIDATE_SITE_FORGOT_PASSWORD_URL]]`</li></ul>
New recruiting operator notification	New recruiting operator notification will be sent to selected recruiting operators when a job requisition is reassigned or goes to the approved state.	<ul><li>`[JOB_REQ_ID]]`</li><li>`[[JOB_REQ_NAME]]`</li></ul>
Recruiting agency	Email is sent to agency user to inform the user when a job has been posted to the agency.	<ul><li>`[[AGENCY_NAME]]`</li><li>`[[COMPANY_NAME]]`</li><li>`[[JOB_TITLE]]`</li><li>`[[POSTING_START_DATE]]`</li><li>`[[POSTING_END_DATE]]`</li><li>`[[AGENCY_POSTING_URL]]`</li><li>`[[AGENCY_PORTEL_URL]]`</li></ul>

Table 9.1 Standard Email Notification Templates Relevant for Recruiting and Their Supported Tokens (Cont.)

Notification	Description	Tokens Supported
Recruiting event interviewer notification	Email is sent to employees to notify them of a recruiting event group interview assignment.	■ [[RECRUITING_INTERVIEWER_NAME]] ■ [[EVENT_NAME]] ■ [[RECRUITING_INTERVIEW_DATE]] ■ [[LOGIN_URL]] ■ [[SIGNATURE]]
Recruiting imminent candidate purge notification	Email is sent to candidates that their profile is about to be purged on purge_date due to inactivity.	■ [[RECRUITING_CANDIDATE_FULLNAME]] ■ [[PURGE_DATE]] ■ [[RECRUITING_CANDIDATE_SITE_URL]] ■ [[SIGNATURE]]
Recruiting interviewer notification	Email is sent to employees to notify them of a recruiting candidate interview assignment.	■ [[RECRUITING_INTERVIEWER_NAME]] ■ [[INTERVIEWER_FIRST_NAME]] ■ [[INTERVIEWER_LAST_NAME]] ■ [[RECRUITING_APPLICANT_NAME]] ■ [[RECRUITING_INTERVIEW_DATE]] ■ [[RECRUITING_INTERVIEW_NOTE]] ■ [[INTERVIEWER_INTERVIEW_TEAM_TABLE]] ■ [[COMPETENCIES_TABLE]] ■ [[LOGIN_URL]] ■ [[SIGNATURE]] ■ (Standard and custom tokens are also supported.)

Table 9.1 Standard Email Notification Templates Relevant for Recruiting and Their Supported Tokens (Cont.)

Notification	Description	Tokens Supported
Recruiting manual candidate notification	Email is sent to candidates who are created manually to notify them about account details.	■ `[[RECRUITING_OPERATOR_NAME]]` ■ `[[RECRUITING_OPERATOR_EMAIL]]` ■ `[[RECRUITING_CANDIDATE_SITE_URL]]` ■ `[[RECRUITING_CANDIDATE_FULLNAME]]` ■ `[[RECRUITING_CANDIDATE_USERNAME]]` ■ `[[RECRUITING_PASSWORD_RESET_URL]]` ■ `[[SIGNATURE]]`
Share candidate search	Email is sent to selected persons with whom you want to share candidate search.	■ `[[RECRUITING_CANDIDATE_SEARCH_NAME]]` ■ `[[SENDER_USER_NAME]]`

Table 9.1 Standard Email Notification Templates Relevant for Recruiting and Their Supported Tokens (Cont.)

9.1.2   Enabling System Notifications

If you're implementing SAP SuccessFactors Recruiting Management in an instance that includes other SAP SuccessFactors modules, you'll need to coordinate with the teams responsible for the other modules as to which email templates you enable. Because these are shared notifications, if a notification is enabled for one module, by default, it's enabled for all modules implemented. This could have unintended consequences of sending out automated notifications that are needed by one module but not expected or desired by another module. E-mail notification templates can be enabled or disabled in **Admin Center** under **E-Mail Notification Templates** settings (see Figure 9.1). To enable or disable a shared notification template, you select the checkbox to the left of the templates you want to enable, and then click the **Save Notification Settings** button at the bottom of the screen.

E-Mail Notification Templates

Use this page to edit notification templates.
Use checkboxes to turn email notifications on/off. Email notifications with a check next to them will be sent to users when the related actions occur.

☐ Disabled User Notification ☑ Document Creation Notification ☑ Document Routing Notification	**Document Routing Notification** Document routing notification will be sent to a user when a form instance is available in his/her Inbox.

Figure 9.1 Selecting the Email Notification Templates You Want to Use within the System

The Recruiting-specific email notifications are further down the page, and there are two that are near the bottom, so be sure to scroll through all the templates to make sure you find them all. Figure 9.2 shows the Recruiting-specific templates.

> ☑ External To Internal Candidate Profile Conversion Success Notification
> ☑ Internal To External Candidate Profile Conversion Success Notification
> ☐ New Recruiting Operator Notification
> ☑ Recruiting Interviewer Notification
> ☑ Recruiting Event Interviewer Notification
> ☑ Recruiting Manual Candidate Creation Notification
> ☐ Recruiting Imminent Candidate Purge Notification
> ☐ Recruiting Agency
> ☐ Share Candidate Search

Figure 9.2 Recruiting-Specific Email Templates.

Note that two email templates are always enabled:

- **Recruiting Interviewer Notification**
- **Recruiting Event Interviewer Notification**

While these can't be disabled, you can still update the text for these templates, if you desire. The Recruiting Interviewer Notification template is used if you're using the legacy Set Up Interviewers functionality. Note that if you're using Interview Scheduling, the emails are specified in **Recruiting Email Triggers**. The Recruiting Event Interviewer Notification template is only used if you're using the legacy Event functionality. This is rarely used but is still available.

9.1.3   Modifying System Notifications

After you've enabled the notifications you plan to use, you can determine whether you want to modify the default wording. The predelivered text of email notification templates is deliberately somewhat generic because these notifications can be shared across modules.

Let's look at an example of the predelivered email notification template called Document Routing Notification. Once enabled, this notification is sent to approvers when there is a document waiting for approval in their SAP SuccessFactors **To-Do List**. Documents that can be routed for approval in the context of Recruiting are requisitions and offer approval forms.

The default delivered text for this notification reads as follows:

Subject: [[DOC_TITLE]] Routing Notice

Body:

Please be advised that the document [[DOC_TITLE]] is now available in your Performance Manager Inbox folder for your [[DOC_ACTION]].

This document was last with [[SENDER]] and [[IS_WAS_DUE_ON]]. Comments from [[SENDER]] are:

[[DOC_COMMENT]]

You can access this document at the following URL:

[[DOC_ACCESS_URL]]

[[SIGNATURE]]

When the notification is sent, the tokens are filled, and the final email appears something like this:

Subject: Standard Requisition for Sales Specialist Routing Notice

Body:

Please be advised that Standard Requisition for Sales Specialist is now available in your Performance Manager Inbox folder for your approval.

This document was last with George Jetson and is due on 05/23/2017. Comments from George Jetson are:

"Please approve."

You can access this document at the following URL:

[URL]

You can modify the delivered default text of these shared notifications to meet your needs. For example, most customers change the default text of the Document Routing Notification template to replace the reference to the Performance Manager inbox with more pertinent instructions on where to find the document for approval or to specify the branding set for the SAP SuccessFactors system.

9.1.4   Defining Form-Specific Email Notification

When you modify the standard default text of a shared notification, that updated default text is applied to the forms used in all modules. However, you can also define form-specific text for each email notification template. For example, you may want to have different approval routing templates for your Performance & Goals document approvals versus your requisition approvals.

This can be configured in Admin Center under **E-Mail Notification Template Settings**. To do so, first click on the name of the email notification template you want to modify on the left side of the screen, then select the **Specify Different Template for Each Form** checkbox, and finally click the **Update settings** button. Then use the form dropdown to select the form for which you want to modify the notification, and click the **Switch to** button. The form dropdown contains a list of all active document templates in your SAP SuccessFactors instance.

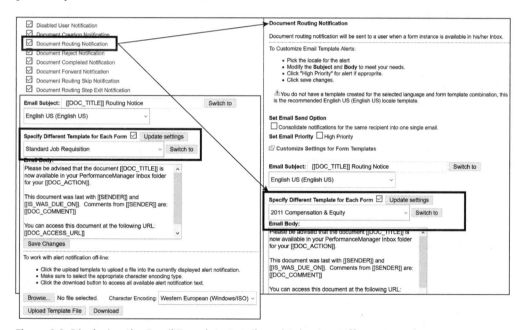

Figure 9.3 Displaying the Email Template Details and Selecting Different Templates to Define Email Text

Figure 9.3 shows how you can specify different text and tokens for the same email template by document type. In the example, the **Document Routing Notification** has been enabled and selected. The details of this notification are displayed on the right side of the screen. You can then tailor the notification to be specific to the selected template. For example, you could include information about the requisition approval process, links to company processes, and so on. This information is very specific to Recruiting, so it wouldn't make sense to include it in a standard notification for all modules.

> **Tip**
>
> When enabling the Document Routing and Document Completed notifications, be sure to change the default text specific to your Recruiting templates because the default text is focused on performance management.

If you have multiple requisition templates, you would repeat these steps for all applicable templates. You can also specify different language for the offer approval detail templates as well. You can do this by selecting the language you want to modify from the **Language** dropdown, click **Switch to**, modify the text, and click **Save Changes,** as illustrated in Figure 9.4.

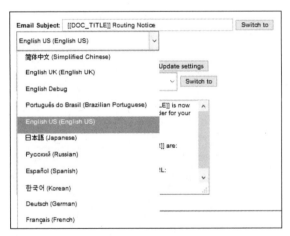

Figure 9.4 Setting Language Translations for Modified Email Templates

9.2   Recruiting Email Templates

You can define a library of email templates for use in Recruiting to help ensure standard messaging and eliminates the need for recruiters to manually create emails each time they need to send a communication to a candidate. These emails are used in various places throughout Recruiting:

- Selected by recruiters when they choose the email candidate functionality
- Tied to an applicant status to send automatically
- Tied to a Recruiting email trigger

Recruiting users can select from this library of templates when sending emails to candidates. These email templates can be configured to be sent out automatically when a candidate's status changes or when specific Recruiting triggers happen. The automated sending of notifications is discussed later in the chapter. Let's take a brief look at how you can work with Recruiting email templates and features such as language translations, copy, and SMS sending options.

9.2.1   Creating and Editing Recruiting Email Templates

You can create and edit your own email templates in Admin Center under **Manage Recruiting Email Templates**. There is no limit to the number of templates you can create. You should, however, put some thought into a naming convention for your email templates prior to creating a large number of them. It's typical for a customer to create more than 30 Recruiting email templates. Some of these will be used with Recruiting email triggers, discussed later in the chapter, and others will be sent either ad hoc or when a candidate's status changes. When Recruiting users accesses the library of Recruiting email templates, the templates are presented in an alphabetical list. A good naming convention will make it a lot easier for your Recruiting users to find the template they need quickly.

Tip

Append the type of email you're defining to the name of the email template for ease of use. For example, start all of the emails that are sent to candidates with "CANDIDATE" such as CANDIDATE: Thank you for applying, CANDIDATE: First Interview Notification, and so on. This will help users quickly identify the email template they are looking for.

From the email template summary screen, click **Create New Template**. Select the language from the **Change Language** dropdown. Enter the name of the template in the **Template Name** field. The template name is what Recruiting users will select from when searching the template library. Be sure to click the **Enabled** radio button next to **Status** if you want Recruiting users to have access to the template. Next, define the **SMS status** and **Cc** and **Bcc** options as needed. The **Subject** will be the title of the email that the candidate sees when he or she receives the email. This is usually different from the **Template Name** and can contain tokens in it to dynamically populate candidate- or job-specific information in the subject line of the email. See Figure 9.5 for an example of the email template input screen.

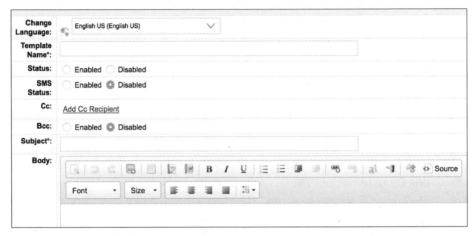

Figure 9.5 Creating a New Email Template

SAP SuccessFactors comes with a rich text editor for notifications that allows a Recruiting user to format the body of the email templates. This includes editing font, font size, and color, as well as inserting images, tokens, and hyperlinks. The rich text editor also allows a Recruiting user to edit the HTML source of the email, thus allowing you to create branded email templates that are more tailored to your needs. Use the **Source** button on the rich text editor toolbar to view the HTML code.

> **Note**
> Email templates can't be deleted after they are created and saved. They can only be enabled or disabled, so use caution when creating them.

9.2.2   Standard Tokens

The system is delivered with numerous standard tokens that are pulled from the applicable recruiting templates involved in the configuration. All standard tokens will display to administrators creating the tokens, regardless of whether those corresponding fields were used in your configuration. It may take some time for users to get accustomed to which tokens to use in the email templates. Tokens can be used in the subject line and the body of the emails. You can view the tokens available in two ways: use the **Show Tokens** link at the top of the page, or use the **Insert Job Requisition Field** toolbar button. Figure 9.6 shows how to insert tokens.

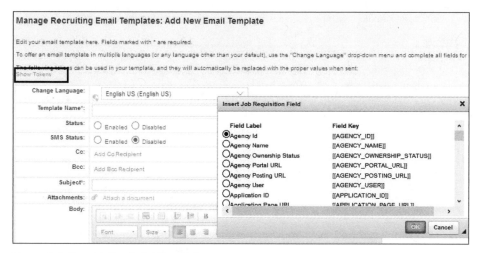

Figure 9.6 Two Methods to View Tokens

You must test specific notifications to ensure the tokens are filled as expected. Table 9.2 provides the tokens for standard fields that can be used.

> **Tip**
>
> You may want to create an email template that is used just for testing your tokens. You can just input all of the tokens you plan to use in all email templates and then generate that email to see what tokens aren't pulling data. This can be less time-consuming than testing every email template for tokens.

Token Name	Token Description
[[AGENCY_ID]]	Agency ID
[[AGENCY_NAME]]	Agency Name
[[AGENCY_OWNERSHIP_STATUS]]	Agency Ownership Status

Table 9.2 Tokens Available to Use in Email Templates

Token Name	Token Description
[[AGENCY_PORTAL_URL]]	Agency Portal URL
[[AGENCY_POSTING_URL]]	Agency Posting URL
[[AGENCY_PWD_RESET_URL]]	Link for Agency Password Reset
[[AGENCY_USER_ID]]	Agency User ID
[[AGENCY_USER]]	Agency User
[[APPLICATION_ASSESSMENT_PACKAGE_TITLE]]	Assessment Package Title
[[APPLICATION_ASSESSMENT_PROVIDER_URL]]	Assessment Provider URL
[[APPLICATION_ID]]	Application ID
[[APPLICATION_PAGE_URL]]	Application Page URL
[[ATTACHMENT_COVER_LETTER]]	Application Cover Letter, rendered as a ZIP file attached to a notification
[[ATTACHMENT_RESUME]]	Application Resume, rendered as a ZIP file attached to a notification
[[BEGIN_REPEAT]] and [[END_REPEAT]] (mandatory)	Posting Begin and End
[[ORIGINATOR_FULL_NAME]]	Originator Full Name (O Role on the Requisition)
[[HIRING_MGR_FULL_NAME]]	Hiring Manager Full Name (G Role on the Requisition)
[[RECRUITER_FULL_NAME]]	Recruiter Full Name (R Role on the Requisition)
[[COORDINATOR_FULL_NAME]]	Coordinator Full Name (T role on requisition)
[[SOURCER_FULL_NAME]]	Sourcer Full Name (S Role on the Requisition)

Table 9.2 Tokens Available to Use in Email Templates (Cont.)

Token Name	Token Description
[[SECOND_RECRUITER_FULL_NAME]]	Second Recruiter Full Name (W Role on the Requisition)
[[VP_STAFFING_FULL_NAME]]	VP Of Staffing Full Name (Q Role on the Requisition)
[[CANDIDATE_FIRST_NAME]]	Candidate First Name
[[CANDIDATE_LAST_NAME]]	Candidate Last Name
[[CANDIDATE_FULL_NAME]]	Candidate Full Name
[[CANDIDATE_ID]]	Candidate ID
[[CANDIDATE_EMAIL]]	Candidate Email
[[CANDIDATE_OFFER_URL]]	Link to Candidate's Online Offer
[[CAREER_SITE_FORGOT_PASSWORD_URL]]	Career Site Forgot Password URL
[[CAREER_SITE_URL]]	Link to Career Site
[[CAREERSITE_USER_NAME]]	Candidate Career Site User Name
[[COMPANY_NAME]]	Company Name
[[COMPETENCIES_TABLE]]	Interview Competencies
[[CURRENT_APPROVER]]	Current Offer Approver
[[DOC_COMMENT]]	Comments Entered during a Status Change (i.e., requisition approval), included in the email notification sent to the next approver
[[DOC_TITLE]]	Document Title, e.g., Requisition Title
[[EVENT_NAME]]	Recruiting Event Name
[[INTERVIEW_DATE]]	Interview Date
[[INTERVIEW_SCHEDULING_CONFIRM_INTERVIEW_URL]]	Link for Candidate to Confirm Interview Schedule
[[INTERVIEW_SCHEDULING_INTERVIEW_DATE]]	Interview Date

Table 9.2 Tokens Available to Use in Email Templates (Cont.)

Token Name	Token Description
`[[INTERVIEW_SCHEDULING_INTERVIEW_LENGTH]]`	Interview Length
`[[INTERVIEW_SCHEDULING_INTERVIEW_LOCATION]]`	Interview Location
`[[INTERVIEW_SCHEDULING_INTERVIEW_TITLE]]`	Interview Scheduling Interview Title
`[[INTERVIEW_SCHEDULING_INTERVIEW_TYPE]]`	Interview Type
`[[INTERVIEW_SCHEDULING_INTERVIEWER_NAMES]]`	Interviewer Names
`[[INTERVIEW_TEAM_TABLE]]`	Interview Team Members Names
`[[INTERVIEWER_FIRST_NAME]]`	Interviewer First Name
`[[INTERVIEWER_LAST_NAME]]`	Interviewer Last Name
`[[INTERVIEWER_FULL_NAME]]`	Interviewer Name
`[[INTERVIEWER_INTERVIEW_TEAM_TABLE]]`	Interviewer Name and Times
`[[INVITE_JOB_POSTING_DATE]]`	Job Posting Date
`[[INVITE_LINK]]`	Invite to Apply Link
`[[INVITE_REFERRER]]`	Referral Link
`[[JOB_ALERT_NAME]]`	Job Alert Name
`[[JOB_ALERTS_LINK]]`	Job Alert Hyperlink
`[[JOB_ALERTS_UNSUBSCRIBE]]`	Job Alert Unsubscribe
`[[JOB_LIST]]`	Job Alert List
`[[JOB_REQ_ID]]`	Job Requisition Number
`[[JOB_REQ_LOCATION]]`	Location (from requisition)
`[[JOB_REQ_TITLE]]`	Job Title

Table 9.2 Tokens Available to Use in Email Templates (Cont.)

Token Name	Token Description
[[JOBREQ_DESC_INT]]	Job Description (internal)
[[LOGIN_URL]]	Link to BizX log in page
[[LOGIN_URL]]	Link to Career Site Used in Career Site Password Reset for External Candidates
[[LOGO]]	Company's Logo (logo used on company's SAP SuccessFactors portal)
[[MICROSITE_LOGO]]	Career Site Logo Assigned to External Career Site
[[NEW_JOBS]]	Job Alert New Jobs
[[NEXT_APPROVER]]	Next Offer Approver
[[OFFER_DECLINE_COMMENT]]	Offer Decline Comment
[[OFFER_EXTENDED_DATE]]	Date of Offer
[[OFFER_RESPONSE_DATE]]	Offer Response Date
[[OFFER_RESPONSE]]	Offer Response
[[POSITION_NUMBER]]	Position Number
[[PREVIOUS_APPROVER]]	Previous Offer Approver
[[PURGE_DATE]]	Date When Candidate Records Are Scheduled to Be Purged
[[RECRUITING_APPLICANT_NAME]]	Candidate Name
[[RECRUITING_CANDIDATE_FULLNAME]]	Candidate Full Name
[[RECRUITING_CANDIDATE_PASSWORD]]	Candidate Password
[[RECRUITING_CANDIDATE_SEARCH_NAME]]	Name of Shared Search
[[RECRUITING_CANDIDATE_SITE_URL]]	Link to Career Site
[[RECRUITING_CANDIDATE_USERNAME]]	Candidate User Name
[[RECRUITING_ERP_GENERAL_POOL_URL]]	URL for general Employee Referrals

Table 9.2 Tokens Available to Use in Email Templates (Cont.)

Token Name	Token Description
[[RECRUITING_ERP_REFERREE_NAME]	Name of Person Referring Candidate
[[RECRUITING_INTERVIEW_DATE]]	Interview Date
[[RECRUITING_INTERVIEW_NOTE]]	Interview Note
[[RECRUITING_INTERVIEWER_NAME]]	Interviewer Name
[[RECRUITING_JOB_EXTERNAL_TITLE]]	Job Title
[[RECRUITING_JOB_TITLE]]	Job Title
[[RECRUITING_MASTER_CANDIDATE_USERNAME]]	Candidate Primary User Name (if merged)
[[RECRUITING_NONMASTER_CANDIDATE_USERNAME]]	Candidate Previous User Name (if merged)
[[RECRUITING_OPERATOR_EMAIL]]	Email of Person Who Manually Added Candidate
[[RECRUITING_OPERATOR_NAME]]	Name of Person Who Manually Added Candidate
[[SENDER_USER_NAME]]	Name of Person Sharing Search
[[SENDER]]	Sender User
[[SIGNATURE]]	Company Signature
[[TODAY]]	Today's Date (e.g., January 31, 2017)
[[TOTAL_JOBS]]	Job Alert Total Jobs
[[USER_SALUTATION]]	Salutation of Person Sending the Email
[[USER_FIRSTNAME]]	First Name of Person Sending the Email
[[USER_MI]]	Middle Name of Person Sending the Email
[[USER_LASTNAME]]	Last Name of Person Sending the Email
[[USER_SUFFIX]]	Suffix of Person Sending the Email
[[USER_TITLE]]	Title of Person Sending the Email

Table 9.2 Tokens Available to Use in Email Templates (Cont.)

Token Name	Token Description
[[USER_ADDR1]]	Address Line 1 of Person Sending the Email
[[USER_ADDR2]]	Address Line 2 of Person Sending the Email
[[USER_CITY]]	City of Person Sending the Email
[[USER_STATE]]	State of Person Sending the Email
[[USER_ZIP]]	Zip Code of Person Sending the Email
[[USER_COUNTRY]]	Country of Person Sending the Email
[[USER_EMAIL]]	Email of Person Sending the Email
[[USER_FAX]]	Business Fax of Person Sending the Email
[[USER_HOME_PHONE]]	Home Phone of Person Sending the Email
[[USER_BIZ_PHONE]]	Business Phone of Person Sending the Email
[[USER_CELL_PHONE]]	Cell Phone of Person Sending the Email
[[USER_CUSTOM01]] – [[USER_CUSTOM15]]	Custom Fields from the User Data File

Table 9.2 Tokens Available to Use in Email Templates (Cont.)

9.2.3   Custom Tokens

The standard delivered tokens don't encompass all potential tokens a company might want to use in notifications. Companies can create custom tokens based on any custom fields defined in their Recruiting templates: candidate profile, application, requisition, and offer approval. The current limit of custom tokens at the time of writing is as follows:

- Requisition: 150
- Application: 150
- Offer approval: 45
- Candidate profile: 45

Custom tokens are configured in provisioning and therefore require professional services support. Best practice is to tokenize all custom fields during implementation, unless there is a risk of using up all available slots for custom tokens. Figure 9.7 shows where custom tokens are defined in provisioning.

Custom Token Setting		
Job Req Application Job Offer Detail Candidate Profile		
Enter the Field IDs from the Job Requisition templates that you want to configure as tokens. The configuration is required only for custom fields.		
Save		
Column Name	**Field ID**	**Token Name**
custom1	cust_positionTitle	JOB_REQUISITON_CUSTOM1
custom2	cust_region	JOB_REQUISITON_CUSTOM2
custom3	custaddRep	JOB_REQUISITON_CUSTOM3

Figure 9.7 Setting Custom Tokens in Provisioning

> **Note**
>
> Don't forget that any new fields added to a template (requisition, application, offer details, or candidate profile) after go-live will need to be tokenized if you want to use them in email templates.

9.2.4   Defining Cc and Bcc Options

Recruiting email templates include functionality that determines whether or not Recruiting users are able to add copied recipients to email templates, either carboned or blind copied. This is a global setting that applies to all Recruiting email templates and is configured in Admin Center under **Manage Recruiting Email Templates**. You can enable or disable the ability to add Cc and Bcc recipients across all templates or by template. When Cc or Bcc is enabled, you can add roles, specific users, or email addresses to the default Cc or Bcc line by editing the email template. Figure 9.8 shows where you can specify the **Cc** and **Bcc** options for the email templates. Note that you can have different options for Cc and Bcc.

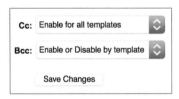

Figure 9.8 Setting the Copy Options for Your Email Templates to Enable Cc and/or Bcc on Emails

This feature is very useful in cases where you need to always send a specific notification to a person or role. If you assign a Cc or Bcc recipient to a notification template (see Figure 9.9), that person or persons will automatically be sent the email when the notification is generated. The Recruiting user will also have the opportunity to spec-ify the Cc or Bcc recipient at the time of sending, provided they are sending an ad hoc notification and not a system-generated notification.

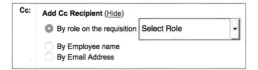

Figure 9.9 Set the Recipients for Your Cc and Bcc Settings

9.2.5   Translating Recruiting Email Templates

After you've created your Recruiting email templates, you need to determine which ones, if any, need to be translated into which languages. You can translate these tem-plates in the same place in Admin Center where you create and edit Recruiting email templates. Click the name of the template you want to translate, and select the lan-guage into which you want to translate the email from the **Change Language** drop-down, as shown in Figure 9.10. Not all customers translate the **Template Name** as this field is only shown to internal Recruiting users, but be sure to translate the **Subject** and **Body** (the message itself) as they are seen by candidates.

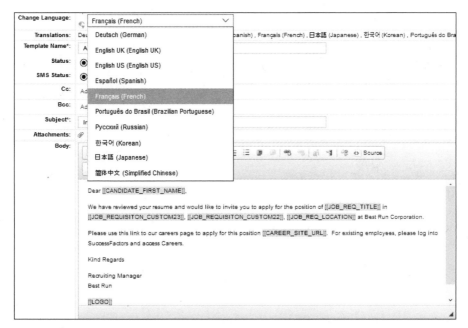

Figure 9.10 Translating Email Notifications in Multiple Languages

> **Note**
>
> Sometimes companies will choose to create new email templates in various languages rather than defining text in the default language and then translating it in multiple languages. This is simply a preference.

9.2.6   Sending Ad Hoc Email Notifications

There are many points in the recruiting process where Recruiting users would like to send candidates an email. For example, requesting additional information from candidates, asking them to send availability for a phone screen, sending them an update on their application, and so on. Ad hoc emails sent to applicants on a requisition are recorded in each candidate's application in the **Correspondence** portlet and can therefore be audited. Ad hoc email notifications can only be sent to candidates. You can't send ad hoc emails from the system directly to hiring managers or other internal users. Noncandidates can be copied on ad hoc emails if the Cc or Bcc functionality is enabled, but they can't be set as the sole recipient. You can send ad hoc emails from the talent pipeline by selecting one or multiple candidates, and then selecting the **Action • Contact Candidate**, or by clicking the **Email** option directly on an individual application, as shown in Figure 9.11.

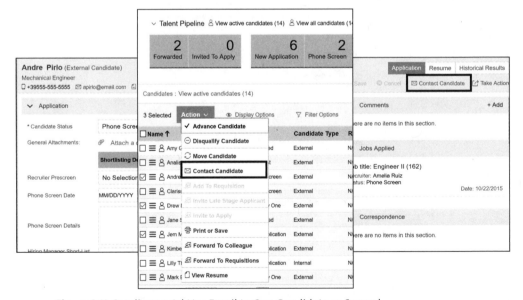

Figure 9.11 Sending an Ad Hoc Email to One Candidate or Several

On the subsequent screen that appears, you can select the language in which you want to send the notification, the template, and Cc or Bcc recipients if those options are available. Note that you can't change the information in the **From** or **Candidate** fields.

After selecting a template from the **Template** dropdown, the **Subject** and **Message** fields will be prefilled with content from the selected template. The Recruiting user can edit the defaulted content. You can also upload and add an attachment that will be sent along with the notification. These additional attachments aren't stored in SAP SuccessFactors but must be uploaded from a user's local computer.

If you want to send an email to one or more candidates through the system so that it's tracked in the **Correspondence** portlet but don't want to use a predefined template, you can do this too. Just follow the preceding steps to initiate the email without selecting a template. You can type in the **Subject** line and the **Message** of the email right in the screen, as shown in Figure 9.12. You can even add tokens in your ad hoc email by using the **Insert Job Requisition Field** button on the toolbar.

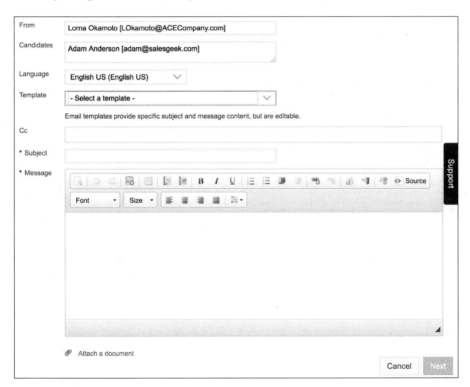

Figure 9.12 Sending an Ad Hoc Email by Typing in the Information without Selecting a Template

9.3   Implementing Email Triggers

Recruiting email triggers allow you to automate the sending of emails at specific points, or triggers, in the recruiting process. The available triggers are predefined by SAP SuccessFactors. You can't create your own Recruiting email triggers at the time of writing, but there are a large number of triggers that can be used.

Recruiting email triggers are similar to the shared email notifications in that they enable you to automatically send emails to candidates at certain points. However, Recruiting email triggers send notifications that are specific to Recruiting and aren't shared by other modules.

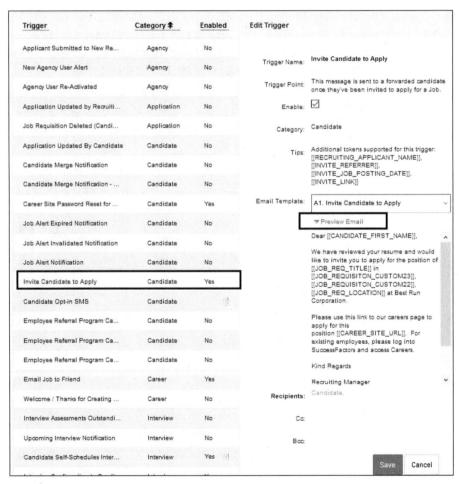

Figure 9.13 Enabling the Email Trigger and Assigning the Email Template to the Trigger

When enabling Recruiting email triggers, you select an email template from the dropdown menu of available templates and preview it. The available email templates you can select from are those you created in **Manage Recruiting Email Templates**, so all of your email templates should be created before enabling the email triggers. Any tokens in the template won't be filled in the preview window. See Figure 9.13 for a preview of the **Invite Candidate to Apply** trigger (you use the **Preview Email** link to see the email defined).

Some email triggers have predefined email templates associated with them. This means when you enable one of these triggers, the predefined email template will be automatically created in the **Manage Recruiting Email Templates** section of the Admin Center. To avoid creating duplicate email templates, it's best to first enable the email triggers you want to use that have predefined email templates. If you accidentally create duplicate email templates, you can simply disable the ones you don't need.

Email templates that are automatically created when you enable the corresponding email trigger include the following:

- Candidate Merge Notification
- Candidate Merge Notification – Master
- Career Site Password Reset for External Candidates
- Employee Referral Program Candidate Added to General Pool Notification
- Employee Referral Program Candidate Referred to a Job Requisition (Existing Candidate)
- Employee Referral Program Candidate Referred to a Job Requisition (New Candidate)
- Import Job Role Tag Notification Success
- Invite Candidate to Apply
- Job Alert Notification

Table 9.3 lists the Recruiting email triggers available at the time of writing along with information on when they are sent.

Trigger	Trigger Point
Applicant Submitted to New Requisition by Agency	Sent when an agency successfully submits an applicant to a requisition

Table 9.3 Triggers to Support Sending Emails at Various Recruiting Trigger Points

Trigger	Trigger Point
New Agency User Alert	Sent to an agency user when a new agency user is created by the system administrator
Agency User Re-Activated	Sent to an agency user when their status is changed from **Inactive** to **Active**
Application Updated by Recruiting Operator	Sent when a recruiting operator (not the candidate) changes data on the application
Job Requisition Deleted (Candidate)	Sent to candidates when a job requisition to which they have applied is deleted
Application Updated By Candidate	Sent when candidates update data on their application after initially applying
Candidate Merge Notification	Sent to candidates whose multiple accounts are merged by the system administrator
Candidate Merge Notification – Master	Sent to candidates whose multiple accounts are merged by the system administrator
Career Site Password Reset for External candidates	Sent to candidates when they reset their password
Job Alert Expired Notification	Sent to candidates when their job alert is left unmodified for X number of days
Job Alert Invalidated Notification	Sent to candidates when the filters specified in their job alert are no longer visible
Job Alert Notification	Sent to candidates according to the schedule defined in their job alert
Invite Candidate to Apply	Sent to candidates who were forwarded to a requisition when they were invited to apply for the job
Employee Referral Program Candidate Added to General Pool Notification	Sent to candidates when they are added to the candidate database via the employee referral program
Employee Referral Program Candidate Referred to a Job Requisition (New Candidate)	Sent to candidates when they are referred to a job requisition

Table 9.3 Triggers to Support Sending Emails at Various Recruiting Trigger Points (Cont.)

Trigger	Trigger Point
Employee Referral Program Candidate Referred to a Job Requisition (Existing Candidate)	Sent to candidates when they are referred to a job requisition
Email Job to Friend	Sent to an external email address specified by a candidate using the **Email Job to Friend** feature in the career site
Welcome/Thanks for Creating Account	Sent to external candidates when they successfully create an active user account
Interview Assessments Outstanding	Sent to an interviewer if the interview assessment form hasn't been completed X days following the interview
Upcoming Interview Notification	Sent to interviewers who have an upcoming interview that was scheduled using Interview Central
Candidate Self-Schedules Interview	Sent to candidates who have been invited to interview, telling them to log in and confirm an interview time (required for Interview Scheduling)
Interview Confirmation to Candidate	Sent to candidates when they've confirmed an interview
Interview Confirmation to Organizers	Sent to the interview organizer when a candidate confirms an interview
Interview Confirmation to Interviewers	Sent to the interviewers when a candidate confirms an interview
Interview Delete Notification	Sent to the candidate, interviewer, and interview organizer when an interview is deleted (required for Interview Scheduling)
Candidate Deleted from Interview	Sent to the candidate, interviewer, and interview organizer when a candidate is deleted from an interview schedule
Interviewer Availability Notification	Sent to interviewers to request they maintain their availability for a certain time (required for Interview Scheduling)

9

Table 9.3 Triggers to Support Sending Emails at Various Recruiting Trigger Points (Cont.)

Trigger	Trigger Point
Interview Cancellation to Organizers	Sent to the interview organizer when a candidate declines an interview
Booked Interview Cancellation to Interviewers	Sent to the interviewers when a candidate cancels a booked interview
Booked Interview Cancellation to Candidate	Sent to candidates when they have canceled a booked interview
Booked Interview Cancellation to Organizers	Sent to the interview organizer when a candidate cancels a booked interview
Booked Interview Reschedule Email to Candidate	Sent to candidates when they have rescheduled a booked interview
Cancel Interview Notification	Sent to all participants when an interview is canceled by interviewers when Outlook integration isn't enabled
Candidate Interview Response Reminder	Sent to candidates in the status of **Not Booked** who have been sent an invitation to interview but have not responded yet (required for Interview Scheduling)
Booked Candidate Interview Update	Sent to booked candidates if details of the interview are changed, for example, location or attachments (required for Interview Scheduling)
Outlook Response to Interview Organizer	Sent to interview organizers when an interviewer or a meeting room responds to an Outlook interview invitation
Offer Approved by All Approvers	Sent when an offer has been approved by all approvers and has no further approvals pending
Offer Received An Approval	Sent when an offer has been approved by an approver who isn't the last approver, and it has been passed to the next approver in the queue
Offer Initiated (Sent For Approval)	Sent when an offer has been sent to the first approver in the queue
Offer Approval Declined	Sent when an offer has been declined by an approver

Table 9.3 Triggers to Support Sending Emails at Various Recruiting Trigger Points (Cont.)

Trigger	Trigger Point
Online Offer Accepted by Candidate	Sent when candidate chooses **Accept Offer** or **Accept & eSign**
Online Offer Declined by Candidate	Sent when candidate chooses **Decline Offer**
Online Offer Canceled by Sender	Sent when an operator has canceled an online offer that was in a pending state
Online Offer Canceled by Sender Candidate Notification	Sent to the candidate when an operator has canceled an online offer that was in a pending state
Requisition Posting Expiration Upcoming	Sent when a job requisition has one or more postings within X days of expiration
Home Page Tile Stalled Requisition Nudge	Sent when a user clicks the **Nudge** feature on the **Home Page** tile on the home page
Requisition Re-opened	Sent when a job requisition has changed from a closed state to an approved state
Requisition Closed	Sent when a job requisition has changed from an approved state to a closed state
Requisition Changed	Sent when job requisition data has been updated
Requisition Posted	Sent when a job requisition is posted (internal, external, internal private, external private, agency/ agencies, eQuest)
Job Requisition Deleted (Internal User)	Sent to internal user (noncandidate) when a job requisition is deleted
Approved Job Requisition Restored	Sent when an approved job requisition is restored

Table 9.3 Triggers to Support Sending Emails at Various Recruiting Trigger Points (Cont.)

To enable or disable a Recruiting email trigger, you first click on the name of the trigger on the left side of the screen and then check or uncheck the **Enable** checkbox. You then select which template to use by choosing an option from the **Email Template** dropdown list, as shown in Figure 9.14.

You can define that these emails are sent to one or multiple recipients based on the role on the requisition, employee name, and/or email address. Figure 9.14 shows where you configure Recruiting email triggers.

Figure 9.14 Setting the Email Trigger Options after the Trigger is Enabled

9.4   Communicating to Recruiting Operators and Candidates via the Candidate Pipeline

There are two ways you can communicate with candidates via the talent pipeline. The first way is to trigger emails simply by placing a candidate in a different status. This can trigger emails to the candidate as well as various players in the recruiting process, such as hiring manager, recruiter, and all other Recruiting roles. The other way is to use the **Next Step Text** field to display on the **Candidate** portlet. Let's look at both of these options.

9.4.1   Assigning Emails to an Applicant Status

As mentioned, you can tag a variety of email templates to various players in the process so that the emails are sent upon the trigger of updating a candidate's status. After all the necessary email templates are defined, you can add these emails in **Edit Applicant Status Configuration** within Recruiting in Admin Center.

As shown in Figure 9.15, you can configure separate email templates to be sent to any role on the requisition, for example, hiring manager, recruiter, recruiting coordinator as well as internal candidate, external candidate, internal candidate's current manager, agency user, and referrer. The email template is automatically previewed for you after you select it from the **Select template** dropdown field. You can hide it by selecting the **Preview** link and collapsing the view.

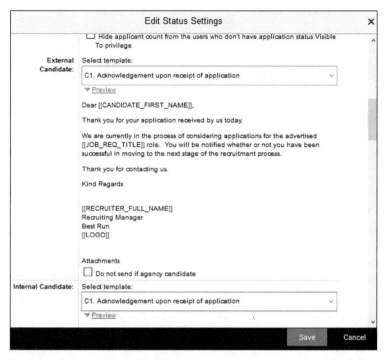

Figure 9.15 Assigning Email Templates to Various Recipients on Each Status

These emails are sent automatically based on configuration and can't be edited at the time of sending. The emails are recorded in the candidate's application in the **Correspondence** portlet.

9.4.2   Using Next Step Text on a Status

The second way you can effectively communicate with candidates is to use the **Next Step Text** field on each status (see Figure 9.16). This is also maintained in **Applicant Status Configuration** in the Admin Center. At the top of each status, you'll define the **Internal Label**, which is what is displayed to Recruiting users within the Candidate Workbench, and the **Candidate Label,** which is displayed to the candidate on the portal. There is also an option to define **Next Step Text** to display next to the **Candidate Label**. This can be used to let the candidate know what action is being taken and what they can expect. Some companies choose to keep this text very generic and handle more specific communication via emails and the personal touch of phone calls.

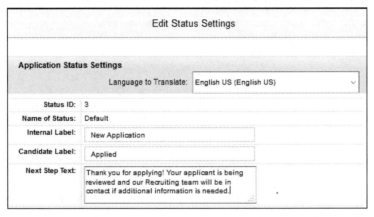

Figure 9.16 Defining a Message to Display to Candidates on the Portal within the Next Step Text

While you may choose to keep this communication to a minimum, it's important to understand that this field does need to be updated when enabling and setting up new statuses, or the candidate will see **[[Not translated in the selected language]]** in this field for each status, which we can all agree isn't a good user experience.

9.5   Offer Letters

Offer letters are treated differently from the other correspondence in Recruiting due to the sensitive nature of their content. There is a separate role-based permission for creating offer letter templates from the permission to create Recruiting email templates.

The ability for Recruiting users to create and view offer letters is permissioned by role on the application template. This ensures that individuals who should not have visibility into sensitive offer information can't access that information. Best practice is to grant permission to the offer letter feature in all statuses where a Recruiting user may need to reference the offer letter. This is typically all statuses that follow the initial status in which the feature was permissioned.

The process for creating offer letter templates is very similar to that of creating Recruiting email templates. You can access the functionality in Admin Center under

Recruiting • Manage Offer Letter Templates. Offer letters are discussed in greater detail in Chapter 8 of this book.

9.6 Summary

A key to keeping applicants engaged in the recruiting process is to keep them informed. This can be overwhelming without the proper tools, but with SAP Success-Factors Recruiting there are numerous ways to keep not only your applicants but also other key recruiting players up to date with the latest information. System email notifications can be enabled or disabled and updated to reflect the templates being used for recruiting. Any number of ad hoc email templates can be built and maintained to serve many different purposes, from being sent automatically when a status is updated, to a recruiter initiating an email in the Candidate Workbench. There are also a large number of email triggers that can be defined as necessary to support your process. Here the email templates are used as well to send detailed information, prepopulated with job and candidate-specific information that replaced tokens.

Finally, offer letter templates are the final tool to communicate very critical information to that successful candidate with details about starting salary, date, and various benefit and bonus details.

In the next chapter, we'll turn our attention to implementing Recruiting.

Chapter 10
Implementing Recruiting Management

You've selected a world-class Recruiting system and are about to embark on the implementation. How you plan for and execute the implementation will either set you up for success or not. From methodology to resourcing to time lines, SAP provides tools that enable customer and partner success.

If you have any SAP SuccessFactors modules implemented in your organization, you're familiar with the methodology, roles and responsibilities, and other aspects of a cloud-based, and specifically a SAP SuccessFactors, implementation. However, if you're new to SAP SuccessFactors, you likely have many questions about what the implementation looks like and what you should expect.

Planning for the implementation is nearly as important as adequately executing the implementation. Understanding the project methodology, schedule, the roles required of your team, the roles that your implementation partner will fill, key activities, and time commitments will help you plan for a successful project. The SAP SuccessFactors Recruiting module contains a tremendous amount of functionality, and your project team may feel overwhelmed with all of the options. Laying a good foundation for them even before the project begins can help allay some of the uncertainty, stress, and frustration that come with any system implementation. If you're implementing the solution in multiple countries, wanting to leverage multilanguages, and considering data migration, these are all elements that will add to the time and resources needed on the project.

In this chapter, we'll discuss the implementation of SAP SuccessFactors Recruiting Management, discuss how to lay a good foundation, look at roles and responsibilities of those involved, understand customer roles versus implementation partner roles, and discuss the implementation process and methodology, including some key project milestones and time lines. Let's begin with discussing how you can lay a good foundation for your project team members and key stakeholders to ensure you start the project off on the right foot.

10.1   Laying the Foundation: Project Planning

Every good construction project begins with a solid foundation. When you have the right resources and materials, you're off to a great start. Starting any project is similar to building a house. The better you plan, the better the project will go. The first thing you should take care of is identifying the right project team members to join the team. The team members should be representative of the key stakeholder groups that will use the resulting system, and they should be empowered to make decisions on processes and configuration. The project will take a considerable amount of time over the course of the implementation, so the project team members should have other job responsibilities distributed so they can devote adequate time to the project. This topic is covered in greater detail in Section 10.2.1.

After your team is identified, you can begin preparing immediately. After they have registered for the customer community, each project team member should avail themselves of the project team orientation training offered by SAP. This online training will provide an overview of the functionality within the Recruiting module, and it's a good introduction to project team members to have before the project begins.

The other large task that your project team can begin even before the official start of the project is to gather current forms, templates, processes, emails, and other content that is in use with your current recruiting processes and systems. This information will be needed when the project begins and is a good starting point when discussing your new recruiting business processes. Any discussions that the team can facilitate internally on areas of process improvement, identifying pain points you want to address with the new system, data required for reporting, and how you want to deal with data in a legacy system will put you that much further ahead when the project officially starts.

Other project planning activities include getting introduced to your implementation partner project resources, scheduling kickoff meetings, and defining the detailed project plan.

10.2   Roles and Responsibilities

Implementing Recruiting Management doesn't differ too greatly from implementing any other talent management solution. It will require heavy involvement from your subject matter experts (SMEs) to influence the processes designed and the system configuration agreed to that supports those processes. When identifying your project team, there are some critical things to address. Let's discuss those from the business's perspective first.

10.2.1   Project Team

As with every systems project, you should begin the effort with an examination of your affected business processes. If you have a geographically dispersed organization, or perhaps different legacy systems or processes in disparate parts of the organization, it will be important to bring key stakeholders from those areas to represent the business concerns. It's not always feasible to have every voice represented on the project, and if that isn't an option for you, then it will be important to get a good representative sample of business representatives. These project team members should be empowered to provide input and to make decisions. For a Recruiting implementation, you'll want to have the following input at a minimum:

- **Recruiters**
  As the "power users" of the system, recruiters not only have the best knowledge of how recruiting processes are carried out currently but also have one of the biggest stakes in how the SAP SuccessFactors Recruiting system will work after go-live. They likely come with a list of pain points and items they'd really like to see the new system support. It's critical to have this input and voice in the project. It's hard to provide the specific number of recruiters that should be involved because this will vary based on each business. Again, the rule of thumb should be to have enough to provide a representative sample of recruiters in your total organization.

- **Recruiting coordinators**
  You may have recruiting coordinators that work in conjunction with recruiters. Coordinators may help schedule interviews with candidates, hiring managers, and others. They also may communicate with candidates throughout the process and manage ancillary processes such as background and drug checks, assessments, and more. These coordinators will often have a different perspective from recruiters and can provide additional input on current processes and what the resulting system should include.

- **Hiring managers**

    Depending on how involved hiring managers are in your talent acquisition process, it's advisable to get some input from this stakeholder group as well. Hiring managers may not be involved in your current talent acquisition process, perhaps because your system doesn't support that, but you likely want them to be involved in the future. Definitely plan to get their input at various points in the project. Although it's not necessary to have hiring managers involved from day one through go-live, having a hiring manager focus group you can call on as needed, and to participate in some testing, will serve the implementation well.

- **Talent acquisition manager**

    These stakeholders likely aren't the power users of the system, but they definitely have ideas, opinions, and needs for data and reporting from the system after it's live. This group is likely involved in the steering committee to provide strategic direction and approvals for the project. Getting their input from the beginning of the project on guiding principles and boundaries and then checking back in on reporting needs is critical.

- **Project manager**

    Depending on the size of the project, it's advisable to have a project manager resource to work with the implementation partner project manager to coordinate your resources and manage the project plan, task completion, milestones, and issues.

- **IT resources**

    Again, depending on the complexity of the implementation and the integrations that may be involved, you'll likely have various IT resources play a role in the implementation. These exact resources and roles will vary by business and project. Some examples include resources that maintain the SAP ERP Human Capital Management (SAP ERP HCM) system for integration with employee data, position management, and new hire integration for talent hybrid deployments.

- **Testers**

    In addition to your project team members, it's advisable to have others involved in testing. Often when employees are involved in every aspect of the project, they can develop "tunnel vision" and not be aware of areas that are difficult to understand or not working exactly as intended. Having some people involved just with testing not only gives you more resources to ensure all the testing activities are completed but also provides valuable insight into the overall process and configured system, as well as areas that may need to be highlighted in training.

While additional resources may be involved depending on your requirements and the modules involved, the preceding roles are what you can expect for Recruiting Management implementations. Let's now discuss the implementation partner team roles.

10.2.2   Implementation Partner Roles

The roles that your implementation partner will fill largely depend on the partner you choose to work with and its model for implementing Recruiting Management. Following are some partner roles that may be involved on a typical Recruiting Management project:

- **Project manager**
  Your partner will likely bear most, or all, of the responsibility for managing the project. As such, they will have an experienced project manager to own the project plan, manage the partner work stream leads, own issue and risk management, and provide regular reporting to your steering committee. This role should be engaged from project planning through go-live and project close-out.

- **Work stream/functional lead**
  This role provides the business process and system functionality expertise necessary to guide you through the process design and configuration workshops. This resource should explain to your team how the system is designed to work, explain specific areas of functionality, and provide business process and configuration best practice guidance. They will complete the configuration of the modules and all testing prior to turning over each iteration to you for testing.

- **Configuration consultant**
  If your project is large in scope, your partner may have one or more consultants assisting the functional lead with configuration. This resource should have much of the same experience with the Recruiting Management module in order to not only configure the system to your specifications but also provide guidance on other options or workarounds, if required.

- **Technical resource**
  If you have custom integrations to ancillary systems in scope, you'll likely need a technical resource to develop the specifications and do any of the development in either Boomi, SAP Cloud Platform Integration, or the Integration Center. If your project has integration with SAP ERP HCM in scope, your partner may provide a resource that can support your implementation of the standard integration packages on the SAP ERP side.

10

- **Testing lead**

  Again, if you have a large project scope, it's advisable to have someone own the test plan and logistics, develop the process-specific test scripts, and support the testing activities throughout the testing cycles. The test lead should also be responsible for tracking identified issues and coordinating with the project manager and functional leads to ensure items are resolved in a timely manner.

Your partner may bring additional resources to the project depending on the scope of your individual project so the preceding list isn't meant to be exhaustive. Additionally, some roles may have more than one member to support the scope of work involved, such as the technical resources. Every project will differ a bit, and the key to success is finding the right balance of business and partner roles and resources to ensure the work scoped can be completed.

Let's now discuss the implementation methodology and project time lines.

10.3   Implementation Methodology and Time Line

Recruiting is implemented with the same methodology as all other SAP SuccessFactors modules. Here again, the partner that you choose to work with may have its own variations on the methodology, but the SAP-approved methodology is currently called *SAP Activate*. SAP Activate is an Agile project methodology that provides a harmonized approach for cloud, on premise, and hybrid implementations. The methodology provides a flexible, scalable, modular approach to accommodate not only today's deployments but also implementations in the future.

SAP Activate is intended to accelerate your project delivery by incorporating SAP Best Practices, fit to standard analysis, and an agile project management. There are comprehensive guided procedures for project managers and other project team members. The framework enables co-innovation with businesses to continually improve the methodology. SAP Activate succeeds both the ASAP and SAP Launch methodologies. In the following sections we will look at the project phases of SAP Activate and then briefly touch upon project timelines.

10.3.1   Project Phases

The SAP Activate methodology contains four project phases:

- Prepare
- Explore

- Realize
- Deploy

Each phase will include key tasks, activities, and deliverables for both you and your implementation partner, and finally a quality gate (Q-gate). Let's look closer at these for each project phase.

Prepare Phase

During the *prepare* phase, the project team performs project planning activities such as identifying the project team members and drafting project plans. Activities preparing for process and system design begin. The business project team attends project team orientation, the SAP SuccessFactors instances are provisioned, and the partner gains system access.

Key tasks in the prepare phase are as follows:

- **Project orientation**
  Several activities are geared toward orienting the business and the implementation partner to the project. These will include introductions of the consultant project resources to the business project team members, as well as introducing SAP SuccessFactors to the business and any technical resources that may be involved from a SAP technical services perspective.

- **Project team orientation**
  The business project team members should complete any project team orientation training provided by SAP SuccessFactors and the implementation partner, as offered. As discussed in the previous section, this online training provides an overview of the modules being implemented. This training is meant as a primer of sorts to give the business project team some basic knowledge going into the project kickoff and configuration workshops.

- **Roles and responsibilities**
  During project planning, there should be discussions and agreements on clear project roles and responsibilities of all team members. All team members should begin the project knowing what their role is, what is expected of them, and to whom they can escalate issues and risks. This is even more critical on large projects that are geographically dispersed as there may be seeming overlapping roles between the business and partner in some areas.

- **Project plan**
  One of the first activities that should commence in the prepare phase is drafting

the detailed project plan. This drives resource scheduling, time line, and key milestone dates. While the project plan is obviously a living document, growing as the project progresses, a baseline should be developed and agreed to by the business and partner. Key elements of the project plan should be presented in the kickoff meeting.

- **Objectives and success criteria**
One area that is often overlooked is discussing, identifying, and confirming the organization's business objectives and success criteria for the project. Projects that don't pay attention to these elements can find themselves far off course very quickly. These items should be a topic for discussion in the kickoff meeting so that each project team member is clearly aware of why the project is even happening and what will be considered success at the end.

- **Schedule kickoff meeting**
Each module should begin with an official kickoff to start the project work. Take time to review project team schedules and get something on the calendar for this important milestone. Communicate the date and time early so that all participants can plan to attend this exciting meeting.

- **Develop strategies for supplementary work streams**
While the main focus of the project activities will be designing business processes and system configuration, several other elements are important to the project running smoothly and being successful. Even before the official start of the project, it's important to have a high-level strategy for how training and communications will be handled throughout the project and in preparation for go-live. Identifying the process for issue and risk management, including defining "issue" and "risk," and having a clear escalation path, is critical to managing these successfully as they arise. Finally, it's never too early to begin planning for testing, including identifying what kinds of testing will occur (functional, integration, user acceptance, etc.) and at what points in the project each will take place.

- **Process definition**
Every implementation is an opportunity to review and redesign business processes to take advantage of best practices and identify areas of efficiency that can be achieved. In the preceding section, we discussed that even before the project preparation, businesses can start planning by gathering current processes and identifying areas of pain and where they would like to improve. If your organization operates in a siloed manner, but you want to define a more global process for all business units and geographies, it's even more critical to begin this work as

soon as possible. Prepare for process definition in this phase by gathering all the key inputs and feedback on business processes so you're ready for detailed discussions in the next phase.

- **Technical integration and data migration**
  Depending on the ancillary systems and processes in scope, you may have some integrations with third-party systems, such as a background check vendor, that will need to be developed. Identifying these touchpoints early and knowing when these activities will begin is helpful for all project team members. It also helps to scope the level of integration. If you want to migrate data from your legacy systems, this is the time to discuss and identify what data will be brought over and how much. Again, this will have an impact on the overall project schedule, so it's important to identify the magnitude of this work now.

Partner deliverables during this phase will include the following:

- Project kickoff presentation
- Project plan
- Project team orientation training and materials
- Configuration workbooks that document configuration decisions and define the configuration roadmap
- Technical workbook(s) (if required service)

Business deliverables during this phase will include the following:

- Attend project team orientation training
- Attend kickoff meeting
- Participate in requirements gathering workshops to define configuration blueprint
- Communication plan
- Training plan
- Test plan
- Post-implementation support plan

Prepare Q-Gate

At the start of the project, the business and the implementation partner review the readiness checklist(s) per module to ensure the business is ready to begin activities.

Explore Phase

In the *explore* phase, the team will perform *fit to standard* analysis to validate the solution functionality included in the project scope and to confirm that the business requirements can be satisfied. Identified gaps and configuration values are added to the backlog for use in the next phase. The business has participated in the kickoff meeting and process design sessions and will provide feedback during the configuration workshops. Also during this time, the project team builds on the strategies for communication planning, change management, training, and testing, and the team starts to develop plans for providing end-user support.

Key tasks in the explore phase include the following:

- **Best practice demonstration of the standard solution**
  Because Recruiting has so many best practices built-in to the solution, it's helpful to begin the explore phase with a detailed demonstration of the tools and capabilities the system provides before diving into the configuration discussions. Often it's been several months since the business has seen the product demonstration, and many project team members may have never seen it. You partner should take as much time as you need to explore the system with your team and talk through questions. This is really a continuation of project team orientation.

- **Identify/confirm requirements**
  Hopefully, you went through a requirements gathering exercise prior to selecting Recruiting as your solution. Take time in the beginning of the explore phase to review and reaffirm those requirements and identify any additional requirements that may have surfaced since the last discussion. It's impossible to build a process and system without knowing your requirements for it. Don't forget this critical part of the project.

- **As-is and to-be process discussions**
  You've gathered your prework and discussed pain points and areas for improvement with key stakeholders, and now you're ready to sit down and hammer out the processes. Take time to review current as-is processes so you understand where you're starting from. Then, with the detailed best practice system demonstration in mind, design your new processes that will be supported by Recruiting. These processes will be enhanced throughout configuration workshops and iterations of configuration.

- **Kickoff meeting**
  Every module should begin with an official kickoff meeting. Here the project team is formally introduced, hopefully in person, and begins to build a working rapport

that will grow throughout the process. All of the work done in the prepare phase to identify project time lines and milestones, identify business objectives and success criteria, and develop the project issues/risks management procedures should be reviewed so everyone involved is aware. Here is where your communication and change management activities commence in getting your key stakeholders engaged and excited about the new processes and systems. Don't underestimate the importance of a well-planned kickoff meeting or the value of taking the time to orient each team member. Invite your core team as well as those that will be involved in testing or providing process input.

- **Configuration workshops**
  After you've kicked off and spent time discussing and mapping out the to-be business processes, it's time to dive into the configuration workshops. Here you'll spend time discussing options for configuring your Recruiting system to support the business processes defined and capturing those decisions in a series of configuration workbooks. This is the meat of the explore phase. Configuration workshops can take several days over the span of a few weeks, depending on how you approach the schedule. Again, don't rush through these sessions. The goal is to identify 60–70% of the system configuration, so take the time you need to understand what's possible and vet these decisions internally. Each configuration workbook will need to have an official "sign off," so take the time to socialize the decisions with your wider stakeholder network and executive team to ensure that there are no show-stopping issues or concerns later in the project.

Implementation partner deliverables during this phase include the following:

- Validate scope
- Fit-gap requirements to solution
- Introduce configuration workbooks

Business deliverables during this phase include the following:

- Customer team enablement
- Sign off on initial workbook

Explore Q-Gate

The business agrees that business needs and requirements stated in the configuration workbook align to their requirements.

Realize Phase

The *realize* phase is all about building the system through a series of iterations to incrementally build and test an integrated business and system environment that is based on the business scenarios and process requirements identified in the previous phase. During this phase, data are loaded, adoption activities occur, and operations are planned.

Key tasks in the realize phase include the following:

- **Configuration of baseline system**
  This is the configuration of iteration 1 based on the decisions documented in the configuration workbooks completed in the explore phase. After the workbooks are signed off on, your implementation partner team will begin configuring the test instance per the decisions identified in the configuration workbook. This workbook will be updated throughout all iterations to capture decisions made.

- **Iterative reviews of configured system**
  After each iteration of configuration, your implementation partner team should review in detail the system configuration. In Iteration 1, the demo will review everything that has been configured. Subsequent iterations may only touch on those things that were changed but should still tie the process together for your team.

- **Execute testing and training strategies**
  You've planned for testing and training throughout the previous two phases, and now it's time to execute on those plans. Coordinating all of the testing activities, whether onsite or remote, should be the focus of executing the test plan. After testing is signed off on, you can train your end users, including Recruiting users, hiring managers, employees, and administrators.

- **Conduct testing (end-to-end, system integration, and user acceptance)**
  Perform all test scripts through all facets and phases of testing and identify issues. Issues should be tracked for resolution or clarification and retested. Ensure all aspects of the test plan are adequately executed.

- **Administrator knowledge transfer**
  If the knowledge transfer process from the implementation partner to your administrators hasn't begun, now is the time to get that going. The goal should be fully functioning administrators at go-live.

- **Review/attend training sessions**
  Executing the training plan may mean your team members serve as master trainers for the end-user training that occurs, or they may need to sit through some training, depending on the role they will play post go-live. The key to successful

user adoption is providing users with the right blend of training to suit their learning style and needs.

- **Administrator training**
  If knowledge transfer isn't adequate to cover all of your administrators' needs, follow up with more in-depth training. This can be consumed from SAP in the form of administrator training courses, job aids, and even some certification programs. In addition, your implementation partner may provide administrator training, depending on your requirements.

Implementation partner deliverables during this phase include the following:

- Configured system, including unit testing
- Provide demonstrations of configured system
- Adjust configuration based on client feedback

Business deliverables during this phase include the following:

- Explore configured system during iterations
- Provide feedback during iterations
- Complete user acceptance testing
- Test scenarios/scripts that align to business process
- Sign off on testing and solution
- User acceptance test plan
- Identify and train those individuals who will be part of your *train the trainers* initiative

---

Realize Q-Gate

The business agrees that the SAP SuccessFactors test environment system, including all aspects of inputs, processing, and outputs, has been tested and found to be functioning as specified in the design documents.

Deploy Phase

During the *deploy* phase, the business prepares for final system deployment. Communication and change management plans are executed, and end users and support teams are trained. The business is supported by its implementation partner through go-live.

Key tasks in the deploy phase include the following:

- Go-live planning and readiness
- Migrate configurations and data to production
- End-user training
- Execution of support plan
- Introduction of customer success team

Implementation partner deliverables during this phase include the following:

- Go-live checklist
- Cutover checklist
- Customer success introduction and transition
- Customer transition document

Business deliverables during this phase include the following:

- Trained and informed users
- Production readiness sign off
- Knowledge transfer plan to the business's support team

Deploy Q-Gate

Business agrees that acceptance testing in production is complete, and the system is accepted for go-live.

Note that the tasks discussed in this section are typical tasks and deliverables. The actual tasks and deliverables will vary depending on the approach the implementation partner you're working with adopts. For example, some partners take on the responsibility of documenting decisions in the configuration workbook while the business retains the responsibility to sign off on the decisions. There can also be additional activities, deliverables, and checkpoints added as necessary depending on your IT project methodology. Table 10.1 provides an example RACI chart for some of the main project activities in the SAP Activate methodology. RACI is an acronym that represents *responsible, accountable, consulted*, and *informed* and helps to represent the level of involvement of project team members for project activities.

Implementation Phase	Deliverable	Partner Responsibility	Customer Responsibility
Prepare	Statement of work	R	C, A
	Project kick off	R	C, A
	Project plan	R	R, A
	Communication strategy	C	R, A
	Risk assessment plan	R	C, A
	Resource plan—project team roles and responsibilities	C	R, A
	Draft testing strategy	C	R, A
	Training plan—training project team training strategy	C	R, A
	Prepare configuration workbooks	C, R	R, A
Explore	Post implementation support plan	C	R, A
	Provide access to system for project team	C	R, A
	Review reports, if applicable	R	R, A
	Document business processes	C	R, A
	Complete configuration workbook for iteration 1	R, A	R
	Update modification requests for iterations 2 and 3 in configuration workbooks	C	R, A
	Create language translation cookbooks (if applicable)	C, R	R, A
	Apply translations to configuration (if applicable)	C	R, A
	Employee data mapping	C	R, A

Table 10.1 RACI Activities by Project Phase

Implementation Phase	Deliverable	Partner Responsibility	Customer Responsibility
Explore, cont.	Ongoing validation of business requirement to support system configuration	C	R, A
	Configure the application and set security roles	R	R, A
	Create employee data files	C	R, A
	Data cleansing and migration (if applicable)	C	R, A
Realize	Unit test the configuration	R	R, A
	Create reports (if applicable)	R	R, A
	Application test	R, A	I
	Data migration test (if applicable)	C	R, A
	System and integration test plans (including acceptance criteria)	C, R	R, A
	Test scenarios and test scripts	C, R	R, A
	System integration test execution	C, R	R, A
	Test issue resolution	R, A	R
	User acceptance test plan	C	R, A
	User acceptance test execution	C	R, A
	UAT issue resolution	R	R, A
	Testing sign-off	C	R, A
Deploy	Quick reference guides	R, A	C, R
	Other training materials/manuals	C	R, A
	Perform user training	I	R, A
	User rollout plan	C	R, A

Table 10.1 RACI Activities by Project Phase (Cont.)

Implementation Phase	Deliverable	Partner Responsibility	Customer Responsibility
Deploy, cont.	Knowledge transfer plan to customer support team	C	R, A
	Production readiness sign-off	R	R, A
	Execute post-implementation support plan	C	R, A

Table 10.1 RACI Activities by Project Phase (Cont.)

10.3.2 Project Timelines

Obviously, project time lines will vary greatly depending on any number of things such as business drivers, resources, competing company initiatives, and others. But for Recruiting Management, a conservative estimate for a successful project is four to five months. This amount of time will leave time for the project team and other stakeholders to really absorb all the functionality available in the module and determine how they will use it, or not, in their business processes. If other ancillary processes or activities such as third-party custom integrations or data migration are in scope, this will increase the project time line. The amount of time will depend on the amount of data being migrated, the effort required to cleanse and format the data for loading into SAP SuccessFactors, and the complexity of the third-party integrations.

Note that these estimates only apply to Recruiting Management. If SAP SuccessFactors Recruiting Marketing and SAP SuccessFactors Onboarding are also in play, the project time line will increase based on the implementation schedule of those pieces.

10.4 Recruiting Configuration Workbooks

As with all modules of SAP SuccessFactors, decisions about how your Recruiting Management functionality should be configured are captured in a series of three configuration workbooks. These are very large Excel files with multiple tabs that fall into three categories:

- Requisitions
- Candidates
- Miscellaneous

Let's briefly discuss the composition of these workbooks and highlight some practical advice.

10.4.1   Requisition

This workbook provides information and captures decisions for everything related to a requisition. From defining the fields on a requisition template, to the field-level permissions, to the route map that a requisition should be attached to, this workbook will gather all of that important information. Additional decisions captured in this workbook are the rating scale associated with each job requisition data model (JRDM) that is used to capture interview assessments. If you're implementing job code entity on your requisition, the requirements for this feature are captured in this workbook along with the questions in the question library and any job role tags that may be used. Figure 10.1 provides an example of the **Requisition Fields** tab of the requisition configuration workbook.

			SF internal field	Requisition Field Labels	Standard or Custom	Type of Field (Text, Textarea, Picklist, Date, True/False, Percent)	Picklist Name (enter values on picklist TAB)	If Picklist, parent picklist	Required	Mobile Req	Auto-populate via Job Code Entity	Job Desc Token
			Template Name:									
			instrInformation	Requisition Information	Custom	Instruction						
			id	Requisition ID		Auto generated						
			filter2	Country		picklist	postingCountry		Yes			
			filter1	Location		picklist	companyLocation	postingCountry	Yes			
			division	Division		derived						
			department	Department		derived						
			location	Location		derived						
			functionalArea	Functional Area	Custom	picklist	functionalArea		Yes			
			addRep	Additional Hire/Replacement	Custom	picklist	addRep					
			costCentre	Cost Centre	Custom	text						
			contractType	Employment Type	Custom	picklist	contractType					
			eeoGroup	Job Level (Required for US only)		picklist	FSLA_Status					
			eeoJobCat			picklist	JobEeoCat					
			keyPosition	Key Position	Custom	picklist	yesno					
			numberOpenings	Number of Vacancies	Standard	Number						
			fte	Total number of FTE for the openings	Custom	text						

Cover Sheet | Introduction | Links | Recruiting Roles | Requisition Sample | **Requisition Fields** | Route Map | Rating Scale | Career Sites …

Figure 10.1 Requisition Fields Defined on the Requisition Fields Tab of the Workbook

The requisition workbook features the following tabs:

- **Recruiting Roles**
- **Requisition Sample**
- **Requisition Fields**
- **Route Map**
- **Rating Scale**

- Career Sites
- Career Sites Search Settings
- Header and Footer
- Job Code Entity
- Job Code Entity Loads
- Picklists
- Job Role Tags
- Question Library
- Standard Fields
- Reference Fields

10.4.2 Candidates

This workbook contains all information pertinent to your candidates, from application field definition, defining the candidate profile and associated permissions for each, to identifying the search criteria for your internal careers page. Additional items discussed in this workbook include the statuses in the talent pipeline and the visible to and selectable by permissions. Figure 10.2 provides an example of the candidate workbook.

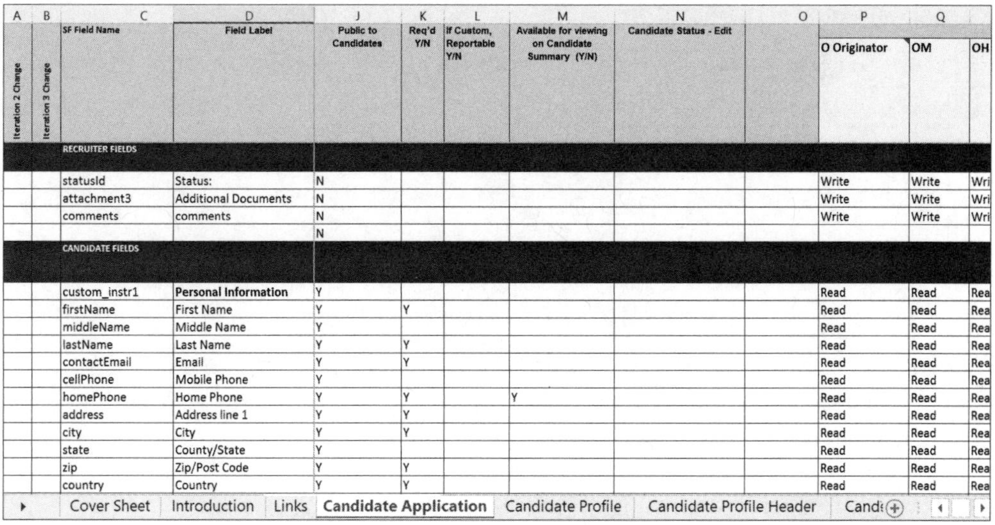

A	B	C	D	J	K	L	M	N	O	P	Q	
Iteration 2 Change	Iteration 3 Change	SF Field Name	Field Label	Public to Candidates	Req'd Y/N	If Custom, Reportable Y/N	Available for viewing on Candidate Summary (Y/N)	Candidate Status - Edit		O Originator	OM	OH
		RECRUITER FIELDS										
		statusId	Status:	N						Write	Write	Wri
		attachment3	Additional Documents	N						Write	Write	Wri
		comments	comments	N						Write	Write	Wri
				N								
		CANDIDATE FIELDS										
		custom_instr1	**Personal Information**	Y						Read	Read	Rea
		firstName	First Name	Y	Y					Read	Read	Rea
		middleName	Middle Name	Y						Read	Read	Rea
		lastName	Last Name	Y	Y					Read	Read	Rea
		contactEmail	Email	Y	Y					Read	Read	Rea
		cellPhone	Mobile Phone	Y						Read	Read	Rea
		homePhone	Home Phone	Y	Y		Y			Read	Read	Rea
		address	Address line 1	Y	Y					Read	Read	Rea
		city	City	Y	Y					Read	Read	Rea
		state	County/State	Y						Read	Read	Rea
		zip	Zip/Post Code	Y	Y					Read	Read	Rea
		country	Country	Y	Y					Read	Read	Rea

Figure 10.2 Candidate Workbook: All the Templates and Attributes Related to Candidates

The following tabs are found within the candidate workbook:

- **Candidate Application**
- **Candidate Profile**
- **Candidate Profile Header**
- **Candidate Profile Settings**
- **Candidate Status**
- **Offer Approval**
- **Picklists**
- **Application Standard Fields**
- **Candidate Standard Fields**

10.4.3   Miscellaneous

This may also be known as the "other" workbook and, as you might expect, serves as a bit of a catchall for the other things that are left over from the other two workbooks. This workbook deals with email templates, offer letter templates, agency portal and access, data privacy and purging, as well as identifying standard and custom integrations that will be included as part of the implementation. Figure 10.3 includes an example of an "other" workbook.

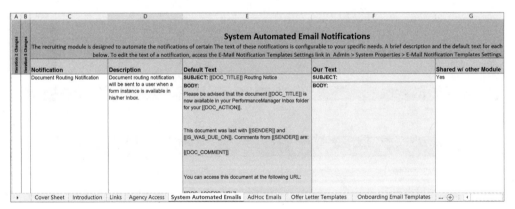

Figure 10.3 Other Workbook: Miscellaneous Collection of Elements to Complete the Configuration

The following tabs are found within the miscellaneous workbook:

- **Agency Access**
- **System Automated Emails**

- AdHoc Emails
- Offer Letter Templates
- Data Purging
- Recruiting Permissions
- Recruiting Settings
- Reports
- RCM to EC integration
- RCM to ONB integration
- RML integration

10.4.4   Working with the Workbooks

The workbooks are large with many tabs and can be very cumbersome to work with. There are columns that are intended to identify if an entry is an iteration 1, 2, or 3 entry (see Figure 10.4). This doesn't always work well, and project documentation commonly suffers if the business isn't diligent about managing version control and how to work with several versions of a document before signing off and submitting it.

A	B	C	D	E
			Template Name:	
Iteration 1	Iteration 2 Change	Iteration 3 Change	SF internal field	**Requisition Field Labels**
			nstrInformation	Requisition Information
			d	Requisition ID
			filter2	Country
			filter1	**Location**
			division	Division
			department	Department
			ocation	Location
			functionalArea	**Functional Area**
			addRep	**Additional Hire/Replacement**
			costCentre	**Cost Centre**
			contractType	**Employment Type**
			eeoGroup	Job Level (Required for US only)
			eeoJobCat	

Figure 10.4 Identifying Your Changes for Iterations 2 and 3 and Noting What the Changes Should Be

Developing and maintaining a good practice for working with and keeping these workbooks updated throughout the project will be critical to overall team success. So many things rely on the decisions that these workbooks capture, including test scenario identification and test script development, the beginnings of integration specifications, and just having good project documentation at go-live.

After the project is live, it's recommended that these workbooks continue to live on and that you capture new decisions in them as releases are deployed that impact configuration and system design. It sounds like a lot of work, and it can be, but if you have good quality workbooks at go-live, keeping them up afterward won't be bad at all and will prove quite worth the effort as issues arise and people come and go from the organization.

10.5   Summary

SAP provides the project methodology to help all customers and implementation partners ensure quality and consistency of implementations. Although the methodology provides for flexibility in phase duration, adding and removing tasks, and deliverables to meet customer-specific situations and partner influences, you can be sure nothing is missed if you follow as closely as possible the SAP-designed framework. Your implementation partner may bring some of its own influences and tools to the project to enhance the SAP Activate methodology, but the key tasks and Q-gates should be included. This methodology may change over time, so it's important to ensure that your project managers are always aware of and trained on the latest version of the methodology.

Begin your project preparation early to ensure your team feels adequately equipped to manage the work that is coming their way. Engage your stakeholders early and keep them excited with effective communications throughout the project. Take advantage of the Project Team Orientation materials SAP provides, and consume any training or knowledge transfer your implementation partner provides. This will serve you well throughout the project and at go-live.

Now let's look at implementing Recruiting Marketing and considerations for integrating it with Recruiting Management.

Chapter 11
Implementing Recruiting Marketing

For job seekers, your career site is often the first impression of you as an employer. Having an engaging, mobile-friendly career site can enhance your employer brand. Making sure you carefully plan and execute your SAP SuccessFactors Recruiting Marketing implementation is one of the first steps.

In the preceding chapters, we've discussed the SAP SuccessFactors Recruiting solution without differentiating much between the two aspects of the solution: SAP SuccessFactors Recruiting Management, which provides applicant tracking capability, and SAP SuccessFactors Recruiting Marketing, which is all about posting jobs through multiple channels and attracting and engaging talent to your organization. However, it's important to make distinctions between them when discussing implementation, as they are implemented a little bit differently

When it comes to Recruiting Marketing, you have two options for your platform. Both platforms result in a robust, responsively designed, mobile-enabled career site, but there are differences in what you can build, how it's built, and how it's maintained that need to be understood. The first platform is a fully custom-built Recruiting Marketing platform that can be 100% customized to your requirements, branding, and other design needs. SAP builds and maintains this platform, and there is no self-service capability. The second platform is a Recruiting Marketing site built and maintained in the Career Site Builder. This option provides self-service capability so that your company (or consulting resources working on your company's behalf) can nearly wholly build and maintain the site.

Career Site Builder comes with many advantages, as compared to the customized Recruiting Marketing platform, that we'll discuss in this chapter. The main disadvantage, though, is that the Career Site Builder won't be a pixel-perfect, agency-grade site. Career Site Builder has a fixed list of components and configuration options that the consultant/administrator can select from when designing the site. No custom components, fonts, styles, Cascading Style Sheets (CSS), buttons, spacing, or code can be added to any Career Site Builder page, unlike in a fully custom site built in Recruiting Marketing. Customers with complex requirements or requiring pixel-perfect branding are ideal candidates for the custom solution. These SAP Professional Services-managed custom career sites may still be purchased and implemented for customers that require 100% customization to their career site. However, it's critical to note that they won't have any ability to leverage the benefits of Career Site Builder. So it's a cost-benefit analysis exercise on how much the customized site is needed over the ability to self-manage the site easily.

In this chapter, we'll discuss implementing the Recruiting Marketing platform, both as a fully customized site built by SAP and as the self-service career site built via Career Site Builder in Admin Center.

We'll begin discussing the fully customized Recruiting Marketing site, covering what is involved in this implementation, the benefits of this model, roles and responsibilities, and time lines. Then, we'll discuss a Career Site Builder implementation, discussing the various elements that are available to build the site, features and functionalities, and the key milestones and time lines. Let's begin by discussing implementing the customized Recruiting Marketing solution.

11.1   Customized Recruiting Marketing Site Implementation Using SAP Technical Services

Prior to the introduction of Career Site Builder in late 2015, there was only one option for implementing Recruiting Marketing. The legacy Recruiting Marketing implementation differs quite a bit from other SAP SuccessFactors modules. For one, it involves engaging with SAP professional and technical services, who are highly skilled in creating beautiful, branded career sites. The technical resources work in a shared-service environment so work is placed into a work queue and prioritized based on "first-come, first-served," and the final project plan and launch date can't be verified until the company completes a lot of prework. Obviously, this means that many tasks are out of the control of the company project team, and the time line becomes critical as the company missing key dates has a domino effect on its priority in the queue, and other work may be prioritized ahead of the company at times. Activities such as gathering assets and completing the readiness checklist, which will be discussed later in the chapter, aren't calculated into the estimated project schedule, as these time lines are dictated by the company's responsiveness.

In this section, we'll cover the following:

- Tools and applications used in a custom implementation
- Implementation methodology
- Project roles and responsibilities
- Key project milestones and time lines

11.1.1 Tools and Applications Used in a Custom Implementation

Several tools and applications are used in Recruiting Marketing implementations that aren't used in implementing other SAP SuccessFactors modules. These tools are used in implementing both Recruiting Marketing platforms; however, they are used much more frequently in the custom solution than they are in Career Site Builder. We'll discuss these tools here and then make reference to them, as applicable, when we discuss Career Site Builder.

- **SAP SuccessFactors instance**
  Configurations such as field mapping to support real-time job sync and posting jobs to strategy pages in Recruiting Marketing are completed in the Admin Center.

- **Provisioning**
  Backend configuration for integrating the SAP SuccessFactors instance with the Recruiting Marketing career site, setting up scheduled jobs, and performing other settings are completed in provisioning.

- **Command Center**
  This is the main configuration platform for Recruiting Marketing. The custom site is built using Command Center. For Career Site Builder, Command Center is used for some initial setup to enable self-service in Career Site Builder. There is a stage and production Command Center, based on which environment is being managed. You can see an example of the stage Command Center in Figure 11.1.

- **QuickBase**
  This is the system where tasks are submitted to the SAP Services team and tracked. This system isn't used with other SAP SuccessFactors modules. QuickBase is used in both types of Recruiting Marketing implementations.

- **Notable**
  This tool is used to gather mockups of web pages and feedback on those pages. Notable is mainly used for custom Recruiting Marketing solutions.

11

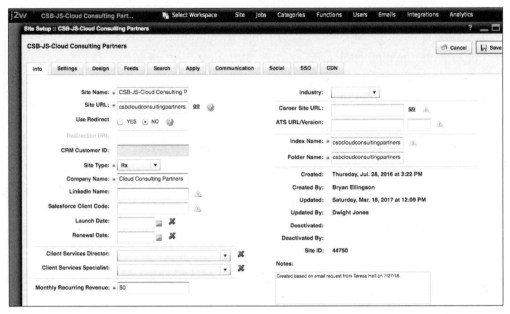

Figure 11.1 Setting Up Self-Service for Career Site Builder and Building Parts of the Custom Career Site in Command Center

11.1.2   Implementation Methodology

Custom Recruiting Marketing implementations follow a fairly rigid and structured process largely because of the multiple handoff points between the consultant operating as the Recruiting Marketing project management, the company, and the SAP technical services team doing the project build. Using the SAP Activate methodology that we discussed in the previous chapter, Recruiting Marketing implementations have different tasks, checkpoints, and sign-offs. In this section, we'll briefly discuss these elements within the SAP Activate phases of *prepare, explore, realize,* and *deploy.* Let's look at the activities and sign-off points in each phase.

Prepare

During the prepare phase, SAP professional services consultants work closely with companies to gather necessary information, scope the project, and plan for the site build. Unlike most other SAP SuccessFactors implementations, Recruiting Marketing implementations are heavily skewed to the prepare phase in terms of company involvement by phase. The prepare phase is therefore key in a custom Recruiting Marketing implementation. Companies must be very focused and diligent during this phase as any mistakes made in the prepare phase will negatively impact the following phases and may lead to increased cost and slipped deadlines.

This phase focuses on getting the project team together and making sure they understand what Recruiting Marketing includes so that they are clear about what they've purchased and what they will be implementing. But it goes much further into actually defining the specific site requirements before the build process starts. Let's take a detailed look at some of the most important aspects of the prepare phase:

- **Gather information and assets**
  The first step in gathering company requirements is to send the company a site design questionnaire and a readiness checklist. The completed questionnaire provides information about the company's vision for its career site. It asks for information about the company's goals and expectations for the site, branding and styling strategy, web design preferences, recruiting strategies, and company culture. The questionnaire lists several examples of Recruiting Marketing career sites, so companies can visit live sites and provide feedback on elements of the sites they like and dislike.

  The readiness checklist is used to collect company contact information, information about graphics and images that will be used in the site, and information on the company's critical hiring needs by job area and location. This document requires some explanation and also will take some time to complete thoroughly. The project consultant should work closely with the company to ensure the company understands the importance of the questionnaire and readiness checklist. The critical job areas and locations for hiring, for example, will form the basis for the featured jobs or strategy pages. Both of these documents are used as key input for the initial site design. Figure 11.2 provides a quick view into some of the topics and questions covered in the readiness checklist.

- **Design consultation meeting**
  The goals for the design consultation meeting are to review the readiness checklist, web style guide, and assets, as well as to discuss the company's design preferences. The following people should attend the meeting:
  - SAP SuccessFactors web designer
  - Consultant
  - Project manager (if one is assigned)
  - Company project sponsor
  - Company project manager
  - Company marketing contact

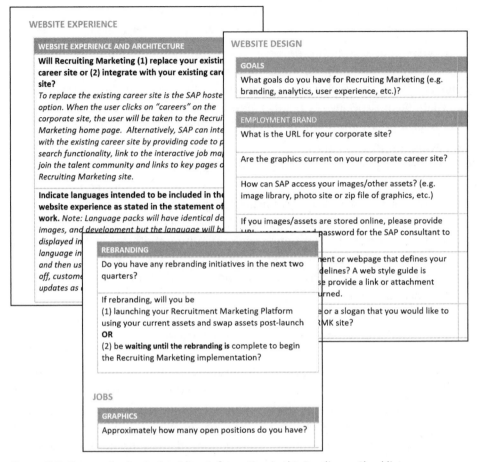

Figure 11.2 Companies Begin Providing Information in the Readiness Checklist

In this meeting, project roles and responsibilities, the project implementation methodology, and the company's design preferences are discussed with the help of the completed site design questionnaire. This is also an excellent opportunity to demo Recruiting Marketing to the core team. Chances are that not everyone on the client team has seen a demo of Recruiting Marketing, or, if they have, it has been some time ago. Reviewing the robust tools and data that will be available from the Recruiting Marketing tool will help build excitement for the implementation as well as allow the company team to start planning their talent acquisition strategies based on their new robust career site.

The readiness checklist should be reviewed and guidance provided to the company team. If you haven't already, start the conversation about the subdomain the company will need to create. For best search engine optimization (SEO) results, we generally recommend either "jobs.companyname.com" or "careers.companyname.com". Some companies have strong opinions internally about which domain is best, so they should start discussing it early in on the process. The design consultation meeting is one of the first meetings held during the implementation. This meeting is a good time to schedule regular check-in meetings with the team to ensure the project stays on track.

- **Site setup/SEO copy**

  SEO is the process of applying specific strategies, techniques, and tactics to increase the number of visitors to a website by obtaining a high-ranking placement in the search results page of a search engine. Choosing the keywords you want to target is the first part of optimizing your website for search engines. It's also the most important aspect of SEO and sometimes the hardest part. The SAP SuccessFactors SEO team has a lot of experience in reviewing company websites and recommending the best copy to use on SEO pages.

  After the design consultant meeting, the consultant submits a QuickBase task to the SAP technical services team to start the site setup. At the same time, the consultant submits another QuickBase task for the SEO team, which includes any special requests from the company. The SEO team reviews the company's current website and comes up with a proposal of a 100–200 word block of SEO text for the company's Recruiting Marketing site. This proposal can be tweaked by the company if they feel it doesn't adequately fit.

- **Create configuration workbook**

  After the company provides its web style guide, employment brand assets, completed readiness checklist, and design questionnaire, the project consultant works with the SAP Shared Services team to develop recommendations for the company site. The project consultant collaborates with the company to complete the Recruiting Marketing configuration workbook, an example of which is provided in Figure 11.3. The Recruiting Marketing configuration workbook is a spreadsheet with many tabs, requiring a lot of input from the company. It's highly recommended for the project consultant to own the initial completion of the workbook, with close cooperation from the company.

  It's imperative that the decisions and text copy are documented carefully in the workbook. This document is the blueprint that SAP Shared Services will use to build the company site. Because it's a SAP Shared Services team doing the build, there is rarely any communication back and forth about the workbook. The SAP Shared Services team will design the site to the exact specifications defined in the workbook. If things aren't clear or contain mistakes, these could impact the project time line and budget.

General Information				
Job Collection: XML Feed or Collection URL		http://www.careersatsap.com/en/CareerCenter.aspx#popUps=0;mainView=search		
Source Tracking Feasible in ATS?		Yes		
Customer Sub-domain		jobs.sap.com		
Recruiting Management Test Instance URL		SAP please provide		
Recruiting Management Production Instance URL		SAP please provide		
Recruiting Management Company ID		SAP please provide		
SSL Set-up in Recruiting Marketing				
Data	Review	Risk Level	SuccessFactors Comments	Requested Customer Action
Location	Locations have standard formatting (Location: City, State, Country; City, Province, Country: or City, Region Country format)	High	Missing Country from locations	1. Add country to location data
Location	In the United States, locations are titled as recognized by the US Postal Service	Medium	Missing Country from locations	1. Add country to location data
Location	Locations are mapped to a specific location (No locations listed as Negotiable/Multiple locations/Nationwide)	Medium	Remote positions included	2. Display primary location for
Titles	Titles are applicable to an external audience	Low		
Titles	Consistent titles for same job	Low		
Fields	Consistent fields used among job descriptions; ATS fields are turned on and are populated consistently	Low		
Cover Sheet 1. Introduction 2. TOC 3. Sign Off 4. Standard Configurations 5. Custom Configurations 6. Job Data 7. Business Cards and TC Emails ... ⊕				

Figure 11.3 Configuration Workbook Capturing Information Related to the Design of the Career Site and Reviewed by SAP

- **Review jobs data**

  The jobs published on a Recruiting Marketing site originate from the company's applicant-tracking system, such as Recruiting Management. The jobs information available in the applicant-tracking system must contain certain elements for the Recruiting Marketing site to function optimally. It's important to verify that these data are included now, in case adjustments need to be made in the applicant tracking system to make best use of the Recruiting Marketing platform.

  If you're implementing Recruiting Marketing at the same time as Recruiting Management, you need to work closely with your Recruiting Management consultant to make sure there are enough real-world examples of job postings that can be used for this jobs data assessment. Most Recruiting Management consultants are aware of the interdependencies between the two modules, but it's a good idea to check in with them early to make sure the fields that will be needed for the jobs feed and analytics in Recruiting Marketing are available in Recruiting Management.

Job posting description best practices recommend the first few sentences of the job posting be specific to the job and not standard boilerplate text about the organization. The first few sentences are what gets displayed on search engines and other online sources. Make sure the job title is applicable to an external audience and not just internal lingo. There are a number of fields that need to be checked in the jobs review:

- Unique **Requisition ID** for each job
- **Job Title**
- **Job Description**
- One primary **Location**
  - Location formatted as either **City**, **State/Province**, **Country** or **City**, **Country**
  - US locations must be recognized by the US Postal Service

The fields needed for job distribution and rule writing for strategy pages are as follows:

- **Job Function/Job Category/Industry**: This is the function, category or industry the listing falls under, such as information technology, healthcare, retail, or other broad descriptions.
- **Location**: Locations are mapped to a specific location (not **Multiple**, **Negotiable**, etc.).
- **Ad code**: This is used if you're using a particular code for a listing that directs the job to a specific page or site or for additional handling information.

The recommended fields to capture analytics are as follows:

- **Department/Organization/Business Unit**: This is the department or work area that describes the job. This is a sublisting under the **Category** field, for example, clinical staff, web development, and so on.
- **Experience/Education** (if applicable): This is the experience or education level required, such as professional, bachelor's degree, and so on.
- **Facility** (if applicable): This is the physical location/branch where the posting is located.
- **Job type** (if applicable): This designates what type of position this is, such as full-time, part-time, or contract.
- **Shift/Schedule** (where appropriate): This designates the job hours, such as first shift, overnight, 8–5, and so on.

Best practice is to make fields required in the applicant tracking system that you need in Recruiting Marketing to avoid having incomplete job data. You also need to keep the formatting of your job postings consistent to ensure they are captured and displayed correctly in Recruiting Marketing.

- **Create site mock-ups**
Recruiting Marketing implementations differ from other SAP SuccessFactors implementations in that the three iterations of the product actually happen in the prepare phase. Companies get three opportunities to provide feedback and adjust the site based on mock-ups of the site. There are no additional rounds of iterations after the site is actually built.

After the initial configuration workbook is created, the consultant creates a Quick-Base task for the SAP Shared Services team to create the first of three rounds of mockups. The pages that are mocked up are the home page, one strategy page, and one job description page.

- **Kickoff call**
The goals of this meeting are to ensure all project team members understand the project phases and to gather initial feedback on the proposed design of the site. A typical agenda for this meeting is to review the goals for the Recruiting Marketing implementation; go over project stakeholder roles, project phases, and methodology; review initial page mockups and gather feedback; discuss page content and site configurations; and then go over next steps.

The initial project plan is also presented in this meeting. A typical traditional Recruiting Marketing implementation takes 16+ weeks after the kickoff call has been conducted.

The busiest time during a Recruiting Marketing implementation is the first 10–15 business day period after project kickoff. Attendance in projects status calls and assistance in aligning the appropriate resources for approval is critical during this phase in the implementation. Marketing plays a key role in this step of the process to provide approval on branding.

- **Feedback rounds on mock-ups**
As mentioned earlier, there are three feedback rounds on the site mock-ups. Like in any other SAP SuccessFactors implementation, there should be fewer changes in each iteration. An online app called Notable, described in Section 11.1.1, is used to collect feedback on the mock-ups. The tool allows multiple reviewers to collaborate on feedback. Each point is documented as to who gave the feedback, and when. Designers use this feedback to update the site mock-ups in each round.

After the third round of mock-ups is completed, the company or consultant needs to update the configuration workbook to document any changes that were made during the mock-up review process. Remember, the workbook is the blueprint the SAP technical services team will use to design the site. They won't be questioning decisions, just building the site.

The culmination of the prepare phase occurs when the company signs off on the mock-ups and the configuration workbook. Only then will the launch date be confirmed, and the realize phase will begin.

Key activities in the prepare phase then include the following:

- Perform a Recruiting Marketing product overview.
- Hold a pre-kickoff call with the company to do the following:
  - Review the web style guide, readiness checklist, and assets
  - Discuss design preferences
- Develop design, content, and approach recommendations to share with the company during the kickoff call.
- Review job data.
- Hold the kickoff call.

Because in this type of implementation, SAP Shared Services resources are engaged to do the build work, it's critical to have certain deliverables completed, signed off on, and submitted to identify the overall project time line and go-live date. The deliverables included in the prepare phase must be completed thoroughly and signed off by the company before being submitted.

The company is required to provide sign-off on these deliverables prior to build:

- **Home, strategy, and job description page mock-up**
  This comprises the design of the site.

- **Configuration workbook**
  This document captures site functionality and scope definition, content, and graphics.

After the project scope is agreed upon as defined in these two deliverables, a detailed schedule, including a launch date, will be provided. This project plan will be built with company input and acceptance before moving forward.

Changes after the prepare phase will be governed by the SAP Shared Services change control process as detailed in the configuration workbook. The site is built to the agreed-upon specifications.

> **Note**
>
> Recruiting Marketing will use mock-up iterations during the prepare phase that differ from iterations during the explore phase in other SAP SuccessFactors module implementations.

Explore

During the explore phase, the main activities center around the career site being built according to the requirements and specifications detailed and signed off during the prepare phase. The SAP technical services team builds the company's career site using Command Center to the company's specifications based on the configuration workbook and the signed-off mock-ups. As part of this process, the company's jobs are imported into the public site.

This phase generally has much less involvement from the company because the SAP Shared Services team is building the site. Key activities in the explore phase include building the following:

- Home page
- Strategy pages
- Content
- Job map pages
- Additional SEO pages
- Mobile site

After these items are built, jobs can be collected from Recruiting Management and mapped to the appropriate strategy pages within the career site. This includes the setup of the subdomain. Activities also focus on preparing for deployment even this early in the process by holding a Recruiting Marketing training intake discussion with the company and introducing Advanced Analytics. There is also a discussion focused on media with the SAP media services team.

Realize

As you would expect, the activities during the realize phase center around testing. During this phase, the SAP Shared Services team ensures that the public site is functioning properly and is built to company specifications. The SAP quality assurance team reviews the site and resolves issues. The project consultant and the company also test the system before the site goes live. At this point, the only changes that will be made to the site are to correct bugs or errors. No new design changes will be incorporated at this point without a change order.

Activities are focused around the following:

- **Stage site quality assurance testing (QAT)**
  - Test cases executed and issues resolved
  - Additional QAT, if necessary
  - Site certified for user acceptance testing (UAT)
- **User acceptance testing (UAT)**
  - Company reviews live clickable site in staging environment to confirm it was built to agreed-upon specifications.
  - SAP SuccessFactors resolves any issues identified.
  - Additional UAT is performed, if necessary.

When UAT is complete, and all issues have been resolved and retested, the company signs off on the stage site, which is the approval to move everything to production. The site is moved to production under the company's subdomain at the end of the realize phase.

Deploy

The final phase in implementing a custom Recruiting Marketing site is the deploy phase. During deploy, the public site is moved from its preproduction environment to production. Some production site QAT takes place where test cases are executed and any issues identified are resolved. This process repeats until the site is certified for deployment, which encompasses the following:

- Company acceptance sign-off
- Site map submitted and job feeds activated
- URLs for back links and widgets delivered

Now that we've discussed the project activities within each phase, let's look at some of the key project roles and responsibilities.

11.1.3   Project Roles and Responsibilities

The typical project team roles for a Recruiting Marketing implementation will have some different types of resources involved than other modules. Some of these roles can be shared from the larger project implementation, such as project sponsors and project manager. But others will be new and unique to Recruiting Marketing. Following are the main roles and some of their responsibilities to the project:

- **Project sponsor**
  The project sponsor may come from the larger pool of project sponsors/stakeholders, but this role may also be someone from marketing or your media/web department. The main responsibilities are as follows: ·
  - Identify and secure support from internal stakeholders.
  - Remove internal obstacles if they arise.
  - Attend project status meetings.
  - Provide final approval for site build.

- **Project manager**
  The project manager may also be the overall partner project manager, but depending on the larger project scope, there may be a part-time project manager dedicated to Recruiting Marketing that works with the project manager and company team to do the following:
  - Coordinate internal deliverables and drive to deadlines.
  - Collect internal feedback on design, copy, and graphics and provide to the build team.
  - Notify SAP SuccessFactors of any potential delays or issues.
  - Confirm the site is built to the agreed-upon specifications during testing.
  - Coordinate and attend project status meetings.

- **Media team representative**
  This representative focuses on major job distribution campaigns that companies undertake and the measurement and refinement of job distribution. Media services must be involved with each implementation.

- **Marketing/communications contacts**
  These contacts usually play a role in a Recruiting Marketing implementation because the end result is a branded website, and they are well suited to provide input and context to the company's style guide and branding themes. These resources will do the following:
  - Provide access to employment brand assets (images, videos, graphics, logos, etc.).
  - Provide web style and brand guidelines.
  - Review and approve mock-ups, copy, and graphics.

- **IT administrator/webmaster**
  This resource will perform the more technical tasks on the company side to do the following:

- Set up the subdomain.
- Set up the Secure Socket Layer (SSL).
- Implement back links to key pages on the SAP SuccessFactors site and appropriate SAP SuccessFactors widgets (search, join map, etc.) on the corporate website/corporate careers site.

- **Functional Recruiting consultant(s)**
  These consultants are also involved in working with SAP SuccessFactors to ensure that Recruiting Management and Recruiting Marketing are talking to each other as required. They will do the following:

  - Adjust the job location or other data as necessary.
  - Make updates to the requisition template as needed.
  - Map fields between Recruiting Management and Recruiting Marketing.
  - Configure candidate single sign-on (SSO) and recruiting.

- **SAP professional services consultant**
  This consultant is usually involved throughout the process to help instruct the company on design considerations and provide overall product knowledge. This resource will be the main point of contact with SAP technical services resources and is responsible to do the following:

  - Guide the company through the implementation process by leveraging in-depth knowledge on product capabilities and best practices.
  - Function as a day-to-day implementation expert and contact.
  - Manage project scope, costs, schedule, and deliverables to ensure a successful deployment.

- **SAP technical services**
  These resources will be responsible for the technical setup of the site wireframe and will also do the following:

  - Provide design guidance, as needed.
  - Build the site.
  - Provide quality assurance.

11.1.4   SAP Technical versus Partner Roles

In the custom Recruiting Marketing implementation model, the consulting partner plays the role of product expert, project manager, and the interface between the client and SAP Shared Services. The SAP Shared Services team is behind the scenes building the site based on the input and specifications provided by the client through the project manager. The consulting partner will be the point of contact to the company on the project. The company rarely directly interacts with SAP Shared Services. As you'll learn in the next section, there are a lot of handoff points between the consulting partner and the SAP Shared Services team. These handoffs are managed in the QuickBase tool, discussed in Section 11.1.1. This tool is the "ticketing" system that manages the work queue for tasks between SAP Shared Services and the partner project resources.

The partner resources will also handle the configuration of the integration between Recruiting Management and Recruiting Marketing, and set up real-time job sync, complete field mapping for job postings, and appropriate recruiter roles in role-based permissions to allow recruiter SSO to the Recruiting Marketing Dashboard.

11.1.5   Key Project Milestones and Timelines

Recruiting Marketing follows the basic SAP launch methodology of prepare, realize, verify, and launch. A high-level view of key project milestones and time lines is as follows:

- **Prepare**
  - Estimated duration is 15 to 20 business days from official project kickoff
  - Key milestones:
    - Formal project kickoff
    - Review of Iteration 1, 2, and 3 of mock-ups
    - Final sign off on mock-ups and configuration workbook
- **Explore**
  - Estimated duration is 25 to 30 business days from sign-off on mock-ups and configuration workbook
  - Key milestone:
    - Site build
- **Realize**
  - Estimated duration is 20 to 25 business days
  - Key milestones:
    - Consultant smoke test
  - Company validation test

- **Launch**
  - Estimated duration is 10 to 15 business days from sign off on stage QA
  - Key milestones:
    - Site live

Several factors can impact these time lines, including if the company plans to implement multiple languages, multiple brands, or is in the middle of implementing other modules at the same time.

The details of each phase are described in the following sections.

11.2   Career Site Builder Implementation

The Career Site Builder product was introduced by SAP in late 2015. Career Site Builder is essentially a self-service tool that allows companies to build and maintain their own Recruiting Marketing site rather than having to rely on SAP to do so. This product has been a huge advancement that allows partners and companies to take control of this activity with minimal setup and involvement by SAP technical services.

Career Site Builder sites are Recruiting Marketing sites that simplify the implementation process and decrease the time line. All Recruiting Marketing features are included within Career Site Builder, so you can build an engaging, fully responsive career site—all from within Admin Center. For example, if your logo or corporate brand elements are updated, you can log in and make the necessary changes to your site in real time. Or, if your company is launching an exciting new initiative, you can quickly create a new page to highlight those jobs or adjust the copy on existing pages. These are things that would need to be funneled through SAP technical services previously, which was not only time-consuming but often expensive.

Keeping content fresh and relevant is an important part of employer branding and will enable you to continue to attract the right talent. Being able to update your career site on your own time line and by your own staff definitely helps in this regard.

In this section, we'll look at implementing Career Site Builder and what tools are available to build an engaging site that attracts the candidates you're looking for. We'll discuss the following:

- How Career Site Builder is implemented
- Features and functionality within Career Site Builder
- Key project milestones and time lines

Let's begin our discussion by looking at how Career Site Builder is implemented.

11.2.1 How Career Site Builder Is Implemented

Career Site Builder implementations of Recruiting Marketing occur in six basic steps. These steps, or groups of activities, are spread throughout the project phases that were discussed in Section 11.1.2. After the site is set up by SAP Shared Services in the Command Center, meaning that the frame of the site is created, the partner consultant will take over and complete some additional setup tasks, making Career Site Builder available in the Admin Center. In Command Center, choose **Select Workspace,** and then find the appropriate site. You'll make or confirm the following settings:

- **Site Setup • Info**
  Confirm the **Site Name**, **Site URL**, **Site Type (RX)**, **Company Name**, **Index Name**, and **Folder Name**.

- **Site Settings • Settings**
  Set the **Framework Type** to **Responsive v3**, and check the box for **Use Career Site Builder**. This is what makes the Career Site Builder tools available in Admin Center. Additionally, confirm the following settings have been made, or make them:
  - **User Intercom.io**
  - **Show Search Filter**
  - **Show Talent Community Subscribe**
  - **Auto Generated Keyword Landing Pages**
  - **Branding On**
  - **Phrase Filter Back: <companyname>**
  - **Active**
  - **Deselect Optimize Jobs (w/Functions)**
  - **Optimize Locations**
  - **Display SEO Fields on Jobs**
  - **Use SSL/Entire Site SSL**
  - **Display Lat/Long in Dashboard**
  - **Display Department Dropdown in Dashboard**
  - **Job Start On (JATS)**
  - **Job Expiration On**
  - **Privacy Policy On**

- – Use Saved Jobs
- – TC User Session Type: Cookie Session Permanent
- **Site Settings • Design**
  Set the **Page Title** and **Default Description**, and then confirm these settings:
  - – Style Sheet: custom.css
  - – Search Results Max: 500
  - – Map Type: Google
- **Site Settings • Search**
  Confirm the search settings, such as keyword and location.

- **Site Settings • Apply**
  Here you make settings related to the talent community signup, on-page business card, business card for mobile apply, and preapply settings.

- **Site Settings • Communication**
  Set the agent email address, the locale to determine jobs presented in agent emails, subscription settings, and talent community emails.

After the basic **Site Settings** have been made or confirmed, and the other integration tasks have been completed, you can set the administrator permissions for Career Site Builder in the Admin Center. From here, all tools within Career Site Builder are available to build the rest of the career site. The implementation will focus on the following:

- **Selecting the career site kit**
  Choose the kit from those available to define the basic of your career site.

- **Selecting the structure of the site**
  Choose the layout and spacing of your career site.

- **Selecting site components**
  Choose the components for your site such as job search and strategy pages.

- **Uploading images**
  Images are uploaded in the Career Site Builder UI and managed in one central image area. Images are hosted on Akamai's Content Delivery Network (CDN) to enable fast delivery.

- **Creating pages**
  Home pages and content pages can be created for each client brand and locale. Each page can have its own set of components, images, and colors. There is no limit to the configuration of components on each page.

- **Site design review**
  After all site elements have been configured, the company can review. Changing images, colors, and components can be done quickly in the Career Site Builder UI.

11.2.2   Variations from Custom Recruiting Marketing Implementations

The biggest difference between a Career Site Builder implementation and a custom Recruiting Marketing implementation is the split of work between the implementation consultant and the SAP Shared Services team. With Career Site Builder, the functional consultant does the bulk of the work, with only minimal hours required from SAP Shared Services to implement Recruiting Marketing. This both speeds up the implementation and can reduce the cost. Another big difference is that the Career Site Builder implementation follows the traditional implementation approach of other modules, with the three iterations for the company to provide feedback and update the configuration workbook after each iteration built and played back. As we discussed in Section 11.1, custom Recruiting Marketing sites are built from the completed configuration workbook, and changes made after submitting the workbook will result in a change order and affect the project schedule and cost.

Because Career Site Builder is self-service, companies can play a large role in building the site, which is encouraged. This is a great time to involve your marketing or website resources to build a world-class career site.

Finally, because Career Site Builder sites are based on predefined site kits, there are no custom elements that can be accommodated at this time. The company needs must be met by the components within the site kit. As we discussed in the introduction of this chapter, this needs to be considered during the sales cycle so that the appropriate product is purchased.

Let's now look at some of the features and functions within Career Site Builder.

11.2.3   Features and Functions of Career Site Builder

Career Site Builder uses site kits, which are best practice templates that can be selected for use as a starting point in building your career site. After you have your site kit, you can customize the components of the kit to meet your specific requirements and branding. There are numerous elements that comprise a site kit. There are a set number of components that can be used in building your site, such as the following:

- Search
- Images

- Customized text, colors, and labels for company branding

The components can be combined and arranged in any order. For example, you may want to overlay some text on the background image and then have another area where text is displayed next to an image, creating a unique and distinctive design for your career site. There are new components begin introduced as the product matures.

Career Site Builder doesn't produce a pixel-perfect, agency-grade site. It has a fixed list of components and configuration options that the company can select from when designing the site. No custom components, styles, CSS, buttons, spacing, or code can be added to any Career Site Builder page to create an exact replica of a client corporate brand.

Configuration of Career Site Builder is performed in the Admin Center under **Manage Career Site Builder**. The configuration tool is divided into the following main sections:

- **Global**
- **Pages**

- **Layouts**

The **Import & Export** menu allows you to export your Career Site Builder configurations from one instance and import them into another. It lists previous configuration versions and allows you to choose which one you would like to export. Figure 11.4 provides an example of the **Import & Export** function. The export and import functionality is especially useful when transitioning from a development instance to test instance and then to production.

Figure 11.4 Exporting Career Site Builder Configuration for Import into Another Instance or as a Backup When Designing

Being able to export and import configurations significantly reduces the chance of manual errors. It also makes it possible to quickly revert to an earlier version of the site if issues are discovered.

Global

The **Global** menu is divided into five submenus, each of which offers numerous options for configuring the site:

- Settings
- Styles
- Search Grid
- Translations
- Locations

We'll look at each of these submenus in the following sections.

Settings

The **Settings** menu, shown in Figure 11.5, allows you to customize features that are shared across the whole career site. Here you can select a predefined site kit if desired, select the social sharing options you want to enable, define any company social links, and define items such as font type, vertical and horizontal padding, header and footer style, meta keywords, and description.

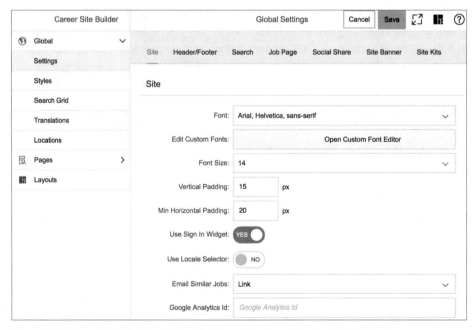

Figure 11.5 Career Site Builder Global Settings Configuration in Admin Tools

Styles

The **Styles** configuration area is divided into the following sections:

- **Global Styles**
- **Headers**
- **Footers**

You can configure global style colors for each brand you want to represent in your career site. You can also configure separate headers and footers, with custom colors and images for each brand. This gives great flexibility for companies operating multiple brands that have distinct colors and fonts. When you configure global styles, you associate each style with a specific brand, and you must configure each brand separately. Figure 11.6 displays the **Global Styles Details** page within Career Site Builder showing configuration of global styles. Note that locales and brands must be defined in Command Center before they can be configured in the Admin Center.

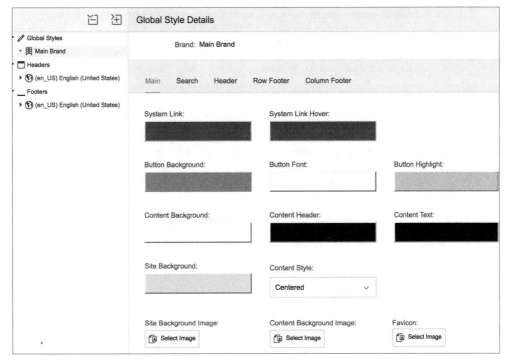

Figure 11.6 Configuring Global Styles in the Admin Center

Search Grid

The search grid appears on all strategy pages, support pages, SEO pages, and search pages. The search grid is used to display the jobs that match a defined search, and it allows candidates to sort through and filter the list to find the jobs in which they are really interested. An example of the search grid is shown in Figure 11.7.

Results 1 – 25 of 49		« **1** 2 »
Title	**Location**	**Date ▼**
Title	Location	Date (m/d/yy) Filter Reset
Channel Content Marketing Sr Specialist Job	Palo Alto, CA, US	Mar 13, 2017
Channel Marketing Sr Specialist Job	Palo Alto, CA, US	Mar 13, 2017
Marketing Execution Senior Specialist Job	Mexico City, MEX, MX	Mar 13, 2017

Figure 11.7 Example of a Search Grid on a Strategy Page

The **Search Grid** configuration area allows you to configure the layout of the grid, including which columns are shown, how many jobs should be shown per page, and so on. You can also define which columns are displayed in the search grid on mobile devices. Because the screen size is much smaller, it's highly recommended to keep the columns to a minimum for mobile.

Translations

The **Translations** area is where you manage the field labels for the standard elements on your site. Here you can change the standard field labels in all languages you've enabled for Recruiting Marketing to meet your company-specific terminology, as you can see in Figure 11.8.

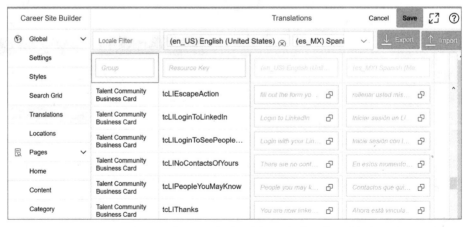

Figure 11.8 Manage Translations for Standard Field Labels for All Enabled Languages for Your Site

This isn't where you translate the copy for your pages. There is also an **Import** and **Export** feature here that allows you to download your field label language configurations and upload them to another site or instance.

Locations

The **Locations** area is where you can define map coordinate overrides if jobs aren't appearing on maps correctly for some locations. The page shows the Google map coordinates per location and allows you to define an override, as you can see in Figure 11.9.

Career Site Builder	Locations				
Global ⌄	Location ⬆	Country	Google Location	Override Location	
Settings	Albuquerque, MO, US, 87109	United States - US	35.1576°N 106.5978°W	35.1576°N 106.5978°W	✏ ↺
Styles	Albuquerque, NM, US, 87109	United States - US	35.159°N 106.5761°W	35.159°N 106.5761°W	✏ ↺
Search Grid					
Translations	Amarillo, TX, US, 79106	United States - US	35.2019°N 101.8949°W	35.2019°N 101.8949°W	✏ ↺
Locations	Amarillo, TX, US, 79106	United States - US	35.2019°N 101.8949°W	35.2019°N 101.8949°W	✏ ↺
Pages ⌄	Arnold, MO, US, 63010	United States - US	38.4317°N 90.4031°W	38.4317°N 90.4031°W	✏ ↺
Home	Atlanta, GA, US, 30344	United States - US	33.6832°N 84.4488°W	33.6832°N 84.4488°W	✏ ↺
Content	Atlanta, GA, US, 30344	United States - US	33.6832°N 84.4488°W	33.6832°N 84.4488°W	✏ ↺
Category					
Landing	Austin, TX, US, 78752	United States - US	30.3317°N 97.7052°W	30.3317°N 97.7052°W	✏ ↺

Figure 11.9 Setting Coordinates for the Job Locations on Your Site

Pages

The **Pages** menu is divided into three submenus, each of which offers numerous options for configuring pages within the site:

- **Home**
- **Content**
- **Category**

We'll look at each of these submenus in the following sections.

Home

The home page is the main landing page of the career site. You can define separate home pages for each brand and locale in your career site. The **Home** menu allows you to select and customize the components used in the page as well as their layout. This is where you define the text that goes on the home page.

You can adjust the style, appearance, and content of each component. You can't, however, control the size of components, or the distance between them on the home page. These are controlled by content and functionality of the components themselves. You can also control which home page components should be enabled by device type—**Desktop**, **Tablet**, or **Mobile**—as shown in Figure 11.10.

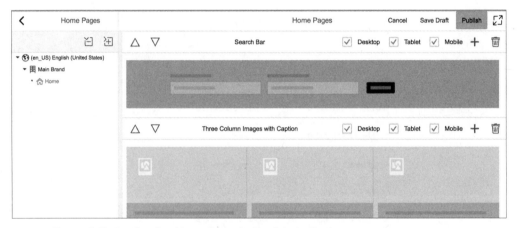

Figure 11.10 Configuring Home Pages in the Admin Center

The **Home Pages** area includes a preview function so that you can see what your page looks like prior to publishing. There is also built-in versioning so that you can view previously published versions of the page and edit them if desired.

Content

Content pages are typically used for company information, such as benefits or company culture, or for event landing pages and media campaigns. Content pages support all Career Site Builder components.

The **Content Pages** area allows you to create pages, add components to those pages, and manage their layout as shown in Figure 11.11. Here you define the actual page titles and text that go onto the content pages.

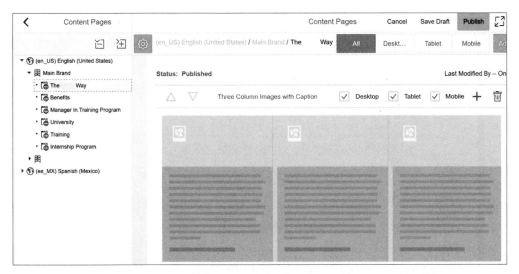

Figure 11.11 Creating Pages to Provide Company-Specific Information to Your Candidates

Just like for home pages, you can control which content page components should be enabled by device type—such as **Desktop**, **Tablet**, or **Mobile**. You also have the same preview and versioning functionality.

Category

Category or strategy pages are jobs pages that target a company's key locations or job types. These pages include a description of the location or job type and a listing of the corresponding open jobs in the company. Category pages each have their own unique URL and are indexed with search engines. This improves a company's SEO and makes it easier for candidates to find your jobs when using a search engine. Candidates can perform natural language searches such as "creative jobs Kansas" and be presented with a category or strategy page as one of the top hits.

When defining the metadata on category pages, the best practice is to use the term "Jobs" or "Careers" in the title. This helps SEO and allows search engines to understand that this is a page that houses jobs, not simply a page about "sales" or "operations," and so on.

The configuration options in the **Category Pages** menu are pretty much the same as those for home pages and content pages. The **Category Pages** screen is displayed in Figure 11.12.

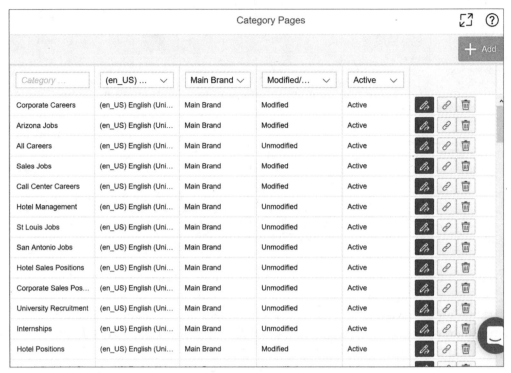

Figure 11.12 Setting Up the Category Pages to Target Specific Jobs

Layout

Layouts determine how data are displayed on a page. Currently, Career Site Builder supports layouts for job pages and custom layouts. Job page layouts will determine how the job data will appear on the site. You can add multiple columns that have different widths, and the components on the job page will fit dynamically within the column widths specified. You can also set up filters so that certain jobs are presented in the layout configured. For example, if you want jobs within a certain department to be presented in the layout you're configuring, you would create the filter accordingly.

Token components can be used to display custom content dynamically. You can see how a layout is defined in Figure 11.13.

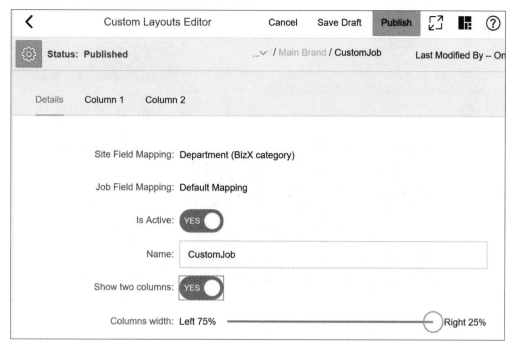

Figure 11.13 Creating Layouts for Jobs Pages or Other Custom Layouts to Determine How Data Are Presented on a Page

In-Product Assistance

SAP has recently released a very nice, user-centric feature within Career Site Builder that provides pertinent assistance on the product. This embedded technology is used to provide informational and instructional videos from product management to administrators managing the career site within Career Site Builder. This in-product assistance is available at the bottom right of each screen where additional information is available. These videos are intended to provide quick overviews of the feature and how it can be configured. It's like having "show-me" videos for your Career Site Builder administrators! This is the first step in the product becoming more consumer-like in overall experience. You'll see more informational videos pop up going forward. Figure 11.14 shows an example of these messages and videos.

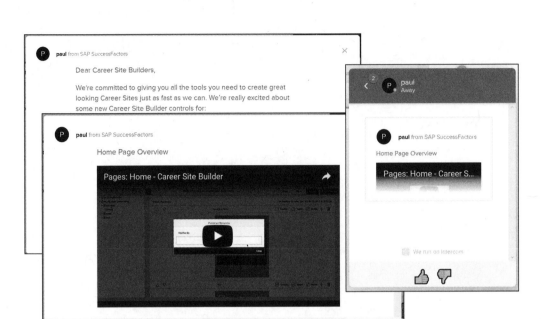

Figure 11.14 Information Videos throughout the Career Site Builder Interface Providing Assistance to Administrators

11.2.4   Key Project Milestones and Timelines

Career Site Builder follows the same basic SAP Activate methodology of prepare, realize, verify, and launch as the custom Recruiting Marketing implementation. However, the work is distributed a bit differently among the phases in a Career Site Builder implementation. Because of the limited effort by SAP Shared Services, companies and partner teams have much more control over the implementation time frame because work isn't being queued. Most Career Site Builder implementations are completed concurrently with a Recruiting Management implementation, and the time lines will be in sync. Let's look at the key milestones and considerations for the project time line in a Career Site Builder implementation.

Project Milestones

Because a Career Site Builder project is more in line with other SAP SuccessFactors modules, such as Recruiting Management, where the partner drives the configuration, the methodology, activities, and milestones will be more familiar than in a custom Recruiting Marketing implementation. The following is a high-level view of key Career Site Builder project milestones:

- **Prepare**
  - Formal project kickoff
  - Site wire frame built by SAP Shared Services
  - Integration with Recruiting Management configured
  - Sign off on iteration 1 of configuration workbook
- **Explore**
  - Iteration 1 build: review and feedback
  - Iteration 2 build: review and feedback
  - Iteration 3 build: review and feedback
  - Job distribution strategy developed with media team
- **Realize**
  - UAT
  - Production readiness sign-off
- **Deploy**
  - Site live
  - Media team task complete
  - Project transferred to advanced analytics team
  - Project close-out

Other milestones may be identified as required and specific to a project, depending on the scope of the work.

Career Site Builder Timelines

One of the biggest advantages of a Career Site Builder implementaiton is that there is very little involvement from SAP Shared Services, so companies and partners have more say in the time line and can also react to things that arise as the project progresses to adjust time lines. SAP Shared Services involvement has gone from more than 100 hours of consulting services in a custom implementation to roughly 20 to 30 hours, at the most. A best practice, English-only implementation of Career Site Builder is estimated to take 16 weeks from formal project kickoff to site launch. This schedule is estimated as follows:

- Prepare phase: 4 weeks
- Explore phase: 8 weeks
- Realize phase: 2 weeks
- Deploye phase: 2 weeks

There are numerous variables that will impact the actual duration of the project. Because Recruiting Marketing is where jobs are posted, it doesn't make sense for it to go live before Recruiting Management. As a result, the time line is greatly dependent on the project schedule for Recruiting Management. Other factors that will impact the project time line include the following:

- Additional languages implemented, resulting in translation activities
- Lack of company-dedicated resources to provide input on site design
- Company providing assets and design input/feedback with the requested time frames

> **Note**
>
> Often resources outside the project are needed for guidance and approvals, perhaps from marketing or the corporate website owners. Tight coordination with these resources is required to keep on track!

- Complex rules or business processes
- Business process or design change requiring rework in the site build

> **Note**
>
> Even though the career site can be easily updated, it's important to manage change control so they don't get out of hand and impact the scope of the project.

Additional Considerations

As you progress through your Career Site Builder implementation, there are a few more things to keep in mind. First, SAP Professional Services is available for general support and troubleshooting on things such as the following:

- Image slicing and optimization
- Page rules creation

- SEO page generation
- Email setup
- Business card setup
- Language pack and locale setup
- Branding setup

In addition, a web designer is available to meet with consultants on Career Site Builder implementations to provide support related to design questions and recommendations, branding questions, or general Career Site Builder layout usage. This support won't be company-facing.

There is also an opt-in service for Recruiting Marketing media services that allows companies to leverage a dedicated team of recruiting analysts and strategists to assist companies in managing and optimizing their online recruiting spend. This team can support companies on two levels:

- Campaign management for short-term, hard-to-fill needs
- Agency of record for annual and ongoing planing, management, reporting, analysis, and execution of their recruiting strategy

This media service is purchased separately from implementation and can be tailored to the company's needs; however, it may not cost anything additional beyond what the company is already spending, depending on the job board.

11.3 Summary

Understanding the similarities and differences between custom Recruiting Marketing and Career Site Builder before you purchase is critical and will determine what your implementation looks like from the breakdown of roles and responsibilities, milestones, and time lines. Most implementations at this point are of the Career Site Builder type. With the ability to build and manage your career site directly from within Admin Center, the advantages to Career Site Builder are great. This allows you to not only control your project time line but also to update your site structure and content at any time without relying on SAP Shared Services resources. Companies find this a great enough benefit to sometimes forgo requirements they would otherwise like to see in their career site. By selecting from predefined site kits and using a set series of components in a user-friendly interface, career sites can be built using Career Site Builder by nontechnical or web designer resources.

If you require a pixel-perfect site or customized components, and those requirements outweigh the self-service benefits, then a custom Recruiting Marketing site is for you. In this implementation, SAP Shared Services resources do all of the work in building the site based on the configuration workbook provided by the company. This work is queued among the SAP Shared Services center resources and will likely drive project time lines. Changes to the site design after the configuration workbook is submitted will require a change request and will lengthen the duration of the project due to the rework involved.

Recruiting Marketing is a powerful tool for attracting and engaging candidates, whether you implement the traditional full-blown Recruiting Marketing or take the Career Site Builder approach. Which option is best for your company really depends on the complexity of your site, your need for pixel-perfect branding, and your company's appetite for managing the career site.

Whichever product and implementation you choose, Recruiting Marketing offers tremendous tools to support your overall talent acquisition objectives and provide insight into where your candidates are coming from and how effective your recruiting dollars are being spent.

In the next chapter, we turn our attention to considerations for migrating legacy recruiting data into SAP SuccessFactors Recruiting.

Chapter 12

Recruiting Data Migration

When you're moving from a legacy applicant tracking system, you may have several years' worth of data that you don't want to lose or can't afford to lose. You want that information easily accessible in SAP SuccessFactors to support the smooth transition to the new system and facilitate reporting. Fortunately, there is an option to migrate legacy data.

One question that often arises in a systems implementation is to migrate or not to migrate data. This is no less true with applicant tracking information. If you've been using a legacy system for a while, you have a lot of data stored in that system that you don't want to lose track of. Often you have no choice because you need it to report on. You also may have a robust candidate database that you want to retain for immediate use in SAP SuccessFactors. And there may be any number of additional business reasons that you need your existing data in your brand new system.

SAP SuccessFactors Recruiting does support migrating legacy data; however, the decision to migrate data and how much to bring over should be discussed thoroughly within the framework of what SAP SuccessFactors supports and the amount of time that it adds to the project.

In this chapter, we'll discuss how SAP SuccessFactors supports legacy data migration and some considerations and best practices for embarking on the task. We'll also discuss migrating recruiting entries and setting up the jobs in provisioning.

12.1 Data Migration Considerations

SAP SuccessFactors Recruiting supports importing data into numerous recruiting templates such as requisition, application, candidate profile basic information, candidate profile background information, candidate tags, and candidate résumés and cover letters. The data are migrated using flat files (.csv files), and the templates are dependent on the configuration of the templates in question. Because the configuration drives the import templates, and SAP SuccessFactors is implemented in an iterative approach, data migration activities really shouldn't begin until Iteration 3 has been identified and signed off. This can be a challenge because many clients want to test their configuration using their own data, creating a chicken and egg situation.

After configuration is signed off, or at least as stable as possible, your implementation consultant will build the data migration import templates in a flat file. The templates themselves are relatively simple, including some required fields for each type of data element being imported, and then the fields from the configured templates. The consultant provides the templates to the business that then works to format its data into the SAP SuccessFactors templates. The completed files are placed on the secure file transfer protocol (SFTP) site associated with the customer instance and the import jobs are created and run from provisioning. The jobs will retrieve the files from the SFTP site and load them into the system. The job will run until it encounters errors up to the error threshold set for the job. Errors are provided in the email to the job owner sent upon job completion and can also be viewed from the job details in the Monitor Jobs tool in provisioning.

Sounds easy, right? In the following sections, let's take a look at some of the limitations of data migration, and you might change your mind!

12.1.1   Data Migration Limitations

It's critical to be aware of the limitations of data migration in SAP SuccessFactors Recruiting to help you decide whether to take on the work, and if you do decide to go ahead, to understand what will be required of your resources during the activity. Following are some of the roadblocks you might face:

- **Only external candidates can be imported.**
  Internal candidate imports aren't supported because internal candidates are your employees and are imported using the employee import feature in admin tools (for non-SAP SuccessFactors Employee Central customers) or using your employee import files if you use Employee Central. This can prove to be a challenge because some applicant tracking system solutions on the market don't easily distinguish your employees from external candidates. It's not an insurmountable obstacle, but it could add even more time to the project timeline if you have to figure out which candidates in your legacy database are external.

- **Data migration imports only create records.**
  It's not possible to update or delete records using a data migration import. Essentially, you get one shot to create your external candidate records, job requisitions, and applications. This can complicate testing, but we'll discuss some ways to get around this later in this chapter. For now, just be aware of this.

- **Imports must be done in order.**
  There is an order to the imports because of the relationships that are built among the data objects in the system. Either requisitions or external candidates can be imported first, but both must be imported and in the system before you can create the associated applications. This is because the application creates the relationship between the candidate and the requisition. Another important thing to be aware of is that you can only import applications against requisitions that were also imported.

> **Note**
>
> You can't import applications against requisitions that have been created manually in the UI or via the SFAPI web service. You can only import applications for requisitions that are also imported.

- **Employee profile data doesn't overwrite.**
  When importing employee profile data, the overwrite feature doesn't apply the candidate profile background elements after the candidate profile has been manually updated. This is due to the way the data are stored when background elements are mapped between the employee and candidate profiles. If an employee profile data import is completed more than once, the additional imports could cause the background elements to be duplicated in the candidate profile.

- **Records are imported slowly.**
  The import job runs very slowly. This means that testing can take a long time, and, if you're importing hundreds of thousands of records, plan accordingly because this time line needs to be added to your production cutover time line.

- **No support is provided for team recruiting.**
  The operatorTeam fields in the recruiting team functionality aren't presently supported in the data migration import, nor will the admin settings populate automatically on requisitions created via the data migration import. In fact, you can't have the recruiting team functionality enabled on the requisition template when you import your requisitions. This will cause the job to fail. For data loading, you'll need to turn off recruiting team settings, import the files, turn recruiting team

back on, and then reset administrator defaults on *each* requisition to make them apply. This also can add considerable time to your cutover schedule.

- **No support is provided for the job code fields.**
  Job code entity `jobCode` field types are also not supported in the data migration import, nor will the values automatically populate from the job classification foundation object. You'll need to get creative here!

- **Imported attachments will appear as a candidate history document.**
  You can't import documents into the two document fields on the candidate profile. Any additional documents that are imported will be available as a candidate history document.

Read on to learn about what you need to watch out for while preparing the templates and testing your imports.

12.1.2   Data Migration "Gotchas"

Now that you know about the limitations of the data migration utility, there are some things that will be helpful to understand as you begin the work of completing your templates and testing the loads, as follows:

- **Time and date stamps**
  Each template will have a series of date and time stamps required for each record. The date/time values are stored in the time zone of your datacenter. For example, for an instance hosted in the US East Coast datacenter, to accurately reflect a last login date/time of January 1, 2016, at 8:00 AM Pacific Time, the value imported should use 2016-01-01T11:00:00. The system is incredibly finicky about these values, and every entry must be formatted precisely, or the job will fail.

- **Picklist fields**
  When importing values into fields that are picklists, first all of the picklist values in the import file must exist in your picklist in SAP SuccessFactors, or the job will fail. Picklist fields should use the picklist label value of the locale specified on the import job. The system will look up the appropriate picklist option ID based on this label and store the ID internally for proper multilingual handling. We'll discuss some tips later in this chapter for importing historical records that may have values no longer in use in SAP SuccessFactors.

- **Cascading picklist validation**
  Parent-child picklist values will be validated during the import, and mismatched values will cause the import to fail. Triple-check your picklist values in the import

file against the values in your picklists in the system. Any variation, such as a stray space, will cause the record to fail.

- **Language translations**
  If you're importing data in various language packs, the data in any one import file must be in only one locale; different locales will require different files.

- **Special characters and import files**
  While we're talking about languages, be very careful how you handle your flat file with special characters in use. Microsoft Excel doesn't handle special characters, so it's advisable to use another program that will generate a .csv file. The system will import what you provide it, including corrupted characters.

- **Working with multiple Recruiting templates**
  If you have multiple templates in your configuration, for example, more than one requisition template, the data for these templates should be imported in different files. This is logical because your different templates likely have different fields in them and different required attribute settings per field.

- **Specifying operators**
  Recruiting operator fields must use the user ID (not username) of the account.

So we've covered the limitations in data migration as well as some things to watch out for. Now let's look at each data object and discuss considerations for importing data against it.

12.2   Migrating Recruiting Entities

As we mentioned, various recruiting data entities may be migrated into the SAP SuccessFactors system:

- Requisitions
- Applications
- Application attachments
- Candidate profiles
- Candidate profile attachments (résumés and cover letters)
- Candidate profile background data
- Candidate tags

Let's discuss each entity and the parameters required to import data against that entity.

12.2.1   Requisitions

Requisitions of all statuses (**Unapproved**, **Approved**, and **Closed**) may be imported. **In-Progress** requisitions, those that are still being approved, will use the route map configured for the particular requisition template and will appear under the first step of the route map. **Approved** and **Closed** requisitions will appear in the system to have used a single-step route map.

Some mandatory fields must be completed and be present in the template for a successful load. Table 12.1 provides information on those mandatory fields.

Field ID	Description	Format	Notes
JobReqGuid	Job requisition ID	Any	This is a unique identifier from the legacy system. This value can be anything, and it's not visible in the UI. If importing requisitions from multiple systems, it's recommended to preface the system in this value (e.g., Taleo_1234).
jobReqTemplateId	The template ID of the template in SAP SuccessFactors	Number	Only one template ID should be imported in a single file.
templateType	The type of template (here, it's a requisition)	JOB_REQ	This value will be the same for every entry.
jobReqLocale	Locale of the content	xx_XX	Import one locale per import file.
formDueDate	Due date of the requisition	yyyy-MM-dd'T'HH:mm:ss	Put the actual date for approved and closed requisitions; put the anticipated date for unapproved requisitions.

Table 12.1 Mandatory Fields to Import Requisitions

Field ID	Description	Format	Notes
jobReqStatus	Status of the requisition	**Unapproved, Approved, Closed**	Provide the status of the requisition in SAP SuccessFactors terms.
creationDate	Date the requisition was created	Timestamp	N/A
lastUpdatedDate	Date the requisition was last updated	Timestamp	N/A
jobOpenDate	Date the requisition was opened	Timestamp	This is mandatory if the requisition is approved.
jobCloseDate	Date the requisition was closed	Timestamp	This is mandatory if the requisition is closed.
Title	Internal job title	Text	This is always required.
extTitle	External title	Text	This is mandatory if posted externally.

Table 12.1 Mandatory Fields to Import Requisitions (Cont.)

There will be other mandatory fields depending on whether you choose to provide posting dates in your import file. This isn't required; in fact, most businesses choose not to import posting dates because they want recruiters to go through each requisition to validate the data imported, make any necessary corrections, and then post the requisitions. In addition, any fields in your requisition template that have been set as required should also be included in the import file.

12.2.2   Applications

Applications are imported after both the requisitions and the candidate profiles because you must reference both in the application import file. Each application needs to have a unique identifier. This can be something you create for import; it's not visible in the UI and is only used for import purposes. Application attachments are handled in a separate import file, so just include application data in this file. The system will take the current candidate information in the system when the application is imported to create the candidate snapshot in the Candidate Workbench.

12

Note that you can't import the responses to prescreening questions because these don't reside on the application. If you have more than one application template, load the applications for different templates in different files. Remember that each requisition template references the application template, so you should have only one application-requisition combination in the same import file.

Mandatory fields for the application import are provided in Table 12.2.

Field ID	Description	Format	Notes
jobAppGuid	Application ID	Any	This is a unique identifier per application that is set by you.
jobReqGuid	Unique requisition ID	Any	This should reference the applicable requisition GUID set in the requisition import file.
candidateEmail-Address	Email address of the applicant	Email address	This ties the applicant to the requisition.
jobAppLocale	Locale of the applicant	xx_XX	This specifies the language pack of the applicant.
applicationDate	Date of application	yyyy-MM-dd'T'HH:mm:ss	This must be in this format down to :ss.
lastModified	Last date the application was modified	yyyy-MM-dd'T'HH:mm:ss	This must be in this format down to :ss.
internalstatusId	Status of the application	Text	Valid options are **Open**, **Disqualified**, or **Closed**.
statusItem	Status of the applicant in the status set	Text	Values are configured by you.

Table 12.2 Application Import Mandatory Fields

12.2.3   Application Attachments

After applications are imported, it's possible to import attachments that candidates may have included with their application in the legacy system. This is completed in a separate file. You can import attachments added by the candidate as well as attachments that may have been added by the recruiter. For example, if a candidate has completed a background check or drug screening, and the recruiter attached the results of that check, this attachment could be imported into SAP SuccessFactors.

Mandatory fields for application attachments include those listed in Table 12.3.

Field ID	Description	Format	Notes
jobAppGuid	Application ID	Any	This is a unique identifier per application that is set by you.
fieldId	Field ID of the attachment field	Text	Must be one of: resume, coverLetter, or the fieldID of a multi-attachment field defined in the application template.
filePath	References where the attachment file is stored	Text	This will always be a URL or file path to the location of the actual attachment on the SFTP server.

Table 12.3 Mandatory Fields for Application Attachments

12.2.4 Candidate Profiles

Candidate profiles store general information about a candidate, independent of the candidate's applications. The profile for import purposes encompasses the live profile data elements. Background data are imported in a separate file. Remember that for importing, we're only considering external candidates. Figure 12.1 shows an example candidate profile with a resume import file.

Any live profile field may be imported into the profile. There are no mandatory fields for the candidate profile. Note that you don't import a candidate ID in the file; this is automatically generated and assigned by the system. Résumés on the candidate profile are imported in this file as well. Be sure to provide the file path or URL to the actual file on the SFTP site.

primaryEmail	contactEmail	firstName	lastName	address	cellPhone	city	state	zip	country	lastLogin	resume
jsuaaa123@yahoo.com	aaa@yahoo.com	Stan	Hetcher	1 Townville Road	(379) 555 5337	Cincinnati	OH	45248	US	2009-01-31T19:01:59	a.doc
jsubbb@yahoo.com	bbbbbb@yahoo.com	Susan	Ghirtey		753-555-1367	Cincinnati	OH	45211	IN	2009-01-31T19:01:59	b.doc
jsuccc@hotmail.com	ccc@hotmail.com	Cynthia	Dalmond	2 Oak Dr		Oregonia	ON	ABC 123	CA	2009-01-31T19:01:59	c.doc
jsuddd@yahoo.com	ddd@yahoo.com	Raymond	McCullirs	3 Geneva Road	49 283 2938192	Maineville		45039	FR	2009-01-31T19:01:59	d.doc
jsueee@yahoo.com	eee@yahoo.com	Marlene	Cruise			Lebanon	PA	45036	US	2009-01-31T19:01:59	e.doc

Figure 12.1 Candidate Profiles with Résumés Imported in the Same File

> **Note**
>
> If you're importing résumés with your candidate profiles, the résumé files referenced within the import template must reside in the same directory on the SFTP site as the import file. If the files aren't in the same directory, the import will fail for that record.

12.2.5   Candidate Attachments

Candidate profiles with résumés are imported in the file discussed in the previous section. If your candidates have a cover letter and additional attachments, they can be imported using the candidate attachment file. Here you can import up to two additional files to associate with the candidate profile. As with the candidate profile import, there are no mandatory fields in the import file. You just need to make sure you have the `fieldId` referenced correctly, identify the candidate to whom the attachments belong, and then provide the URL or file path of the actual file(s) on the SFTP server (see Figure 12.2).

primaryEmail	fieldId	filePath
abc@yahoo.com	coverLetter	coverLetter1234.doc
abc@yahoo.com	candidateHistory	candidatehistory1234.doc
xyz@yahoo.com	candidateHistory	candidatehistory1235.doc

Figure 12.2 Importing Additional Attachments after Candidate Import

12.2.6   Candidate Background Fields

After candidate profiles are imported, you can import data into the various background elements that have been configured on your candidate profile template, for example, education and work history. The format of the candidate background import is very similar to the employee profile import files for internal employees. Be sure that your `CandidateID` in this file matches exactly the value in the `primaryEmail` field. Any date fields that are imported should follow the same date format of `yyyy-MM-dd-'T'HH:mm:ss`.

Figure 12.3 provides an example of how this import file should be formatted. Note that for every row or entry, you must specify the candidate `primaryEmail` and also repeat the background element ID. The first two fields (columns) for candidate background CSV should not be reordered. These carry the candidate ID and the background section ID information. The rest of the columns can appear in any order.

^CandidateId	outsideWorkExperience	employer	startTitle	businessType	startDate	endDate
abc@yahoo.com	outsideWorkExperience	GE	Analyst	Consumer Products	2005-01-01'T'12:00:00	2006-06-30'T'12:00:00
abc@yahoo.com	outsideWorkExperience	ABC Company	programmer	Software	2006-07-01'T'12:00:00	2007-07-31'T'12:00:00
^CandidateId	education	major	country	university	otheruniversity	degree
abc@yahoo.com	education	Engineering	United States	UC Berkeley		Bachelors
^CandidateId	languages	language	speakingProf	readingProf	writingProf	
xyz@yahoo.com	languages	Spanish	Intermediate	Intermediate	Intermediate	
xyz@yahoo.com	languages	Chinese	Beginner	Beginner	Beginner	
^CandidateId	certificates	name	description	institution	startDate	endDate
abc@yahoo.com	certificates	CPA	Certified Public Accoun	CPA Institute	2007-07-01'T'12:00:00	2008-07-01'T'12:00:00

Figure 12.3 Format of the Candidate Background Element Import File

12.2.7   Candidate Tags

You can import candidate tags after the candidate profiles have been imported and created. In the UI, tags are created on an ad hoc basis by recruiters. When imported, however, the tags must be created first and then assigned to candidates. In the candidate tag file, be sure to include the tag, the locale of the tag, and the userID of the user who created the tag.

After the tag file is imported, follow this by the candidate tag assignments file. This file will contain the same three fields as the first file with the addition of adding the candidate email address to make the assignments. Enter a row for each candidate and each tag.

12.2.8   Employee Profile Data for Internal Candidates

Although you can't import internal candidates into Recruiting because they already exist as employees, you can import background data into their employee profile, which will flow over to their candidate profile (assuming sync has been configured). This can create a better user experience for your internal candidates when they visit their candidate profile (and employee profile) and see data already there. To import data into the employee profile, you the use the **Import Extended User Information** feature in Admin Center. Choose the **Background Information** option, browse for the file, and then select **Import Extended User Data File**, as demonstrated in Figure 12.4.

Admin Center

Back to Admin Center

Import Extended User Information

Extended User Information is the extra information that forms the employee's user profile. You can add the extra user information by uploading (importing) a data file. If this is your first time, download the data import file template so you can see how it's formatted. Please note that some imports may take up to a few minutes depending on the size of the file.
SuccessTips:
- Import files in CSV format only. You can edit the file in MS Excel, then save it with the *.csv extension.
- Only import files for a single locale at a time.

File Name::   Browse...   No file selected.

Specify the Type of Information You Want to Import
○ Personal Information
○ Trend Information
◉ Background Information

▷ **Specify How You Want User Information Updated**

▷ **Specify Additional File Options**

| Download Data Import File Template | Import Extended User Data File |

Figure 12.4 Importing Internal Candidate Background Data into the Employee Profile

The background import can also be managed from provisioning as well. Set up the job(s) as shown in Figure 12.5. These import files typically have massive amounts of data, so it's advised to run these from provisioning rather than via the Admin Center. The Quartz scheduling engine is better able to handle large files with large amounts of data.

Job Definition

* **Job Name:**	Internal_InsideWork History
* **Job Owner :**	SF F Admin ⊚ Find User...
	The Job Owner will be used to authenticate all submitted jobs. They will also be the default user to receive E-mail notifications.
* **Job Type:**	Live Profile Import
Job Parameters:	* Live Profile Type:
	○ Personal Information
	○ Trend Information
	◉ Background Information
	Supported Locales: English US (English US) ⌄
	Character Encoding: Unicode (UTF-8) ⌄
	☐ Stop Import If Invalid Users Found
	☐ Overwrite Existing Data
	☐ Upload attachments along with Data.

Figure 12.5 Running Background Imports from the Quartz Scheduler in Provisioning

12.3   Setting Up the Jobs in Provisioning

After your import files are prepared, they will be loaded to your SAP SuccessFactors SFTP site, and jobs are run from provisioning to execute the imports. Jobs are created, edited, scheduled, and run from **Managing Job Schedule • Manage Scheduled Jobs**. When you pull up this page, you'll see all of the jobs that have already been created, whether they are submitted or not submitted. To create your recruiting import jobs, select the link at the top that says **Create New Job**. Choose the type of import from the list provided in the **Job Type** dropdown, as illustrated in Figure 12.6.

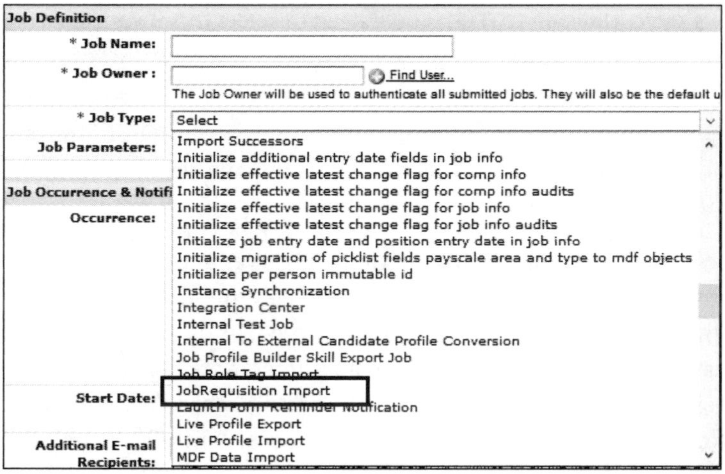

Figure 12.6 Select the Type of Recruiting Import from the List in Job Type.

There are several **Job Types** used for migrating Recruiting data. We'll examine them in the next section, starting with the **Candidate Profile Import** job.

12.3.1   Jobs to Import Candidate Profile Data

This job is used to import data into all the candidate-related entities. Depending on the entity, you'll select the appropriate parameters. In addition, you'll enter the following information for each candidate import job you create:

- **Job Name**
  It's suggested that you make this very descriptive as this section of provisioning can get very crowded, and searching for your job may prove difficult.
- **Job Owner**
  Here you'll select an active user from the user database to "own" the job. This user

423

will receive emails when the job starts, when it completes with results, and if there is an issue with the job running.

- **Job Type**
  From the dropdown menu, select the type of job you're running. The job type you select will drive the job parameters that are set.

- **Supported Locales**
  Select the appropriate locale for the data contained in the file. Remember that each file imported should contain only one locale.

- **Character Encoding**
  It's best to always select **Unicode (UTF-8)**; you'll need to select this if your file contains special characters for languages other than English.

- **Threshold for Failed Job Records**
  Select from the predefined list how many record fails the job will take. It's recommended to set it to more than the number of records in your file, or to 10,000 if you have more than 10,000 records.

After you've set the job information, you'll enter the SFTP server information and the username and password to access the server. You'll then determine if the job should be scheduled or run once. For these types of data loads, you'll likely run them manually so you don't have to worry about setting dates and times. Note that when you're testing and loading data into production, you may want to schedule some of the imports to run automatically so that your data can load consistently 24 hours a day until all data loads are complete. Figure 12.7 illustrates setting up the **Candidate Import** job.

Figure 12.7 Job Parameters for Importing Candidate Profiles

You can see in the **Job Parameters** section in Figure 12.7, that the candidate import job is used for loading candidate profiles as well as the background information, additional candidate attachments, and tag definitions and assignments.

12.3.2   Job to Import Requisitions

The parameters for the **JobRequisition Import** job are much simpler, as you can see in Figure 12.8. Here you'll just set the **Job Name**, **Job Owner**, and then the **Supported Locales**, **Character Encoding**, and **Threshold for Failed Job Records**. Again, make sure this is set high enough so your entire job runs without erroring out due to the threshold being met. All other details are the same as discussed in the previous section.

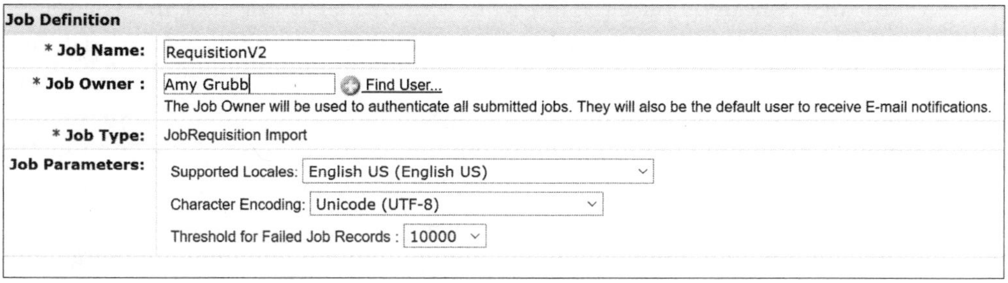

Figure 12.8 Parameters for the JobRequisition Import Job

The **Application Import** job will run after the job requisitions and the candidate profiles are loaded. Here the parameters are choosing whether you're importing applications or application attachments and can be seen in Figure 12.9. Again, you'll set the appropriate **Supported Locales**, **Character Encoding**, and **Threshold for Failed Job Records**.

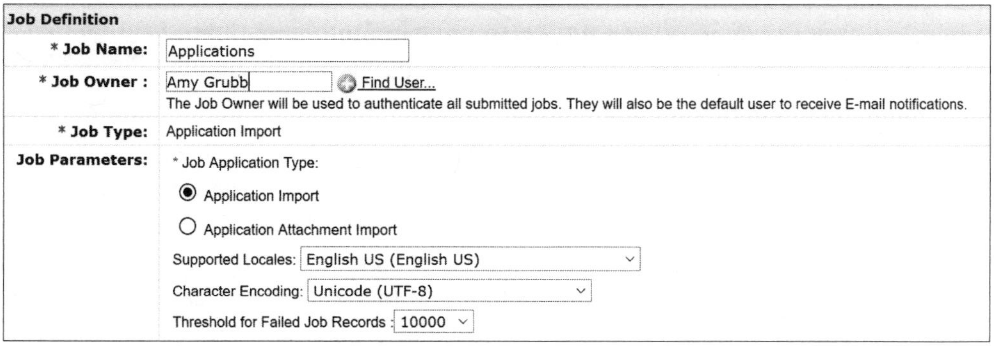

Figure 12.9 Application Import Parameters

If you have multiple files to load due to high volumes of data to bring over into SAP SuccessFactors, you may want to create several jobs for each type of import and consider scheduling some of them.

12.4   Data Migration Considerations and Best Practices

If you decide to import legacy data into your SAP SuccessFactors systems, there are some practical lessons learned and best practices that may prove valuable. We'll review some of those in this section:

- **Timeline**
  The first consideration is the impact to your overall project timeline. You should never underestimate how much time it's going to take to get your legacy data into the format and to reference the values you've configured in SAP SuccessFactors. Plan your time and then double it, at least! The testing process is very iterative, and you should test files with just a few records in them first to make sure you identify the issues you're going to have before you start trying to load a file with 10,000 rows. Because the import script is a `write` and not an `update` script, you can date stamp your template-specific GUIDs so you can use the same files over and over, which still creates new records. For example, if you want to test your requisition import file, and you have a `jobReqGUID` of `12345`, you can reuse this one record by adding a date stamp to the end, something like `12345_03102017`. Each time you want to run the file, update the date stamp, and you can be on your way. Repeat this with your job applications and candidate files as well.

- **Email address**
  Remember that the candidate's email address is his unique identifier for the system. You'll definitely want to date stamp the candidate IDs so that you don't have live email addresses in your test instance. This could have disastrous results if you decide to start testing emails using imported candidates.

- **Historical data**
  If you want to import historical data that may have values no longer in use, and if those values reside in a picklist field, you'll run into issues trying to work with the picklist and importing those values when they aren't included in the most recent configuration. For this purpose, you'll likely want to add the historical values to your impacted picklists, load the files, and then make the picklist values **Obsoleted**.

- **Planning for cutover**
  When you have all of your files tested and have ensured that they will run without errors, you should plan how many files for each template are needed and then test how long it takes the system to process the files. This will be critical for scheduling enough time during cutover to get all of the data loads done in time for go-live. Run a few files at different times of the day, and mark down how long it took the files to run at various parts of the day.

- **Legacy data**
  Sometimes, your legacy or historical data doesn't contain all of the data that you design to capture within SAP SuccessFactors, but it's still valuable data that you collected and that you want to retain for reporting purposes. In this case, you may want to consider making all of the fields on all impacted templates nonrequired so that you can load the data without any data in certain fields. After the files are processed, you can reapply all of the required attributes to the impacted templates.

- **File paths**
  When importing attachments, the actual files referenced in the attachment column in the import file must exist in the same directory on SFTP as the import file. The path then will reflect that as it might be */incoming/SJones.doc* if you're importing a résumé. The path would mean that the file and the import file would both sit in the */incoming* directory on the SFTP site. If the files to be imported and the import file aren't in the same directory, the job running the file won't find the files, and the record will fail.

- **Breaking up data**
  If you have a lot of data to import, it's advisable to break up your data by entity into multiple files. For example, if you have 100,000 candidate profiles to import, you may want to break up the data into four files of 25,000 records each. As we discussed, the job that runs the file and loads the data into the entities runs slow and is impacted by server activity. Breaking up the data into more manageable files will improve the speed of the files being processed somewhat.

These are just a few considerations and best practices gleaned from years of experience. While this list is by no means exhaustive, it hopefully provides some foundation and also some pitfalls to avoid when attempting this time-consuming and labor-intensive activity.

12.5 Summary

Migrating legacy historical data is a time-consuming, laborious process. After the decision is made, it's important to determine how much data you'll bring over and begin estimating the amount of time necessary to complete the related tasks. Knowing the limitations of the SAP SuccessFactors systems for the desired data will help set expectations and give everyone a clear picture of what can and can't be done. With so many different types of data involved in SAP SuccessFactors, there are certainly options for making the most of your existing data. However, the amount of time involved to cleanse the data and test the loads may prove too costly to the timeline and budgeted resources, as well as impact your ability to meet your planned system launch date. Given all of the considerations discussed, you may decide to forgo this activity altogether.

We've mentioned locales and languages a few times in this chapter, and in the next chapter, we'll turn our attention to discussing language translations and their impact on Recruiting.

Chapter 13
Language Translations

In today's global economy, organizations need to provide support to their employees and others in multiple languages, especially when hiring within a global or multinational organization. Candidates will want to see job postings in their language and expect systems to support those needs. SAP SuccessFactors has the multilanguage support that global organizations need to hire candidates in all geographic areas.

Organizations that operate in multiple countries often have a need to make the recruiting system available in multiple languages for their users. These users include both internal users of the system, such as recruiters, hiring managers, and HR representatives, and both internal and external candidates searching and applying for jobs. Sometimes organizations post jobs in multiple languages in different geographic markets to appeal to a wider applicant base. Other times, companies have business operations in countries that have requirements around local languages. An example of this is providing systems in French for employees and candidates in Quebec, Canada. In these situations, companies need to find solutions that support their business and regulatory requirements for language support.

Being a robust, global system, SAP SuccessFactors Recruiting offers multiple language support for organizations to provide a true global recruiting solution. In this chapter, we'll discuss what language support features Recruiting provides and some considerations for evaluating how to leverage these features within your Recruiting deployment. Specifically, we'll discuss the following:

- Language packs
- Recruiting languages
- Considerations for implementing language support

Let's begin with a discussion of the language packs supported in Recruiting.

13.1 Language Packs and Recruiting Languages

One of the early decisions a company makes when implementing SAP SuccessFactors Recruiting Management is which languages to enable. Language packs are the means by which SAP SuccessFactors controls language versions. These language packs will provide predelivered standard translations for navigation and some other standard elements of the system. Let's look at the language packs available and how users can update their language preference. We'll first discuss the languages available.

13.1.1 Available Languages

SAP SuccessFactors provides language packs that will translate the user interface (UI) into particular languages. Nearly 50 different language packs can be enabled within provisioning and made available within the instance. In some cases, there are multiple language packs for a single language to accommodate nuances in language based on country. For example, there are language packs for Spanish, both for Spain and Mexico, and French for France and French Canadian, among others.

Language packs don't need to be licensed individually. They are all available for all you to enable as needed. The language packs available within SAP SuccessFactors are provided in Table 13.1. It's important to note that these language packs aren't specific to Recruiting. The language packs apply to the entire SAP SuccessFactors suite and will translate every module in play within your landscape.

Language Pack	Language Key
Bahasa Indonesia (Indonesian)	bs_ID
Bahasa Melayu (Malay)	bs_BS
Català (Catalan)	ca_ES
Čeština (Czech)	cs_CZ
Cymraeg (Welsh)	cy_GB
Dansk (Danish)	da_DK
Deutsch (German)	de_DE
English Debug	en_DEBUG
English Debug Apostrophe	en_DEBUG_APOS

Table 13.1 Language Packs Available within SAP SuccessFactors

Language Pack	Language Key
English Debug Apostrophe RTL	en_DEBUG_APOS_RTL
English RTL (English US)	en_RTL
English UK (English UK)	en_GB
English US (English US)	en_US
Español (Mexico)	es_MX
Español (Spanish)	es_ES
Français (French)	fr_FR
Français canadien (Canadian French)	fr_CA
Hrvatski (Croatian)	hr_HR
Italiano (Italian)	it_IT
Magyar (Hungarian)	hu_HU
Nederlands (Dutch)	nl_NL
Norsk (Norwegian)	no_NO
Norsk bokmål (Norwegian Bokmål)	nb_NO
Polski (Polish)	pl_PL
Português (Portuguese)	pt_PT
Português do Brasil (Brazilian Portuguese)	pt_BR
Română (Romanian)	ro_RO
Schweizer Hochdeutsch (Swiss High German)	de_CH
Slovenčina (Slovak)	sk_SK
Slovenščina (Slovenian)	sl_SI
Srpski (Serbian)	sr_RS
Suomi (Finnish)	fi_FI
Svenska (Swedish)	sv_SW

Table 13.1 Language Packs Available within SAP SuccessFactors (Cont.)

Language Pack	Language Key
Svenska (Swedish)	sv_SE
Tiếng Việt (Vietnamese)	vi_VN
Türkçe (Turkish)	tr_TR
Ελληνικά (Greek)	el_GR
Български (Bulgarian)	bg_BG
Русский (Russian)	ru_RU
Українська мова (Ukrainian)	uk_UA
עִבְרִית (Hebrew)	iw_IL
العربية (Arabic)	ar_SA
हिंदी (Hindi)	hi_IN
ภาษาไทย (Thai)	th_TH
한국어 (Korean)	ko_KR
日本語 (Japanese)	ja_JP
简体中文 (Simplified Chinese)	zh_CN
繁體中文 (Traditional Chinese)	zh_TW

Table 13.1 Language Packs Available within SAP SuccessFactors (Cont.)

13.1.2   Updating Language Preference

When languages are enabled, users within SAP SuccessFactors can choose to change their language to display the interface in that new language on the **Options** tab, as shown in Figure 13.1.

As soon as the language preference is saved, the screen refreshes, and the UI is immediately presented in the new language. The language pack will translate all navigation throughout the system. Any custom content isn't included in this translation and must be done within the particular module or feature. For example, any custom tiles that have been defined to display in English will still be displayed in English unless an administrator provides the translation into the languages available. You can see the UI translated into French after the language preference is updated in Figure 13.2.

Options

Password

Start Page

Sub Tab Configuration

Notifications

Change Language

Compensation Number
Format

Forms

Accessibility Settings

Proxy

Groups

Change Language

Changing Language will redirect you to the Homepage.

- ○ Deutsch (German)
- ○ English UK (English UK)
- ○ Español (Spanish)
- ○ Português do Brasil (Brazilian Portuguese)
- ○ 한국어 (Korean)
- ○ 简体中文 (Simplified Chinese)
- ○ English Debug
- ◉ English US (English US)
- ○ Français (French)
- ○ Русский (Russian)
- ○ 日本語 (Japanese)

Switch

Figure 13.1 Changing Language Preferences on the Options Tab

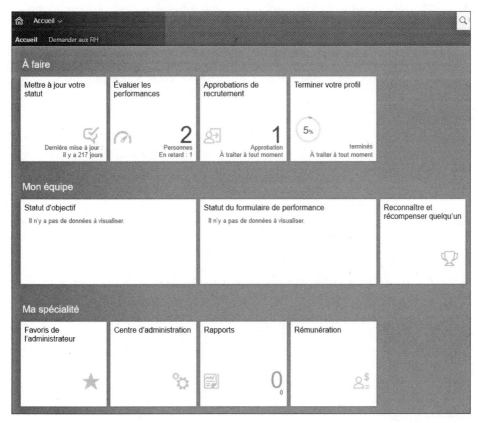

Figure 13.2 The SAP SuccessFactors System Translated into French after Updating Language
Preferences

13.2   Language Translations in Recruiting

Deciding to implement language translations in Recruiting is a bit more of an involved discussion than whether you want to make language packs available to your users. In Recruiting, all of the field definitions are defined in a series of templates maintained in provisioning. It's common to have many custom fields defined in Recruiting in addition to using the standard Recruiting fields available. All of the translations for all languages implemented must be configured into all templates within Recruiting. Figure 13.3 provides an example of a requisition template that includes translations in US English, UK English, and German. Each language that is translated will have its own space for every field definition in every template. This can represent a significant amount of work and increase the overall project timeline, especially if you implement several languages. Additionally, when updates are required, they must be made within the template and then uploaded into provisioning. As a result, it's not something you can maintain yourself.

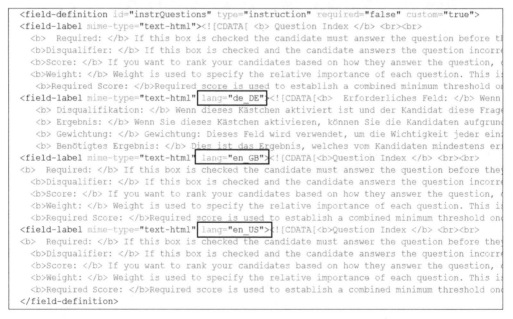

Figure 13.3 Each Language Pack Requires Its Own Translation in the Requisition Template

In addition, you have to consider that there are different consumers of your Recruiting data and different types of data—internal candidates that access job openings directly from within SAP SuccessFactors where they may view the interface in their local language, and external candidates who are consumers of job postings on job boards and your external career site. Both types of consumers have different entry points and will view different data. Are you going to provide your career pages in additional language translations or choose to hire in one language? Will you translate job descriptions or just the interface of the careers pages? How will translations impact postings on job boards?

As you can see, several questions need to be thought through before deciding whether or not to implement languages within your Recruiting system. There is no one right answer, and companies should understand the implications of choosing to move forward so informed decisions can be made.

13.2.1   Setting Recruiting Languages

Regardless of what you decide to do around implementing Recruiting in multiple languages, it's necessary to enable and establish at least one Recruiting language. If you don't do this, you won't be able to set up your applicant status set (**Talent Pipeline**) in Admin Center because it's required to specify at least one language.

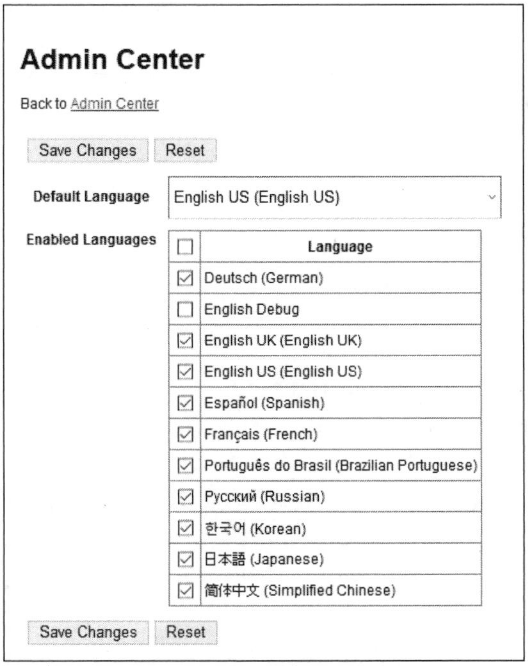

Figure 13.4 Setting the Recruiting Languages and the Default Language

To set at least one Recruiting language, you must enable it in **Manage Recruiting Languages** within Admin Center. Within **Manage Recruiting Languages,** you'll see a list of all the language packs that have been enabled in your instance. You'll also see the selection for the **Default Language**. The default language determines which language will be shown to users in cases where fields have not been translated into their specified language. Make the necessary selections under the **Enabled Languages,** and save your changes. Figure 13.4 provides an example of enabling Recruiting languages.

13.2.2   Choosing Which Language Packs to Implement

When you implement Recruiting as part of a larger overall SAP SuccessFactors project, it's likely that the decision of which languages to implement will be influenced by the other modules that are being implemented. The first obvious step in deciding which languages to deploy is to look at the countries in which you operate and the languages spoken there. Another consideration is planning for the future and looking at whether you'll be expanding into other regions or countries in the near future.

After you have the list of languages where you currently operate and plan to operate, you need to consider language variants. For example, if you operate in both the United Kingdom and the United States, will you implement the US English language pack, the UK English language pack, or both? Though the differences are often subtle, they do exist and are impactful to users. If you choose to implement two language packs for the same language, there are some nuances of which you need to be aware. Let's assume you implement both the US and UK English language packs, but primarily do your configuration in US English. There will be some considerations that will need to be factored into the work as described next.

Email Notifications

With multiple language packs, you'll need to provide translated versions of notifications in both US and UK language variants. If you're a recruiter with UK English as the preferred language and want to send an email to a candidate, by default, the system will show you only those templates that are available in UK English. This is the case even if there are more templates available in US English that are relevant for the UK. To send those other emails, you'll need to change the language dropdown to select a template in US English, or translate the template into UK English as shown in Figure 13.5. Maintaining the same content in two variants of the same language adds to the maintenance burden and can result in templates not being updated properly in both languages.

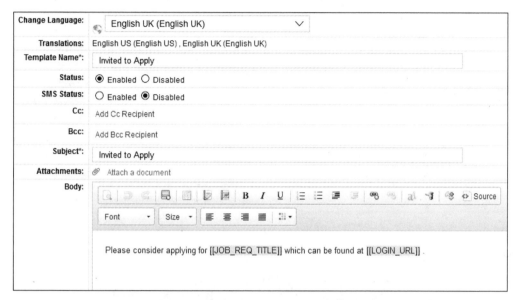

Figure 13.5 Maintaining Notifications in All Applicable Language Packs for the Best Candidate and Recruiter Experience

Applicant Status Maintenance

We discussed the maintenance of the applicant status set in Chapter 8. When language translations are involved, there is additional maintenance that needs to occur on each status to ensure you're communicating appropriately to your candidates. As you can see in Figure 13.6, all of the Recruiting languages enabled are available to translate on each status. You'll want to be sure to provide translations for the **Candidate Label** and **Next Step Text** for each status so you can ensure your candidates' needs are being addressed. If you don't translate these labels into each language, the candidate is apt to see them displayed as **[Not Translated in selected language]**, which we can all agree isn't a good candidate experience.

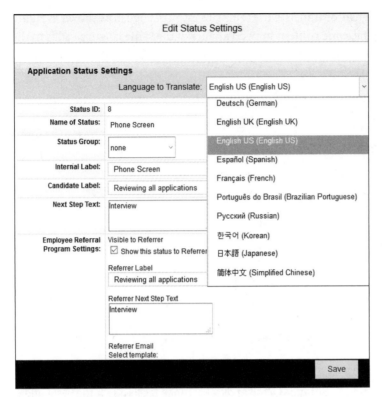

Figure 13.6 Translating Each Applicant Status in Recruiting Languages

The **Next Step Text** will display as blank if that text hasn't been maintained in the language variant in which the candidate is logged in. For example, the technical status name for the initial status a candidate lands in when they apply is **Default**. If you don't maintain the candidate label in a language, that is how it will display to candidates logged in in that language. If you define a **Next Step Text** for candidates to help them know where their application is in the process but don't translate it, the field will appear blank. Figure 13.7 shows an example of the candidate's view of their application if they are logged in with UK English.

Jobs Applied						
Job Title ↓	Actions	Req ID	Date Applied	Status	Status Date	Next Step
Project Manager	Select ∨	2122	11/11/2016	Thank you for your application! You've been short listed for a phone interview.	11/11/2016	We will be in contact with you in the next 5-10 business days.

Figure 13.7 Candidate View of Jobs Applied with Translations in UK English

13.2.3 Choosing What Areas of the System to Translate

After you decide on your language packs and Recruiting languages, another important decision to make is what parts of the system you want to translate into which languages. You can translate all parts of the system in all languages, or you could break it down and translate parts of the system in all languages or parts of the system in a subset of languages. For example, you can choose to make the UI available for translation via a language pack and provide translated job descriptions so candidates can review them in their local language, but leave the **Requisition** and **Application** fields in the default language. Translating only parts of the system will save time and money, but there are some things you need to consider with the approach.

Some clients, for example, have a standard global language used internally, such as English, but they want to advertise positions in different languages and allow candidates to apply in those languages. In these cases, the clients make the decision to only translate candidate-facing parts of the system and keep the rest in English. If you decide to take this approach, be sure that your recruiters are able to read and understand applications that are submitted in other languages. For example, if you translate the system into Japanese and post a position in Japanese, recruiters processing those applicants will need to understand Japanese.

There are some drawbacks to translating either only the internal-facing parts of the system or only the external-facing parts. Because translations in Recruiting are partly based on standard translations that are delivered in language packs as well as on translation of custom fields and recruiting content, this approach can lead to a mixture of languages on screens. Figure 13.8 shows an example where the Dutch language pack was applied, but custom fields weren't translated. As you can see, the standard parts of the system appear in Dutch, with some English fields mixed in.

A more common approach to translating parts of the system is to look at the individual components outlined in the following list and determine which make sense to translate into which languages. For example, prescreening questions that only apply to certain countries only need to be translated into languages where the questions will be used. Clients may also have correspondence templates and offer letters that only apply to a specific country or countries as well. These would not need to be translated into all languages.

Figure 13.8 Candidate Profile with a Dutch Language Pack with Custom Fields in a Default Language

Some elements that can be translated are as follows:

- **Recruiting templates**

  These include the candidate profile, requisition, application, and offer approval.

- **Custom help text**

  This is field-level help that can be defined for fields on Recruiting templates.

- **Standard fields**

  Standard fields come predelivered with translations, but some can be relabeled and translations changed to meet your business needs.

- **Picklist values**

  These are values shown in dropdown lists. Some picklists come pretranslated by SAP SuccessFactors. Any custom picklists must be translated by the business.

- **Correspondence**

  This includes Recruiting email notifications, offer letters, as well as email notifications shared between modules.

- **Applicant status sets**
  This includes internal and external status labels, candidate next step texts, and referrer texts.

- **Prescreening questions**
  These are added to the requisition and presented to candidates in the application process.

- **Route maps**
  These include approval step names and instructional texts.

- **Rating scales**
  These are used in Interview Central by internal Recruiting users to describe the scale used when evaluating candidates after an interview.

- **Career sites**
  This refers to the navigation and landing page of the career sites. The internal and external career sites can be treated independently when it comes to translations. In other words, you can translate one and not the other if desired.

- **Data privacy consent statements**
  These are relevant only for businesses that have configured data privacy consent statements.

13.3   How Recruiting Elements Are Translated

As mentioned, adding translations into Recruiting has various parts and touches many different areas of the system. Translations can be made in the following:

- Provisioning
- Templates
- Admin Center
- Recruiting external site
- Data such as job descriptions, competencies, and picklist values

When translations are in scope, the work begins after the configuration is stable. It's recommended not to begin translation work until the configuration of the system is signed off because any change in the configuration will impact the translations in process or that have already been applied to the system/configuration. The businesses are responsible for providing the actual translations for any fields and areas of the system that aren't covered by language packs. After the final configuration has been signed off, the recruiting implementation consultant will prepare a translation workbook. The translation workbook is usually prepared as a spreadsheet document and includes all fields that can be translated, separated into tabs by template and element. An example translation workbook is shown in Figure 13.9. When prepared, the workbook will have all fields to be translated and what the values are in the **Default Language** and then columns for all the languages in which each field will be translated. These columns will be blank until the translation work is complete.

The client is responsible for either translating the workbook or having it translated by a translation agency. After the translations have been completed, the client hands the translation workbook back over to the consultant who configures the translations in the system. When the consultant completes the translations, the business verifies the translations are correctly configured.

	English US	English UK	French	Japanese	Korean	Spanish
1	English US	English UK	French	Japanese	Korean	Spanish
10	Default Language	Default Language	Langue par défaut	Default Language	Default Language	Default Language
30	Job Posting Language	Job Posting Language	Langue de la description de poste	Job Posting Language	Job Posting Language	Job Posting Language
40	If you are not the budget owner please click the "Add Approver" button and select your budget owner to approve this Req. If you do not know who your budget owner is please contact your Manager.	If you are not the budget owner please click the "Add Approver" button and select your budget owner to approve this Req. If you do not know who your budget owner is please contact your Manager.	Si vous n'êtes pas le/la responsable du budget, veuillez cliquer sur le bouton « Ajouter un approbateur » et sélectionner le nom du/de la responsable du budget pour approuver le poste à pourvoir. Si vous ne savez pas qui est votre responsable de budget, communiquez avec votre gestionnaire.	If you are not the budget owner please click the "Add Approver" button and select your budget owner to approve this Req. If you do not know who your budget owner is please contact your Manager.	If you are not the budget owner please click the "Add Approver" button and select your budget owner to approve this Req. If you do not know who your budget owner is please contact your Manager.	If you are not the budget owner please click the "Add Approver" button and select your budget owner to approve this Req. If you do not know who your budget owner is please contact your Manager.
50	Please make sure to verify Internal Equity before approving this req.	Please make sure to verify Internal Equity before approving this req.	Assurez-vous de vérifier l'équité interne avant d'approuver ce poste à pourvoir.	Please make sure to verify Internal Equity before approving this req.	Please make sure to verify Internal Equity before approving this req.	Please make sure to verify Internal Equity before approving this req.
60	<table frame="border" width="100%"><tr><td style="background-color:#EE8013" valign="bottom"><b>Requis	<table frame="border" width="100%"><tr><td style="background-color:#EE8013" valign="bottom"><b>Requis	<table frame="border" width="100%"><tr><td style="background-color:#EE8013" valign="bottom"><b>Détails	<table frame="border" width="100%"><tr><td style="background-color:#EE8013" valign="bottom"><b>Requis	<table frame="border" width="100%"><tr><td style="background-color:#EE8013" valign="bottom"><b>Requis	<table frame="border" width="100%"><tr><td style="background-color:#EE8013" valign="bottom"><b>Requis

Figure 13.9 A Completed Translation Workbook

Tip

When working with completed translation workbooks, don't use Microsoft Excel. It doesn't support special characters, and the translations will likely be corrupted. Use a spreadsheet program other than Excel for all work with language translations, including picklists. Just be sure to save the files as .csv before importing.

Translations of fields in Recruiting templates, such as the requisition, candidate pro-file, application, and offer approval are generally configured directly in the XML tem-plate during implementation. This method allows you to configure translations for multiple fields in one template at one time. This is done by configuring the `field-label` element in the XML, which determines the field label displayed on the screen. A separate `field-label` element must be added in the template XML for each custom field and language as shown in Figure 13.10. Here you see two requisition fields that have translations for nine languages. Notice that each language must be declared as a separate line with the necessary label. The first `field-label` definition is for the default language and is equally as important as the individual language packs. Remember that if a user has a language preference set that hasn't been translated, the user will be presented with the default language.

```
<field-definition id="cust_targetEquity" type="currency" required="false" custom="true"
<field-label><![CDATA[Target Equity]]></field-label>
<field-label lang="de_DE"><![CDATA[Zielanteil ]]></field-label>
<field-label lang="en_US"><![CDATA[Target Equity ]]></field-label>
<field-label lang="es_ES"><![CDATA[Capital objetivo ]]></field-label>
<field-label lang="fr_FR"><![CDATA[Actions cibles ]]></field-label>
<field-label lang="it_IT"><![CDATA[Quote azionarie target ]]></field-label>
<field-label lang="ja_JP"><![CDATA[エクイティターゲット ]]></field-label>
<field-label lang="pt_BR"><![CDATA[Target na Participação das ações ]]></field-label>
<field-label lang="ru_RU"><![CDATA[Целевой бонус ]]></field-label>
<field-label lang="tr_TR"><![CDATA[Hisse Senedi Hakedişi ]]></field-label>
<field-description><![CDATA[Target Equity]]></field-description>
</field-definition>
<field-definition id="cust_otherAllowance" type="text" required="false" custom="true">
<field-label><![CDATA[Other Allowance]]></field-label>
<field-label lang="de_DE"><![CDATA[Weitere Zuschüsse ]]></field-label>
<field-label lang="en_US"><![CDATA[Other Allowance ]]></field-label>
<field-label lang="es_ES"><![CDATA[Otra prestación ]]></field-label>
<field-label lang="fr_FR"><![CDATA[Autre indemnité ]]></field-label>
<field-label lang="it_IT"><![CDATA[Altre agevolazioni ]]></field-label>
<field-label lang="ja_JP"><![CDATA[その他手当 ]]></field-label>
<field-label lang="pt_BR"><![CDATA[Outra concessão ]]></field-label>
<field-label lang="ru_RU"><![CDATA[Другие надбавки ]]></field-label>
<field-label lang="tr_TR"><![CDATA[Diğer Teşvikler ]]></field-label>
</field-definition>
```

Figure 13.10 Requisition Fields Translated in Multiple Languages

After a client is live, the client may choose to update translations themselves using the **Manage Templates** functionality in Admin Center. Navigate to **Admin Center • Manage Templates**. From there, select the template that includes the field that needs to be translated, and then select the field itself. Click **Add More+** under the **Field Label** field to add or update translations as shown in Figure 13.11 and Figure 13.12. Note that while this is supported, you may experience issues saving the translations. If this occurs, try using a different browser, or work with your professional services partner to update the translation.

Figure 13.11 Finding the Recruiting Field in Manage Templates in Admin Center

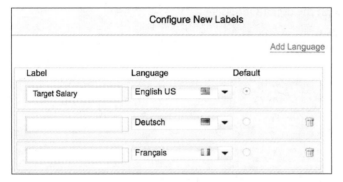

Figure 13.12 Adding Multiple Language Translations per Field with the Add Language Feature

13.4   Other Considerations

There are a few other aspects you need to take into consideration when you choose to translate your Recruiting system into multiple languages. You should keep in mind the language of the requisition, the language spoken by your recruiters, impacts to picklists, and reporting. Let's discuss each one of these in a bit more detail.

13.4.1   Requisition Language

When you define your Recruiting languages in Admin Center you need to specify one language as default. If you deploy multiple languages, you can choose to enable the setting **Use originator's preferred language as the default language of a new job**

requisition. This setting is found in **Admin Center • Recruiting Settings** under the **Job Requisition** section. Enabling this setting means that the Recruiting default language is ignored when a new requisition is created, and instead the Recruiting user's preferred language is used. Obviously, enabling this setting should be thoroughly understood and communicated before enabling.

Recruiting users need to ensure they then pay attention to the posting language regardless of whether this setting is enabled or not. If the setting is enabled, by default, the requisition posting will be set to the language in which the requisition was created. So for example, if a recruiter in Russia has her preferred language set to Russian, anytime she creates a requisition, the posting language will be set to Russian by default. This means that any candidate viewing the posting will see it in Russian. If she is recruiting for a position located in the United Kingdom, she will need to add UK English as the posting language so that English-speaking candidates will be presented with the English posting.

A common early mistake by businesses is to assume that the language in which the candidate accesses the system determines the language of the job posting they see. A posting must exist in the corresponding language variant for an applicant to access the posting in that language.

13.4.2   Language Spoken by Recruiters

Another consideration is the languages spoken by your recruiters. If a job is posted in multiple languages, the recruiters working on that requisition will need to understand all of those languages to evaluate applicants. This is one reason why many companies choose to have an official language for recruiting purposes and present job postings and templates in that language. Another option for dealing with this is approaching multilanguage postings with a team of recruiters that can cover all of the possible languages applicants may speak.

13.4.3   Reporting

When language translations are in scope, it's always important to remember the impact that translations may have on reporting. While it may seem obvious, many businesses are surprised when they run reports and don't see translations! Remember that reports will only be output in those languages for which you have translations. If you haven't provided picklist translations for French, don't expect to see picklist fields on a report in French. They will be displayed in the default language. Reporting on free-text fields will be output in the language in which they are maintained. There is also the case sometimes where a business's foundation objects are maintained in a single language, which results in fields that you may expect to be translated appearing in the single default language. The impact on reporting should be included in the discussion when deciding whether to implement languages. In fact, reporting may be important enough to drive the decision to implement certain languages.

13.4.4   Picklists and UTF-8

You need to be thoroughly trained in maintaining picklists for a multilingual system and understand the impact of any updates prior to maintaining the picklists. It doesn't matter if you're only changing or adding English picklist values. You can easily cause negative consequences to all picklists if you don't understand what you're doing. Picklist management in general is outside the scope of this book; however, we'll discuss it in general terms in relation to translations.

First, as mentioned when discussing translation workbooks, picklist files should always be managed in a program other than Excel. Many a business has uploaded picklist values with corrupted characters by downloading the picklist file, opening it in Excel, and then importing it back to the system. When managing translated picklists (or really any picklists), you should work with only one picklist at a time. This reduces the risk of unintentionally impacting other picklists. Download the full picklist file, and save it as an original. Open the file in a non-Excel program, and delete all other picklists besides the one you need to maintain. Keep your original file so you can revert back, should the need arise. Make the needed updates, save as a .csv file, and reimport into the system.

To manage special characters and formatting, picklist files should always be downloaded in UTF-8 Unicode formatting and imported with this option as well. Be sure to make this selection when you export and import. Figure 13.13 shows selecting **Unicode (UTF-8)** when exporting a picklist.

If you don't have translations for all language packs, simply copy and paste the default language values into the corresponding language columns.

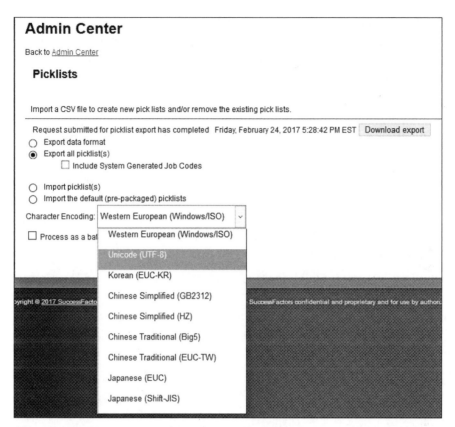

Figure 13.13 Selecting Unicode (UTF-8) as the Character Encoding before Exporting and Importing Picklists with Translations

13.4.5 New Languages Post Go-Live

Adding a new language after you're already live with Recruiting requires some thought and planning. It will be important to maintain good documentation of what has already been translated and keep this up to date as changes are made, so that you can consider the current scope of languages and don't cause any negative impacts to those already in use. As we discussed in Section 13.2.2, you'll need to determine which parts of the system will be translated into the new language. You should also be conservative when estimating the time it will take to implement the new language. While a translation workbook may not need to be created from scratch, one should be prepared. Build in time to have the translations completed either by internal resources or a vendor. Then remember that all translations should first be applied in the test instance, tested thoroughly, and signed off on before moving to production. Depending on what elements are translated, this could be a project in its own right. Plan accordingly!

13.5   Summary

SAP SuccessFactors Recruiting supports recruiting efforts in countries across the globe in multiple languages. While it may seem like an obvious decision to implement languages, there are many things that need to be considered before moving ahead. Understanding the different parts that language plays within Recruiting and how it impacts the consumers of your system, both internal and external, is critical to making the right decisions for the organization.

After the decision is made to use language translations and how they will be incorporated into Recruiting, this work will need to be built into the overall project time line. Remember that most partners, or SAP Professional Services, won't do the actual translating of the words. This will need to be done by internal resources or a vendor based on a workbook that is prepared by the consultant supporting you.

After translations are in place, it's critical to thoroughly communicate the impact of languages and how they are addressed within your landscape to your Recruiting users so they understand that what they do in creating and posting requisitions can impact what a candidate can see. This topic can be confusing to some, so take the time to make sure everyone is on the same page.

Finally, take the time to keep your translation documentation up to date! You'll appreciate the time invested when you need to make an update or choose to introduce a new language into your configuration.

Now let's turn to a discussion on integrating Recruiting with SAP SuccessFactors Employee Central and SAP ERP Human Capital Management (SAP ERP HCM).

Chapter 14

Integrating Recruiting with Employee Central and SAP ERP HCM

Many companies leverage SAP SuccessFactors Recruiting to support their talent acquisition processes without implementing SAP Success-Factors Onboarding. In this instance, there are integration points to and from Recruiting and the human resource information system (HRIS). If you use SAP SuccessFactors Employee Central or SAP ERP Human Capital Management (SAP ERP HCM) to maintain your core HR processes, there are standard integrations you can use. If you're looking to implement SAP SuccessFactors Recruiting standalone, read on!

Several scenarios call for SAP SuccessFactors Recruiting data integrating with your core HRIS. Whether you're using positions in HRIS to drive open requisitions or simply passing new hire data to your system of record, there are two main system touchpoints that may be involved to integrate Recruiting with the HRIS. With Recruiting, standard integration is available for Employee Central for companies that run core HR processes in the cloud, as well as integration with SAP ERP HCM for those companies that run HR processes on premise.

Integrating Recruiting with Employee Central is contained solely within the SAP SuccessFactors suite. There is no other technology required to implement this integration. Depending on whether you're implementing position management or new hire integration, configuration is handled nearly completely in the SAP SuccessFactors Admin Center. Integrating Employee Central position management with Recruiting provides numerous benefits:

- Create a requisition form a position in the position org chart and automatically derive the job profile and specified data values of the job:
  - Create on the current date to open a requisition immediately.
  - Schedule creation of the requisition on a future date, and the system will create the requisition when the date is reached.

- Show assigned job requisition or position requisition processing request on the position title (with v12 of the position org chart).
- Show more job requisition data in the **Position** side panel.
- Use the rules engine to derive the job requisition template to be used for the new requisition.
- Use the rules engine to define field mapping between the position and the new requisition.
- Use the job scheduler to automatically create the job requisition from request objects.
- Automatically assign the candidate from the requisition in pending hires in Employee Central to the position linked to the requisition.

Of course, creating requisitions this way increases the integrity of the data on the requisition and ensures that only open positions are being filled. This isn't only a time savings for those who create requisitions, it's a check for the hiring needs within the organization.

For companies that manage HR processes in SAP ERP HCM, there is also a standard integration package that supports creating requisitions in Recruiting when a position is opened or vacated in SAP ERP HCM. The same benefits of data integrity and time savings that are gained with Employee Central position management also apply here. SAP ERP HCM communicates with Recruiting via SAP Process Integration (SAP PI) middleware to pass a series of reports that will send position data to SAP SuccessFactors to generate the creation of a requisition and keep it updated throughout the talent acquisition process as changes occur. Then it will pull data from Recruiting when candidates have been identified for hire. The data are staged in SAP ERP HCM and reviewed before processed as a new employee master record.

Implementing SAP ERP HCM positions to Recruiting integration requires implementation of the SAP PI middleware as well as configuration of both SAP ERP HCM and Recruiting. You'll need resources that are familiar with your SAP ERP HCM configuration to undertake those setup and configuration tasks. Sometimes there are configuration changes that will be required to accommodate the integration, and depending on business requirements, you may need to implement Business Add-Ins (BAdIs) within SAP. Likewise, there are configuration requirements on the SAP SuccessFactors side to add standard fields within the integration package to accommodate the data transfer between systems.

In this chapter, we'll discuss the integration points between Recruiting and Employee Central, covering prerequisites, basic setup, and configuration, as well as field mapping. We'll also discuss the standard integration package between SAP ERP HCM and Recruiting to trigger requisition creation. We'll also review the prerequisites in both systems and discuss the configuration at a high level. You should refer to the standard package documentation maintained by SAP for detailed information on how to configure SAP ERP HCM to support this integration.

We'll also review the backend integration points of sending new hire data from Recruiting to Employee Central to support the hiring action. We'll cover how to set up the integration and complete the field mapping so data flows from Recruiting to Employee Central. This is in the absence of the SAP SuccessFactors Onboarding module. We'll discuss integration with Onboarding and Employee Central in Chapter 21.

We'll then discuss the standard SAP ERP HCM new hire integration package available from Recruiting. This integration package will queue new hire data from Recruiting to your SAP ERP HCM system so hires can be processed. This is also in the absence of Onboarding. Refer to Chapter 21 for a discussion of integrating Onboarding with SAP ERP HCM.

Let's start our discussion by looking at Employee Central position management integration with Recruiting.

14.1   Employee Central Position Management and Recruiting Integration

In the previous section, we highlighted some of the benefits of integrating position management with Recruiting to increase the integrity of your data by eliminating the need for requisition originators to fill in fields, many of which they may not know how to complete. The mapping of data already maintained on the position to the requisition isn't only a time savings for users, it ensures that the correct values are selected. It also queues up the position for easy hiring of the successful candidate after the recruiting process is concluded. In this section, we'll discuss position management integration with Recruiting to create requisitions and cover the following:

- Prerequisites and initial configuration
- Configuring the integration
- Testing the integration

Let's being by discussing the prerequisites for this standard integration.

14.1.1   Prerequisites and Initial Configuration

To use Employee Central position management integration with Recruiting, you must have the relevant modules and features configured. Many companies run Employee Central but don't have position management configured, so they aren't able to use this integration. If you have position management and Recruiting implemented (or are working on it), then you've met the first prerequisite.

To enable the integration, you must update the **Position Management Settings** in the SAP SuccessFactors Admin Center. You need to enable the integration and set up rules for both deriving the requisition template the system will use to create the requisition as well as mapping fields between the position and requisition. It's recommended that you first create the business rules because these are specified in the integration settings in position management.

To create the first business rule, navigate to **Admin Center • Configure Business Rules • Create New Rule**. Find the options related to position management. There are two choices, as you can see in Figure 14.1:

- **Derive Job Requisition Template in Recruiting Integration**
- **Map Fields from Position to Job Requisition in Recruiting Integration**

You'll need to create at least one rule for each setting.

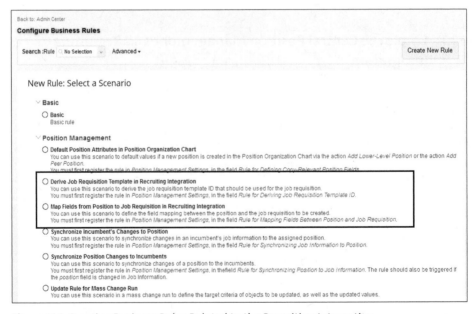

Figure 14.1 Creating Business Rules Related to the Recruiting Integration

Let's look at the job requisition derivation rule first.

Derive Job Requisition Template

To create the business rule to derive the job requisition template, from the **Configure Business Rules** page, select the relevant radio button under **Position Management**.

A dialog will appear to the right of the screen where you enter the following information (see Figure 14.2):

- **Rule Name**
  This field is required and will be the name of the rule displayed within the **Position Management Settings** screen.

- **Rule ID**
  This field is also required. The system will default the rule name here, and you can keep that value or change it, based on your needs.

- **Start Date**
  This field is required and is the effective date of the rule. You may want to use the system start date here.

- **Description**
  This is an optional field used for descriptive purposes.

Select **Continue** when you've entered the requisite information.

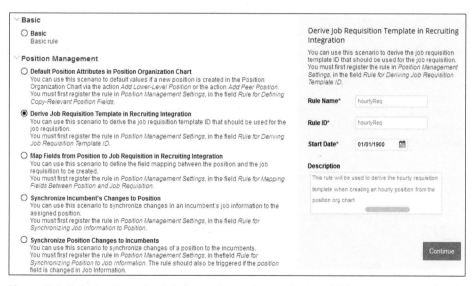

Figure 14.2 Entering Some Basic Information to Create the Requisition Derivation Rule

In the next screen, you'll build the business rule by adding "If" and "Then" statements that specify the parameters of the business rule. For example, in Figure 14.3, you can see that the rule has an "If" statement that reads:

If Position.Department.Code is equal to Text HR, Then Set Recruiting Parameter.Job Requisition Template to be equal to Text Hourly Job Requisition.

It's possible to add additional **If** and **Then** statements to the rule. For example, if you have multiple requisition templates, you can create all the if-then statements to derive each requisition template.

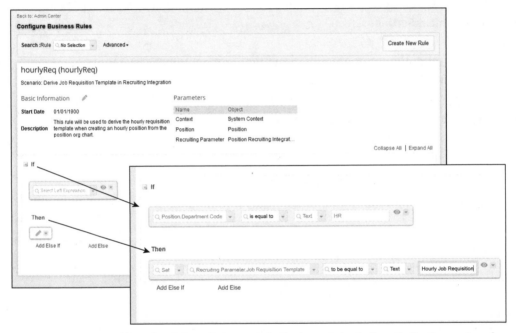

Figure 14.3 Adding If and Then Statements to Business Rules to Specify the Parameters for Deriving Requisition Templates

---

Tip

When creating the job requisition derivation business rule, choose an **If** parameter that is broad enough to encompass all the variables under which a particular requisition template should be selected. While it's possible to build complex rules, this will just make configuration and testing that much more involved.

Map Fields from Position to Job Requisition

You also need to create a rule to map the fields from the position object to the fields on the requisition template. From the **Configure Business Rules** screen, select **Map Fields from Position to Job Requisition in Recruiting Integration,** and enter the same information as we added in the first business rule:

- **Rule Name**
- **Rule ID**
- **Start Date**
- **Description**

Select **Create** and begin building the **If/Then** statements on the next screen, as shown in Figure 14.4. Add the **If** statement, and then create the **Then** statements to specify field mapping. You'll need a **Then** statement for each field that should be mapped from the position to the requisition. Continue adding **Then** statements until all fields are mapped. Save your rule.

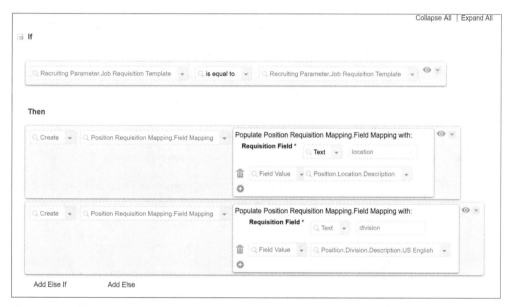

Figure 14.4 Add Then Statements for Each Field That Needs to Be Mapped from the Position to the Requisition

Note that if you want to map data from the position to custom fields in the requisition, you must ensure that the custom="true" attribute on the field definition is correct, and the custom fields are visible. If the custom attribute isn't set correctly, you won't be able to map data into these fields. This is possible because provisioning will only provide a warning if custom attributes aren't set properly.

It's also necessary that the requisition have the following standard fields defined:

- `numberOfOpenings`
- `positionNumber`

These fields don't need to be mapped in the business rule because the system recognizes them as standard in this integration, and they will be automatically populated.

> **Tip**
> You need to make sure that all required fields of the corresponding job requisition template are mapped with a value. Otherwise, the job requisition can't be created. If you want to create the job requisition without all required fields filled, you need to add an additional mapping to the rule with **Requisition Field = is Draft** and **Field Value = true**.

14.1.2   Enable Integration and Register Business Rules

After the business rules have been created in **Configure Business Rules**, you can update the **Position Management Settings**. Navigate to that area of Admin Center, and select the **Integration** tab. You'll find three fields:

- **Use Recruiting Integration**
- **Rule for Deriving Job Requisition Template ID**
- **Rule for Mapping Fields Between Position and Job Requisition**

Select **Yes** in the **Use Recruiting Integration,** and then search for the two business rules created in the previous section in those corresponding fields, as show in Figure 14.5. **Save** your settings.

Figure 14.5 Enabling Recruiting Integration and Registering the Business Rules

Set Role-Based Permissions

After the settings have been saved, your business rules have been registered, and the system is in the default setting. This means that no user is allowed to create or view job requisitions in the position org chart. You must first set role-based permissions for users that should be able to view and create requisitions from the position org chart. From the Admin Center, choose **Manage Employees • Set User Permissions**. Find the affected roles, and edit them so that are granted these permissions (see Figure 14.6):

- **View Job Requisition in the Position Organization Chart**
- **Create Job Requisition in the Position Organization Chart**
- **Select Job Requisition Template in the Position Organization Chart**

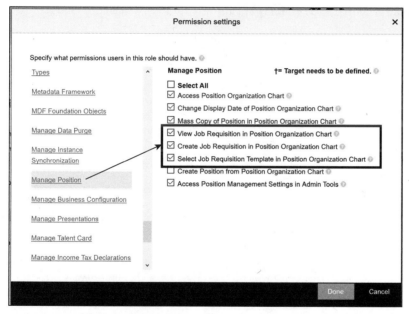

Figure 14.6 Adding the Relevant Permissions for Job Requisitions in the Position Organization Chart

Schedule Recurring Quartz Job

If you plan to use the job requisition scheduling feature to create job requisitions in the future, be sure that the corresponding Quartz job is set up in provisioning. This will need to be completed by your implementation partner because companies don't have access to provisioning. The scheduled job is shown in Figure 14.7. Within **Manage Scheduled Jobs**, create a new job with these parameters:

- **Job Name**

  Name the job in such a way that you'll recognize it from the list. This field is required, but any value may be entered.

- **Job Owner**

  Select a user from the user database to "own" the job. This user must remain active; if the job owner is made inactive, the job will fail.

- **Job Type**

  From the dropdown list, select **Position Job Requisition Processing**. This field is also required.

- **Occurrence**

  Set the job to be **Recurring,** and set the frequency and time it should run. For example, you can schedule it to run **Daily** at **1** am, as you can see in Figure 14.7.

Select the **Create Job** button to save it. You can submit the job from the main menu so the job runs on the recurrence established.

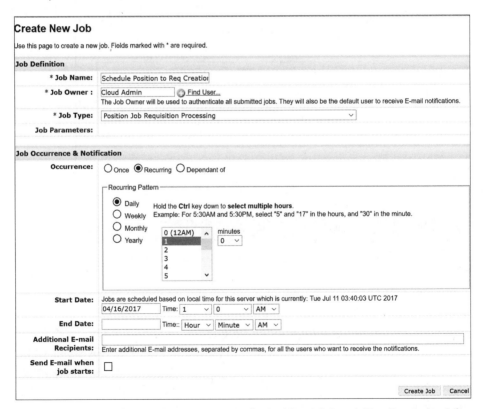

Figure 14.7 Entering the Parameters to Create the Position Job Requisition Processing Job

The job will run per the recurrence set up in the job parameters, and the Quartz scheduler will send the job owner email notifications with the results of the job each time it runs. If there are no requisitions scheduled for creation, the job will run, but no action will occur. If there are issues with requisitions being created, these errors will be provided in the email confirmation to the job owner. Additional email addresses can be added to the job so other users besides the job owner can be notified.

> **Tip**
>
> It's recommended to create a generic user that can "own" the jobs in the Quartz scheduler. This way jobs aren't interrupted if a user is made inactive. You can also set the user's email address to a shared mailbox that can be monitored by several people.

Configuring the Candidate to Employee Integration Template

After a candidate is selected for hire, the data gathered in Recruiting needs to be transferred to Employee Central for processing into an employee record. The Recruiting to Employee Central integration provides a seamless way to transition the external candidate record into a new employee account. The integration is supported by a candidate to employee integration template that is configured in XML and imported into provisioning, as shown in Figure 14.8.

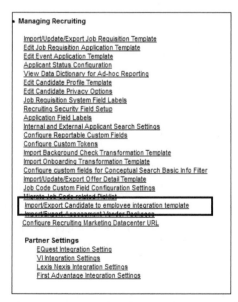

Figure 14.8 Managing the Recruiting to Employee Central Data Transfer in Provisioning

Here you build mapping between the Recruiting fields defined in the job requisition data model (JRDM), candidate data model (CDM), and offer letter, and then map them to corresponding fields in Employee Central. An example of this integration template is provided in Figure 14.9.

```xml
<object-mappings source="RCM" target="EC" integration-type="CandiDateToEmployee">
    <entity-details-mapping>
        <mapping-attribute>
            <source refid="customLong1" entity-type="offerletter"/>
            <target refid="personInfo.person-id-external"/>
        </mapping-attribute>
        <mapping-attribute>
            <source refid="budgetedAccountNumber" entity-type="jobrequisition"/>
            <target refid="jobInfo.division"/>
        </mapping-attribute>
        <mapping-attribute>
            <source refid="firstName" entity-type="application"/>
            <target refid="personalInfo.first-name"/>
        </mapping-attribute>
        <mapping-attribute>
            <source refid="middleName" entity-type="application"/>
            <target refid="personalInfo.middle-name"/>
        </mapping-attribute>
        <mapping-attribute>
            <source refid="lastName" entity-type="application"/>
            <target refid="personalInfo.last-name"/>
        </mapping-attribute>
        <mapping-attribute>
            <source refid="contactEmail" entity-type="application"/>
            <target refid="emailInfo.email-address.P"/>
        </mapping-attribute>
```

Figure 14.9 Configuring Field Mapping between Recruiting Templates and Employee Central in the Integration Template

The integration template can pull from the candidate application, job requisition, and offer letter. To maximize data transfer, please make sure the requisition, application, and offer details XML templates are configured to include the Employee Central fields supported in the SAP SuccessFactors Recruiting Management–Employee Central transformation template.

Because the **Manage Pending Hires** list is populated based on offer approval information, a candidate must go through an approved offer approval prior to being set to **Ready to Hire (Hirable)**.

Test the integration by sending a candidate to the Employee Central pending hires queue and processing the hire action.

> **Note**
>
> After the candidate has been hired, you can sync the external candidate profile data to the employee profile to convert all of the data stored there. You can't send background information to Employee Central; it must be synced directly from the candidate profile to the employee profile.

14.1.3   Creating a Requisition from the Position Org Chart

When the integration has been set up, and the business rules registered, you can test the integration. Navigate to the position org chart by choosing **Home • Company Info • Position Org Chart**. Search for a position by selecting **Positions** or **People** from the **Search By** field. After you've selected this criteria, you can search for the specific value in the **Search** field as shown is Figure 14.10. Find the position for which you want to create the requisition.

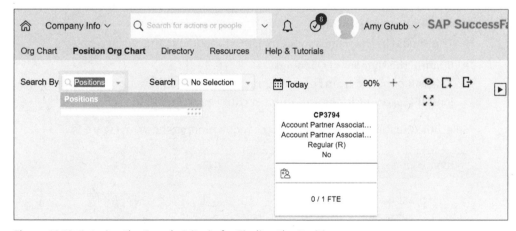

Figure 14.10 Entering the Search Criteria for Finding the Position

From the position details, click the **Position** tile to activate the position details, as shown in Figure 14.11. In the top right of the details screen, there are three lines, select this icon to activate the actions. Choose **Create Job Requisition**.

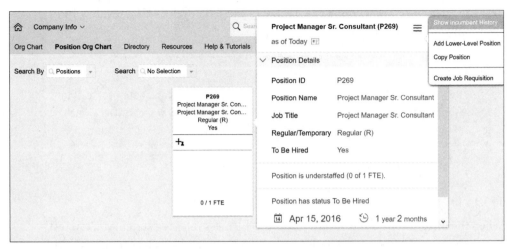

Figure 14.11 Choosing the Action Menu to Create Job Requisition

The system will display a dialog where you can update the following fields:

- **Date of New Job Requisition**
  Leave the date unless you want to schedule the creation for a future date.

- **Job Requisition Template**
  This should be the requisition template configured in the business rule.

- **Confirm the Number of Openings**
  This will populate from the position; if you maintain multiple full-time equivalents (FTEs) on positions, this number could be greater than 1.

Select the **Create** button to generate the requisition, as shown in Figure 14.12.

Figure 14.12 Confirming the Information or Entering a Future Date to Create the Requisition

When the system generates the requisition, it's accessible from the originator's requisition dashboard on the **Recruiting** page. From there, you can do several things, as follows:

- View requisition fields mapped from the position.
- Complete any additional fields that weren't mapped from the position, such as the headers and footers and Recruiting Marketing posting details.
- Add the job profile to the requisition.
- Complete the **Operator** fields that will be involved in approving the requisition.
- Add prescreening questions.
- Add **Interview Guides**, as applicable.
- Add a **Hiring Manager Note**, as applicable.

> **Tip**
>
> While you're configuring the position to requisition integration, you may want to update the JRDM so all fields aren't required. This will allow you to work with the business rule one field at a time and work through any mapping issues. After the mapping is done, and data are passing from the position, you can update the JRDM so the appropriate fields are required again.

When the requisition fields are completed, the requisition can be sent through the route map for approval. From this point, the requisition behaves just like a requisition created from **Browse Families and Roles** or created from a blank template.

While the requisition is being actioned, there are certain details that can be viewed from the **Position Details** on the position org chart. At any time, you can view the following:

- Requisition ID
- Job Title
- Requisition Status
- Number of Openings
- Candidates

- Job Requisition Originator
- Hiring Manager
- Job Requisition Created date
- Days Requisition Open

The **Job Requisition Details** are shown in Figure 14.13.

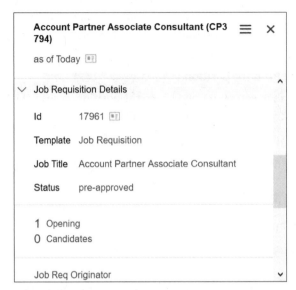

Figure 14.13 Viewing Highlights from the Requisition in Job Position Details

As you can see, configuring the Employee Central position management to Recruiting integration is fairly straightforward. As long as there are no issues, the integration can be configured in a few hours. This allows company administrators to easily modify the business rules as requirements change over time.

In the next section, we'll discuss configuring the position integration from SAP ERP HCM to Recruiting.

14.2   SAP ERP HCM and Recruiting Integration

For companies that maintain core personnel administration processes in SAP ERP HCM and maintain open positions, SAP provides standard integration packages that will trigger the creation of requisitions in Recruiting when a position becomes open in SAP ERP HCM and another integration package to process new hires. The process involved will depend on how each company manages positions within their organization and how the position object is configured in SAP ERP HCM. Let's look at how the process could work:

1. **Create a vacant position in SAP ERP HCM.**
   This is the first step in the Recruiting integration process. An open position is

created in Transaction PPOME. Some companies may not use the vacancy Info-type; in this case, it will be created manually.

2. **Trigger the job requisition creation.**
   SAP ERP HCM runs the Create and Update Job Requisitions report to select any vacant position in SAP ERP HCM from Infotypes 1007 and 1107. Position, organizational, and job information will be passed to SAP SuccessFactors, and the job requisition creation is triggered. We'll discuss this in greater detail in the next section. A requisition is created in **Preapproved** status.

3. **Send the requisition ID to SAP ERP HCM.**
   The Create and Update Job Requisitions report will read the requisition ID in SAP SuccessFactors and will send this information to SAP ERP HCM to update Infotype 1107.

4. **Update the job requisition.**
   The Create and Update Job Requisitions report will again run and will update the job requisition with any updates to the position from SAP ERP HCM.

5. **Send the job application data from Recruiting to SAP ERP HCM.**
   The Import Recruiting Data report will pick up all candidates in Recruiting that have a status of **sendToSAP** and will transfer them to SAP ERP HCM. When the transfer is successful, the report will update the candidate status in SAP Success-Factors to **transferredToSAP**.

6. **Process the job applications in SAP ERP HCM to complete the hire action.**
   Run Transaction HRSFI_RCT_HIRE to trigger the personnel action so the administrator can complete the hiring process in SAP ERP HCM.

7. **Update the position vacancy in SAP ERP HCM.**
   During the hire action in SAP ERP HCM, the vacant position is closed. The administrator runs the process job applications transaction to send the updated job requisition information to Recruiting to trigger the closing of the requisition.

8. **Update the candidate record and status.**
   The user ID of the new employee record is transferred to SAP SuccessFactors; the candidate record is updated, and the applicant status on the requisition is changed to **Hired in SAP**.

9. **Convert candidate data to the employee master file.**
   Run a sync to transfer candidate data captured in the SAP SuccessFactors candidate profile to the employee master record in SAP ERP HCM. Transaction HRSFI_SYNCH_EMP_DATA makes the data visible to the employee and manager.

14

14.2.1   Integration Overview

Five basic groupings of activities are necessary to implement both integration packages:

- **Set up basic settings**
  - Import metadata from SAP SuccessFactors.
  - Activate vacancy Infotype 1107.
- **Recruiting basic configuration**
  - Activate additional functions.
  - Assign SAP SuccessFactors talent solutions objects to field sets.
  - Map SAP SuccessFactors fields and SAP ERP fields to each other.
  - Check field sets for required fields and correct, as necessary.

Tip

SAP provides best practice templates that contain the required SAP integration fields for the following Recruiting items:

- Job Requisition Template
- Job Application Template
- Ad Hoc Report for New Hires

- **Configuration for transfer of job requisitions (SAP ERP to SAP SuccessFactors)**
  - BAdIs for transfer of job requisitions (SAP ERP to SAP SuccessFactors); there are three BAdIs that can be implemented to created requisitions in SAP SuccessFactors:
    - The Determination of Job Requisition Template from SAP SuccessFactors BAdI can use custom logic for determining the template ID for job requisitions in SAP SuccessFactors.
    - The Mapping of SAP ERP Infotype Fields to SAP SuccessFactors Fields BAdI is used to create custom logic for reading SAP ERP HCM fields. This needs to be implemented if you use the mapping value of **Mapped via BAdI**.
    - The Mapping of SAP ERP Infotype Fields to SAP SuccessFactors Fields—Change of Mapping Results BAdI is used for further processing the mapping of an SAP ERP HCM field to SAP SuccessFactors fields, for example, sending data from one SAP ERP HCM field to multiple fields within SAP SuccessFactors.

- Define **Value of Job Requisitions Status** used in SAP SuccessFactors.
- Specify handling of existing vacancies during data transfer.
- Display Infotype SFSF Job Requisition in Organizational Management (OM) applications.
- Correct the status of job requisitions in SAP ERP.

■ **Configuration for transfer of job applications (SAP SuccessFactors to SAP ERP)**

- BAdIs for transfer of job applications (SAP SuccessFactors to SAP ERP); there are also three BAdIs that can be implemented to transfer job application data from SAP SuccessFactors to SAP ERP HCM:
  - The Mapping of SAP SuccessFactors Fields to SAP ERP Infotype Fields BAdI is used to create custom logic to map fields from SAP SuccessFactors to SAP ERP HCM fields. A separate BAdI implementation is needed for each field mapping.
  - The Mapping of SAP SuccessFactors Fields to SAP ERP Infotype Fields— Change of Mapping Results BAdI is used for further processing the result of mapping SAP SuccessFactors fields to SAP ERP fields, similar to what was discussed previously for the requisition integration.
  - The Determination of Further Data for Recruiting Scenario BAdI is used to derive the country grouping and one or more personnel action types from the recruiting data that are transferred from SAP SuccessFactors.
- Change the application status values used in SAP SuccessFactors.

■ **Further process of imported applications**

- Define additional display fields.
- Define names of SAP SuccessFactors fields.
- Change the print form used for the PDF overview.
- Choose options for deriving SAP SuccessFactors user ID from SAP ERP HCM.

The details of these settings are outside the scope of this book, but you can refer to the documentation on these standard integration packages maintained by SAP for the most up-to-date information.

Let's discuss how these standard integration packages work, beginning with the job requisition trigger integration.

14

14.2.2   SAP Job Requisition Trigger Integration

The SAP job requisition trigger integration is the standard package that connects SAP ERP HCM position management with Recruiting. When a vacant position in SAP ERP HCM is identified as "ready for hire," certain position details can be transferred to Recruiting to create a requisition. Depending on how a company manages positions, irrespective of the system behavior, some positions may still be filled with an incumbent, but the vacancy is pending. When a position in SAP is marked vacant, SAP creates Infotype 1007 per standard SAP functionality. For companies using the requisition trigger integration, a new Infotype 1107 is created when the position is marked vacant and then closed when the position is filled. SAP does this automatically as part of the integration. This new Infotype, 1007, is what triggers the job requisition created in SAP SuccessFactors.

> **Note**
>
> Companies that don't use vacancies in SAP can trigger Infotype 1107 manually to create the requisition in Recruiting.

When configuring the integration, a scheduled report is set up to run regularly to trigger the creation of requisitions in SAP SuccessFactors. Every time the report runs, any position with an Infotype 1107 will be queued into the report to be sent to SAP SuccessFactors.

Report Processing

The position to requisition integration is facilitated by a standard report in SAP ERP HCM and an ad hoc report in SAP SuccessFactors. The SAP ERP HCM report is Create and Update Requisitions (Transaction HRSFI_RCT_DATA_IMP). This report pulls all of the positions that have Infotype 1107 populated and queues the data to be sent to Recruiting to create requisitions and then periodically to update requisitions when information has changed in SAP ERP HCM. The report will pull all positions with Infotype 1107 every time. It will then look for positions that don't have a **New** flag and compare the extract to the last extract stored on Infotype 1107. When the next report runs, all positions with an Infotype 1107 are selected. Any positions that have changes are selected for processing to update the requisition in SAP SuccessFactors. Note that the following fields on the position aren't updated for Recruiting reasons:

- title and extTitle
  These fields won't be updated after the requisition is created because they are published in the internal and external postings. The field sapPositionName will be updated and will contain the HRIS job title.

- listingLayout and extListingLayout
  These fields aren't created on the requisition; instead, these fields for the job description must be updated after the requisition is created in SAP SuccessFactors. Because the integration doesn't create them, they can't be updated.

> **Note**
>
> If you have Job Profile Builder deployed in your organization, the standard job description fields aren't used in the requisition. The job profile is instead attached to the requisition either manually or by creating the requisition from **Families and Roles**.

- The originator field is transferred during the creation of the requisition but isn't updated. Depending on the route map defined in Recruiting and data maintained on the position, originator may not even be used in the requisition routing.

- The jobReqStatus field isn't an explicit field in the job requisition XML, but it's very important to the function and field level permissions on the requisition. This is the **Preapproved**, **Approved**, and **Closed** statuses in a requisition lifecycle. Requisitions created from SAP are created in **Preapproved** status. The status is required when opening and closing the requisition and is represented as <urn:jobReqStatus>1</urn:jobReqStatus>. The values for the statuses are as follows:
  - **Preapproved = 0**
  - **Approved = 1**
  - **Closed = 2**

- The Status field is only considered in closing and reopening requisitions. The statuses must be added to the applicable requisition status picklist in SAP SuccessFactors:
  - **SAPClosed**
  - **SAPReopened**
  - **SAPDeleted**

- The dateCreated field is sent with the initial transfer that creates the requisition. This is the system date on which the requisition is created.

14

- The dateClosed field is sent when the requisition is closed after a successful hire. This represents the system date when the requisition is closed.

> **Tip**
>
> You can't update the requisition in the integration report to change the requisition template used. If a different template is needed, you'll need to close the vacancy in SAP ERP HCM, create a new one, and then proceed with the new requisition.

The trigger report will run regularly, multiple times per day, looking for positions with Infotype 1107 to create new requisitions and identifying any updates that need to be sent to SAP SuccessFactors. At the end of the process, when the requisition is filled in SAP SuccessFactors, and the new hire data are transferred to SAP ERP HCM for hiring, the report will update the requisition with this information so the requisition can be closed in SAP SuccessFactors.

In Recruiting, an ad hoc report is built to extract the candidate and associated application data to send to SAP ERP HCM. This ad hoc report is actually triggered by a Transaction HRSFI_RCT_DATA_IMP in SAP ERP HCM. The ad hoc report should be built in SAP SuccessFactors to filter candidates that are in the **SendToSAP** status, indicating they are ready to transfer to SAP ERP HCM for further processing. You do this by applying a filter to the ad hoc report that is equal to the **SentToSAP** applicant status. This report will also be run regularly, often numerous times per day depending on the volume of hiring that occurs in your organization.

Create a Vacancy in SAP ERP HCM

To start the position to requisition process in SAP ERP HCM, follow these high-level steps:

1. In SAP ERP HCM, activate Transaction PPOME.
2. Select the header **Details for Position <Position Name and Number>**.
3. From the list of positions within **Organization and Staffing Change**, find the position for which a vacancy should be created.
4. Highlight the object, and select the **Copy** button from the toolbar. Enter the details to copy the position object.
5. Select the **SFSF Job Requisition** tab, and view the **To Be Created** status. This is the status that flags this position to be sent to Recruiting to create a new requisition.

6. When the data are transferred to SAP SuccessFactors, and the requisition is created, you can see the updated status is changed to **Created** on the **SFSF Job Requisition** tab on the applicable position (see Figure 14.14).

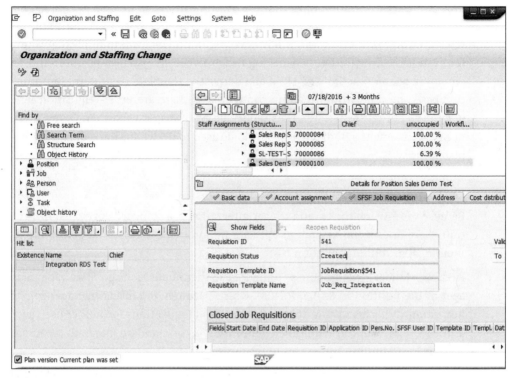

Figure 14.14 Requisition Status Updated to Created after the Requisition Exists in Recruiting

Requisition Created in Recruiting

After the trigger process has run, and the requisition is created in Recruiting, it's available in the requisition queue of the hiring manager for the particular requisition. This is determined by the manager of the position in SAP ERP HCM. The hiring manager will then review the requisition, complete any additional fields not populated from the position by the integration, and populate the operator roles involved in the approval process of the requisition within SAP SuccessFactors. When the requisition is saved, the route map approvers are inserted, and the requisition can continue on in the approval workflow.

From here, the recruiting process is carried out just as if the requisition were created directly in SAP SuccessFactors. Report HRSFI_RCT_TRG_JOBREQ will continue to run, and the requisition will be updated as necessary based on changes to the source data on the position in SAP ERP HCM. This occurs until the requisition is filled, the new hire is transferred to SAP ERP HCM for hiring, and the requisition is closed.

For the trigger integration to work properly, the SAP SuccessFactors job requisition template ID must be available in SAP ERP HCM so that they system can derive the job requisition in SAP SuccessFactors. If your configuration includes multiple requisition templates, the integration will distinguish between a manager position and an employee position in SAP ERP HCM and derive the template ID from that information based on the settings that are configured. If there are other requisition templates, or your templates aren't distinguished by manager versus employee, you'll need to implement a BAdI to define the logic used to derive the job requisition template.

Key Points to the Trigger Integration

Because the SAP job requisition trigger integration is a standard developed integration, there are several key points that are important to understand before implementing it in your organization.

First, the standard integration is configured so that requisitions go first to the manager of the position in SAP ERP HCM, which becomes the hiring manager role in Recruiting. If this isn't your process, you can send requisitions to another user, such as the recruiter, but this requires customization of the standard integration package and could add time and resources to the project effort.

Second, the standard integration contains predefined minimum required fields that are included, as well as a set of fields that are commonly used in company configurations. If you have other fields that you want to be included as part of the integration, you can include these and also remove any fields that are present in the integration but not used in your configuration.

This integration uses SAP PI as middleware, as you might imagine. Setting up the integration successfully will require resources that are knowledgeable in all three products: SAP ERP HCM, Recruiting, and SAP PI.

If the SAP new hire integration is being used (see Section 14.2.2 for more information), the information from the new hire integration is cross-referenced against the open job requisitions. If the operation fails, the candidate status is updated in SAP SuccessFactors to **TransferredToSAPError**. From here, data can be updated in SAP

SuccessFactors, and the new hire can be resubmitted by changing the candidate status to **SendToSAP** again to queue the candidate to SAP.

Closing and Reopening Requisitions

When a candidate is selected, successfully transferred to SAP ERP, and hired into SAP
ERP HCM, the final step in the recruiting process is to close out the requisition. This
requires a status change on the requisition from **Approved** to **Closed**. Sometimes,
there is a need to reopen a requisition that has previously been closed to accommodate changes in the requisition or hiring need. Both of these scenarios are handled by
the trigger integration. When a candidate is hired into the position opened, the trigger integration will send an update to trigger the closing of the requisition in SAP
SuccessFactors. This occurs when the state of Infotype 1107 changes from **Open** to
Closed. The application programming interface (API) supporting the integration will
send a message to SAP SuccessFactors to update the requisition status accordingly.

The message sent is `<urn:jobReqStatus>2</urn:jobReqStatus>`. This will update the
status in SAP SuccessFactors and generate a message that is passed back to SAP,
which is similar to "`Internal status changed from <1> to <2>`".

Two things are updated when this process is complete:

- SAP stores the status of the requisition before it was closed (this is **Approved**).
- The SAP SuccessFactors job requisition status field is updated to **SAPClosed**.

When a requisition needs to be reopened, which means the status changes from
Closed to **Open**, the state on Infotype 1107 will need to be updated to **Open**. This will
trigger the update in the trigger integration, and the requisition status in SAP SuccessFactors will be updated to **SAPReopened**. The requisition is then returned to the
state in which it was at the time of closing. This could be either **Approved** or **Preapproved**, if the requisition is closed while going through the approval workflow.

Now that we've discussed the frontend integration from SAP ERP HCM to Recruiting
to trigger the creation, update, and closing of requisitions from the position object in
SAP ERP HCM, let's turn our attention to the new hire integration.

14.2.3   New Hire Integration

When the candidate is selected and has a status of **SendToSAP**, the new hire integration picks up to transfer the candidate data to SAP ERP HCM for processing and hiring

into the position. A report is built in SAP SuccessFactors ad hoc reports to gather the candidate data necessary to support the hiring action in SAP ERP HCM. The transaction in SAP ERP HCM triggers the ad hoc report to run and pull data into the SAP ERP staging table for review.

There is a prebuilt Recruiting ad hoc report that is available for download from the Recruiting rapid-deployment solution (RDS). This report definition can be uploaded into ad hoc reports and used to support the integration. However, you can also build the report within Ad Hoc Report Builder. Be sure it includes the fields in Table 14.1, at a minimum.

Ad Hoc Folder	Columns
Applications	<ul><li>Application ID</li><li>Application Status</li><li>Template ID</li><li>First Name</li><li>Last Name</li><li>Gender</li><li>Date of Birth</li><li>SAP Position ID</li><li>Other fields mapped to SAP ERP</li></ul>
Last Offer Details	<ul><li>Start Date</li><li>Other fields mapped to SAP ERP</li></ul>
Requisitions	Company-specific fields mapped to SAP ERP for the new hire integration

Table 14.1 Fields That Need to Be Included in the Ad Hoc Report in SAP SuccessFactors to Send New Hire Data to SAP ERP

To send new hire data from SAP SuccessFactors to SAP ERP, build an ad hoc report in the Ad Hoc Report Builder.

Select **Create New Report**, and choose the **Report Type**:

- **Single Domain Report**
- **Multi Dataset Report**
- **Cross Domain Report**

For the new hire ad hoc report, select **Single Domain Report**, as shown in Figure 14.15. Select **Recruiting V2** in the **Report Definition type** dropdown.

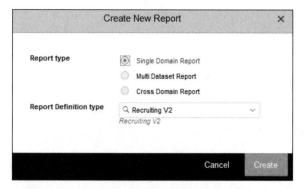

Figure 14.15 Creating the New Hire Report as a Single Domain Report

Select **Create** and open up the report. Give the report a name and a description (optional), as shown in Figure 14.16, and tab through the options across the top of the page:

- **General Info**
- **Columns**
- **Configuration**
- **Filters**

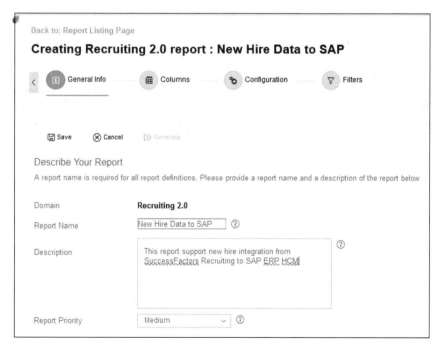

Figure 14.16 Giving the Report a Name and Description

Select **Columns** and add the fields outlined earlier in Table 14.1, at a minimum. You need to add fields from the application and last offer details and any requisition fields you'd like to include. Filter the type of data in the far left column, display the available columns in the middle, and select the checkbox to add fields to your report on the right, as shown in Figure 14.17.

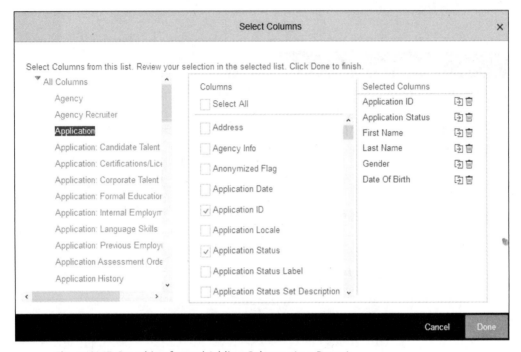

Figure 14.17 Searching for and Adding Columns to a Report

The final step is to add the filter so that only candidates in the status **SendToSAP** are included in the report. Choose the **Filter** tab, and add the **By My Selection** filter, as shown in Figure 14.18, so you can search for the correct status. Find the **SendToSAP** status, select it, and click **Done**.

Figure 14.18 Adding a Filter for the SendToSAP Status

When the report is built, you can preview it to ensure you've selected the correct columns and that the filter is working. Save your report, and you're all set.

14.2.4   Prerequisites to Configuring SAP ERP HCM

There are several prerequisites to configuring the integration between SAP ERP HCM and Recruiting:

- Configured SAP ERP HCM system
- Configured SAP PI middleware
- Installation of the Integration Add-On
- Configuration of the Recruiting module, including an updated Data Dictionary
- Implemented standard SAP SuccessFactors employee profile integration with SAP ERP HCM
- Implemented standard SAP SuccessFactors Recruiting integration with SAP ERP HCM

Note that the employee profile and integration package can be implemented concurrent with this integration, if you're just beginning your SAP SuccessFactors journey, and this isn't already in place. After these prerequisites have been fulfilled, the integration can be set up and tested.

14.2.5   Basic Settings

The first step in configuring the integration is to set up the basic settings in SAP ERP HCM. Within the IMG, navigate to **Integration Add-On for SAP ERP HCM and Success-Factors Bizx • Integration Scenario for Recruiting Data • Basic Settings**. Here you'll perform the following functions (Figure 14.19):

- **Define Authorizations (Recruiting Data)**
- **BAdI: Authorization Check for SFSF Integration**
- **Importing Metadata from SuccessFactors BizX**
- **BAdI: Determination of SAP ERP Personnel Numbers and SFSF User IDs**

Under **Settings for Middleware**, you'll perform these functions:

- **Store Credentials for Transferring Recruiting Data in Secure Storage**
- **Define Package Size for Transfer of Recruiting Data**

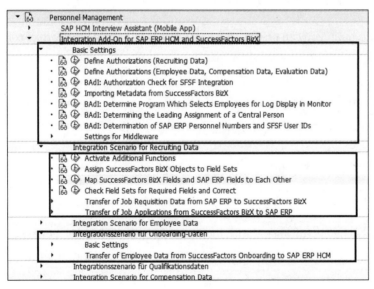

Figure 14.19 Basic Settings for the Integration in the Integration Add-On for SAP ERP HCM and SAP SuccessFactors BizX

After the **Basic Settings** are updated, navigate to **Integration Scenario for Recruiting Data,** and complete the following:

- Activate **Additional Functions**.

- Map SAP SuccessFactors suite fields and SAP ERP HCM fields to each other in **Basic Settings • Map SuccessFactors HCM Suite Fields and SAP ERP HCM Fields**. We'll discuss this action in greater detail in the next section.

- Check field sets for required fields and correct; there are two field sets that map fields from SAP SuccessFactors to SAP ERP HCM. **SAP_DEMO_01** has fields with lists of values, and **SAP_DEMO_02** has the fields as text fields. Additionally, you can transfer application data two ways:
  - Transfer job requisition data from SAP ERP to SAP SuccessFactors BizX
  - Transfer job applications for SAP SuccessFactors BizX to SAP ERP

Transferring Application Data Only

You can transfer application data only from SAP SuccessFactors to SAP ERP HCM. If you use this scenario, no contents are transferred from the SAP ERP system to SAP SuccessFactors for the fields in the field set. Users must make manual entries in these fields.

Transferring Applications with Requisition Data

If, in addition to the scenario for transferring applications from SAP SuccessFactors to SAP ERP, you also use the scenario for transferring job requisition data for positions from SAP ERP to SAP SuccessFactors, field contents are transferred from the SAP ERP system to SAP SuccessFactors for these fields.

For more information and detailed steps, refer to the relevant documentation on the SAP Support Portal related to configuring this integration package.

Let's now discuss how data are transferred from Recruiting to SAP ERP HCM.

14.2.6   Transferring Data from Recruiting to SAP ERP HCM

When configuring the integration between Recruiting and SAP ERP HCM, there are several actions in SAP ERP HCM that need to be set up:

- Map SAP SuccessFactors suite fields and SAP ERP HCM fields.
- Assign objects to field sets.
- Use the Mapping of SAP SuccessFactors Fields to SAP ERP Infotype Fields BAdI.

Let's discuss each one of these actions in the following sections, beginning with mapping Recruiting fields to SAP ERP HCM.

Map Recruiting Fields to SAP ERP HCM

Mappings are available for certain data, such as the following:

- Personal information, such as name, address, disability, marital status, and national ID information
- Organizational information such as division, department, and location
- Job information such as title, job code, and pay rate
- Race/veteran status

Field mapping is completed in **Basic Settings • Map SuccessFactors HCM Suite Fields and SAP ERP HCM Fields**. This transaction will define what data will be imported from SAP SuccessFactors Recruiting and is required for candidate data using the SAP SuccessFactors Simple Object Access Protocol (SOAP) API.

To map fields, double-click the **Fields and Mapping Modes** folder to display the field sets that can be mapped. Find the field set for Recruiting, and select the **Field Description** to activate the field set. Here you'll find the fields that can be mapped from Recruiting. Scroll through to find the fields you want to map. Select the field, and then double-click the **Mapping to Infotype Fields** folder, as shown in Figure 14.20.

When the **Mapping to Infotype Fields** screen is opened, find the infotype to be mapped using the dropdown list. Complete the **Subtype** and **Field Name** fields, as necessary, and save the mapping. The infotype screen is displayed in Figure 14.21.

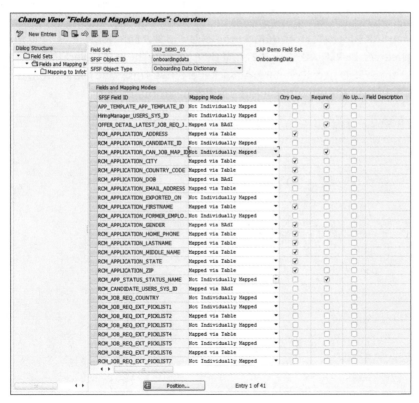

Change View "Mapping to Infotype Fields": Details

⬚ New Entries 📋 🔛 ⟲ 📑 📄 📑

Dialog Structure		
▾ ☐ Field Sets	Field Set	SAP_DEMO_01	SAP Demo Field Set
▾ ☐ Fields and Mapping M	SFSF Object ID	onboardingdata	OnboardingData
• ☐ Mapping to Infot	SFSF Object Type	Onboarding Data Dictionary ▾	

SFSF Field ID	RCM_APPLICATION_CITY
Mapping Mode	Mapped via Table ▾
☑ Country Dep.	

Mapping to Infotype Fields

Ctry Grouping	99 Other Countries ▾
Infotype	0006 Addresses ▾
Subtype	1
Field name	ORT01
IT record no.	

Figure 14.20 Selecting the Infotype to Map to the Recruiting Field

Change View "Fields and Mapping Modes": Overview

⬚ New Entries 📋 🔛 ⟲ 📑 📄 📑

14

Dialog Structure		
▾ ☐ Field Sets	Field Set	SAP_DEMO_01	SAP Demo Field Set
▾ ☐ Fields and Mapping M	SFSF Object ID	onboardingdata	OnboardingData
• ☐ Mapping to Infot	SFSF Object Type	Onboarding Data Dictionary ▾	

Fields and Mapping Modes

SFSF Field ID	Mapping Mode	Ctry Dep.	Required	No Up...	Field Description
APP_TEMPLATE_APP_TEMPLATE_ID	Not Individually Mapped ▾	☐	☑	☐	
HiringManager_USERS_SYS_ID	Not Individually Mapped ▾	☐	☐	☐	
OFFER_DETAIL_LATEST_JOB_REQ_J...	Mapped via BAdI ▾	☐	☑	☐	
RCM_APPLICATION_ADDRESS	Mapped via Table ▾	☑	☐	☐	
RCM_APPLICATION_CANDIDATE_ID	Not Individually Mapped ▾	☐	☐	☐	
RCM_APPLICATION_CAN_JOB_MAP_ID	Not Individually Mapped ▾	☐	☑	☐	
RCM_APPLICATION_CITY	Mapped via Table ▾	☑	☐	☐	
RCM_APPLICATION_COUNTRY_CODE	Mapped via Table ▾	☑	☐	☐	
RCM_APPLICATION_DOB	Mapped via BAdI ▾	☑	☐	☐	
RCM_APPLICATION_EMAIL_ADDRESS	Mapped via Table ▾	☐	☐	☐	
RCM_APPLICATION_EXPORTED_ON	Not Individually Mapped ▾	☐	☐	☐	
RCM_APPLICATION_FIRSTNAME	Mapped via Table ▾	☑	☐	☐	
RCM_APPLICATION_FORMER_EMPLO...	Not Individually Mapped ▾	☐	☐	☐	
RCM_APPLICATION_GENDER	Mapped via BAdI ▾	☑	☐	☐	
RCM_APPLICATION_HOME_PHONE	Mapped via Table ▾	☑	☐	☐	
RCM_APPLICATION_LASTNAME	Mapped via Table ▾	☑	☐	☐	
RCM_APPLICATION_MIDDLE_NAME	Mapped via Table ▾	☑	☐	☐	
RCM_APPLICATION_STATE	Mapped via Table ▾	☑	☐	☐	
RCM_APPLICATION_ZIP	Mapped via Table ▾	☑	☐	☐	
RCM_APP_STATUS_STATUS_NAME	Not Individually Mapped ▾	☐	☑	☐	
RCM_CANDIDATE_USERS_SYS_ID	Mapped via BAdI ▾	☐	☐	☐	
RCM_JOB_REQ_COUNTRY	Not Individually Mapped ▾	☐	☐	☐	
RCM_JOB_REQ_EXT_PICKLIST1	Not Individually Mapped ▾	☐	☐	☐	
RCM_JOB_REQ_EXT_PICKLIST2	Mapped via Table ▾	☐	☐	☐	
RCM_JOB_REQ_EXT_PICKLIST3	Not Individually Mapped ▾	☐	☐	☐	
RCM_JOB_REQ_EXT_PICKLIST4	Mapped via Table ▾	☐	☐	☐	
RCM_JOB_REQ_EXT_PICKLIST5	Not Individually Mapped ▾	☐	☐	☐	
RCM_JOB_REQ_EXT_PICKLIST6	Mapped via Table ▾	☐	☐	☐	
RCM_JOB_REQ_EXT_PICKLIST7	Not Individually Mapped ▾	☐	☐	☐	

◀ ▶

📑 Position...   Entry 1 of 41

Figure 14.21 Selecting the Appropriate Value from the Mapping Mode Column

Return to the **Fields and Mapping Modes** screen, and select the correct value in the **Mapping Mode** field under the **Mapping Mode** column. The values are as follows:

- Mapped via Table
- Mapped via BAdI
- Not Individually Mapped

Save the settings, and repeat these steps to map all the fields from Recruiting into the correct infotypes in SAP ERP HCM.

It's recommended that you begin the mapping exercise by mapping one or two fields and then testing to see if the mapping was configured properly. After you've confirmed that data are passing from Recruiting to SAP ERP correctly, you can complete the field mapping.

Assign Objects to Field Sets

After the Recruiting fields have been mapped to Infotypes, as described in the previous section, you'll assign Recruiting objects to field sets in SAP ERP HCM. This is completed in **Map SAP SuccessFactors HCM Suite Fields and SAP ERP HCM Fields**. Find the Recruiting field set, **ZHREF_ADHOC_1021**, and then activate the **SFSF Object ID** field. In Figure 14.22, the **SFSF Object ID** value is **AdhocReport_681**. This value comes from the Data Dictionary that was imported before you began the mapping.

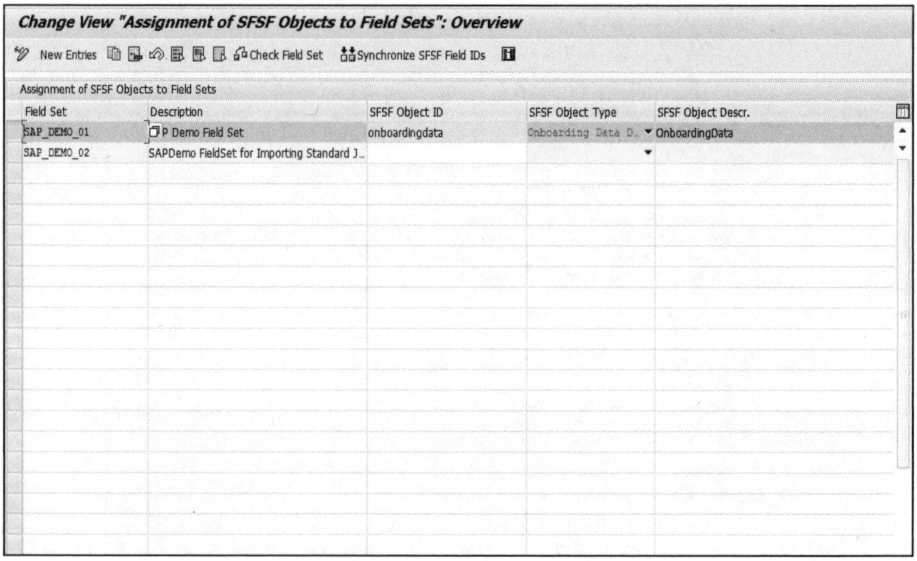

Figure 14.22 Associating the Object ID from Recruiting to the Field Set in SAP ERP HCM

BAdI Mapping of Recruiting Fields to SAP ERP HCM

BAdIs can be used to map data from Recruiting to SAP ERP HCM. If you do this, you'll need a separate BAdI implemented for each field that is mapped. BAdIs are used when you require more complex mapping than that provided by the standard template. For more information on this topic, refer to the applicable documentation provided by SAP.

After the settings have been made, the integration can be tested by scheduling the new hire report discussed in Section 14.2.2 and running through the hire process.

14.3   Summary

Connecting a Recruiting system to your HRIS provides robust functionality to not only share data from one module to another but also increase data integrity throughout the process. Using data that are maintained in position management to create requisitions eliminates the opportunity for hiring managers and other Recruiting users to input incorrect data when initiating the job requisition. SAP provides standard integrations to both Employee Central and SAP ERP HCM to Recruiting. These frontend integrations leverage data on open positions to fill fields on requisitions. The Employee Central position management to Recruiting integration is configured solely within the SAP SuccessFactors suite and doesn't require any additional tools or middleware. If SAP ERP HCM is your HR system of record, SAP PI is used as the middleware to pass data from your on premise SAP system to Recruiting.

When the successful candidate is selected, the data collected in Recruiting needs to be passed back to the HRIS for the hire action to be completed. SAP again provides standard integration packages to support new hire data passing to the HRIS to complete the process. Recruiting data are mapped to Employee Central using the candidate to new hire integration template. This XML document maps fields from Recruiting to corresponding fields in Employee Central and queues the candidate data to the pending hires in Employee Central. With SAP ERP HCM, candidate data are extracted from Recruiting via an ad hoc report that is triggered by the SAP PI integration. The report passes the candidate data for those marked with the **SendToSAP** status and queues it to a staging table in SAP ERP HCM. The HR administrator reviews the data, identifies and corrects errors, and then processes the new hires.

Let's turn our attention to integrating Recruiting to various third-party vendors in Chapter 15.

Chapter 15

Integrating Recruiting with Third-Party Vendors

A robust recruiting solution often involves one or more ancillary systems that are integrated into the talent acquisition process to provide the best solutions for recruiters. SAP SuccessFactors Recruiting offers an open platform that makes working with third-party systems to support various business processes an easy proposition.

A bevy of recruiting applications are included in a talent acquisition process beyond an applicant-tracking system, from candidate assessments to background checks to custom onboarding solutions. SAP SuccessFactors Recruiting can integrate with pretty much any external system to provide add-on services to companies to extend their talent acquisition process.

The integrations fall into two categories: standard-delivered integrations and custom integrations. Standard-delivered integrations are those that SAP SuccessFactors has put development resources into providing prebuilt components that allow Recruiting to talk to the other system.

SAP SuccessFactors has partnered with several companies to provide these standard integrations:

- LinkedIn (candidate profile/application completion)
- eQuest (job board posting)
- First Advantage (FADV) (background checks)
- SHL Talent Measurement Solutions and PeopleAnswers (assessment integrations)
- DocuSign (electronic signature)

In addition to the standard integrations, companies can integrate with any other vendor by developing a custom integration. This can be done using the Integration Center or middleware such as Boomi or SAP Cloud Platform Integration.

> **Note**
>
> Integration with third-party vendors only impacts Recruiting Management.

In this chapter, we'll discuss the standard integrations and the options for approaching a custom integration. Let's start by looking at the standard integrations and partners with LinkedIn.

15.1   LinkedIn for Candidate Profile/Application Completion

SAP SuccessFactors supports integration with LinkedIn in two ways: by allowing candidates to create profiles and apply for jobs using data from their LinkedIn profiles, and by sending externally posted requisitions, associated applications, and status updates to the LinkedIn Recruiter and Referral products. Note that this integration is dependent on LinkedIn continuing to support it. Let's look at these two integration points.

15.1.1   Apply with LinkedIn Profile

When a candidate maintains a professional profile on LinkedIn, you have the option of allowing them to leverage information from their LinkedIn profile while applying for jobs in SAP SuccessFactors. With this option enabled, there is an option from the job search page to Apply Using LinkedIn™. When candidates select this option, they are presented with a screen that prompts them to log in to their LinkedIn profile and retrieve a code. This code is then entered into the **Enter LinkedIn Security Code** window where their profile information can pass into SAP SuccessFactors, as shown in Figure 15.1.

After candidates successfully connect their LinkedIn profile, they can pass their work history and educational information from LinkedIn to the corresponding portlets on the candidate profile within SAP SuccessFactors, as illustrated in Figure 15.2. This can be a useful time saver for candidates who have likely built work and education history into their profiles, similar to the résumé parsing feature.

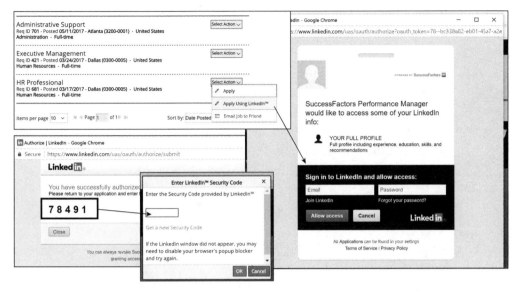

Figure 15.1 Accessing LinkedIn Profile Information after Retrieving a Security Code

15.1.2   LinkedIn Recruiter and Referral Integration

If you use the LinkedIn Recruiter or LinkedIn Referral products, you can enable integration from SAP SuccessFactors to send requisitions for externally posted jobs, application, and status update information. Before the integration can be set up, you must review and accept the terms and conditions, as provided in Figure 15.2.

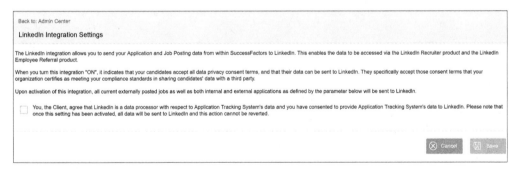

Figure 15.2 Reviewing and Accepting the LinkedIn Integration Settings Terms before Continuing to Set Up the Integration

When the agreement is accepted, additional fields are provided to map data between SAP SuccessFactors and LinkedIn, as shown in Figure 15.3 and described here:

- **LinkedIn Company ID**
  This is the ID assigned to your company by LinkedIn. Contact LinkedIn for this information if you don't already have it.

- **Applications created on or after this date will be sent to LinkedIn**
  Enter a date in this field. Only the applications that are created on or after the date specified will be sent to LinkedIn.

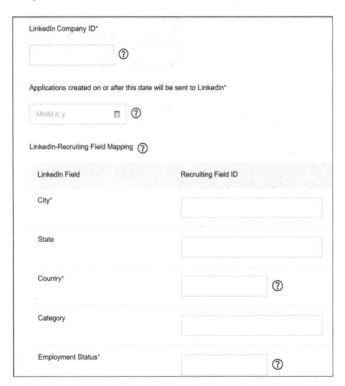

Figure 15.3 Mapping Fields from Recruiting to LinkedIn

- **LinkedIn-Recruiting Field Mapping**
  Map the job requisition data to the job posting data that will appear on LinkedIn. The supported field types are text, enum, and picklist.

- **City**
  Map the standard city (`refid=city`) field in Recruiting or any other field that may contain city values.

- **State**

  Map the standard state (refid=stateProvince) field, or any other field that may contain state values. This field is optional and will be sent to LinkedIn as part of the **Location** field.

- **Country**

  Map the standard country (refid=country) field or any field that contains a two-digit ISO country code. This field must be configured as **Label** if it's of the picklist and enum field types, and **Text** if it's of the text field type.

- **Category**

  Map any field that contains the category of a job requisition. This is also an optional field.

- **Employee Status**

  This field must be a picklist field type only. Although this field can be labeled to suit company needs on the requisition, the values in the picklist must match the following:

  - **Value** = 1/LinkedIn = FULL_TIME
  - **Value** = 2/LinkedIn = PART_TIME
  - **Value** = 3/LinkedIn = CONTRACT
  - **Value** = 4/LinkedIn = TEMPORARY
  - **Value** = 5/LinkedIn = VOLUNTEER
  - **Value** = 6/LinkedIn = OTHER

The picklist values for these fields in SAP SuccessFactors will then look like Figure 15.4. Notice that the value set in column **E** should match the values in the preceding list. Note that value 6 can be set to whatever other category you need. In our example it indicates a seasonal employee.

A	B	C	D	E	F	G	H	I
^picklistId	OptionId	minValue	maxValue	value	status	external_code	parentOptionId	en_US
EmployeeStatus		-1	-1	1	ACTIVE			Full Time
EmployeeStatus		-1	-1	1	ACTIVE			Part Time
EmployeeStatus		-1	-1	1	ACTIVE			Contract
EmployeeStatus		-1	-1	1	ACTIVE			Temp
EmployeeStatus		-1	-1	1	ACTIVE			Voluntary
EmployeeStatus		-1	-1	1	ACTIVE			Seasonal

Figure 15.4 Setting Up the Employee Status Picklist Referencing the LinkedIn Values

- **Department**

  Map the standard department (`refid=department`) field or any other field that contains department values.

Saving the data triggers the transfer of data for all externally posted jobs and all applications linked to those requisitions that are after the defined date in the setting mentioned earlier. A recurring job is also triggered to run every 30 minutes to manage incremental changes. The first recurring job will run 2 hours after the initial data transfer.

Once you have completed the mapping between the LinkedIn profile and the candidate profile, the integration will populate data from a candidate's LinkedIn profile to their candidate profile, as you can see Figure 15.5.

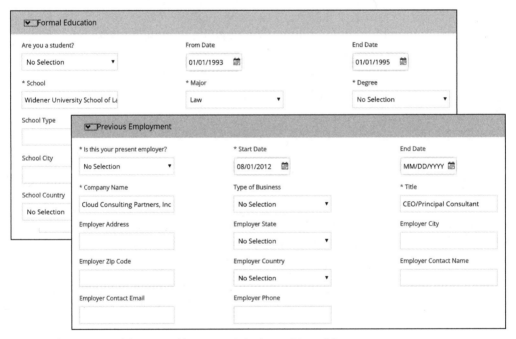

Figure 15.5 Fields Mapped between LinkedIn and Recruiting

Note

Using this integration, the **Past Applicants** in LinkedIn will show recruiters that a LinkedIn member is an existing applicant in their SAP SuccessFactors database. This is subject to the following:

- Applicant must be a LinkedIn member.
- Due to the index process at LinkedIn, there may be a delay of one week for all applicants to display.
- Applicants won't show in the spotlight if they have any association to the same company as the recruiter.

For LinkedIn Referral, there is validation to ensure that candidates can't be referred from LinkedIn if they already have a SAP SuccessFactors profile. This validation follows this logic:

- If there is no current ownership for the candidate in SAP SuccessFactors, the referral from LinkedIn is valid ownership.
- If there is current ownership for the candidate in Recruiting through other sources (e.g., agency or employee referral), then the existing ownership is retained, and LinkedIn ownership isn't registered in Recruiting.

Tip

The **Source** column in the Candidate Workbench will show **LinkedIn** and the **Candidate Source** column will show as **Employee Referral**.

15

15.2   eQuest Integration

Recruiting companies can post jobs automatically to job boards and to multiple job boards simultaneously using the eQuest integration. eQuest is a job board aggregator that provides job posting services to companies to push their jobs to multiple external job boards.

If you have a contractual relationship with eQuest to purchase postings, you can post your requisitions from the Recruiting **Job Postings** page to post the job to various job boards via eQuest. Postings can be purchased from eQuest in bulk packages or with the eCommerce solution offered by eQuest. After you've contracted with eQuest, you'll receive a username and password, which are required to set up the integration with SAP SuccessFactors Recruiting.

Tips

A few things to note about posting jobs to eQuest:

- The **Posting Start** and **Posting End** date fields don't show on the **Job Requisition Detail** page. The only place to access these fields is via the **Job Postings** page. This is the same for all posting methods.
- You can't permission READ access to the intranet and corporate start and end dates. All users with the same recruiting role have the same access to these fields. This means that if a user has access to the **Job Postings** page, that user can post to all available posting methods.
- Job board postings access is controlled solely through the **Job Postings Permissions** admin page.

Now let's discuss the steps to set up the integration and configure the job requisition data model (JRDM) to support eQuest postings from Recruiting.

15.2.1   Set Up eQuest Integration

Configuring the eQuest integration doesn't take long and is very straightforward. It involves some provisioning settings, configuration of the JRDM, and some set up in Admin Center, as follows:

1. Start by enabling the integration in provisioning.
2. From provisioning **Company Settings**, ensure that the **Enable Job Board Posting** setting is checked.
3. Return to the main provisioning page.
4. Navigate to **Partner Settings,** and select the **EQuest Integration** setting.
5. Enter the URLs the system needs to talk to eQuest (see Figure 15.6). These URLs vary by datacenter and are provided in the Recruiting Implementation Guide. Example URLs for a company on the Arizona datacenter are as follows:
   - **EQuest URL**: *https://successfactors.equest.com/post/*
   - **Return URL**: *https://performancemanager4.successfactors.com/rcmequestpost*
   - **Candidate Response URL**: *https://career.successfactors.com/career?company= companyID&career_job_req_id={requisition_number}&career_ns=job_listing& jobPipeline={pipeline_id}*

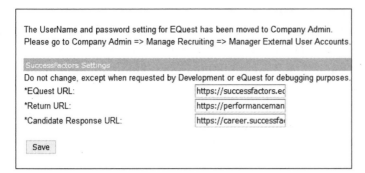

Figure 15.6 Setting the URLs for eQuest Integration under Partner Settings

6. After the provisioning settings are made, complete the setup in the Admin Center. Navigate to **Recruiting • Manage External System Accounts**. Here you'll import/ export a flat file with the user account information for those who can post to eQuest.

7. Choose the option to **Export all external accounts** to get the template to complete.

8. You need to enter information for all of your recruiters who will post to eQuest.

9. Complete the file, save it, and then import it into the same page.

To avoid duplicate job postings, it's recommended that only one eQuest login should be configured per company. However, multiple eQuest logins are supported. Accounts can be mapped to a single user to allow that user to use the account, or they can be mapped to all users by using the asterisk (*) in the upload file. The following settings in the Admin Center need to be addressed:

- **Recruiting Settings**
  Navigate to **Admin Center • Recruiting • Manage Recruiting Settings** to enter company contact information that will display on external postings.

- **Set Up Job Board Options**
  Navigate to **Admin Center • Recruiting • Setup Job Board Options** to configure the values for the standard enum fields on the JRDM needed to support the eQuest postings.

- **Industry Values Setup**
  The options configured here map to the industry field in the requisition XML. From this page, admin users can select the industries applicable to the company's business. The fields selected appear in the dropdown list when the industry field is shown or edited on the job requisition XML.

- **Country and State/Province Values Set up**

  The selections made here map to the `country` and `stateProvince` enum fields in the requisition XML. Admin users can search from a list of countries, states, and provinces to find the appropriate selections as shown in Figure 15.7.

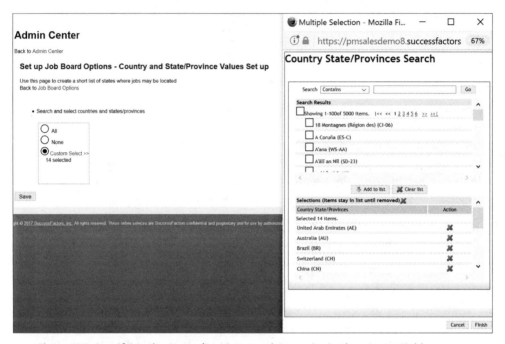

Figure 15.7 Specifying the States/Provinces and Countries in the eQuest Fields

15.2.2   Configure the Job Requisition Data Model

After you've set up the necessary values in the Admin Center, you need to add some configuration to the JRDM. These fields will be used by eQuest when posting the jobs on the various job boards. eQuest has worked with all of its partner job boards to identify the information necessary to support postings. That information is consolidated and captured in the following eQuest fields:

- **Classification Type** (`refid` "`classificationType`")
  - **Permanent**
  - **Contract**
  - **Contract to Permanent**
  - **Intern**

- **Classification Time** (refid "classificationTime")
  - **Full-Time**
  - **Part-Time**
- **Industry**
- **Function** (Note this field is a text field with restricted values. It has a *quickfind* function so that you can start typing the function of the job requisition, and the quickfind lists only the functions with that text in the function name.)
- **City** (refid "city")
- **State/Province** (refid "state")
- **Postal Code** (refid "postalcode")
- **Country** (refid "country")
- **Recruiter Name** (refid "recruiterName")

Classification Type, **Classification Time**, and **Country** are also enum fields with a short list of options. The short lists for these additional enums are built in to the application, so no additional configuration (other than adding them to the JRDM) is required.

After the eQuest standard fields are configured, the field permissions need to be configured per role for each requisition status, as discussed in Chapter 2. It's recommended to set eQuest fields to **Required** for the **Preapproval** status to ensure values are provided, but read and edit permissions can be assigned to meet the needs of the company.

15.3   Background Check with First Advantage

The integration between SAP SuccessFactors and First Advantage (FADV) allows clients of both companies to initiate and receive results of background checks and drug screens on candidates directly from the Recruiting system. The client must have an existing contract with FADV and should obtain the URLs and credentials necessary to set up the integration. With the integration in place, recruiters can queue candidate data from Recruiting to the FADV system to begin the background check or drug screen process. As that process proceeds, progress and results can be tracked from within SAP SuccessFactors.

This integration creates a better candidate experience because the data entered into Recruiting on the application and candidate profile is fed to FADV, and candidates don't have to reenter the same information. It also creates a better recruiter experience, as recruiters can initiate and monitor the process in one system.

In the next sections, we'll discuss how to enable the integration and configure the JRDM to enable the initiation of background checks from the Candidate Workbench.

15.3.1   Setting Up the FirstAdvantage Integration

As you might expect, there are settings that are required in provisioning and some configuration updates necessary. To enable the integration from provisioning, navigate to **Company Settings • Recruiting • Enable Background Check • First Advantage Background Check Integration**. Check the **First Advantage Background Check Integration** box, and save the setting. Next, find **Managing Recruiting Partner Settings • First Advantage Integration Settings**. Here you'll enter the following URLs provided by FADV, as shown in Figure 15.8:

- **Request URL for DA**
- **Order Status URL**
- **View Report URL**
- **Candidate Order Status URL**
- **Get Accounts URL**
- **Get Packages URL**

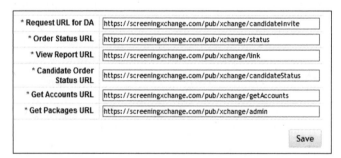

Figure 15.8 Setting the Necessary URL Values in Provisioning to Enable the First Advantage Integration

When the URLs have been set and saved, it's necessary to enable the API. From provisioning, select **Company Settings • Enable SFAPI Webservices**. Set the password login exceptions.

Next, you'll log in to the SAP SuccessFactors suite, and from the Admin Center, find **Password Policy Settings • Set API Login Exceptions • Add**. Enter the IP addresses that the OData (Push) status responses are sent from and a minimum password age of **-1**. For example, you can share the URL pattern for OData access with FADV: https://<hostname>/odata/v2/upsert.

15.3.2 Configure the Job Requisition Data Model

After the settings are enabled and saved, you need to add some configuration to the JRDM. Add the field definition for the FADV account package first. This is standard and looks like the code in Listing 15.1.

```
<field-definition id="fadvAccountPackage" type="derived" required="false"
custom="false">
<field-label><![CDATA[Fadv Account Package]]></field-label>
<field-description><![CDATA[Fadv Account Package]]></field-description>
</field-definition>
```

Listing 15.1 Defining the FADV Standard Field in the JRDM

This should be done for all JRDMs from which you wish to initiate background checks.

15.3.3 Update Permissions

When the field definition has been added, be sure to permission it appropriately for any impacted recruiting operator role and add the feature permission, as shown in Listing 15.2. Upload the updated JRDM(s) to provisioning, and test your changes.

```
<feature-permission type="backgroundCheck">
<description><![CDATA[R can initiate Background Checks]]> </description>
<role-name><![CDATA[R]]></role-name>
<role-name><![CDATA[G]]></role-name>
<status><![CDATA[Offer]]></status>
</feature-permission>
```

Listing 15.2 A Feature Permission in the JRDM to Enable Background Check Initiation

Role-based permissions should also be updated to add the necessary permissions to relevant roles as follows:

15

- Select **Administrator Permissions • Manage Recruiting • First Advantage Background Check Integration Settings**.

- Select Under **Administrator Permissions • First Advantage Background Check Settings**.

- Update the API user to have the OData API permission from **Administrator Permissions • Manage Integration Tools • OData API Permission**.

15.3.4   First Advantage Integration Settings

After permissions have been updated appropriately, you need to make the settings for the integration. Navigate to **Admin Center • Recruiting • Configure First Advantage Background Check Integration Settings**. Make the following settings:

- **Email applicant**
  This is a two-step process where SAP SuccessFactors sends applicant data to FADV, and FADV contacts and invites the candidate to fill out the missing background check data.

- **Allow account and packages to be selected at the application level**
  Users with the appropriate permissions can add, edit, or remove account and package combinations from the job application page. All updates will be reflected on both the job requisition and job application fields.

- **Accounts and Packages**
  Synchronize accounts and packages from FADV.

- **Parent Field Selection**
  Select a job requisition picklist field as a parent field for the FADV account field. This refines the list of selectable accounts based on the parent field data selection.

- **Job Requisition**
  Map job requisition fields from each JRDM to the corresponding FADV fields. Note: You can't map the user-defined fields **Due Date** or **Post Job Language** in the job requisition.

- **Job Application**
  Map job application fields from each job application XML template to the corresponding FADV field.

- **Candidate Profile**
  Map candidate profile fields from the candidate profile XML template to the corresponding FADV fields.

- **Background Elements**
  Map additional information from the candidate profile to FADV to send these fields to FADV when a background check or drug screen order is submitted.

- **API Credentials**
  Enter FADV API credentials (provided by FADV).

You can also grant users the ability to view or initiate background checks. Navigate to **Admin Center • Recruiting • Recruiting Permissions • Background Check Initiate Permissions**. For companies who use different unique identifiers between SAP SuccessFactors and FADV, map SAP SuccessFactors employee usernames to the employee usernames entered in FADV in **Admin Center • Recruiting • Manage External User Accounts**.

This is the same file that is used to set up eQuest permissions. Export all accounts, add the necessary information as shown in Figure 15.9, and import back into the system. The fields in the file are as follows:

- **USER_NAME**
  SAP SuccessFactors users' usernames who need permission to the FADV system.

- **EXTERNAL_PARTNER_CODE**
  Enter "FADV" for all users.

- **PARTNER_USERNAME**
  This is the employee's username in FADV.

- **PARTNER_PASSWORD**
  Leave this blank because it isn't needed.

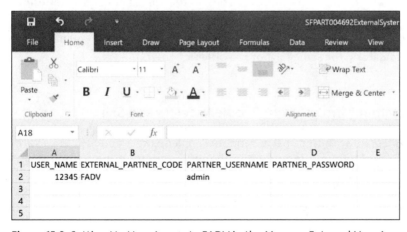

Figure 15.9 Setting Up User Access to FADV in the Manage External User Account File

Be careful not to impact the permissions for other users for other integrations. If you're using another integration such as eQuest, ensure that you have the appropriate passwords for the accounts included in the exported file. Uploading this file without passwords for the existing accounts deletes the existing passwords and prevents users from being able to use the other integrations. All new FADV companies should use the same unique identifiers between the two systems. Companies who follow this don't need the additional configuration step.

15.3.5   Initiating a Background Check with First Advantage

You associate background check packages with job requisitions and then initiate the background check for candidates. When you're creating a job requisition, select one or more account and package combinations. Configure the selectable account and package using **Admin Center • Managing Recruiting • First Advantage Background Check Integration Settings**. During the job requisition creation process, configure one or more account and package combinations for the job requisition.

When a candidate is in a **Background Check** applicant status, the Recruiting user sees an **Initiate Background Check** option at the top of the application page. Click this option to select a background check order creation method.

After choosing a creation method, the Recruiting user sees a pop-up of all configured accounts and packages for the job requisition. You can only select one account and package combination per requisition.

After the background check is initiated, Recruiting users can see background check results in the **Background Check Status** portlet on the application. Click **Refresh** to update the information on the portlet. Click **View Report** to see the FADV report for the candidate. Users can resubmit the same package and account combination for the same candidate on the same job but as a different order.

15.4   Assessment Integration: PeopleAnswers and SHL

Clients can integrate with third-party vendors PeopleAnswers and SHL to perform candidate assessments. Using this integration, companies can do the following:

- Assign assessments to job requisitions.
- Prompt applicants to fill out the corresponding assessment.

- View assessment statuses and results in the assessment portlet within the application.

- Configure hard stops in the process to keep candidates from moving forward in the pipeline until assessment results are registered.

Companies that want to use this integration must have a separate contract with the particular vendors. If you want to opt-in to the assessment integration and configure it, Recruiting users will see a section on the requisition that allows them to assign an assessment package to the requisition. Multiple assessment packages on one requisition aren't supported.

The Recruiting integration with PeopleAnswers and SHL requires either Boomi or SAP Cloud Platform Integration. Companies must have appropriate licensing to use the assessment integration. The company's Boomi account must be provisioned for access to integration packs and the Atom Cloud where they will be deployed. If the company uses SAP Cloud Platform Integration, the account must be provisioned for access to integration flows. Refer to the Implementation Guide specific to enabling this integration for more details.

In the following sections, we'll discuss the prerequisites for setting up this integration, how to manage assessment packages and configuring the JRDM, and setting necessary permissions.

15.4.1   Prerequisites

Provisioning of the account is directly tied to the SKU used to purchase the integration. The company account must have an environment created and attached to the Boomi Cloud. The Recruiting system must be configured for assessment integration before configuring the third-party integration via Boomi or SAP Cloud Platform Integration. You also must manage vendors to upload vendor packages into the Admin Center. The first step is enabling the integration in Provisioning by choosing **Company Settings • Recruiting • Enable Assessment Integration (Required Candidate Workbench)**.

- Next, you must manage vendors to enable uploading of vendor packages. First, grant permissions to the applicable role(s) by choosing **Admin Tools • Set User Permissions • Manage Permission Roles • Recruiting Permissions • Manage Assessment Vendors Permission**.

Users with **Manage Assessment Vendors** permissions can upload vendors by navigating to **Admin Center • Import/Export Assessment Vendors**.

For the first vendor import/export, export the CSV file to generate a sample CSV file with required fields. The following fields are mandatory:

- externalPartnerCode (SHL or PeopleAnswers)
- clientId (corresponds to client being implemented and comes from the assessment vendor)
- active (Y/N)

You must manage the vendors first before you can import the assessment packages. You'll get an error if this isn't done properly. You can export CSV templates for both imports from Provisioning.

15.4.2   Manage Assessment Packages

After the manage assessment vendors file has been uploaded as described in the previous section, you can manage the assessment packages in Provisioning under **Import/Export Assessment Vendor Packages** (see Figure 15.10). Assessment vendor packages are provided by the third-party vendor.

Figure 15.10 Manage Assessment Vendor Packages in Provisioning

For the first vendor package import/export, export the CSV file to get a sample CSV file with required fields. The following fields are mandatory:

- vendorId
  Identifies the assessment vendor the package uses. The only supported values are SHL or PA.
- packageCode
  ID that identifies an assessment solution to use for the order. This is generated by PeopleAnswers or SHL.

- `shortName`
  Shortened name of the package for use on the candidate summary page. The complete label appears everywhere else.
- `label for each locale`
  The combination of the country and location code for each language the assessment will be display in, for example, `en_US`, `fr_FR`, and so on.

The following columns/fields are included in the template but aren't used for PeopleAnswers or SHL and may be left empty:

- `Reportpackagecode`
- `ComparisongroupID`

The only supported values for `vendorId` are `PA` (PeopleAnswers) and `SHL` (SHL).

Let's now discuss how to configure the JRDM to support this integration.

15.4.3   Configure Assessment Field and Permissions

As you may expect, after the integration is enabled in provisioning and the initial settings have been managed, some maintenance of the JRDM is required. You must first configure the assessment field ID in the job requisition XML and then permission it appropriately. The assessment field ID can be permissioned in the same way as all other job requisition fields. The field will display on the job requisition page in the same order it's configured on the template. See the XML sample in Listing 15.3 in the next section for an example of how to declare the assessment field and grant feature permissions.

15.4.4   Configure the Alert Subscription

To configure the alert subscription, follow these steps:

1. Grant user permissions for the SFAPI integration user in **Admin Center • Set User Permissions • Administrator Permissions • Manage Integration Tools • Enable "Access to Event Notification Subscription"**.

2. Grant the SFAPI assessment permissions in **Admin Center • Set User Permissions • Manage Permission Roles • Recruiting Permissions • SFAPI Retrieve Assessment Order and SFAPI Update Assessment Report Permissions**.

3. Navigate to **Admin Center • Event Notification Subscription**. Click the **Subscriber** tab, and click **Add Subscriber** to add or edit a subscriber, as shown in Figure 15.11. For each new subscriber entry, enter the following:

   - **Subscriber Id**: For Recruiting Management, the value can be either **PA** or **SHL**. Companies can also use custom assessment vendors.

   - **Name**: Provide a description.

   - **Status**: The value is either **Active** or **Inactive**.

   - **Client Id**: This should match the `externalPartnerCode`.

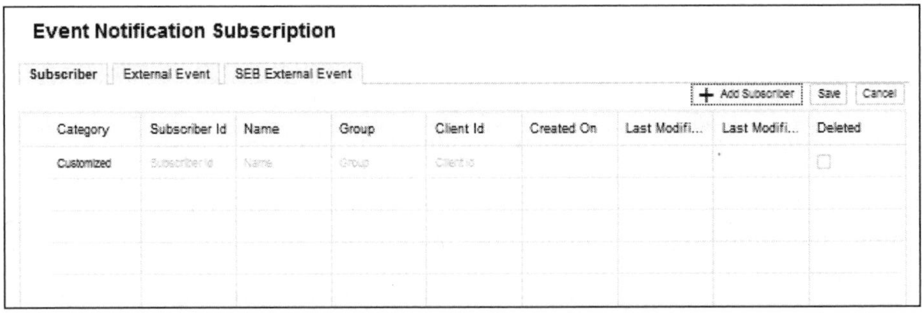

Event Notification Subscription

	Category	Subscriber Id	Name	Group	Client Id	Created On	Last Modifi...	Last Modifi...	Deleted
	Customized	Subscriber Id	Name	Group	Client Id				☐

Figure 15.11 Adding a Subscriber to the Event Notification Subscription Page

Tip

If you want to use a new custom assessment vendor, you must file a JIRA ticket to have the new vendor added to the system. After a vendor has been added, other companies can use that vendor without additional configuration.

4. In **Admin Tools • Event Notification Subscription**, click the **External Event** tab, and then click **Add** to configure a new subscription as shown in Figure 15.12. To add the Boomi process as a subscriber, enter the following information:

   - **Event Type**: Enter "rcm_assessment_alert".

   - **Subscriber**: Chose either **PA Assessment Subscriber** for PeopleAnswers or **SHL Assessment Subscriber** for SHL; these are the only valid options.

   - **Protocol**: Choose **SOAP_OVER_HTTP_HTTPS**.

   - **Endpoint URL**: Enter either the Boomi web service URL or SAP Cloud Platform Integration web service URL.

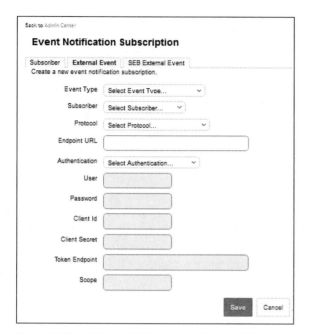

Figure 15.12 Adding or Editing Subscriber Notifications

Once you have completed the previous steps to configure the alert subsection, be sure to update the requisition XML shown in Listing 15.3, which shows two configurations, as follows:

- Field declaration with permissions.

- Feature permission to view the **Assessment** portlet in the applicant profile. In this example, the **Assessment** portlet will be visible only when the application is in **Default** and **Phone Screen** status.

```
<field-definition id="assessment" type="derived" required="true"
custom="false">
<field-label><![CDATA[Assessment assocication]]></field-label>
<field-description><![CDATA\[Assessmentasso]]></field-description>
</field-definition>
<field-permission type="write">
<description><![CDATA[job code permissions]]></description>
<role-name><![CDATA[R]]></role-name>
<status><![CDATA[pre-approved]]></status>
<field refid="assessment"/>
```

505

```
</field-permission>
<feature-permission type="assessmentIntegration">
<description><![CDATA[Operators with below roles can see Assessment
detail report for the applicant when the application is in Phone Screen
Status]]></description>
<role-name><![CDATA[S]]></role-name>
<role-name><![CDATA[T]]></role-name>
<role-name><![CDATA[O]]></role-name>
<role-name><![CDATA[R]]></role-name>
<role-name><![CDATA[G]]></role-name>
<status><![CDATA[Phone Screen]]></status>
</feature-permission>
<feature-permission type="assessmentIntegration">
<description><![CDATA[Operators with below roles can see Assessment
detail report for the applicant when the application is in New Application
Status]]></description>
<role-name><![CDATA[S]]></role-name>
<role-name><![CDATA[T]]></role-name>
<role-name><![CDATA[O]]></role-name>
<role-name><![CDATA[R]]></role-name>
<role-name><![CDATA[G]]></role-name>
<status><![CDATA[Default]]></status>
</feature-permission>
```

Listing 15.3 Field Definition and Feature Permission in the JRDM

You can edit the assessment after the job requisition is posted, but this configuration isn't recommended. If a Recruiting user edits the assessment field after candidates have applied to the job (e.g., requiring a more rigorous skills screening than was previously asked for), two sets of candidates with different assessment criteria will be created. Permissions for the assessment field are the same as any other field-level permission.

The admin can also create an email template for assessments using the same procedure for all Recruiting email templates.

15.4.5 Configure Hard Stop Field

A **Hard Stop** status ensures the applicant won't proceed in the application pipeline past a certain status until the results for that assessment order are returned on the applicant record. A **Hard Stop** status field is configured on the job requisition template as a standard field.

On the **Job Requisition Detail** page, the **Hard Stop Status** dropdown consists of a list of active **Default**, **In Progress**, and **Onboarded** statuses available in the application status set associated with the job requisition.

After this is configured, when the recruiter moves the applicant to a status past the **Hard Stop** status, the system checks for any assessment triggers for the applicant and whether all of them are completed. If yes, the status change is allowed; otherwise, the candidate can't move past the status until all assessments are complete.

The assessment **Hard Stop** field can be configured in the job requisition template and permissioned the same as all other job requisition fields. This field is configured as a standard picklist field, as shown in Listing 15.4.

Although this standard field is configured as a picklist, and a picklist ID is provided, the field behaves as a derived field and displays the **Default**, **Onboarded**, and **In Progress** statuses of the job requisition, according to the application status set ID associated with the requisition.

```
<field-definiteion id="hardstopStatus" type="picklist" required="false"
custom="false"><field-label><![CDATA[Hardstop Status]]></field-label>
<picklist-id>jobReqStatus</picklist-id></field-definition>
```

Listing 15.4 Hard Stop

The system doesn't check the selection of the **Hard Stop** status against the status configured for the assessment. Users should not configure a **Hard Stop** status that would exist in the workflow before the status associated with the assessment. This would prevent the candidate from moving through the system without being sent an assessment.

15.4.6   Assessment Integration Known Behavior

The following items are known behavior of the assessment integration:

- **Uploading and managing the vendor assessments**
  You can upload the vendor assessment to Recruiting and change the display name of previously loaded assessments by uploading a new list with the new display names. You can't remove uploaded assessments or remove them from the picklist on the requisition.

- **Adding assessments to a requisition**

  The **Assessment** field on the requisition has a link that allows you to add multiple assessments to the requisition. However, PeopleAnswers and SHL only support one assessment per requisition. It's recommended either to use Custom Help Text or configure an instruction field on the requisition to alert Recruiting users to this limitation.

- **Using multiple assessment vendors**

  The fields, configuration, and workflows used with this integration are only valid for PeopleAnswers and SHL. Integrating with any other vendor requires a custom integration. Any custom integration won't use the same fields, configurations, or workflows so the user experience will differ for applicants.

- **Candidate forwarding**

  In Recruiting, if you move a candidate from one requisition to another requisition and into a status after the assessment trigger status, the system won't send an assessment request to that candidate. You should move the candidate to a status before the assessment trigger status in the new requisition.

- **Adding assessment score to applicant summary view**

  Data for PeopleAnswers and SHL are stored in different fields, and the two vendors don't share a common score field that can be permanently added to the applicant summary page. To view the score for all applicants, you must add the individual vendor score field to the applicant summary view for each requisition.

- **Boomi failure message**

  The Boomi standard integration for assessment integration requires that all the fields used in the integration pack are available in your requisition data model. If you get a failure message in Boomi with the pattern **Exception=[SFAPI Domain Error!] Error Code=[INVALID_FIELD_NAME] Error Message=[Field <field name> is not defined]**, check your data model for missing fields. For example, the **Gender** field is used in the integration pack. You must have this field in the JRDM, but it doesn't have to be permissioned for any user, so it never displays.

15.5   DocuSign for Electronic Signature

One of the newer third-party integrations offered by SAP SuccessFactors is with Docu-Sign to support electronic signature. Within Recruiting, you can use DocuSign integration to support electronic signatures on offer letters. This is a welcome integration as many companies don't feel the electronic acceptance feature is enough to support their needs.

To enable **Online Offer with eSignature**, a company must have a DocuSign account. This feature isn't supported with other eSignature vendors. For new DocuSign clients, contact *sales_successfactors@docusign.com*. Indicate that you're an SAP SuccessFactors Recruiting company who would like to sign up for a new business or enterprise account. Provide a system administrator email and password to DocuSign. The admin user is the primary account for the integration and can update DocuSign account preferences.

DocuSign refers to transactions as envelopes, which are equivalent to offer letters (or the act of sending an offer letter) in SAP SuccessFactors. This feature includes only the candidate eSignature process to be assigned via the SAP SuccessFactors system. However, additional signers can be added on demand within the DocuSign portal.

The **Online Offer with eSignature** option follows the existing online offer functionality. For example, if a Recruiting user creates a new online offer with eSignature while an existing offer is pending, the existing offer and eSignature request expire. The DocuSign system triggers any emails specific to the eSignature functionality. You can't modify the branding and content of these emails in the SAP SuccessFactors system.

15

Tip

If there is a limit to how many users can be linked to your DocuSign account, SAP SuccessFactors can't override the limit, and no additional users will be added. If additional users are required, contact DocuSign.

Recruiting users see a warning if they attempt to create an online offer letter for a candidate who already has an offer letter for another job at the same company. When candidates view their online offer, they will see an option to **Accept & eSign**, along with the options to decline the offer or email the recruiter. If candidates select **Accept & eSign**, they can choose to sign the offer at a later time. If candidates don't want to eSign the offer, they can decline the eSignature and contact the recruiter to sign a hard copy of the offer.

After candidates accept and eSign the offer, the Recruiting user can view the eSignature offer or eSignature certificate by clicking on the appropriate link in the **Offer Letter** portlet. You can also view the candidate response and eSignature response status separately. ESignature is reportable. All other fields follow online offer reportability.

Let's look at working with DocuSign integration from both the recruiter and candidate perspectives.

15.5.1   Online Offer with eSignature for Recruiters

Recruiting users with the appropriate permissions can create an offer letter from the application record toolbar for candidates in the **Offer** status. When an online offer with eSignature is configured, you can select **Online Offer with eSignature** to trigger DocuSign to display an iFrame in SAP SuccessFactors. The candidate's email address is used to populated the **To** field.

Don't edit the candidate email address directly in this field. This causes the DocuSign integration to fail. The candidate's email address and name must match exactly in the DocuSign system and SAP SuccessFactors. This includes middle name or initial. If a candidate has a middle name or initial in one system, the name must match exactly in the other system. The offer letter **Message** field populates with the offer letter template name. You can edit this field in the iFrame. The Recruiting user can then drag and drop tags onto the offer letter. Add additional signers in the **To** field. These signers aren't asked to sign in to SAP SuccessFactors before signing the document but will arrive directly in DocuSign. For additional signers, the Recruiting user must assign additional tags on a per person basis.

Signers are tracked in the certification document available from the **Offer Letter** portlet. The **Offer Response** status doesn't update based on the additional signers. To view the response from additional signers, click **View Certificate**. To return to the **Offer Method Selection** page, click any of the following:

- **Cancel eSignature Offer**
- **Go Back**
- **Save Draft** (draft mode isn't supported so selecting **Save Draft** will result in a Recruiting user losing the work they attempted to save)
- **Discard Changes**

Clicking **Send** sends the candidate an email from DocuSign and displays a success message to the Recruiting user. The Recruiting user can select **Continue to Candidate** to return to the candidate profile. After the offer letter is sent, Recruiting users with appropriate permissions see an entry for the offer letter in the **Offer Letter** portlet. Individual fields in the portlet can't be permissioned.

Following are the **Offer Letter** portlet fields related to eSignature:

- **Send Mode**
  This includes a link to view the offer letter in DocuSign.

- **View Certificate**
  This includes a link to view the DocuSign certificate of the audit history of the signing process.

- **Offer Extended On**
  This is the date the Recruiting user sent the offer.

- **Candidate Response**
  Possible values are as follows:

  - **Accepted**

  - **Declined**

  - **Expired** (displays when an offer has expired because a new online offer was created)

  - **Canceled**

- **Candidate Responded On**
  This is the date the candidate responded to the offer. This isn't always the date of the eSignature response.

- **eSignature Response**
  Possible values are as follows:

  - **Pending with Candidate**

  - **Declined by Candidate**

  - **Declined** (implies additional recipient added, not candidate)

  - **Completed**

  - **Expired** (eSignature has expired because a new offer was created)

  - **Canceled**

> **Note**
>
> The cancel functionality isn't supported. To cancel a current offer, the Recruiting user must send a new offer. Sending a new offer will alert the candidate to the voided and new offers.

By default, all DocuSign notifications for candidates and Recruiting users are enabled. Individual users can change these settings to manage their notifications.

15

Additionally, a Recruiting user can enable email notifications when a candidate chooses to accept or decline an offer via Recruiting email triggers.

15.5.2   Online Offer with eSignature for Candidates

After the Recruiting user sends the offer letter, the candidate receives an email from DocuSign requesting an eSignature. Upon receiving the email, the candidate clicks on the **View Documents** link in the email and arrives on the sign-in page for the internal or external career site, based on the candidate type. Candidates don't need a Docu-Sign account to give their eSignature.

After the candidate signs in to the career site, the details of their offer display on the **My Offers** tab.

When candidates view the online offer, they can accept and eSign the offer, decline the offer, or email the recruiter. If candidates select **Accept & eSign**, the DocuSign pop-up displays. The candidate then sees a disclosure statement, which is configured in the DocuSign admin. The candidate can do the following:

- **Review Document**
- **Decline** (the eSignature status updates to **Declined by Candidate**)
- **Finish Later**

Candidates can return to the **My Offers** tab and initiate the eSignature process later. After choosing **Review Document**, candidates can choose their signature.

After candidates choose their signature, they can sign and complete the document. Candidates can view their list of offers from the **My Offers** tab when signed in on the career site.

> **Note**
>
> The DocuSign portal is translated to the candidate's locale. The candidate can over-ride this function by selecting a language on the DocuSign site.

15.6   Summary

Using the standard integrations developed with SAP SuccessFactors vendor partners, integrating ancillary systems to SAP SuccessFactors Recruiting Management is rela-tively straightforward and can be done quickly. It does require time and effort on the vendor side as well, but neither effort should be extensive. Using these vendor relationships will facilitate ancillary processes such as background checks and assessments within Recruiting. Electronic signatures via DocuSign offer robust functionality where eSignatures can be captured on offer letters. Sharing information between SAP SuccessFactors and LinkedIn provides a user-centric experience by leveraging candidate profile data.

When a company has a relationship with a vendor that isn't an approved vendor partner of SAP, it's possible to create a custom integration to that system from Recruiting in a variety of ways. Having the ability to pull the ancillary systems into the overall landscape of your talent acquisition process and systems provides the most robust candidate and recruiter experience.

In the next section, we turn our attention to SAP SuccessFactors Onboarding.

15

PART II
SAP SuccessFactors Onboarding

Chapter 16
Onboarding Overview

*More than two-thirds of all new hires fail to meet their first perfor-
mance milestones, and the attrition rate among new hires is twice as
high in the first year of employment than in their succeeding years.
Getting your new hires connected and contributing isn't just critical to
their individual success, it's critical to overall company success. The
first few days, weeks, and months of the employee's employment are
crucial to their (and your) long-term success.*

You've worked hard to attract, engage, and select the best candidate possible for your
critical positions. Now what? With research overwhelmingly showing that many new
hires decide to leave their new jobs within the first few months, the pressure is on to
make the most of your recruiting investment to help make your new hires productive as quickly as possible. There are many business drivers for which customers
might buy an onboarding solution, including the following:

- Manage paperwork and manual tasks more efficiently
- Get new employees productive more quickly
- Increase employee engagement
- Improve employee retention
- Assimilate new hires faster and more efficiently

Statistics show it can take up to six months for new hires to reach the break-even
point where they start contributing to the performance of the company. If you lose a
new hire within those first six months, you've lost every bit of investment made in
that new hire up to that point, and you're in the hole. This is where SAP SuccessFactors Onboarding comes in to provide the complete set of tools that you need to get
your new hires productive as soon as possible.

In this section of the book, we turn our attention to onboarding, both as a business
process and specifically looking at the SAP SuccessFactors Onboarding module. We'll
talk about trends in employee onboarding, offboarding, and crossboarding, as well as

ways that companies may want to approach these critical business processes as they not only seek to engage new hires but also transition out exiting employees and make inter-organization transfers more seamless.

In this first chapter of Part II of this book, we'll discuss the philosophy behind the design of the Onboarding module and the ways in which SAP SuccessFactors approaches this critical business process area. We'll discuss some of the features geared toward new employees and hiring managers, talk about collaboration options, and touch briefly on some administrative features. Let's begin by discussing how SAP SuccessFactors approaches onboarding.

16.1   The SAP SuccessFactors Approach to Onboarding

Many people are usually involved in onboarding new hires: hiring managers, HR, IT, security, facilities, and others. Each of these represents key players in getting a new employee sorted to begin working on the first day. Activities include getting critical paperwork processed, assigning office or desk space and making sure the needed equipment is available, and making sure the employee gets his badge on day 1. All of these activities are time-consuming and take a lot of coordination. And then you have the new hire, who is facing starting with a new company, meeting a new manager and new coworkers, and getting used to a new work space, geographical location, and company culture. This can be overwhelming! Every one of these players, including the new hire, has a part to play in making the new employee successful.

SAP SuccessFactors views onboarding new employees like mountain climbing. New hires are expected to scale the mountain to reach the top and succeed, but do they have the right equipment and training? SAP SuccessFactors Onboarding is focused on equipping new hires with what they need to reach the top of the mountain. From the moment they log in, they can immediately start connecting with the people and information they need to be successful on their first day and beyond. With a personalized experience, new hires connect with their mentors, teammates, and other peers and get access to critical content and resources. The Onboarding experience adapts with new hires to help them assimilate and develop.

The focus is threefold:

- Guide
- Connect
- Develop

Onboarding *guides* both new employees and hiring managers through easy-to-follow steps using a series of wizards. You want your new employees to have the best possible experience as they surf waves of paperwork, government forms, benefit elections, and payroll information as their first real introduction to their new company. Likewise, onboarding may be something hiring managers do once per month, or maybe once per year. Some hiring managers excel at it, and others need more support. Making the onboarding experience as easy for the hiring manager as it is for the new employee increases the overall effectiveness of the process.

By guiding each key player through important steps and tasks, you increase process efficiency while reducing legal risk with higher compliance returns—all while giving them a user-focused experience in a central location for all users.

SAP SuccessFactors recognizes that it's important to *connect* new employees with the company and that the more connected they are, the faster they are on the road to productivity. Even before their first day on the job, Onboarding provides a social platform for new hires to meet and interact with their new team members, manager, and company. Extending features of the SAP SuccessFactors platform such as SAP Jam and the employee profile, you can personally welcome each new hire to the company, provide critical information, and reduce the fear of the unknown they would otherwise face on day one. Provide a point of contact by assigning a new hire "buddy" on whom they can rely for the questions they may be afraid to ask. Robust collaboration options within Onboarding give new hires the opportunity both to meet their new team and introduce themselves. By beginning to complete their profile, recording their name, and providing a short bio, new hires can tell their new team who they are and what their background is.

Then, Onboarding helps to *develop* the new hires right from the beginning by empowering them with integrated talent management. Of course, Onboarding is a natural fit from SAP SuccessFactors Recruiting, but it also fits with goal setting, development, performance, and learning. From the first day, new hires can discuss what is expected of them in their new role with their new managers and set their first performance goals captured on the new hire goal plan. Reviews at the 30-, 60-, and 90-day mark are easily supported in SAP SuccessFactors Performance & Goals, and SAP SuccessFactors Learning knows exactly who they are and what role they fill to assign training to the learning plan automatically. No longer will your new hires sit around waiting to find out what training they are expected to take while the days tick away of their first week. Increasing an employee's time to contribution improves employee satisfaction, which in turn increases retention.

16

Onboarding recognizes that companies which excel at onboarding can see quite significant improvements in first-year retention and employees meeting first-year performance metrics, so it's geared to help customers excel at this often-neglected business process. Studies show that companies that do onboarding well can see over 90% retention in first-year employees and over 60% of those employees meeting first-year milestones. On the reverse, companies that struggle with onboarding see numbers as low as 30% in first-year retention and less than 20% meeting first year goals.

Those statistics are staggering. With all the time, money, and resources spent finding the right candidates, it's critical to continue the hard work through the onboarding process to help equip new hires with the tools they need to be successful. An effective onboarding process can lead to the following, among other things:

- Higher job satisfaction and performance levels
- Organizational commitment
- Career effectiveness
- Lower turnover

Let's now take a look at the experience of the new employee within Onboarding.

16.2   The New Hire Experience and Team Collaboration

Onboarding is mainly centered around creating a positive experience for the new hire and engaging them with their new company using a variety of collaboration mechanisms. In this section, we'll discuss the new hire experience within Onboarding, the Employee Portal or pre-day one activities, using Onboarding to complete necessary paperwork, beginning to build out performance expectations on the new hire goal plan, and other collaboration mechanisms within the module. We'll start with the new hire experience.

16.2.1   New Hire Experience

The candidate has made it through a possibly arduous recruiting experience—interviews, assessments, background checks—and has made it to accepting the offer. It would be nice if that would be the end of the climbing, but, in many ways, it's just the start. They still have very far to go to reach that mountain peak to productivity. Let's think about some of the many things that a new employee may be confronted with when starting a new job:

- Completing reams of paperwork
- Reading and acknowledging company policies and procedures
- Being assigned equipment and a work area
- Meeting new colleagues
- Dealing with a new commute, how to get there, where to park, and how to access the building
- Adjusting to a new role with possibly more or different responsibilities
- Learning and assimilating to a new company culture

Then they can be faced with meeting with their new manager to discuss performance expectations, set goals, and complete training. It's daunting to even consider. With tools such as new hire buddies, the Employee Portal, and the employee profile, Onboarding can ease the burdens placed on new employees by giving them a consolidated place to connect and learn.

Onboarding is focused on giving new hires a personalized experience even before they show up for their first day; you want to give them a look into what their first day on the job will be like to alleviate the natural stress that comes with starting a new job. Figure 16.1 demonstrates how hiring managers can set personalized messages for their new employees. With social collaboration tools that allow them to see what their new manager and peers look like and the ability to learn a little about them through their employee profiles, and giving them access to critical information and resources, they can show up on day one feeling more confident in what the day will hold. This results in more relaxed new hires who can begin to engage and learn right away.

In SAP SuccessFactors, the Onboarding experience can adapt with the new hire. Linkages to other elements of talent management within the suite such as the goal plan and SAP SuccessFactors Learning, and connecting with internal social networks via SAP Jam create a very personal experience for each new employee. The whole goal is

16

to help the new hires hit the ground running with the right equipment to scale the mountain.

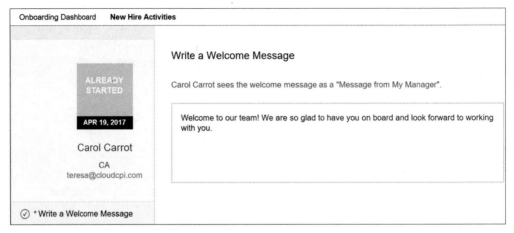

Figure 16.1 Greeting New Employees with a Personalized Message Set by the Hiring Manager

16.2.2   Employee Portal and Pre-Day One Access

There are two options to introduce new employees to their Onboarding experience: the Employee Portal and pre-day one access. Both of these tools will help guide new hires through all of the resources available to them while they are being onboarded to the company. The Employee Portal is based on SharePoint technology and provides access to this portal prior to new hires being hired within SAP SuccessFactors Employee Central. Pre-day one access gives your new hires access to SAP SuccessFactors Platform even before the hiring action to complete the necessary steps in the onboarding process. So the difference is that with the Employee Portal, new hires are accessing a SharePoint platform, whereas with pre-day one, they are logging in to SAP SuccessFactors. Let's look at the features of each one.

Employee Portal

This portal is available to new hires within the first numerous weeks or months of employment, but it can be set for longer periods of time. Some customers have robust onboarding processes that can span the entire first year of employment. To allow new hires to engage even before their first day, you can give them access to the Employee Portal before they are actually hired into your human resources information system (HRIS).

The Employee Portal can be branded to your company color scheme, with your logo and company-specific graphics so that the new employee feels welcomed from their first experience as shown in Figure 16.2. Because the Employee Portal is built on SharePoint technology, filters are available to enable you to create customized content for different groups of new hires based on data such as location or job code. For instance, you could create a look and feel for new employees in the United States, a different one for new employees in France, and still another experience for new employees in Australia. This could also fall along lines of business (IT, finance, engineering, etc.). This helps you create targeted experiences for new hires in different locations, business units, and kinds of jobs.

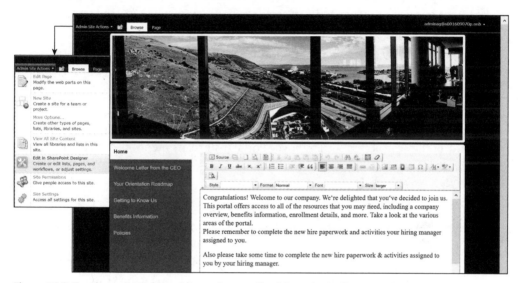

Figure 16.2 Employee Portal Providing a Personalized Experience for New Hires

Documents make up an important component of the Employee Portal. Information such as benefits offerings, employee handbooks, company policies, and the like are examples of documents that can be accessed in the Employee Portal. All of the documents you want to make available there must first be loaded to the Employee Portal server before they can be accessed. They will then be accessible via the web browser. The Onboarding administrator has access to modify the Employee Portal to make it as engaging and informative as possible and to keep it updated over time. One way to ensure you're always providing the most engaging experience for your new employees is to survey them about their onboarding experience. Take their feedback and funnel it back into improving the experience. Not only will it enhance your process, but it will also help new employees feel they are making an important contribution from the start.

Within the Employee Portal, you can provide Flash files and YouTube videos with engaging and personalized content for a better experience than just reading through documents. Adding a video welcome message from the CEO, for example, is a great way to engage your new hires and help make them feel valued. Provide some pictures from recent company events or perhaps a marketing video on ways the company is involved with the community. There really is no limit to the options, and you should approach building the Employee Portal with an open mind and lots of creative ideas. Perhaps ask recent new hires what would have made their onboarding experience more engaging or what some of their previous employers included in onboarding. With the flexibility of the tool, you can always update and improve.

When the Employee Portal is used in your onboarding process, the new hires will receive an email invitation welcoming them to the portal and providing instructions on how to access it. After they select the link to access the portal, they will first be directed to create a password. If the Employee Portal is used as part of an onboarding process, new hires will have the option to complete their paperwork through a wizard, or they can access the Employee Portal instead. As mentioned, after their paperwork is complete, they will access the Employee Portal when logging in.

Pre-Day One Access

Very similar to the Employee Portal, with a different access point for new employees prior to their first day of employment, is the pre-day one feature. As part of the pre-day one functionality, new hires log in directly to the SAP SuccessFactors platform to access their new hire activities. These activities are set up by the hiring manager and should be personalized to the new employee. Managers can set up any number of activities such as the following:

- Provide a welcome message
- Provide recommended links
- Schedule meetings with the new employee
- Assign a buddy
- Create an onboarding checklist

When new employees log in to SAP SuccessFactors, they will see the **Onboarding Tour**. This feature appears on the home page for the first 30 days the new hire is with the company. It displays as a carousel across the top of the home page, and new employees can access different information about the company and their new team.

The Onboarding tour will highlight for employees the tiles that are available to enhance their experience such as Onboarding tiles, SAP Jam, the status of their paperwork, and other customized information. The **Onboarding Tour** is displayed in Figure 16.3 to show the **People to Meet** tile where new employees can get introduced to their buddy and other key people the manager thinks are important for the employee to connect with. As you would expect with SAP SuccessFactors, this is graphical and engaging for new employees, providing pictures of each key person so they can get to know these key contacts even before their first day in the office.

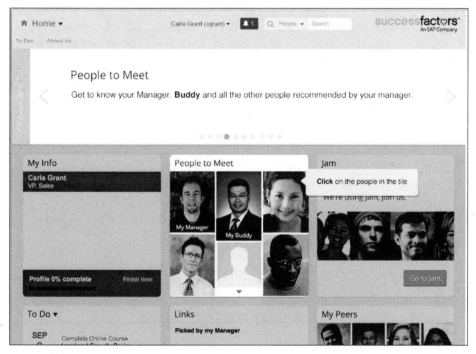

Figure 16.3 Onboarding Tour Providing Important Information and New Hire Activities Set Up by Managers of New Employees

Onboarding Tiles on the Home Page

Several tiles can be enabled for new hires to access on the SAP SuccessFactors home page. These tiles each provide specific information to new employees and easy access to other features in their onboarding experience:

- **Paperwork**
  This tile provides an inventory of the paperwork that the new employee has completed or still needs to complete. If there are pending items, these are easily accessible from this tile.

- **Welcome Message from the Manager**
  Presented as a type of postcard in special handwriting font, the welcome message allows the manager to provide a very personalized message to the new employee. This is one of the first things the employee sees after logging in to SAP SuccessFactors.

- **People to Meet**
  While the manager is creating the new hire activities, the manager can assign the new employee a buddy as well as other key contacts that are recommended. When you select a person's photo, you can view profile information as well as the reason the manager recommended that person.

- **My Peers**
  This tile is similar to the **My Team** tile that managers have access to, but this tile displays an employee's peers with photos and available employee profile information to get acquainted with new team members.

- **Picked by my Manager**
  Here new employees can access various links that the manager may create while setting up new hire activities. These can be anything from information on key initiatives, company events, links to the intranet, or helpful information on the surrounding area.

- **Create Your Profile**
  In this tile, new employees have access to a wizard the first time they access their home page. This also provides an overview of key things they will need to pay attention to such as the **ToDo** tile and the **About Us** page.

- **Employee Portal**
  If the Employee Portal is in use, you can create a custom tile to display on the home page where new hires can access the portal.

Any, or all, of these tiles can be deployed to provide the best user experience for your new employees. Figure 16.4 provides an example of some of these available tiles.

Figure 16.4 Tiles with Specific Onboarding Information to Create an Enhanced Experience for New Employees

16.2.3   Completing Necessary Forms and Electronic Signatures

One of the most tactical and valuable features of the Onboarding module is the ability to automate filling out and signing various forms that are always a part of starting a new job. From government tax forms to direct deposit information to reviewing and acknowledging company policies and procedures, there always seems to be a mountain of documents to review, fill out, and sign. This can prove to be a nightmare for both the new hire and those in HR responsible for coordinating the effort. Often hiring managers get involved in these activities, trying to follow up with new hires after they start.

Onboarding not only eliminates the back and forth and paper involved in onboarding, it takes care of the compliance aspect too. HR and the hiring manager can all log in and track who has completed what and which steps and documents are still outstanding, and then follow up as appropriate. And all the documents are stored in one location, which is always accessible. Figure 16.5 provides an example of completing a form in the system. The system requests information in a way that is easy to understand and outputs it into a completed form that meets government standards. It couldn't be a better user experience for new hires.

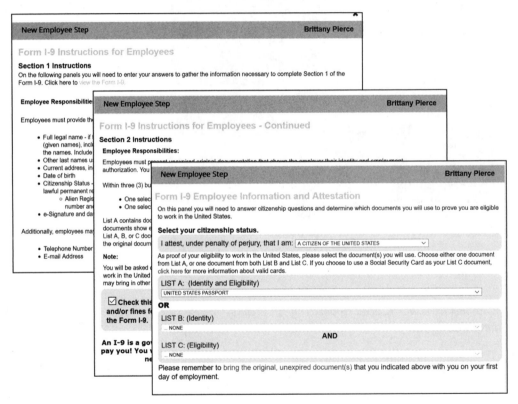

Figure 16.5 Screens Asking New Employees for Information Used to Populate Necessary Forms

Throughout the process, managers and HR can keep tabs on how each new hire is progressing through the process and can provide assistance as needed. All of the forms are presented for electronic signature at the end of the process and are stored in the Document Center or can be downloaded locally or printed, as the need arises.

New employees are stepped through an easy-to-follow wizard that asks questions and captures information that can then be formatted into preconfigured forms. Government forms for various countries are maintained as standard in the Onboarding module that can be deployed to capture necessary tax and other information required of new employees. Figure 16.6 is an example of how an employee in the United States can use Onboarding to complete tax forms that are then signed and submitted for processing. Additional information is also available to assist the employee in completing the forms, as provided.

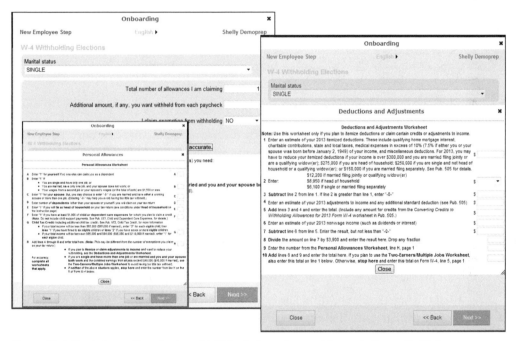

Figure 16.6 Tax Information Captured within Onboarding and Properly Formatted into a Government Approved Form

New employees continue through numerous panels to complete all necessary paperwork and forms. Often businesses will solicit emergency contacts as well as direct deposit information that will be passed to Employee Central with the hiring action. After all paperwork is completed, the forms are presented for review and signature. Employees can electronically sign by entering their password and a PIN, as shown in Figure 16.7. Additionally, integration with DocuSign is available so that electronic signatures can be captured on all necessary forms.

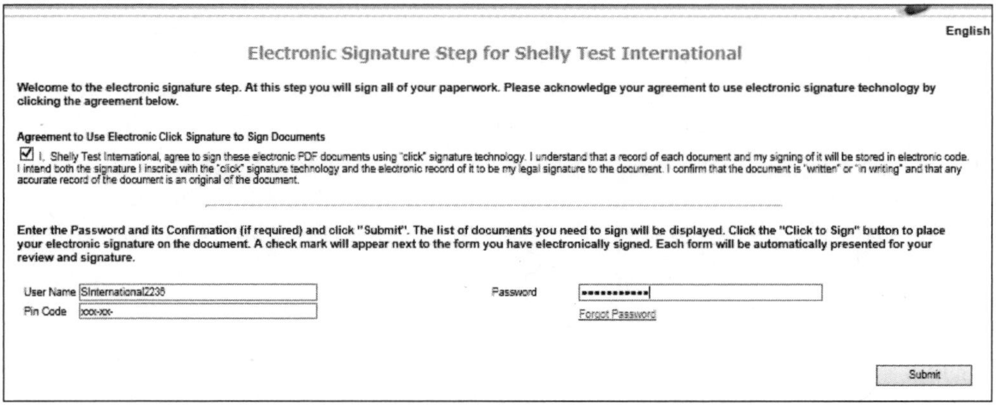

Figure 16.7 Entering a Password and PIN to Sign Documentation

16.2.4   New Hire Goal Plan and Training To-Do Items

One of the most important elements of setting up new employees to succeed in their roles is to communicate the expectations for their performance and set goals for their first few weeks and months on the job. Statistics show that new employees who have clearly defined and communicated performance goals and targets are the most successful within the first year and are more likely to stay in their jobs. One of the advantages of the SAP SuccessFactors suite is the built-in integration among the modules. With Onboarding, you can integrate with SAP SuccessFactors Performance & Goals and make available a new hire goal plan where new employees can work with their managers on setting the first performance goals as displayed in Figure 16.8.

All of the functionality within Performance & Goals is available via the Onboarding platform to support the goal setting of new employees in the first few days of employment. One of the first meetings new employees should have is a performance discussion with their new manager to set goals for them to focus on while their Onboarding experience plays out. After they are hired in the HRIS, they can maintain their goals from the **Goals** tab within the platform. If pre-day one is in use, the **Goal** tab may be available even before an employee's first day.

Training can be assigned to new employees and be made available for completion during their pre-day one activities as well. These are assigned in Learning and available in the **ToDo** tile, or the **Learning** tile, directly from the home page. Having new hires get started on required training even before their first day on the job is a great way to increase their productivity in their first weeks of employment. While this isn't always possible, many new employees appreciate the opportunity to take care of some of these more tactical activities before they start their job.

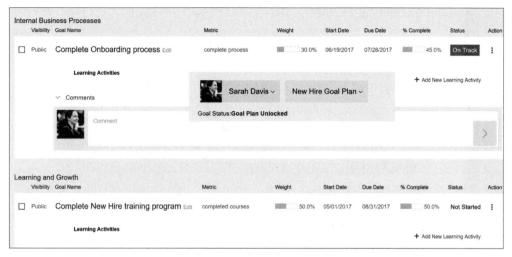

Figure 16.8 Integration with Performance & Goals to Maintain New Employee Goals within the First Months of Employment

16.2.5   Team Collaboration Options

Any effective onboarding process will include opportunities for the new employee to meet and collaborate not only with their direct team members but also with others within the company who can contribute to their success. We've seen a few of these collaboration opportunities in the **My Peers** and **People to Meet** tiles that introduce new employees to key contacts they need to know. Other ways to provide new employees the opportunity to collaborate—either with each other or valuable company contacts—is via SAP Jam groups. Common examples of collaboration via SAP Jam include new hire groups that connect new employees despite geographic location or role. Here they can access important information, view videos and other resources on company events and culture, and ask questions and receive responses from other new employees or other group administrators.

16.3   Hiring Manager Experience

Research shows that hiring manager involvement in the onboarding process is critical to the overall success of the new employee. Onboarding is geared toward the hiring manager taking a front-and-center role, and there are several activities that the hiring manager can drive and complete to make onboarding as engaging and meaningful as possible for the new employee. Hiring managers may complete onboarding after a month or after a year. Some are going to be excellent at onboarding, and others are going to need some help to make sure all the bases are covered. Emphasizing that guiding principle, Onboarding offers the hiring manager easy-to-follow steps in wizards, just as it does for the new employee.

In the previous section, we saw the output of the manager's setting up new hire activities. Here the manager creates a very personalized experience for each new employee, as shown in Figure 16.9. These new hire activities can include some or all of the following and can be updated throughout the onboarding process:

- Writing a welcome message that is displayed to new employees when they log in
- Assigning a new hire buddy
- Recommending people the new employee should connect with
- Scheduling meetings
- Recommending links to critical information or resources
- Setting goals
- Furnishing equipment
- Going through a checklist of items

Figure 16.9 Managers Setting Up Activities for Each New Hire

Hiring managers can drop in and out of activities as needed to make changes or updates. This capability is provided via the web browser and the mobile app so they can continue onboarding on the go.

Hiring managers can scroll through a carousel of new hires assigned for them to onboard, with critical information provided such as name, start date, location, and position by selecting the ‹ or › buttons (see Figure 16.10). Below each new hire's information is the space where the manager can complete the list of activities for that new hire. They can keep track of what has been completed, what is still outstanding, and what is required.

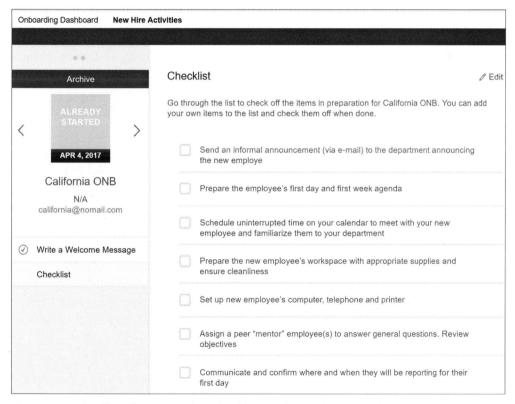

Figure 16.10 Checklist of Activities That Should Occur during the Onboarding Process

There is some best practice content for the hiring manager checklist activities available from the Success Store. These templates provide a good starting point for creating the first hiring manager activities and can be built on from there. Let's briefly look at several components of the hiring manager activities, as follows:

- **Welcome Message**

  This message is seen by the new employee when they enter Onboarding. Hiring managers can create their own message for each new hire, or an administrator can provide a template message that is displayed to all hiring managers and new hires. This default welcome message only supports tokens and may not be the personal touch desired. New employees will also see this welcome message on their phone on day one.

- **Schedule Meetings**

  One of the convenient features of Onboarding is the ability for managers to schedule meetings with their new employees. Administrators may configure a list of recommended meetings that display to managers in the **Schedule Meetings** activity. These will have a default **Subject** and **Agenda** for each type of meeting. Any orientation scheduled by HR will appear as well, so the manager doesn't schedule conflicting meetings. You can configure the types of meetings being recommended to suit your needs.

- **Assign a Buddy**

  Managers can assign each new employee a buddy that will be their go-to person for questions and other support as they are onboarded. In this activity, the manager can select from a carousel of possible buddies that are pulled from the new employee's peers. They can also search from the employee directory. Note that the system only supports one buddy, but the **Recommended People** activity can be used to assign additional support for the new hire.

- **Recommended People**

  This features allows managers to connect the new employee with more than just one buddy and helps build their social network from day one. Managers can search the employee directory to add each recommended person and then enter a reason they are being recommended. Recommendations are assigned a status of **Relevant** or **Mandatory**.

- **Checklist**

  This is a list of reminders for managers to make sure they know what they need to do when and that they don't miss anything. This is an important activity and should be included in your process.

Business rules can be used to drive certain manager activity assignments. For instance, you may want to have a different collection of hiring manager activities in two different locations or business units within the organization. If business rules aren't used, then all hiring managers will have the same activities within the system.

16.4   Delivered Forms versus Custom Panels

Onboarding comes with numerous forms standard depending on what country is in scope. These forms will capture various information required by the government as well as other information such as where to deposit paychecks and emergency contacts. Not all countries have forms delivered as standard. For those countries that don't have standard forms, you can build custom panels that can capture the information necessary for onboarding employees in a specific country. The countries and forms provided as standard are shown in Table 16.1.

Country	Form Type
Australia	<ul><li>Tax file number declaration</li><li>Superannuation standard choice form</li></ul>
Canada	<ul><li>Federal and provincial tax forms</li></ul>
India	<ul><li>Transfer Claim form</li><li>Provident Funds Declaration and Nomination Form</li></ul>
United Kingdom	<ul><li>Starter Checklist</li><li>P45 – Details of employee leaving work</li></ul>
United States	<ul><li>I-9</li><li>W4</li><li>8850</li><li>I-9 Reverification</li><li>State withholding forms</li><li>Federal W-4 for States and Military Spouse Residency Relief Act Forms</li><li>State tax withholding forms</li><li>California Wage Theft Protection Act</li><li>New York Wage Theft Protection Act</li><li>Pennsylvania Residency</li></ul>
Standard Hiring Forms	<ul><li>Direct Deposit</li><li>Pay Card Acknowledgement</li><li>New Employee Summary Form</li><li>EEO Information (US)</li><li>Emergency Contact</li></ul>

Table 16.1 Standard Delivered Onboarding Forms by Country

16

16.5   Administrative Functionality

As with other modules within the SAP SuccessFactors suite, Onboarding has robust administrative capabilities. Since its introduction several years ago, nearly all of the module configuration has been moved into the Admin Center. This is great news because you can now build and maintain onboarding, offboarding, and crossboarding processes as needed to support your business after initial implementation. Within Admin Center you can do the following:

- Manage the Employee Portal
- Set up and maintain the new hire activity planning process
- Manage notifications
- Maintain Onboarding settings
- Manage security
- Design panels
- Maintain the Data Dictionary
- Manage home page tiles
- Manage the work queue

Figure 16.11 demonstrates how administrators can manage notifications for Onboarding.

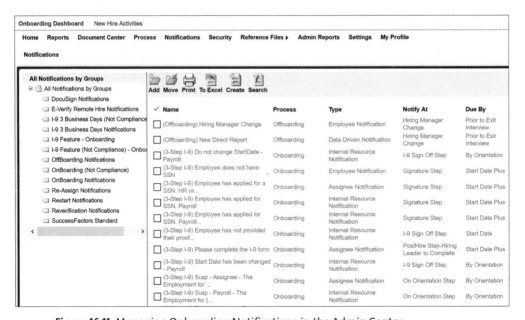

Figure 16.11 Managing Onboarding Notifications in the Admin Center

You can also see some of the other features available such as reference files, admin reports, and other settings. You can even process employees manually for onboarding, offboarding, and crossboarding from the **Process** tab. Figure 16.12 demonstrates an offboarding process being initiated.

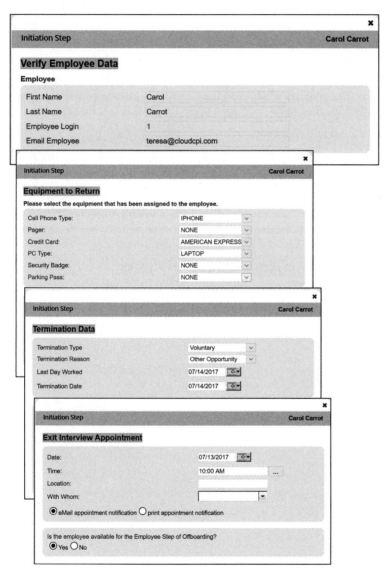

Figure 16.12 Initiating Offboarding from the Onboarding Dashboard

We'll discuss Onboarding administrative features in greater detail in Chapter 18.

16.6   Summary

SAP SuccessFactors Onboarding is designed around the two most critical players in the onboarding process: the new hire and his or her manager. By guiding, connecting, and developing new employees, companies can increase their engagement while decreasing their time to productivity, helping to create longer retention of their workforce. The Onboarding module is geared toward providing new employees with an engaging and collaborative experience where they can complete burdensome tasks such as completing paperwork and connect with key contacts that will help create an effective and impactful experience. Whether new employees log in to the Employee Portal or experience the pre-day one activities, their experience can be personalized, helping them feel valued and special.

By not only including managers in the onboarding process but also having them develop and guide the process, they play one of the most critical roles in getting new employees acclimated to their new environment and effective in their jobs. Managers can use numerous tools such as welcome messages, buddies, links, and checklists to create the best possible onboarding process for all involved. By leveraging other modules within SAP SuccessFactors, such as Performance & Goals and Learning, you're able to focus on employee performance from even before their first day, providing them with the tools they need to hit their stride in their new job.

Now let's look at the various processes that can be supported by the Onboarding module.

Chapter 17

Onboarding Processes

"The oldest and strongest emotion of mankind is fear, and the oldest and strongest form of fear is fear of the unknown." H. P. Lovecraft most certainly wasn't thinking about employees when he made this statement. However, it's certainly very applicable to new employees beginning a position with a new company, moving to a new position within the same company, or venturing out to new opportunities. The more we can alleviate employee fear, the better we can support their success.

We began this book with a brief discussion of onboarding at a glance and discussed several key statistics relevant to new employee effectiveness and retention. As we saw, the onboarding process plays a significant role in a worker's success, and it's critical to get new employees engaged and productive as quickly as possible. However, this doesn't just apply to onboarding employees but also the processes commonly referred to as crossboarding and offboarding. But what do these terms really mean, and what do these processes look like?

In this chapter, we'll take a deeper look at the onboarding process and how to structure an effective and engaging onboarding process to support your new employees. We'll also define both crossboarding and offboarding, and consider what these processes may look like.

Let's start with discussing a well-designed onboarding process.

17.1 Onboarding

Onboarding is a system of processes for integrating new employees into the social and performance aspects of their new jobs as quickly and smoothly as possible. The sooner new employees can feel assimilated into their new company, culture, and job responsibilities, the better they will perform, and the greater the odds of their retention with the company. After an effective recruitment process, onboarding is one of the most important and impactful ways an organization can improve the effectiveness of their overall talent management strategy.

Companies that engage in formal onboarding by defining and implementing detailed processes for new employees are more successful than those who don't. The long-term benefits of formal onboarding include not just higher retention rates but also increased job satisfaction, performance levels, and career effectiveness. A formal onboarding process should strive to achieve the following:

- Begin before day one of employment
- Engage others in the process such as hiring managers and peers
- Facilitate the paperwork associated with starting a new job
- Communicate and set performance expectations early
- Communicate the culture often
- Give new employees time to hit their stride
- Provide open channels of feedback

Let's begin our discussion of an effective onboarding process by discussing how to start even before the employee's first day on the job.

17.1.1   Begin Before Day One

The highest-performing companies will begin onboarding new hires before their first day. With engagement high during the recruiting process, it can send the wrong message to stop interacting after the offer letter has been accepted and expect new employees to show up on their first day excited to get started. Build on the momentum of the hire process so your new employees maintain excitement about starting their new job. This could be as simple as a welcome message from the hiring manager or someone in HR or even a video message from the CEO. Continue to communicate important information between offer acceptance and day one so new hires aren't coming in completely blind.

Introducing new employees to their manager, their new team members, the organization structure, and other elements of their department as well as their HR business partner can help foster engagement in the period between accepting the offer and the start date. Effective ways to begin for day one can include starting the process of collecting that critical paperwork, and communicating job responsibilities, performance expectations, and training needs so employees know what to expect. Some companies may even facilitate employees taking some of that required training before day one.

Of course, SAP SuccessFactors Onboarding offers an employee-focused system to support this engagement and communication between new employees and all players in the process. Traditionally provided through the Employee Portal, new hires can be greeted with a personal message from their new manager, perhaps view a welcome video from the CEO, and begin getting acquainted with their new team. Figure 17.1 provides several views of the Employee Portal.

Figure 17.1 Messages and Panels with Information on the Employee Portal

The Employee Portal can be leveraged in any number of ways to engage your new employees and help build excitement for their new job. Based on SharePoint technology, the Employee Portal must be built and maintained by the business. As of early 2017, SAP is encouraging businesses to use the pre-day one functionality, which allows new hires to log in to the SAP SuccessFactors platform rather than the Employee Portal. Here new hires can view the **Onboarding Tour** page where the hiring manager message is displayed, along with other things such as meetings scheduled for their first few days of employment.

17.1.2   Engage Others in the Process

No one person can communicate everything a new employee needs to know. HR knows what's necessary for compliance, the new manager knows what performance expectations await, coworkers can speak to the day-to-day of the job, and IT knows how to get access to the right systems and equipment. Involving players from all of these areas not only reduces the burden on onboarding a new employee from the HR business partner or the manager but also increase the immediate network the new employee can access to get acclimated.

A common way to engage the new hire and spread the tasks of onboarding is to assign a mentor or a new hire "buddy" in Onboarding. This is the person the new hire can go to for questions as simple as how to work the coffee maker to more serious questions such as how to communicate with the manager. This go-to mentor gives new hires a sense of security in a new and uncertain environment and a channel to get questions answered without feeling as if they are overburdening their new manager. It also takes a great burden off of HR, who often plays this role in an unofficial capacity. Having a point of contact such as a mentor or new hire buddy can alleviate a tremendous amount of stress new employees can experience in their first days and weeks on the job, which can negatively impact their productivity.

Another successful method of increasing engagement and employee productivity is to connect new employees with veteran employees in various departments. Set up meetings or schedule lunches or coffee breaks to get the new employees face time with some of your long-time employees to help new employees see how their role fits in the big picture. It can foster collaboration between departments and establish working relationships that can facilitate cross-department projects in the future.

Finally, it can be advantageous to connect new employees with other new employees. New hires often run into the same challenges and can feel a sense of comradery with other new employees facing the same uncertainty and questions. Many companies will connect new hires in facilitated meetings in the first day and plan activities that keep these new hires connected throughout the first few months of employment. Within SAP SuccessFactors, you can create any number of new hire SAP Jam groups that create social collaboration venues for new hires to connect with each other and other key players in the Onboarding process. These SAP Jam groups are accessible from within Onboarding.

17.1.3 Facilitate the Paperwork

Employee handbooks, payroll forms, nondisclosure agreements, and tax documents are all a part of the great amount of paperwork that accompanies starting a new job. Surveys of HR professionals show that as much as 80% of onboarding paperwork is completed by the new employee in person on their first day on the job, either alone at their new desk, or in a conference room in a new hire orientation session. All of this paperwork can be daunting and even overwhelming, and it cuts into valuable time that new employees could spend in training, meeting with their manager, or getting connected with their peers. Not to mention that it puts a great burden on HR of collecting, tracking, and storing all of those paper forms!

Using Onboarding, businesses can automate the distribution and completion of all of this paperwork, gather electronic signatures, and track the completion of all that necessary paperwork at every step in the process. Giving new employees the freedom to complete this paperwork over time in the privacy of their home can help them deal with often overwhelming amounts of information and source documentation that is required to complete this critical piece of a new job. Best of all, it frees them up on their first day to focus on real value-added activities.

17.1.4 Set Performance Expectations Early

Statistics show that nearly 60% of companies don't set any goals for their new employees. Vagueness in role responsibilities, performance objectives, and norms are dangerous in general but especially so with new employees. Starting a new job already comes with uncertainty and ambiguity that result in stress. Adding to that stress by not communicating what is expected of their performance can increase the uncertainty that accompanies a new job. Expecting new employees to expend time and effort without working toward anything specific can cause new employees to feel quite aimless.

One of the first things managers can do to support the success of new employees is to discuss their immediate performance objectives, setting up a new hire goal plan that is accessible by new employees and their manager throughout the onboarding process. Give new employees clear targets and then give them access to the tools to help them achieve those targets. A good new hire goal may be something such as "Complete 50% of sales training by the end of week two." Longer-term performance

17

objectives and role-specific competencies can be discussed after new employees have had time to show what they can achieve when given the right tools. In addition, probationary performance reviews can be completed to continue giving feedback to employees to help them be successful in the long term.

New hire goals may be consistent for all new hires within the company or a business unit. Others will be more specific to the individual employee. Use Onboarding integration with SAP SuccessFactors Performance & Goals by setting up a new hire goal plan and making it accessible within Onboarding. You can communicate these goals to employees before their first day, and then the new hire can expand on them in deeper conversations with the manager. This plan can then be updated and tracked during the first three, six, or nine months of employment, depending on what is customary in the organization. Giving new hires clear direction on what tasks they should be focused on will increase their likelihood of success.

17.1.5   Communicate the Culture Often

Would it surprise you to learn that nearly 90% of hiring failures are related to poor cultural fit? Assuming recruiters adequately assess a candidate's skills and experience, new hires aren't going to fail because they are unable to do their job. They are more likely to fail because their personality, beliefs, or work habits aren't homogeneous with the company culture and workforce. While you can use screening techniques and assessments to compare a candidate's qualities against the company culture, there will be new employees that are hired that don't fit in right away. What should you do? Make a concerted effort to communicate the company's culture during the recruiting process by providing information about the company, its mission and values, and other aspects of the culture prominently on the external **Careers** page so potential candidates have this information available all throughout the recruiting process. Reiterate company culture throughout the interview process and then continue the culture message throughout the Onboarding process. Onboarding offers tools such as the **Pre-Day 1** or **Employee Portal** pages and SAP Jam groups to help reinforce messages about company culture.

Managers should reaffirm culture during new hire goal setting discussions and explaining roles and responsibilities. These culture conversations can include the following:

- Meeting protocol within the company
- Skills most valued in employees, for example, creativity or analytical skills

- Whether the company fosters social collaboration with sports leagues or other activities
- The importance or role of community service
- Collaboration environment of teams

Giving candidates and new employees an honest picture of the culture can assist them in understanding how, or whether, they fit.

17.1.6 Give New Employees Time to Hit Their Stride

It can take anywhere from 6 to 12 months for new employees to become fully productive in their new roles. After the paperwork is checked off the list, team members are introduced, and managers set clear expectations and performance targets for new hires, it can still take them time to reach full productivity. It can be a fine line between giving employees time to prove themselves in their role and expecting them to produce results. Speeding up the onboarding process so employees can start producing can be tempting. However, speeding up onboarding can be harmful to the development and integration of the new employee and can affect new employee retention. Although it may seem counterintuitive, employees who are exposed to a longer onboarding process actually reach full productivity faster than those who are sped through. Remember that new hire integration into the organization will take time, and the best results occur when new employees are given the tools necessary to be successful.

With Onboarding, you can design a robust and flexible process that includes various touchpoints and steps that can begin before the new hire's first day and go all the way through the first several months of employment. With integration points throughout the SAP SuccessFactors suite, new employees can track their performance goals in SAP SuccessFactors Performance & Goals, keep up to date with their learning requirements in SAP SuccessFactors Learning, create and manage development objectives in SAP SuccessFactors Succession & Development, and perform other critical onboarding activities at any time.

17.1.7 Provide Open Channels of Feedback

Soliciting feedback is not only applicable to new hires but is always a good idea to foster employee satisfaction overall. If employees feel they have a safe and open feedback mechanism, they are more likely to provide feedback that can be critical to improving processes and culture. New hires are likely to notice things in the onboarding process that can be improved or have unique suggestions as an outsider to the organization, but they aren't likely to openly express that on their first day on the job. Providing several avenues for honest feedback will encourage your newest employees to provide feedback and solutions on problems you may not even be aware of.

New employees come into the organization with fresh perspectives and, if asked, are usually willing to share their feedback. If that feedback is incorporated and acted upon, your new employees will feel heard, and you've improved a process or resolved an issue. That is a win all around.

17.2   Offboarding

If a company has a defined onboarding process, it's typically focused on those employees entering the organization while those leaving are often left to their own devices. Leaving a job can produce nearly as many questions and stresses as starting a job. What is offboarding? It's the strategic process for transitioning employees out of the organization, and it's equally as important as onboarding to a company's overall success. Let's examine why offboarding is so important and what elements go into a strong offboarding process.

17.2.1   The Value of a Strong Offboarding Program

Departing employees have power because they leave with their years of industry experience, company knowledge, and intellectual property earned through their service with the organization, and they can freely share their opinions of the company with whomever they choose after they leave. They can be your best advocate or your worst detractor. To ensure they are advocates, companies need to understand that offboarding is much more than turning in a badge and a computer. Offboarding is the chance to create a positive voice in the marketplace. We live in the digital age where social networks run rampant, and individuals are connected through numerous communication channels. While you can never guarantee former employees won't post scathing comments about the organization, you can significantly decrease that likelihood with a strategic offboarding process.

17.2.2   Show Them They Are Valued

Employees leave for various reasons, but unless they are terminated for cause, they represent a valuable member of the team who has made contributions to the success of the organization. Simply remembering this will help ensure they are treated with respect and care as they depart for other opportunities. You never know whether they will become a customer or competitor, or possibly even a return employee. Leaving a good impression with them will help ensure they are champions of the organization long after they are gone.

17.2.3   Have a Process

How are departing employees transitioned out of the organization? Is there a process in place to ensure that all the paperwork is collected, their equipment is returned, all nondisclosure and other agreements have been reviewed and signed, and they are aware of their benefits postemployment? All of these details, and others, make the difference between a positive and negative offboarding experience. While the list will vary by business and industry, and it can be quite comprehensive, there are several things that should be included in the process. With Onboarding, you can define an offboarding process to support transitioning employees out of the organization. Let's look at things that should be covered in an offboarding process:

- **Have a knowledge transfer plan and follow it**
  Who will assume the duties of the departing employee, and will they have the information and tools necessary to do so? Having a defined knowledge transfer process in place and ensuring it's followed is critical to successful offboarding. We'll review this element in more detail in the next section.

- **Final paycheck and other financial matters**
  Monetary matters are always at the forefront of any employee's mind, especially as they leave. How will their last paycheck be processed and when? What should they know about their retirement accounts, insurance policies, pension, and other accounts? Have information available to address these questions, and even someone to speak with for more complex conversations. Don't leave this to their last day. Often these important questions can distract the employee from any transition activities that need to occur. With Onboarding, you can capture the address where your outgoing employees wants their final check sent.

- **Health insurance coverage**
  This will vary by country, but employees will need to know what to expect after they transition out, especially if there is a gap in their employment. An offboarding process within SAP SuccessFactors can provide COBRA or continuation health insurance information to your terminating employees. Have them enroll in any needed coverage and complete forms right in the system before they move on.

17

- **Returning physical equipment**

  Many organizations issue laptop computers, tablets, smartphones, and other equipment that is necessary for employees to complete their job duties. It's imperative that all pieces of equipment are returned to the company, signatures obtained, and receipts provided to document the transition. Just as you can use Onboarding to issue physical equipment to incoming employees, you can likewise use the system to provide a checklist for the hiring manager, IT, and HR to ensure that all issued equipment is returned. This can also provide the employee with a sense of security knowing they have checked all the necessary boxes before moving on.

- **Intellectual property transition**

  Just as important as physical property is the intellectual property of the company. Ensure your employees are aware of their responsibilities and any restrictions on their handling and use of intellectual property as they are transitioning out. Just as you can manage a checklist of physical equipment that is returned, you can likewise manage checklists and sign-offs within Onboarding to ensure that employees are aware of their responsibilities where intellectual property is concerned and that they have a detailed list of what needs to be returned or transitioned to others.

- **Noncompetition and nondisclosure agreements**

  If you have these types of agreements, either during employment or upon terminating, it's critical that employees be reminded of their responsibilities and understand them. Have HR or someone from the legal department available to answer questions and ensure there are no misconceptions in this important area. Make sure employees sign any agreements necessary before their last day, and provide them with copies of all signed agreements for their records. Distributed as part of an offboarding process, this can happen early in the termination process so employees have plenty of time to review the documents and ask questions.

- **Conduct the exit interview**

  Many organizations don't take advantage of the opportunity to receive feedback from the exiting employee on their experiences while employed as well as their transition from the company. Just as new employees can provide valuable insights as outside participants to processes in place, so exiting employees can help identify issues the organization is unaware of. This can be done face to face or via an online questionnaire, but don't miss the opportunity to hear from your soon-to-be former employees.

Having a defined process for ushering employees out of the organization in an efficient and timely manner creates goodwill that can last way beyond the last day. It also communicates how the organization values all employees, before, during, and after employment. The result is most often positive advocates in a volatile marketplace.

17.2.4   Communication and Knowledge Transfer

When an employee tells a manager he's leaving, or the decision has been made to let a worker go, there's a temptation not to communicate the change internally immediately. Some want to wait for answers to all the questions such as the last day of employment, who will take over responsibilities, and so on. However, the longer the organization takes to address those questions, the more likely that employees will start determining their own answers and possibly spreading misinformation. There is no better way to ensure that a valuable employee leaves with no goodwill, or desire to one day return, than to let questions go unanswered and possibly cultivate their coworkers thinking they were terminated when they are leaving for a new career opportunity.

Managers and HR should be working in concert from the moment the resignation is tendered to support the employee in their transition and working to ensure the team can function during and after that transition. Many organizations prohibit their departing employees from speaking about their departure or even saying goodbye to their colleagues. This only breeds rumors and disintegrates team confidence.

The offboarding process should begin immediately upon acceptance of the termination or delivery of the termination notice. The first thing addressed should be the knowledge transfer plan. Employees who are long-time contributors are likely leaving with years of institutional knowledge in their heads. Don't let them walk out the door without sharing this invaluable experience with those that remain. While this issue goes far beyond offboarding to issues of succession planning, it's critical to continued organizational success to ensure that a defined plan is in place to transfer as much knowledge as possible, even if you haven't yet identified their replacement.

Define the Plan

One of the first things the manager and employee should do after resignation is to sit down and define the knowledge transfer plan. This should include specifics such as the objectives of the plan, timing, and to whom the knowledge will be transferred. It's always helpful to define the who, what, when, where, and how. Having as much time as possible is always preferred. If the departing employee hasn't accepted a new job yet or has flexibility in negotiating the start date, talk with the employee about staying on until the knowledge transfer is complete. Of course, this isn't always possible, and, if time is short, you need to identify the most critical elements of the employee's knowledge that need to be transitioned. If there is no immediate successor in place, then perhaps including several employees in the knowledge transfer plan is the answer. The important thing is to document the plan and make sure it's followed.

Encourage Employees to Share Their Knowledge

Having a plan in place is only helpful if the employee is an active participant. If the employee leaving is somewhat disgruntled or disillusioned, this could prove challenging. Sometimes, employees don't really know how to transfer their knowledge and don't realize how valuable their knowledge is. They may think of it as just the way they do the job, rather than a valuable contribution to the organization. This is where the manager and HR should work together to enable the employee to be successful in the knowledge transfer.

Have knowledge transfer sessions facilitated with identified note takers. Ask probing questions of the employee as to whom they contacted and why to resolve certain situations or what their thought process was in addressing an issue. If you can get them talking then the session is more a conversation than a difficult documentation task. Importantly, try to avoid having the employee document the job duties in painstaking detail. This has proven only marginally successful and relies on the written communication skills of the employee. Documentation is only usually valid for a point in time.

Maintain the Relationship

If the employee is leaving on good terms, the best way to ensure you retain the employee's knowledge is to maintain the relationship. In this way, as questions arise after employees have departed, they are usually open to answering them and being of help. This not only makes them feel valued but also leaves the relationship open to future engagements or even hiring them back one day. Setting the right tone during the transition helps foster that advocate we discussed in an earlier section. The worst thing a company can do is make the employee feel disloyal or mistrusted for pursuing a new opportunity. Employees want to feel good about the organization they are leaving, and how they are treated during this knowledge transfer period can set the tone for the entire offboarding experience.

> **The Bottom Line**
>
> Just as they are now dedicated to creating a positive onboarding experience for new recruits, companies must be equally committed to engendering goodwill among outgoing employees. Ultimately, no one understands a company—its values, its culture, and the way it does business—more than the people who've earned a living there. When this understanding is shared in a positive light, it can only contribute to the success of the company.
>
> Research suggests that nearly 70 percent of companies can make improvements in their offboarding processes. These programs aren't created overnight and aren't always the same for every departing employee. Companies can plan strategies and identify milestones that should be achieved to ensure success, but they should also be flexible to review and improve these programs continually. Understanding why, when, and how departing employees can be advocates of the company after they leave is the key to successful offboarding.

Now let's look at our final process: crossboarding.

17.3   Crossboarding

Transitions don't just occur when an employee joins, or leaves, an organization. They also occur when an employee moves from one part of the organization to another, to a different geographic region, or even to a new role within the organization. The process for transitioning existing employees internally is known as crossboarding. Let's discuss some considerations that might drive defining a crossboarding process and touch on how Onboarding can support this critical process.

17.3.1   Transfer from One Business Unit to Another

In large organizations, it's common for employees to change jobs that take them from one line of business to another. These changes can be accompanied by different job duties and requirements that may necessitate completing paperwork but most often with new training and development requirements. If the organization is regulated by a government agency, the criticality of these requirements and ensuring they have been met may be quite strong with severe consequences if they aren't completed properly. Having a process defined to ensure the employee, manager, and HR representative are all aware of the important elements involved is important. Employees will need to know what is expected of them to complete, what information they may need to provide, documentation of certifications or training they need to present, and what new training they will be required to complete.

Managers will need to understand what gaps the employee may have coming into the new business unit and what their role is in supporting the employee in closing those gaps. They should also be made aware of any time limits or particular requirements for doing so. Having the ability to track the completion of the new requirements will make the manager's job that much easier and also eliminate the risk of noncompliance due to lack of data or reporting.

Likewise, HR should also be made aware of the time lines involved in documenting the employee's fulfillment of the requirements or ability to close any gaps, and the consequences of noncompliance.

17.3.2   Transferring to a New Country

When an employee moves to a new geographic location, there can be nearly as much paperwork, possibly more, than onboarding a new employee. And with changes such as a new manager, HR team, and colleagues, there are also changes in language and country customs. Having a defined process in place to support employees through this transition will increase the likelihood of a successful move and ex-patriate experience for both the employee and the organization.

This crossboarding process can be very similar to an onboarding process conducted in the particular country. Ensure all the necessary paperwork is included, such as new policies and procedures, and any relocation information that may be needed. Connect the employee to a network in the new location as early as possible so the employee can be a part of the transition, and the team rapport and networking can begin before the employee arrives. Provide additional resources as needed. Hopefully, at this point, you can see how useful Onboarding can be with these types of activities and tasks, from connecting employees with their new manager and team members, to communicating role requirements and assigning training that will be needed, to supporting employees with completing cumbersome paperwork. SAP SuccessFactors helps alleviate much of the stress that can accompany moving to a new, unfamiliar country.

17.3.3   Transitioning to a New Role in the Organization

Transitioning to a new role with increased responsibilities can bring new challenges in a different way than starting with a new company. Businesses don't always think about defining a process for helping employees transition to positions with significantly new responsibilities, but this should not be overlooked. Employees moving to a leadership or management role for the first time will need support to be successful. They will often need training on things such as giving feedback, settling disputes, and often specific HR or compliance training.

It's not uncommon for this type of transition to have specific performance and development goals for employees, so integrating Onboarding with SAP SuccessFactors Performance & Goals and SAP SuccessFactors Succession & Development provide the employee and manager with powerful tools to facilitate these activities. Using Onboarding to support these kinds of career transitions will provide very useful information to employees on what to expect within the first few weeks and months of their new position. Having a clear process with checkpoints along the way will ensure that important components of transitioning to a new role aren't missed.

17.4   Default Process Steps

Within SAP SuccessFactors Onboarding, there are three default process steps, as follows:

- Post-hire verification
- New employee
- Orientation

Each process is geared toward capturing different information from different users. Let's briefly discuss each default process step.

17.4.1   Post-Hire Verification Step

In this process step, the corporate representative user (typically an HR user) will either confirm data already entered into SAP SuccessFactors Onboarding or will enter the data themselves. This data is job-related information such as the organizational information on where the new hire will work, information on salary and benefits, and any equipment provisioning that may be needed. If SAP SuccessFactors Recruiting is in place and integrated with SAP SuccessFactors Onboarding, most, if not all, of this data will be passed from SAP SuccessFactors Recruiting into SAP SuccessFactors Onboarding. In this scenario, the corporate representative will review the information for accuracy and make updates as required. If SAP SuccessFactors Recruiting is not place or if you have a need to onboard a new employee that isn't being passed into the system from SAP SuccessFactors Recruiting, the corporate representative will enter the information directly into SAP SuccessFactors Onboarding in this step.

17.4.2   New Employee Step

In this process step, the newly hired employees will enter any personal information that was not already captured during the recruiting process. The new hire may be presented with data passed from SAP SuccessFactors Recruiting, such as the organizational or job-related information mentioned in Section 17.4.1, but they will also enter additional information such as their national identification number (such as a SSN in the US), complete government and other tax forms, and enter direct deposit information for payroll. Additionally, they may be asked to provide emergency contact information as well as review and sign company policies and procedures.

This process step will contain panels and forms that you configure within the SAP SuccessFactors Onboarding processes that you define in your configuration workshops.

17.4.3   Orientation Step

In this process step, you can have both the new employee and the corporate representative enter data into SAP SuccessFactors Onboarding. This step can be used to gather additional information, such as gathering information that requires further certification or acknowledgement, such as proof of receiving a certain degree or a certification applicable to the new employee's position. Some organizations require new employees to present certain documentation on their first day, such as a driver's license, passport, or visa. Within the orientation step, the corporate representative can review the information provided by the new hire and sign off on its accuracy. They could also acknowledge having viewed the documentation presented by the new employee.

17.5 Summary

Studies have shown that the better new employees' onboarding experiences are, the less time to productivity they experience and the more likely they are to have longevity with the company. Onboarding will often begin before an employee's first day and should involve numerous players and extend well into the first year of employment. Effective onboarding processes will go beyond facilitating paperwork completion and will include engaging numerous players from the hiring manager, HR, IT, and peers. Everything you can do to communicate roles and responsibilities, explain performance expectations, and reinforce the company culture will enable your new employees to embrace their role and assimilate into the organization. Finally, giving new hires adequate time to hit their stride while providing them open channels of communication will also go a long way to increasing the longevity of your new employees. Onboarding provides numerous tools and features that will support every aspect of your onboarding process.

Organizations should take care to define not only their onboarding experiences but also an effective and positive experience for those employees that leave. Onboarding can be leveraged to support an offboarding process to facilitate important tasks that need to be completed by departing employees. Using the system to communicate important information and gathering signatures on agreements such as confidentiality and noncompetition, as well as checking off the return of physical equipment, will increase the efficiency of offboarding employees while making them feel valued and building a sense of goodwill as they move on in their careers. Remember that your former employees can be your best advocates and should be treated with care.

Finally, don't underestimate the value of a good crossboarding process to support your existing employees as they transition to a new country, business unit, or role within the organization.

Let's turn to look at some of the administrative features within Onboarding.

17

Chapter 18
Onboarding Administrative Features

Onboarding can be maintained nearly 100% from the administrative features built-in to the SAP SuccessFactors Onboarding module itself, which places a great amount of configuration control in your hands during and after go-live.

As with other SAP SuccessFactors modules, there are many features and functions that can be maintained within the administrative interface of SAP SuccessFactors Onboarding. Onboarding actually has several places where administrative features are managed:

- SAP SuccessFactors Admin Center
- Onboarding Super Admin platform
- Onboarding Dashboard

Within these three areas, you manage a variety of settings and access various functions from initial settings to actually building panels and mapping data among SAP SuccessFactors Onboarding, SAP SuccessFactors Recruiting, and SAP SuccessFactors Employee Central.

Other areas of administration that are used frequently include the Document Center, work queue, and the Employee Portal.

In this chapter, we'll discuss these administrative features as well as the three areas provided to manage them. We'll start with SAP SuccessFactors Admin Center.

18.1 SAP SuccessFactors Admin Center

This will be familiar from Part I of this book as we discussed the many administrative features within Recruiting. Many of these options will take you to other areas within Admin Center or Onboarding to carry out the functions. The Onboarding administrative features are as follows:

- **Configure New Hire Activity Planning Process**
  In this step, you configure the steps that will be included in the **New Hire Manager Activities**, as shown in Figure 18.1. You can set the number of days the process should complete prior to the new hire start date as well as how many days to notify hiring managers when the process is stalled.

Figure 18.1 Configure the New Hire Manager Activities

- **Maintain Number of Active Days for Onboarding in Home Page**
  This will take you to the **Manage Home Page** area of the Admin Center where you can set the period in days for how long Onboarding tiles will appear on the SAP SuccessFactors home page. You can see this in Figure 18.2.

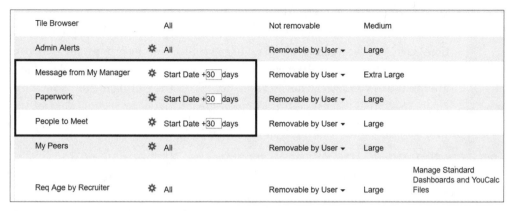

Tile Browser		All	Not removable	Medium
Admin Alerts	⚙	All	Removable by User ▾	Large
Message from My Manager	⚙	Start Date +30 days	Removable by User ▾	Extra Large
Paperwork	⚙	Start Date +30 days	Removable by User ▾	Large
People to Meet	⚙	Start Date +30 days	Removable by User ▾	Large
My Peers	⚙	All	Removable by User ▾	Large
Req Age by Recruiter	⚙	All	Removable by User ▾	Large	Manage Standard Dashboards and YouCalc Files

Figure 18.2 Manage Home Page Tile Settings

- **Manage Employee Portal**

  This feature will take you to the Employee Portal page within Onboarding. Here you can set up and manage the Employee Portal, if you choose to use this over the pre-day one feature. The Employee Portal is built in SharePoint, and you can brand it to your corporate colors and logos. Use the **Admin Site Actions** menu to access the SharePoint editing tools, as shown in Figure 18.3.

Figure 18.3 Editing the Employee Portal Using SharePoint Editing Tools

- **Manage Onboarding Notifications**

  This link will take you to the Onboarding Dashboard and directly to the **Notifications** page. Here you can view and manage notifications by groups, such as **Docu-Sign Notifications** and **Restart Notifications**. Related notifications are placed into groups. When you select a notification, you access the editing menu, as shown in Figure 18.4. We'll discuss notifications in greater detail in Section 18.3.1 of this chapter.

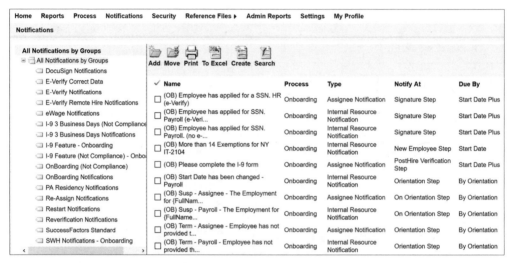

Figure 18.4 Accessing Notifications from the SAP SuccessFactors Admin Center Menu or Directly from the Onboarding Dashboard

- **Manage Onboarding Reference Files**

  Selecting this from SAP SuccessFactors Admin Center will land you on the **Reference Files** page of the Onboarding Dashboard. Here you'll access items such as the corporate structure, data lists, provisioning, forms, banks, and container forms.

- **Manage Onboarding Security Settings**

  This feature will also jump you to the **Security** tab of the Onboarding Dashboard. We'll discuss this in more detail in Section 18.3.

- **Manage Onboarding Settings**

  Selecting this option will take you directly to the **Security** page in the Onboarding Dashboard. We'll cover this area in Section 18.3.

- **Onboarding Mapped Data Review**

  In this feature, you can run a validation of mapped data within the Recruiting and

Onboarding configuration such as fields from the requisition, application, and offer. You can also validate data from the applicant status configuration as well validate background elements from the candidate profile for the Recruiting to Onboarding to Employee Central integration. This is shown in Figure 18.5.

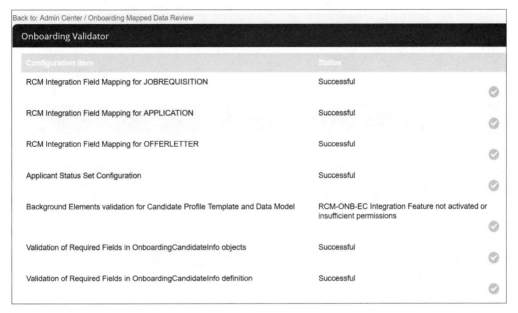

Figure 18.5 Validating the Integration and Mapping of Data among Recruiting, Onboarding, and Employee Central

Let's next discuss the Onboarding Super Admin platform.

18.2   Onboarding Super Admin

The main administrative platform for Onboarding is referred to as Super Admin access. This is similar to provisioning access for SAP SuccessFactors in that it requires special access by partners. Each consultant needs to be granted Super Admin access for each Onboarding implementation on which the consultant works. Here is where the Onboarding module is configured and managed. Until recently, many of the features available in Super Admin weren't available to businesses. SAP recognized the value of enabling businesses to build and maintain their Onboarding processes, so much of the administrative capability of Super Admin has been brought into the Onboarding module and is accessible from the Onboarding Dashboard.

Each consultant will have an account on each SAP SuccessFactors server, just as they do for provisioning access. Then they request access to each customer's Onboarding instances. They may have numerous instances within their account on each server. Figure 18.6 displays the login screen for Super Admin as well as what consultants see when they log in.

Figure 18.6 Consultants Logging into Super Admin to Access Onboarding Instances

> **Note**
>
> Customers can't access Super Admin; this is only available to SAP Professional Services and partner consultants. Consultants must be granted specific permission by their customers before SAP will grant Super Admin access.

When you log in to the Super Admin platform, there are several links where you can manage the following features:

- **Accounts**
- **Site Forms**
- **Site News**
- **Site Options**
- **Site Config**
- **My Profile**
- **Global Search**
- **Audit trail**
- **Debug Site files**
- **Global Assignment Report**

Each link will give you access to the areas shown in Figure 18.6. Note that these features aren't available in the Onboarding Dashboard. Before Onboarding processes can be built, some technical configuration must be done in Super Admin:

- Configure at home/on-site options
- Activate features
- Set up Pretty Good Privacy (PGP) encrypting (optional)
- Manage passwords for corporate users or new hires
- Activate E-Verify in QA mode (only in the United States)
- Set self-service account options

18.2.1 Configure At-Home/On-Site Options

This feature determines if new hires will be allowed to complete their paperwork at home or in the office in the first days on the job. Options for this feature are as follows:

18

- **At Home**
- **On-Site**
- **Both (Manager will choose at PHV step)** (PHV refers to Post Hire Verification)

This feature is very straightforward, and you just need to select one of the options and save, as you can see in Figure 18.7. For maximum flexibility, it's recommended that you choose **Both**.

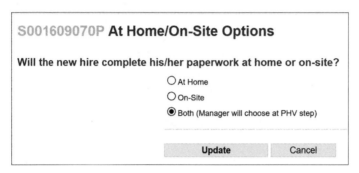

Figure 18.7 Setting the At Home/On-Site Options to Govern Where New Hires Can Complete Their Paperwork

18.2.2   Activate Features

Before you can begin building the Onboarding configuration, several features need to be activated. These are accessible from the **Account • Features** menu. The features are categorized as the following:

- **BizX Integration**
- **Integrations**
- **Misc**
- **Portals**
- **Standard Forms**
- **US Compliance**
- **WOTC Vendor Integrations**

The recommended features to activate are shown in Table 18.1. You can see the **Feature** menu in Figure 18.8.

Feature	Description	Status
BizX Integration		
SF_BizX_Connection	Sets BizX instance connection information.	Active
SF_Goal_Management	This feature enables panels for Goal Management system.	Inactive
SF_Notifications	This feature enables sending messages to BizX.	Active
Integrations		
CustomNewHireDataExportFeature	This feature enables Custom New Hire Data Export feature.	Inactive
DocCenterStandardExportFeature	This feature enables Document Center Standard Export.	Active
Foundation Import	This feature enables foundation data synchronization between XpressHR and SuccessFactors.	Active
NewHireDataExportFeature	This feature enables New Hire Data Export feature.	Active
Misc		
Internal Hire	This feature allows to create a process for internal hire, who is a candidate being selected from the existing workforce to take up a new job in the same organization	Inactive
Orientation Manager	This feature enables panel to set a manager for the Orientation.	Inactive
Portals		
ONB_DocumentCenter	DocumentCenter.	Active
ONB_EmployeePortal	Employee portal.	Active
Standard Forms		
KMS_8850Form	This feature enables KMS 8850 Panel and Form.	Inactive
KMS_DirectDepositForm	This feature enables KMS Direct Deposit Panel and Form.	Inactive
KMS_EmergencyContactForm	This feature enables KMS Emergency Contact Panel and Form.	Active
KMS_NewEmployeeEeoInformationForm	This feature enables KMS New Employee EEO Information Panel.	Active
KMS_NewEmployeeSummaryForm	This feature enables KMS New Employee Summary Form.	Active
KMS_PayCard	This feature enables Pay Card Panel and Form.	Active
KMS_PoliciesList	This feature enables KMS Policies List Panel.	Active

Figure 18.8 Activating Features before Building the Onboarding Processes

Feature	Description
SF_BizX_Connection	Specifies the name of the Onboarding instance and other settings specific to integrating with BizX
SF_Notifications	Enables the sending of notifications to SAP Success-Factors
KMS_Policies_List	Enables the **KMS Policies List** panel
SF_Document_Center	Enables the Document Center
Foundation Import	Enables foundation data synchronization between XpressHR and SAP SuccessFactors
SF_EmployeePortal	Enables the Employee Portal

Table 18.1 Several Features That Should Be Activated before Configuration of the Onboarding Processes

18

Feature	Description
SF_DrugTest_BGCheck_Education	Enables the **Background Check**, **Drug Screen**, and **Education Check** panels
SF_PaperWorkDone_Message	For sending **Paperwork Done** messages; required for Onboarding to Employee Central and SAP ERP Human Capital Management (SAP ERP HCM) integrations

Table 18.1 Several Features That Should Be Activated before Configuration of the Onboarding Processes (Cont.)

Additional features can be activated as needed in your processes. The features in Table 18.1 are the base recommendations.

18.2.3   Set Up PGP Encrypting

Depending on your Recruiting and HRIS landscape, you may need to export data from Onboarding for various reasons. Because this information is often confidential, some businesses choose to encrypt the data using PGP encryption. This uses a private key to encrypt the data before it's exported from Onboarding. The data can then only be decrypted with the private key.

To set up encryption, in **Super Admin,** go to **PGPKey**. Select **Encryption Mode** and choose to **Generate Key**. For data that are exported from Onboarding, you need to enable encryption at each feature level. From the **Features** menu, select the feature you've enabled that you want to encrypt. Choose the checkbox, and save your settings.

18.2.4   Manage Passwords for Corporate Users and New Hires

You can set password policies for the corporate users and new hires in your Onboarding system. Following are some important things to note about passwords in Onboarding:

- Minimum length is eight characters.
- The default lockout period is three hours; custom time frames can be configured in **Super Admin • Account Options • Security • UserUnlockTime**. When setting this, a value of "0" means lockout periods aren't in use.

- You can enable a forgot password feature that allows users to be sent a reset link via email one time. These are both set up in **Super Admin • Account Options • RecoverPasswordByMail** and **PasswordRecoveryMode.**

- When security questions are used, users can only attempt to answer them a maximum of three times. If they don't answer correctly, they can't try again for at least one hour.

- If you change the password settings, you can force users with passwords that don't comply to change their password on the next login.

- When users log in for the first time with an automatically generated password, they will be prompted to change it.

- After they've reset their password, the new hires should select **Start New Employee Wizard** to move to the next step.

18.2.5 Activate E-Verify in QA Mode

For businesses in the United States, it's possible to activate E-Verify in the test environment to simulate E-Verify checks without actually connecting to the E-Verify system. This is very helpful in allowing businesses to see how Onboarding will behave with E-Verify. To activate E-Verify in test mode, from the **Super Admin** menu, choose **E-Verify Options**. Enter dummy data in the **Client Company ID** and **Submitter's Phone Number** fields. Under **Account Type**, make sure that you select **Test Account**, as shown in Figure 18.9.

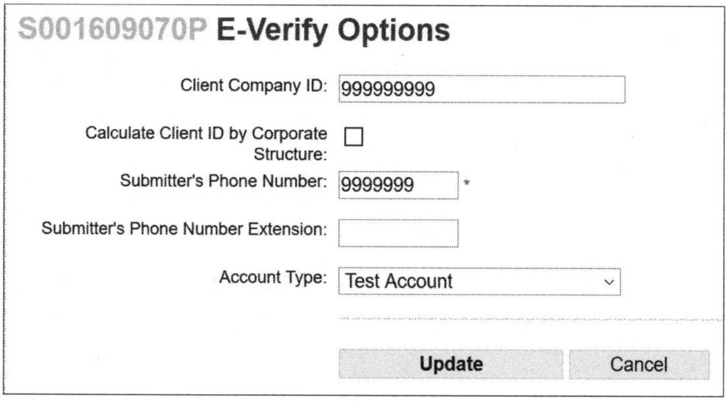

18

S001609070P E-Verify Options

Client Company ID:	999999999
Calculate Client ID by Corporate Structure:	☐
Submitter's Phone Number:	9999999 *
Submitter's Phone Number Extension:	
Account Type:	Test Account ⌄

Update   Cancel

Figure 18.9 Setting Up E-Verify in the Test Instance to Simulate How Onboarding will Interact with E-Verify

18.2.6   Self-Service Account Options

The self-service tools enable business administrators and partner implementation consultants to configure Onboarding. Many keys are available within the **Account Options** to make various settings. These are spelled out in detail in the Onboarding Implementation Guide maintained by SAP. Refer to this document, available on the SAP Support Portal, for more detailed information on these settings.

18.2.7   Enabling and Building Processes in Super Admin

Super Admin comes with several default processes that can be enabled, as shown in Figure 18.10. To continue configuring Onboarding in the Onboarding Dashboard, you must first enable or build one process within Super Admin. These processes are all disabled at first, and you'll need to enable the processes that are required for your configuration.

If you're company has operations in the United States, you'll need to enable the following processes:

- **Onboarding** (this is the I-9 sign-off step)
- **I-9 3 Business-Days**
- **I-9 Reverification**
- **E-Verify**
- **E-Verify Correct Data**

Processes							
Process Description	**Step 1**	**Step 2**	**Step 3**	**Index Fields**	**Due Dates**	**Status**	
Onboarding	PostHire Step-Hiring Leader to Complete	New Employee Step	I-9 Sign Off Step	Index Fields	Due Dates	Enabled	Disable
I-9 3 Business-Days		I-9 3 Business-Days Step		Index Fields	Due Dates	Enabled	Disable
E-Verify	Initial Verification	Secondary Verification	Third Verification	Index Fields	Due Dates	Disabled	Enable
I-9 Reverification		Reverification Notification Step	Reverification	Index Fields	Due Dates	Enabled	Disable
Forms On Demand	Forms On Demand	Forms On Demand	Forms On Demand	Index Fields	Due Dates	Disabled	Enable
Offboarding	Initiation Step	Employee Step	Exit Interview	Index Fields	Due Dates	Enabled	Disable
E-Verify Correct Data	Setup	Section 1	Section 2	Index Fields	Due Dates	Disabled	Enable
eWage	Initial Step	Employee Step		Index Fields	Due Dates	Enabled	Disable
Pennsylvania Residency	Initial Step	Employee Step		Index Fields	Due Dates	Enabled	Disable

Figure 18.10 Default Processes in Super Admin

For companies with operations outside the United States, you should build a custom process. You can do this by selecting the **Add Process** link under the **Tasks** menu, as shown in Figure 18.11.

After these processes are created and/or enabled in Super Admin, the rest of the configuration can be accomplished within the Onboarding Dashboard.

Figure 18.11 Adding Custom Processes for Companies with Operations Outside the United States

18.3 Onboarding Dashboard

The third area where Onboarding administrative functions occur is really where most of the work is done. This is the Onboarding Dashboard accessible from the **Onboarding** menu to those with the correct Onboarding privileges. You can see the **Onboarding Dashboard** in Figure 18.12. We've already discussed the Onboarding Dashboard in several previous chapters of this book and in Section 18.1, where you saw how the Admin Center has convenient "jump to" links to various areas of the **Onboarding Dashboard**.

The main administrative menus that can be maintained here fall into these categories:

- **Notifications**
  At various steps in the process, notifications can be automatically sent to all internal and external resources. Notifications go beyond just emails and have various types of triggers.

- **Security**
  Permissions for each user are maintained here.

18

- **Reference Files**

  Maintain the corporate structure, data lists, provisioning, forms, and banks in the **Reference Files** area. Reference files are used throughout Onboarding to update various components of configuration, but we won't discuss those items in this chapter because they were discussed in Chapter 17.

- **Admin Reports**

  Generate reports with Onboarding metrics and report on security in this section.

- **Settings**

  The **Settings** menu houses the **Logos, Password Security, Manage Employees, Data Dictionary, Data Lists, Panels, Forms, Mail Queue**, and **Audit Trail** tools. This area is also used extensively in configuration during implementation and isn't the focus of this chapter. Many of these functions were discussed in Chapter 17.

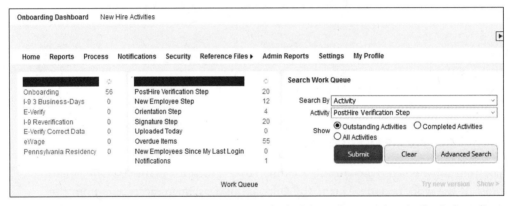

Figure 18.12 Managing Process Activities and Administrative Functions in the Onboarding Dashboard

Within this section, we'll discuss the **Notifications, Security, Administrative Reports, Document Center**, and **Work Queue** areas. Let's begin by discussing the ways Onboarding notifies key players in the process.

18.3.1   Notifications

Communicating with participants in the Onboarding process is a critical piece of a successful Onboarding experience. The ability to keep all the various players in the process informed of what is required of them and what actions have occurred is critical. In Onboarding, it's possible to craft different types of notifications that can be used to automatically communicate with each internal and external resources involved in an onboarding process. These notifications are much more than just emails, and they can relate to completing tasks such as completing drug testing or background checks, ordering uniforms, planning access to facilities, having a badge created, and assigning equipment. In this section, we'll review the ways in which Onboarding supports notifying users, as well as how to configure the module to support the necessary notifications.

Using Notifications in Onboarding

The Onboarding module contains four functional types of notifications:

- Email notifications
- Work queue notifications
- Reminder notifications
- Notifications executed by schedule

The notifications may be assigned by group and by process (i.e., onboarding, offboarding, etc.). Each type of notification is further defined by the intended recipient. The Onboarding module has nine recipient types that can be used in a notification:

- **Employee**
  Notifications are sent to the new employee in the new hire record.

- **External**
  Notifications may be sent to resources outside the organization such as background check vendors or others.

- **Internal**
  Notifications are sent to internal users such as HR, IT, facilities, and others.

- **Hiring managers**
  Notifications are sent to the manager listed in the new hire record.

- **Recruiters**
  Notifications are sent to the recruiter listed in the new hire record.

- **Employee download and track**
  Used when an employee needs to either download a file or a document's status needs to be tracked that it was received or opened.

- **Assignee**
  Notifications are sent to the person assigned to an activity.

- **Supervisor**
  Notifications are sent to the employee's supervisor. Note that this is different from the hiring manager.

18

- **Data driven**

  Notifications are sent to the email address contained in the Equal Employment Opportunity (EEO) data or other tables for the new hire.

Notifications can be sent at any step in an onboarding process. There are default **Notify At** steps that are available as well at either the completion of a step or when the **Close** button is selected. These default **Notify At** steps are as follows:

- Step completion:
  - **New Employee** step
  - **Orientation** step
  - **Signature**
- When the **Close** button is selected on any panel of the particular step:
  - **On PostHire Verification** step
  - **On New Employee** step
  - **On Orientation** step
  - **On Notification** step
- Failed message
- Undelivered message

Additionally, there are notification steps available if E-Verify is used for onboarding processes in the United States. You can enable notifications for a status change, or if the employee contests a tentative nonconfirmation from either the Department of Homeland Security (DHS) or the Social Security Administration, and finally when the DHS verification result is received.

Configuring Notifications

As you might expect, notifications are configured in the Onboarding Dashboard and can be accessed directly from the dashboard or via the jump to link from **Admin Center • Manage Onboarding Notifications** in the Admin Center. In the **Notifications** area, you'll create a new notification and enter necessary data in the **Main Properties** tab. Besides entering the notification name and opting to assign a wizard's panel to the notification, requiring the recipient to use the wizard to complete an activity, there are numerous settings addressed as described in Table 18.2.

Option	Description
Create Activity in WQ	This option places the activity in the work queue.

Table 18.2 Notification Settings

Option	Description
Notify At	Select the step of the process that causes the notification to be sent on completion of the step.
Due By	Set a due date for the notification by selecting an option from the **Due By** dropdown.
Post Controller	Set the parameters here to execute an automatic operation after a notification activity is completed.
Secured Wizard	If a wizard is attached to the activity, this setting forces users to enter their user ID and password to access the notification's wizard panel.
Attach logo, Send Email or Print	Attach a logo to a notification, send an email, or print the notification.
Send with iCalendar Event	Send the notification with an .ics file, which allows recipients to add the activity to their calendar.
Enable Notification	Activate the notification.

Table 18.2 Notification Settings (Cont.)

Tip

If you make **Manage Onboarding Notifications** a favorite in the Admin Center, it will be available as a link on the **Admin Favorites** tile on the home page. Here you can jump directly to the **Notifications** page in the Onboarding Dashboard. See Figure 18.13 for an example.

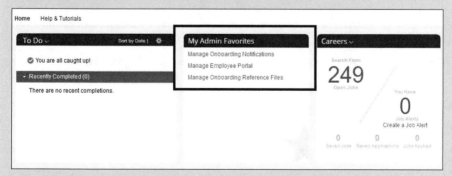

Figure 18.13 Making Onboarding Activities Favorites on the SAP SuccessFactors Home Page

18

Note that there are additional settings on the **Main Properties** tab, so be sure to fully review this area when configuring a notification. Figure 18.14 demonstrates the information that is entered on the **Main Properties** tab, as well as the other tabs available to enter data for the notification.

Figure 18.14 Enter All Data on the Various Tabs When Creating a New Notification

Once established, you can add various settings to notifications such as the following:

- Set advanced conditions
- Attach files to the notification
- Add forms that require an e-signature
- Build or modify the notification text
- Create custom triggers
- Organize notifications into groups

Detailed steps for every component of managing notifications are covered in the Onboarding Administrator's Guide. Be sure to check there for step-by-step instructions.

18.3.2   Onboarding Security

Security roles and groups are maintained within the Onboarding admin interface. Role-based permissions within the SAP SuccessFactors interface will govern which roles and people can access the Onboarding administration. This is similar to other modules of SAP SuccessFactors, such as SAP SuccessFactors Learning. Role-based permissions determine who has access to the Onboarding module and configurations in the Admin Center. Onboarding security determines who has access to what tools within Onboarding. Table 18.3 provides a side-by-side comparison of role-based permissions and Onboarding security.

Onboarding Security	Role-Based Permissions
Onboarding has 10 fixed roles that can't be modified. No custom roles may be added.	No predefined roles and businesses create roles that meet their requirements.
A role has specific permissions, defining what parts of the system users have access to and what they can do.	Roles have specific permissions assigned to them, defining what users have access to and what they can do.
A user may belong to more than one security group.	A user may belong to more than one role-based permissions group.
A security group can be assigned to one Onboarding role.	A role-based permissions group can belong to more than one role-based permissions role.

Table 18.3 Onboarding Security versus Role-Based Permissions in SAP SuccessFactors

Onboarding Security Groups

In Onboarding administration, you can set up groups of users to have permissions to do certain things. Onboarding security is comprised of roles and groups, in a similar concept to role-based permissions. Onboarding roles determine the types of permissions you may assign to your group. For each group of users in Onboarding security, you can assign the following functions as shown in Figure 18.15:

- **Allow view glance**
  Allow users to view data entered through the Onboarding process steps.

- **Allow delete HRData**
  Allow users to delete an activity from the work queue.

- **Allow restart/edits**
  Allow users to restart or edit a step in the process that has been completed. Note that only the last step completed can be restarted. You can't send new employees back to any previous step.

- **Report Permissions**
  Allow users to create and view reports within the Onboarding admin feature.

- **Reassign Activity**
  Allow users to reassign an activity to another user from the work queue, for example, from the hiring manager to HR.

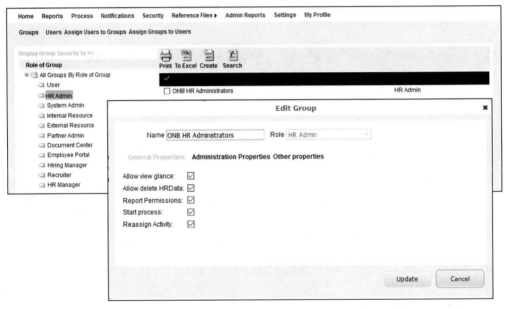

Figure 18.15 Security Roles Maintained in Groups by Role

If no permissions need to be assigned to a group, you can skip this step and just create the group. However, activity, monitoring, and document permissions can also be assigned. You can assign users to groups or assign groups to users.

It's possible to have user security within Onboarding based on the corporate structure. If this is the case, the relations between the hierarchy levels will automatically populate from the corporate structure.

Onboarding Security Roles

As mentioned previously, there are 10 predefined roles within Onboarding:

- **User**

  Members are provided permissions to onboard a new employee and execute or monitor any or all steps of the Onboarding process.

- **Hiring manager**

  Members are assigned to execute or monitor onboarding activities depending on whether or not you're the assigned hiring manager for the new hire's record.

- **Recruiter**

  Same activities as the hiring manager, as long as you're the assigned recruiter in the new hire's record (determined by Recruiting).

- **HR manager**

  Members may execute and monitor onboarding activities as the HR manager included in the new hire's record.

- **Internal**

  Members have access to execute additional activities to complete the new hire's process *inside* the company.

- **External**

  Members execute additional activities to complete the new hire's process *outside* the company.

- **HR admin**

  Typically, administrators are responsible for maintaining the notifications, security, reference files, and other account settings.

- **Document Center**

  Members assigned to this role have access to view, upload, and print documents stored within the Document Center.

- **Employee Portal**

  Members have access to view and configure the Employee Portal.

- **System admin**

  Typically, administrators have access to manage Onboarding settings such as wizards, user controls, HR data, PDF forms, and configuration settings.

Roles that have access to the entire Onboarding process have the following types of permissions:

18

- **Activity permissions**
  Configurable permissions to execute an activity under certain conditions, such as location, gender, age, start date, and so on.

- **Activity steps permissions**
  Configurable permission to execute any or all steps of a process.

- **Monitoring permissions**
  Configurable permission to monitor an activity under certain conditions, for example, location, gender, age, start date, and so on.

- **Monitoring steps permissions**
  Configurable permission to monitor steps of a process.

- **Document permission**
  Selectable permission to view documents from the work queue.

Onboarding Security and Syncs

When changes are made to Onboarding security, whether you've created new groups, added users to groups, or made other changes, it's necessary to run a sync so that SAP SuccessFactors and Onboarding have the right permissions set. There are several syncs, and they must be run in this specified order:

- HRIS USER SYNC (this is only needed if you're importing from an HRIS other than Employee Central)
- ONSTARTDATE PROCESS
- USER SYNC FROM SF HCM TO ONB
- SECURITY SYNC

The DELTA USER SYNC will send all users from SAP SuccessFactors to Onboarding the first time it's run and then only delta changes thereafter.

18.3.3   Admin Reports

Within this section, you can generate reports that provide Onboarding metrics, information about activities, and data about security within the module. The reports are predefined and include the following:

- **Post Hire Verification Step** average
- **New Employee Step** average
- **Orientation Step** average

- Activities list and their status
- List of security groups with assigned users

These reports are really intended for administrator use, but you may want to consider granting some of the these to other users such as hiring managers. An example of an **Activities** list report is provided in Figure 18.16. You can enter various filter criteria to limit the scope of the data.

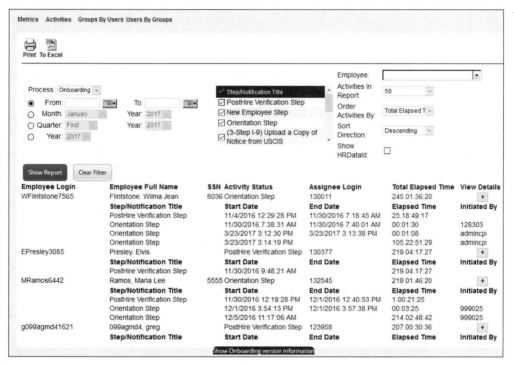

Figure 18.16 Reports from the Onboarding Dashboard Used to Display Metrics, Activities, and Groups of Users

18.3.4   Document Center

The Document Center is the storage component for complete and signed documents. It's provided for companies that don't have their own storage solution or for companies that may want to maintain a separate storage for Onboarding compliance documents. Documents stored in the Document Center are saved at the completion of an Onboarding process and remain there until purged. It's intended to only store documents for Onboarding; you can't use it to store other documents from other modules of SAP SuccessFactors.

Within the Document Center, you can search for documents using a simple search, or you can search for documents by name of the document or by first or last name of the new employee completing the document. There is an advanced search where you can search document fields, operators, or condition values. Searches can be saved for easy reuse in the future.

In this section, we'll discuss uploading and downloading documents into the Document Center, as well as the document purge.

Uploading and Downloading Documents

A bulk upload/download feature in the Document Center allows you to work with multiple documents at once. When uploading documents, you can use the bulk upload feature to select multiple files from your computer, and you can also upload an index file that contains various fields such as the following:

- Physical file name
- Document Center internal field name
- Field title
- Field value
- Field data type

The index file should be in comma-separated format in a .csv flat file.

When you've selected the files to upload, and they have been uploaded, you can edit the index fields from the index file by double-clicking on the index field, entering a new value, and pressing ⌈Enter⌋. You can access a full list of field definitions and a template for the .csv file from within **Instructions** and accessing the **Bulk Upload** window. After you've finished updating the fields, click **Update Indices** and **Finish**. Maintaining these index fields will aid tremendously when searching for your documents.

You can also download the documents associated with new employees stored in Document Center. Search for the new hire and then use the bulk download utility. Use this feature to download all of the documents of the same type or that meet other criteria when you use the advanced search. Using the bulk download utility in the UI, you can download a maximum of 100 documents. The utility is intended for one-off downloads and not meant to download all of the documents in the Document Center.

The default system forms in the system can be searched by text, but you can't search documents added by individual users automatically. You can choose to make these searchable at the time of upload, which is recommended.

Finally, there is an Onboarding application programming interface (API) you can use to create scheduled bulk download jobs that can run at regular intervals. Details on this feature and the full list of metadata are available in the Onboarding API documentation provided by SAP.

Document Purge

You can configure a document purge to automatically delete documents on a scheduled basis, depending on what your company policies are. There will be retention minimum periods depending on the type of compliance form. For example, I-9 forms have a minimum period of time. After this time, you can delete the forms. This purge feature is similar to the data purge in Recruiting where you can configure the system to purge application and candidate profile data after a specified period of time.

The document purge job runs four times per day. The updates will appear in Onboarding within 24 hours after the purge job. You'll configure document purge rules that control the document delete process. This feature is only available for users in the HR admin security group with associated permissions and should be controlled tightly. You should set up the purge rules carefully and test them extensively.

> **Tip**
>
> Be mindful that the document purge is a complete delete. After documents have been deleted, they can't be retrieved, so use this feature sparingly.

18

18.4   Work Queue Refresh

The Onboarding work queue has a new UI available to manage the items in the work queue. This feature has several benefits including the following:

- Localization support
- SAP SuccessFactors theming support
- Consistent user experience across modules
- Improved user experience

- Default filters
- Page reload performance enhancements

This page works very similar to the Admin Center in BizX in that after it's enabled, you can choose to view the page in the legacy view or select the link to view the new UI. Use the **Switch to Old Work Queue** link to toggle between the two views. See an example of the new work queue in Figure 18.17.

Data from the work queue can be exported to a .csv flat file. Use the **Export** feature to view the data and help you run reports to understand the Onboarding status better.

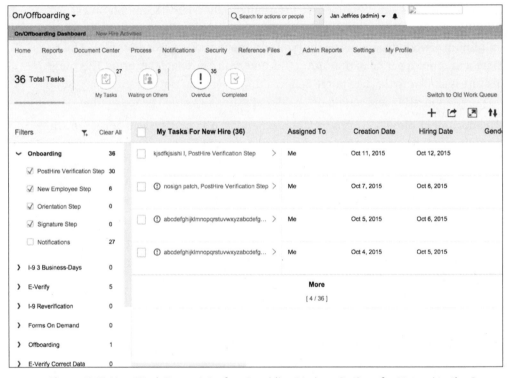

Figure 18.17 New Work Queue Interface Providing Various Options for Managing the Queue

18.5   Employee Portal

We discussed the Employee Portal in Chapter 16 and the important role it can play in your Onboarding process. Administrators manage the Employee Portal completely within the Admin Center. Details on how to complete all of the administrator tasks are provided in the Onboarding Administrator Guide. In this section, we'll briefly discuss these features. You should refer to the Administrator Guide for step-by-step instructions as this guide is maintained by SAP and is updated after each quarterly release to reflect the most up-to-date information.

One of the main purposes of the Employee Portal is to distribute documents easily. Documents such as policies and procedures, forms in addition to those included in the **New Employee** wizard, and other various employee handbook-type documents. To make documents available to the Employee Portal they must first be uploaded to the Employee Portal server. This includes videos and graphics as well.

Documents can be uploaded singly, or multiple documents can be uploaded at one time, as you can see in Figure 18.18. New documents that have been uploaded are indicated with a **New!** flag.

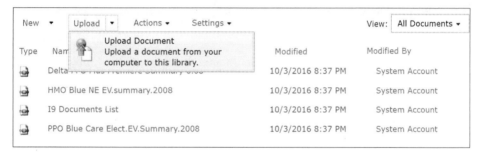

Figure 18.18 Uploading Documents Either Singly or in a Batch

Tips for Working with the Employee Portal

Change the **Get Started** link in the body of the page of the Employee Portal to **@Link-toNEW@** in the URL field when you edit the page.

If you have multiple onboarding processes configured, the **Getting Started** link to begin the **New Employee Step** will require additional configuration to work properly.

If you use Internet Explorer to manage the Employee Portal, you'll need to make some settings in **Tools • Compatibility Settings** and add *www.successfactors.com*. Note that if you make these compatibility settings, PDFs won't display in the **New Employee Step**.

The pages within the Employee Portal contain all of the content in the portal. Before configuration, the Employee Portal is just a shell similar to the wire frame of the Recruiting Marketing website. With the shell, you can add or modify content contained in the portal through the UI in the Admin Center. The Employee Portal is based on a SharePoint site and uses familiar Microsoft editing tools.

Other things you can do to manage the Employee Portal include the following:

- Add data keys to a web page such as {LocationAddress}
- Create a link to a document
- Create a link in an email
- Create a link to Onboarding
- Create a link to an external website
- Create additional web pages and parts
- Manage navigation menus to create new menus and submenus and also to edit existing menus
- Manage videos by inserting Flash videos in a web page or YouTube videos
- Manage the branding of the Employee Portal with logos, colors, and other graphics

In addition, remember our discussion in Chapter 16 regarding the Employee Portal versus pre-day one capability when you're deciding whether to use this feature.

Let's now discuss user access to Onboarding.

18.6 User Login Access

Users can log in to Onboarding in two ways. They can enter **Account**, **User Name**, and **Password** on the login page, or they can be authenticated via single sign-on (SSO) and access the link somewhere on an intranet page. You can control the access point for users with custom attributes in the user profile. For example, a user can be granted permission to access Onboarding via login page, SSO string, or both.

The attributes that determine a user's login method are as follows:

- Login.SSO.Enabled
  Allows authentication from the corporate intranet site via SSO.
- Login.Interactive.Enabled
  Logs users in by entering username and password.

The default value to allow access is "1". When the value is "0", the related Login (SSO or interactive) is disabled. If SSO is used, these attributes are automatically added to the user profile.

You can reset user passwords for external resources that don't have access to SAP SuccessFactors. You can also do it to facilitate staged users for testing. For all corporate users, passwords should be managed from SAP SuccessFactors or Active Directory, if SSO is enabled.

18.7 Summary

There are three main administrative interfaces for the SAP SuccessFactors Onboarding module. Super Admin access is reserved for SAP Professional Services or partner consultants and is very similar in concept to the provisioning interface for SAP SuccessFactors. Access is tightly controlled by SAP, and each consultant must be granted access to their customers' instances to their Super Admin account on each server. From Super Admin, there are initial setup steps that are made to enable default processes or create a base process and to enable self-service features. From there, the Onboarding module can be maintained from within the Onboarding Dashboard by users with the appropriate permissions. The Admin Center provides easy jump to links to various parts of the Onboarding Dashboard and using the favorites feature will even make these accessible from the home page on login.

Within these administrative interfaces, businesses and consultants can build processes; configure field mapping among Recruiting, Onboarding, and Employee Central; and manage security and notifications. The Document Center allows access to all of the completed documents that Onboarding stores, and purge rules can be maintained to purge old documents that are no longer needed, after applicable retention periods have expired. Finally, a new work queue interface is available for users to access that provides a more consistent feel across the suite and provides support for theming.

As new functionality is released within the Onboarding module, the administrator functions will continue to be expanded. Be sure to refer to the administrator manuals provided and updated by SAP for all the step-by-step details on how to perform all the administrative functions within Onboarding.

In the next chapter, we'll turn our discussion to implementing the Onboarding module.

18

Chapter 19
Implementing Onboarding

New tools available within the SAP SuccessFactors Admin Center now make implementing SAP SuccessFactors Onboarding much more flexible and allow you to develop processes on your own. When you understand how to work with the tools and where fields are mapped, you can unleash a powerful tool to increase the reach of onboarding, offboarding, and crossboarding within the organization.

If you're thinking of implementing SAP SuccessFactors Onboarding, either in conjunction with SAP SuccessFactors Recruiting or on its own, there are some considerations unique to the Onboarding module that you should keep in mind. As the development of the Onboarding module has progressed, there have been great strides in access to the tools needed to implement the module. Many of the features that were previously reserved for Super Admin access, similar to provisioning access with special access requirements, are now available in the administration interface within Onboarding. This opens up all kinds of possibilities for partners and businesses to share the load in implementing and expanding this feature-rich tool.

We covered methodology in an earlier chapter in this book, and the same methodology used to implement Recruiting is used to implement Onboarding. The same project phases, tasks, deliverables, and quality gates (Q-gates) remain consistent across both modules. Time lines will vary based on whether you're implementing multiple modules. As we've discussed in the previous two chapters, processes are very important in the Onboarding module. They become particularly important when defining the project time line, as the more processes that are built, the longer the development and testing phases are likely to be. In addition, you must consider the integration required with Recruiting and Employee Central, or your human resources information system (HRIS), when planning your project. If these modules are already live, some rework is likely needed to get the integration in place and working

19

smoothly. In this chapter, we'll look at some of the nuances of implementing Onboarding, as distinct from other modules within the SAP SuccessFactors suite. We'll discuss the following in particular:

- Process definition
- Roles and responsibilities
- Defining the corporate structure
- Working with panels and forms
- Key project milestones and time lines
- Testing the configuration and integration with Recruiting and Employee Central

19.1 Onboarding Process Definition

Defining the processes at play is just as important an activity in Onboarding as it is with Recruiting and any other talent management module. As we discussed in Chapter 17, Onboarding processes have a unique twist in that what gets configured is referred to as a *process*, and you can have many processes that make up a configuration. For example, you may define a process to onboard employees in the United States in English, another to onboard employees in Mexico in Spanish, and, finally, an offboarding process for all employees. In Onboarding terms, these are three processes that will be configured. Each of these then has an actual process of business activities that need to be completed by various players such as the new hire, the manager, HR, IT, and others.

This can cause a lot of confusion among the project team until everyone gets their heads around this concept. When you're planning for your Onboarding implementation, it's very important that you identify the number of Onboarding processes to be configured that are in scope. After you know this, you can begin the actual process design discussions about how you would like to improve onboarding within your organization, what steps it should include, information it should gather, and what best practices you'll incorporate. Remember that implementing a system is the perfect time to reevaluate how and why you do things the way you do today and design for a more efficient tomorrow. Onboarding is no different; you just need to approach it from a unique viewpoint. And don't forget all of the tools Onboarding provides to allow you to design a state-of-the-art onboarding process geared toward guiding your new employees through each step with the ultimate goal of getting to productive work as efficiently as possible.

19.1.1   Process Design

Onboarding may be conducted differently within various business units or geographies within your organization. Maybe you're a large company with disparate business units that operate somewhat independently and have their own "flavor" of onboarding new employees. Or, you may be a multinational corporation with offices all over the world, which necessitates different onboarding processes because of differences in culture and government regulation. Perhaps you haven't really thought about how you onboard your employees or the value you can add to the organization by having an efficient and well-planned process for your new employees.

Whatever your situation, it will be very important that you thoughtfully consider the process you want to see played out in SAP SuccessFactors and what people you'll want to be involved. There is much you can do with the Onboarding module, from covering your compliance and internal paperwork to full-on collaboration and socialization before day 1 and into their first weeks and months of employment. Having a plan for what to include and understanding what employees, besides the new hire, it will impact is critical to your success.

As you're talking through and designing your recruiting processes, also include the touchpoints with Onboarding. Identifying at what point in your recruiting process you want the chosen candidates to begin their Onboarding journey, and what data they will need from Recruiting, is the first step in designing the beginning of your Onboarding process. If you're new to an onboarding system and are coming from a completely manual process, you may want to pace yourself and just focus on the most critical and value-adding components of an automated onboarding process. Perhaps just getting the reams of paper completed online with e-signatures instead of managing copies and wet signatures, making sure everything gets turned in, will be a huge win for the organization. If you're implementing Recruiting simultaneous to Onboarding, be sure that you discuss both areas thoroughly. You may have different team members focused or involved in these two work streams of the project, so take the time for join discussions and design sessions to ensure the handoff between Recruiting and Onboarding is smooth.

If you already have Recruiting in place when you implement Onboarding, it will be important to understand what recruiting processes have been defined and are in place and what candidate data are already being captured to identify any additional data needs or process areas that will need to be adjusted in Recruiting to accommodate Onboarding. Note that changes are often needed in an existing Recruiting configuration, such as capturing additional data from candidates that will be needed in

19

Onboarding or adding a status or two to facilitate communication between the parties after Onboarding is integrated. You should account for this in your project planning to ensure you have the appropriate resources from your partner as well as internally to make any modifications to existing configurations. This can also have an impact on the time line, so understanding this up-front will help you make sure there is adequate time in the project schedule for this work as well.

19.1.2   Knowing What to Expect

Because of the flexibility and increased capabilities in the Admin Center, it's very possible for your Onboarding administrators to change and grow the processes configured during the implementation to contain additional steps. You can also build additional processes and deploy them, even cloning an existing process and making needed changes. With the right training and support, your onboarding administrators will become incredibly savvy and can extend the onboarding presence in many ways.

Don't feel pressured to nail down every step of every process you could ever possibly need. Start out with a manageable onboarding process that is achievable, not just from a configuration/systems perspective but also from an organizational perspective. Then grow into the onboarding culture that you desire to be. The system will be there to support your needs when you're ready for it.

If you're implementing Recruiting and Onboarding at the same time, whether you intend to configure one simple Onboarding process or multiple processes with different languages or process steps, you definitely want to have those discussions right up-front with Recruiting processes. Often businesses that haven't had any onboarding automation are used to managing "onboarding" activities within their applicant-tracking system configuration. Talking through the entire prehire process from requisition to completing all onboarding activities will identify where data are captured, where handoffs occur or will be needed, and who will be involved. These discussions could impact the scope of configuration of either module, and knowing this from early on in the project will be of huge benefit. Both the Recruiting scope and Onboarding scope will dictate the project timeline, which we'll discuss in Section 19.5.

19.1.3   Considerations When Designing the Process

Certain crucial topics and questions should be covered when discussing the to-be onboarding process that will be designed within Onboarding. Keeping these in mind and ensuring you address them in the early stages of the implementation will increase the overall success of the project and the eventual onboarding experience for your new hires. Let's review these now, in no particular order:

- Capture and review all onboarding activities across the organization, including all business units and geographies; best practice is to design a common global process to the lowest common denominator and then customize as needed for business operations and country-specific differences.

- Gather all the paperwork, forms, policies, and procedures new hires are currently completing. Revise any internal policy or procedure documents prior to including them in Onboarding so they represent the most current version.

- Review all documentation, and assess what, if anything, can be removed; likewise, identify what documentation isn't currently captured that should be.

- What are the roles that will be involved in your new Onboarding process and what will they do? Will there be any training required for any players in the process? If so, what will that include and when will it be delivered? How will this be sustained ongoing?

- How much collaboration with extended team members will you include in your process? Will you use the buddy and recommended people components within Onboarding? If so, what are the expected responsibilities of these roles and how will you communicate them to those who fill these roles?

- When do you want new hires to begin their Onboarding experience, will this be before their first day on the job or just start on day one? The answer will impact the timing of certain activities within Onboarding.

- Will your Onboarding process simply capture paperwork, or do you want to introduce integration with other processes such as SAP SuccessFactors goal setting and SAP SuccessFactors training? If the latter, how and when will you integrate those modules within the Onboarding process?

- How long will your onboarding process last? What post-hire activities and expectations are there for your new employees, and how will Onboarding support those?

These items and questions are certainly not exhaustive. However, if you ensure these items are discussed, you can be confident that your baseline process is well thought out, and the discussion will likely lead to other important topics as well.

Now let's discuss the roles and responsibilities included in implementing Onboarding.

19.2   Implementation Roles and Responsibilities

Because the same methodology is used to implement all SAP SuccessFactors modules, the roles and responsibilities will remain consistent when implementing Onboarding with what we discussed in Chapter 10. You'll remain responsible for providing subject matter expertise on the company's current onboarding process, such as it is, and be largely responsible for designing the new process in Onboarding, with support from the partner, key stakeholders, and other subject matter experts (SMEs) as necessary and appropriate. IT involvement will be dictated by whether you're implementing with Employee Central or SAP ERP Human Capital Management (SAP ERP HCM). Definitely plan for heavier IT involvement if integrating with SAP ERP HCM because they will be responsible for necessary configuration and testing in that system.

Let's review again some of the roles you may see involved in your Onboarding project, as follows:

- **Hiring managers**
  SAP SuccessFactors is designed around hiring managers owning the Onboarding process and connecting with their new employees right away. If you'd like to have your hiring managers be a part of the onboarding process, it will be critical to have them involved in designing the processes and providing input to the configuration. Just as you may have a focus group of hiring managers provide input to Recruiting, you may want to do the same for Onboarding. This could be the same group of managers or different ones, depending on your needs. Use this opportunity to discuss with your hiring managers what has worked well in past onboarding experiences, either within your company or elsewhere. In addition, discuss what hasn't worked well. Often, you can learn much more from things that haven't gone well than from those that have! Solicit input from this group on what role they feel managers can play in onboarding new employees and what they can do to set those new employees up for success.

- **Human Resources**
  HR always plays a critical role in onboarding new employees. HR professionals have to track down all the required forms that need to be completed and understand the nuances of certain state and federal government regulations. Likely, systematizing onboarding is going to have the biggest impact on your HR department by eliminating much of the burdensome manual work they do and freeing them up to be more strategic. Getting their input into the overall process

and program as a whole is invaluable. Understanding how managers and HR will work together during onboarding, what the hand-offs are, and how communication between these two critical roles will be managed, is paramount to a successful process. Because HR typically bears the burden of onboarding in most organizations, introducing managers into the process will be a change to HR players, and the change management impacts of this should not be underestimated.

- **Executive leadership steering committee**
  This group of stakeholders is always important to transformation projects, but if you're trying to introduce or build a culture focused on socialized onboarding that goes beyond filling out paperwork, then this group will be critical in signing off on the overall design of the process, helping to build excitement for the coming change, and being your champions within the organization. Don't limit your steering committee to just executives in HR or talent acquisition. Branch out and find executives that believe in what onboarding can do to bring value to their business.

- **Project management**
  Just as with Recruiting, either your partner will cover project management or you'll own it jointly. If your project is tackling both Recruiting and Onboarding together, it's probably a good idea to own this jointly with your partner project manager to help coordinate all of the internal resources. Testing activities should be planned well and tightly coordinated between Recruiting and Onboarding processes after integration has been configured.

- **IT resources**
  As mentioned previously, if you're integrating with SAP ERP HCM for new hire data from Onboarding and then again to SAP SuccessFactors to create the new employee record, you'll have IT involvement on the project. Typically, companies maintain their own SAP ERP HCM landscape and will need to own the configuration needed on the on premise side of the integration. If you use another third-party HRIS, you'll need to send new hire data from Onboarding to the HRIS, and often IT can be of help in these activities as well.

- **Testers**
  Testers will be incredibly important in testing the integration points and ensuring that all the data are flowing as required. If possible, coordinate your testing activities between Recruiting and Onboarding so that the data can begin being built in Recruiting and then carry over into Onboarding. Whether you maintain the same tester group for both modules or bring in new resources for Onboarding, having adequate numbers to test will be critical.

- **Recent newly hired employees**

  Something you may want to consider is including a small group of recently hired (and onboarded) employees who can provide valuable input on their experience and how it could have been improved. Because these employees have just walked through the process, they are perfectly positioned to help you design the new process and provide input on what additional collaboration or resources would have made their onboarding experience even better. They can even be great testers.

Throughout the implementation, the activities of these roles will ebb and flow, so having a clearly defined project time line with resource needs called out in each phase of the project will provide clarity and set expectations with all those involved. This is especially important with those who aren't involved throughout the entire project. If you use managers and even recent new hires in a focus-group way, be sure to keep them in the loop on progress throughout so they feel their input was valuable, and they can be champions for the process at go-live and beyond.

In the next section, we'll look at one of the most important foundational aspects of the Onboarding module—the corporate structure.

19.3   Corporate Structure

When a new employee is hired, certain information is needed to define where that new hire will work within the organization, as well as specific information about the employee's position. When Onboarding works in conjunction with Recruiting, the information about the new hire's position will come from Recruiting to Onboarding and will be driven by how the data are already set up in Recruiting. If Employee Central or SAP ERP HCM is in play, the organizational information is likely being driven by those systems and then being passed into Recruiting in various ways, either through position integration or via job code entity. If you happen to be implementing Onboarding standalone, you'll define the corporate structure within Onboarding itself. The corporate structure in Onboarding is used for the following reasons:

- There is a need to select or change the work location or position for the new hire from what was specified in Recruiting.

- In the absence of Recruiting, the work location and position need to be selected within Onboarding.

- There is a need to assign activities to a user (called a "corporate user") so that only this user can see or execute activities for the user's location or department. This is important to the security model of Onboarding because, in the absence of corporate or other filters, a corporate user can see all activities. This is fine for a small organization or to have a "super" corporate user. But if you want to distribute this capability throughout an organization, you'll want to restrict this user access to specific parts of the organization.

- The corporate structure will assign the corporate address and any identification number to government forms.

Let's look at the components of the corporate structure, beginning with levels.

19.3.1   Levels

The corporate structure has four levels available that can be used independently or in conjunction. The number of levels you use in Onboarding is one of the first things you decide in configuration workshops and is foundational to your Onboarding configuration. Again, if you're using Recruiting, the levels will be determined within the Recruiting configuration and values will be set on the requisition level. Levels can be configured and managed in the **Reference Files** area of Onboarding, as shown in Figure 19.1, and will correspond to the corporate structure.

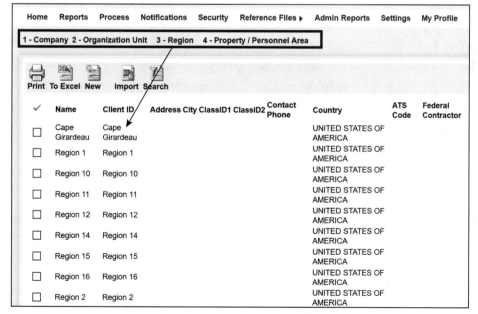

Figure 19.1 Example of a Four-Level Corporate Structure Managed in Reference Values

While an administrator can maintain the corporate structure manually, it's most often imported into Onboarding on a regular schedule. This will sync the reference file data containing your corporate structure with Recruiting or your HRIS on an ongoing basis.

Each organizational unit within the corporate structure can have a different set of property values. The Onboarding module has commonly used fields for all organizational units, and there is a flexible set of property values that can be used to meet customer needs. The standard fields are as follows:

- Company
- Division
- Department
- Location
- Position

The **Division**, **Department**, and **Location** fields should be familiar if you're an existing SAP SuccessFactors user, as these are also standard fields within the SAP SuccessFactors platform. If you run Employee Central or SAP ERP HCM, you'll likely have a company or legal entity structure as well. The labels for these fields can be changed to reflect your terminology, similar to Recruiting. You can see this displayed in Figure 19.1 as the **Company**, **Division**, **Department**, and **Location** values are defined as **Company**, **Organization Unit**, **Region**, and **Property/Personnel Area**.

19.3.2   Corporate Structure Relations

When the corporate structure is defined, you can set relationships among and between the levels. Organizational levels can be structured various ways to meet your needs:

- Hierarchical structure is when each level is dependent on the level before.
- Nonhierarchical is when all levels are independent of each other.
- A mixture of hierarchical and nonhierarchical occurs when you can have some levels dependent on the level before while others are independent.

In a hierarchical structure, the values will be presented in a parent-child relationship where **Division** fields are associated to a particular **Company**, each **Division** has a set of assigned **Departments**, and each **Department** has one or more **Locations**. Users are then limited to the set of dropdown values in the wizard panels based on the **Company** value they select first. In a nonhierarchical structure, at every level, the values for that level are always available to select. This is very similar to having picklist fields that bear no relationship to any other.

In the mixed corporate structure, you may have two or more fields that are related, while the remaining fields are independent. For example, perhaps you have **Departments** associated to **Divisions**, but there is no relationship between **Division** and **Company**. And **Locations** could either be associated with **Departments** or be independent as well. This flexibility allows you to define the corporate structure that will work best within your organization.

When building the corporate structure, there are two main tasks:

- Create the base information about the organizational unit such as name, address, identification numbers, contact information, whether e-Verify will be activated (for United States), and others.

- Create the relationship between each of the levels, if you're using the hierarchical structure.

To build or edit the corporate structure within Onboarding, you can import the information or do it manually. If you're importing the corporate structure, you shouldn't edit the information manually as this may cause issues when the sync is run. To import your corporate structure data, from the Onboarding Dashboard, you'll select **Reference Files • Corporate Structure • Import**. Browse for the file, and then select the file format, **CSV** or **XML**, as shown in Figure 19.2. Be sure to choose the **Delimiter** if you use a CSV file. Follow the steps in the import wizard to import the corporate structure.

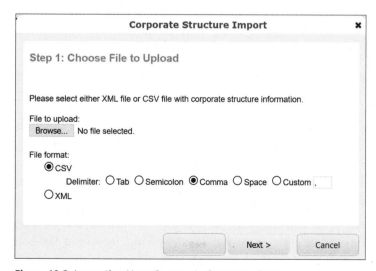

Figure 19.2 Importing Your Corporate Structure Data

If you want to build or edit the corporate structure manually, follow the same main menu path: **Onboarding Dashboard • Reference Files • Corporate Structure**. Select the **Level** that you want to create or edit. Figure 19.3 provides an example of how to create a company in the corporate structure. Continue this method for each value within each level.

Figure 19.3 Adding the Applicable Information to Be Defined on Each Level of the Corporate Structure

You can also set up relationships between the values in the levels. Select the value you want to relate, check the box to select it, and then click the **Relations** button. To add a relation, click the **Add Relation** button in either the **Parents** or **Children** area. Select the **Level**, and then search for the unit you want to relate. Repeat these steps until you've finished adding relations.

After the corporate structure is configured, the processes defined in configuration workshops can be built against it. Let's now discuss working with forms and panels. If you are implementing Onboarding with Recruiting, you will not relate the corporate structure, as your structure will be determined by Recruiting.

19.4   Working with Panels and Forms

Within Onboarding, users will walk through a series of panels where a wizard guides them through questions that capture information that is then populated in various forms that are signed at the end of the process. These panels capture personal information such as name, address, government identification number, dependents, tax withholding information, and banking information, among other data. In addition to the information on panels, we'll also briefly look at how forms are populated in this section.

19.4.1   Panels

In the following sections, we'll look at the types of panels, how the wizards that are part of your onboarding process hold the smart data entry panels, and the panel designer.

Panel Types

Three types of panels are used within the Onboarding module that serve different purposes and collect different data:

- **Compliance panels**
  These panels are used to collect data for standard government-issued forms, such as US federal and state forms, including Form I-9, W-4, and state withholding forms. Figure 19.4 is an example of a US compliance panel. Other compliance panels for other supported countries are also available, as discussed in Chapter 16. These compliance panels can't be deleted, disabled, or edited by the Onboarding administrator and are only updated by SAP Engineering when there are needed forms changes. SAP will continue to increase the compliance panels that are available for various countries as the module further develops. In the meantime, if you have a need to capture compliance information for a nonsupported country, you can create a user-defined panel.

- **Standard panels**
  These panels are used to collect data for standard corporate forms delivered with Onboarding such as the direct deposit and emergency contact forms. Figure 19.5 shows an example of a standard panel used to gather a new employee's organizational information. These panels may be disabled and enabled but not modified. If you need to use a standard panel but want to make changes to it, you should copy the panel and then modify the copy of the panel in panel designer.

19

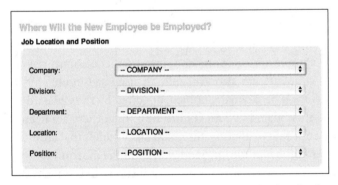

Enter Your Name and Social Security Number

It is our company's policy that each employee must have a social security number for payroll reporting purposes only.

Do you have a social security number? ⦿ Yes   ○ No

Please enter your SSN: [   ]

Please enter your name as it appears on your social security card.

First Name: [   ]

Middle Name: [   ]

Last Name: [   ]   Suffix: [⬍]

Please enter your date of birth.

Date of Birth: [   ][📅] (mm/dd/yyyy)

☐ I have verified that this is my correct SSN and that my name is as it appears on my Social Security Card.
☐ If your last name differs from that shown on your social security card, check this box.
☐ I acknowledge that I must call 1-800-772-1213 to obtain a new or replacement Social Security card.

Figure 19.4 A Compliance Panel Used to Onboard Employees in the United States

Where Will the New Employee be Employed?

Job Location and Position

Company: [-- COMPANY -- ⬍]

Division: [-- DIVISION -- ⬍]

Department: [-- DEPARTMENT -- ⬍]

Location: [-- LOCATION -- ⬍]

Position: [-- POSITION -- ⬍]

Figure 19.5 Standard Panel Used to Gather Organizational Information for the New Employee

- **User-defined panels**

  These custom panels are built to collect business-specific data, most often to populate business-specific forms. Figure 19.6 provides an example of a user-defined panel built to capture a new employee's preferences and sizes for company logoed shirts and other items.

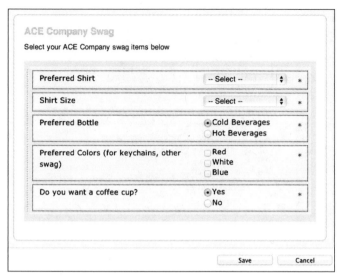

Figure 19.6 Building Custom, User-Defined Panels to Meet Any Number of Customer-Specific Requirements

The Onboarding administrator can create and edit these panels in panel designer to meet specific requirements. These panels can also be exported and imported using XML files. When you import a panel XML, the system will check the import package for conflicts. For the panels to be imported, the panel names, data keys, and list items must all be unique.

Wizards

A wizard holds the smart data entry panels that are used to collect data from new hires throughout the onboarding process. Your onboarding processes will contain one or more wizards. If you create a new panel in your process, you need to first make sure you're working in the wizard that panel will belong to. Each step in your Onboarding process is assigned one wizard by default. You can add new wizards or copy existing wizards and modify them, and then move or create panels within that particular wizard. Wizards can be assigned to notifications as well.

Wizards are available from the Onboarding Dashboard, under **Settings • Panels • All Wizards**. You can view the components of each wizard, or you can copy a wizard if you'd like to make changes to it by selecting the wizard and using the **Copy Wizard** button as shown in Figure 19.7.

19

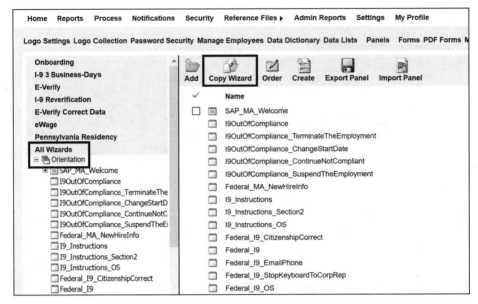

Figure 19.7 Viewing and Copying Wizards within the Panels Area of Settings

When copying a wizard, it's recommended to choose a smaller wizard such as the **New Hire Activities** wizard.

Panel Designer

Panels are accessed, created, and edited in the **Panels** area under **Settings**. You can navigate through the various types of panels on the left navigation window. Here the panels are organized into groups of related panels. Search for the panel you want, and select it to display the panel in the right window. You can see in Figure 19.8 that we're viewing the **SAP_Standard_NewHire_Setup** panel. There is also a copy of this standard panel that has been made to modify it. In Figure 19.9, you can see that when that panel is selected, it can be edited from the standard panel. Use the **Editing** menu to the left of the panel to make the necessary changes to fit your process and requirements.

When you design panels within Onboarding, keep in mind the experience of the end user as well as system performance. While it may seem better to include numerous fields on a panel and keep the clicks down, it's actually recommended to create more panels with fewer fields on them. Best practice is to include no more than six to eight input fields on a single panel. When you're adding picklists, include no more than four per panel to ensure performance isn't negatively impacted.

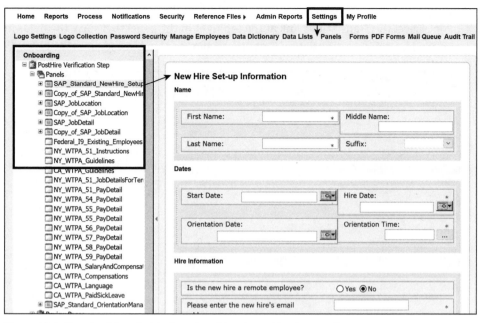

Figure 19.8 Standard Panels Displayed and Previewed in the Panel Screen

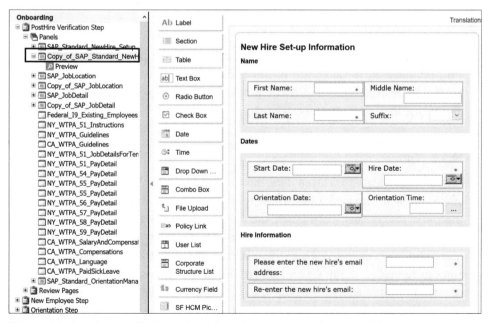

Figure 19.9 Copying Standard Panels and Making Changes Using the Editing Menu

19

If language translations are in scope, you can set the translations on each copied panel. Select the **Translations** link at the top right of the panel to display the fields in that panel, provide all translations, and then save the panel (see Figure 19.10).

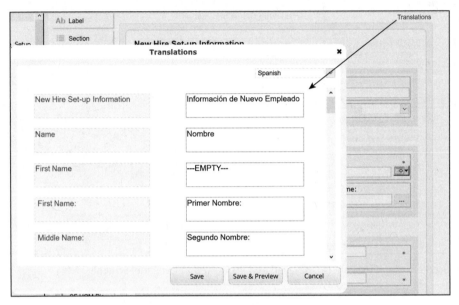

Figure 19.10 Including Translations for Each Field on the Panel

If more than one language is in scope, be sure to set the translations for each language by selecting the language at the top right of the panel. In Figure 19.10, you can see that **Spanish** is being viewed. You provide the translations for each field, save the inputs, and then select the next language.

19.4.2   Forms

Forms are populated with the data captured in the wizards on the panels we discussed in the previous sections. These forms are most often electronically signed at the end of the process. Just as there are **Compliance** and **Standard Corporate** panels, there are compliance and standard corporate forms that are populated with the corresponding data collected. Then there are business-specific forms that are custom and can be uploaded into Onboarding for distribution, consumption, and acknowledgement. These custom forms can also be edited using a PDF editor to either change or add fields for additional data collection.

Any field that isn't included in the compliance or standard corporate form must be included in the Onboarding Data Dictionary and then properly mapped so to be used in the process. If a business has policies and procedures it wants to include in its process, those policies can be added to a custom **Policy** panel and distributed to new hires.

Advanced conditions can be set up to determine under what conditions a form will be displayed to a new hire. Examples might be union forms or various country forms. PDF forms are part of form groups, which not only store related forms but also have conditions that will apply to all forms within a particular group. Administrators can create new form groups, edit or delete existing groups, and assign forms to groups. Your group list can be printed or exported to Microsoft Excel. After a PDF form has been assigned to a group, an administrator can view or edit the form attributes. You should have a forms group for all the corporate forms that are uploaded into Onboarding.

To add a custom form to Onboarding, five main steps need to be completed:

- Identify the initial form specifications, including the following:
  - Know who will complete the form to identify the process step in which the corresponding panel will appear.
  - Know who will sign the form to determine the signature step.
  - What type of signature will be used: electronic or wet signature?
  - Will the form need to be printed?
  - How many copies of the form should be printed by default?
- Identify the fields on each PDF form that should be populated with data.
- Ensure any fields on the forms are included in the Data Dictionary; if missing, they will need to be created.
- Add the fields to be populated to the form with a PDF editor such as Adobe Acrobat.
- Upload the form into the Onboarding module.

This was a brief overview of the kinds of panels you can define and add to wizards and the forms that are output of the data collected. Implementation partners and customers should work together on extensive knowledge transfer on how wizards and panels can be configured to support each process defined within Onboarding.

Let's now discuss the key project milestones and the time line for implementing Onboarding.

19

19.5   Key Project Milestones and Time Lines

Your Onboarding implementation will have similar project milestones to Recruiting or any other SAP SuccessFactors module. We discussed the project methodology, SAP Activate, in detail in Chapter 10. As a brief reminder, the project phases in SAP Activate are as follows:

- Prepare
- Explore
- Realize
- Deploy

Refer to Chapter 10, Section 10.3, for a detailed discussion of the project methodology and overall time lines, with an example RACI chart. In this section, our discussion will focus on some things that are unique to implementing the Onboarding module, both in conjunction with Recruiting and on its own.

19.5.1   Project Timelines

If you're implementing Onboarding in conjunction with Recruiting, configuration of Onboarding will start right around the start of Iteration 2 of Recruiting. Because of the integration and the heavy reliance of Onboarding on receiving critical candidate data from Recruiting to support the onboarding of your new employees, you should focus on getting the Recruiting module going and the configuration about 70% set before the Onboarding configuration begins. Of course, you can begin your process design, project orientation training, and high-level configuration decisions going much sooner, and you most certainly should as we discussed in Section 19.1 of this chapter.

A big influencer on the time line of your project is the scope of work to be configured and rolled out at go-live. As you might expect, the more processes that are configured and need to be integrated with Recruiting, the longer the project time line will take. If multiple language translations are in scope, this can also increase the project time line. As we discussed in Chapter 13, adequate time must be planned for the translations to be provided by either internal resources or the translation vendor. The translations must be made to all applicable fields within the various processes, and then, of course, all of those translations must be tested.

As we mentioned previously, you now has a tremendous amount of control over configuring additional processes in the administrative interface of Onboarding. Because of this, it's possible to spread the work of configuration across the implementation partner and your administrators. Not only can this contribute to getting all of the configuration complete, it's also a great way to ensure detailed knowledge transfer occurs so you're prepared to sustain the module at go-live.

Another factor impacting project time line is the integration points with Recruiting and either Employee Central or SAP ERP HCM. The integration with Employee Central and Recruiting is fairly straightforward and can all be set up within those respective modules and the Onboarding module. However, if you run core HR processes in SAP ERP HCM and need to integrate back with new hire data, there is a lot of configuration and set up on the SAP ERP side that will need to be factored into the project time line. This will also have an impact on configuration and testing resources. Consider all of these factors when developing the project plan. We'll discuss testing considerations in Section 19.6.

19.5.2 Key Tasks and Milestones

We provided a detailed discussion of key milestones within the SAP Activate methodology in Chapter 10. A brief review of those milestones by phase is provided next.

Prepare Phase

As the phase name suggests, the *prepare* phase is all about planning for the project, and activities are focused around identifying and planning for the work that is coming. This is when the business team attends any Project Team Orientation training provided by SAP for the Onboarding module and begins gathering current practices and documents for Onboarding.

Key tasks in the prepare phase include the following:

- Create the project plan
- Define processes
- Perform technical integration

Explore Phase

The *explore* phase is focused on designing processes and beginning to discuss the configuration. Gaps should be identified and noted to be discussed in the next phase. Ancillary work streams focused on communication, change management, and training will also begin in this phase. Additionally, preparing for the testing in the next phase should begin.

Key tasks in the explore phase include the following:

19

- Identify/confirm requirements
- Discuss as-is and to-be processes
- Hold kickoff meeting
- Have configuration workshops
- Perform initial planning for testing, communication, change management, and training

Realize Phase

The *realize* phase is all about building the system through a series of iterations to incrementally build and test an integrated business and system environment that is based on the business scenarios and process requirements identified in the previous phase.

Key tasks in the realize phase include the following:

- Configure the systems
- Perform iterative testing and configure the system
- Build and begin executing testing and training strategies
- Conduct all testing
- Conduct administrator knowledge transfer
- Conduct and attend applicable training, as needed

Deploy Phase

The *deploy* phase is about preparing for go-live and deploying the system to end users. Key tasks in the deploy phase include the following:

- Perform go-live planning and readiness
- Migrate configurations and data to production
- Conduct end-user training
- Execute the support plan
- Introduce the customer success team

To reiterate the material in Chapter 10, the tasks and activities just discussed are typical of implementing Onboarding. Actual tasks and milestones will vary for each individual project.

Let's now discuss testing Onboarding configuration and some unique considerations you should prepare for.

19.6   Testing Onboarding

When you're putting together the testing plan for your Onboarding implementation, you'll need to keep the following in mind:

- Have scenarios that test each process configured within Onboarding that have steps for each role in the process.

- Have a checklist of the panels in each process, especially the modifications made to the standard panels, the user-defined panels, and any custom panels that were copied from **Compliance** panels.

- Test the integration from Recruiting to Onboarding, ensuring the mapped fields are passed correctly, including the mapping of picklist data.

- Test the integration from Onboarding to Employee Central, again focusing on the mapped data to ensure it's passing from Onboarding to Employee Central as expected.

- If language translations are in scope, test the scenarios and mapped data in each language by testers that speak the language.

- Don't forget to test the Recruiting settings made related to updating data in Recruiting; if you've selected to pass updated data from Recruiting such as the hiring manager change, be sure you include a scenario to test these settings as well.

- Often companies will have different groups of testers for Recruiting as they do for Onboarding. If this is your case, remember in your planning that this needs to be tightly coordinated with Recruiting testing so there is data to work with in Onboarding. This will also apply to testing Employee Central integration.

- Plan adequate testing time during your iterations to step through each panel that is part of each process so you can identify as many needed updates as possible prior to the integration between Recruiting and Employee Central. Your configuration should be fairly set prior to integrating the modules in question.

19.7   Summary

Implementing Onboarding will be very similar to other SAP SuccessFactors implementations in many ways, with the same methodology employed and familiar phases and Q-gates. Approaching the design of your Onboarding processes and systems at the same time as you design Recruiting will greatly increase the harmonization of these two modules and reduce the amount of rework that may need to be done. There may be a few different roles in the Onboarding implementation, for example, managers may take a larger role in implementing Onboarding than they do in Recruiting. Take the opportunity to gather input from both managers and recently hired employees on the current Onboarding experience, and incorporate that feedback into the processes defined during implementation.

Understanding the foundational elements within Onboarding, such as the corporate structure, will be important during the process and configuration workshops. Additionally, the project team should take time to learn about the relationship between panels and forms so that these critical elements of Onboarding can be properly designed to support the processes.

Finally, keep in mind the relationship of Onboarding to both Recruiting and Employee Central when planning for testing to ensure that the timing of Onboarding scenarios is coordinated with both touchpoints. Having adequate data available in Onboarding means sending candidates from Recruiting, which impacts testing timing. Likewise, the same considerations impact Employee Central integration.

Now let's turn our attention to how the Recruiting and Onboarding modules are integrated with each other.

Chapter 20

Integrating Recruiting with Onboarding

When you have both Recruiting and Onboarding implemented in your landscape, data are easily transferred from the Recruiting module into Onboarding to facilitate an efficient and user-centric process for onboarding new employees. This not only saves time and resources otherwise expended in manual tasks, but it also makes for a better new hire experience.

Businesses that implement both SAP SuccessFactors Recruiting and SAP SuccessFactors Onboarding in their landscape will integrate the two databases so that new hire data captured during the recruiting process flows seamlessly into Onboarding. This integration will replace any previously existing integration with a third-party onboarding vendor, or integration directly from Recruiting to SAP SuccessFactors Employee Central if this predates the implementation of the Onboarding module. As Onboarding is one of the newer modules within the SAP SuccessFactors suite, it's very likely that many businesses choose to implement it into their existing Recruiting to Employee Central environment.

If Onboarding is implemented in your landscape after Recruiting and Employee Central, there are a few things that you need to be aware of. Best practice is to pass new hire data from Recruiting to Onboarding and then to Employee Central to complete the new hire process. You can't send data from Recruiting to Employee Central directly and then send additional data to Employee Central from Onboarding after the new hire has been through the process.

With certain types of new hires, you might need to send data on from Recruiting in two different workflows. For example, new hourly employees may not need to go through Onboarding, so you may want to send their data directly to Employee Central. This would be supported if a separate requisition template is configured for this need. This would then allow for the Recruiting to Onboarding to Employee Central workflow for other candidates hired against a different requisition template configured for that purpose.

This chapter will focus on the integration points between Recruiting and Onboarding. Specifically, we'll discuss the following:

- Setting up the integration in provisioning and the configuration
- Mapping data between Recruiting and Onboarding
- Testing the integration

Let's begin our discussion with looking at how to configure the integration.

20.1   Setting Up the Integration in Provisioning and Configuration

To send data captured during the Recruiting process to the Onboarding module to support that process, several steps need to be set up. As you would expect, the integration process begins with enabling settings in provisioning. This sets up the gateways for the databases to talk to each other and makes the necessary features available via the Admin Center. There is also some amount of configuration that needs to occur in the job requisition data model (JRDM) templates within Recruiting. In this section, we'll look at the following:

- Prerequisites
- Enabling the integration
- Setting permissions in role-based permissions
- Onboarding settings

Let's begin by discussing the prerequisites to setting up the Recruiting to Onboarding integration.

20.1.1   Prerequisites

There are a few prerequisites to enabling the Recruiting to Onboarding integration:

- Enable the V12 framework
- Enable role-based permissions

New Recruiting business users will have the V12 framework and role-based permissions enabled as part of the SAP SuccessFactors foundation implementation. While most long-time Recruiting users have likely upgraded to the V12 framework and role-based permissions, there are still a few businesses that are still on the legacy permissions model. This is an excellent opportunity to be on the latest release of security so you may also take advantage of other features such as the **Upgrade Center** in the Admin Center and all other new features. For new users, these prerequisites will already be met. These settings are set up in provisioning.

20.1.2   Enabling the Integration

After the prerequisites have been confirmed, there are several settings in provisioning that must be made to begin the integration. These steps are detailed in the Implementation Guide maintained by SAP, but we'll review them at a high level here.

Provisioning

First, to enable Onboarding integration, from provisioning, find the appropriate Company ID and then navigate to **Company Settings • Recruiting • Enable Onboarding Integration • BizX Onboarding Integration**. Select **Enable Onboarding Integration**, as shown in Figure 20.1, and save this setting.

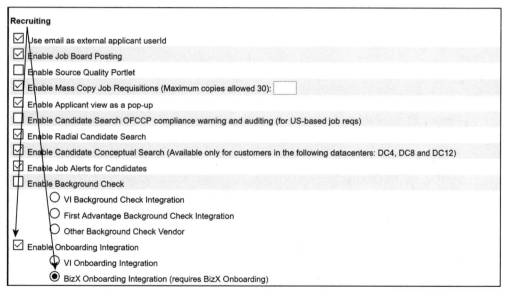

Figure 20.1 Enabling the Recruiting to Onboarding Integration in the Recruiting Settings in Company Settings

While in **Company Settings**, navigate to **Enable Onboarding Application**. You'll find this setting higher up in the **Company Settings** than the Recruiting settings. It's best to search for "enable onboarding" to easily find these settings. Here you'll confirm if the Onboarding module has been set up by SAP Operations. For new business users just purchasing Onboarding, these settings should be made by SAP during the instance provisioning process. If you don't see any settings made in this section, you'll need to log a support ticket to have this enabled by SAP. Figure 20.2 provides an example of what you should see when Onboarding has been provisioned and enabled.

☑ Enable Onboarding Application — requires "Enable Generic Objects", "Version 12 UI framework (Revolution)" and "Enable the Attachment Manager"
   ☑ Enable Onboarding Tour
   ☑ Enable External ATS-ONB-EC Integration
   ☐ Enable MDF-based new hire activity planning (refer to Onboarding Config Guide for details)
   ☐ Enable Pre-Day1 Experience for new hires
      ☐ Use the Same User ID for Pre-day1 User and the Employee
   ☐ Make future dated users active after EC hire process
☐ Enable Offboarding Application — requires "Enable Intelligent Services", "Enable Generic Objects" and "Enable the Attachment Manager"
   ☐ Enable Offboarding EC Writeback-requires "Employee Central V2"

On/Offboarding settings

Account ID	C0007438927P
Environment	DC8 Stage ⌄ Path (e.g., ONB, ONBPREM) ONB
WebService URL	https://onboarding4preview.sapsf.com/ONB
Enter KMS Web Services credentials	
Username	C0007438927P_ws
Password	C0007438927P$ws
Enter KMS Rest Web Services credentials	
Username	C0007438927P_ws
Password	C0007438927P$ws

Figure 20.2 Onboarding Settings Made during the Instance Provisioning Process

Configuration

Setting up the Onboarding and Recruiting integration requires initial configuration of templates and field mapping between the two modules to facilitate information passing from one system to the other. Onboarding is accessible to users in Recruiting via a *feature permission* configured in the JRDM. Remember that feature permissions define operator access to certain special functionalities such as offer approval, offer letter, and Onboarding, as we discussed in Chapter 2. This permission setting will make the **Initiate OnBoarding** action accessible in the specified status(es) within the talent pipeline, as you can see in Figure 20.3, and must be granted separately for each status users will need to perform the **Initiate OnBoarding** action for.

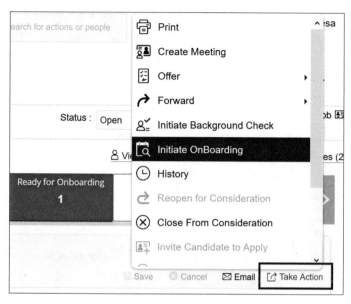

Figure 20.3 Feature Permissions Making the Initiate OnBoarding Action Available in the Talent Pipeline

To configure the Onboarding feature permission, go to provisioning and download all applicable JRDM templates. You'll need to configure the appropriate feature permission for each status for which you want to make **Initiate OnBoarding** available, in each requisition template. Feature permissions are set in the <application-status-config> section of the JRDM, where you also enable offer and interview functionality. An example of the Onboarding feature permission is shown in Figure 20.4. You can enable the feature permission for multiple roles in the same <feature-permission>, but if you want Onboarding to be available in more than one status, this needs to be for each status.

```
<feature-permission type="onboarding">
  <description><![CDATA[The following roles can initiate Onboarding.]]></description>
  <role-name><![CDATA[R]]></role-name>
  <role-name><![CDATA[G]]></role-name>
  <status><![CDATA[Hired: Start Onboarding]]></status>
</feature-permission>
```

Figure 20.4 Feature Permissions in the JRDM Showing the Recruiter and Hiring Manager Can Initiate Onboarding in the Hired: Start Onboarding Status

20

20.1.3   Settings in Onboarding

After you've ensured the necessary provisioning settings have been made, and you've set up the feature permissions as required in each affected JRDM, you'll need to make settings in the Onboarding module. To do this, you must assign the field to its entity so the mapping tool knows on which tab the fields should appear. To do so, follow these steps:

1. Go to **Onboarding • Onboarding Dashboard**. From there, navigate to **Settings • Data Dictionary**.

2. Select the **Entities** folder in the navigation area on the left, as you can see in Figure 20.5, and select the **Fields** button.

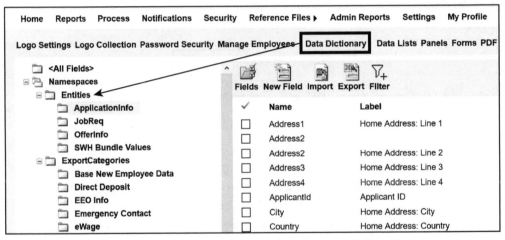

Figure 20.5 Assigning Fields to the Correct Entity in the Data Dictionary within Onboarding

3. Select the appropriate type of data from the options available, such as: **ApplicationInfo**, **JobReq**, or **OfferInfo**. Select the **Fields** button to display the fields available for the entity data chosen. Ensure you have **Entities** selected in the **Namespace** field. Here you can select fields available and add to or remove them from the entity using the arrow buttons. You can see this in Figure 20.6.

4. After fields are added to the entity, you can also reorder the fields by using the **Up** or **Down** buttons.

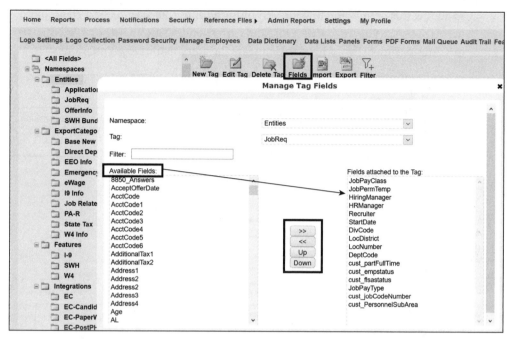

Figure 20.6 Making Fields from Onboarding Available to Various Recruiting Entities in the Data Dictionary

20.1.4   Set Permissions in Role-Based Permissions

Several permissions need to be enabled for the Recruiting to Onboarding integration at any time after the provisioning settings have been updated or confirmed, as discussed in Section 20.1.2. You'll need to permission the appropriate admin users to access the **Setup Onboarding Integration** feature in Admin Center. Individual users will also need to have the permission to **Initiate OnBoarding**. These permissions are shown in Figure 20.7. This is in addition to configuring the feature permission in the JRDM discussed in Section 20.1.2.

Often, companies will create new roles within role-based permissions that address Onboarding, rather than impacting existing roles. There is some advantage to this because you can finitely manage the role assignment this way. For example, you may have certain administrators who only maintain the Onboarding module, and you don't want them to have additional permissions that would come with adding Onboarding to an existing administrator role. Likewise, you may not want your Recruiting administrators to be able to access the Onboarding administrative features,

20

so adding this permission to your "recruiting admin" role(s) won't be a viable option. In this scenario, you can create a role and corresponding group within role-based permissions to support your need to delineate the administrative permissions.

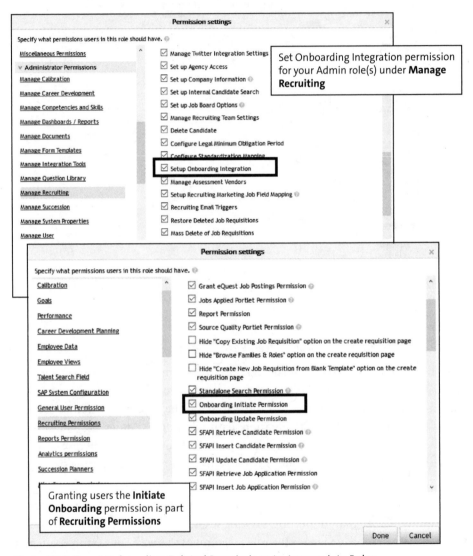

Figure 20.7 Grant Onboarding-Related Permissions to Appropriate Roles

Many companies, however, will just add these permissions to existing roles. A good example is adding the **Onboarding Initiate Permission** to the existing recruiter role(s)

because recruiters are the likely ones to perform this function. There isn't much sense to creating a new role just for that when it can easily be incorporated into an existing role.

However you choose to set it up, it's important to ensure that any new roles or new permissions to existing roles follow the convention already set up for managing your security model.

> **Tip**
>
> Don't forget to add the role-based permission configuration to your testing scenarios and scripts to ensure this isn't missed!

20.1.5 Onboarding Settings

There are a few settings related to Onboarding that need to be made in the Recruiting settings within Admin Center to ensure that data are sent over to Onboarding correctly. Let's look at each of these.

Integration Settings

The Onboarding integration settings allow enabling Onboarding for all requisition templates or specific templates, if you have multiple JRDMs in use. From within **Onboarding Integration Setup** on the **Settings** tab, enable Onboarding according to your needs. Onboarding may only be limited to requisitions based on one field or criteria, and this needs to be kept in mind when configuring the integration. By way of example, if you use Recruiting globally but use Onboarding only in the United States to start, you would set up the criteria so that Onboarding options are only available on requisitions for jobs in the United States. Figure 20.8 provides an example of the settings. You can see when you select to **Apply Onboarding to Job Requisitions that meet the following criteria** that you must select the appropriate requisition field and add it to the **Assigned Values**.

You can also restrict Onboarding for applicants who have already been onboarded in the past number of days. This settings specifies a number of days after which a candidate could be eligible to be onboarded again. This would apply if for some reason a new hire started onboarding, but it wasn't completed for some reason. This setting could be restrictive so you should take care when deciding how many days to set and also test all business scenarios thoroughly.

20

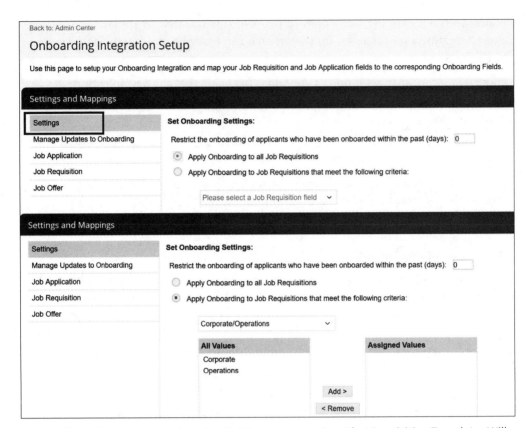

Figure 20.8 General Onboarding Settings to Determine What Requisition Templates Will Send Data to Onboarding

Manage Updates to Onboarding

On the **Manage Updates to Onboarding** tab (see Figure 20.9), the settings determine if data updates can be sent from Recruiting to Onboarding after it's already been initiated, for example, if Onboarding has begun, but there is a change to a new employee's start date or if the position has somehow changed. You can also choose to have the system reassign activities in Onboarding if the hiring manager is changed in Recruiting. This could feasibly happen if there is an unexpected reorganization or if the current hiring manager terminates or is promoted.

When deciding how to make these settings, it's advisable to discuss where data changes should be managed in relation to the overall talent acquisition process. There may be no need to make changes to the data within Recruiting and just choose to update the information in Onboarding and keep the process moving. Consider the impact to Recruiting reports in making this decision.

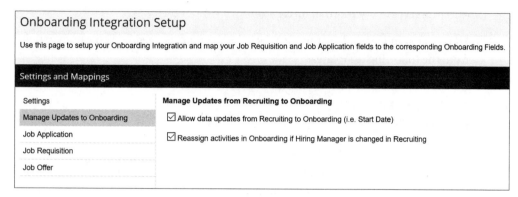

Figure 20.9 Determine How to Manage Data Updates within Onboarding

The other settings in this area deal with mapping fields between Recruiting templates and Onboarding, which we'll cover in the next section.

20.2   Mapping between Recruiting and Onboarding

Part of what makes Onboarding a win for the business and the new hire is the ability to have data in Onboarding that was captured in Recruiting during the requisition approval, application, and candidate evaluation process. There are several elements that need to be mapped from Recruiting to Onboarding:

- Field mapping from requisition templates
- Mapping picklists
- Mapping the corporate structure

We'll look at each of these in the following sections. Let's start with mapping fields from Recruiting templates to Onboarding.

20.2.1   Setting Up the Field Mapping

There are a few standard fields in Recruiting that are passed to Onboarding by default:

- `JobReqId`
- `ApplicationId`

20

- `CandidateId`
- `InternalHire` (true/false)
- `EmployeeLogin` (for internal hires)

The other standard and custom fields can be mapped as needed. You can map fields from the following templates:

- Job Requisition
- Job Application
- Job Offer Details

You can see an example of the field mapping in Figure 20.10. If you use multiple templates in Recruiting, you should repeat the field mapping for each template for which Onboarding integration is being configured. If you already have Recruiting in place when implementing Onboarding, it may be necessary to reconfigure some Recruiting fields to put them on the entities (templates) available for mapping to Onboarding. This should be taken into account in the overall implementation plan and time line.

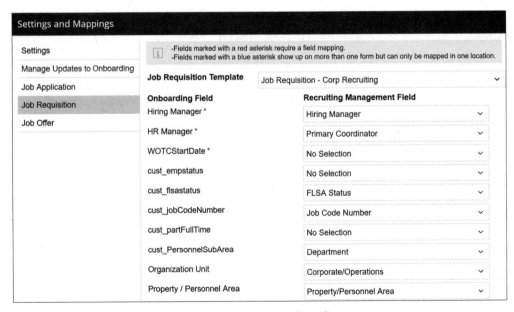

Figure 20.10 Map Fields Used in Recruiting to Onboarding

> **Note**
>
> You can't map fields from the candidate profile or any other Recruiting entities. This should be taken into consideration when implementing Recruiting to ensure that all data that you want to pass to Onboarding is captured on a template that can be mapped to Onboarding.

Before beginning the field mapping from Recruiting to Onboarding, you should first ensure that all the fields that require mapping are available. It's recommended to check the fields in **Manage Onboarding Settings** • **Data Dictionary** • **Namespaces** • **Integrations** • **RX**. Here you'll find all the fields that are available to be mapped from Recruiting to Onboarding. You can see the **Integrations** area of the **Data Dictionary** in Figure 20.11. You may need to update these according to your requirements by selecting **Fields** and then reviewing and maintaining the applicable entities.

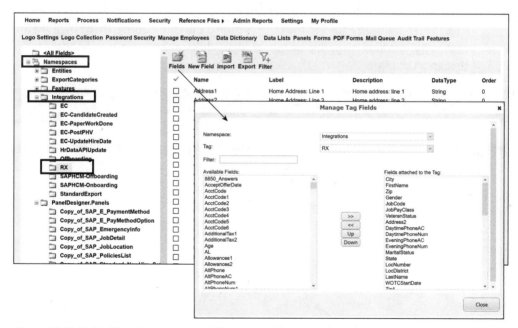

Figure 20.11 Fields That Can Be Mapped from Recruiting to Onboarding in the Data Dictionary

After you've confirmed that all fields are in the Onboarding Data Dictionary, you're ready to map the fields. Let's discuss how that works in the next section.

20.2.2   Mapping Fields between Onboarding and Recruiting

After you've confirmed the fields in the Data Dictionary, you can do the mapping from **Manage Recruiting • Set up Onboarding Integration**. When you're talking about Recruiting integration with Onboarding, what you refer to as a template in Recruiting is called an entity in Onboarding. Choose the appropriate Recruiting entity on the left, such as **Job Application**. Then select the appropriate template from the dropdown on the right. All the fields made available in the Onboarding Data Dictionary will appear here, and you can do the mapping between the **Onboarding Field** and the corresponding **Recruiting Management Field**. This field mapping exercise is very similar to mapping fields between Recruiting Management and Recruiting Marketing as well as mapping fields to support résumé parsing in **Configure Standardization Mapping**. The fields that are available to be mapped are displayed with dropdown fields in the next column.

There will likely be some fields that don't have a corresponding mapping. Additionally, you may see different fields between templates within an entity. For example, if you use different fields on an hourly and salaried requisition template, and the custom fields have been added to the Data Dictionary in Onboarding, then you'll see differences in the field mapping in Onboarding. Additionally, there may be some fields that aren't mapped.

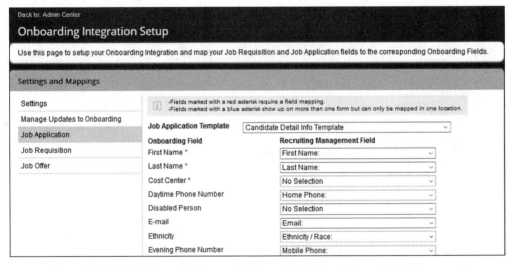

Figure 20.12 Fields Mapped between the Recruiting Templates and the Corresponding Onboarding Field

The fields that are marked with a red asterisk are required, as you would expect. You'll also see fields marked with a blue asterisk, such as the **Cost Center** field in Figure

20.12. This is used to indicate that this field is used on more than one template in Recruiting. However, these fields can only be mapped to one location in Onboarding. It's important that you don't map these fields to more than one template.

> **Best Practice for Mapping**
>
> When setting up the integration between Recruiting and Onboarding, start by mapping all the fields that are required. Test the mapping, and after it's working appropriately, add the additional fields that are needed.

Note that there are 54 fields hard-coded in the Onboarding module that aren't dependent on customer-specific configuration. These fields will appear on the **Job Requisition** and **Job Application** entity tabs.

The field mapping from Recruiting to Onboarding is one of the biggest areas to focus testing on during the implementation.

20.2.3   Types of Dropdown Lists and Integrating Picklists

Within Onboarding, there are several types of dropdown lists, or picklists, that can used in the configuration: data lists, provisioning lists, and SAP SuccessFactors picklists. Let's briefly review these types of list fields before we discuss the mapping.

Types of Dropdown Lists

When configuring the Onboarding module, especially the integration of picklist values, it's important to understand the types of dropdown fields and how they are used:

- **Data lists**
  These are used in dropdown fields on panels within Onboarding. There are up to four different list types:
  - Lists: All data lists in this list type are stored in the same table (e.g., corporate structure). This list type supports multiple properties and localization. The user can create and maintain these lists.
  - Global DB: This type will display countries and other global database lists.
  - Provisioning: All provisioning lists are shown in this list type.
  - Table mapped: This will display table-mapped data lists such as countries and states. In addition, it will display custom tables as custom data lists.

- **Provisioning lists**

  These allow you to create and manage the standard dropdown list values within Onboarding. Examples of these include gender and marital status. This is managed in **Onboarding • Reference Files • Provisioning** as shown in Figure 20.13.

- **SAP SuccessFactors picklists**

  These are the preferred method of handling fields with dropdown lists in Onboarding to facilitate the mapping of data from Recruiting. Use these picklists over the data lists and provisioning lists whenever possible. SAP SuccessFactors picklists are created and maintained in **Admin Center • Picklist Management**. Here you can export existing picklists, make modifications and reimport, and also create new picklists. This is where all picklists used throughout SAP SuccessFactors are managed, so you'll have access to all picklists, not just those used in Recruiting and Onboarding. Refer to Chapter 8 for more detailed information on managing SAP SuccessFactors picklists.

Home	Reports	Process	Notifications	Security	Reference Files ▶	Admin Reports	Settings	My Profile

Provisioning

Print   To Excel   Create   Delete

✓	Provision Code	Name	Display As
☐	AUTFNTitle	AUTFNTitle	Drop Down List
☐	BankAccountType	Bank Account Type	Drop Down List
☐	CA_WTPA_Language	CA_WTPA_Language	Drop Down List
☐	CA_WTPA_RegularPayDay	CA_WTPA_RegularPayDay	Drop Down List
☐	CellPhoneType	Cell Phone Type	Drop Down List
☐	CreditCardType	Credit Card Type	Drop Down List
☐	DirectDepositAmountType	Direct Deposit Amount Type	Drop Down List
☐	DirectDepositCountries	DirectDepositCountries	Drop Down List
☐	EC_AccountType	EC_Account Type	Drop Down List
☐	EmergencyRelationship	EmergencyRelationship	Drop Down List
☐	Ethnicity	Ethnicity	Drop Down List
☐	FLSAStatus	FLSA Status	Drop Down List
☐	FontType	FontType	Drop Down List
☐	Gender	Gender	Drop Down List
☐	MaritalStatus	Marital Status	Drop Down List

Figure 20.13 Managing the Values within Standard Dropdown Lists in Reference Files

> **Tip**
>
> Data lists and provisioning lists that are delivered with your Onboarding system should not be removed or modified.

Integrating Picklists

When creating fields to be used in a picklist, you'll have to select the type of integration that will be used. There are three different types of picklist integration:

- **Suite integration**

  As the name implies, Suite integration uses the same picklist in multiple modules. This is the recommended type of integration for Recruiting to Onboarding to Employee Central integration when two conditions exist. First, Recruiting and Employee Central use the same picklist; second, there isn't an external or third-party applicant-tracking system or Human Resources Information System (HRIS) in place. When Suite integration is used, the **System ID** value is sent from Recruiting to Onboarding, and the value then sent from Onboarding to Employee Central is considered the option ID. If the picklist is the same for all three modules, no mapping is necessary. If the picklists aren't the same, you'll need to map the picklists in Admin Center.

- **Code based integration**

  Code-based integration was previously referred to as externalized integration. This integration may be used if there is a third-party applicant-tracking system or HRIS in place, and the picklist value already has a value in the **external_code** field, as you see in Figure 20.14. This type of integration allows the reuse of the external codes with external systems.

- **Label-based integration**

  In this type of picklist integration, communication among modules will use the localized label of the picklist value. This type of integration was previously referred to as localized integration. In this type, locales are represented in the picklist file beginning in column I, as you can see in Figure 20.15. There may be several columns if multiple locales are in use. The labels for the picklist options in the specified locale should not be empty and should be unique. Systems will communicate using display text. Both Onboarding and the external HRIS should use the same display text values.

20

	A	B	C	D	E	F	G	H	I	P	Q
1	^picklistId	OptionId	minValue	maxValue	value	status	external_code	parentOptionId	en_US	fr_CA	es_ES
2	ONB_Building		-1	-1	-1	ACTIVE	Bldg_A		-1 A		
3	ONB_Building		-1	-1	-1	ACTIVE	Bldg_B		-1 B		
4	ONB_Building		-1	-1	-1	ACTIVE	Bldg_C		-1 C		
5	ONB_Floor		-1	-1	-1	ACTIVE	Floor_First		-1 First		
6	ONB_Floor		-1	-1	-1	ACTIVE	Floor_Second		-1 Second		
7	ONB_Floor		-1	-1	-1	ACTIVE	Floor_Third		-1 Third		
8	ONB_Floor		-1	-1	-1	ACTIVE	Floor_Fourth		-1 Fourth		
9	ONB_Floor		-1	-1	-1	ACTIVE	Floor_Fifth		-1 Fifth		
10	ONB_Floor		-1	-1	-1	ACTIVE	Floor_Sixth		-1 Sixth		
11	ONB_Quadrant		-1	-1	-1	ACTIVE	Quadrant_First		-1 First		
12	ONB_Quadrant		-1	-1	-1	ACTIVE	Quadrant_Second		-1 Second		
13	ONB_Quadrant		-1	-1	-1	ACTIVE	Quadrant_Third		-1 Third		
14	ONB_Quadrant		-1	-1	-1	ACTIVE	Quadrant_Fourth		-1 Fourth		

Figure 20.14 External Codes Assigned in Column G of the Picklist File to Communicate with External Third-Party Systems

Note

Don't confuse "localized" with translations. Picklist values can be translated in any of the three integration methods discussed.

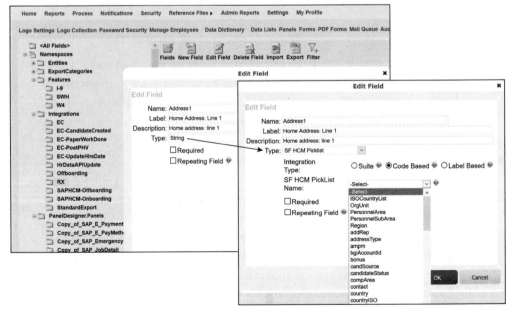

Figure 20.15 Choosing the Integration Type for Each Picklist Field in the Configuration

To map the picklists, you navigate to the **Integrations** section of the Onboarding Data Dictionary. Select **RX** to display the Recruiting fields, and then select the field for which you want to map the picklist. As you can see in Figure 20.15, by choosing **SF HCM Picklist** in the **Type** field, you're presented with the three integration types we discussed earlier. The data entered depends on the type of integration. If you select **Suite**, you reference the **Ext Code Key,** and if you select **Code Based**, you're presented with an option to select the **SF HCM Picklist**. Finally, **Label Based** also asks for the **SF HCM Picklist,** but it also solicits the **Locale**. Make the appropriate entries, and save your settings.

Repeat the mapping for each field until all picklist fields have been set up to map data from Recruiting to Onboarding.

20.2.4 Mapping the Corporate Structure

As we've mentioned, one of the values of the integration between Recruiting and Onboarding is carrying over data maintained or captured in Recruiting and passing it to Onboarding so it doesn't have to be reentered. The corporate structure in Recruiting contains critical information about the job such as organizational data, location, salary grade, and other data. We map the corporate structure to Onboarding so that these data are passed with the new hire and can drive specific paperwork or forms to be completed, as well as location-specific policies. Managers in certain parts of the organization can also be allowed to drive the onboard process.

If the corporate structure is mapped, the data on the requisition are carried to Onboarding along with the new hire's personal data. If you don't map the corporate structure, when Onboarding is initiated for a new hire, Onboarding takes the first value listed to populate the Level 1 information. For example, if the first value listed is the Division of Finance, then every new hire onboarded will be placed in that division in Onboarding. While this can be changed in the **Post-Hire Verification** step, this is an unnecessary update that can be avoided by simply setting up the integration correctly.

20.3 Summary

Having both Recruiting and Onboarding modules offers you tremendous benefit in reducing manual processes and collecting paperwork that is often arduous and time-consuming. Setting up the two modules so that the data maintained and captured during the Recruiting process are available and passed with the new hire to Onboarding is a huge benefit of the modules. By taking time to think through the data that should be shared from Recruiting to Onboarding and then setting up the mapping, you're offering your recruiters, HR business partners, hiring managers, and new hires tremendous value in eliminating time and effort during the onboarding process.

Several types of data are mapped to pass from Recruiting to Onboarding, and you must ensure that the proper setup has been made in both the Recruiting and Onboarding modules. If you've previously implemented Recruiting and are now implementing Onboarding, there are likely some configuration changes that will be made in Recruiting to make sure data are captured in the correct entities so that the data can pass to Onboarding.

Now let's turn our attention to discussing integrating Onboarding with SAP ERP Human Capital Management (SAP ERP HCM).

Chapter 21

Onboarding Integration with Employee Central and SAP ERP HCM

You've worked hard to recruit a great candidate who has been evaluated and given an offer of employment. Next is getting the candidate through your onboarding process and then into the HRIS for official hiring. With a robust suite of offerings, whether you run SAP SuccessFactors Employee Central or SAP ERP HCM, passing data from SAP SuccessFactors Onboarding to HRIS is seamless and efficient.

After new hires have been queued from SAP SuccessFactors Recruiting to SAP SuccessFactors Onboarding, with all pertinent data captured in the recruiting process sent to with them to support their Onboarding experience, they will complete the process as it has been designed and configured. After completing the necessary paperwork, the employee record can be created in the HR system of record to complete the lifecycle of the new hire. Onboarding integrates with SAP SuccessFactors Employee Central very easily through standard integration settings. However, there is also standard integration between Onboarding and SAP ERP Human Capital Management (SAP ERP HCM) for businesses that maintain their core HR processes on premise.

By this point in the talent acquisition process, we've gathered much valuable data about the candidate in both Recruiting and Onboarding, and we want to mine that data for completing the new hire record in the HR system of record. This provides the optimal user experience for the new employee, his manager, and the HR professionals processing the action.

In this chapter, we'll look at how Onboarding integrates with both Employee Central and SAP ERP HCM. Specifically, we'll discuss the following:

- Integrating Onboarding with Employee Central
  - Enabling the integration

- – Repeating fields
- – New hire processing
- – Supported entities in Onboarding to Employee Central
- – Mapping data from Onboarding to Employee Central
- Integrating Onboarding with SAP ERP HCM
  - – Prerequisites to the configuration
  - – Basic settings
  - – Transferring data from Onboarding
  - – Hiring options in SAP ERP HCM
  - – Testing the integration

We'll begin our discussion with integrating Onboarding with Employee Central.

21.1   Integrating Onboarding with Employee Central

Onboarding to Employee Central integration allows you to convert candidates into employees, with or without an integration with Recruiting. In most scenarios, the integration will be Recruiting to Onboarding to Employee Central. There are two integration scenarios that are supported among Recruiting, Onboarding, and Employee Central:

- Onboarding to Employee Central (with or without Recruiting in place)
- Onboarding to Employee Central integration *and* Recruiting to Employee Central integration working simultaneously

The most common integration scenario is the first, where data are captured in Recruiting and mapped to Onboarding to support that process—gathering additional information during Onboarding such as national identification and date of birth information—and then the new hire data are passed on to Employee Central. We discussed Recruiting to Employee Central integration in Chapter 14. Refer there for additional information on that scenario. Remember that if you have a business need supporting that scenario, such as using Onboarding to process internal transfers and promotions, you must have a separate requisition template that will be used to support this need so that the data can be sent directly from Recruiting to Employee Central.

Candidate data are wholly extracted from either Recruiting or Onboarding and sent to Employee Central. You can't pull some data from Recruiting and some from Onboarding for the same candidate. If you want any Onboarding data sent to Employee Central, then you must pass any Recruiting-related data into Onboarding to pass through to Employee Central.

The goal with the integration among these modules is to exploit the data already residing in the system and reduce the amount of data users need to enter to complete their Onboarding experience. Not only does this create the best possible user experience, it also increases data integrity by eliminating the need to duplicate data entry introducing the likelihood of mistakes. For example, you'll want to pass the job-related information that began in Recruiting on the requisition into Onboarding and then back into Employee Central. This information may include title, salary and pay grade information, benefits, organizational data, and location. It's critical that these data are correct when processed in Employee Central because it can impact an employee's organizational data as well as compensation.

In the next sections, we'll look at how this integration is enabled, configured, and tested. Let's begin by discussing how to enable this integration scenario.

21.1.1   Enabling the Integration

To enable the Onboarding to Employee Central integration, you first must establish SAP SuccessFactors message notifications. There are three notification messages available to enable:

- **CandidateCreate message to BizX once new-hire is created.**
- **PostPHV message to BizX after PHV is completed.**
- **PaperWorkDone message to BizX after NES is completed by new-hire.**

These messages are enabled in Onboarding Super Admin under **Accounts • Features • BizX Integration • SF_Notifications**.

After the notifications are enabled, as you can see in Figure 21.1, make sure the Onboarding fields are available for mapping. This was likely completed when setting up the Recruiting to Onboarding integration, as discussed in Chapter 20. However, if you don't have Recruiting in your landscape, you'll need to perform this activity. It's recommended to verify the field mapping before you begin the integration effort in

21

earnest. Fields need to be updated in the Data Dictionary within Onboarding and then mapped in the Admin Center.

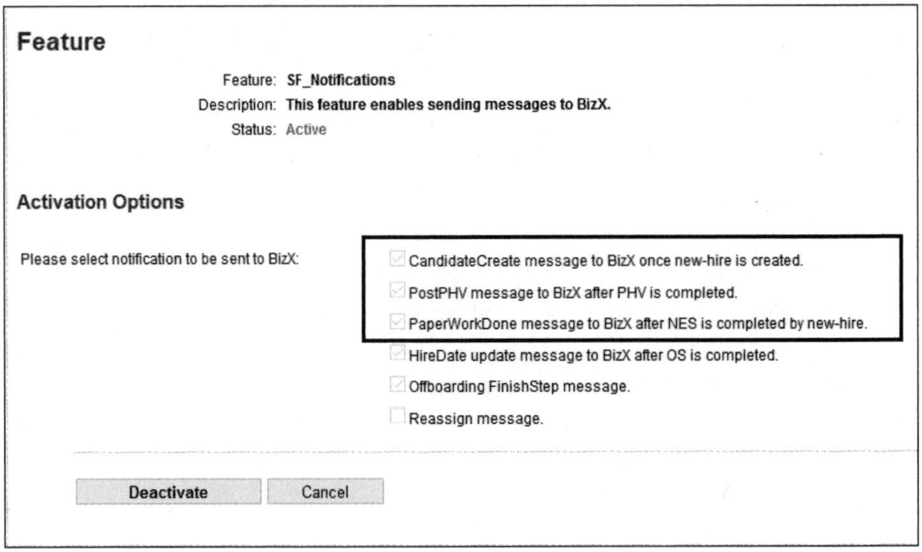

Figure 21.1 Activating Notifications in Super Admin as the First Step in Enabling Employee Central Integration

Updating the Data Dictionary

Before fields can be mapped from Onboarding, they must first reside in the Data Dictionary. Fields need to not only be available but also be of the same field type in Onboarding and Employee Central. This should be the first step in preparing for the integration. Do this in **Onboarding Dashboard • Settings • Data Dictionary • Namespaces • Integrations • EC**. Here you'll find all the fields that are available to be mapped from Onboarding to Employee Central. You can see the Employee Central **Integrations** area of the Data Dictionary in Figure 21.2. You may need to update these according to your requirements by selecting **Fields** and then reviewing and maintaining the applicable entities. Notice that there are several **EC** folders under **Integrations**:

- EC
- EC-CandidateCreated
- EC-PaperWorkDone
- EC-PostPHV
- EC-UpdateHireDate

You'll want to peruse each folder to check all fields that may be used. Note that in the **EC** folder, there are numerous pages of fields.

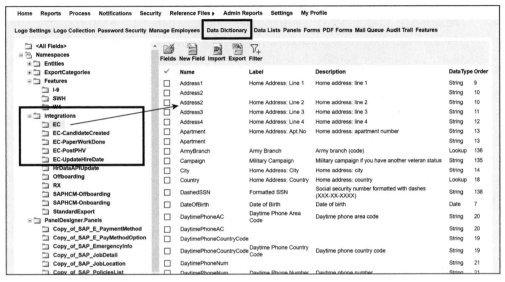

Figure 21.2 Checking and Updating Fields in the Data Dictionary to Prepare for Mapping Data from Onboarding to Employee Central

There are some fields that won't map from Onboarding to Employee Central:

- Any I-9 fields that begin with **I9**
- W-4 fields that begin with **W4**

These fields should not be mapped from Onboarding to Employee Central and should not be included in the **Fields Attached to the Tag List**. Note that Employee Central cannot accept W4 fields for tax information in the United States.

> **Note**
>
> For businesses using Recruiting and Employee Central, the field type must be the same among the three modules in the field definition. For example, if the field being mapped from Recruiting to Onboarding is a string field in Recruiting, it must also be a string field in Onboarding, and likewise in Employee Central. In addition, the field value must match exactly, including case.

21

Repeating Fields and Multi-Panels

Repeating fields allow you to send multiple values for a single field from Onboarding to Employee Central. For example, when capturing new hire dependents, there may be several entries, and the system will allow multiple names from records of the same field. Think of these as portlets in Employee Profile where you can have multiple entries within one portlet. There are four types of repeating fields that can be configured:

- Emergency contacts
- Dependent information
- Work permit
- National ID

To configure repeating fields for these field types, you must first enable the Employee Central **Enable Dependents Management** setting in **Provisioning • Company Settings**. You can see this setting in Figure 21.3. The configuration is the same for all four field types listed. Note that you must configure **Emergency Contact**, **Dependents**, and **Work Permit** as repeating fields even if you're only sending one value.

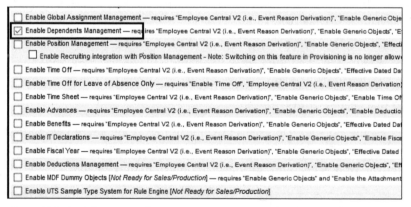

Figure 21.3 Enabling Dependent Management in Employee Central Settings to Configure the Repeating Fields

After the repeating field types are configured, you need to create a multi-panel in Onboarding. If you're using emergency contacts, there is an existing panel that should be copied called SAP_EmergencyInfo. For dependent or work permit information, you'll need to create a new multi-panel. To copy the standard SAP_EmergencyInfo panel, follow these steps:

1. In the Onboarding Dashboard, navigate to **Settings • Panels • All Wizards**. Find the **NewEmployee** wizard and highlight the panel group. Don't expand the group to display the individual panels within the wizard.

2. The panels within the **NewEmployee** wizard will display on the right, as you can see in Figure 21.4. Tab through the pages until you find the **SAP_EmergencyInfo** panel.

3. Check the box to select the panel, and click the **Copy Panel** button when it becomes available.

4. Choose the wizard into which you want to copy this panel, and then choose the **Copy** button.

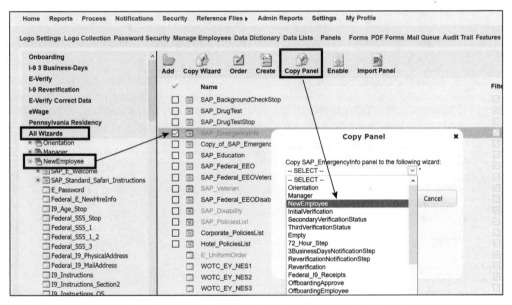

Figure 21.4 Copying and Assigning Standard Panels to the Appropriate Wizard

If you need to configure multi-panels for other than emergency contact information, such as dependent or work permit, from the **Settings • Panels** menus, select **All Wizards • NewEmployee**. Choose the **Create** button, and then follow these steps:

1. For the **Is this panel a password panel?** option, select **No**.

2. Enter a **Name** and **Description** for your panel, if applicable. Note that your panel name should not have spaces in it.

3. For the **Is this panel an editable panel after completion?** option, select **No**.

4. For the **Is this panel a stop panel?** option, select **No**.

5. For the **Show review page for this panel?** option, select **Yes**.

   For the **Is this panel a multi-panel?** option, select **Yes**.

   When you select **Yes** for the **Is this panel a multi-panel?** option, you'll be presented with additional fields:

   – For the **Show Add More Panels question?** option, select **Yes** or **No** depending on your needs.

   – Select the **Number of Panels** within the multi-panel.

   – Select the **Start Index** to specify the panel on which the workflow begins. The recommended value is "0" for this field.

   – For the **Show Delete button?** option, select **Yes** or **No** depending on your needs.

   – For the **Validate duplicated information?** option, select **Yes** or **No** depending on your needs.

6. Select the **Create** button.

These settings are displayed in Figure 21.5. Note that not all the settings in the preceding list are contained in this figure.

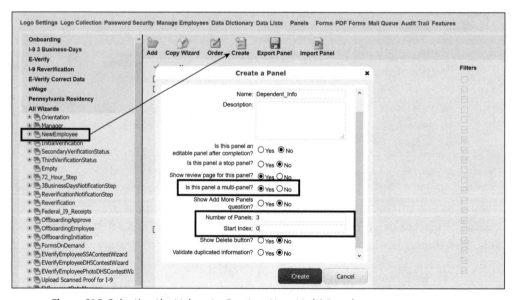

Figure 21.5 Selecting the Values to Create a New Multi-Panel

After the panels are copied or created, enable the **Repeating Field** setting in the Data Dictionary for each panel by following these steps:

1. Navigate to **Settings • Data Dictionary**, and find the panel that was created or copied.

2. Select the field within that panel, and choose **Edit Field**.

3. Select **Repeating Field,** and click **OK** (Figure 21.6).

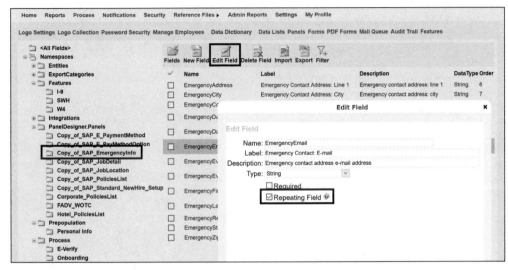

Figure 21.6 Enabling the Repeating Field Option for the Fields in the Multi-Panel

Repeating fields can also be configured in the XML; however, it's best practice to use the Admin Center tool. An example of the XML mapping is provided in Listing 21.1.

```
<mapping-attribute>
<source multi-valued="true" refid="EmergencyFirstName"/>
<target variant="" refid="emergencyContactPrimary.[#].name"/>
</mapping-attribute>
```

Listing 21.1 Example Configuration of Repeating Fields in an XML Template

21.1.2 New Hire Processing

After the integration has been enabled and any repeating fields have been configured, you need to set up the transformation of data between Onboarding and Employee Central. This can be done in one of two ways:

- Configure an XML transformation template and upload it in provisioning
- Set up the data transformation in the Admin Center

The first option is to configure an XML transformation template and upload it via provisioning in **On/Offboarding Settings • Import Export for EC Integration Template**. If this option is chosen, you must include a `mapping-attribute` for each field for which you want to send data from Onboarding to Employee Central. A sample Onboarding transformation template is provided in the Onboarding to EC Integration Implementation Guide and can be copied for reuse. An example is shown in Figure 21.7.

```xml
<?xml version="1.0" encoding="UTF-8" standalone="yes"?><objectMappingsType mappingXML-createdBy="UI"><entity-details-mapping>
    <!-- Personal Info -->
    <mapping-attribute><source multi-valued="false" entity-type="ApplicationInfo" refid="FirstName"/>
        <target variant="" refid="personalInfo.first-name"/>
        <processes><process>onboarding</process></processes>
    </mapping-attribute>
    <mapping-attribute><source multi-valued="false" entity-type="ApplicationInfo" refid="LastName"/>
        <target variant="" refid="personalInfo.last-name"/>
        <processes><process>onboarding</process></processes>
    </mapping-attribute>
    <mapping-attribute><source multi-valued="false" entity-type="ApplicationInfo" refid="MiddleName"/>
        <target variant="" refid="personalInfo.middle-name"/>
        <processes><process>onboarding</process></processes>
    </mapping-attribute>
    <mapping-attribute><source multi-valued="false" entity-type="ApplicationInfo" refid="Suffix"/>
        <target variant="" refid="personalInfo.suffix"/>
        <processes><process>onboarding</process></processes>
    </mapping-attribute>
    <mapping-attribute><source multi-valued="false" entity-type="ApplicationInfo" refid="EMail"/>
        <target variant="P" refid="emailInfo.email-address"/>
        <processes><process>onboarding</process></processes>
    </mapping-attribute>
    <mapping-attribute><source multi-valued="false" entity-type="ApplicationInfo" refid="DateOfBirth"/>
        <target variant="" refid="personInfo.date-of-birth"/>
        <processes><process>onboarding</process></processes>
    </mapping-attribute>
```

Figure 21.7 Configuring the Onboarding to Employee Central Transformation Template and Uploading in Provisioning

Note

If you choose to configure the XML transformation template, it's necessary to specify the source entity-type if the data are sent from Recruiting to Onboarding and then on to Employee Central. For any data that are entered directly into Onboarding, this attribute is left blank.

The second option and recommended option to configure the transformation template is completed in the SAP SuccessFactors mapping tool. This is found in **Admin Center • Field Mapping tool for Onboarding to EC Integration**. This is basically an XML frontend interface that makes changes in the XML file based on the values entered. To complete the mapping, first find the appropriate Onboarding field, and enter the following information (see Figure 21.8):

- **Category**
  Select from the list.

- **Field Mapping**
  Based on the **Category**, select the corresponding Employee Central field.

- **Variant**
  Based on the field being mapped, select the correct variant. Not all fields will have a variant. Fields such as email or address will have a **Business** or **Home/Personal** variant.

- **Process**
  Select the correct Onboarding process for this mapping.

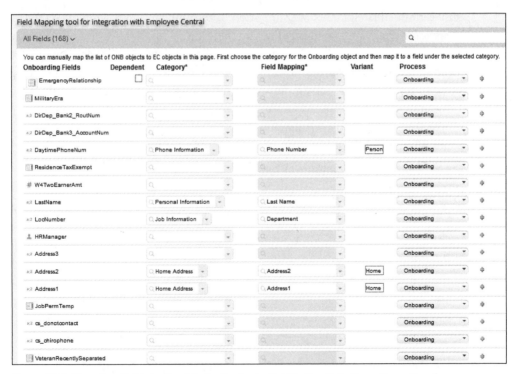

Figure 21.8 Mapping Fields in the Admin Center to Set Up the Data Transformation from Onboarding to Employee Central

Do this for all fields that need to be mapped. At the bottom of the screen there are two options:

- **Validate**
  Choose this option if you just want to make sure the mapping is correct.
- **Validate and Save**
  Choose this option if you want to validate and save in one action.

> **Note**
>
> If propagation rules are configured in Employee Central, these rules will overwrite data that are coming into Employee Central from Onboarding.

21.1.3   Supported Entities

Only certain HRIS elements are supported in the Onboarding to Employee Central integration. These are provided below and there are no additional elements available for use. It's recommended that for any field in the Employee Central data model, the required attribute (required="true" or required="false") should match among Recruiting, Onboarding, and Employee Central configurations. In other words, if the data element is required in Employee Central, it should also be required in Recruiting and/or Onboarding. Any mismatch in field definition in these modules will cause issues with the hire data as it's passed through the system.

The available data elements are as follows:

- personalInfo
- globalInfo
- nationalIdCard
- homeAddress
- employmentInfo
- jobInfo
- payComponentRecurring
- payComponentNonRecurring
- phoneInfo
- employmentInfo
- jobRelationsInfo
- emergencyContactPrimary
- workPermitInfo

21.1.4   Testing the Mapping from Onboarding to Employee Central

Just as we discussed in Chapter 14, when you're setting up the integration, it's best practice to map one or two fields, test, and then proceed with updating the configuration as necessary or finish mapping the additional fields. Good examples of fields to test the mapping with are name and address fields. Testing the mapping means that you need to have new hires in Onboarding that are through the process and are ready to be queued to pending hires in Employee Central. This testing is time-consuming because new hire data needs to start from the beginning. If you have Recruiting in your landscape, this means beginning the testing in Recruiting, gathering the appropriate data there, passing it successfully to Onboarding, gathering additional data in the Onboarding process, and then passing it to Employee Central.

A good practice in configuring and testing the integration among modules is to spend some time up-front creating test data so that it's ready when you have configuration to test. Following the mantra that "you can't test too much," take the time to stage 20 to 30 new hires, if not more, before you begin testing the integration. If you're a consultant who has implemented SAP SuccessFactors for any length of time, you'll appreciate that configuring and testing is very repetitive, but necessary.

After your new hire data are staged within Onboarding and the new hires have been queued to Employee Central, the testing process picks up with the **Manage Pending Hires** action in the Admin Center. Here, users with appropriate permissions will view and access the new hires that need to be processed in Employee Central, completing the hiring process. An example of the **Pending Hires** queue is provided in Figure 21.9. By selecting the **Hire** button, HR users can begin the conversion of candidate records into employee records.

Figure 21.9 Pending Hires Queue Displaying Candidates Ready for Hire

Selecting **Hire** will begin the **Add New Employee** process, and the user will be presented with the following four main areas where information is pulled in from Onboarding as well as entered manually, as required (see Figure 21.10):

- **Identity**

  This data identifies the employee by name, date of birth, country of birth, and other identifying data.

- **Personal Information**

  This section includes email, address, phone numbers, emergency contact information, and additional business-specific configured fields such as gender and marital status. The information included here is completely dependent on your configuration within Employee Central.

- **Job Information**

  This area specifies information about the job the employee is hired into, including organizational information, job code, pay grade information, and employment details such as hire date.

- **Compensation Information**

  This area captures data regarding employees' salary and bonus.

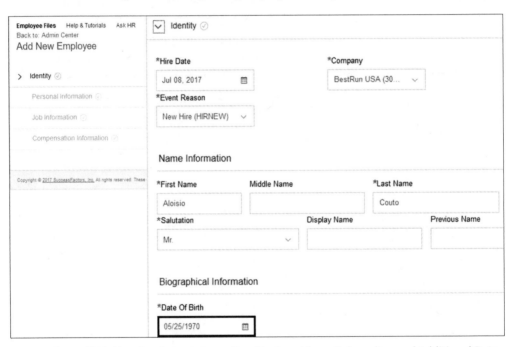

Figure 21.10 New Employee Information Displayed from Onboarding and Additional Data Entered as Necessary to Complete the Hiring Process

> **Tip**
>
> As you test the integration, if you find fields that should have data but don't, first check to ensure that the particular data was completed within Onboarding. Many

times, integration testing is impeded by data that aren't being sent because they don't exist. If you ensure the fields are required in both Onboarding and Employee Central, this shouldn't occur, but it should be a first step in troubleshooting.

After you've walked through each area in the **Add New Employee** action and confirmed that all data are populating from Onboarding correctly, you've confirmed that the integration is working.

Now, let's turn our attention to integrating Onboarding with SAP ERP HCM.

21.2 Onboarding Integration with SAP ERP HCM

For companies that maintain core HR processes—Organizational Management and Personnel Administration—in SAP ERP HCM, SAP supports standard integration between Onboarding and your core HR system on premise to allow data to flow between the systems. In this integration scenario, it's important to decide when you need to have SAP ERP HCM updated in the hiring process. This will drive when the data flow is triggered and from where. If you don't need employee data in SAP ERP HCM until the new hire has completed the onboarding process, the integration can be configured so that the Onboarding process is triggered from Recruiting. This is the scenario we discussed in Section 21.1 of this chapter when covering integrating Onboarding with Employee Central. If you need to have employee records in SAP ERP HCM earlier in the process, the integration should be from Recruiting to SAP ERP HCM, and then Onboarding will be triggered from SAP ERP HCM.

If you're triggering Onboarding from Recruiting and then sending new employee data to SAP ERP HCM, the candidate must be flagged as readyToHire in Onboarding. This is the trigger the system uses to know what data to send to SAP ERP HCM. The readyToHire flag is set to Yes by the system when the **PaperWorkDone** notification in Onboarding is sent when the **New Employee Step** is completed by the new hire. These flagged records are then imported into SAP ERP HCM. These data imports are done via scheduled import jobs that are configured in SAP ERP HCM. The import job is usually scheduled numerous times per day. You can configure this based on your business requirements and the volume of new hire records that need to be processed. SAP recommends an interval of every 30 minutes when scheduling the job. If your hiring volume isn't large, you may want to extend this time. Obviously, if you schedule the import more frequently, and there are no records to be imported, there is no impact.

21

Tip

When scheduling your new hire import from Onboarding into SAP ERP HCM, keep in mind that the larger the data set of records being imported, the longer the job will take to run.

When the import job has run and the candidate data are in SAP ERP HCM, the administrator reviews the data and makes any corrections that are necessary before posting the data to the employee master data record. This is important to remember because the data from Onboarding isn't written into SAP ERP HCM automatically. The administrator must review the data and trigger the process to create the employee data record. It's possible for administrators to set up recurring jobs in SAP ERP HCM for the data replication and then monitor any errors that occur. Candidate records that have errors can be pulled before writing the rest of the data to SAP ERP HCM.

When employee data are written into SAP ERP HCM, and the hire action is complete, there is no communication from SAP ERP HCM to Onboarding. Any communication that occurs to new employees from that point will come from Onboarding and will be based on data available within SAP SuccessFactors. It's strongly recommended that businesses implement the standard employee data integration package from SAP ERP HCM to SAP SuccessFactors for new employee data, so new employees are able to log in to SAP SuccessFactors to either complete the onboarding process or complete any other talent processes such as goal setting and completing training.

In this section, we'll review the configuration required to integrate Onboarding to SAP ERP HCM. In particular, we'll discuss the following:

- Prerequisites to configuring SAP ERP HCM
- Basic settings
- Transferring data from Onboarding
- Hiring options in SAP ERP HCM
- Testing the integration

Let's first discuss the prerequisites needed to configure integration with SAP ERP HCM.

21.2.1 Prerequisites to Configuring SAP ERP HCM

There are several prerequisites to configuring the integration between SAP ERP HCM and Onboarding:

- Configured SAP ERP HCM system
- Configured middleware SAP Process Integration (SAP PI)
- Installation of the Integration Add-On
- Configured Onboarding module, including an updated Data Dictionary
- Implemented standard Employee Profile integration with SAP ERP HCM
- Implemented standard Recruiting integration with SAP ERP HCM

Note that both the Employee Profile and Recruiting integration packages can be implemented concurrent with this integration if you're just beginning your SAP SuccessFactors journey, and these aren't already in place. After these prerequisites have been fulfilled, the integration can be set up and tested.

21.2.2   Basic Settings

The first step in configuring the integration is to set up the **Basic Settings** in SAP ERP HCM. Within the IMG, navigate to **Integration Add-On for SAP ERP HCM and SuccessFactors Bizx • Integration Scenario for On-/Offboarding Data • Basic Settings** (Figure 21.11).

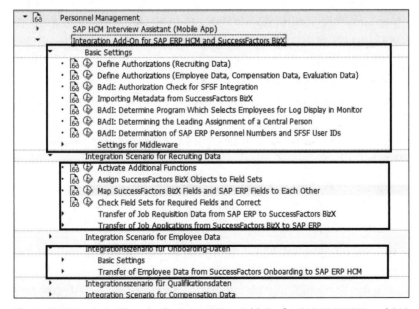

Figure 21.11 Basic Settings in the Integration Add-On for SAP ERP HCM and SAP SuccessFactors BizX

Here you'll perform the following functions:

1. Begin by defining authorizations by working with your Basis team.

2. Import metadata from Onboarding by running the Import DDIC report. Transaction RH_SFI_IMPORT_ONBOARDING_DDIC for this report will import the XML file that is exported from the Onboarding Data Dictionary. You must first configure Onboarding and define the fields in the Data Dictionary as we've discussed at length in Chapter 19. The **Object Name** to reference is **ZOnboardingDD**, as you can see in Figure 21.12.

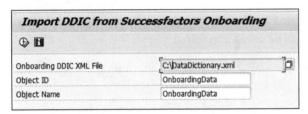

Figure 21.12 Importing the Data Dictionary from Onboarding to SAP ERP HCM

3. Store the credentials for transferring Onboarding data in secure storage.

4. Map SAP SuccessFactors suite fields and SAP ERP HCM fields to each other in **Basic Settings • Map SuccessFactors HCM Suite Fields and SAP ERP HCM Fields**. We'll discuss this action in greater detail in the next section.

5. Assign SAP SuccessFactors objects to field sets, which contain multiple Onboarding fields that can be mapped to SAP ERP fields.

6. For more complex field mappings, create one of the following Business Add-Ins (BAdIs):

   – BAdI: Mapping of SAP SuccessFactors fields to SAP ERP Infotype Fields (HRSFI_B_FIELD_MAPPING)

   – BAdI: Change of Mapping Result (HRSFI_B_CHANGE_MAPPING_RESULT)

7. Configure the action type.

8. Configure the action type reasons.

This chapter isn't meant to cover the configuration of SAP ERP HCM in detail. For more information and detailed steps, refer to the relevant documentation on the SAP Support Portal related to configuring this integration package. Let's now discuss how data are transferred from Onboarding to SAP ERP HCM.

21.2.3   Transferring Data from Onboarding

When configuring the integration between Onboarding and SAP ERP HCM, there are several actions in SAP ERP HCM that need to be set up:

- Map SAP SuccessFactors suite fields and SAP ERP HCM fields.
- Assign objects to field sets.
- Use BAdI `HRSFI_B_FIELD_MAPPING` (Mapping of SAP SuccessFactors Fields to SAP ERP Infotype Fields).

Let's discuss each one of these actions in the following sections, beginning with mapping onboarding fields to SAP ERP HCM.

Map Onboarding Fields to SAP ERP HCM

As you learned when setting up the Onboarding to Employee Central integration, to map data between systems, you must first make sure the fields have been added to the Data Dictionary. We saw in the previous section that one of the **Basic Settings** is to import into SAP ERP HCM the XML file containing the Data Dictionary via **Onboarding Dashboard • Settings • Data Dictionary**. Just choose the **Export All** button, and then select the format of the export. To enable the integration with SAP ERP HCM, the Data Dictionary must be exported in XML format, as shown in Figure 21.13.

After the Data Dictionary has been imported, the relevant fields must be mapped. There are mappings available for certain data, such as the following:

- Personal information, such as name, address, date of birth, gender, disability, marital status, and national ID information
- Organizational information such as division, department, and location
- Job information such as title, job code, and pay rate
- Race/veteran status
- Direct deposit information for up to three banks
- Emergency contact information

Field mapping is completed in **Basic Settings • Map SuccessFactors HCM Suite Fields and SAP ERP HCM Fields**. This transaction will define what data will be imported from Onboarding and is required for candidate data using the SAP SuccessFactors Simple Object Access Protocol (SOAP) API.

21

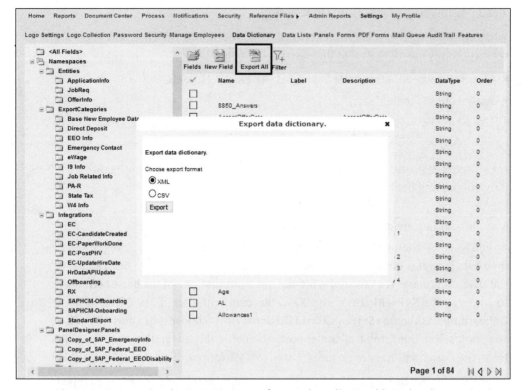

Figure 21.13 Exporting the Data Dictionary from Onboarding Dashboard and Importing into SAP ERP HCM

To map fields, double-click the **Fields and Mapping Modes** folder to display the field sets that can be mapped. Find the field set for Onboarding, and select the field **Description** to activate the field set. Here you'll find the fields that can be mapped from Onboarding. Scroll through to find and select the fields you want to map. Double-click the **Mapping to Infotype Fields** folder, as shown in Figure 21.14.

When the **Mapping to Infotype Fields** screen appears, find the infotype to be mapped using the **Infotype** dropdown list. Complete the **Subtype** and **Field name** fields, as necessary, and save the mapping.

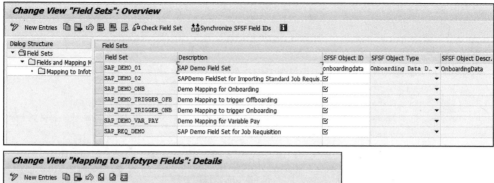

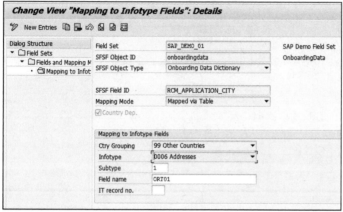

Figure 21.14 Finding the Field Set to Map and Selecting to Map the Infotypes

Return to the **Fields and Mapping Modes** screen, and select the correct value in the **Mapping Mode** field under the **Mapping Mode** column. The values are as follows (Figure 21.15):

- **Mapped via Table**
- **Mapped via BAdI**
- **Not Individually Mapped**

Save the settings and repeat these steps to map all the fields from Onboarding into the correct Infotypes in SAP ERP HCM.

21

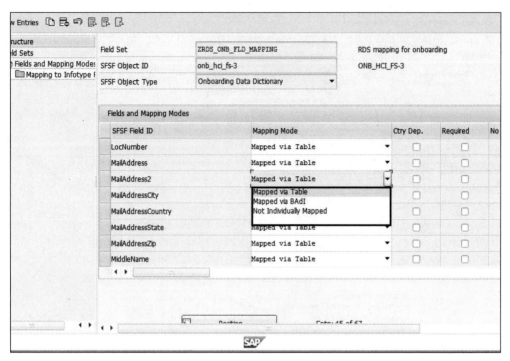

Figure 21.15 Selecting the Appropriate Value under the Mapping Mode Column

As we discussed in Section 21.1.4, it's recommended that you begin the mapping exercise by mapping one or two fields and test to see if the mapping was configured properly. After you've confirmed that data are passing from Onboarding to SAP ERP HCM correctly, you can complete the field mapping.

Assign Objects to Field Sets

After the Onboarding fields have been mapped to SAP infotypes as described in the previous section, you'll assign Onboarding objects to field sets in SAP ERP HCM. This is completed by mapping SAP SuccessFactors suite fields and SAP ERP HCM fields. In the **Assignment of SFSF Objects to Field Sets** screen, find the Onboarding **Field Set**, **ZRDS_ONB_FLD_MAPPING**, and then activate the **SFSF Object ID** field. In Figure 21.16, the **SFSF Object ID** value is "onb_hci_fs-3." This value comes from the Data Dictionary that was imported before beginning the mapping.

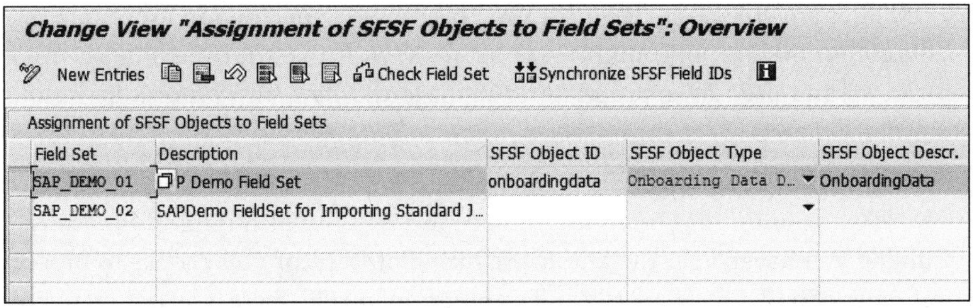

Figure 21.16 Associating the Object ID from Onboarding to the Field Set in SAP ERP HCM

BAdI Mapping of Onboarding Fields to SAP ERP HCM

BAdIs can be used to map data from Onboarding to SAP ERP HCM. If you do this, you'll need a separate BAdI implemented for each field that is mapped. BAdIs are used when you require more complex mapping than that provided by the standard template. For more information on this topic, refer to the applicable documentation provided by SAP.

Now let's discuss how the hiring action is handled in SAP ERP HCM.

21.2.4   Hiring Options in SAP ERP HCM

After the new employee data are brought into SAP ERP HCM from Onboarding, there are two ways to process the new hire transaction: automatically or in a mass transaction. How the hiring action is configured will depend on each the company's business processes related to managing employee data. The specifics on how to configure the hiring options in SAP ERP HCM are outside the scope of this book. Refer to the standard documentation provided by SAP to determine how to configure the hiring options with Onboarding integration. Let's briefly look at each option available.

Automatic Hire

With Integration Add-On 3.0 SP06, the report **Import Onboarding Data from Success-Factors HCM Suite** includes a parameter that allows you to automatically hire applicants when the data are brought over. This automatic hire option can be restricted, as needed, by specific countries, groups of countries, company codes, personnel areas and subareas, and employee groups and subgroups. If no restriction is specified, then all new hires are processed automatically. This can be a good option for certain segments of the new hire population. However, it's advised that the constraints be studied closely and used as appropriate to manage the new hire process in various countries and parts of the organization.

Mass Hire

Assuming you haven't set the automatic hiring process, or you choose to process some types of hires automatically and do others manually, there is an option to process those hires in a mass function. Using Transaction HRSFI_ONB_HIRE (Process Applicants Imported from or Exported to Onboarding), you can select a group of records to process for hire. This is also a time-saving option that prevents an administrator from processing each new hire record individually.

21.2.5   Testing the Integration

In the previous section, we discussed some guidelines for testing Onboarding integration with Employee Central, and many of these same guidelines will apply when testing the integration with SAP ERP HCM. Testing will involve processing the hiring of test candidate data from Onboarding into SAP ERP HCM. You'll need to set up adequate test user sets within Onboarding to send to SAP ERP HCM via the import transaction. This will include beginning from the Recruiting process with creating external candidate data and processing them through your recruiting configuration, into Onboarding and through that process, and then on to SAP ERP HCM.

After the data is in SAP ERP HCM, the testing process will depend on the business process in place at your organization and the roles that are involved in hiring employees. It's recommended that the data that comes into SAP ERP HCM has several records with errors so you can test the error processing before continuing with the hiring action. If you're using both the individual hire and mass hiring options in SAP ERP HCM, you should test these scenarios as well.

As you encounter data errors, remember to first check to ensure that the fields have data in Onboarding before troubleshooting the error in the configuration. Many errors that arise in testing the integration are data related.

Because integration with SAP ERP HCM also involves employee data being sent from SAP ERP HCM back into SAP SuccessFactors via the Employee Profile integration after the hire is processed, this data transfer also needs to be included in the testing scenarios and scripts. This integration isn't within the scope of this book. If you already have the Employee Profile integration implemented in your landscape, the introduction of the Onboarding integration shouldn't impact this. However, it should be tested to close out the new hire process. Again, remember that you cannot test too much.

21.2.6   Known Issues with Onboarding to SAP ERP HCM Integration

There are a few known issues with enabling the standard integration from Onboarding to SAP ERP HCM, and it's wise to understand these as you begin your implementation so they can be fully addressed.

Pre-Day One Functionality

We've previously discussed the pre-day one feature within Onboarding that provides access to the SAP SuccessFactors suite to new employees before they have an official employee record. See Chapter 16 to recall this discussion. When you've enabled pre-day one within Onboarding and plan to integrate to SAP ERP HCM, there is some additional work that needs to be taken into consideration. When the pre-day one feature is in place, Onboarding creates a temporary user in SAP SuccessFactors so that new employees can access the suite prior to having an employee record. When the integration from Onboarding to SAP ERP HCM is run, this temporary user needs to be synced from the employee data replication in one of two ways:

- If you're using a middleware-supported integration, such as SAP PI, to replicate the employee data, the temporary user ID created through the pre-day one feature must be manually disabled before the integration is processed.

- If you integrate via a file-based integration, this must be enhanced to include an **ONBOARDING_ID** column in the file that identifies the temporary ID and should be populated with the Onboarding ID of the temporary user when the employee data is replicated to SAP ERP HCM.

Legacy Data in Onboarding

If you already have Onboarding implemented and are just implementing the SAP ERP HCM integration, you may have legacy data with internal hires that don't have the Hired flag set to True in the candidateInfoObject. To avoid having this legacy data pass into SAP ERP HCM, you'll need to configure the integration by setting a filter for the import report so these records aren't included. With this in place, SAP ERP HCM will only read data that was created after the integration was activated.

SAP SuccessFactors API Limitations

The import program in SAP ERP HCM expects to import only candidate data with the readyToHire status. But there is a limitation in the SAP SuccessFactors API that doesn't allow the data to be filtered. To work around this, administrators will need to manually check Onboarding to ensure that the candidate in a transaction has the correct status before processing. To support this, you can enable the field CurrentStatus in Transaction HRSFI_ONB_HIRE in SAP ERP HCM. You'll also need to add this field to the list layout of the transaction. You'll then need to note the values in this **Current Status** field before you start the action. Candidates that are in **New Employee Step** are still engaged in the Onboarding process. Candidates that have a status of **Orientation Step** will be ready to process.

21.3   Summary

Whether you maintain your core HR processes in Employee Central or SAP ERP HCM, SAP has provided for streamlined sharing of necessary data between Onboarding and the HRIS of record to provide you with a fully integrated talent acquisition-to-hiring system landscape. In this chapter, we've discussed the ways in which Onboarding integrates with Employee Central for sending candidate data to complete the hiring process. We covered the steps involved in configuring the integration, including the following:

- Updating the Onboarding Data Dictionary
- Mapping data fields between Onboarding and Employee Central
- Setting up repeating fields and multi-panels in Onboarding to capture multiple rows of information such as dependents

We also discussed how new hires are processed in Employee Central after data are sent from Onboarding, and where data can be populated from the candidate record versus data that are entered manually in the hiring action. Finally, we provided guidelines and considerations for testing the Onboarding to Employee Central integration.

In Section 21.2 we discussed the standard integration package to integrate Onboarding with core personnel processes in SAP ERP HCM. While we didn't cover the configuration steps in detail, we discussed several components of the integration:

- Prerequisites to configuration
- Making basic settings in SAP ERP HCM

- Options for transferring data from Onboarding to SAP ERP HCM
- High-level steps involved in configuring the data mapping

We then covered the hiring options available in SAP ERP HCM to hire employees individually as well as in a mass transaction. The way in which candidates are hired in SAP ERP HCM completely depends on the business processes in use at each specific business, as well as the configuration of the SAP ERP HCM system being integrated. Testing the SAP ERP HCM integration will likely involve a few different players to ensure that the processes in place on the SAP ERP HCM side aren't negatively impacted by the Onboarding integration.

Finally, we highlighted a few known issues with the Onboarding integration to SAP ERP HCM. These known issues impact the pre-day one functionality within Onboarding, how the integration handles legacy data in Onboarding when the integration is enabled, and some limitations in the SAP SuccessFactors API.

For additional detailed information about the Onboarding to SAP ERP HCM integration, refer to standard SAP Help documentation. This documentation will contain the latest information based on SAP SuccessFactors releases and SAP ERP service packs.

This book has provided information about the functionality provided by SAP SuccessFactors Recruiting and SAP SuccessFactors Onboarding and how they can support your talent acquisition strategic objectives to identify, attract, and retain the best talent. We hope you've found this information helpful as you either implement these solutions in your organization or consider how they can support your talent acquisition strategies.

21

The Authors

Amy Grubb is the CEO and principal at Cloud Consulting Partners, Inc., an SAP SuccessFactors consulting partner and full-service HCM consultancy focused on implementing cloud solutions. She has consulted in the HCM space for more than 18 years, focused on SAP SuccessFactors for the last 10 years. She is the coauthor of *SuccessFactors with SAP ERP HCM: Business Processes and Use, 2nd Edition.*

Kim Lessley is a director of Solution Management at SAP SuccessFactors and is currently responsible for the SAP SuccessFactors platform topics of Intelligent Services and cloud security. She has been working with SAP and SAP SuccessFactors products since 1990, focused on the human capital management (HCM) space and in particular on Recruiting and Onboarding.

Index

O

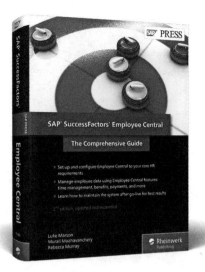

- Set up and configure Employee Central to your core HR requirements

- Manage employee data using Employee Central features: time management, benefits, payments, and more

- Learn how to maintain the system after go-live for best results

Luke Marson, Murali Mazhavanchery, Rebecca Murray

SAP SuccessFactors Employee Central

The Comprehensive Guide

Get the most out of SAP SuccessFactors Employee Central! Use its extensive HR functionality, from hiring, termination, time sheets, and benefits programs to integration with SAP ERP and third-party cloud applications. Set up position and workforce management, and maintain payroll and tax information with Employee Central and configure critical HR functionality for your processes with step-by-step walkthroughs. Get everything you need for Employee Central!

approx. 675 pp., 2nd edition, avail. 11/2017
E-Book: $69.99 | **Print:** $79.95 | **Bundle:** $89.99

www.sap-press.com/4480

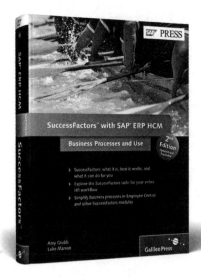

- SuccessFactors: what it is, how it works, and what it can do for you
- Explore the SuccessFactors suite for your entire HR workflow
- Simplify business processes in Employee Central and other SuccessFactors modules

Amy Grubb, Luke Marson

SuccessFactors with SAP ERP HCM

Business Processes and Use

Looking to better your HR workflow? Discover the potential of SAP Success-Factors, SAP's HR cloud solution, with this introductory guide. Updated and revised, this edition covers new integration packages, additional SAP HANA Cloud Platform information, details on the Metadata Framework, and a look into the new Job Profile Builder. Discover what SAP SuccessFactors is, how it works, and what it can do for you.

644 pages, 2nd edition, pub. 12/2014
E-Book: $59.99 | **Print:** $69.95 | **Bundle:** $79.99

www.sap-press.com/3702

- Integrate SuccessFactors with SAP ERP, SAP ERP HCM, and third-party applications

- Explore SuccessFactors deployment models through in-depth case studies

- Implement SuccessFactors APIs and standard integration templates

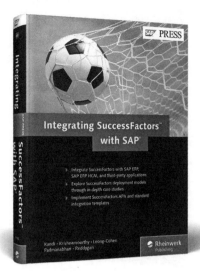

Kandi, Krishnamoorthy, Leong-Cohen, Padmanabhan, Reddygari

Integrating SuccessFactors with SAP

Whether you're making the jump to SAP SuccessFactors all at once or in parts, explore your deployment options and how to integrate this cloud-based functionality into your HR landscape. Learn to apply prepackaged or planned integration scenarios and walk through case studies that model the use of templates and APIs. With SuccessFactors, the question isn't what to aim for—it's how to get there.

551 pages, pub. 05/2015
E-Book: $69.99 | **Print:** $79.95 | **Bundle:** $89.99

www.sap-press.com/3723

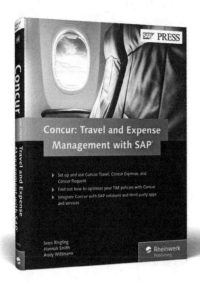

- Set up and use Concur Travel, Concur Expense, and Concur Request

- Find out how to optimize your T&E policies with Concur

- Integrate Concur with SAP solutions and third-party apps and services

Sven Ringling, Hannah Smith, Andy Wittmann

Concur: Travel and Expense Management with SAP

New York. Tokyo. Dubai. If your business is on the go, learn how to get the most out of Concur Travel, Concur Expense, and Concur Request! Set up this cloud solution to reflect your travel policies so you can plan trips, settle expenses, and manage critical approvals. Analyze your T&E spending with standard and custom reports and then integrate Concur with SAP solutions and third-party apps. With this guide, you'll make your T&E processes quick and effective!

322 pages, pub. 04/2017
E-Book: $69.99 | **Print:** $79.95 | **Bundle:** $89.99

www.sap-press.com/4262

- Learn how to work with the SAP ERP HCM architecture and data models

- Program for custom enhancements, reports, performance, and more

- Understand what SuccessFactors, SAP HANA, SAP Fiori, and HR Renewal mean for you

Dirk Liepold, Steve Ritter

SAP ERP HCM: Technical Principles and Programming

Your SAP ERP HCM system needs more than just a pretty face—get the information you need to work with your backend system! This book will help you to master the technical aspects of SAP ERP HCM, starting with the basics of its architecture, and moving to more advanced concepts like authorizations and performance programming. With the help of screenshots and detailed instructions, you'll acquire new skills in no time flat. In addition, get the latest updates for SAP HANA, SAP Fiori, and HR Renewal.

863 pages, 2nd edition, pub. 12/2014
E-Book: $69.99 | **Print:** $79.95 | **Bundle:** $89.99

www.sap-press.com/3698

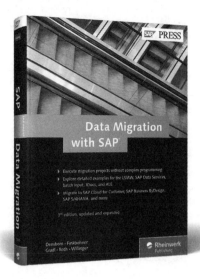

- Plan and execute migration projects without programming

- Explore detailed examples on LSMW, SAP Data Services, batch input, IDocs, and ALE

- Learn what data migration means for SAP Hybris Cloud for Customer, SAP Business ByDesign, and SAP S/4HANA

Densborn, Finkbohner, Gradl, Roth, Willinger

Data Migration with SAP

When it comes to data migration, choosing the right approach for your organization can be overwhelming. This comprehensive guide not only leads you through project planning, but also gives you step-by-step instructions for executing your migration with LSMW, SAP Data Services, the batch input technique, and more. Whether you're moving to the cloud, migrating to SAP S/4HANA, or replacing a legacy system, let us smooth the way.

563 pages, 3rd edition, pub. 04/2016
E-Book: $69.99 | **Print:** $79.95 | **Bundle:** $89.99

www.sap-press.com/4019

Interested in reading more?

Please visit our website for all new book
and e-book releases from SAP PRESS.

www.sap-press.com